SUCCESS...

is peace of mind that is a direct result of self-satisfaction in knowing that you made the effort to become the best you are capable of becoming.

John R. Wooden

John R. Wooden, Head Basketball Coach, Emeritus, UCLA

PATIENCE
ood things
e time

TIVE
ESS
st when
needed.
ent
allenge.

INTEGRITY
purity of
intention

CONFIDENCE
Respect without fear.
May come from being
prepared and keeping
all things in proper
perspective.

RELIABILITY
creates
respect

TEAM SPIRIT
A genuine
consideration for
others. An eagerness
to sacrifice personal
interests of glory for
the welfare of all.

f and the
perly and
ecute the
prepared
very
etail.

HONESTY
in thought
& action

INITIATIVE
Cultivate the ability to
make decisions and
think alone. Do not
be afraid of failure,
but learn from it.

INTENTNESS
Set a realistic goal.
Concentrate on its
achievement by
resisting all tempta-
tions and being deter-
mined and persistent.

SINCERITY
keeps
friends

LTY
and to
pending
ep your
spect.

COOPERATION
With all levels of your
co-workers. Listen if
you want to be heard.
Be interested in find-
ing the best way, not
having your own way.

ENTHUSIASM
Brushes off upon
those with whom you
come in contact. You
must truly enjoy what
you are doing.

OF SUCCESS

THE
JOHN WOODEN
PYRAMID OF SUCCESS
REVISED SECOND EDITION

*The Authorized Biography, Oral History, Philosophy and
Ultimate Guide to Life, Leadership, Friendship and Love
of the Greatest Coach in the History of Sports*

NEVILLE L. JOHNSON

Published by
Cool Titles
12121 Wilshire Blvd., Suite 1201
Los Angeles, CA 90025
www.cooltitles.com

Cover and book design by Lisa Wysocky, White Horse Enterprises, Inc.

Photo Credits:
Photo of Wooden in coaching outfit by Joe Kennedy, *Los Angeles Times*, ©1967;
photo of Wooden with great granddaughter by Anacleto Rapping, *Los Angeles Times*,
©1990; interior and cover photo of Wooden on UCLA track by R.L. Oliver,
Los Angeles Times, ©1974

Second edition published April 2003

The Library of Congress Cataloging-in-Publication Data Applied For

Johnson, Neville, 1949—
The John Wooden Pyramid of Success, Revised Second Edition
p.   cm
ISBN 0-9673920-2-0
1. Biography 2. Sports/Basketball 3. Self Help/Motivation I. Title
2003

Printed in the United States of America

3 5 7 9 10 8 6 4

For information regarding special discounts for bulk purchases,
please contact us at
www.cooltitles.com

Dedication

For my parents,
Barbara and L. Richard Johnson

Overview

This is the second edition. The first edition quickly sold out. This version has been updated, edited further, and corrected. The book is divided into seven sections. The first chapter summarizes John Wooden's achievements both on and off the court; the second, three times the size of that in the first edition, profiles his life and career.

The third chapter contains the "guts" of the book: John Wooden's speech about the Pyramid of Success, including its substance and elements, edited and approved by him, and improved since the first edition.

The fourth chapter is an interview with Coach, directed primarily towards his motivations in creating the Pyramid of Success and methods for applying its tenets.

Chapter Five contains a collection of his essays, and "Woodenisms": thoughts, favorite maxims and poems, that are relevant to the concepts he articulates. Many new "Woodenisms" have been collected and added to this edition.

The sixth chapter contains interviews, recollections and comments about Coach Wooden and the impact of the Pyramid upon those who have come in contact with him: his family, historians, and those he's influenced as we travel through Indiana to Los Angeles. New to this edition are interviews with H. R. "Bob" Haldeman (former Chief of Staff of United States President Richard Nixon) with whom Wooden maintained his friendship, even during his incarceration; Jack Tobin, the co-author of Wooden's autobiography, *They Call Me Coach;* and Andy Hill, a former UCLA player who went on to be a top entertainment executive and who co-authored with Wooden the recent best-seller, *Be Quick But Don't Hurry.*

We are fortunate to have the inner thoughts of many sports legends who were taught by Coach Wooden, including the six greatest players he ever coached, Kareem Abdul-Jabbar, Bill Walton, Willie Naulls, Walt Hazzard, Gail Goodrich and Sidney Wicks. You will meet Ann Meyers-Drysdale, one of the greatest female basketball players in history and certainly the best to play at UCLA. You will see his incredible impact and influence, that he is the true to life version of *Goodbye Mr. Chips*, James Hilton's lovely novella of a British school teacher and his boys, who as men acknowledged and carried on his example. We are lucky to have a rare look into the home life of Coach Wooden, as his children, grandchildren and brothers let us into their happy world.

Finally, in the seventh chapter, we have a look at Coach interacting with some of the stars who played for him.

Table of Contents

Wooden created this beautiful concept as a contribution to charity for the American Heart Association. The original hangs in Geoffrey's Restaurant, on the Pacific Coast Highway in Malibu, California.

Introduction

We all want to better ourselves. Advice on doing so is abundant, but few courses, books, or aids offer a definitive methodology for attaining "success" that embraces all forms of the human condition: mental, moral, physical, and spiritual. Fewer still have been proven to work. John Wooden's "system," his Pyramid of Success, is the exception.

John Wooden is far more than the greatest basketball coach in history. He is also the designer of a philosophy for living that is logical in its approach, brilliant in its simplicity, non-sectarian and pragmatic. Most importantly, his Pyramid of Success is effective. During the success of the UCLA basketball program throughout the "Wizard of Westwood's" era, the one constant in the equation was John Wooden. He is the paradigm. Both professionally and personally, Coach has emerged victorious time and time again by virtue of his virtue. He is widely recognized for his kindness, humility, integrity, and honesty. As you will see in this book, he is more successful as a person—as a husband, parent, friend, teacher—than as a coach. In our current world, where winning at all costs too often is the code by which the athlete lives by in order to "succeed," realize this: no one in the history of basketball is more synonymous with winning than John Wooden. And, no one has done it in as gentlemanly, more honorably a fashion.

But Coach's contributions to this planet are far greater than just the spectrum of basketball. Rather, it was basketball that became the proving ground for his ultimate achievement and legacy: The Pyramid of Success. For many years, the Pyramid has been a grassroots phenomenon that has swept through much of the country. The primary carriers of that message were his players, who were among the first to hear his wisdom. The effect of the words were so profound that almost to a man, every student who played for John Wooden upon graduation would return to discuss their meaning, ramifications and implementation. "Sometimes it would be a year after graduation, sometimes ten," notes Coach. But they would always come back.

In 1953, Wooden allowed Vic Kelley, the UCLA sports information director, to issue a press release Wooden wrote wherein he explained the Pyramid, but there is no evidence it was ever reprinted. In that version, Wooden observed that, "a winning record can be built up by adroit scheduling, better facilities, low university entrance requirements that give a coach a clear shot at more players in many other ways. But I agree with George Moriarity, the great major league umpire, who said, 'Giving all, it seems to me, is not so far from victory.'"

In the 1960s, the Pyramid was published in several magazines, garnering a large response. *Guideposts*, a Christian periodical, featured the Pyramid in an article. Shortly thereafter, Coach Wooden received 15,000 handwritten requests for copies of it. Once a year in Southern California, sports fans could hear Wooden lecture on the Pyramid on his local television show about UCLA basketball. However, the publication of John Wooden's autobiography, *They Call Me Coach* (1972), followed the next year by a *New York Times Sunday Magazine* story featuring the Pyramid graph on the cover, were the two events that made society at large take notice. As the Pyramid became known, the business world began to recognize the blessings of his philosophy, and John Wooden became and still remains one of the most sought-after dinner and motivational speakers in America. From savings and loan groups to sports clinics, churches and clubs to community events, Coach passed on his knowledge and insights with aplomb and enthusiasm. As might be expected, UCLA has always had an affinity for the Pyramid; it is prominently displayed on campus at the John Wooden Athletic Center, as well as in the UCLA Athletic Hall of Fame. On a visit to UCLA in 1985, Wooden was frequently stopped by students, and to his surprise, "almost every one of them mentioned the Pyramid to me." Still, due to Coach Wooden's requests not to commercialize the Pyramid, and until the publication in 1997 of *Wooden*, a slim volume containing the Pyramid lecture and some of Coach's favorite sayings, it was relatively unknown and generally unavailable to most of the world. It is now becoming widely known as an international treasure.

Here are the complete, updated philosophies of Coach John Wooden, what has kept audiences, athletes, friends, family and students rapt for years. These pages contain the ingredients for success in all fields. Here are the stories of those who love Coach, and why.

Many consider *It's a Wonderful Life*, Frank Capra's heart-warming movie starring Jimmy Stewart, to be the all-time feel-good movie, if not the greatest movie of any genre. The same values espoused in that movie—friendship, the joy and blessings of family life, love, integrity, honesty, and hard work—are what Coach Wooden is about. He's the real-life embodiment of George Bailey, the protagonist of that movie. But John Wooden is no fictional character, which makes his life and history all the more fascinating. Somebody does exist who has had an unblemished and remarkable career, but who as a human being exceeds those accomplishments. How and whom he has touched—from basketball greats to the student managers of basketball teams—is remarkable in breadth and duration. How rare it is that a high school teacher or coach is remembered, sometimes over seventy years, as the greatest influence on a large group of men.

Basketball provides the tableau of this book, but it is really a road map, with all directions clearly indicated, enabling you to reach your fullest potential in all aspects of life. Enjoy the journey. This is a case study. You will learn about the Pyramid of Success by examining the life of its inventor, who has tried to follow it, and those who have been influenced by it and him. You will find the results astonishing, heart-warming, human, real, and inspiring. As you read this book, you will find yourself performing a self-evaluation so that you can learn from this master teacher, the *sensei* of sport, Coach John Wooden.

This is a book for both sexes. It is about the human condition, love, marriage, relationships in business, family and romance, and generally how to get along in life, both internally and socially. It is the story of the glory of love, strength in the face of adversity, joyfulness, of a man whose reach exceeded his grasp. We are not allowed to say that what John Wooden did attain exceeded that of everyone else by a country mile because, as you shall learn, it is not appropriate to compare. John Wooden may now be elderly, but his concepts are bursting with energy. This is a book of and about wisdom, what it is based upon, and why it came to be. Legendary editor, Norman Cousins, said in 1975 that "Wisdom consists of the anticipation of consequences." Wooden's advice and life have always met this criterion. A great man is someone who never reminds us of anyone else. That, too, is Coach.

Alcindor/Abdul-Jabbar and Walton's numbers are retired.

THE JOHN WOODEN PYRAMID OF SUCCESS

Chapter One

John Wooden's Legendary Achievements

We live in a "show me" society, skeptical of any advice, constantly vigilant to disprove or displace a hero. Many are cynical. This is a world with few lasting contemporary heroes. Rock stars, movie stars, athletes and politicians enter and recede from our consciousness with regularity. Precious few possess that most intangible of qualities: staying power—the ability to achieve, then maintain a level of extraordinary accomplishment. Even fewer can attain this level without some notoriety plaguing their personal lives, interfering with the esteem in which they are held. John Wooden is the rarity. We're inundated with motivational speakers and writers, some of whom have much to contribute, but none of them come close to having credentials on a par with John Wooden. In the last decade, many of these motivational speakers have taken to calling themselves "coaches" or "personal coaches."

Many have borrowed liberally from the philosophy, ideas and sayings of Coach Wooden. Anthony Robbins is a good example; he calls himself a coach, quotes Wooden, and sells a tape of an interview he conducted with him. John Wooden is the real coach.

For those requiring proof of heroic achievement and the presence of greatness, consider the following evidence.

AWARDS AND ACHIEVEMENTS

John Wooden is considered by many to have been the greatest coach in the history of modern sport. That he is the greatest coach in the history of college basketball is not debatable. There are but two other contenders who could be argued to have been the greatest coach in all of basketball: Red Auerbach, who coached the Boston Celtics, a professional team that won nine straight National Basketball Association (NBA) championships, 1959-1966, and was voted in 1980 by the Professional Basketball Writer's Association of America as the greatest coach in the history of the NBA; and Phil Jackson, who formerly coached the Chicago Bulls, achieving six NBA championships in his nine years there, and now three with the Los Angeles Lakers.

Jackson can now claim the most coaching victories in NBA playoffs, 156-54, with a percentage of .743, followed by Pat Riley (155-100; .608) and Red Auerbach 99-69; .589.) (Auerbach supposedly griped—when Jackson won his third in a row championship in June, 2002—that Jackson had it easier with superstars Michael Jordan and Scottie Pippen when he led the Chicago Bulls, and with Shaquille O'Neal and Kobe Bryant of the Los Angeles Lakers. Wooden, of course, would never so react should any of his records fall.)

Jackson is lauded for his "Zen-like" style and approach to the game. He is the closest in temperament and style to Wooden. Those who argue that Wooden is the greatest always observe that Auerbach (and now Jackson) led teams where the players returned season after season, whereas Wooden always had a new crop who could never play longer than three years. Wooden was able to win with "little" teams and others with "big men." He adapted his strategy and played varying styles to manage his assets, winning nineteen conference championships in his twenty-seven seasons at UCLA, the record of which he is most proud. Another astounding record about which Wooden was unaware when this author brought it up to him in 2000, was that Wooden's teams won 149 of the 151 games coached by him in Pauley Pavilion, the Bruin's home court. In August of 1999, a 48-member panel created by ESPN, the cable sports channel, selected the ten greatest coaches of the century. They are in descending order:

1. Vince Lombardi, Green Bay Packers, professional football
2. John Wooden, UCLA, basketball
3. Red Auerbach, Boston Celtics, professional basketball
4. Dean Smith, University of North Carolina, basketball
5. Bear Bryant, Ohio State, football
6. John McGraw, New York Giants, baseball
7. George Halas, Chicago Bears, football
8. Don Shula, Baltimore Colts and Miami Dolphins, football
9. Paul Brown, Cleveland Browns, football
10. Knute Rockne, Notre Dame, football

Blair Kerkoff in *The Greatest Book of College Basketball* (1998) rates Wooden as the greatest coach, followed by Dean Smith of North Carolina, Bobby Knight of Army and Indiana (and now Texas Tech), Adolph Rupp of Kentucky, and Hank Iba of Northwest Missouri State, Colorado and Oklahoma State. Peter C. Bjarkman's history of basketball, *The Biographical History of Basketball* (2000) observes that if any fan is ever asked to name the top three greatest coaches of all time, Wooden will always be one of the three. Bjarkman concludes that Forrest C. "Phog" Allen of the University of Kansas, "invented the profession of basketball coaching. Rupp and Auerbach first defined the standards for dynasty rule in the cage sport, but it was the Wizard of Westwood who fashioned the greatest winning legacy of them all."

Of the major universities, Adolph Rupp (1931-72) had the winningest record on a percentage basis (876-190 for a percentage of .822), followed by

Roy Williams of Kansas (305-72, for a percentage of .809), and Jerry Tarkanian of Long Beach State (709-170 for a percentage of .807). Wooden is fourth at 664-162, for a percentage of .804. Dean Smith of North Carolina (1962-97) has the most overall victories (1962-97) with a record of 879-254, and has the fifth best percentage (.776). Wooden's percentage during the twelve-year dynasty was .938.

Denny Crum, Wooden's former player and assistant coach, who went on to coach championship teams at the University of Louisville, says in his 1999 autobiography, *The State of The Game*, that no one has had the impact on the game that Wooden has. "Not only in style, but in terms of how he approached the game. The way he dominated college basketball for so long is mind-boggling. You look around and no one can come close to doing what they did at UCLA. And of course Coach Wooden was the architect of all that. He is as probably as versatile as teacher as anyone I have ever seen."

This is John Wooden's legacy as a coach.

UNEQUALED RECORDS

1. **88 Consecutive Victories.** During a three-year period (1971-1974), UCLA won 88 consecutive games. The next closest streak is 60 (University of San Francisco 1955-60). Wooden also holds the record for most appearances in the Final Four, 12 (next is Dean Smith, North Carolina, 11); most consecutive appearances, 9 (next is Mike Krzyzewski, Duke, 8); and most victories, 21 (next is Adolph Rupp, Kentucky, 9).

2. **10 NCAA Championships.** 1964, 1965, 1967, 1968, 1969, 1970, 1971, 1972, 1973, and 1975. Ten national championships in collegiate basketball. No other school in the history of the sport has more than four, that being Kentucky under Adolph Rupp.

3. **7 Consecutive National Championships.** An extraordinary feat, considering no other school has won more than two in a row.

4. **38 Consecutive Sudden Death NCAA Tournament Victories.** From 1964 until the 1974 finals—an unbelievable ten year string — Wooden's UCLA teams won every sudden death, life-on-the-line playoff game in national competition. No other school has won more than 13.

5. **4 Perfect Seasons.** 1964, 1967, 1972, 1973. No other coach has done this more than once. (The last perfect season by a major school was in 1976, Indiana, coached by Bobby Knight.)

6. **8 Undefeated PAC-8 Championships.** No other school in UCLA's home conference has ever gone undefeated in this league. His 12 NCAA regional championships is another unequaled record.

OTHER AWARDS AND HONORS

One of Two Persons Ever Inducted Into the Basketball Hall of Fame as a Player and as a Coach. In 1960, Wooden was inducted as a player. In 1973, he was inducted as a coach. Until 1999, he was the only person so doubly honored. (The other is Lenny Wilkens, who, other than the Olympics, only coached professional teams.)

All-American. In 1930, 1931, 1932, Wooden was an All-American basketball player at Purdue, and the first player to be a three-time consensus All-American.

Player of the Year/The John Wooden Award. In 1932, John Wooden was voted college basketball player of the year due to his outstanding season at Purdue. That year, he also was bestowed the Big-10 Award for Proficiency in Scholarship and Athletics, graduating 19th academically in a class of 4,675. Ironically, the distinction for Player of the Year would later be renamed the John Wooden Award, given by the Los Angeles Athletic Club. The John Wooden Award was created in 1976 for college basketball. Its first award was in 1977, and it is voted by the major sportswriters in the United States, as is the Heisman trophy for college football.

All-Time All-American. In 1943 with the Helms Athletic Foundation Basketball Team, Wooden was elected an All-Time All-American. The Helms Bakery in Los Angeles, out of business since the 1960s, had a wonderful foundation and museum honoring American athletes and it was a great honor to be inducted.

Indiana Basketball Hall of Fame. Wooden was inducted in 1964, in the first group.

NCAA College Basketball Coach of the Year in 1964, 1967, 1969, 1970, 1972, and 1973.

Sportsman of the Year. In 1970, Coach Wooden was selected for this honor by *Sporting News Magazine*. In 1973, *Sports Illustrated* gave him this distinction, an award he shared with tennis great Billie Jean King.

The John Wooden Classic is played each year in Anaheim, California, and the **John Wooden Tradition** occurs each year at the Conseco Fieldhouse in Indianapolis. Both are doubleheader college invitational events of national prominence.

In 2000, *Sports Illustrated* ranked the greatest sports figures from each state. John Wooden was listed as the greatest sports figure ever to come from Indiana for his contributions as a player and coach, with basketball legends Larry Bird and Oscar Robertson, ranked two and three, respectively.

But again, the real measure of John Wooden's legacy begins off the court. His humanitarian awards include: **California Father of the Year** (1964), (awarded by California Father's Day Council); **Coach of the Century** from the Friar's Club (1971) [quite an award considering there were twenty-nine years to go]; the **Whitney Young Urban League Memorial Award for Humanitarian Service** (1973); the **Christian Church Humanitarian Award for Service to Mankind** (1973); **UCLA Honorary Alumnus of the Year** (1973); **Campbell College Honorary Doctorate of Humanities** (1973); first recipient of the **James Naismith Peach Basket Award** for outstanding contributions to basketball (1974); the first **Layman's Leadership Institute Velvet Covered Brick Award for Christian Leadership** (1974) [Wooden was particularly proud of this award as it related to Christian service]; the **John Bunn Basketball Hall of Fame Service Award** (1974); **California Grandfather of the Year** award by National Father's Day Committee (1974); **California Sports Father of the Year** award (1975); resolution in his honor in the **United States Senate** (1975); **John R. Wooden Day** proclaimed by governor of Indiana (December 13, 1975); **House of Representatives General Assembly of the State of Indiana** resolution in his honor (1975); **Commendation from Los Angeles City Council** (1975); **John R. Wooden MVP Award** created and given to the most outstanding player of the McDonald's All-American Game, a yearly tournament where the best athletes in high school basketball compete in a tournament (1978); first sports figure to be honored with the **Bellarmine Medal of Excellence** (1985) (previous recipients include Walter Cronkite and Mother Teresa); **Sportslink Pathfinder Award** to the Hoosier who provided service to the youth of America (1993) (a "Hoosier" is an Indiana native); an inductee into the **GTE/Academic All-American Hall of Fame** (1994); **40 for the Ages** award by *Sports Illustrated*; the **Landry Medal** for inspiring youth of America (1994); the **Frank G. Wells Disney Award** awarded by the Walt Disney Company for service as a teacher (1995) (another award he particularly enjoyed because he considers himself a teacher first and foremost); the **Lexington Theological Seminary Service to Mankind Award** (1995); the **Reagan Distinguished American Award** (1995); the **AYA Humanitarian of the Year Award** (1995); the **NCAA Theodore Roosevelt Sportsman Award** (1995); six **Victor Awards** from the City of Hope, the last coming in 1996; the **ICON Award** from the UCLA Center on Aging (1996); **"Coach Wooden Keys** to Life Award" created to be given at the annual Legends of the Hardwood Breakfast, presented to a member of the college or professional basketball community who exemplifies outstanding character and leadership on and off the court, and given in the host city of and at each Final Four (1996); **Corvette Award**, St. Vincent's Medical Center (1998); **San Pedro Boys and Girls Club Service to Youth Award** (1999); **Naismeth Men's College Coach of the 20th Century** (2000); **University of Louisville Honorary Doctorate of Public Service** (2000); and the **Pac-10 Hall of Honor**, essentially the Pac-10 Hall of Fame, which commenced in 2002 (each school picks one inductee, UCLA selected Coach).

In December 2002, UCLA announced that the basketball court at Pauley Pavilion would be named "The John Wooden Court."

A Marine Corps scholarship is named after Coach, as is the John Wooden Recreation Center on the UCLA campus. The Nell and John Wooden Humanitarian Award for Lifetime Coaching Achievement was created in 2002 by the World Sports Humanitarian Hall of Fame, to be given annually to a coach, at any level, who exhibits many of the qualities Wooden used in his career. His textbook, *Practical Modern Basketball* (1966), now in its third edition, is the definitive work on the subject, and has been translated throughout the world. If you find yourself in Martinsville, Indiana, be sure to drive along John Wooden Drive over by the hospital. Few individuals have had as lasting and profound an impact on sports and life as Coach Wooden.

Chapter Two

Biography of John Wooden

John Wooden quietly radiates dignity, grace, and sincerity. After having met Wooden, the mother of Lew Alcindor (now Kareem Abdul-Jabbar) described him as "more like a minister than a coach." A rival coach, after losing a recruit to Wooden and UCLA, lamented, "We thought we had a kid sewed up, but then Jesus Christ walked in. How do you recruit against Jesus Christ?"

Sid Ziff, a sportswriter for the *Los Angeles Times*, wrote, "John Wooden is an unexciting intellectual whose teams play wildly exciting basketball."

John Wooden is an almost shy, unaffected, polite gentleman who is not flamboyant in dress (Midwest conservative), personality (calm, pleasant), speech (flat, even, direct), or manner (modest and straightforward). Although not egotistical, obviously he is proud of his legendary accomplishments. Wooden is man of simple pleasures, who in his terms, and by the standards of most, has had a marvelous, invigorating, healthy and interesting life.

Wooden is the first to admit that he's not perfect and there are those who are not fond of him, but the mistakes are few and minor and the detractors fewer. All aspects of his life considered, the natural and inescapable conclusion is that John Wooden is a man of enormous skill, integrity and kindness. He rose to the top of his profession, and decades after his retirement is still considered to be the greatest basketball coach in history. But John Wooden is no enigma; there's nothing mysterious about who he is and how he got to where he wanted to go. He worked hard to climb his mountains, which were the highest peaks around, doing so with an organized plan and a great *joie de vivre*, leading a happy and fulfilled life. The reason for this, he believes, is that he kept his priorities in order, placing his wife and family before basketball or anything else. He earned the best of both: a happy family and winning teams. On the subject of placing his family first, Wooden comments, "I don't think I should, but I think the Lord will understand, and maybe the Lord had a hand in my doing this." Summed up, John Wooden is a great, but unpretentious, man with simple passions, enormous discipline, and uncommon logic. He is an extraordinary achiever.

THE EARLY YEARS

Born October 14, 1910, into a tenant farmer family, in the tiny town of Hall, Indiana, John Wooden grew up happy and healthy, the second of four brothers. His father, Joshua Hugh Wooden, of Dutch and Irish descent, later became a mail carrier. When John was eight, the family moved to a sixty-acre farm near Centerton, Indiana, which his mother had inherited. The farm raised wheat, corn, alfalfa, tomatoes and watermelons; and standard stock, including cows, pigs and chickens. Unfortunately, Joshua Wooden ran into difficulty running the farm and lost it in 1924. As a result, the family moved ten miles down the little road to Martinsville, Indiana, located thirty miles southwest of Indianapolis, where Joshua Wooden, for the next twenty-five years until he retired, worked in the bath house, and as a masseuse at the Homelawn Sanitarium, known for its therapeutic artesian wells.

John Robert Wooden was a happy child, the biggest influence on his life being his father who read the Bible daily, didn't swear, and was an honest man—characteristics his son also acquired. Wooden believes the word "gentleman" (pronounced by him as "gentle man") was "coined for someone like my dad." Joshua Wooden, Wooden reminisced, "was a wonderful man, a kind person, a gentle person, gentle but firm. When he said something, you could bank on it. But he never said an unkind thing about anybody. He never complained."

Wooden looked up to his father as a man of "great faith and patience," who "was far more interested in character than in reputation. He had many misfortunes in regard to material things; but he never complained nor compared himself with those who seemed to be more fortunate. In my opinion he came as close to living the philosophy of The Golden Rule as any person that I have ever known. I attribute my emotional balance, which I feel is critical to playing and coaching success, to my father," said Wooden. Joshua Wooden, by all accounts, was a very fine, kind, nice person. "He always had compassion for others, especially those who were infirm," Wooden wrote in his autobiography, *They Call Me Coach*. His father wrote and read inspirational prose, and Wooden still carries with him words given to him by his father. In 1956, the *Los Angeles Times* reported that Coach Wooden had given what he called "My Last Lecture" to UCLA students, wherein he discussed what his father had given him.

> *If this were to be my last opportunity to advise young people, I would want to speak of things that have not only been meaningful to me but which might apply to all. Years ago when I was the age of you, my father gave me an Adopted Creed, which I have always carried in my wallet. The six points are listed as follows:*

> ### 1. Be True to Yourself
> *You will remember what Polonius said to his son Laertes (in* Hamlet), *"This above all to your own self be true and it must follow as the night the day thou canst not be false to any man." Remember that.*

THE JOHN WOODEN PYRAMID OF SUCCESS

2. *Make Each Day Your Masterpiece*

Merely try to do your best, every day. Do not put things off. True success can come only from the satisfaction one gets from knowing you did the best you are capable of doing.

3. *Help Others*

Remember, the Bible says, "Do unto others as you would have others do unto you." And there is an anonymous quotation, "A man there was and they called him mad, the more he gave, the more he had."

4. *Drink Deeply from Good Books*

Remember Alexander Pope's advice, "Know then, thyself, presume not God to scan, the proper study of mankind is man." You can learn a man from reading Shakespeare, Gray—read Lloyd Douglas and find out what the "Magnificent Obsession" was.

5. *Make Friendship a Fine Art*

Look at what Abraham Lincoln did with friendship. You can if you will.

6. *Build a Shelter Against a Rainy Day*

That is not difficult. It means only to practice moderation and look forward to the future.

My father also gave me a quotation, which I have carried on the back of this card listing the Adopted Creed. The Quotation says: "Four things a man must do if he would make his life more true; to live without confusion clearly; to love his fellow men sincerely; to act from honest motives purely; to trust in God and Heaven securely."

If all of us could mold our lives after this quotation and the mentioned creed, think what the world would be. Are you familiar with the poem by Leigh Hunt, About Ben Adhem? "He was blessed with the love of God because he loved his fellow men." Isn't that all any of us really needs to do, have a genuine love for our fellow men?

Too many of us are concerned with building a reputation or obtaining material possessions. We should be more interested in building character within ourselves. Your reputation is merely what others consider you to be, but your character is what you

> *KNOW yourself to be. Material possessions can't bring content-*
> *ment, peace of mind, happiness, or true success. . .*
>
> *One final word of advice: BE A DOER! You are now at a*
> *wonderful, curious age where courage should predominate over*
> *timidity and the spirit of adventure over the love of ease. Don't be*
> *afraid of making mistakes. Instead, profit and learn from your mis-*
> *takes and those of others. He who makes no mistake does nothing*
> *and contributes nothing and we are all here to contribute some-*
> *thing, one way or another.*

The creed Wooden espouses today has a seventh statement: "Pray for guidance and counsel and give thanks for your blessings each day." The creed is part
of what Wooden refers to as "timeless wisdom from a godly father," and
includes the "two sets of threes" taught by Joshua Wooden: "Never Lie, Never
Cheat, Never Steal," and "Don't Whine, Don't Complain, and Don't Make
Excuses." Wooden carries the creed and two sets of threes with him at all times.

John's older brother, Maurice "Cat" Wooden, now deceased, said in 1969,
"I attribute John's success to the fact that he was always motivated. Our father
was one of the poor people in town, but he always was very interested in athletics."

Wooden was always a good student, industrious and fun loving. Centerton,
Indiana, where his family lived until Wooden was fourteen, was a typical rural
town with not much more than a water tower and a general store. He loved to
read, especially the *Leatherstocking* series, *Tom Swift* and *Modern Mechanics*.
He palled around with Cat, going to neighborhood dances in a barn, the music
supplied by an organ. As a boy, John Wooden loved sports, especially baseball,
at which he was an exceptional player, and basketball, where he was nonpareil.

NELL

Wooden attended Martinsville High School and during his freshman year at
a carnival he met ninth grader Nellie Riley (her father dropped the "O'"), who
became his lifetime love. The story told is that Nell faked the ability to play cornet so she could join the school band and watch Wooden play basketball. She
would later become his cheerleader. (In 1931, when Wooden played for Purdue,
Nell reportedly got so excited at an important conference game at Elkhart,
Indiana, that she fainted and didn't get to see the exciting finish when her beau's
team won.) She lived next door to his high school coach, who imposed a no dat-

ing rule on his players, but that didn't get in their way. Theirs is a classic American romance. From the time they met they were devoted to each other, and according to Wooden, "knew we were in love."

Mary Schnaiter, privy to the storybook love affair, reminisced, "I was Nell Wooden's best friend. She was cute, with a turned-up nose. I remember when she first met John. She thought he was cute, cute, cute. Her first romance was wonderful. She got him and that's all there was to it. One time I got her to go on a date with another boy. John Bob was all right—that's what everybody called him. He was the greatest player. He was never stuck up at all."

Wooden told Tommy Hawkins in 1992 about this great love, "We were high school sweethearts, and I can't explain it, but we fell in love almost immediately. . . She had tremendous influence. In high school I was very shy, and she got me to go to speech class to help me overcome that."

Nell said in 1980 that when "he came to see me at my home he was always polite and my parents liked him, but he was so bashful he could hardly hold his head up to say, 'How do you do?' to them. In his senior year, his high school coach was afraid we might be foolish enough to get married and that John would not go to college. He lived right behind us, which was unfortunate, because John wasn't supposed to have any dates during basketball season. I remember Coach Curtis saying to my mother, 'You wouldn't want Nell to marry somebody who would never make over $25 a week.' Mother thought to herself, 'If he ever makes $25 a week, I'll be surprised.'"

Schnaiter's sister, Judy Savournin, whose wealthy father, Clifton Schnaiter, owned a lumber business and grain mill in Martinsville, remembers the teenage John Wooden as "a nice guy. In those days everyone had an excellent relationship with the Wooden family. The Woodens weren't exactly poor, but they were of moderate circumstances and great people. You couldn't say one thing [negative] about any of them. I remember John Bob from walking home. He was just a very wholesome person to know. You just felt like you'd like to know him. The other girls were jealous when Nell got him. When she made up her mind, that was it, and she got him." She confirms that Nell was "cute," "feisty," and that "wherever he went, she just stuck by him."

In *They Call Me Coach*, Wooden recounts the occasion when Nell and some friends came to watch him plow the fields because she was sweet on him, and Wooden ignored them because he was too bashful. The next day after that encounter, when Nell asked why he didn't come over, Wooden replied that he was "dirty, and I thought you'd make fun of me." Nell responded, which brings tears to his eyes if he is asked about it, "I would never make fun of you." It was the defining moment when he said he "knew" she was the one.

In an interview for this book in 1991, Wooden was queried about the love of his life.

I've been asking a lot of the people about your relationship with Nell and a lot of people have commented on it. Can you tell me what made her so special?

It's very hard to say. Nellie and I met when I was in my second year in high school. She was a freshman. Who could tell? It's hard to figure. I lived on a farm, from which I always commuted eight miles to town. She was probably the most popular girl in her class and I was a nobody. And yet there seemed to be a spark there. Somehow I think we fell in love immediately. I never dated another girl. [Mary Dohn who attended Purdue the same years as Wooden, confirmed this in 2002: "He never brought a girl to any dance, but mostly stood off to the side and occasionally would dance with another fellow's girl. Everybody knew he was going with his high school girlfriend."] But she did. She was very popular. She dated other fellows, but I was the one who she loved. I knew that, too. I didn't have money to take her places and do things, but I turned down the appointment at West Point when she said, "If you go, I'm not waiting six years." [West Point, the military academy for the U.S. Army, had recruited him for his senior year; the rules then permitted him to play another four years.]

You were going to go to West Point?

I had an appointment and I wanted to take it, she said she wasn't going to wait six years, she'd join a convent.

She wasn't serious about that?

Yes she was. I think she was. I never questioned her seriousness about anything she said. She was Irish, she was outspoken, I knew where she stood all the time. I was extremely jealous of her, but I loved her. And she always stood by me. She helped me . . . as I say, I came from a farm and was an extremely shy person. Her parents said I was the shyest boy they'd ever seen. And she got me to go to speech and public speaking classes to help overcome that. When I was discouraged at Purdue—purely and simply there was no athletic scholarship—and my folks had no money and I considered dropping out and getting a job, she encouraged me to stay. In the early years, she was extremely supportive all the time. You probably have read *They Call Me Coach*, and I talk about us losing the money that I'd saved for us to get married. She was always supportive. She never put any pressure on having more things. When I had a couple of extremely lucrative offers to leave, I talked with her, and my children said, "You'll have a lot more things if you take that." She didn't want me to. There's never been a finer wife and mother than Nellie.

And you just were interested in each other and everything she had to say and do and it was fun and intellectually stimulating?
I didn't agree with her on everything, but. . .

Did you ever raise your voices at each other? Did you ever quarrel?
Yes. Yes, we had some spats, but it all turned out great in the end.

Wooden's dedication in his autobiography states simply and elegantly his deep feelings: "This book is gratefully dedicated to my wife Nellie. Her love, faith and loyalty through the years are primarily responsible for what I am—be that good or be it bad."

Wooden played varsity basketball for three years, beginning in 1926, at Martinsville High. The games were the primary pastime for the small town. Basketball was so revered there that the arena in which the team played held more fans than there were residents of the town (5,200 to 4,800, a statistic that made its way into *Ripley's Believe It or Not*). All three teams on which Wooden played went to the final game for the state championship, and in Wooden's junior year the team won the state championship.

Wooden also participated in high school track events. During his senior year, Wooden came in sixth in the state meet for the 100-yard dash, running it, he remembers, in "under 10 flat."

Always industrious, Wooden worked a variety of mostly manual labor jobs during his youth, including stints canning tomatoes and peas, working on high tension lines to plant poles, in an ice cream factory, boxing groceries, in the wheat fields, and as a garbage collector. Between his junior and senior years in high school, in 1927, Wooden and a teammate, wearing their state championship letters which would help them catch rides, hitchhiked to Kansas and worked in the fields traveling up through the Dakotas. They had hoped to work in Lawrence, but the wheat was not ready for harvest, however, they caught the attention of Phog Allen (who got his name because his voice sounded like a foghorn), one of the greatest coaches prior to Wooden, who got them jobs pouring concrete for the Memorial Stadium then being built, and let them sleep in the campus gym. In 2001, Wooden, considering the stadium was still in use, commented with amusement, "I think I did an excellent job." During that summer, Phog Allen offered Wooden a spot on his team, but Wooden turned it down, preferring to stay in Indiana for his college years.

WOODEN FIGHTS RACISM

That Wooden escaped being a racist is particularly salutary given the environment and culture in which he was raised. He had plenty of opportunity. The Ku Klux Klan was a powerful, important presence in the 1920s in Martinsville and throughout Indiana, reaching into business and all aspects of government. In 1924, the Indiana Klan had an estimated membership of at least 250,000 in a state of three million inhabitants. In 1925, 27 percent of the white male inhabitants of Morgan Country, where Martinsville, the county seat, is situated, were members of the KKK. Its tentacles of terror reached throughout the state, including the virtual take-over of the Republican party, and the election of Klan puppet and sympathizer Ed Jackson as Governor of Indiana on November 4, 1925. That year, the KKK took over the state government, also electing the Lieutenant Governor, the Secretary of State, a majority of the state legislature, and all but one of the congressional seats. Jackson, who served one term, was a crook as well as a bigot. The influence and menace of the KKK had seriously waned by the end of the Roaring Twenties, but Indiana's (particularly the Southern part) sad history of racism cannot be ignored. Indeed, in 1967, a march by the KKK through various Indiana cities concluded in Martinsville.

Martinsville historically has the worst reputation for racism of any town in Indiana, with black columnist James Patterson writing in May, 2002, for the *Indianapolis Star* that Martinsville was "where black folks traveling on State Road 37 know better than to stop after dark."

Two weeks previously, another journalist for that paper who was analyzing Martinsville's reputation observed, "If you're black and if you must drive [near Martinsville], the conventional wisdom is this: Make sure your car is in good working order; have plenty of gas in the tank." There were but eleven blacks found in the 2000 census of the town's 11,698 inhabitants, who are overwhelmingly Christian and Republican. There were reports of racist conduct at sporting events by fans who shouted epithets at visiting players of color during basketball games, and of a generally racist attitude by fans against non-white visitors at high school football games in Martinsville in the 1990s.

In January 2002, the *New Yorker* published a lengthy article on Martinsville's reputation for racism, and the lingering cloud dating back to the 1968 unsolved murder of a young African-American woman, Carol Jenkins. In May of 2002, her alleged killer, Kenneth C. Richmond, who had never lived in Martinsville, was arrested for the crime, turned in by his daughter, and a major story on the case was reported in the *New York Times*, under the headline, "After Arrest, Indiana Town Shamed by a 1968 Killing Sees a Chance for Renewal." Richmond was scheduled for trial in October 2002, but died of cancer in August of that year.

However, racism gained no influence on John Wooden as he grew into his teens, and you will see in interviews that follow numerous examples of Wooden fighting against it. The African-American population thinks enough of Wooden that in 1973 he was given the Whitney Young Urban League Award, presented by its then executive director, Vernon E. Jordan, Jr., who went on to become former president Bill Clinton's best friend. It was not and is not not just lip service by Wooden about equality, it was preached—more importantly, it was practiced. Coach gave an interview to *NOMMO*, a black newspaper in the 1970s, answering the question of his relationship with black players: "If you ask me right now how many black players we have on this year's team," Wooden said, "I could not answer that question. Of course, I can sit here and count the players on my fingers. What I mean is, color makes no difference to me. As long as they are a good citizen, a good student, and a good athlete, they have the opportunity to play for UCLA, regardless of color."

In a 1992 interview for this book, Wooden explained why racism never had a chance in his life.

One of the subjects that I found interesting is the color blindness that you had towards everyone. I'm interested to know how and why you had such feelings given that Indiana in the early twenties had a lot of racism and the Ku Klux Klan was very active.

Well you couldn't help but be somewhat aware of it. My father tried to teach us that no one is better than anybody else.

It's my understanding that to this day there has been only one black family ever in Martinsville.

When I was going to high school I only knew of two. There were two and they had no family. They were just individuals. One was Hobo Mitchell. I don't know what his first name was it—he was just Hobo Mitchell. He was in school and some say that he could have been the best athlete in school but he didn't participate. The other was Lionel Blankenship who worked around the barber shop cleaning up and shining shoes—a very nice person. Now at the particular time that I was there it never entered my mind that there were no other black people there. That never entered my mind at all, but I think that is because of my early environment.

Did you see many overt or subtle signs of racism?

Never! You are talking about my high school days now since I went to South Bend. Later on I saw it at my first teaching position. I never saw it through college at all, despite the fact there were hardly any black athletes. Then I took my first teaching job in Dayton, Kentucky and I definitely saw it there. Some parents weren't going to let one of my teams participate against a team in Cincinnati because they had black athletes. I just said, "They don't participate here they don't participate at all." They were through as far as I am concerned as long as I am the coach. I saw it then and I saw it in other things in Northern Kentucky and South Bend. I never saw any in Northern California but taking my team South, playing at Washington one time, and when I had one or two black players on my team at that time we couldn't go in a restaurant with them so I wouldn't eat at all there. So I saw it. I even saw it at Indiana State. I took the first black player to ever play in what was known then as the NAIA Tournament in Kansas City. About four or five years later the two teams that played for the champion were all black. I had some problems with that. I refused the invitation my first year at Indiana State because he couldn't go and it wasn't because he didn't help the team because he was probably the twelfth man on a twelve man squad. But, I felt that everybody had to be treated alike, and then the next year I refused again. [The NAIA relented and] our team was invited back and we did extremely well that year . . . and though the NAACP and his parents felt it would be good that we did go, he couldn't stay with us at the hotel in Kansas City. He stayed with the minister and his wife and he ate with us. However, we had to eat in a private room but we usually did that anyway so that wasn't particularly a problem as far as our meals were concerned, but he couldn't stay with us in the hotel at night. [In 2000, Wooden told an interviewer that "three years later a whole black team won that one. They're still mad at me."] So I experienced it before and here I experienced it when I took the first black player to Kentucky and I saw the treatment that black players received when we played at Duke, and I saw it in Houston. Pete Blackman [see interview that follows] said something about it in Houston. He was very funny; he left something on the blackboard where we stayed: "They laid me out on the rack and only half my name is black."

At UCLA there were Johnny Moore and Willie Naulls. You had to find them housing in the Jewish fraternity in Westwood.

That's correct! At that particular time. But a lot of strides have been made since then. Not as much as there should have been, but there were a lot of good strides.

You don't believe Martinsville was particularly racist when you were there?

I never saw it if it was there. I didn't see it. No! I never saw it. I never saw a sign or action toward the two. Well I hope I mentioned I wasn't there.

You didn't hear disparaging remarks?

Never!

About black people?
Never! Never! Never!

And you weren't aware of the KKK then?
I heard rumors—while I was there, there was a lynching. The KKK involved in Marion, Indiana. There were lots of things in the paper about that. That's about the only thing that I remember about the KKK in Indiana.

Where is Marion?
It's quite a ways from Martinsville. [It's 107 miles north of Martinsville.]

In 2000, Wooden was asked of what he was most proud. He replied, "After we'd won a national championship game, a reporter asked one of my players (Curtis Rowe) what kind of racial problems we had on the team. The player looked at the reporter and said, 'You don't know our coach, do you? He doesn't see color, he sees ballplayers.' And he turned and walked away. That's what I'm proud of."

In the 1980s, at one of his talks on the Pyramid of Success at Carnegie State College in Nebraska, Wooden was asked who was harder to coach, black or white athletes? Steve Nester, there that night, remembers Wooden "sat there and put his hand on his chin and smiled, and then all of a sudden said, 'Seniors,' to roaring applause."

Wooden's refusal to submit to or participate in any form of racial prejudice is one of the hallmarks of his life and career. Since the 1930s, in his quiet, determined way, by action and example—such as walking out en masse with high school teams of restaurants that discriminated, refusing to play in tournaments that would not allow athletes of color to play, by finding athletes housing in the 1950s segregated Westwood—Wooden stood his ground firmly and peacefully, Gandhi-like in his approach, the personification of Atticus Finch, the Southern small-town lawyer in *To Kill a Mockingbird*, who stood up to a crowd mentality. This awareness of, sensitivity to and rebellion against racism is his most heroic but least known contribution to sport, indeed America and the world.

Basketball was slow to integrate. Although African-American athletes eventually came to dominate the sport, it was a long, hard road. Don Barksdale, from UCLA, played on the 1948 U.S. Olympic team, but there were no athletes of color on the 1952 squad. The Big-Ten, southern and southwestern schools resisted integration, though the rest of the conferences, became more open in the 1950s, but white schools did not recruit black high schools during that era. In 1957, legend Wilt Chamberlain was subjected to a burning cross on a vacant lot across from where he stayed in Dallas for the NCAA Western Regionals.

According to the definitive work on race relations in sport, Arthur Ashe's *Hard Road to Glory* (1988), these coaches, besides Wooden, deserve our respect and gratitude for their respect and openness to having black players: Dean Smith at North Carolina, Bobby Knight at Indiana, Al Maguire of Marquette, and Denny Crum of Louisville.

Wooden was fortunate to come to UCLA to where he could promote his goal not just of racial harmony, but equality and acceptance, as that institution was the first in its conference to play integrated teams in varsity sports. Baseball great Jackie Robinson played at UCLA, going on to become the first African-American to play professional baseball, breaking the color barrier in 1947 when he played for the Brooklyn Dodgers. UCLA is likewise proud of Ralph Bunche, who played football, baseball and basketball during the 1920s, graduating summa cum laude and as valedictorian. Bunche achieved fame as a U.S. diplomat who served as under-secretary general of the United Nations and won the Nobel Peace Prize for his successful negotiation of armistice agreements between Israel and four Arab states. In 1949, Sherrill Luke was elected as the first black student body president of UCLA. Racial acceptance could prosper and be promoted at UCLA during this period, but Los Angeles and the United States had a long way to go. "Restrictive covenants" in deeds that were racially discriminatory were outlawed by the United States Supreme Court in 1948 in Shelley v. Kramer, but court orders do not erase years of imbued intolerance, and Los Angeles then and now suffers, as all urban cities do, from racism.

Wooden had no players of color his first two years, and only one, Bobby Pounds, in the 1950-51 season. The following season there were two black players, the next year one, the next year two, and thereafter, from 1954 until Wooden's retirement in 1975, there were always three to four African-American players on each 13-15 man squad. By 1963, in conformity with University of California policy, UCLA was not playing Deep South teams because it would not allow segregation to be practiced against its teams,

Because Wooden played integrated teams as soon as he got to UCLA, other universities in the NCAA had to likewise do so if they wanted to successfully compete. Other great coaches of the day and those who preceded him, Adolph Rupp of Kentucky in particular, fielded only white teams and resisted integration, playing black athletes only when it became impossible not to do so and then not in the same numbers as would Wooden.

One clear example occurred in 1966 for the NCAA national championship, when Texas Western University (now University of Texas at El Paso), an all black team, trounced Adolph Rupp's Kentucky 72-65. Among the black community, the University of Kentucky was known as the "Blue Grass Bigots." For its part, Texas Western had an enrollment of 250 blacks out of 10,000, and school athletic officials referred to the former by the "n" word and were astounded when they sought better conditions. Sadly, as of 1980, only 20 percent of those African-Americans who went on to play for the NBA graduated from college. Through the 1960s, a quota system was in place to ensure that there weren't too many dark faces on pro teams.

Rupp coached the Kentucky Wildcats from 1930-72, winning four national championships, and twenty-seven Southeastern Conference (SEC) championships with a win percentage of 82.2 percent. He was at best indifferent to racism, but most probably was racist, given various reported incidents of his having used the "n" word and having made racist comments in private. He did not allow a black athlete on his team until 1970. He certainly did not do anything volitionally to integrate basketball as Wooden so valiantly did. His bedside manner was abrupt, if not downright nasty. Bill Spivey, a Kentucky star in the 1950s, told the *Atlanta Journal and Constitution* in 1997, that "Rupp wanted everybody to hate him and he succeeded. He called us names some of us had never heard before."

Former player Tommy Kron told the *Detroit Free Press* in 1996 that "Adolph would never allow himself to get close to the players. He was a tough-guy kind of guy who would verbally abuse his players to get them to play harder." (The most unpleasant athlete in any team sport—no one approaches fighter-biter Mike Tyson as an individual athlete—was baseball great Ty Cobb, as misanthropic and difficult as he was terrific at hitting and stealing bases with his reputed sharpened spikes so as to cause intentional injury. Tommy Lee Jones portrays him in all his nastiness in 1994's *Cobb*.)

College basketball did not begin to integrate in the ACC (Atlantic Coast Conference), SEC and old Southeastern Conference until 1965, with some schools resisting until 1972. Consider this sad list of racism detailing when the following institutions first allowed African-Americans to play: Houston (1965-66, which team starred Don Chaney and Elvin Hayes, the latter who was chiefly responsible for beating UCLA in the so-called Game of the Century at the Astrodome in 1968); Maryland (1965-66); Duke (1966-67); Texas Christian (1966-67); Baylor (1967-68); North Carolina (1967-68); Vanderbilt (1967-68); Wake Forest (1967-68); Arkansas (1968-69); North Carolina State (1968-69); Texas (1968-69); Auburn (1969-70); Rice (1969-70); Texas Tech (1969-70); Alabama (1970-71); Clemson (1970-71); Georgia (1970-71); South Carolina (1970-71); Florida (1971-72); Louisiana State (1971-72); Mississippi (1971-72), Tennessee (1971-72); Texas A&M (1971-72); Virginia (1971-72) and

Mississippi State (1972-73). The foregoing is hard evidence that racism was a very big problem at many very big schools. But not for Wooden and other coaches, administrators and athletic directors of like-mind, that bloc would not have been broken until much later, and Wooden was a general in that war to promote peace, love, and understanding

Conservative in his dress, manner, style, and politics but far in front of the rest of his contemporaries when it came to promoting racial integration and equality, Wooden has had a strong, enduring impact on the values concerning race of those he coached and encountered. Wooden's living what his conscience dictated has been a life-changing example that instilled and fortified in his players the same humanistic unprejudiced approach at the core of Wooden's psyche. This leadership against racism also welded and melded individuals into teams that fought not just on the court, but anywhere the integrity of the team was challenged and forged friendships that have lasted lifetimes. Wooden sometimes got hate mail for his stance against racism, which did not deter him. Another measure of the man is that Wooden has never trumpeted his courageous, and in retrospect, heroic conduct, a contributing factor as to why Wooden's activities in this regard have been virtually unreported until now.

Consider the by-product of Wooden's love for fellow man, and what it did for him; not only did it help him produce winning teams, but this love spread throughout the teams he coached, and to competitors' teams.

PURDUE

In 1928, Wooden entered Purdue University in Indiana, then and today a top university located in West Lafayette, about ninety miles north of Martinsville. During the next four years, he worked to support himself hashing (serving food) at fraternities, waiting tables, selling concessions (sandwiches, apples, doughnuts and cigarettes) on trains and taping the ankles of football players. He also wrote copy and sold ads for Purdue's basketball program, hiring others to hawk them. Of course, he played varsity basketball, and graduated an honor student with the best grades of any player in the Big-Ten.

He says today, in 2002, that "I'm more proud that I'm in the Academic Hall of Fame than I am in the Basketball Hall of Fame. I earned that. [Having been inducted into] the Basketball Hall of Fame, I had some great players with me and great coaches and as a coach I had great players." His academic record is indeed phenomenal, 19th in a class of 4,675, putting him in the top one-half of 1 percent of his class, graduating with degrees in English and physical education, all while working to support himself through school, and becoming the finest player of basketball in the nation. He was an All-American basketball player each of his three years and in 1932, the year he graduated, was voted Player of the Year, the best athlete in college basketball. As an athlete, Wooden was renowned for his determination, aggressiveness and superb conditioning. He was nicknamed "The Indiana Rubber Man" because of his gutsy style of play, which often had him bouncing off of fans and floors. Wooden led the Purdue Boilermakers to the Big-Ten and NCAA championship in 1931-32, with a 17-1 record. His team won the Big-Ten crown the year before. With 15 points per game, Wooden set the record for points scored during his senior year. Wooden was the captain of both teams. During his sophomore year, Purdue kept its opponents to scores under 20 per game, while averaging 42 for its team.

Ben Miller, who played for Indiana University at Bloomington, remembers Wooden having "uncanny speed. He was built low, with a center of gravity close to the floor, and he had a change of pace and direction that was remarkable. He was hard to guard."

Doyal Plunkett, from the University of Iowa had similar experiences. "If we got close out on the floor, he'd go around us," he said. "If we didn't get close he'd shoot over our heads. As a guard, John Wooden was the best we've ever had, and one of the smartest. He wasn't a big person, but for his athletic ability, he was probably number one. I remember when I was guarding him one time and I was staying close to him. He could shoot the long shot and go around me before I ever knew where he had gone. He was such a fast dribbler and passer and shooter, and on defense he would just stall around the player. He's probably the fastest dribbler that I ever knew."

His brother, "Cat," in 1980, described Wooden's abilities to Marv Dunphy who was writing his thesis for a doctorate in education on Wooden. "John was not particularly fast, he wasn't a sprint champion, but they couldn't guard him. He was very quick and a split second is worth more than all the speed in the world. He was good on defense, an excellent dribbler, and very competitive, but his chief stock in trade was his change of pace."

Kenneth Watson, four years younger than Wooden, grew up in Martinsville, and remembers that when Wooden "was in college, he had a very unusual thing he did. He would drive down to the foul circle, and he'd change directions, cause he's like a cat anyway. He would change directions and go either way and he could confuse everybody. That's where he got a lot of his fouls, and lots of shots, changing his direction there real quick at the foul circle because he was very fast, and he was a good ball handler with it."

Watson confirms that Wooden was "our ideal" and "hero" for any aspiring basketball player in Martinsville. "To the people of my generation, John Wooden means a lot . . . He was a real role model to me and the people of my generation. He never let us down. He never did anything that anybody would have to apologize for."

Wooden was idolized as a player then, just as today's star athletes are. Wooden is today regarded as one of the one hundred greatest players in the history of basketball according to the 1997 Naismith Memorial Basketball Hall of Fame book on the subject.

Commenting on his own abilities, Wooden said in 1980, "It's hard to be objective but I think I had good quickness and was able to control my quickness, I also felt that due to the models that I had when I was a youngster I possessed the necessary emotional balance."

Wooden also holds the dubious distinction of being hospitalized every year on Christmas Day during his years at Purdue. As a freshman, he contracted scarlet fever, as a sophomore he hurt his leg in an "argument with a truck," in his junior year, while practicing, he hit a loose board and hurt his leg, and as a senior he had his tonsils removed.

Wooden wistfully describes the road that took him to coaching. "I was raised on a farm in Southern Indiana. There wasn't much to do, so we'd take one of mother's old cotton socks and sew it up and fill it with rags and make a basketball out of it. That's when I first started playing—with a peach basket up against the barn door and I just got interested in it. We had a grade school basketball team and baseball team and they've always remained my favorites, although I like them all. I had a little God-given talent: quickness, which I feel is the most important ability a player must have. And I liked it. . .

"I went to high school eight miles south of the farm where I lived. After high school, I went to Purdue, but there were no athletic scholarships at the time. I wanted to be a civil engineer, and Purdue was a fine engineering school. But I had to work in the summers, too, and in civil engineering you had to go to summer school and summer camp all three summers between the freshman, sophomore and junior years. I found that out at the end of the freshman year. So I changed to the School of Forestry and found out that you had to go to summer ranger camp, so I decided to take a teaching course and major in English, which I did, with no intention of getting into coaching. It wasn't until maybe the upper division in my junior or senior year that I began to thinking about teaching and coaching. Coach Lambert was the one who counseled me to consider physical education and I took all my electives in that area. I followed his advice and from that time on I started keeping a notebook on coaching."

From this point forward, Wooden was a vacuum for knowledge on the fundamentals and techniques of coaching. He never stopped learning as much as he could about his chosen profession, and was constantly updating, examining and investigating. By the time he coached his first high school team, he was thoroughly grounded in the fundamentals of coaching as well as playing.

"Upon graduation, I almost stayed at Purdue," Wooden said. "I became good friends with the head of the English department . . . and he wanted me to stay on with a fellowship and turn into a college English teacher. But Nellie said, 'If you do that we would have to postpone getting married for awhile.' So we got married. I took a coaching and teaching job where I coached football, basketball, baseball and track and taught five English classes a day and I was director of athletics."

TEACHING AND COACHING

John and Nellie became engaged during the spring semester of his senior year, and their marriage on August 8, 1932 was a near disaster. Wooden had lost his life savings, $909.05, a few days before because of a bank failure. Fortunately, a family friend lent them enough to start their life.

Unable because of the Depression to find work in Indiana, Wooden's first position was in Dayton, Kentucky. "They didn't have coaches in my day," he said. "I was hired as a teacher. You coached because you loved it. I was an English teacher. All the coaches I knew in my day all taught. Today, I think they should all teach. They would have a better concept that would help deflate some egos and give them a better standing on the faculties and a better understanding on why the youngsters are there to begin with. I think they'd do a better job coaching because coaching is teaching, nothing more."

That first season was Wooden's only losing season as a coach (six wins, eleven losses). He never had a losing season as a player. During this period, showing remarkable energy and stamina, Wooden (along with his brother Cat) also played professional basketball throughout the Midwest—it was really semi-pro—for such teams as the Kautsky Grocers of Indianapolis and the Hammond Professional Basketball Team. The circuit, restricted to weekend play, included Sheboygan and Oshkosh, Wisconsin; Pittsburgh, Pennsylvania; Heron, Montana; and Detroit, Michigan. Wooden once successfully completed 138 free throws without a miss, which probably still stands as a professional record. John Wooden made fifty dollars a game, and once got a hundred dollar bonus when he hit one hundred free throws. He scored 67 points in one game for the Kautskys, led the nascent National Basketball League (NBL) in scoring during his first year (1932-33), and was the second highest scorer two seasons later still playing for the Kautsky's in the MidWest Basketball Conference. Two years later, again in the NBL, he was the second highest scorer for the Whiting, Indiana team.

South Bend, Indiana, 137 miles north of Indianapolis, is most famous for being the home of Notre Dame University. In 1934, Wooden went to work for the South Bend school district, teaching and coaching at South Bend Central High School, and continuing to play professional basketball. (Brother Cat also coached high school basketball, his teams playing three games against brother John, but they decided it wasn't a good idea to compete against each other, and Cat gave that up.) His load included teaching English classes; being the comptroller; and coaching, as an assistant, basketball, baseball and tennis. In 1937 he became head coach and took the high school team, the Bears, who were getting whipped by everybody, to the top. In 1938, they were ranked number one in the state. During one stretch, they built up a thirty-game win streak against four traditional rivals. When you get to the South Bend interviews later in this book, many of those whom he affected will testify to the incredible impact he made on their lives.

One story of those days sticks in the memory of Ed Powell, who played under him at South Bend Central High. "One of the starters—and the son of the vice-principal—had missed the team bus for a game, though he eventually made it to the venue prior to its start. He did not play, and though his team won, it would have done so easily had he been involved. Wooden was called into the vice-principal's office the next day. "We really thought he was going to catch it," Powell relates, "but the vice-principal just wanted to shake John's hand for teaching his son a lesson. He appreciated Coach Wooden's actions because he could handle everybody else in school, but he couldn't handle his own son."

Wooden throughout his career was constantly on the prowl to learn all he could about coaching. "In those years I talked with as many coaches as I could about basketball and coaching in general," Wooden related in 1980. "I talked with Dr. Carlson, the great coach from Pittsburgh, and I remember Frank Leahy letting me observe his practices. I was teaching in South Bend when he got the football coaching job at Notre Dame. I got acquainted with him and he invited me to attend his practices, which was almost unheard of. He wouldn't even let football coaches attend his practices. I learned [a] considerable [amount] about practice organization, which was important to him. Everything was right down to the detail, and my practices became more that way after observing him."

During this first year of teaching at South Bend Central High in 1934, at the age of twenty-four, Wooden began working on the Pyramid of Success. He began thinking about the issue of success when one of his teachers, Lawrence J. Shidler, a math teacher at Martinsville High School, asked his students for their definition of success, and suggested that the appropriate answer was not the attaining of prestige or material wealth, but peace of mind from doing your best.

THE JOHN WOODEN PYRAMID OF SUCCESS

Glenn Curtis, who Wooden played under at Martinsville High School, used what he called *A Ladder of Achievement*, to inspire teams and Wooden incorporated five elements from that into his Pyramid. The Pyramid would undergo many evolutions over the next fourteen years until it reached its final form. It was designed to help Wooden become a better teacher, and to assist his students and their parents in understanding that grades were not the only indicia of gauging self-worth. The Pyramid was created solely by John Wooden, but he lists as influences the great philosophers. He admits to having read or been influenced by the teachings of motivational pioneer Dale Carnegie and the Rev. Norman Vincent Peale, who was a nationally known Protestant minister famed for his television and radio broadcasts, but the Pyramid is an original, not derivative, work. A deeply religious Christian, Wooden has always been active in church.

HEROES

Wooden's heroes are the great poets of history: Scott, Tennyson, Shelley, Byron, Coleridge, Poe, Whittier, Whitman, Longfellow, Shakespeare and Saint Francis of Assisi. Asked about T.S. Eliot, Wooden once said, "I am not fond of the modern poets." His favorite American is Abraham Lincoln, and he quotes him more than anyone else.

When asked in 1992 whether he believes that man by nature is inherently good, Wooden replied affirmatively, "My favorite American, Abraham Lincoln, said 'It is better to trust and be disappointed occasionally than to distrust and be miserable all the time.'" Why is Lincoln his favorite American? "For statements of that sort and statements like: 'The worst thing you could do for those you love are the things they could and should do for themselves.' 'Most anyone can handle adversity, but to test a person's character give them power.' For saying, 'Am I not getting rid of an enemy when I make him a friend.'"

He greatly admired Helen Keller, who was an American hero for leading a productive life despite being blind and deaf, and he read what she wrote. (The movie and play, *The Miracle Worker*, are about Keller's life.) A picture of Mother Teresa, whom he says is his favorite person, is framed in his home. Asked in 2002, who he would invite to a dinner party, Wooden wished for Christ, Mother Teresa, and Lincoln.

Four men have influenced him the most in his life. The first is his father. Next is Earl M. Warriner, his grade school principal and first coach, whom you'll meet in the interview section of the book, and whom Wooden credits for "instilling a sense of motivation."

Wooden wrote of Warriner in 1966, at the dedication of Pauley Pavilion, that, "There were no 'stars' or privileged few in his eyes. Everyone was given the treatment that he or she earned and deserved. He would not compromise his principles for the sake of convenience. He recognized the right to a difference of opinion and was man enough to admit being wrong without rationalization or alibi. He commanded respect.

"From him, as much as anyone else," Wooden said in 1980, "I got the idea of not having stars and importance of togetherness. Through his consistency and the principles that he stood for, he earned our respect."

Wooden's next mentor and hero, chronologically, is Glenn Curtis, his high school basketball coach, whom he describes as a "brilliant fundamentalist, psychologist and handler of young men. He had a tremendous talent for inspiring individuals and teams to rise to great heights. He demanded perfection in the execution of fundamentals and was a master strategist." Wooden recounts, in his autobiography, walking off the Martinsville basketball team his sophomore year because he believed Curtis had wrongly sided with a young man with whom Wooden had engaged in fisticuffs. Wooden was also resentful that Curtis had not played his older brother, Cat, when he was on the team, which Wooden believed was a mistake. They made up, obviously, and Wooden says in his book that "this incident accounts for the fact that throughout my coaching career I tried to understand the young men who stood up to me. That's why I listened to their side, and why I almost always took back a boy who had walked off the team." Wooden loves poetry, and Curtis would sometimes quote some to make a point, which further solidified their bond.

Wooden praises Ward "Piggy" Lambert, his basketball coach at Purdue, as "one of the truly great coaches in the history of the game, he was considerably ahead of his time. . . Although he was a fierce competitor while a game was in progress, he was a man of very high principles and refused to swerve from what he believed to be right regardless of potential personal gain, recognition or glory.

"I probably got most of my ideas about basketball and coaching [from him]," Wooden said in 1980, adding, "He was also a great motivator, but in a different way than Curtis. He believed in the individual technique. It was amazing how much he did by just talking to you for twenty seconds." Wooden, in his autobiography, wrote that Lambert "always had options, as he never wanted to take away a man's initiative; he merely wanted to direct it within the bounds of his attack."

Wooden remembers Lambert, saying, "he noticed the little things that make the difference between a great player and an ordinary one. I think I learned my attention to detail from him. He was also a man of very high moral caliber, very honest. He believed in a day's work for day's pay."

THE JOHN WOODEN PYRAMID OF SUCCESS

After the outbreak of World War II, Wooden enlisted in the Navy; was commissioned a Lieutenant, junior grade; and assigned as a fitness officer training combat pilots. Due to a ruptured appendix, he missed the first ship on which he was to have sailed. The man who replaced him died in a kamikaze attack, which nearly destroyed the ship. Old friend and former assistant coach Ed Powell kids Wooden that he must not have been much of a sailor as he used to refer to "parking the boat" instead of "docking the ship." Wooden suffered a back injury during the war, which occurred when he fell playing basketball, and since then he has walked with a slight stoop to his five-foot-ten, 180-pound frame. Due to the war, Wooden was unable to keep up his house payments and lost it.

Wooden returned to South Bend at the end of 1945, and to Central High the following January. All told, Wooden spent eleven years coaching high school basketball before moving in 1946 to Indiana State Teachers' College (now Indiana State University), in Terre Haute, where he began to coach the basketball team. He left a distinguished high school coaching record in his wake, winning 218, losing 42, for a percentage of 83.9.

According to Wooden, "Had it not been for World War II, I would never have left South Bend, I'm quite certain, but while I was away in the service, several things happened. The main thing is I lost my home. When I came back, we just couldn't find an appropriate place to live and get located. Then I wasn't happy about the way that I felt the community school system, which I had been just practically in love with before I went in the service, was treating some of my friends—returning service men—who had been coaches. I had no complaint about myself. They were wonderful to me and everything came back just as they said it would when I left, but some good friends didn't get their coaching jobs back. Those were war times. In most cases they didn't get their jobs back, they gave them a teaching job, but they wanted to coach. I didn't like them treating people that way and I went to bat for a couple of very good friends of mine who were in the coaching professions, and said if they didn't do that, I didn't want to stay and work for them. I had opportunities at two very fine high schools in Indiana, in cities that I thought a lot of, and they had huge high school gymnasiums. While I was thinking about which one to take, my high school coach, who'd gone on to Indiana State, left to take a pro job and the president wanted me to take his place. So I decided, 'Well, shucks, since I've decided I'm leaving South Bend, I'll try college. If I do well, I'll get opportunities at other places. And if I don't do well, I have a lifetime superintendent/principal/English teacher's license and there are other things I can do.' I never worried about not having a job or anything. That didn't bother me. So I took it there and then. Purdue tried very hard to get me, but I didn't like the way they were treating the man I was replacing, so I decided I didn't want to go for them."

During his stint at Indiana State, Wooden earned a graduate degree in education, writing his thesis on poetry. He greatly enjoyed his time there. Indiana State won the conference in 1946, the first season Wooden coached, and thereby qualified for the NAIA (National Association of Intercollegiate Athletics) tournament in Kansas City, then the preeminent championship for smaller colleges, but as previously discussed, Wooden refused to let the team compete because blacks were not permitted to play, another courageous stance against racism. [The first important championship "league" was the National Invitational Tournament (NIT), which was established in 1937 by national sportswriters, its tournament held in Madison Square Garden in New York City. The NCAA (National Collegiate Athletic Association) was established in 1938 at Northwestern University, but it was not until the late 1940s that it became the preeminent league and championship contest.]

The NAIA relented and the next year blacks were allowed to play. Indiana State went to the tournament, and Wooden with his team broke the color barrier, and were runners-up for the tournament. Because Indiana State won its conference that second season as well, Wooden was in great demand as a coach. Wooden was ready to move because he wanted to coach at the Big-Ten level. Purdue offered him the job if he would wait another year, but he didn't like the way Purdue was handling the situation as they could change their mind the next year. The University of Minnesota and the University of California at Los Angeles (UCLA) both tendered positions. UCLA had offered the job to Wooden's friend, Branch McCracken, then the coach at Indiana University. McCracken declined, and recommended Wooden to Wilbur Johns, athletic director of UCLA.

Dutch Fehring, a former teammate from Purdue and then football line coach at UCLA, suggested Wooden, as also did Bob Kelly, the broadcaster for the professional football team, the Los Angeles Rams, who had seen Wooden's magic at South Bend Central High, so the offer was made.

Wooden intended to accept the Minnesota position, but due to a snowstorm that delayed the contact to whom he was to convey his acceptance of the Minnesota offer, he ended up accepting the UCLA offer and signed a contract for three years. Fate brought Wooden, at age thirty-seven, west, though for him, Indiana will always be home. "I have never been comfortable, I guess I could put it that way, with the big cities," he said. "Having been raised and born on a farm in a little town, I feel at home, more comfortable there. I'd say I'm far more recognizable in Indiana even now, and I left there to come here in '48. It's because they're so nutty about basketball."

THE JOHN WOODEN PYRAMID OF SUCCESS

Wooden offers this comment about the mania for basketball in Indiana. "If you go back to the origin of basketball, and high school basketball in particular, at one time there were dozens of high school gymnasiums in the state that seated more than any college gymnasiums in the country. There was a time that Amos Alonzo Stagg held a national high school tournament, but they wouldn't let Indiana high school teams in. They could send their so-called 'B' teams, but they were just too far advanced over others." Wooden believes his fellow Hoosiers are somewhat over the top regarding basketball. "You don't think so at the time when you're going through it, but you when you look back and reflect on it, I'd say it's out of line, taking it all that seriously. After all, it's still just a game." He continues, observing that when he was in high school, "everything shut up when there was a game. Every kid in high school had to get a season ticket for the basketball games. They were given to the homeroom teachers who were responsible for the payment of the number of season tickets for everyone in their room. Now they couldn't all pay, so they'd arrange pie socials or box socials or cookie sales to raise money, and some of the people who could pay more would pay extra. But imagine doing something like that in a California high school. It'd be impossible. I don't think they do it back in Indiana now, not that they're still not crazy about it."

UCLA

Although Wooden decided on UCLA, "there was no allure. They'd never won a conference championship and didn't have a good facility," Wooden told *Indiana Sports Weekly* in 1982. "There were things about UCLA that had I known about at the time, I wouldn't have gone. For instance, I was paid by the student body." UCLA was, however, a class act as institutions go. It, and the Berkeley campus, were the jewels of the University of California.

The Southern Branch of the University of California commenced operations in September of 1919, opening on Vermont Avenue, about four miles west of downtown Los Angeles, and offered two years instruction in Letters and Science and four years in the Teacher's College. The first year's enrollment was 1,338, with women outnumbering men six to one. In 1927, the school was officially renamed the University of California at Los Angeles, and its nickname went from the Grizzlies to the Bruins. That year it joined the Pacific Coast Conference, where the bigger West Coast schools competed. The Westwood campus—located in the undeveloped rolling hills of Los Angeles, just seven miles east of the Pacific Ocean, was dedicated in March of 1930.

By the late 1950s, UCLA took only the most highly qualified students scholastically, and since then has been one of the top schools in the United

States. The University of California has widely been considered as the finest state-run university system in America since the 1960s. UC-Berkeley and Stanford University are the only West Coast schools in the same league as UCLA. UCLA is today one of the top ten research universities in the nation: thirty-one of its Ph.D. programs are ranked in the top twenty in their field— third best in the country; since the 1960s, UCLA has usually been ranked in the top universities in America. Its destiny to become a major intellectual institution was a major motivating influence on Wooden's decision, he recollected in 1991. "I felt that it was going to be a fine university from the educational point of view, which was probably one of the reasons that I accepted the opportunity to go there, because I didn't foresee it being any basketball power at all," he said. "And yet I was hired as a basketball coach, when I could have gone to other places where I thought basketball would be held in much higher esteem." Wooden knew he had to start from scratch with that program, but "I didn't mind that . . . Never in my life have I felt pressured about a job. I think I can go get a job. I always felt that I could get a job. I had a lifetime teacher/administrative license. I often had many offers with businesses for far more money than I could ever make in teaching, which I never would accept, but that may be one of the reasons that I never worried about win/loss records or anything."

The young married Woodens found Southern California more than a bit intimidating. Nell Wooden was quoted as saying, "We got on the Pasadena freeway, and it almost scared us to death. We'd never seen a freeway before. I remember John getting all upset and saying. 'What are we doing here anyway?'"

Starting with a team that the press predicted would finish last in the 1948-49 season, UCLA won its Pacific Coast Conference the first season that Wooden coached, finishing with the finest season UCLA had ever had. UCLA was undefeated on its home court, winning 13; the Associated Press placed them 15th in the nation. The following season, UCLA again finished first in its division and won the conference title. At the end of his second year at UCLA, Wooden considered accepting a position at Purdue, but decided to stay, even though the UCLA administration gave him permission to break his three-year contract. Purdue flew three executives to pitch him with a higher salary and blueprints for a pavilion to be built that would seat 20,000, a family membership in a country club, a new car every year, a home on campus, and a large insurance policy,

"I agreed to go back to Purdue providing I could be released graciously from my contract out here," Wooden admitted in 1972. "I have never been one to break contracts and I didn't want to create trouble . . . It was back home and

THE JOHN WOODEN PYRAMID OF SUCCESS

[I] was not here long enough really to become sold on California."

After the NCAA tournament that second season, Wooden asked to meet with the two men who had hired him, Wilbur Johns, director of athletics, and William Ackerman, executive director of the ASUCLA, the entity (the student body) that had hired him. They in turn requested that Wooden bring his wife because "they knew what I wanted to talk about."

"So I explained the situation to them—that I thought it was a much better area for basketball back there, and that when I came out here, I was led to believe, not promised, led to believe, that there would be a place to play on campus within three years." In 2002, Wooden confirmed that UCLA had even shown him plans for a new pavilion on campus that would be ready within two years. "Now, I had been here two years and there was not the least sign of a place to play on campus. I could see the handwriting on the wall, the number of stumbling blocks towards getting one. I thought it would be difficult to do as well as I would like to do without a home place." Johns and Ackerman "pointed out that I was the one who had insisted on a three-year contract and felt I should honor it," Wooden has recounted. "They made me feel like a heel for even considering leaving."

"We thought you were an honorable person and we expected you to live up to it as we would live up to it. But if you insist on pulling out, we will permit you," Johns and Ackerman told him.

"I was irritated to say the least. Though I understood their position at the time, I thought it was unfair," Wooden remembered in 1972. "I wasn't very happy about it and I am ashamed to say it is true. But I fulfilled my contract. At the time, in the back of my mind, I said 'Yes, I'll fulfill it; then I'll probably fly the coop.'"

In 1991, Wooden explained how difficult those times were. "My biggest problem with UCLA, what people don't understand, was for seventeen years we didn't have a home court in a sense. Yet we won our first two national championships under those adverse conditions. Conditions were very difficult, and I almost left after my three-year contract ran up because I had been led to believe that we were going to have a place to play by the time of my third year of the contract. And I could see that it wasn't coming. We eventually got it after seventeen years."

Wooden had other reasons for staying at UCLA other than his contractual relations. He liked working with athletic director Wilbur Johns and his staff, saying in 1991, that "Primarily, after being here three years, I didn't want to take my children and move them again to another school or back to another area of the country. We had become a little bit settled by that time, and so I stayed without at the time feeling that there was any great future as far as basketball was concerned." In 1972, Wooden acknowledged that he'd had offers from "just about every school in the Big-Ten and all over, but after about [my first] three years I sort of had the attitude that I'll stay as long as they want me."

The initial period after Wooden's move to Los Angeles was not glamorous. "My first four years at UCLA, I worked in the mornings at a dairy from six to noon, then I'd come into UCLA," he said. "Why did I do it? Because I needed the money. I was a dispatcher of truck in the San Fernando Valley and was a troubleshooter. After all the trucks made their deliveries and came back, I would call in the next day's orders, sweep out the place and head over the hill to UCLA."

Wooden is one of the major reasons basketball caught on in Southern California, and in 1956 he knew it was going to happen, advising UCLA Sports Information Director Vic Kelley for a press release:

> *I don't see how it can miss. This is an outstanding sports community. In addition, from the spectator point of view, virtually no sport can compare with basketball. It has great continuous action, it's played with a large ball that's easy to follow, the fans are seated closer to the action, and the game is such that the "uninitiated" can understand it readily. It's fun for the fans because of the closeness and the fans have a good opportunity to get to know the players personally, as it were. I believe no game has quite the interest.*

In another draft of the press release, Wooden argued that "basketball is one of the fastest of all games ever devised. Hockey is the only game that's faster. Also it's played on a comparatively small area where all the action can be seen easily." Wooden also noted that in every other section of the country except Southern California, the sport has wide acceptance to both men and women and by folks of all ages. Further, Wooden pointed out that basketball games are completed in a comparatively short length of time compared to football, baseball, golf, or tennis, yet it holds a lot of suspense because of the action. Finally, Wooden pointed out that "basketball is a game in which the underdog has a better chance than in most all other sports. Teams won't run as to true to form as in other activities." Thus, Wooden asserted "because of the speed, timing and split-second teamwork that's needed, basketball is the most unpredictable of all human sports." Wooden's words explain the essence of the attraction of basketball for him and fans everywhere.

In 1972, Wooden said, "People recognized from the beginning that our style of play was a little different. It was more entertainment. That's not necessarily to say it was better, but it was definitely more entertainment. I think that's the way basketball should be."

In 1952, Wooden offered these insights into the game to Kelley:

I consider feet and legs just about the most important items in basketball. A performer can once in a while get by with other deficiencies but you can never be top player without strong feet and legs. Basketball is a game of running and you can't run faster than the next fellow if you have weaker limbs. The team that is in best condition usually wins. Even a team of lesser ability still has a good chance to win if it is in better condition than its opponent.

Wooden wrote a draft of a column on the Pyramid of Success in June of 1953, but there is no record it was ever published. It contains much of the lecture contained in the next chapter and these interesting asides:

[W]ho is a greater personification of self-control than National Open Golf Champ Ben Hogan? His emotions are under control at all times. In other words, he doesn't become over-exuberant and careless in his shot making. Nor does he become discouraged or angered when he misses a shot, only to give a half-hearted effort subsequently. He's whipped himself, so that now he can whip other competitors. And he has an almost fanatic concentration on his one purpose—to win. . .

In describing this Pyramid of Success, friends have asked me to name a few athletes I've known that I've considered as successes. Oddly enough, some are still in the continuing process, but they all possessed most or all of these attributes in great quantity.

I mentioned Hogan, possibly the greatest athletic competitor who ever lived. I'd also include Ty Cobb, despite the ideas of some folks who believe he was not a great team man. He must have been, however, since he realized that his team must win if he were going to win.

George Mikan was without peer in basketball. He would practice literally thousands of shots per day to perfect certain techniques. And, since he was inclined to put on weight, he had to work especially hard to stay in condition, something that took great moral and mental fortitude.

Between 1948 and 1964, UCLA never had a losing season, but the fans took their time arriving, and as late as 1952, even though Wooden was already being called the "Miracle Man," the 2,500 seat Men's Gym was only half full for home games. Wooden continued to refine his coaching methods. In 1956,

Wooden explained his technique, "On our team, the system is devised so that theoretically every man on the floor can have an equal number of scoring opportunities. If you can present a five-man good scoring team, it's awfully hard for the opponents to concentrate their defense on your strong point. On our UCLA team, the man or men who work hardest, who move quickest, who get open most and who are the hottest are the ones who are supposed to score the most. And the offense is designed to give each man the same chance. This also keeps the performers happy since they know they'll get the same opportunity their teammates get."

It took fifteen seasons under Wooden before UCLA achieved a national championship, but his teams were systematically improving. In the 1955-56 season, UCLA was undefeated in its conference, winning 17 consecutive victories in PCC competition, and including the previous year, 27 consecutive victories, attaining a conference record. The following year at the close of the season, UCLA broke more conference records, 34 consecutive victories in league play, and a 22-4 record, the best in UCLA history. [The PCC league was dissolved in 1959 and replaced by the Athletic Association of Western Universities (AAWU), which later added Washington State, Oregon and the University of Oregon, and thereafter was commonly referred to as the Pac-8.]

Still, despite his winning seasons in the conference, Wooden was not at his peak. He knew he needed to improve if he was to obtain his grail, the NCAA championship, and figured out why he was not where he believed he could be in terms of achievement. "A place to play, the things I had to do for practice, the fact that for a long time I never had even one full-time assistant, just had part-time assistants. All these things I permitted subconsciously I believe for a long time to prey on me and I had developed somewhat of a persecution complex," Wooden revealed in 1988. "I think I realized this about 1959 or '60. And I believe I changed, because I did admit it to myself and recognized it and I think our whole thing improved from that point on."

We learn a lesson here, the value of a positive mental attitude, that one must not let the fact that one does not have everything desired to accomplish a task stand in the way of success. Wooden did the best he had with what the opportunity presented to him. He wanted a nice stadium, he needed a full-time assistant, but he was coaching in the big leagues at one of the greatest universities in the world, and it was bound to improve. Wooden did not gripe or mope or permit himself to get self-defeated, he got on with the task. We all face similar situations in our lives. Wooden viewed obstacles in a positive light, as a challenge. The foregoing is an interesting admission by Wooden—that at one point his attitude was inappropriate. The attitude of the teacher must not be self-defeating. The teacher must be motivated, he has to believe he can "outscore his opponent," and he has to make do with what is presented. Problems are not hindrances but challenges to be met. Wooden had a "can do" attitude.

UCLA won its conference in the 1961-62 season, but lost in the NCAA semi-finals. Two years later, UCLA won the national championship and the UCLA dynasty began. The team was undefeated during that season despite the fact that it was a "short" team, the shortest of Wooden's ever to win the NCAA. Wooden's innovative utilization of the full-court press—a defense attack where the opponent is constantly pressured—was a visual, visceral, and exciting experience. When a player from the opposing team tried to pass in a ball from the sidelines, UCLA was closely "pressing" each player of the other team, so that they could not perform what was ordinarily routine. It would simply appear at times and paralyze the opposing team, while energizing the crowd.

In the 1963-64 semi-finals, against Kansas State, UCLA was down 75-70 with 7:28 to go. The zone press was put into operation causing three quick turnovers and accompanying baskets, along with a free throw, and three minutes later the Bruins had scored eleven points, leading ultimately to victory, 90-84. UCLA then faced Duke for the championship, where the press confounded a big team with two six-foot-ten players that at one point allowed sixteen points in just 2-1/2 minutes, for a final verdict of 98-83. It was breathless to take in, magic before everyone's eyes.

That victory closed out a perfect season, 30-0, and the dynasty was underway. Wooden says that team was his favorite because it came "as close as humanly possible to achieving its full potential." The records that year fell like rain, including: most points scored by a UCLA team in one season (2,866) and game average (88.9); most wins in one season as well as the most consecutive (30); most points scored in a NCAA playoff game (98 to Duke's 92), and the breaking of the scoring records at Stanford, Berkeley, and Washington State.

NORMAN AND THE FULL-COURT PRESS

The full-court press was reportedly first conceived by Coach Phog Allen of Kansas State in 1936, but was rarely used, and then only as a desperation measure. Lambert used a form of it at Purdue. Wooden had successfully implemented it at South Bend Central High and Indiana State. Pete Newell of the University of California at Berkeley refined it further in the 1950s, as you will read in his interview. The full-court press allowed UCLA to control the tempo of play, forcing errors by the other side. Prodded by his then-assistant, Jerry Norman, and based on techniques Wooden had learned from his Purdue coach, Ward "Piggy" Lambert, Wooden tried it because, "You've got to have imagination." In Wooden's mind, "You've got to try. The team that makes the most mistakes will probably win," he said, reiterating a phrase often stated by Lambert. Even though the press had worked in high school and at Indiana State, Wooden had been reluctant to use it at the Division I level. He now feels that reluctance was one of his greatest mistakes.

Norman, who was Wooden's first full-time assistant, believes he was not given due credit for the utilization of the press. Though Norman is unwilling to say so directly, it is evident from the tone of his interview that follows and from interviews conducted for this book with those who are close to Norman that he feels this way. But there are instances where Wooden clearly did, and publicly, credit Norman. In the February 5, 1969, *Los Angeles Times* article, "Bruins' Wooden Fought Against Installing Press," Wooden clearly credits Norman (who the year before had left coaching), stating that Wooden "decided to install the press after much prodding by his former assistant Jerry Norman. 'One of my greatest strengths is that I've had good assistant coaches. Jerry wasn't a 'yes man' by any means. We haggled for a long time over whether we should use the press.'" In his textbook, *Practical Modern Basketball*, Wooden also credits Norman for his work with Lewis Alcindor (now known as Kareem Abdul-Jabbar) and overall as an assistant coach.

Wooden is complimentary of Norman in *They Call Me Coach*, his autobiography, first published in 1973. It discusses Wooden's serious clashes with Norman as a player, whom he kicked off the team for insubordination. He accepted Norman back, and wrote that Norman was a "strong competitor, full of fire and drive, and with a great innate basketball sense. Jerry ultimately accomplished all the goals I had set for him . . . " In the book, Wooden praises Norman for having a "fine basketball sense and was an excellent recruiter," but does not credit Norman for the pressing defense. Instead, Wooden says, "I played the press at Purdue under Lambert. It wasn't a zone press, but it was a pressing defense with zone principles. At the time I didn't know of any other coach using it." Wooden concluded his comments on Norman by calling him a man of strength who had overcome obstacles, and was pleased to report that "he never uses profanity anymore," which is condescending to Norman, who denies ever being profane. [Former teammate and lifetime friend of Norman, Eddie Sheldrake, says Norman never used vulgarities.] The relationship between Wooden and Norman was at times tempestuous, but they clearly respected the other and got the job done. Like a great songwriting partnership that ran its course, they ultimately split up, but their records live on.

Relations between Wooden and Norman are strained. Norman does not visit with Wooden at UCLA games both attend; they are polite to each other when they interact. At a gathering of UCLA players in the summer of 2000, 150 former players, coaches, managers and their wives reminisced as the microphone was passed around to each table. Wooden spoke last and as he did Norman would not even look at his former boss. There are a handful of Norman supporters—mostly former UCLA players and equally fond of Wooden, who criticize—most not for attribution—what they perceive has been Wooden's failure to fairly acknowledge Norman's contributions to Wooden, in creating and refining the full-court press and for his recruiting efforts.

Norman must also be credited for being a superb recruiter. Bill Putnam, in 1980, confirmed that "Jerry became very interested in recruiting, did most of the work, and then John would step in and finalize."

Norman says that Wooden "was as good as anyone one-on-one."

In an interview for this book in 1991, Wooden was asked about lingering criticism by Norman's supporters, and the following exchange occurred:

I'm going to ask you a tough question. There's been criticism, some talk that you have not given perhaps sufficient credit to the people who helped you on the coaching staff. How do you react to that?

You surprised me a little by saying that—that's why I'm a little reluctant to answer.

You don't have to give an answer, and I'll ask you another time.

No, no. I'm trying to think of . . . as far as I know, I only had one who ever sort of indicated that. And that would have to be Jerry Norman. Jerry got a little upset one time at me . . . I never felt it was Jerry, I think he was influenced by somebody else, but he said after we lost to Houston in the Astrodome in 1968, that when we played them again, he wanted to go to a box and one defense if we ever played them again. And I said, "No, I would never go to a box and one because that would take Alcindor away from the basket." From his saying that, I suggested that I might consider a diamond and one. And we went and worked from the diamond and one just in case we met them again, and we used it the next time we played them. Someone, a reporter I think, after that, had mentioned us using the diamond and one, and said, "How come you went with a zone that you've never used?" I said, "Well, actually, my assistant Jerry Norman suggested we go to a box and one and I said I wouldn't consider going to a box and one because it would take Alcindor away from the basket." But from that suggestion, I did work on a diamond and one and we used it. If he hadn't suggested the box and one, we probably would not have used the diamond and one.

But you do give Norman great credit for helping you on your teams?

Oh, my, yes. I think I have. When I met Denny Crum, I've often said that he was born to coach and was great. I don't want you to feel that we didn't have disagreements, but I wanted that. I don't think you learn from a "yes" man. I think they just inflate your ego. But they must understand that you have to make the decisions and you won't always agree with them any more than they're always agreeing with you. But I don't believe I ever knew him or any of my assistants feeling that I hadn't given them credit.

Other topics were then brought up, but the subject of credit and recognition given to assistants bothered Wooden—he knew of the "controversy," if one can call it that, about Norman—so he steered the interview back to him:

Somebody was commenting that you wanted to actually teach English when you went to UCLA. Is that right?
I would have liked that.

You asked them if you could, right?
No, I don't think I ever did that. In talking with them, might have talked about the possibilities of it. But I don't think I ever requested it, no.

Getting back to the point that I made a while ago, Jerry was a fine assistant. I always tried to give him credit, but perhaps it was not what he wanted or needed. I thought I was giving him credit for it when I said that he suggested a box and one. And at that time, I don't think Jerry had ever heard of a diamond and one. It was his suggestion of a box and one that made me come around and use the diamond and one, with us working it out together. I thought I'd given him credit for that, but I guess he didn't feel I had.

And of course, as far as the pressing defense was concerned, if he says he suggested that, I don't remember it. I think he suggested that I stick to it. I had used the pressing defense somewhat when he played because he played on the first teams when I came here and I was using the press. I'd used it in high school and I'd used it at Indiana State, but I wasn't using it here. I tried it a little bit and didn't think I had the personnel to make it work. When he graduated, I thought Jerry had a good mind as a player. They may have told you he gave me a little trouble because of he profanity. He was very profane. And I just can't stand that and I probably kicked him off the floor more times for profanity than all the rest of the players that I've ever had put together. And one time, the last time, I just said, "This is gonna be for good." Eddie Sheldrake, he was close to me, talked me into taking him back, and his father came and talked to me. He was afraid he was gonna end up out of school and maybe in trouble with some of the friends he had. So I did take him back and he got over it where he didn't use it anymore and I think that's very good. And then later I recommended him, when he graduated, for his first job. My brother (Cat) was the principal at West Covina High School. And I got him to take him in as his coach. From there I brought him to UCLA later. I knew Jerry was strong in his opinions, but no stronger than Denny Crum was.

With Denny Crum, we would discuss things pretty strongly, but then when the decision was made, we'd do it. Denny is the one that I said when he played, he was the only player I've ever had who I said was born to coach. That's just what he wanted to do. He asked more questions. He wanted to know more why we did things than any player I ever had. When I had Denny Crum and Gary Cunningham as the assistant, I had a wonderful setup.

I wouldn't want any better than I had with Denny. They weren't "yes" men. We disagreed and that's all right. But I have to make the final decision, the coach does, and I didn't agree with everything any more than they agreed with everything. When I made the decision, they accepted it, and that's the only thing that really matters. Doug Sale was also a very loyal assistant.

Wooden leaned heavily upon and learned from his assistant coaches. Norman admitted in 1980 that he was encouraged to bring creative and imaginative ideas to meeting, adding, "Coach was a great person to talk with in that respect because he was very open-minded. He'd challenge you on a lot of these things—he was very challenging—but not on whether he like it or not, but how much you're sold on it."

An assistant coach would be required to defend his suggestion. If he could not or would not do so, it was given less serious consideration. "I would make a suggestion," said Frank Arnold in an interview in 1980, "and he would rip it to shreds. I felt very insecure about that. Then I found out that it was simply his way of testing me to see how much I believed in the suggestion."

Marv Dunphy, who interviewed Wooden's assistant coaches for his dissertation, confirmed that Wooden wanted, sought and employed individuals who prodded him with suggestions and were encouraged to do so.

"I never had formal conferences with my assistants to evaluate their work. I thought that was an ongoing thing," Wooden told Dunphy in 1980, explaining "I had certain responsibilities for the assistants that I went over with them when they first came. I wanted assistant coaches who were ambitious to become head coaches, otherwise they might just go through the motions. And yet I wanted extreme loyalty, but also one who made suggestions. On the floor I tried never to correct an assistant in front of the players. There would be things that we would discuss in private. If he wasn't teaching something the way I wanted it taught, I did not want to embarrass him. If he was on the floor so I could talk to him without putting him down in front of the players, I'd do it then, otherwise I would discuss it with him later. We all have strength and weaknesses and it is a little easier for us to analyze our own strength. We are more reluctant, perhaps, to see our own weaknesses. I felt that the assistants would help me in overcoming my own weaknesses. If you don't listen to them, then they just become yes men and really aren't doing a job, so I tried to make them feel free to make suggestions and the same time understand that only one can make the final decision. If I overruled them on something, or didn't go alone with a suggestion, I tried not to make them feel bad about it. I believe in the positive approach more so than a negative approach, although the negative things certainly have to be pointed out. So I did try to be honest in my workings with my assistants."

Wooden sought out assistants who had personalities that were compatible with his, those who "weren't afraid to contribute," a "little more fiery perhaps," he let on in 1980. When he needed someone to assist on the academic side of sports, he wanted someone who was a graduate of UCLA who could advise from experience. He was thorough before hiring someone, for example, spending two days interviewing assistant Doug Sale about his philosophies before offering him the job.

Wooden has made it clear to this author that he is pained by the estrangement from Norman and the criticism whether he gave him enough credit, does not think he deserves it, and is sorry if he does.

Norman does deserve great credit for insisting on the implementation of the full-court press and for his recruiting efforts; his disaffection is not surprising as Wooden's success would have cast a long shadow for anyone who was under him but he is the only assistant who has indicated any disenchantment with Wooden. By analogy, Wooden was the lead singer of the biggest band in history with a constantly changing cast of players who were the focus of attention, and Norman could never be more than a side-man.

Norman and some of his supporters claim Wooden simply did not understand the defense strategy proposed and ultimately implemented by UCLA. Wooden, when queried on the subject, says he certainly understood what Norman proposed, but admits that maybe he didn't completely, but, only in the sense that anything is possible. Norman, interviewed in 2002 for this book, said that he suggested to Wooden a defense that did not incorporate taking Alcindor away from the basket, that there was "no name" for this strategy and thereafter the press began to call it a "diamond and one." Norman said that Wooden did not think in terms of strategies, and that Wooden did not suggest a "diamond and one defense" as "there is no way I would have suggested taking Alcindor away from the basket." When it was suggested that assistant coaches ordinarily did and do not receive credit, particularly in those days, Norman agreed.

Norman said Wooden told him a year before he left that he received a call from Notre Dame asking if Norman was interested in coaching there, and that he turned the offer down as he did not want to move to South Bend. Norman said he left coaching for two main reasons: poor pay, and primarily, having to be away from his family so much. "I never got home until nine o'clock at night and never got to put my girls to bed," Norman recalled in 2002. Norman added that he received inquiries about returning to basketball as a coach after entering the business world, but by then he had made his decision to leave basketball.

Given Wooden's total mastery of the game, it is hard to believe that Wooden did not comprehend all nuances of whatever strategies he put into play. Wooden describes in *Practical Modern Basketball* his understanding of a "diamond and one" defense, which focused on Alcindor staying near the basket as an intimidator. Whether Norman deserves more recognition for his contributions is arguably a tough call, but after all, he was the assistant coach, and the press as a whole is not interested in those who occupy such positions. Norman probably could have moved on to a head coaching position at another university, but chose not to, and there were none attractive to him at the time. Moreover, Norman found the business world inviting.

In Norman's defense, he was brilliant and indefatigable in recruiting— which Wooden greatly disliked—and as a strategist, and but for his prodding, it is doubtful the full-court press would have been implemented to the extent it ultimately was. Norman then and today remains close to players he coached, and he and Eddie Sheldrake, a UCLA great from the 1950s who has been a friend of Norman's since high school, are promoters of irregular events where players from all UCLA teams (1940s to present) gather every few years. Norman, after leaving coaching, went on to make a fortune working in asset management and especially in putting together syndicates that invested in real estate for mobile homes.

Opponents were confounded and stymied by the full-court press, which demonstrated Wooden's tenet, "I've always said it's defense that wins games." The country was fascinated by "the full-court press—a phrase which then entered and has remained a part of the national vocabulary for any situation where a person, team or entity goes "all out"—and even those usually disinterested in sports began to take notice. In 1966, Wooden told *Sport* magazine that "the press isn't specifically designed to steal the ball. The by-products of the press are just as important. These include tiring your opponents and forcing them into wild passes and other errors of commissions, and omission."

Wooden told Jeff Pugh of the *Los Angeles Times* in 1969, "You force the other team to make mistakes and it's only human nature that people hurry to correct those mistakes. And when you hurry, you get careless. We try to take advantage of that carelessness."

Sports Illustrated even ran a cover story on how to beat this maneuver which, when utilized by UCLA, was as innovative as Knute Rockne's invention of the forward pass in football. Wooden recalled, "I said, after looking at this article, 'Boy this is good, because they can't agree on how to break it.'"

Another defense was invented to break the full-court press—the stall. With played keep-away with the ball to stave further damage by UCLA. But Wooden and Norman, Pete Newell explains in his interview, were diabolical in using the press. They would modify it, especially after they'd played a team once before. Opponents didn't know what to expect, and were often psychologically devastated by the formidable press which was exceedingly difficult to combat, as UCLA was unrelenting in forcing errors made by their opponents.

Of the 1963-64 team, Stanford basketball coach Howie Dallman quipped at the time that the Bruins were so skilled that they "pressed you from the time you left the dressing room."

Here is what Wooden wrote about the press in 1966 in his typically direct and perfect prose:

UCLA'S ALL-COURT PRESS
by John R. Wooden, UCLA Head Basketball Coach

The full value and effectiveness of the full-court press, which has proved so successful at UCLA over the last two years, is difficult to assess, but there are some principles to be kept in mind that give one an insight into how it operates and what it can do.

First to be remembered is that the press is a gambling type of defense, and requires continued effort and limitless patience if it is to pay dividends.

All players must be well grounded in the individual defensive fundamentals. Since I feel that these must be taught through the use of the man-to-man defense, our freshman team uses only a man-to-man press, but does use the principles of the zone defense when away from the ball.

The press can speed up the game and, perhaps, force an opponent out of their normal style of play. Thus, it also can cause disharmony and disunity in the team play of the other team. As a matter of fact, the principal value may come from demoralizing the opposition and upsetting their game.

I coach my UCLA players not to reach in to attempt to take the ball away from an opponent, but play position and force errors when the opponent hurries. This cuts down fouling and helps to establish the proper philosophy.

We try to permit only lob or bounce passes forward. Passes back toward your offensive basket will not hurt, but crisp passes the least bit forward toward the basket you are defending can cause trouble.

Our players are taught to turn and sprint toward the defensive basket and to pick up the man in the most dangerous position whenever the ball passes their individual line of defense. Strong side men should be alive to "two-time" as they go back, and the weak sidemen should be alert to intercept.

However, I would like to stress that we do little "two-timing" as far as trying to take the ball away, but stress body position to force errors.

Regardless of the type of zone that we set up initially (2-2-1, 1-2-1-1, 1-3-1, 2-1-2), we use tight man-to-man principles if the man in your zone has the ball, and floating man-to-man principles, depending upon how far from the ball your man is in the other areas. If no opponent is in your zone, move closer to the zone that is being attacked.

Results often come in spurts, so apply immediate pressure after acquiring the ball through an error. Often they will try to make up the loss by "hurrying" and will make more errors. Our 1964 team had at least one "spurt" in a period of approximately two minutes duration in all 30 games in which we outscored the opponents from 10 to 20 points. Sometimes it did not come until the middle of the second half, but we would usually have at least one spurt before the end of the first half.

Players must realize the necessity and value of and be willing to make the necessary sacrifices to attain and maintain top condition.

In addition, they must also be unselfish in regard to scoring, since oftentimes the scorer, when you capitalize, will not necessarily be the player who caused the error.

It's interesting that the requirements for the No. 5, or deep, position are about what all coaches look for in all players. An outstanding player at this position is essential. He must be quick, alert, courageous, unselfish, and able to "read" the man with the ball, be very good at handling the deep defense when outnumbered and a fine rebounder who can get the ball out quickly. He must be very aggres-

sive, with judgment that prevents committing himself too soon, and—above all—a player who really loves a challenge.

Sportswriter Carl White of the *Santa Monica Evening Outlook* captured the nature and effect of the press at that time:

Why does a team's morale break down eventually when it faces the full-court press, as applied by John Wooden's UCLA Bruins? The press is an insidious thing. We have watched the Bruins closely since they first began using it so successfully at the start of the season a year ago as an offensive defense, or as a defensive offense, if you choose to label it that way. No matter what you call it, it has the same effect.

Quite often the opposition sails down the floor to their forecourt with ease, even though the press is on. At other times there is no press. Generally speaking, it is applied only after the Bruins have scored. If it is broken, the Bruins show no disappointment and drift back to their normal defensive positions.

Once it succeeds in forcing an error to let the Bruins steal the ball and go in for a score, those on the sidelines can almost feel the viciousness with which it is applied again. Often it results in a batch of scores without retaliation that has become the keynote of the UCLA teams of this year and last.

Sometimes it is a sophomore who breaks down under the pressure. More often than not it is a junior or senior. No one seems to be immune. One error compounds another. Almost before the opposition coach can call a time out, the game is almost beyond recall.

Decades later, Jerry Norman reminisced about the press he created with Wooden, saying, "Some things evolved out of it and we had no idea when it would happen. Teams would just start to make mistakes. They'd make three or four mistakes and it would snowball. They'd make eight or nine before they got under control. They would get frustrated. There would be a lack of concentration. Look at most of our games and there would be one period—not necessarily throughout the game—when we would run up ten, twelve, fourteen, sixteen points in a row."

UCLA won its first two championships without a home court. (The championship playoffs are always referred to as the Final Four.) "We never had a permanent home. We played home games at Santa Monica City College, Venice High, Long Beach City College, Long Beach Auditorium, Pan Pacific Auditorium, Shrine Auditorium, Olympic Auditorium and even one time in

Bakersfield," Wooden recollects. "We practiced at our on-campus gym with no private dressing room or private showers. We had only two baskets, and we shared the gym with gymnasts and others [wrestlers] who worked out around us. We climbed three floors to get to the gym." There were other distractions besides that. "The gym was co-ed and I certainly wasn't against that. But the women would wear leotards and it was tough to get the attention of my players on occasion." He noted, 'We had no private shower or locker rooms.'

Besides being cramped, "For years, I didn't have a full-time assistant, and helped the team's managers sweep up and mop the floors. It was hard not just for us in those days, but for all the sports at UCLA." Wooden and his managers swept and mopped the floors in the Men's Gym (which was nicknamed by some, the "B.O. Barn") before practices for seventeen years. "Before every practice, we'd sprinkle it and mop it because there'd be so much dust that would accumulate during the day . . . I had special mops made. They were six feet long, and we'd wrap towels around them. I'd get a bucket of water and just like you were throwing corn to the chickens, I'd throw water and mop it up."

That Wooden participated in such menial work is circumstantial evidence of how he instilled camaraderie and loyalty from the team and its managers. When something had to be done he didn't just supervise, he participated. The playing surface needed to be clean. Wooden with his special mops was there with his crew—and with his mop—to ensure this as the first order of business before every practice. Team spirit is a natural by-product when the team leader is in the trenches along with everyone else.

Los Angeles was not exactly quick to catch on fire to UCLA basketball, though it ultimately did. When UCLA beat Washington for its twentieth straight victory that first championship season, there were but 5,000 fans in the Los Angeles Sports Arena, which held at least three times as many. Eventually basketball fever caught hold and virtually every home game thereafter coached by Wooden was a sell-out. Dedicated in November 1965, Pauley Pavilion, the Bruins' basketball stadium, was built in the center of the campus, and it was and still is gorgeous and intimate. Wooden fondly recalls that first championship team of 1963-64, "I remember everybody in Kansas City talked about what a fine little team we were, then picked Duke, except for one coach from Czechoslovakia who'd been with us for a week, and with Duke and with several other teams. 'UCLA win. UCLA is team,' he said. That was about as fine a compliment as a coach can receive from another coach." [Coach, or more probably the reporter responsible for the quote, got his facts wrong. The coach, Aleksandar Nikolic, was from a place then known as Yugoslavia.]

UCLA's win streak continued relentlessly, with Wooden and the university breaking and eventually establishing records that have become virtually insur-mountable. The Bruins were so invincible that by 1968 there was serious debate as to whether they could beat a professional team in the NBA. Wooden offered this analysis at the time, "A great team could have a chance to beat any other team on a particular night. I mean if the team under discussion is really great. Any other team could include a professional team." However, Wooden acknowledged, "Most every team in the NBA has to be better off than mine in depth except for five or six of our players, and maybe I'm exaggerating that all the teams would have an edge on us. But remember, every player on a pro team was a college star."

Wooden hardly ever recruited, though his staff did. He only went to twelve homes of a prospect during his twenty-seven years at UCLA. He methodically built and forged his championship teams so that UCLA became the school of choice for high school athletes because of its star attraction—John Wooden, the master coach. But unlike many universities and colleges, UCLA's basketball program was modest. In 1972, for example, UCLA had only three freshmen on scholarship for basketball, however, almost all of those who played major var-sity sports at UCLA during the first half of 1970s received "grants-in-aid," their tuition was covered and they received a living allowance, certainly a reasonable trade-off for the enormous revenues sports made for the university.

Wooden did not like to visit homes of recruits because he "felt that visita-tion was pressuring them . . . and I didn't believe in that." Wooden preferred that "student-athletes" (a term commonly used by him and UCLA Athletic Director J.D. Morgan) visit the campus, and talk to players to get an idea of what lay ahead.

"We preferred to have the players and/or parents come to his office; that way it would be on his grounds, not theirs, and made us feel that they were more genuinely interested, than if we were always pursuing them," remembered former assistant coach Jerry Norman in 1980.

While Wooden was clearly an asset in recruiting, some of his former assis-tants say he was also a handicap. Given his philosophy, there was no recruiting at basketball camps where other recruiters commonly descended to find talent.

An out-of-state recruit had even less of chance, according to former assis-tant coach Frank Arnold. He explained in 1980, "Coach Wooden was a liabili-ty from the standpoint that he allowed you to recruit absolutely nobody from outside the state of California unless that young man wrote John Wooden a per-sonal letter or called him personally and said, 'I'm interested in UCLA.' Only then would we actively pursue the prospect. Jerry Norman got around it and suggested I do the same thing by going behind the scenes and through the back door to contact [some of] these kids, their coaches or some associate of that player and tell them of Wooden's restriction. And so he spent as many hours as did I in recruiting a kid to write to John Wooden."

In 2002, Wooden advised that then, as he would wish today, he was after "kids who would want an education," continuing that, "Coaches and teachers must do a better job of impressing on them the value of an education." He would "want to know everything about the family." In a lighthearted manner, but making it clear he was serious about what followed, Wooden added that although he didn't "want to step on anyone's toes and please forgive me, but I sure wouldn't recruit one of these guys who has tattoos up and down him. I think I wouldn't. I never recruited one with long hair." One potential recruit was not offered a position because Wooden observed him being disrespectful to a parent. When explaining his beliefs and philosophy, Wooden often does so in a humorous manner. For example, when he tells the story of advising Bill Walton that his haircut had to go, he tells the story dryly, then with impeccable comic timing, holding the punch line to the last moment, rushes out that he told Walton if he didn't cooperate, "We're sure gonna miss you," which always brings a laugh.

Basketball exploded as a sport in 1968. The biggest sporting event of the year was the Bruins' 71-69 loss to Houston at the Astrodome on January 20th that year, witnessed by 55,000 fans, referred to then, and today, as the "Game of the Century." The Bruins' 47-game winning streak had ended, though it was not really a fair fight as Alcindor/Jabbar played with an injured eye in that game. When the team lost, Wooden told the national television audience, "We've been winning a long time. The only thing I think is worse than losing too much is winning too much and maybe we've been winning too much." That game, that recognition, was the result of Wooden's skill in building and maintaining the UCLA machine.

There were 9,800 seats for the general public at Pauley Pavilion, and 3,000 for the students, a total of 12,800 seats. Tickets were so coveted they were reportedly the subject of divorce settlements and wills. Hundreds of students would camp overnight outside the box office to obtain tickets. Wooden and UCLA basketball were the common bond, the catalyst for the UCLA student experience; good clean fun during a time when there were many less savory alternatives. UCLA basketball appealed to hippies and conservatives alike.

THE ALCINDOR YEARS

By 1969, Wooden was longing for a time "when I can coach to win again instead of not to lose."

"All the teams that we played, they had an emotional advantage. We weren't supposed to lose and they had nothing to lose. We were the only ones who had anything to lose," commented Kareem Abdul-Jabbar (known during his collegiate years as Lew Alcindor) at the close of his college career in 1969.

During the Wooden dynasty, it was a foregone conclusion that UCLA was going to win the game, for the fans it was by how much, for the players, according to Lynn Shackelford, one of Wooden's greats, the issue was "who was going to get to play the most."

UCLA won every national championship, except two (1966 and 1974) between 1964 and 1975. That's ten out of twelve consecutive years. No other collegiate team has ever come close to such an impressive record, and only Red Auerbach's Boston Celtics compare in the pros for so many championships during such a short period. At the center, the heart of the hub, was John Wooden: intense, methodical, coherent and clever. Teams and players came and went, but the coach, his standards and style, remained. Compare the difficulty of starting from scratch each year with an amateur team, with any professional sport where players can be recruited with money, and, moreover, are allowed to work as a team for as long as they can meaningfully contribute. Wooden is noted for adapting his strategy around the strengths and weaknesses of his various teams. For example, when Lewis Alcindor began to play varsity basketball at UCLA during his sophomore year in 1965, Wooden completely changed his offense plan to effectively use the talents of this seven-foot-one basketball great. Alcindor was so good that the freshmen team on which he played beat the varsity team at a preseason exhibition by 15 points, and the varsity consisted of a number of veterans of the previous team which had won the national championship the year before! A crack at the time was that "UCLA is number one in the country and number two on its own campus."

Mike Warren, who was on the varsity, remembered in 1987, that the frosh ran by their dressing room after the game, chanting "'We're number one.' It was a quite humbling experience, to say the least."

Alcindor could dunk a basket at will, and arguably because of him (it was referred to as the "Alcindor Rule"), between his sophomore and junior years, in 1968, the NCAA rules were changed to prevent dunking in college games. In March of 2000, Wooden said that Alcindor "didn't cause the change. The NCAA Rules Committee outlawed the dunk because of hanging on the rim, rims bending back, boards breaking and glass down." Alcindor/Abdul-Jabbar believes otherwise, commenting that it "was an attempt to legislate against me." That rule change, Wooden told Alcindor at the time, would only, and did, make him a better athlete. In 1977, dunking was again permitted.

Actor Tom Selleck, a center for USC during the Alcindor era, confided to him years later that he was told to imitate this awesome, menacing talent at practices by waving two tennis rackets.

Wooden and Alcindor/Jabbar have a special relationship and respect for each other. When Jabbar was inducted into the National Basketball Hall of Fame in 1995, Wooden made his feelings apparent. "I learned more from Lewis, as I called him then, than from any other player I ever had. I am not talking about basketball now, but about man's inhumanity to man. People would say the most hurtful things, call him a freak in his hearing without thinking about it. Even some referees would unfairly allow opponents to rough him up. He was subjected to things that, had it been me, I would have really flared up. But he didn't. He had amazing self-control. He was the most valuable player the college game has ever had, on or off the court."

Alcindor's name surfaced when Wooden was asked in 1992 for this book whether he was interested in other motivational philosophies. Coach replied, "Of course I am. I was always concerned about learning. You never learn enough. You learn from others. You learn from reading. You learn from listening. I learned from all my players and associates. I learned from all the assistants I had. Different things, different ways. The player from whom I learned more than anyone else was Lew Alcindor. I learned more from him about many things, more than I ever did from any other player," including, "a better understanding of someone of that unusual height. I saw in restaurants that he'd always have to be on the end with his feet out. I saw him uncomfortable in most planes. Could hardly ever have window seat, the aisle seats had more leg stretching room. [Many] hotels now have teams in [and] have extra-long beds. They didn't have them at that time. We'd have to get him a King-size and he'd have to sleep sideways in that. I saw that he couldn't go into a store and buy clothes that you and I could. I saw how people would treat him. I saw people make remarks. I saw a woman say, 'Look at that big black freak.' Things like that. I saw him being criticized for not signing autographs, when all he had been doing was signing autographs. I tell him, 'Now we gotta go. The rest of the team is waiting,' and he'd say, 'Sorry,' and walk along. The kids would be running after him and the adults would say, 'Look at the big guy too good to sign autographs' and that's all he'd been doing. I never took the time to see a lot of these things before. I just didn't realize it. I would talk with him when he might have some problems and tell him that you have so many blessings and we have to count our blessings. The seventh point of the creed that my father gave me is 'give thanks for your blessings and pray for guidance every day.'"

It was this sensitivity that enabled Wooden to coach, nurture, protect and analyze the needs of Alcindor effectively; Alcindor could not have asked more from a mentor. Inside that unusual physique has always been a sensitive, intelligent human being. Wooden's goal was developing the person inside, rather than just exploiting the athlete who so interested the masses. Wooden knew how to help Alcindor cope with the attention, to put his life in perspective, to provide a nurturing relationship while allowing Alcindor to blossom as a player, but more importantly, as a person. He was "my kind of guy, very direct, very honest. He had a sense of humor, but he was about discipline," Alcindor said in 1987. "I identified with all of those values. He put it in terms he didn't expect us to do anything that he didn't do. He was an A student and an All-American."

During the Alcindor years, UCLA amassed the incredible record of 88 wins and 2 losses. Jabbar wrote about Wooden in equally respectful terms in his 1990 book, *Kareem*, that Wooden "understood the game totally. He eliminated the possibility of defeat. It was genius."

The genius of Wooden was being able to take a talent such as an Alcindor, or another giant in both stature and talent, Bill Walton, and inducing them to do their best without subordinating the best interests and goals of the team. Alcindor and Walton were extraordinary players, yet Wooden taught them to play unselfishly, and their teams were invincible. Coach stated in 1995, that Alcindor was "*perfect*—unselfish, hardworking, on time, just a great talent. Walton was exuberant and seemed more active, but he was no more unselfish than Kareem. Both were great team players."

But Wooden coached teams won—stars or no stars. Wooden did a tremendous job with average players, and was equally superb with superstar athletes. His first championship teams were small and used the press and a running attack, featuring guards Walt Hazzard and Gail Goodrich. With Abdul-Jabbar, Wooden changed UCLA's offense and defense to fit his amazing abilities, and after he departed, used a different game with subsequent teams. Before his retirement in 1975, Wooden won thirteen of the previous fourteen conference championships, with eight perfect seasons. No other team in the conference can claim even one perfect season.

Moreover, Wooden's teams during the championship years entertained the nation, which Wooden once admitted in 1969, was one of the purposes of basketball. "We have an obligation not only to try to win, but to entertain the customers, especially here in Los Angeles, where there are so many other attractions," he said. "When people cease to be entertained, they'll go elsewhere." In 1975, Wooden admitted, "I like to feel that my style of play—not me, my style of basketball—made basketball a little more entertaining. I think my style of play caused other coaches to make their style a little more entertaining. I feel that my style helped build up basketball."

THE JOHN WOODEN PYRAMID OF SUCCESS

In 1982, Wooden commented further on this subject, "Anyone that takes a position that puts them in the public eye in the first place has to have an inordinate amount of ego. But I don't like to see it expressed on the court or sideline. As a coach, I wanted people to some and see my team play. I wanted my team to provide the entertainment. I didn't want them to come to see me and I think there are announcers today that think the viewing public is more interested in them than the players. And there are many players that are more concerned with executing a fancy dunk than they are in just getting the ball through the basket. I personally do not like it. Now, I know it is show business to a certain extent. That is true. But I don't think there is anything more beautiful than the perfect execution of a pass or a good block, a nice shot, a good stop and turn, a change of direction, I don't think it has to be fancy. Those who watched my teams know that I did not permit things of that sort. I personally do not favor the dunk because I believe it takes away from team play."

As Wooden became successful as a coach, as a person he stayed unaffected: a modest, decent, hard-working family man.

"We were having undefeated seasons and to know and see and interact with Coach Wooden, you would have never dreamed it, never guessed it," said Keith/Jamaal Wilkes, a former star player, in 1987.

A typical example occurred during October 11-13, 1969, when some 100,000 Hoosiers turned out for the Morgan County Fall Foliage Festival, where Wooden was king of the festival. His comment at the time was typical Wooden: "Naturally, I'm very pleased and flattered, but without any attempt at false modesty, I feel my hometown has a number or natives sons more deserving than I." That understatement and modesty, such a rarity then and now in any sport or profession, is why Wooden has always been so loved as a champion.

A current athlete with the same temperament and style, who has accomplished at the same level as Wooden in terms of achieving records is Tiger Woods, the professional golfer. Wooden and Woods are friends and mutually admire the other, one can deduce, because neither has the need or desire to gloat. They go about their business quietly, show respect for others, are humble and soft-spoken. What is not to like about such persons? By simply being a gentleman, Wooden won the nation over.

We can learn from this conduct in business. We want to "outscore our opponents," of course. That's the nature of competition. There is going to be a victory and a loss in courtrooms; that is why they exist. Life is about competition in many respects. There have to be winners and losers in many endeavors, but there should also be respect at all times for the adversary. The intelligent lawyer knows that 99 percent of all cases that are set for trial ultimately settle. The lawyer who "gets personal" and antagonizes his opponent does himself and his client a disservice when settlement talks are warranted. When other malevolent emotions are invoked, achieving a good result becomes more problematic.

Wooden did not antagonize opposing teams and coaches. Had Wooden become a lawyer, the judge, the jury, opposing counsel, and even the party on the other side would have loved him. Wooden understood the dynamic of graciousness, of true sportsmanlike conduct. Wooden was never a sore loser, nor was he ever a jerk when he won. Being collegiate and gracious is all the more difficult when you are a superstar, as Wooden was during the dynasty. There was no notable change in him, if anything, he was more modest publicly—and the same way in private, what you saw was what you got.

Nell was always at his side. She traveled on the road with him most of the time. Like a Norman Rockwell painting come to life, they would signal each other before a game with their thumbs and index fingers forming an "O.K." sign, and with nods, winks, smiles and kisses. True love. Wooden was known for his habit of never letting go of a rolled-up program during any game.

"On the program, which many people did not notice, I would have many little facts and reminders to myself," Wooden said. "For example, one of the things I would have on there, which coaches don't like to admit, would be the names of the poorest free-throw shooters on the other team and the best one. I would want to know whom we would play more aggressively, not foul intentionally, because we would never want to know that. This was their perspective: "When you come on the basketball floor each day for practice, to me you are a basketball player. In a sense you are no longer a person or a student at UCLA, you are a basketball player, and I want to relate to you and your teammates as basketball players and from this group I want to develop the best team that we can have. As soon as practice is over, the very instant practice is over, you're a student."

Not widely known is that during games Wooden held in his left hand a small metal cross. The cross featured the Alpha and Omega, the beginning and end of the Greek alphabet on each end of one stem, the sun and the moon on the ends of the other, worn smooth over the years. The cross was given to him by a minister in 1942, before he entered the Navy. His reason for the cross? "If I am able to control myself, perhaps it will help my boys to control their emotion and play up to their true potential. I know that I have faltered at times, but I also know that it has been most helpful. It gave me a certain peace, a serenity," Wooden says. "Now I keep it in my hand whenever I'm speaking." Nell Wooden held a similar, smaller cross during all the games as well, and Wooden has carried both since she passed away.

THE JOHN WOODEN PYRAMID OF SUCCESS

Wooden has no regrets about his habits that brought him luck. "Subconsciously, certain rituals may give you a little more peace, a little more calmness, a little more serenity, and that, in turn, may make you play a little bit better," Wooden said in 1980. "I don't believe in superstitions as such, but certain things of that sort I'd go along with. If you have a feeling that doing a certain thing is going to be helpful to you, then it probably will be, not because of that reason alone, but because your feeling that way gives you a little more confidence and that may give you a little more poise. If you have a little more poise and confidence, a little more self-control, you're going to execute a little better. I don't believe in jinxes, I felt that it was more difficult to play in certain places because of physical factors, real factors, and not due to a jinx. The jinx may come in if you permit yourself to be afraid because of the physical factors. I think it is wrong when you become involved, concerned, and worried about things over which you have no control."

Ed Powell described Wooden's ritual: "He'd start by pulling up his socks, then he'd spit on the floor and rub it out, then turn and wave to Nell."

Denny Crum observed that Wooden "had a little rubbing stone he kept in his left pocket, that he always rubbed before a game—I guess for good luck. Also, anytime he would find a coin he'd put it in his left shoe and keep it there for at least the day."

Wooden enjoyed the Southern California suburban life, and spent plenty of time with his family. Marjorie Ashen, married to freshman basketball coach and UCLA scout Donald Ashen, remembers those good old days. "We lived at the beach, and they used to come down and bring their family," she said. "Nell was a lot of fun, she had a good sense of humor, and used to tell jokes. It was a very close family life that they had. They were just a joy to be around, they brought happiness wherever they went."

Diane Bragg, wife of All-American Don Bragg, who graduated in 1955, put it this way, "How could you not love a man who was so devoted to his wife? He was so considerate of her whenever you saw them."

Wooden was an intense competitor who rarely lost his temper. He was always mature about his victories and his defeats. Nell Wooden once observed, "I know of course the game's outcome but I can never tell from John's sitting around the house whether we won or lost. He's not hilarious when we win." (In 1957, Nell did admit that her husband became a bit difficult to get along with when UCLA had to play Stanford.) Nor was he one to let a loss get him down.

Frank Arnold, an assistant to Wooden from 1971 to 1975, recounted in 1981 one reaction to a heckler, which paints him as the "Shane" of basketball: "We were walking out after the game and they've got the cops and ropes lining the court, but we had to go right though the corridor to get downstairs to the dressing room. People were lined five and six deep. As we're walking down the corridor, they are vicious; they're cursing and swearing and hollering at Coach Wooden. This one guy right on the rope was particularly vengeful and Coach stops, turns around and walks back to this guy. He didn't show any emotion whatsoever, just turned around as pointedly as he could. Coach says, 'I'm sorry, sir, I didn't hear exactly what you said. Would you mind repeating it for me?' The poor guy just crawled into his shell. He stammered and stuttered, looked around and walked off. Wooden didn't smile; he didn't say anything. He just turned around and walked into the dressing room."

Wooden's conduct after he once lost his cool is instructive. In late January 1973 at South Bend, Coach Wooden, upset by what he perceived was unfair conduct by Notre Dame forward John Shumate, walked down to the Notre Dame bench and told Dick "Digger" Phelps, the opposing coach, "If he doesn't knock it off, I'll send Nater in for Walton and he won't take that."

Phelps snapped back: "It's a two-way street." Believing he had acted wrongly, four days after the game Wooden wrote:

> *Dear Digger,*
>
> *I owe you and John Shumate an apology and hope you will accept it in the spirit it is offered.*
>
> *I acted hastily without thinking clearly and taking all things into consideration and as usual actions from emotion are seldom with reason.*
>
> *John Wooden*
>
> *P.S. Please convey my feeling to John. He is a fine young man and an outstanding basketball player and I did him an injustice.*

Clear, crisp, direct, honest, and plain-spoken, Wooden acted upon his wrongful conduct in an appropriate manner. According to Swen Nater, the following practice "was the same as any other." Wooden's loss of temper was so rare, it was even reported. In the final game of his career, for the championship, Wooden was angered that an official had called a technical foul on Bruin Dave Meyers, and was held back by the player and another official. After the game, asked about this display of temper, Wooden said, "It's not good to show that kind of emotion," though he was "annoyed, very annoyed." And what were his feelings at having won his tenth national championship? He responded with characteristic understatement that it was "pleasing."

Nicknamed "Saint John" and "The Wizard of Westwood," appellations he greatly dislikes, Wooden played and coached fairly and cleanly. The violations of NCAA rules he admits to between 1949 and 1975 are for bailing basketball players out of jail, paying rent money for a player whose wife was ill and in the hospital, and inviting players who didn't return home to Christmas and Thanksgiving dinners.

Wooden never had a technical foul (these are given for unsportsmanlike conduct) called on him as a player, and only three as a coach, none of which, he notes, "had any effect on the game," even though they were for criticizing officials. One of the fouls was for saying "goodness gracious sakes alive" too loudly in a game in the 1950s against San Francisco State. As to another, Wooden in 1999 told *Referee* magazine (which rarely departs from interviewing other than an official), that the other foul "really wasn't called on me. The official thought that I said something that somebody behind me said. But I kept it. I didn't have any confrontation with him at all in any way." Dr. John Berberich, in his interview for this book, recounted an instance where Wooden asked for a technical to be called because of perceived unfairness in officiating.

Wooden discounts those, who during his early coaching years, called him a referee-baiter. "Somebody got on that kick and its been picked up," he once commented. "When I left Indiana to coach UCLA in 1948, I got many letters pointing out I'd never been on officials in comparison with most coaches. I yelled at officials to protect my players, but I never used profanity. About the only time I really got on somebody was on the rare occasion when I thought the official did a bad job. (Wooden was a member of the rules committee for many years.) I always admonished the people on the bench, too, the trainers and managers and such, to let me handle any situations involving officials, particularly when we had the ball, because I didn't want to give it up through a technical."

In 1982, Wooden denied he was out of line: "I have been depicted by newspapers on occasion—and it has sort of amused me—on the bench all cupped up, looking really mad and yelling, and it might have been a game when I at no time was ever perturbed. But they snapped a picture when I was yelling at a player to get back on defense, or something of that sort. Oh yes, I yelled at officials! But it was only in the sense of asking them to call the game at both ends."

Of course, when John Wooden chewed an official out, he did so with the best grammar in the league. In 1986, Wooden criticized the histrionics of the increasing number of coaches who were vehement on the sidelines during games, saying, "I see coaches who have stopped coaching so they can become actors and get the TV cameras turned on them. Most of them have forgotten what the game and their responsibilities are all about." In 1994, Wooden's complaint about basketball was, "There is so much taunting—you always had that, but it used to be the rare player. Now it is at every level."

Gene Collier of the *Pittsburgh Post-Gazette* in 1995 was very critical of modern coaches whose antics he suggested resembled those of the Worldwide Wrestling Federation, and longed for the days of John Wooden. "This isn't to say John Wooden never badgered an official," said Collier. "In fact, quite the opposite was true. But he managed to do it in a way that strongly suggested his mental age matched or exceeded his chronological age."

An intelligent diplomat, Wooden, after half time, occasionally would apologize to a referee for having bawled him out in the first half, saying, "Everyone makes mistakes, I know you were only doing your best." The effect of such a statement would leave the referee quizzical as to whether he had made a mistake, thus leaving Wooden's team with a potential benefit of the doubt on the next close call, and the official believing Wooden to be a gentleman because of the "apology." When he criticized a referee, the bite was wryly delivered. For example, "Your eyesight wasn't as good tonight as it was last week." Instead of shouting that a referee was favoring a home team, Wooden would say, "Don't be a homer."

He was always learning, adapting, and not just about basketball. In 2002, he suggested that he "learned more and was a better teacher in each succeeding year not so much [in a] technical [sense as to] how to work with people." Wooden says he attended so many classes on psychiatry that had he been enrolled he almost could have attained a Masters degree in the subject, and that he kidded his players at the time that he knew more psychiatry than basketball.

Wooden stated in 1992, "I always took a lot of courses in psychology. Just on the side, not for any degree or anything. [I have] studied and read books on psychology because I think that is important when you're in a position where you are dealing with other people . . . you've got to study psychology." Former assistant Doug Sale said in 1980 that Wooden "was a master of group psychology." "The thing I learned from John Wooden was not so much the X's and O's," said former assistant coach, Frank Arnold. "Everybody knows the X's and O's; there are no secrets. It's how to implement, how to teach, how to get kids to do things do them well consistently that really counts."

According to former assistant Ed Powell, "John oftentimes thought he saw something extra in certain individuals, and more often than not, he was correct."

One technique Wooden used was having the players rate the other players by position. This, said former assistant Jerry Norman, was very useful because sometimes the players would rank a member of the team much higher than staff, thus pointing out an undervalued asset.

Wooden watched his student-athletes intensely and avidly. "I was always trying to use the feelings of my assistants in every way possible. That included the trainer and sometimes the manager," Wooden said in 1980.

Another interesting technique of Wooden was rarely to appoint a captain for the season, doing so only three times. Wooden, in 1980, revealed his thoughts on the subject: "The captain that I appointed must be an individual that other players look up to. He must be one that is setting a proper example . . . off the floor as well as on the floor. He must work hard on the floor, setting a good example by working hard and paying attention and one that's going to behave himself on trips. That is where he provides the leadership. I don't think his influence goes beyond those types of things."

Advising players if they were going to play was handled on an ad hoc basis, depending on the temperament of the player. One might not be told until the game was about to start so he would not sulk during the warm-up period. Others might be told in private, or the information would be conveyed before the warm-up started.

"My discipline was, in essence, a denial," says Wooden. "I don't believe in physical punishment. I wanted my players to feel that the worse punishment I could give them would be to deny them the privilege of practicing or playing. They knew that my philosophy was to deny them a certain amount of time and I never told them in advance how much time."

Any player late for practice without notifying him in advance had to explain why, before he could dress for practice. "Any profanity on the floor meant dismissal from the practice for the day—just for the day," continued Wooden. "I liked to start over the next day and not hold it over their heads."

In Marv Dunphy's doctoral thesis on Wooden's coaching technique, the assistant coaches polled stated that the need for discipline was quite uncommon. "He could also get his message across by the tone of his voice, by being humorous, witty, or maybe even sarcastic," wrote Dunphy, who captured Wooden's philosophy in his dissertation: "Coach Wooden believed that players committed two types of errors. Taking a poor shot, throwing a bad pass, or traveling were errors of commission. If a player was not aware that he was continually making those types of errors, Coach Wooden would enlighten him. By and large, he felt players needn't be reminded of those errors. Failure to perform, like not blocking out, not screening or not running in the right lane, were errors of omission and Coach Wooden was very good at correcting errors of that nature."

"I think he was a master at making correction when players didn't do something," summarized former assistant coach Denny Crum for the dissertation. Crum also told Dunphy of Wooden's philosophy during games, "When they're winning, get on them real hard. When they're losing, be very positive with your reinforcement."

Dunphy captured from former assistant coach Frank Arnold this classic story. Two starters were badgering a teammate during practice, which caught the attention of the two assistant coaches. At the conclusion of practice, Wooden discussed the elements that had led to the downfall of civilizations, and advised his players, "In the history of mankind, all civilizations have crumbled from within and the only thing that can possibly destroy this team is ourselves." Coach could and did put it all into perspective; he has to be the only basketball coach who used ancient history to make a point on the court.

Because his players would be more nervous than usual before a playoff game, he would suspend his no-dunking policy during practice, allowing each player two attempts at doing so. Gary Cunningham, in 1980, remembered, "Guys were going in and reverse dunking and different things and it kind of loosened up the team. Occasionally, I'd say maybe once a year, he would do something like that."

When Wooden did discipline, according to former assistant Ed Powell, the discipline was "immediate and fair, and he never wanted to bruise the dignity of the person who was being disciplined. In that regard, Coach Wooden preferred to discipline in private and reward in public." One knew he was angry when he said, "Goodness gracious sakes alive."

Wooden, in 1980, allowed that he was "one of the first coaches to employ the acknowledgment of teammates during a game, particularly after a score. I did that when I was coaching in high school and I don't think anyone else was doing it at that time. To my knowledge, no one was doing it out here when I came west. Now you see it all over; it's a very common thing, pros and all levels." This marvelous innovation was a super-glue for creating team spirit and cohesion.

Wooden, at games, believed strongly in his psychological methodology. For example, he "talked to individuals a lot during time-outs," Wooden stated in 1980. "There were certain things that I said to the team as a whole, but I did a lot of coaching with individuals. I think that one of the greatest assets of my college coach was his ability to get across to individuals . . . He did that at all times—practice, time-outs, between half—a tremendous individual coach."

Wooden dealt with the team after a game by saying "very little . . . I didn't believe in hashing it over immediately afterward. If your players are down, bring them up. If you think they're feeling too good, try to get their feet back on the ground. There are two things that can hurt a person: not reacting and over-reacting . . . I never want my players to feel that winning a basketball game was any great accomplishment, and losing a basketball game was nothing to be too dejected about."

Wooden would find out about a player's family life by having them fill out questionnaires. He wanted to know their birthdays, their brothers and sisters, their parents, and a little of their family background. But Wooden, while cordial and friendly to them, did not encourage or allow parents of players to get too close. One, perhaps primary, reason was simply to be fair to those athletes whose parents lived far away, so that he would not socialize more with those who lived in the vicinity of UCLA. He would only contact parents if a player was in trouble scholastically.

Wooden was a master of managing people of diverse personalities. The 1963-64 Bruins, who won the first championship are one example. Walt Hazzard was an immensely talented star player with Harlem Globetrotter skills that the crowd loved. He "used to get kicked out of practices all the time," according to teammate Keith Erickson. "He was sort of this wild guy that threw passes over his shoulder and though his legs. . ."

Flamboyant Jack Hirsch played steady, great basketball, and was the team clown with a wealthy background. He'd make fun of Coach Wooden behind his back, and got kicked off the team for a short time. "He was always abrasive—and he might be to me," said Wooden. "Maybe one of the few I ever had as a player who'd call me 'John.' Well, I never asked the players to call me 'Coach' or 'Mr. Wooden,' but he's the only one who ever did," Wooden said in 1989. Fred Slaughter, Gail Goodrich and Keith Erickson, also on that team, were on more of an even keel.

Hazzard, in 1975, explained: "Coach Wooden had a way of getting to me when he thought I wasn't playing up to my ability. Once, in a regional game, he called time-out and spent the entire time on me. It was a real tirade. When I went back out on the floor, I was smoking. Smoke was flying out of my ears. I glanced back at the bench and he was sitting there, smiling."

In 1995, Wooden admitted doing so. "By the time I had Hazzard and Goodrich, I had learned, according to the temperaments they have, I'm going to have to pat Goodrich on the back more, and, in a sense, I'm going to have to slap Hazzard a little lower and a little harder. I had to make Hazzard almost mad at me at times—show me! And if Goodrich gets that treatment, he'll sulk." He treated his players so that each got "the treatment that each individual deserved," Wooden stated. "And if your players learned to know that, know that you're doing that, you've solved a big problem immediately. And I learned to listen, which I'm sure I didn't do to well at first. I learned much from my players just by listening."

Wooden mastered his own emotions, but at the same time, knew what prompts were necessary to get the result desired from individual athletes. He explained in 1992 what enabled him to keep his emotions in check and his technique for teaching:

Getting back to the issue of this calm demeanor that you have. Do you think that evenness is a trait that you were born with or something that you learned?

I think I learned that from my mother and dad. You would find the same trait in my three brothers too. I think it has to be from my early home environment, which I always felt has more influence on what becomes later than almost any other single thing. We never had much in material things, but we were always happy. That is the way we were brought up. To accept things and not blame others. I can give you some examples of my senior year. Back in Indiana, you have to understand winning the state high school basketball championship is the epitome. It's not right, but it is true. My senior year we lost the state championship in the final game by one point—a most unusual situation. My teammates cried, I didn't cry. I've seen players cry over losing a game. I never cried. I did the best I could; we got whipped. Usually you get whipped because the other team plays a little better than you.

You talked before about raising your voice with a player in practice. Was that done out of anger or as a legitimate technique?

I learned a lot about my players. I studied them. I tried to analyze them very carefully and they would try and do self-analysis too which is perhaps a lot more difficult then analyzing someone else. Either one can be valid. For example, I couldn't yell at Gail Goodrich. He would go into a shell if he got yelled at. There were other players that I would have to yell at. Hazzard was one. I would have to yell at him. If I could make him mad at me he would play better. He would show me, he was going to show me. If you would do that to Gail he would go into a shell. So different players you have to stroke different ways because they are all different.

Yet one of the mistakes I made early in my teaching career was telling players that I loved them all the same. I liked them all same and would treat them all the same but I never did like them all the same. I have had players I could hardly stand. And they didn't like each other all the same and they didn't like me all the same. I used to tell them that I hope I loved them all the same, but I know I won't like them all the same. It would be no different than my own family. There are times I don't like them, I will always love them. My two children, you couldn't treat them the same way. I used to tell my players that I would treat them all alike and I never did. When I got a little older and a little wiser I hope

I'd say I am going to try and give you the treatment you're going to deserve, but I am human and I am not perfect and I can make mistakes on that. But I have to make a judgment and that's what I am going to try and do. I think the surest way of showing partiality is to treat everybody alike. Yet we say treating everybody alike is being impartial. No it isn't! People don't earn and deserve the same treatment. The surest way of showing partiality is treating everybody alike.

In 1972, Wooden discussed the psychology of coaching, "Whenever you bring together a group of intelligent, highly motivated individuals, you are going to have conflicts. My job as coach is to convince the players that these conflicts cannot get in the way of what the team has to do."

In *Practical Modern Basketball*, Coach describes his philosophy this way: "The coach much come (be present), see (diagnose), and conquer (correct). He must continuously be exploring for ways to improve himself in order that he may improve others and welcome every person and everything that can be helpful to him. A wise motto might be 'Others, too, have brains.'"

On the shelf of Wooden's den is *The Art of War* by Tse-Sun, the classic study of how to succeed in combat. Wooden doesn't miss much when it comes to serious thought, be it philosophy, psychology, even actual physical combat.

Benchwarmer players who saw little action were never referred to as substitutes, but always as members of the team. It was an honor to be such a member on Wooden's teams, articles were even written about what it was like to sit on the bench for Wooden. Gary Franklin told Jeff Pugh of the *Los Angeles Times* in 1972 in an article titled, "Benchwarmer's Blues: It's an empty, tormenting existence, this substitute's role, even when waiting your turn to play with national champions," that he had two goals: to know where he stood with the coach, and to prove himself. Wooden was quoted in that article about how he viewed the issue. "Many of our players who are upset will come to me and say I don't understand their feelings. They tell me. 'You're the way you are because *you* never had to sit on the bench.' I tell our players I've been in coaching long enough to know what the feeling of being a substitute is like." Wooden didn't believe in regular scrimmaging during practices because it might take the competitive edge away from those who did play a lot, but always did so on the Mondays following a game for those who did not get to play much.

In his textbook, Wooden explained what was expected of those who sat on the bench: "They must be taught to cheer, encourage, instruct, warn and advise the playing teammates on occasion, but refrain from making remarks to the officials, opposing players, or spectators. They should study the game and pay particular attention to the man they are most likely to guard, the man who is most likely to be guarding them, and all situations from which advance knowledge may enable them to do a better job if and when they are called upon. They are not spectators, but students of the game." Wooden sought to try "to develop the feeling the player who may be called upon for very little actual playing time may be very important in the overall picture and he must be ready when he is called upon."

Many, perhaps most coaches, concentrate their attention on their starters, and especially their stars. Not Wooden, who explained in 2002, that "If a player didn't get to play very much, some didn't like me. I understood that. . .(but) I wanted them to feel they were wanted and understand their role. I would tell them this slogan, 'I will get ready and then perhaps my chance will come.' But if you're not ready when it comes, it is not going to come around your way again quickly in all probability." Wooden made it clear to his players at the first meeting of the team in October each year that his philosophy was to play seven or eight players until games were won or lost. "I hoped we had games won early so that they all got to play a lot . . . I would tell them that if they couldn't face up to that, they had to decide in a hurry. It was understood that no scholarships would be taken away . . . We never had any problems once this was explained, but I think that sometimes I subconsciously would forget to give attention to the . . . ones who didn't get to play very much. Sometimes I got so engrossed in the top seven or eight that I failed to give others the recognition, a pat on the back, the things they deserved. I think that is something a coach must keep in mind."

"I wanted it to be clear that every player served a purpose," Wooden explained in 1980. "I liked to make this analogy: at times we're like a machine. The engine is probably the most expensive to replace and I might mention one player who was a real standout, that he's sort of the engine, and I might mention another player that maybe played a lot who was not a star in that sense. I might explain that this player is a wheel. But what can the machine do if we don't have four wheels? You have to have them all. Then I'd say another player that gets to play even less; now you're in a sense, kind of like a nut that holds the wheel in place. But where are we going to go if we don't have a wheel? Where are we going to go if we don't have the engine? Some are more difficult to replace, but everyone has a role so I don't want you to feel unwanted."

Virtually everyone who was lucky enough to sit on the bench for Wooden, today realizes that opportunity was invaluable as they were trained by a master of the business of life and love.

THE NAYSAYERS

Over the years, there have been some grumblings about Wooden; some coaches who competed against him have said not for attribution that "St. John" was not as wonderful as he was made out to be, but such criticism is hard to find, and comes second-hand. Chalk it up to rivalry and sour grapes. Digger Phelps of Notre Dame has probably been the harshest on Wooden, and once claimed that officials at Pauley Pavilion were partial to UCLA, and called him bush league. Wooden commented in 1975, "That's his personality. He's known to be very brash, controversial, and he probably did it—I believe he told somebody, well, this is show business, something to attract attention. In fact, I know he told somebody that I'm probably much less vocal than the vast majority. For instance, no player, no coach, has ever heard me use profanity. But you can hear Digger. That is his nature. He's very profane. Woody Hayes is a great coach but he storms, and raves and curses. But he's not a bad person at all, he's a very, very good person. I do yell at officials, but my yelling primarily is, 'Watch the traveling' or 'Give me some protection,' or 'Watch the three-second.' It's meant to keep them on their toes about certain things in the game."

In 1995, Wooden told sportswriter Bob Ellison his reaction when Phelps, years before, wrote a book accusing him of shouting profanities at his players. "I've got lots of faults, but profanity is not one. No player has ever heard me use profanity. And I didn't like that, to write that I did. When I talked to Digger about it, he said, 'It sold books'—that really burned me up!. . . I don't have any anger in me, but I still feel the same way about it." As for Digger, he could show class at times. When the 1975 squad threw a surprise party for Wooden, Phelps happened to be in the same restaurant, and made a point of visiting with Wooden to congratulate him on his final championship and retirement.

In 1973, two sportswriters for the *Los Angeles Times*, Dwight Chapin and Jeff Pugh, published *The Wizard of Westwood*, a biography of Coach Wooden. (The book was done without the cooperation of Wooden; Wooden's autobiography, *They Call Me Coach*, was written in large part as a reaction to the former.) With painstaking effort, they ferreted out all negative commentary about and conduct by John Wooden. Finding little to complain about, those authors went away satisfied that Wooden is an amazing and wonderful individual, the consummate professional. For the record, here is what "negative information" ever surfaced about John Wooden. One athlete, a second stringer, once called him a "cold, tough guy" who was "set in his ways." Another disgruntled second stringer criticized Wooden for a "lack of communication." (Wooden would later help this player get a job.) Others have suggested that he did not relate to his players and that he was old fashioned. The authors quote Wooden as calling his team during a time out when they trailed Long Beach State "nothing but a bunch of All-American women chasers and hopheads."

One unnamed Bruin on the 1968-69 Bruins complained to *Sport* magazine in April 1969 that Lew Alcindor was given preferential treatment and not disciplined as others would be. "No one can knock Wooden," the anonymous critic allowed. "He's a genius as a coach. But we all wonder how he got this kindly grandfather image. To the outside world, he's always smiling and very modest, like a nice old man. But we see him as he really is when he plays the role of the coach. He can be tough, uncompromising, totally humorless." Another unnamed athlete complained, "The coaches want you to always say yes. If you don't, you have a 'bad attitude.' What bothers most of us is when coach throws in his 'going through life' philosophy, and tells us this is how we should run our lives. We feel it's a little outdated."

Player Bill Seibert blistered Wooden in 1969 in a speech at the annual banquet for graduating players, asserting that Wooden treated reserves unfairly, compared to starters. Though he was booed at that event, Wooden's basketball family did, and does, have its detractors, though many have come back into the fold. In 2001, Andy Hill, who saw little play as a Bruin in 1969-72, published *Be Quick—But Don't Hurry*, a personal account of his relationship with, and what lessons he learned from, Coach Wooden. Hill for many years resented not having played much at UCLA. He later achieved substantial success, became the president of CBS Productions, and authorized and supervised the production of television series, including the long-running *Dr. Quinn, Medicine Woman* and *Touched by an Angel*. Hill's best-selling book is a touching story of his reconciliation with Wooden, and broke new ground as it exposed that there had been seriously disgruntled players, some especially bitter that they had not had the opportunity to play more. Hill told not only his story, but also that of another teammate, John Ecker, who also reconciled with Wooden.

Steve Patterson, who played for UCLA and went on to a pro-career, told the *Cleveland Plain Dealer*, "We expected more of him because of what he does on the basketball floor. He is flexible on the basketball floor, but he seemed inflexible when he interfered with our private lives. It was a grandfatherly approach, but we resented it. We were out in the public eye so much that people would call him and say we were seen in a bar or with a girl. There isn't an athlete today who doesn't drink beer and go out with girls—in season. He said we weren't taking care of ourselves. He said we were victims of a permissive society. He'd lock us in hotel rooms the night before games." Patterson tells the story of the Vietnam protest. In the fall of 1970, Patterson and Wicks asked permission to participate in an anti-Vietnam War rally, "He asked us if this reflected our convictions, and we told him it did. He told us he had his convictions too, and if we missed practice it would be the end of our careers at UCLA." Yet Patterson couldn't help but be admiring. "He's got all the platitudes on the tip of his tongue. He's always humble, always saying just the right thing, always ready with the perfect quip. He's just plain folks. But he's so calculating. He channels the conversations. He never lets it get into areas he knows nothing about. . . . If I was coaching, I would attempt to emulate his philosophy and do it exactly like he does." Patterson later became a coach.

Wooden didn't allow reporters in the locker room after games. The NCAA required coaches to do so in championship play-off games in 1973, and Wooden waited twenty-four (instead of ten) minutes after the game, allowing players to shower and dress before opening up the room. Long Island's *Newsday* called this "self-serving arrogance" on the part of Wooden.

Wooden had his reasons for excluding the press from the dressing room. He explained why in 1980 in Marv Dunphy's doctoral thesis: "I never felt that the dressing room was a place for reporters. Following games, we had some problems because reporters have deadlines and were in a hurry and they didn't want to wait to talk after. But I still felt that it was no place for them. Dressing rooms were always small and cramped, players were showering and coming out wet and naked, and reporters only wanted to talk with one or two individuals, consistently ignoring the others. I never thought it was best for the team, and never permitted it, even in tournament play, up until the time the NCAA passed a rule that teams at the tournament had to permit the press in dressing rooms following the game. I disagreed with the rule that you had to do it."

Some reporters complained that Wooden was too restrictive in allowing the press to communicate with his players, and that UCLA's sports information director had an unlisted phone, then, when journalists got through to him, requests for interviews uniformly were declined.

William Gildea of the *Washington Post* wrote this negative, overly touchy, assessment, "Concluding his post-title game interview on national TV, the coach presented a copy of his book *They Call Me Coach*, to a momentarily startled announcer. In the promotion of books, that move ranks as the equivalent of Jabbar's backhanded stuff on the court. The jingle of cash registers was almost audible in bookstores throughout the land."

The meanest article we could find was written by Frank Dolson for Knight News Service in December of 1973, with the title "The Other John Wooden, Baiter of Referees." Here's a generous sample:

> *[H]ow about the other John Wooden? The one who sat on a folding chair before near midcourt last Saturday afternoon* [at a game in St. Louis the week before the famous Game of the Century in Houston]. . . *and did things and said things that were totally inconsistent with the Wooden image, the Wooden philosophy.*

I wonder what Fred Hickel, the referee from the Atlantic Coast Conference, thinks about the John Wooden who kept screaming at him Saturday, kept accusing him of favoritism. . . and incidentally kept pleading with the Pacific 8 ref, Louis Soriano, on a first-name basis.

I wonder how many college basketball coaches should have verbally abused an official the way Wooden did without receiving a single warning, a single rebuke, a single technical.

Wooden, of course, doesn't do it the way some of the referee-baiters (intimidators) do. He doesn't jump up and wave his arms and make a scene, he sits there, with barely a change of expression, and goes to work.

From a seat in front of your TV set, or a seat in the stands, you'd never suspect what John Wooden is really like while a game is going on.

From a seat a few yard away, it's a revelation.

"Watch 'em pushing away. . . Lookit the elbow. . . That's an offensive foul. You called that offensive foul on us. . . Oh, for crying out loud! Bad call. Bad call. . . Lookit him push off. . ."

A steady stream, all directed at the "enemy" official in the split crew. Always Wooden waited until the man was close enough to hear.

"Feeling good," the UCLA coach hollered after State's David Thompson had been awarded a two-shot foul early in the second half. "You should be."

And then, barely 30 seconds later, after a Thompson jump shot had trimmed UCLA's lead to six: "Call 'em, please. Not just at one end, for goodness sakes."

And finally, just before the Bruins blew the game open, the strongest verbal attack of all, in which Wooden accused the ACC referee of being a disgrace.

Consider Peter C. Bjarkman's excellent history of basketball, *The Biographical History of Basketball*, published at the beginning of 2000:

Johnny Wooden's success in manufacturing his own mythical persona as coach and inspirational leader was almost as complete as his decade-plus run at manufacturing NCAA championship victories. As other respected historians of the sport have already noted, the methods that coach Wooden piously espoused once he stood atop the sports world were not always exactly those methods that originally had gotten them there. The coach's advocacy of patience, faith and self-control always seemed at odds with his own personal impatience with losing, his not-infrequent sideline temper-laced outbursts, and his constant scathing cajoling of officials and opponents during heated game action. The carefully crafted image was always more real than the man himself. And yet that image is easily the most luminous in the entire history of a sport seeming always built upon larger-than-life personalities.

Wooden did sometimes lose his temper, and no doubt was not perfect all the time, but his deportment on and off the court personified class, and as previously noted, Bjarkman believes that Wooden was the greatest coach of all time, in large part because of his consistency in molding teams of all sizes and personalities with a constantly revolving roster, whereas Auerbach had some players for six or more years.

This critical commentary is extremely unusual, and rare in that it accused Wooden of unsportsmanlike behavior. To be sure, Wooden was no potted plant when it came to protecting players and seeing that the game was fairly judged. But in more than 175 interviews conducted for this book, and intense research into anything ever written about him, these comments are the only public blasts against his deportment. That's it, the major complaints about Wooden over the past ninety-two years! This was a man who was watched, covered, and combed-over by a press looking for peccadilloes, warts, errors, and aberrational personality traits. Nothing was ever found. There was, as can be found anywhere, plenty of temptation, as Wooden noted in 1978 on the topic of collegiate recruiting, "The coaching profession is comparable to any other," he said. "A lot of people in the highest office in our land are up for income-tax evasion and other things. Coaches are no different. There's no way you can legislate against cheating or stealing. You can try, by putting in rules, regulations, law. But human nature is such that you are always gonna get some cheaters."

Bobby Knight, terminated in September 2000 at Indiana University after years of unsportsmanlike conduct, including physically accosting players, and throwing a chair onto the basketball court during a game, represents the antithesis of Wooden's deportment. Knight was controversial year-in, year-out, always in the news; there were no "incidents," not one during the entire career of Wooden which caused any mar on his record.

The overwhelming majority of those who played for and worked with Wooden are delighted and proud to have been associated with the man. Former players critical of Wooden are virtually non-existent. Indeed, the man's integrity, earnestness and kindness are fabled. One example of Wooden's forgiving nature occurred when Mike Lynn, a player who had been in trouble with the law, returned to the team after having been suspended. Wooden, rejecting those who wanted to make the suspension permanent, told an assembly, "There's not one person in this room who hasn't made a mistake at one time or another. At least you [Lynn] have admitted yours and done something about it."

Adolph Rupp, who coached at Kentucky, a contemporary and peer of Wooden, who comes close to him in equaling his records, paid him this compliment, "He's one of the outstanding coaches this nation has produced. Hell, the nation didn't produce him. He produced himself."

Shortly after he retired, Wooden looked back on his career and commented, "The thing I may be ashamed of more than anything else is having talked to opposing players. Not calling them names, but saying something like 'Keep your hands off him' or 'Don't be a butcher,' or something of the type." There is one other sin—during the off-season, he even used to smoke, but "I was ashamed to let my players see me." He gave up smoking (he would quit on his birthday, each October 14th until the end of the season) and for good in 1955.

It was also rare for his players to show emotion. Says Wooden, "I didn't want them to. When critics said we played mechanically, I considered it a compliment. I wanted us to be robot-like in a sense. . .cool, calculated, methodical, but aggressive and ready to play at the same time. I've seen players who were running over the court every second and never got anything done." Wooden attributes this style in part because it was all right to want to win, but "not to want it too much. I eventually learned that you must treat an NCAA game like any other, and not to put any undue pressure on your players."

COOLNESS UNDER PRESSURE

In 1969, one player related Wooden's pregame talks. Wooden would "tell us that no team can beat us, but that we can beat ourselves. We've heard that before every game this year, but then he'll stop talking and there's silence. He looks at everybody, and then he says in, in a low voice, 'Let's go.' That's what really psyches me up. We all feel like smashing right through the wall."

As to playoff games: "In his own subtle way," former assistant coach Frank Arnold said in 1980, "and he never stated this verbally, he would let the team know that he expected to win. Not hoped to win. And they were here for a purpose; we're the best team in America."

J. D. Morgan, athletic director at UCLA during the dynasty, in 1980 likewise confirmed Wooden's skill during playoffs. "Coach Wooden knew how to coach. You can say that it's all basketball, and it's all games, and that's true; but playoff basketball is different than regular season basketball. Coach Wooden is the greatest playoff coach in the history of the game. By a wide, wide margin,

I've never seen players so ready to play and so aware of what it meant to win a game in the playoffs, without him ever saying 'We have to win this game,' He had a knack of knowing how to approach playoff games."

Former assistant coach Frank Arnold echoes this opinion: "I never heard him say less than the perfect thing. That's the one thing that has probably awed me more than any other thing. He is absolutely eloquent before a game, at half-time, and after a ballgame. He'd always say the right thing. I would marvel at how good he was. In the four years I was with him, I never heard him use the word 'win' one single time."

Former assistant Ed Powell says Wooden "was not the Knute Rockne type who believed in a rah, rah approach."

Bill Walton, interviewed in 2000 by Charlie Rose for a show about Wooden, remembered, "It was so intense. It was a symphony because he was a caged tiger . . . He was up and down that sideline. And remember, this was one of the greatest players ever, not just a coach. And he was so quick and that was what his game was all about . . . More important than Coach's [then] physical quickness . . . was his mental quickness because that's what he really taught you. He taught you how to win with your mind and with your heart. It was nothing to do physical capabilities . . . He would out-think everybody, and that's what Coach Wooden taught us to do."

Wooden writes in his textbook "that for every mental, emotional and physical peak there will be a corresponding valley," and therefore "the coach should not attempt to get the players too high for any particular game. The importance of the game itself should be enough stimulation and any artificial method used by the coach is not likely to have a positive effect that will not be negated by a corresponding negative effect."

Wooden coached winners even when the times they were a'changing. The Vietnam War divided the country from 1963 to 1974. There were demonstrations on every campus, and UCLA's student body was as aggressive as any other. Center Bill Walton, the greatest college basketball player at the time, participated in and was arrested in one demonstration, causing Wooden to give this, perhaps his most caustic interview, in 1975, where he stated he was "glad I didn't have Walton another year. And here he is a great player. But just so many things—through no fault of his own, he brought on many problems. He's a very strange person. He was not sheltered here. He sheltered himself. Other players were jealous of him. Well, that's something I have to handle."

Wooden's thoughts on Walton-the-rebel were substantially mellower in 1991 when he told ESPN that athletes had a responsibility to get involved in social issues. "They have to not be afraid to let their own actual feelings be known, if they really believe in them," said Wooden. "Back in the time that Walton was playing for me, he was anti-establishment, but he had every right to be. . . If everybody agreed on everything it would be a very dull, monotonous world."

Walton didn't like talking to the media when he was at UCLA because it put him in the limelight and he thought it made his teammates jealous. Wooden agreed, "He's a team player. He's unselfishly oriented. But he was inconsistent in some things. Some things he'd think he'd have absolutely the right to do because this was his choice. But what I tried to point out to him was that's all right to a degree, but when it starts affecting the rights of others, then it is no good. If you go and lie down on Wilshire Boulevard (a main artery by UCLA, where a demonstration against the Vietnam War was held) and stop traffic, you're affecting the rights of others. When Walton told me, 'I need an opportunity to express my feeling,' I said, 'Certainly, you have every right, but not at the expense of others. You're doing the same thing now to others that you're protesting about somebody else doing. Sometimes that's hard to understand.'"

In any event, Bill Walton has long been one of the players closest to Wooden. Walton was so enamored of Wooden that he visited him constantly during the off-season. Assistant Coach Frank Arnold said that the one player who spent far more time with Wooden than any other was Walton. "Bill was not awed, I guess. He was that kind of guy. Bill had a great love and warmth for Coach Wooden that you could only see from the inside." After Walton's final game in 1974, Arnold remembers that the star player "just picked Coach up right off his feet and said, 'I love you, Coach Wooden.' And then put him back down. That was one of the very few signs of emotion in that respect that you'd ever see from Bill."

Walton calls Wooden weekly, as do many others who keep in regular communication with him. Wooden once bragged that Walton "once even called me from Paris." The relationship today between Wooden and Walton is touching. Walton has matured into one of the finest commentators in basketball. In 2002 he was one of three network play-by-play announcers for the NBA playoffs and championship after overcoming a lifetime problem of stuttering. He wrote in 2000 for *UCLA*, the alumni magazine, that his home is "a shrine to UCLA and John Wooden, with memorabilia, the Pyramid of Success and pictures of him everywhere. I have taken my four sons to his house to receive the same great lessons of life that I received. I am closer today to John Wooden than I have ever been. . . He remains the same teacher, the same positive force he has always been, the person we would all like to become, only better. The joy in John Wooden's life today comes, as it always has, from the success of others.

THE JOHN WOODEN PYRAMID OF SUCCESS

He regularly tells me what he learned from his two favorite teachers—Abraham Lincoln and Mother Teresa —is that a life not lived for others is not a life. By that measure, John Wooden's is a giant life. He is still our guide in so many ways, with us each day to push, shape, mold, challenge, and drive us to be better. I thank John Wooden daily for all his selfless gifts, his lessons, his time, his vision, and especially, his patience."

(In March 2002, Wooden told admirers visiting his home that Walton's mother had called recently to say how happy she "was that the speech therapists and broadcasters had taught him how to speak, but they didn't bother to teach him how to stop.") Credit for Walton overcoming his speech impediment must in part be attributed to what he learned from Wooden. A listener can't even tell today that he has one. It's one thing to stop stuttering, amazing when such a person goes on to become an Emmy-award winning announcer, as Walton has.

UCLA's basketball teams during the Wooden era were known for their confident style of play, and for their ability to take advantage of opportunities as they arose. The UCLA teams under Wooden rarely lost clutch games. They played clean, fair basketball; Wooden even exhorted the fans to always be "behind the team, not against the opponent."

"I wanted the crowd at UCLA to be wildly enthusiastic about us and to stay off the other team," Wooden commented in 1980. "It is not just impolite and discourteous, but I think against the concept of the game itself. I believe the advantage of playing at home is that the home crowd encourages its own team and makes them play better rather than it hurts the other team's play. I think it's the better play of the home team that makes the other team appear to not do as well. I think the coaches have a responsibility in regard to spectator control, as does the athletic director and the president."

When the going got tough, the team didn't get flustered or down, it dug in. Competitive greatness is what Wooden calls this ability to truly love a hard battle, to realize that nothing of worth comes easy, that adversity can be enjoyable. "One of my players once said that I ran my basketball team like a machine," Wooden related in 1982, using a favorite analogy. "Now he was being a little critical, but I took it as a compliment. That is the way that I wanted them to be, like a well-oiled machine. I felt this had to be accomplished during the week of practice, not during the games. I don't think there is a tremendous amount of strategy involved during the course of a game if your job has been done during the week. If your job hasn't been done during that time, there probably is more strategy needed, but it won't be too successful. You'll often see a team ten points behind with a minute to go and the coach calls a time out and, boy, is he just telling them everything! Now, how in the world is he going to pick up ten points in a minute, against a team that in thirty-nine minutes has accumulated a big lead? It is just impossible."

"One point at a time," was Wooden's understated exhortation to his teams in the fifties. That message is what Barry Chasen, a Wooden player who today reminds Art Alper, his doubles partner in tennis and former basketball teammate, when they face a challenge on the clay court.

And when the teams won, as they almost invariably did, they acted like gentlemen. "Quiet and business-like, that's how I expect them to go out on the floor," Wooden related in 1964. Wooden allowed no histrionics after important victories because it was important that players learned to control their emotions—whether they won or lost. "I don't want them jumping around, no dancing on the floor like fools," is what Wooden instructed his players when they met Houston for a rematch in the 1968 NCAA tournament after the "Game of the Century" (where UCLA's winning streak ended). Nor did UCLA show it when they exacted revenge to the tune of 101-69. Likewise, there was no belly-aching after defeats. Dignity was required at all times, along with perspective. There was much more to life than fame.

UCLA basketball, fundamentally, was coolness under pressure. "Anybody who doesn't put pressure on himself is not worth much," Wooden has stated. "But if we permit outside pressure to influence us very much, we wouldn't be worth very much." Wooden's legacy is the quality and standard of play and sportsmanlike conduct he brought to basketball. What is the ideal player for Wooden? "If I could choose the ideal player," he said, "I'd choose someone who could play defense, offense, was quick, unselfish, team-oriented, no problem on or off the court and a good student. Why not just take Keith Wilkes and let it go at that?" Finally, "I've always felt that quickness is the most important physical asset an athlete can have. Naturally, you want as much size as you can get to go with the quickness, but if I had to sacrifice one for the other, it would be size every time."

The players came from diverse backgrounds, and "we didn't hang around together off the floor," star forward Keith Erickson recollected, "but once on the floor, everyone got along together like a glove on a hand."

To promote team spirit, Wooden did not allow team members to belittle their colleagues. He was always handing out mimeographed sheets of maxims, his philosophy, expectations, and motivational thoughts. When a season ended, the returning players and potential squad would receive a letter from him to guide them through the summer. In his 1970 letter to the team, players were instructed to show up for practice with their feet tough and in condition, with no facial or long hair, to remember they were representatives of UCLA and thus set an example, and to maintain the determination to meet the expectation sought by the player, the coach and the team. Wooden closed the letter as follows:

Please come in and chat with me whenever you feel like it, but remember that it isn't necessarily lack of communication if we fail to agree on your position or the position of another on the team. I am and always will be interested in you and your problems, but do feel that one should never become too dependent upon others for the solution of personal problems. Talking them over, however, to a friendly ear can be of help. I have found prayer to be the most helpful when I am troubled, and believe that all prayers are heard and answered, even though the answer is no.

Have a pleasant and productive summer.

Wooden's favorite spectator sport is baseball. One coach he greatly admired was the late Walter Alston, who coached the Los Angeles Dodgers to be World Series champions. Wooden used to attend about half their home games in Southern California. Their temperaments were similar, and Alston was one of the most respected coaches in his sport, which made them likely candidates for friendship. Like Wooden, Alston rarely raised his voice. Asked about this similarity, Wooden replied, "That's one thing I try not to do. I try to be very firm. You may have to raise your voice a little but yelling is a definite weakness. I think it's like the use of profanity. I think it's a weakness if you have to use it to get your point across."

On another occasion, Wooden spoke of his admiration for Alston, "He's a patient man, patient in bringing along his players. Oh, he's gone through his problems. You can't help but have problems when you've got twenty-five men who just want to play. But just as in basketball, you'd have to do what you think is right. You don't hear Walter Alston blast players, nor does he blast critics. He's firm, without being bull-headed. I admire that quality. He makes decisions with reason and the knowledge and information available. But he could tell you Buckner's average against a certain left-handed pitcher just like that. I heard a heckler ask him once if it wasn't tougher to manage when you were down on the list than fighting for the pennant and he very calmly said, 'No, just more disappointing. I just do the best job I can all the time. There are many things the manager has no control over, others he does. . .'"

Alston was equally complimentary. In December of 1973, Alston agreed with a reporter from UPI press service that Wooden may be the greatest coach in any sport, ever. "Why, you stop and think about it, they're going for their seventy-eighth consecutive victory," Alston observed of what would become eighty-eight consecutive victories. "It sounds absolutely incredible. I don't care what kind of teams you're playing, or even if they're only exhibition games, seventy-eight straight games without a defeat is something you just don't see happen in an ordinary lifetime. That coach of theirs has to be the best I've ever seen."

Wooden was an all-round athlete as he aged. Kareem Abdul-Jabbar recalls Wooden watching several of his players demonstrate their finesse at billiards, then his being handed a cue and dropping seven balls in a row, including long angles and combinations. When Jabbar kidded him about his skill, Wooden joked, "Misspent youth." Gail Goodrich observed Wooden routinely sink twenty consecutive shots during practices.

Bill Walton, in 2000, marveled at Wooden's fitness, that he "would warm us up every day, and he would put his hands out to shake the wrists and the fingers loose, he was so quick. When I played for him—he was in his mid-60s at the time—and his hands would disappear." Wooden also played golf, though he had to give it up when his back injury from World War II gave him trouble.

"I would say being in good condition sets a better example for those whom you are teaching, but it not an absolute essential quality," Wooden opined in 1980. "Any person in good physical condition has an advantage whatever their profession is," he added.

PRACTICES AND PLANNING

Wooden was always prepared as a coach. His practices were fast-paced and organized. Using 3" x 5" index cards (on the back of which he made notes) that contained the day's drills—which were five to eight minutes in length, Wooden's practices ran 1-1/2 to 2 hours, less than many other teams drilled, and *never* went overtime. There were many drills in the practices because "I don't want it to become monotonous for them. I want them to respond to each drill. I've found that if you extend any one thing very long, certain individuals with short attention spans will become careless." Wooden would say about his practices that he didn't work his teams as long or as often as some other coaches did, "but we got a great deal accomplished. It's like the saying that goes 'Don't mistake activity for achievement.'" His players were probably the best conditioned of the time. He didn't waste time in practice, kept it interesting for them, while teaching the fundamentals.

"I feel that one of my strengths was practice organization; we moved quickly from one drill to another," Wooden said in 1988. "I didn't try and condition my players through just running. I wanted to condition my players through fundamental drills. Every drill that we did I wanted to do quickly, I wanted to move position quickly. We're getting our condition through our movement in the drills we would have. In a sense I wanted to kill two birds with one stone."

But Wooden didn't work them too hard, explaining in his textbook, "Since it has been established that the learning processes are closely related to physical, mental, and emotional fatigue, it is not wise to continue past the point where such a condition becomes apparent. This is particularly true once the team has attained good physical condition. In your early season practices it may be advisable to continue conditioning drills a few minutes each day past the point where they are tired but never try to teach past that point." After a practice, Wooden would "sit down with my assistant immediately after practice and before my shower and briefly analyze and discuss the practice of that day."

Players were not allowed to interrupt practices, and hence the rhythm of the same. "Players now feel more things should be explained to them completely," Wooden told the *Los Angeles Times* in 1971. "Well, that's always been part of my teaching method, explaining the purpose of a thing to get the best result. But now some might even like to debate an issue with you. Discussion is all right, but I don't think it's right on the practice floor. I have my practices planned meticulously, and if I take time out for this, I won't have time for that. If they have complaints and want to talk to me afterwards, that's perfectly all right." Wooden was clearly in command at his practices, as evidenced by his tone of voice, which could sometimes be sharp. In 1972, Wooden agreed, "I believe a sharp commanding tone of voice gets better results when you're not there working on things together. It makes you snap, be a little more with it. When you're talking with players privately, I think a calm, pleasant, almost comforting approach is better except for rare individuals."

"All this was done in the subtlest of ways," Bill Walton wrote in 1999. "While our practices were the most demanding endeavors that I've ever been a part of, so physically, emotionally, mentally and psychologically taxing, there is always the sense of joy, of celebration and of people having fun playing a simple game. Always positive, always constructive, John Wooden drives us in ways and directions that we are not aware of, always with the goal of making us better. It is never about him, never about the struggle for material accumulation, but always about individual skill and personal development within the framework of the team, the game and UCLA."

One of Coach's favorite quotes is by Robert Louis Stevenson: "To travel hopefully is a better thing than to arrive, and the true success is to labor." Another is by Cervantes, that "the journey is greater than the inn."

"Well, I sort of equated that. . . I always, from the beginning, enjoyed planning my practices and conducting my practices more than I did the game," said Wooden. He improved his teaching and strategy every year. He was meticulous, teaching the small necessities and the big picture. The first practice of each year included a demonstration on how to tie shoe laces, and as a result, "I never had a player who had a problem with blisters," explained the coach. A few practices in, the players would hear about the Pyramid of Success.

In 1972, Wooden explained that "there are three parts to every season. The first part of the season is the early practice state, between the start of practice and the first game. At that time, I am trying to determine the top seven players, maybe eight, the ones who will play until the games are won or lost. I want five men who play together as a team, and sometimes those are not the most talented five you have. This is the part of my thinking which is often the most difficult for the players to understand. But I have to look out for the good of the whole team and this means that certain individuals are disappointed. The next part of the season are the early games when you put into practice the things you have been learning in the workouts. That's where I, as a coach, must try this group of players against foregoing opponents and make any adjustment." The third part of the season, of course, is the formal season where "we hope we will have another part," but "we do not anticipate NCAA competition. We are only sure that we are going to play the first three parts of the season, so we concentrate on that."

In 1980, Wooden stated that, "I sometimes considered the season to be like a play. Perhaps it's because of my English background in teaching some of the plays, Shakespeare in particular. I would say that the first part of the off-season, your recruiting is like getting a cast ready, getting players. Practice starts on October 15, but prior to that you're trying to get players ready and attempting a story, a plan for the season, a rough plan, a practice. Then you start practice on October 15 and it's like a rehearsal to begin with. You're tying to decide on the cast, and what roles they're going to fill, what part they are going to play. I like to feel that the first games, the games though December, were like dress rehearsal. Then the actual play itself is to get feeling for the audience and to find out if my casting may have been a little incorrect. I might have to change a position or character. I am determining this through the conference game in December. Then the conference starts the first of January and that's putting the show on the road. Our cast has been assembled, we've rehearsed, we're prepared, everything is all set. Now it's good enough to go on the road. That's the conference, now we hope that we're going to be so good there's going to be an encore. The encore is going to be the NCAA tournament."

Jack Tobin, who co-wrote with Coach, *They Call Me Coach*, and covered the Bruins for *Sports Illustrated* and other publications, recalled that in 1963, "I went out one day to see him, just walking in. 'Do not disturb' was on the door. The door had never been closed in my memory. I walked over to the secretary and asked if the Coach was in there and she said, 'He can't be bothered. I can't even phone him.' I came back when the door was open and asked what it was all about? There he was going back over every single day of his coaching career, his cards and notes to find out what he was missing, why they hadn't won the NCAA. He finally concluded that there was only one thing he could see that might be wrong. He usually played five people together all the time. When the team got in trouble was when someone got hurt during the game or if somebody got in foul trouble, and one or two people off the bench had to be in there, they didn't mesh the way he wanted them to. The gist of his discovery was that he would thereafter decide at the outset the seven or eight people who were going to play basketball for UCLA that year, barring injuries. He would previously rotate ten players. That is why the 1963-64 team fell into mesh and won, and one of the reasons for the streak."

This is an example of how Wooden's mind worked in his business context; he learned from his failures. "Good things take time," is one of Wooden's favorite phrases, Wooden noted in 1975, along with it's complement, "Be quick, but don't hurry." He continued, "At the beginning of this year, I said, 'We're going to be a good basketball team, and it's going to take a lot of work. Good things take time. Good things should be difficult to acquire. So we're gonna have to work hard, and it's going to take time, and we're gonna have to show patience,' and I try to use this as an approach. . ."

In 1980, Wooden discussed how he came to this conclusion: "I consider cohesion to be extremely important. I believe three things are vital for team success: the ability to quickly and properly execute the fundamentals, team play and team spirit, and consideration for others. That's cohesion, working together and being considerate of others. It is most important in any team activity or any group activity. Cohesion is one of my reasons for believing that only seven or eight players are going to play the vast majority of the time until the game is won or lost. Why? Because I think those that have had more playing time together are gong to function better as a group. If you start out having ten or twelve men play equal time, there's no way that any five you put together could function that well together.

His coaching philosophy is simple, "Get the players in the best of condition, teach them to execute the fundamentals quickly. Drill them to play as a team."

At his press conference after winning the semi-final game against

Louisville in 1975, Wooden revealed his technique, "Our teams are always in good condition. I'd try to talk them into it if I don't work them into it. I try to get them to thinking. I feel that part of my philosophy is to tell my teams at the beginning of the year—I've done this for a long time [at the] first meeting I have with them before practice starts—that one of the things we intend to do is be in better condition than any team against whom we'll participate. I explain how that can be done. I can do my part on the floor. They'll have to do their part between practices. I want to get them thinking they're in better condition. I guess it's the power of positive thinking to some extent, although not entirely, because we work 'em without a lot of wasted time. They're not unusually long but we keep them working."

Wooden believes that a "thorough proficiency in the fundamentals enables each player to adjust quickly and counteract whatever the other team might throw at us. That way we can execute something without thinking too long about how we're going to do it." For Wooden, "Repetition is the last law of learning," the method by which the fundamentals become rooted.

In 1998, Wooden described his approach this way. "First of all, I never talked to my players about winning in the general sense that most people consider winning," he said. "My whole philosophy is based on trying to get them to never think about their opponent, just think about themselves. I say never compare. It is impossible to compare accurately and validly, so just concentrate on improving yourself day by day. You don't do it in great leaps and bounds, but just try to do a little bit everyday and if you do that everyday, just a little bit. . . it eventually adds up to a considerable amount. . ." He did permit his players to think about their condition in relation to the other team. "Never think of your bruises or fatigue," he would tell them. "If you are tired, think of how 'all in' your opponent may be."

Bill Bertka, in 1972, operating the largest scouting bureau for collegiate basketball, observed that he received few scouting requests about UCLA. "One reason," he said, "is that everything they do is so predictable."

On the other hand, Wooden was no fool and he played close to the vest to thwart his competitors. For example, in 1980 Wooden advised that, "The out-of-bounds plays that we used in non-conference games would not be the ones we used in the conference. I didn't want to show what we used in the conference. I would not show certain things when we were winning easily in a conference game. I wanted to have certain things at our disposal when we were in tight situations or tough games. We may have need of them in the first game, but we tried not to show everything early." Wooden literally kept opposing teams on their toes.

Wooden says, "I am not a strategy coach, I am a practice coach." Wooden habitually states that "I loved practices far more than I ever loved games. The games were an exam. I could see whether I had done things in practice right."

UCLA, under Wooden, could be expected to ruin the tempo and style of any opponent, doing so by a constant running attack and a ball-grabbing, hand-waving, unrelenting, harassing defense. Wooden would reiterate to his teams, "Don't panic, they'll break." Wooden did very little scouting of his opponents. His teams used fundamentals that worked on any team.

In 1980, Wooden stated his opinion of scouting opponents: "I probably scouted opposing teams less than any other coach in the county. That doesn't mean I didn't scout. I want to have a general idea of the other team. I think over-scouting can be as harmful as over-coaching. I think there's a lot of both. I wanted to have a general idea about the other team but I did not want to know all the little intricacies and habits of each individual and have a player of mine waiting for some player to do something he might not do. I considered the main thing to be the development of my own team. If I knew the other coach, I'd know if he used a zone, fast break, press, etc. I'd know his offensive and defensive styles of play, which was all I really need to know. A couple of times a year I liked to have a scouting bureau scout UCLA and send me the report as if they were scouting UCLA for someone else. Maybe they'd see something that might be of benefit to me, that I had overlooked for being too close to the picture."

Bill Walton confirms, "John Wooden was a practice coach. Everything was accomplished on the practice floor. At UCLA we did not have single set play that could be identified by a number or signal. Our offense was simply to get the ball to certain players in certain spots on the court and let them go to work. Everything was flow. . .rhythm. . .mechanical reproduction of memorized moves, set up by creative decision making, a skill developed in practice through countless repetition of anticipated situations. When the defense did nothing, we did another. When they overplayed, we backdoored. When they sagged in, we shot from the perimeter. John Wooden did not believe in taking time outs. They were an admission of defeat, where somehow, some way, the other team was able to accomplish something that you were unprepared for. And, as we all know from living with John Wooden for all these years, failing to prepare is preparing to fail. In all my years at UCLA we *never* called time out. Not once. It just gave the other team a chance to catch its breath."

Conditioning by Wooden was physical, mental and emotional, where athleticism and skill met judgement, where doing the right thing became routine. His players were trained to think and anticipate, not just jump, shoot and rebound. Yet they could pace themselves playing "all out" as they were physically fit. They were conditioned to be organized, and to enjoy playing as a team. Wooden's genius was motivating players to motivate themselves to motivate others on the team. He motivated everybody involved with the team: starters to those who didn't play much, the managers, those in the business office, the press, the fans—anyone who could help the team outscore its opponents.

Wooden was and is an organized man. His textbook, *Practical Modern Basketball* is a marvel to read, and offers tremendous insight into his strategy, methodology, and philosophy. Unlike other textbooks on athletics, the first 78 pages of the 452-page tome are devoted to the philosophy and general concerns of coaching, such as the attributes of assistant coaches and team managers, how a squad is selected, public relations, and trip organization. He lays out his defensive and offensive strategies, including how to break the press, and his many drills. As he notes, "There are no real secrets to the game, at least not for very long." It is an education in basketball, teaching, and how to be organized. All aspects of coaching are covered, every little detail, with remarkable precision and grace of writing style; plain-spoken, direct, yet elegant. His introduction to his coaching philosophy is a perfect example:

> *Psychiatrists tell us that two of the possible symptoms of insanity are delusions of grandeur and delusions of persecution. Since all coaches are subject to delusions of grandeur when their teams on occasion may accomplish what did not seem possible and subject to delusions of persecution when every close call and every break seem to go again them, they must be philosophically inclined to accept such event with calmness and composure and continue to make decisions in the clear light of common sense.*

No subject was unimportant, even game uniforms. "A neat attractive game uniform," Wooden wrote in his book, "can be an asset in the development of pride. The uniforms should be colorful without being gaudy. Some coaches feel that dull game uniforms induce dull play. Although this isn't necessarily true, attractive and well-fitting clothes always seem to add spirit to the wearer." He then goes on to describe in detail the perfect pants (full cut, tackle twill material with an attached belt and elastic back) and shirt ("a fine quality of tightly knit rayon Durene appeals to me," with eight inch numbers on the back and six inch on the front.)

Another example was his dictate as to how the players were to assemble during a time-out:

> *Position. I have conflicting ideas about this, but usually have the playing five form a semicircle in front of me with their hands on their*

knees. The trainer wipes off the back of their necks with a damp towel, and the manager cleans the soles of their shoes. The other players form a semicircle behind the playing group.

I want the undivided attention of the players and want no one else to talk to them at all.

Occasionally, I have the playing five take seats alongside each other, and I have them with the others standing behind them.

Wooden had rules for post-game procedures, the first being: "See the opposing coach and congratulate him in a nice manner if you lose, or make yourself available to graciously accept his congratulations if your team was the victor." Then, the players were to be seen to give them a "lift" or "get their feet on the ground" and to check for injuries. The coach should then meet with reporters. After the players have showered and dressed, a short meeting should be held, followed by food for the hungry players.

With fundamentals also came perspective. His players were told, "You've come here for an education. That comes first." Basketball comes second, "because that is paying your way. You have to have some kind of social activity. But if you let your social activity take precedence of your education and athletic activity, you are not going to do well." This was emphasized by Coach and virtually every player graduated and went on to do great things, to be a productive member of society.

The 1960s saw the creation of "affirmative action" programs at virtually every campus in the nation. Students of color or from disadvantaged backgrounds who may have tested well verbally but not in math, or vice versa, or who demonstrated great ability in the arts, or as athletes, were given preference in admission. Those who availed themselves of this were almost entirely black. In the 1960s, UCLA's Academic Senate, which helped set the admission and educational boundaries, was deeply concerned about the quality of students entering. "Special admissions" were limited to 2 percent of those entering as students, about 120 per year, which was later raised to 4 percent (half of which would have to be used for minority students). One-fourth to one-third of these admissions were for athletic prowess. In 1962, for example, of 1862 male athletes, 90 were specially admitted (one of them being Arthur Ashe). There were those who made Wooden's teams, but Chancellor Franklin Murphy remembers that Wooden's comment on those who got in was, "By God, they are going to graduate." Virtually all of them did.

"If they weren't bright, he didn't want them," remembers Norman Miller, vice-chancellor of student affairs at UCLA from 1970-79, and a former professor of Kinesiology at UCLA. "He didn't think they were teachable or coachable."

Wooden wanted graduating seniors, student-athletes, well-balanced individuals on and off the court and those who could keep up academically, as UCLA was not a "mick" school. It took brains and effort to pass, and there were many professors who were not interested in giving any breaks to athletes. One had to do the work to be bright and diligent as a student to graduate from UCLA. Wooden first looked for players who could make the team, then "the first thing we wanted to find out was whether he had the grades to get in. Then the next thing I would want to find out would be how quick he is in relation to others in the position he would be playing in college. I consider quickness to be the most important physical asset of an athlete. Second to quickness I wanted to know what kind of person he was; was he a team player?"

Wooden always closely monitored the academic efforts of his players. Most did graduate. A study in 1961 showed that of the 1955-56 team, 12 of the 15 players earned their degree; the grade point average for all male undergraduate students above freshman standing in 1960-61 was 2.49; Wooden's players averaged 2.33. Wooden's average is remarkable, considering the four years preceding 2002, the graduation rate for UCLA's basketball team was 36 percent.

Thus, a large part of Wooden's talent and skill was his ability to know who to recruit, who would fit in with the team, who would respect him, the team, have the adequate motivation and intellectual wherewithal to complete UCLA's fairly difficult scholastic requirements.

Here follows the handout Wooden gave to the members of his teams:

1. *You are in school for an education. Keep that first in your thoughts, but place basketball second.*

2. *Do not cut classes and do be on time.*

3. *Do not fall behind and do get your work in on time.*

4. *Have regular study hours and keep them.*

5. *Arrange with your professors in advance when you must be absent.*

6. *Do not expect favors. Do your part.*

7. *Arrange for tutoring at the first sign of trouble.*

8. *Work for a high grade point average. Do not be satisfied by merely meeting the eligibility requirements.*

9. *Do your assignments to the best of your ability, but never be too proud to seek help and advice.*

10. *Earn the respect of everyone.*

Intelligence, skill and poise typified the Wooden teams. Wooden's low-profile and self-effacing, dignified nature downplayed this achievements and those of his teams, but by the early 1970s, UCLA drove such a juggernaut that some coaches questioned whether UCLA's continuing domination was good for the sport. Consider this sampling from 1973. Glenn Dicker of the *San Francisco Chronicle* wrote, "It's a sad thing what has happened to college basketball. UCLA makes everybody else play for second place."

L. H. Gregory wrote in the *Portland Oregonian*, "Gets rather monotonous, doesn't it? UCLA week after week, month after month, season after season, winning every basketball game it plays."

"What John Wooden has done in college basketball is to wreck it. What used to be a tingling spectacle has become, when the Bruins are in town, any town, like feeding time at the zoo. You don't really expect the bone to bite back at the lion, but there is a certain fascination in watching him crack it with his teeth," posited George N. Meyers in the *Seattle Times*.

There was serious debate as to whether UCLA could beat professional teams, with Wooden agreeing that on a given night against a given team, UCLA could probably outscore an opponent. Wooden had a calm reply for the critics. "The same thing was said about the Yankees in baseball years ago," he said. "Whether it's an individual or a team, whenever you reach a plateau of excellence, there are always people who want to reach your plateau of excellence, there are always people who want to see you knocked down. Then when it happens, they don't know what they were really complaining about. There were those who wanted to see Joe Louis get whipped when he was heavyweight champion all those years. Then when he did, many of those same people were sorry. How many fans are mourning for Arnold Palmer right now because he's in a tremendous slump? A tremendous number."

Ruminating at the height of the UCLA epoch, Wooden commented, "No, I don't think we've created a monster by winning so much. Rather than calling what we achieved a dynasty, I prefer to think of it as a cycle. And I believe all cycles come to an end. But certain things can make the cycle extend longer than normal. Little things, such as attentiveness to detail. Things that don't show up in the box scores. Things that help a player shoot better, rebound better, switch men on defense better. They're only minor things but they mean a great deal."

It was this attention to detail that got UCLA and Wooden to the pinnacle of success, all of it done in a methodical, thorough manner. "Positive aggressiveness" is what Wooden termed his style, based on Piggy Lambert's theory, oft-repeated by Wooden, "that the team that makes the most mistakes will probably win," because "if you're not making mistakes, you're not doing anything. I might not go as far as Lambert, but I'm positive that a doer makes mistakes. . .

I'd rather have a 50 percent shooting average with 100 shots than 80 percent of 60 attempts."

THE END OF THE DYNASTY

Felled by a heart attack in 1973, which forced him to miss his first game in thirty-eight years of coaching, Wooden quickly recovered and the team, undaunted, won the NCAA championship that season. By then, the pressure from all quarters—fans, alumni, the press, the past— on Wooden and his UCLA teams was enormous. "I don't know whether always winning is good," Wooden said in 1972. "It breeds envy and distrust in others, and overconfidence and a lack of appreciation very often in those who enjoy it." Wooden began to long for the days when he could "play to win, instead of playing not to lose." It was stressful on Coach. He usually had no problems sleeping before a game. In 1991, he admitted that, "After almost every game, I hardly slept at all, I'd play the game over and over in my mind, looking at all the things we did right or wrong. Even if you win by twenty points, you can do a lot of things wrong."

On March 29, 1975, Wooden ultimately prevailed in a semi-final game with Louisville—against a team helmed by his former assistant, Denny Crum. At the pre-game news conference (which took place some two hours before Wooden announced his retirement to a startled press), Wooden admitted he was sometimes nervous, but didn't want to display it before, during, or after an important game. "I try not to show it," he explained. "I don't want it to affect my players. If I show nervousness, and too much anxiety, too much spirit, too much temperament, it might carry over to my players, so I try to keep that much control as much as possible. I've long ago embraced the philosophy that I do the best I can. I make mistakes, but I can live with them now. Once they bothered me a lot, but now I know I make 'em and they don't bother me later on."

At that same press conference, Wooden dismissed any negative feelings about Crum, any of his other former assistant coaches, or Gary Cunningham, his then assistant. He explained that he disagreed with all of his assistants on many subjects, but that didn't mean they weren't close and respected, that any "disagreement is no different [than one] between man and wife. The love continues."

Nell Wooden didn't mince words in 1974, "These should have been the best years of our lives, but they haven't been. Nine national championships in ten years is great. So are the winning streaks. But the fans are so greedy. They've reached the point where they are unhappy if John wins a championship game by only five points. If he even loses a game they're going to say that he's too old and he's lost his touch. You learn to prepare yourself for the worst and then hope it doesn't happen. They can stretch the rules and let him stay until he's sixty-seven but I wonder if it would be worth it. What more does my husband have to prove?"

The heart attack revealed that Wooden had 65 percent blockage in two coronary arteries. He then began a program of walking five miles a day, doing so in one hour's time, at 6:30 a.m. around the UCLA jogging track. He said at the time, "Some people ask me if I like it. I ask them if they have ever seen the Listerine commercial. Walking is good for me, but I hate it. Until I get breakfast in me, I'm tired and mean. I guess you could say there are some things I enjoy about the walking. I enjoy watching the sunrise. I keep myself occupied during the time I'm walking by reciting poetry and sometimes I hum. I find that helps to ease the monotony."

A year later, in 1974, Wooden modified this comment. "What I mind is the getting here. I like to get up early—always have—but I was used to having a leisurely breakfast and reading the papers, then going about my business. I can't eat before I walk, I have to eat afterwards. In the fall, it's beautiful out here. Each time I come around the track, the sun is a little different. I often wish I were an artist, so I could really paint the sunrise. I'd like to know if other people see it the same way I do. It makes you wonder."

A typical day during the season, after the walk, would be followed by breakfast, and a nine-thirty a.m. meeting with his assistants to plan practice for the day. Wooden would then take care of correspondence (personally responding to the two to ten letters he would daily get from fans once the dynasty began), have lunch, and then, "I wanted to be the first one at practice." Wooden made notes of the players at every practice, and had with him what each player had done in the same practice given at the same time in previous years, if they had been juniors and sophomores under him, so he could observe what changes and improvements had been made. This is a prime example of his attention to detail.

Wooden loved to learn, and during the off-season, he became an autodidact. Two to four weeks after the season was over, "I chose a topic of the game, such as rebounding, or zone press, or some fundamental of the game [to research]. It might be a fast break, the jump shot, free throw shooting, defensive footwork, zone attack, zone defense," Wooden revealed in 1980. "[I would] get every book on the subject from those I respected and were proficient at this element." He would then go through all the issues of *Scholastic Coach* and *Athletic Journal* and single out all articles on that topic. "Once I had selected the appropriate literature, I'd take ideas out of every one. Then I'd start a process of crossing-out and making a composite list. Toward the end of the summer I'd have a pretty good composite theme on the topic. If someone has something that's been very good, let's say free throw shooting, I'd try to talk to that individual and get further information as to his ideas. If some coach seemed to attack zones really well, I'd contact him. If all coaches agree on one thing, it must be pretty good. If someone has done real well in a specific area, why? I want to know why. I did that for about twenty of my twenty-seven years at UCLA, I took a different topic every year.

"When Alcindor came, I never had anyone that size," said Wooden, "so I contacted (NBA great) Wilt Chamberlain and other tall players to see what I could do to help the group as a whole. I would then call their coaches, and make one composite of all I had learned. I learned much from others, especially from those who disagreed with my philosophy."

Wooden would likewise help any coach who sought advice from him, and many high school and junior college coaches did, but not too many from the university level, which he thought was "unfortunate" as he "had no hesitancy about contacting Adolph Rupp."

Every year after the close of the season, Wooden would have a meeting to go over the season just passed and think of ways to improve the program. A list of issues would be developed. "We might talk about special situation like protecting a lead, the changing of a press, the trap, out of bounds, half-time procedures," Wooden said in 1980.

Although Wooden had many opportunities to coach professional basketball, some of which would have tripled his salary, he never chose to do so because both he and his family preferred college ball, and there was no other team that could entice him away from UCLA. "I was interested in the pros at the time because it seemed like such a big thing," he said. "Financially, as I told my family, it was a tremendous opportunity, and I could do a lot more for them personally if I took the job. But I left the actual decision entirely up to my wife and children. They talked things over among themselves and decided it would be best for me to stay at UCLA. Of course, I knew when I asked them what their answer would be!" In 1998, Wooden commented further, "There's one reason at all to go and that's money. And if you make money by God, you're going to be unhappy. True happiness comes from things that can't be taken away from you, and all material things get away from you. I wouldn't have liked the traveling. You're away from home, it would have been rough on family life. There are so many problems in the families of professional athletes because they're away so much. Also, in the NBA, the players can get you fired if they don't like you. You're not really in control, some general managers are in control, sometimes it's the owners, sometimes it's both or either, and I wouldn't like that. . ."

THE JOHN WOODEN PYRAMID OF SUCCESS

His interaction with Lakers owner Jack Kent Cooke must have helped him make up his mind. Wooden was Cooke's dinner guest at a King's hockey game. "It was right after we had beaten Houston by about sixty-five points in an NCAA game. Cooke came up to me and said, 'Can you believe how Elvin Hayes choked?' And I said, 'No, Mr. Cooke, I don't think he choked. I just think he had a subpar game.' And Cooke said, 'Well, I think he choked.' And I said, 'I don't think so.' And he said, 'Listen, you're my dinner guest, and I think Elvin Hayes choked.' I don't think I would have lasted long working for Jack Kent Cooke."

"Cooke was a funny man," Wooden commented years later, about visiting him with Nell. "We went over to his house—a big, gated place. Cooke was in this huge den behind a big desk. He sat there and just looked at me. We sat for quite a while that way. Finally, he said, 'Why do you want to coach the Lakers.' I said, 'Mr. Cooke, I believe something is wrong here. I never said I wanted to coach the Lakers. Mr. Schaus (general manager of the Lakers) wanted me to come out because you said you wanted me to coach the Lakers."

Cooke responded, "Anyone would want to coach the Lakers," and showed Wooden his offer, "What do you think of that?" Wooden replied, "No one's worth that, but I won't take that."

Cooke cajoled, "Well, tell me how much you do want."

Wooden was unmoved, "It isn't just that, Mr. Cooke, I don't think I'd be the person to coach pro basketball, I'd have to be away from home all the time."

"Tell me how much you want," Cooke insisted.

"It isn't the money," Wooden stated.

"Get out," said Cooke.

"So we got up and left," recounts Wooden. Another reason, and one as important, is that Wooden liked college ball better. He told the AP in 1969: "I'm not saying there's no finesse in the pro game, but mainly brute strength."

In 1980, Wooden said, "I think that professional basketball can be good; it is just that I do not like the play too much. I would rather see a good college game any day. If you want to just see individual play, go see the pro game because you will see lots more of that. I do not believe there is nearly the amount of team play in the professional game that you see in the collegiate game. So it sort of depends upon what you are looking for and I happen to appreciate team play a little more." Wooden thus followed the Pyramid, he did what he loved, coaching college ball.

In an interview for this book in 1991, Wooden was questioned about his feelings about money.

Why didn't you care about making money in business? You must have realized how much money you were making for UCLA, particularly in the seventies.

Why didn't you negotiate a big fat salary at that time, the way the coaches are getting right now?

I can honestly say that money has never been my goal. My life, I've put my family first, and I hope my Lord second, and then my profession.

But it's not something you want to ignore, either.

No. I wanted to make a good living for my family. I'd be lying if I'd say that I didn't. But I wouldn't violate certain feelings that I had in order to do that. For example, I wouldn't take a large contract. . .to force my team to wear a certain shoe. I'm not critical of those who do, that's all right. I just happened to look at it differently. I don't believe in that. I'm gonna make my players use the shoe that I think is the best. I'm gonna make that decision, not because somebody's paying me to.

So your point about money is that you always had enough and you were happy with what you were doing.

It depends on what people think is enough.

Do you think you have been a great businessman?

I never, I never . . . no, I would have been a lousy businessman.

Oh, come on! Don't you think you would have been successful at anything you would have gone into?

I have no idea. I might have been better in some type of personnel work. I could have done something of that sort. As far as being a businessman for investments and things of that sort, no . . . I don't think so, I grew up where we had very little, so I never wanted a lot. And my wife, bless her heart, was the same way. We were always happy with what we had and were not worried or thinking about what someone else had. Part of the reason for my Pyramid of Success is my father who said, "Never try to be better than somebody else, but never cease to try to best that you can be." When you start worrying about what other people have, or wanting what other people have, that's when it affects yourself, and that eventually became my whole philosophy of coaching and teaching. Never compare yourself with others. These people you've talked to probably told you that they disagreed on this. Jerry [Norman] disagreed, Denny [Crum] disagreed. They thought I should scout more, and I didn't believe in scouting. They thought I should visit more prospects. I wouldn't do it. They disagreed, but that's all right. As I've said over and over, if you surround yourself with "yes" men, you're gonna be in trouble. I just hoped they'd realize that I had to make the final decision, and that's not easy.

Accumulating wealth has always been a secondary consideration for Wooden. He would rather do what he loves.

THE JOHN WOODEN PYRAMID OF SUCCESS

SAM GILBERT AND THE NCAA

There was never any scandal associated with Wooden, though there was talk that one booster, Sam Gilbert, might have broken NCAA rules by brokering tickets, and giving gifts and financial inducements to certain players, but nothing was ever proven, and he was shunned by Wooden.

Gilbert was a nuisance, if not a menace, to the sports department, as he "was contemptuous of NCAA regulations relating to what an athlete could receive," according to Byron Atkinson, vice chancellor of UCLA from 1958-80. This necessitated J.D. Morgan to call Gilbert to his office as he was "constantly trying to get him to keep his hands off our kids. J.D. was aware students were selling their tickets and turned a blind eye, but he wouldn't do anything shady."

"It isn't so bad what they were doing, selling tickets," averred Robert Fischer, Morgan's chief assistant.

In reality, there was no way to stop players from selling their seats. It is a given at virtually every arena where the sport is played in college, but Gilbert's involvement and danger to UCLA sports, accurately caused him to be viewed as a pernicious influence.

In 1992, Wooden commented for this book about his feelings toward Gilbert:

Sam Gilbert has to be the most controversial figure ever in UCLA Basketball. He was indicted [shortly] after he passed away for things unrelated to UCLA Basketball. But some people say that he had an undue influence over some of the players and was involved in unethical activity—loaning them money. Did you ever have any relationship with Gilbert?

Yes, I had a relationship with him, but I worried about him. I warned my players about him. But you can't pick their friends. You can warn them—you just absolutely can't pick their friends. If they are guilty of some things that you know about then you can take a certain action. But you can't act on suspicions. I warned my players. I knew that he latched on, but he never latched on until after we won the championship. There are a lot of people that latch on when you start winning championships. They'll leave you like a sinking ship, like rats will leave a sinking ship when you get down the other end. But I warned my players and I was worried about him. Yes I was worried but I've read things and heard things and I have been in his home and everything and never was anything true with that at all.

Did he ever try to initiate of a friendship with you?
Yes, I would say.

What did you do?
I just as politely—as courteously as I could—cut it off.

Because you felt he just wasn't your type of fellow?

Yes. I felt he meant well, but I felt that he was a person that was be wrong as far as the NCAA was concerned and he could be influential detrimentally to [the] program. Mr. Morgan talked with him. The director of athletics talked to him. I knew him. I would speak to him. He came to the games. I suspected he got his tickets from the players. He probably paid more than face value. But you can't even sell them for face value so that wouldn't make any difference.

Wooden was criticized for not being more observant or turning his back in the face of evidence, but little evidence was proffered, other than that some of the black players were sporting similar new coats and boots on one occasion, hardly a smoking gun. Wooden admits he worried about Gilbert, but all he could do was warn his players not to be associated with any illegality. After Wooden left, Gilbert continued to be a disturbing influence, for instance, creating a dispute with Larry Brown, UCLA's head basketball coach, in 1980. The NCAA banned him, ruling he could not associate with players. Gilbert apparently was a crook, and four days after he died in 1987 was indicted for laundering drug money by a Florida Grand Jury unaware of his death. During the Wooden era, Gilbert did ingratiate himself with a number of UCLA athletes, predominantly black, some of them to this day, such as Sidney Wicks, defend him. There probably were some violations of NCAA rules such as scalping of tickets, and gifts of clothing, nothing Wooden could control, as this was outside of his knowledge. This author is aware of at least one athlete who got a job from a booster where he got paid but didn't have to show up for work. In 1989, Wooden even had kind words to say about Gilbert: "He felt whatever he did was right, even if it was against the rules." In any event, Gilbert never had anything to do with recruiting, never had any opportunity to interfere with Wooden and the way he ran his operation, and Wooden could not have done more than he did without becoming Big Brother.

Wooden was also asked about the general integrity of NCAA basketball:

You had no knowledge of anybody getting paid off? (The question refers to whether he thought there was any truth to any rumors of any of his players having received any gratuities or favors in violation of NCAA rules.)

Not only no knowledge of it, I don't believe it. I still don't believe it. I can honestly say that I don't believe to the best of my knowledge in my twenty-seven years at UCLA I ever broke a single rule in the recruiting of an athlete, not a single one. After they were there I know some rules that I broke but I would stand up for every one that I broke and justify it.

THE JOHN WOODEN PYRAMID OF SUCCESS

What rules did you break?

Having kids over at my house for dinner—at Christmas or Thanksgiving.

You were not allowed to do that otherwise?

You weren't then—I don't think you still are. On two occasions I had youngsters that were picked up for traffic violations. I bailed them out of jail and that's against the rules. I'm not going to leave them in jail over the weekend. And I [would] tell them when I pick[ed them] up that they are going to have to pay it back. Deep down, I probably didn't expect for them to ever pay it back, but I [would] tell them that and I know it is against the rules. I know I did that.

During all the years since then there have been a number of schools that have been busted for NCAA violations. Isn't this a common or very prevalent practice for these kids to get inducements to play in violation of NCAA rules?

All I knew [were] rumors. Most rumors I don't believe. I would have no fact of basing that on other than I just might be suspicious. But I know that coaches are like lawyers, doctors, salesman. Not all are honest, but the vast majority are. A vast majority of people are good in whatever profession they're in.

You admit you violated some rules. Doesn't that go against your credo of being honorable at all times?

Yes, perhaps I'm a hypocrite. But only in the way that I think I was helping someone really in need, then I would have stood up for it. I didn't. Not to get a kid there. I would never do that.

As the dynasty continued, admiration for Wooden increased. The press of that period, and since, has treated him with respect and admiration, if not reverence. It's pretty much a love-fest, and there have been innumerable articles on Coach since he retired. He's always asked for his opinion about the latest trend or event in basketball, and writers all want to know how and what he is doing.

A typical example is an article in the *Long Beach Press Telegram* in March of 1998, where Wooden held court on a variety of basketball topics, including who was the greatest basketball player of the 20th century. "As you know," he said, "I've never been a man to rate all-time teams or all-time players, but since Michael Jordan has come to the Chicago Bulls after he was gone a while playing baseball, he's played at a level no person ever has in this game. He's definitely the best basketball player I've ever seen."

How does he rate college ball today? Wooden said in 1986, "To me it suffers from two things—too much physical contact that interrupts the flow of the game and too much individual showmanship. I'm interested in teamwork, in the rhythm of the game, in the beauty of watching a play unfold that eventually leads to a basket. If you're big enough and strong enough, anyone can slam-dunk. It isn't hard, and it calls attention to the man doing it. What I see mostly are too many individuals out on the court and not enough team play."

To another reporter in 1998, Wooden said if he could change one thing in basketball, "it might be to abolish the dunk. It's the most exciting thing as far as fans are concerned—fans roar then there's a dunk. And yet, they make a real good play, like a screen-and-roll or a nice give-and-go where there is teamwork involved and you'll get a smattering of applause. I think there's too much show-manship today. When I coached, a behind the back pass, or behind the back dribble meant you went to the bench. I think that has hurt the game. This is just an opinion now, it doesn't mean it's fact." Wooden's comments are an echo of the early days of the sport. As far back as 1895, basketball players were called cagers because there was so much fan interaction that chicken wire had to be erected around the court to prevent the same.

Wooden offered this commentary on basketball in February, 2002. "I think the athleticism of athletes today is out of this world, it's absolutely remarkable. But as the athletes individually have gotten better, in my opinion, the teamwork has not. I think maybe the reason for this is that they are so good individually, the coaches let them go out on their own because they can do so much individ-ually. I think Phil Jackson's greatest accomplishment for the (Los Angeles) Lakers and originally from the (Chicago) Bulls was the way he got the other players on the team to accept their roles and to accept (superstar Michael) Jordan and (Scottie) Pippen, and Shaquille (O'Neal) and Kobe (Bryant, the lat-ter two are the two Laker stars). It's getting the others. He has to convince the other players that they can't get along without Kobe and Shaquille, but Kobe and Shaquille can get along with other players other than (them), because there are a lot of other players available near the level of the other players on the team, but there aren't others available with the level of talent of Shaquille and Kobe. To some degree I had that when I had Lewis—uh—Kareem. I wanted all my players—and I failed miserably in some cases—to feel needed and wanted, even though some might be just a nut that holds the wheel on, but you have to have that wheel, and the nut holding the wheel, then what good was the pow-erful engine that was Alcindor? When I was working with Andy Hill on his book, I found out I failed miserably."

When Wooden learned a few years back that Jackson used Zen teachings to coach, Wooden read several books on the subject to educate himself, to see what might be useful to him—though he had long since left coaching—to bet-ter himself as a teacher and person

THE JOHN WOODEN PYRAMID OF SUCCESS

One doesn't think of Wooden as being a businessman, but of course he was. He knew that basketball was a leisure-time activity for most. He needed an audience, and deserved it. He was there to outscore his opponents, and be the best basketball coach he could be. He knew he had to market his product and he did. He took care of business when it came to dealing with the press, and he enjoyed it for the most part. But he was wary, advising in his textbook, "Never condemn the press as a group because you might occasionally find one who will betray a confidence."

A master of pubic relations, Wooden's philosophy was to just be himself. "The best thing you can do in public relations is just to be a polite person that has interest in other things as well as your own profession," Wooden said in 1980. "Too often we get lost so much in our profession that we forget that other people have a job to do. The more interest that you can show them, the more interest they will show you in you and your particular program. I tried to work from that angle. During the off-season I had many speaking engagements, but I tried to limit my commitment during the actual season, I did go to the weekly writers' meeting and weekly sportscasters' meeting. I tried to be as honest as I could with the questions, tying to keep in mind that they're doing a job just as I'm trying to do a job . . . I always believe that the product sells itself. Good teams were the best method you could possibly have to sell a program. Then if your good teams conduct themselves in a courteous manner, then you further sold it. I've seen some teams win national championships that I would have been ashamed, if I had been the coach, of the conduct that they had following and sometimes during the tournaments. I felt that they lost a little of what they had a chance to gain. I think I see a lot of it in professional sports, too. Coaches certainly have a responsibility along that line in public relations, and you can do an awful lot for your sport and your department."

The lesson we learn from the foregoing is the importance and value of curiosity. By being curious, one just might learn something, have a good laugh, make a new friend, have something or someone other than one's self to discuss with loved ones, friends and acquaintances, and business associates. Wooden has always been genuinely interested in other people. It's obvious to anyone who meets him. He loves meeting people, and not because of the praise he so often gets. He just likes to be engaged in life; doing so wards off and prevents boredom, can be exciting, is interesting and rewarding in many ways, for it broadens the experience simply of being a part of the planet. What use is there in the alternative, being withdrawn, cold, closed, only interested in one's own agenda? One learns by meeting others.

We are talking about social skills, and Wooden by this discourse reveals one of his special techniques—being genuinely interested in the other person. A person can tell when one is making conversation just to do it or when it is for real. Those who meet Wooden lock eyes with him, he is focused and ready for any gambit, quip, piece of information or dialogue there to be invented. Because he so conducted himself in his business, he earned the respect of those with whom he interacted. And it wasn't just with the press—fans, alumni, students all felt the same warmth and gave it back to him. He did it because being friendly brought him happiness. The reward, corny as it sounds, was a little bit of love, camaraderie, a sharing of experience, something by which to give meaning to what Wooden did. After all, the press was there because he was there and his teams won. If they were interested in him, why shouldn't he be interested in them? They were, in a more cosmic sense, part of the same team, united in a common love of sport. They needed each other and Wooden understood that dynamic and made it pleasant for them. It wasn't just a job for any of them but a common endeavor which multiple parts, variables, highs and lows, its own set of politics and pressures. During the dynasty, everybody wanted to talk to Coach Wooden. The amazing thing is that Coach *wanted* to talk to everybody. It was and still is his way of having fun and relaxing. And he didn't just do it in business, but has always done so with everyone he meets in life.

Wooden was doing what he wanted, being a part of a team. That is what companies are, only Wooden had a new team, new "workers" every year. His assistant coaches came back, but student players graduated. It was solid management by UCLA's coaching staff. Their business was playing basketball, teaching young men how to play in two-hour practices, while ensuring their player's well-being in the test of their lives. When it came to doing the best job economically, here's another example. "I don't believe there's been a coach since I retired that went out with a trainer when they were on the road to find where they could get a better deal on meals," stated Wooden. "They don't give those things a thought. And they don't have to, and I'm not saying they should, mind you, but I'm just saying those are just some of the things that when they say they have it tough. Oh, to me, they don't know what it is to have it tough."

J.D. MORGAN

Wooden got on well with his superiors, Wilbur Johns, his first director of athletics, and J.D. Morgan, who succeeded him. Morgan, according to Wooden, "was a very strong person, a man of enormous retentive memory. I dare say he's the only director of athletics at any major university that would know by name and know something about every athlete in every sport. He would know them all. And he was a businessman. He kept UCLA in the black by astute scheduling. Dominant, domineering. A lot of people didn't like him for that. I liked him, and we got along fine." In his textbook, Wooden stated that it was necessary to have the cooperation of those in administrative positions, "Be loyal to them and they will be with you. Remember that an ounce of loyalty is worth a pound of cleverness. Your success or failure will also reflect on them and you would not have the job if they were not with you."

It is fair to describe Wooden as a genius, which the dictionary defines as one who has an exceptional natural capacity of intellect, but he also worked very hard and diligently at exploiting his natural and learned abilities. Besides coaching teams, Wooden also comprised part of a team that managed teams, the UCLA Athletic Department. It all came together for Wooden and UCLA basketball in 1963-64, when they won the first championship. But the back-office team played just as important a role as the team Wooden fielded, helped by another genius who assisted in bringing all together, J. D. Morgan, who succeeded Wilbur Johns on July 1, 1963.

Johns, who had hired Wooden, was a "very fine, very nice person" and "easy to get along with," remembered basketball trainer and track coach Ducky Drake in 1979.

That did not matter to Franklin Murphy, chancellor of UCLA from 1960-68, who declared in an oral history for UCLA in 1982, that he replaced Johns "because his business-administrative operations were inadequate."

The genesis of the problem went back to Robert Sproul, president of the University of California for three decades from 1930 on, who, said Murphy, believed that "athletics [were] not part of the basic program. It was student oriented, and therefore all the intercollegiate programs on the several campuses would be managed by the student organizations. This, of course, was ironic and quite mistaken in my view, because here was the chancellor on campus, charged with the responsibility of everything there, and yet the associated students were charged with a very important part of the program. I got curious about this, and after looking into it, I discovered that in effect, it was a financial shambles. The intercollegiate program was in the red. They were using funds to pay current bills on the basis of ticket subscriptions for the following years. [In 1959-60, the athletic department had $437,00 in revenue and $610,442 in expenses.] The first thing I did was to urge the regents to change the rules and put the intercollegiate athletic programs under the chancellor of the particular campus. This was accomplished finally [in July of 1960]."

Murphy wanted sports to be housed and seen on campus. When he arrived there was no arena for basketball, swimming, or track, and it would need a great deal of money to provide for, which he did not want to do "until I had the basic department properly organized with proper leadership." He also wanted to broaden the minor sports—those other than football, basketball, track and baseball—so he assigned Charles Young, who would succeed him as Chancellor in 1968, to help him pick the next athletic director. After consultation with those in the athletic department, Young became convinced that J.D. Morgan, UCLA's tennis coach, was the right person.

Morgan mentored—and remained very close thereafter—to Arthur Ashe, the gentle, polite tennis champion who broke the color barrier in tennis and led an exemplary life until his tragic passing in 1993 from AIDS, the result of a tainted blood transfusion administered to him.

"To convince my father that I could come to a place 3,000 miles away, he had to convince my father he would take care of me. J. D. took care of me," Ashe said in 1987.

Under Morgan, Ashe became the first prominent African-American male tennis player to become a superstar in college and professional tennis, winning the NCAA singles title in 1965, and with Ian Crookenden, the doubles title the same year. As a pro, Ashe took the U.S. Open in 1968, the Australian Open in 1970 and the 1975 Wimbledon championship. He was *Sports Illustrated's* 1992 Sportsman of the Year.

Morgan's career as a coach was equally distinguished. His teams won the NCAA championship, seven (1952, 1953, 1954, 1956,1960, 1961, 1965) out of the eleven years he was head tennis coach (through 1966). His teams placed second four times, and he produced four NCAA singles champions and five NCAA doubles team champions.

Morgan had attended UCLA as a student, where he played tennis, working his way up to number one on the team, and fought in World War II as a PT boat commander, assigned next to future United States President John F. Kennedy's squadron. Morgan, a great kidder with a good sense of humor, was worldly and seemingly knowledgeable about almost everything and everywhere—including where to stop on the road to get the best watermelon, the quickest route to any location, where to stay and to dine.

"J.D. always gave the impression he was in full control of the situation— even when he wasn't," said Charles Pasarell, one of his talented tennis stars.

Young ran his nomination by Wooden, who readily concurred.

"I have always said it was one of the best appointments I ever made," recounted Murphy.

When Morgan came, Pauley Pavilion became the priority. "Wooden was a powerful speaker and he'd impressed on everybody—the chancellor, J.D., the committees and faculty, they could not expect to have a great program without a decent facility," remembers former Vice Chancellor Byron Atkinson, UCLA's Vice-Chancellor from 1958-80. The process to get it built was underway at the time, but until 1965, UCLA's athletic department was housed in pathetic Quonset huts—semi-cylindrical metal shelters having end walls, more suitable for barracks or storage sheds.

Morgan, big-boned at 240 pounds on a 5-foot-11 frame, possessed of a deep, rough, loud voice was an imposing, powerful, feared, no-nonsense individual who knew what he wanted, how to get it, and almost always did. Morgan was way ahead of everyone else in knowing how to promote and get publicity for athletics. He was "knowledgeable, shrewd and would present an argument in its most favorable light," reminisced Atkinson. In public, Morgan presented the audience information slowly, dramatically and eloquently. With his friendly demeanor he could and would recruit when called upon by a coach.

"J.D. liked to talk to every prospect," Wooden recalled, adding that, "he wanted to know something about every youngster that was going to be potentially a performer in the more visible and income producing sports. However, I think he wanted to do it whether it would be track, baseball, swimming, tennis, golf or in any other non-income sport." Wooden remembered that Morgan "wanted to personally talk to every recruit when they were brought to the campus for a visit," to have "as much advance information about them as possible," that he "always liked to talk to them alone, too." Wooden cannot recall anyone who Morgan can particularly take credit for bringing to UCLA, but, he said Morgan met with all of the recruits, and presumes he was a helpful force, noting that once they signed on, Morgan wanted to be apprised of how they were doing at all times, that they were making normal progress to a degree, not just eligibility.

Morgan was unimpressed with Wooden's efforts at recruiting, believing he should have done more of it, visited more homes, contacted prospects first, that he didn't not spend enough money from the budget doing so.

Morgan, who had encyclopedic knowledge of sports, is a legend among sports cognoscenti for his ability and skill in executing the business of sports, and during his working years was widely considered as one of the top two or three athletic directors in the nation.

Wooden describes Morgan as a "very dominant, aggressive type of person—very outspoken and forceful," though he was a "little pompous, which alienated certain people. But he was just so positive in his own particular thoughts and believed in them so much that he came on very strong, which come people did not like . . . Someone might make a suggestion, and he might put them down, almost to the point of making you feel like only an ignoramus would suggest something of that sort. Now he wouldn't say that in so many words, but his manner would give that impression. And that would happen even on occasion to some of his coaches. There were certain coaches with whom he never got along too well. And he had some real 'run-ins' with some of the coaches that could be heard down the hall. But that would be one day, and then that's over, that's past, that's gone. He didn't carry things over." In Wooden's opinion, Morgan "was extremely forceful and knowledgeable, but I think you had to know him . . . To me he was not arrogant but . . . supremely confident and he backed it up.

"I'd say J.D. had it very much like a dictatorship," Wooden adds, "and a dictatorship is good, in my opinion, if the dictator is good. But the dictator better be good. I would say, even as a form of government, a dictatorship, with a dictator that was truly a dictator with the interest of the people, might be the most effective form of government. It might not, too. But that's saying [you have] the proper dictator. Now, I don't favor it, but because I don't think you can get the proper one, but I think the UCLA athletic department under J.D. was pretty much that. I think he was in sole and complete charge, and being extremely capable, did a great job for the UCLA department of athletics."

Wooden praises Morgan for being interested in everything, "in the prevention of problems more than the cures. There would be less cures if we do more for prevention."

Morgan was the perfect athletic director, equally interested in all sports, and he wanted to be competitive in each of them. Morgan, in 1980, stated that Wooden "was as fine a representative as any man could be of UCLA," noting that "the student body worshiped him." It should have, as Wooden was so open and inviting.

Gary Cunningham commented, "If students would ask him to do something, [if] what they were asking was not unreasonable, he would usually accommodate them. I know he spent hours and hours with students that would come in and want to maybe do a research project or just come in and chat with him. He was very good about that."

As UCLA basketball took off, Morgan knew what to do with it as a business; he made the University a fortune by being able to exploit the dynamic brought about by Wooden's teams. Wooden and Morgan put college basketball on the map in terms of national interest and importance so that today it is exceeded only by the Super Bowl and professional basketball. Basketball has now taken off around the world and may even eclipse soccer as the dominant world sport. During the Wooden years, it can justifiably be argued that UCLA and college basketball were second to professional football only in terms of national interest. UCLA basketball meant excitement, the energy from the teams lit up Los Angeles, the city felt good during the dynasty. Any locale would under similar circumstances.

Under Morgan, the budget was balanced and he didn't need the help of the students in playing any supervisory role. Eventually, jurisdiction over athletics was completely wrested from them, and placed under the aegis of the chancellor. A review of the UCLA budgets during the Morgan era reveals that he came within budget virtually every year, always and apparently intentionally underestimating by roughly 10 percent the income UCLA would earn during any fiscal year. Morgan had it together: he understood and was excellent at the business of sports, he loved business and all sports.

After World War II, Morgan accepted an accounting position with the ASU-CLA in 1946, and as assistant tennis coach. He ultimately was promoted to associate business manager for the university, and became director of intercollegiate athletics in 1963. Norman P. Miller, who joined the Kinesiology Department at UCLA in 1949, and who was Vice Chancellor of Student and Campus Affairs from 1970-79, recalled in 1982 that the Student Representative Fee Advisory Committee, when it controlled athletics, typically "pound[ed] the person speaking and the budget. J.D. never gave them the chance to do that. Either J.D. wouldn't bother to submit the budget or he wouldn't show up. If he did, it would only be because the chancellor requested it. Then J.D.'s approach would be to come very organized and prepared with a lot of facts. By the time he got through with his presentation and analysis, there was no reason to ask a question. All of the arguments they normally had would be dissipated, or J.D. would say 'Well, I have to go now,' and just get up and leave. Then they'd all sit there and say, 'How does he get away with it?'"

A workaholic night owl, Morgan usually took work home, went to bed at two o'clock in the morning, and never ate or went out to lunch. Morgan's strength was being thorough.

"He had a mind like a calculator," observed Robert Fischer, who started on the business staff at UCLA athletics, becoming Morgan's assistant director in 1964 (and succeeded him as athletic director when Morgan, suffering ill-health, was forced to retire at sixty-one in 1980). Fischer discussed at length in 1982 his insider's view of Morgan, and said that he ran a "tough, tight ship, [a] disciplinarian, but fair." Morgan would not allow UCLA to play schools he did not consider prestigious. Track and field, volleyball and tennis prospered during his reign—for he ran his department as a king. His door was always open, "but he didn't want surprises, didn't want to hear first about a problem in the press," recalled Fischer.

The entire department met once or twice a year, when Morgan updated them on new NCAA rules, problems, and finances. Important meetings with coaches were behind closed doors. Otherwise, Morgan would roam around the department, and when his deep voice was heard echoing the hallway, the common remark was "the lion is loose."

"We didn't have many formal meetings," says Wooden, "but he'd drop in the office at least a couple of times a week to chat for a while, sometimes more during the weeks we would have important games coming up."

Other than the annual Christmas party, the department did not socialize much, those at the top saw each other at games—football, basketball, track and others—throughout the year and that was plenty social enough for everybody. At work, Wooden was a pleasure to be around. Sports Information Director Vic Kelley wrote in 1975, when Wooden retired, about his "cheerful smile and salutation every morning, the enthusiasm and thoughtfulness evident in all his dealing with people or problems."

James Bush succeeded Ducky Drake as head track and field coach in 1964 (Ducky remained as trainer), and won four NCAA championships and seven Pac-10 conference tournaments. He recalled in 1982 that, "I didn't love [Morgan], but I sure respected him," for he could be the "meanest man in the world, but he had a heart." He cited as an example his first year at UCLA when he was just able to make his spousal and child support payments and did not have enough money for food. Morgan heard about Bush's predicament and told him to eat dinner four nights a week at a restaurant Morgan had selected until he was back on his feet, with the bill taken care of by Morgan.

Morgan met his match in Wooden. "Not too many people told John Wooden he could not do something," recalled Bush. "We laughed about it. I know he tried to control John Wooden, and there's no way he was going to control John Wooden. Very seldom did I really see John Wooden upset with J.D., although I think he is the one who got the rule passed to keep the athletic director off the bench during any basketball games. J.D. would keep quiet on any subject,and he insisted on sitting on the bench with Wooden during games." Wooden denies having lobbied for or having anything to do with the passage of such rule.

Fred Hessler, sportscaster for the football and basketball Bruins, continues the story. "Bob Boyd [head basketball coach at University of Southern California, UCLA's number one rival] came into the men's room after the [NCAA] meeting and was talking to another coach. [He] said, 'Boy, after that rule was passed outlawing athletic directors from [sitting on the] the bench, J.D.'s going to shit he when hears about this,' A voice from one of the stools [Morgan] said 'that, gentlemen, is exactly what he is doing.'"

THE JOHN WOODEN PYRAMID OF SUCCESS

Morgan was a major baiter of referees, especially on the road. He traveled with the basketball team through the entire dynasty, and once, to his and everyone else's chagrin, had a technical foul called on him, though he sat in the stands.

Morgan was considerate of the special needs of his athletes, said Wooden. "He immediately arranged, when he took over, that in spite of the fact that it cost more money to fly the team first class, he felt that was essential because of their size. There have been times when there weren't enough first-class seats available, and I, he, the trainer, and others might sit in the coach seats, but he wanted the tall players in the first-class seats." Of course, the basketball teams were one of the two breadwinners for the athletic program during his tenure.

As Wooden knew how to work with basketball players, Morgan knew how to work with—and select—coaches. Tennis ace Charles Pasarell recounted in 1982 the time when a group of players in the early 1960s argued over what was the most that the most important quality of a good coach—was it being a teacher, or having been a good player? The discussion ended with Morgan's pronouncement that "the most important quality of a good coach is to have the best players." Morgan's half-serious motto was "Winning solves all problems." Morgan could tell if a coach was up for game. Chancellor Murphy gave Morgan free rein. If alumni wanted to complain about the football coach, they were directed to Morgan.

Wooden, during his tenure at UCLA, was never pressured to win. "No, never," Wooden said in 1991. "Absolutely no pressure did I ever feel at any time. Fortunately, we won a lot of conference championships before we ever won an NCAA. But we had been contenders and had been to the Final Four and we'd won the conference more than anybody else. I'm not sure, we might have won it more than all the others put together. We just never did well in the tournament for a long time. But never did I ever feel any pressure. Not at all."

When he was pressed further on the subject, whether he felt his job was on the line if he didn't have winning teams, that wouldn't termination be the inevitable consequence at any major university, Wooden replied, "I never had a college team in which we lost more than we won. I never had but one team that came close, and that year we won 14 and lost 12, and that's the worst year I ever had. So, why should I be thinking in terms of . . . I never felt we had to win any more than we were winning. And it's quite possible that the year we won 14 and lost 12 might have been one of my better jobs, because we weren't expected to break even that year at all. So, no, I never felt any pressure about the job in any way at all. Not the least, and I'm being completely honest about this."

Morgan did not set policy for the teams. If Wooden didn't allow beards, mustaches or excessive sideburns, that was the rule. But Morgan might talk to a player about such an issue, as he did with star Sidney Wicks, counseling him that shaving his beard wouldn't be so tough as he would soon be out of school and playing professional ball and could then look as he pleased. Though a thorough detail man, Morgan could not delegate. This became increasingly a problem for the university in the latter years of his run as athletic director because of the increasing complexity of administering the athletic program.

"You had to see him for every detail," complained track coach Bush.

Charles Young, who became chancellor in 1968, commented that Morgan was a "seat of the pants administrator" who ultimately "began to show weaknesses."

Morgan became seriously ill, retired at age sixty-one on June 30, 1980, and died December 16, 1982. He would be proud of his legacy today: 86 NCAA team championships (men and women), the most of any university, with *Sports Illustrated* naming it in April, 1997 as the No. 1 "jock" school. During Morgan's seventeen-year span as athletic director, UCLA teams won an unprecedented 30 NCAA championships in basketball (10), volleyball (7), tennis (6), track and field (4), and water polo (3). Prior to becoming athletic director, Morgan was associated with seven more as assistant or head tennis coach.

Allen Scates, head volleyball coach at UCLA, whose teams have won 18 NCAA championships (certainly something to rival Wooden's notches), commends Morgan for making volleyball a national sport. "When J.D. saw 5,000 paying customers in Pauley Pavilion," Scates said in 1988, "he decided he wanted volleyball to become an NCAA sport because we were already strong at the time. It took him five years, but in 1970, volleyball did become an NCAA sport. We won the first three championships."

Scates almost lost his job because of a Wooden edict. In 1965, Keith Erickson, a starting forward, was not a dedicated student. Wooden forbade him from playing varsity volleyball. Erickson and Scates wanted him to compete in the championship playoff. He did that and 300 saw the team play at Santa Monica City College. Scates, who had prevailed upon the press not to mention that Erickson had participated, later worried he'd be found out, and told Morgan he felt bad about having done so, and offered to resign. For his part, Morgan was worried that Wooden would not let Erickson play as a result and said he'd talk to Wooden about it. Scates later found out that Wooden had prevailed in preventing Morgan from firing Scates, though the two never spoke about the incident. In 1987, Scates called Wooden "the greatest coach this country ever produced." (In 1990, Erickson, who went on to a career in the NBA, and then as a broadcaster, was shocked to learn that Wooden had that year called him the finest athlete he ever coached. "I think he could have been an all-star big league shortstop, an all-star in the NFL because he's fast . . . a leading money winner on the tennis or golf circuit. He was a great surfer . . . pool, anything.")

Douglas S. Hobbs was the UCLA faculty representative to the Pac-8 and Pac-10. "I'm not exaggerating when I say what J.D. wanted, J.D. got, in the Pac-10," Hobbs argued in 1982. "This was due to the fact that J.D. always did his homework and knew more than his would be adversaries. He knew the history behind everything, then he just went out and did his homework. He made sure he anticipated every argument. Then in terms of personality, there were not many people that were not steamrollered by J.D. on one occasion or another. J.D. could just intimidate people. J.D., in a sense, was the Pac-10, the dominant figure in the Pac-10."

Hobbs noted that "half the schools were bailed out every year by the spread of the Rose Bowl money." In 1966, for example, when UCLA played Michigan in the Rose Bowl, Michigan received $506,925, and the universities in the Pac-8 divided among themselves a like amount, each receiving, $56,222. According to Hobbs, because Morgan was "knowledgeable, shrewd and would present an argument in its most persuasive light," he became the point man for the Pac-8, for negotiating the Rose Bowl, all television contracts for the conference, and generally the dominant force in the Pac-8 and Pac-10 conference.

Chancellor Franklin Murphy, there at the beginning, remembered that "J.D. discovered and reported to me that the quality of leadership in the conference in terms of the business acumen, negotiating skills, was very, very inadequate. I urged him to try, to the extent he could, to take leadership in this regard. Within a very few years, he clearly became the leader among all the conference athletic directors, in terms of negotiating with the networks for television revenues. They just skyrocketed under his leadership. As a matter of fact, without it being explicitly stated, the one that the conference always turned to matters of negotiating with the Rose Bowl people, with the networks for football, in the beginning, then basketball. He became so successful that he quickly became the leader in the NCAA as well."

Morgan also sat for many years on the NCAA Basketball Committee, understandable since Coach Wooden was the consistent champion when he did so. Morgan spearheaded the enlargement of the Pac-8 into the Pac-10 in the 1978-79 season, with the admission of the University of Arizona and Arizona State, which had a substantial, positive economic impact for the conference with the increased audience that naturally resulted.

His acumen in dealing with basketball bears close scrutiny for any would-be sports entrepreneur. When UCLA played at home, Morgan initiated having the game played on a delayed basis, as UCLA was so hot a team that fans would wait up late. When the team played away, Morgan initiated televised coverage of these games, another first for college ball. The "Game of the Century" in 1968 at the Astrodome was one of the greatest promotions of all time. The idea was to break the attendance record for an indoor basketball game. 54,463 people turned out and it was a smashing success, putting college basketball on the map, as the major networks had eschewed becoming involved.

Eddie Einhorn, a budding entrepreneur who had put together an independent television network for UCLA basketball, TVS, made a fortune out of that involvement, and the game at the Astrodome gave him national prominence. It was also "the" career-making move for sportscaster and television play-by-play announcer, Dick Enberg, the voice of the Bruins. Enberg went on to become one of the top sports broadcasters in America. For Al Michaels who also broadcast the television games in 1973-75, UCLA basketball was likewise the rocket that took him to national stardom as a sports broadcaster. Einhorn continued thereafter as a hugely successful television producer, ultimately selling his company, TVS, Inc., in 1973 to a company controlled by Dun & Bradstreet. Einhorn is currently the vice-chairman and an owner of the Chicago White Sox baseball team, after having been its president and chief operating officer for ten years. By 1974, the televised rights for the Notre Dame-UCLA game at Pauley Pavilion went for $40,000; that same year, individual games against Providence and St. Bonaventure went for $30,000 apiece. These monies were split between the competing teams, and did not include the television rights in the home arena area.

Wooden, in 1982, said he "didn't like playing the game in the Astrodome because I thought it was making a spectacle out of the game. I love the game of basketball, and I did not like to see a game turned into a sideshow. I didn't think the Astrodome was any place to play a basketball game and still don't—under the conditions we played in down there. They put a floor in the middle of a huge area, with the nearest spectators rather far away. I didn't think it was good. But [Morgan] pointed out how much money we were going to make for it and how that would help other sports. He had good and sufficient reasons for doing it."

The next year, after the "Game of the Century," Morgan proposed to Wooden another game with the University of Houston at the Astrodome, but Wooden demurred, believing it would just be exploitive of the game. Morgan backed off and the game was played at Pauley Pavilion.

Another example of Morgan's prowess was scheduling and negotiating games. College basketball has always been a double-header event at New

York's Madison Square Garden, with one exception, UCLA. There was such interest in Lew Alcindor's team that Morgan, who had no desire to split fees if he did not have to, scheduled two single games at that arena, one against Holy Cross, the other Boston College, and both sold out. Morgan wrote those contracts and went home with $60,000, an enormous sum in those days. He negotiated the televised opening of Notre Dame's Convocation Center in 1968 for $25,000, when UCLA's national-rival would have been happy with $7,000. The games against Notre Dame were so successful that Morgan negotiated playing the Irish twice a year. Morgan pulled off a fee of $125,000 for one game against Indiana. The reason he could do this, make all this money, was because "college basketball was an orphan until Wooden," says former Morgan aide Robert Fischer. Wooden made it happen on court, Morgan brought it to the masses, and returned with more loot than anyone had imagined.

Morgan would "tell me after it was done" about scheduling, says Wooden, and was not consulted in advance except on rare occasions. Once, Wooden had verbally committed to and wanted to play Chicago Stadium, because "I'd like to go back there with a team even in the years we don't have a good team."

According to former Vice-Chancellor Byron Atkinson, Morgan retorted, "John, if you don't have a good team, they don't want you," common sense to Wooden's egalitarian naivete.

"A lot of the scheduling I didn't agree with. He made the schedule and I didn't have to do it," Wooden commented in 1991. "I never liked to go into Chicago and play a doubleheader in Chicago or play the second game of a doubleheader, and then go on to Notre Dame and play at one o'clock the next afternoon, which was twelve o'clock [with the time difference]. But that's where the television money came in, and he was a great budgeter and he did a great job. And we did all right with all the scheduling. I really couldn't complain from that point of view."

In the 1960s and 1970s there were few arenas that could seat 10,000 or more fans. Morgan knew where they were and to book them; today there are hundreds of arenas, due in large part to the spread in popularity of the sport.

UCLA basketball was the hugely profitable cash cow that kept seventeen other sports going. More than that, there was a surplus in some years, with the money given back to UCLA for the student health clinic, residence halls, and other capital improvements. In the 1972-73 season, UCLA's athletic department had revenues of $2,887,000 against expenses of $3,127,000; when broken down, football, with a budget of $1,323,000 made a net profit of $690,300, whereas basketball, with a budget of $297,000, made a net profit of $235,000. (In 2002, the budget was in excess of $30 million and the athletic program pays for itself.) Those two sports were then, as now, the engines that pulled the athletic train. Not included in these revenues are the sweatshirts, tee-shirts, pennants, knickknacks, doodads, and memorabilia sold in the student store. On these items the blue and gold colors of UCLA were emblazoned throughout the world. The campus and that store became a tourist destination, due in great part to the reputation of UCLA basketball. From France to Japan, UCLA's insignia became the chic emblem of choice around the world in the 1970s and 1980s. Wooden, because of the success of his teams, has to be given much credit for this. In 1962, the student union at UCLA had a small merchandising section; go there today and it is the size of any major department store when it comes to sportswear, all of it promoting UCLA.

UCLA's athletic headquarters today are housed in impressive quarters, the J.D. Morgan Athletic Center, a deserved honor for the man who brought, if not pulled, UCLA into the forefront of sports during the last half-century. Morgan played a major role in bringing to fruition Pauley Pavilion, which was built out of money from student activity fees, the State of California, alumni donations, and a matching grant of $1 million from wealthy oil magnate and University of California regent Edwin Pauley. There were over 700 schools in the NCAA in 1980 when Morgan retired, and UCLA was then called the "Athens of Athletics" because it had so many championship teams, such a well-run system. Franklin Murphy's dreams were largely fulfilled. UCLA had completed three first class arenas during Morgan's tenure, Jackie Robinson Field for baseball, located at the nearby Veteran's Administration; Drake Stadium (named for Ducky) for track and field; and Pauley Pavilion, though Morgan was never able to muster support for a football stadium.

Every school in the NCAA benefited by the ten national basketball championships and the television package. Those ten national championships were integral "to the success of the operation," asserts former faculty representative for athletics, Hobbs, "because you can't have maximum interest unless you've got the New York Yankees, the Green Bay Packers, or the Boston Celtics or UCLA. A dynasty is critical to success, because everyone either wants them in or wants them out, but they're interested."

There were even bigger residual benefits due to Wooden's wins and Morgan's skilled exploitation of the dynasty, relates Hobbs. "UCLA achieved higher visibility. It takes ten to twenty years for academic accomplishment to be recognized, but this is not true with intercollegiate athletics. Sports were followed more closely than academic achievement. J.D. was prepared to argue, 'Look, much of the foundation and federal largess that UCLA received from the East owes something to John Wooden's ten national championships'. It put the name UCLA in the public eye, and that, on the margins, has a lot to say about 'where do we award the grant?' You starting winning ten national championships and [some] people start to say, 'I wonder what kind of school it is?' Well, if they find out it's a good school, that is something that pays off."

Wooden remembers Morgan as "a great director of athletics. Tremendous for everyone. It's a great memory and a very nice one." Morgan smoothed the way for Wooden to do what he did best. "By all means he helped me," says Wooden. "I'll never forget the first year he became director of athletics. He came into my office. It was in the spring, near the end of the basketball season. I had a lot of papers, and was working on the next year's budget. He said, 'What are you doing?' And I replied, 'I'm working to get . . . trying to get next year's budget ready.' That included everything—equipment, travel and everything we'd have. Mr. Johns always wanted it by the first of April. He came over and he took all the papers that I had and took them, wadded them up, threw them in the wastebasket and said, 'I'll take care of the budget. You get out of line, you'll hear from me. And if you've got any extra expenses, heavy expenses or anything, you talk to me in advance beforehand.' Well, I never had to work on a budget from that time on. And prior to that, I had. Furthermore, in addition to that, he said, 'I'll do all scheduling from now on.' Now prior to that, I had to do all the scheduling. And to do the scheduling, I've got to contact other teams, and then I've got to find out what they'll give us to come there, or what we'll have to give them to come here. Then I'll have to go get an approval from the director of athletics and it was a chore. From that time on I had no say whatsoever in the scheduling. Now, a lot of coaches wouldn't like that. I did. It took a great load off my back. I could concentrate more on the other things."

No longer saddled with scheduling, budgeting, purchasing equipment and myriad other details of administration that detracted from what Wooden did best, practice and games, Wooden's full concentration was finally turned solely to trying to outscore his opponents.

THE ULTIMATE TEAM

Morgan's ascension to athletic director in 1963 coincided with one other critical event in the creation of the dynasty. Jerry Norman became Wooden's assistant coach for the 1959-60 season, but it was not until 1963 that he became Wooden's first full-time assistant. (When Norman left in 1968, Wooden then got two full-time assistants, Denny Crum and Gary Cunningham.) Norman, as discussed previously, was his own man and a serious thinker about the sport, notably in relation to promoting the full-court press and especially as to recruiting, which Wooden greatly disliked. With Norman aboard, Wooden had someone from whom he could bounce ideas off, and more importantly, and without denigrating the contribution of all of Wooden's many fine assistants, Norman was bouncing ideas—notably the full-court press—off of Wooden that ultimately went beyond cleverness to revolutionary.

Add to this mix Elvin "Ducky" Drake, the trainer for the basketball team and, for 18 years, the head coach of the track and field team. Born in 1903 in Friend, Nebraska, Drake grew up on a farm, went to a country school there, and attended high school in Fort Morgan, Colorado, where he played basketball, football and ran the mile. He settled with his family in West Los Angeles, and matriculated at the precursor of UCLA, the Southern Branch of the University of California, at its old campus on Vermont Avenue.

Like Wooden, Drake was a disciplinarian and a devout Christian, a Methodist who met his wife at church. Drake was tough as nails, soft of heart, street-smart and innately born to coach and assist someone like Wooden. Drake was the perfect sidekick and they grew to love each other. The Woodens lived with the Drakes their first week in Los Angeles. "We were very close," Drake recounted in 1979, in part because they used to room together on basketball trips for away games and would have many discussions about what went wrong when Wooden's teams would lose. "I can remember a lot of nights in a lot of cities all over the country when we would take long walks because it was hard for him to settle down," Drake recalled in 1980. "But," he continued, "I never gave him any advice. I couldn't give Coach Wooden any advice." Whether that was because he did not believe Wooden wanted it, or he had nothing to give, is unknown.

Drake had much success as head track and field coach; he was coach of the year in 1956 when his team won the NCAA championship. That year he was also trainer for the U.S. Olympic team, where UCLA athlete Rafer Johnson (who also played for Wooden) won the silver medal in the decathlon, and four years later won the gold, with UCLA teammate C.K. Yang collecting a silver. Drake had the same "fight" as Wooden, and would tell athletes with whom he interacted that, "Fear is your greatest enemy, desire your greatest weapon. Those who reach real success are constant workers. Act as if it were impossible to fail and give 100 percent. No one can ask more of you." "Desire and confidence," Drake would repeat to his athletes, were the greatest attributes of a champion.

Rafer Johnson, in a written tribute to Drake upon his retirement in 1972, described Drake as a "kind, gentle, yet forceful man; a gentleman in every respect," and "a thoroughly nice human being." Addressing Drake directly, Johnson told him that, "You knew each boy as an individual. You knew his strength and weaknesses, and never seemed to demand beyond what was best for him. You got more out of the boy than they ever thought they had. We should try, you said, first for the world record, then the national record, then the school record; and if all these were missed, to try for an individual best. Many were surprised by what they found they could do. But you just said, 'I knew all along you could do it.'"

Ducky, who ceased acting as the head coach in track and field in 1964, was very involved in the mechanics of getting the basketball team to function on schedule and with efficiency. He was in charge of bed checks, head counts, feeding of the team, and their general physical well-being. Thus, in Ducky Drake, Wooden had the perfect full-time trainer; in Jerry Norman, a first-class and *full-time* assistant; and as to J.D. Morgan, probably the best athletic director in the country. Drake, who was associated with UCLA as a student-athlete, track coach and athletic trainer for over sixty years, died in Los Angeles of a heart attack on December 23, 1988, at age eighty-five.

Perspective and judgment are integral components for the supervision of any successful athletic program and of the individual sports thereat. Wooden and his management team understood its role in relation to the athletic department, the university, the press, the public, and of most importance, to the basketball team. The team understood, recognized and implemented all that was necessary to effectuate team play, and that basketball was but one component of their scholastic environment. The education from Wooden was macro (life) and micro (basketball).

When it came to basketball, "he showed you the rationale, the reasoning, and what was to be gained. Eventually, you are thinking that . . . it's really your idea and so you're doing what you want to do," commented former assistant coach Ed Powell in 1980.

"He asked [the players] to do things which were basically of value and realistic in terms of our goals," was former assistant Gary Cunningham's assessment in 1980.

Wooden in 1980 confirmed that he tried to educate his players in all aspects of the game: "That's my idea of teaching also—the whole/part method. Take the offense, for example, I'd present it as a whole, and then break it down and teach it in parts . . . I also felt it was very important to educate players on the roles of their teammates, though not 100 percent. For example, we'd have certain set plays for each individual. The guards are going to initiate these for the most part. There might be a certain cut-back play for a forward to shoot. There might be one forward that I didn't want to get that shot, but I don't want to tell him 'You'll never get this shot.' I would just tell my guard also set it up this way so it would be set up on the opposite side. I might and I might not take them into my confidence . . . I wanted them to know all about the rules, and practically every other aspect of the game that would be important."

Wooden had an open door policy for his players, and "some would talk to me on a consistent basis, others never came," Coach said in 1980. They had his home number, but only a few players ever came to his home. "He was close to the players, but not that close. He had a closeness that was very meaningful," explained former assistant coach Frank Arnold. "They weren't fearful of him; I think a better way to put it is that they were in awe of him. They talked with Ducky Drake more than anybody."

Here again, we learn another lesson: a coach, a supervisor, must always maintain a certain distance from the player or employee; it is part of the natural order and hierarchy of discipline and supervision. When the student-teacher relationship is ongoing, the coach and student are not friends, but the coach is available for advice and counseling. When the final season or job ends, a more typical friendship can commence. Andy Hill, in his interview that follows, delights in explaining how this happened between himself and Coach. Now that all the seasons are over, Wooden can be just a regular guy with his former players, though of course, he will always be the legend. The interviews that follow reveal and explain how seamlessly Coach has allowed this transition from supervisor-coach to friend to occur with his many players. It is touching and an example to all of how things can go right.

Wooden and Morgan knew how and when to keep their distance from the press, and what was appropriate. Likewise, both felt that the "Bruin Hoopsters" club was a necessary evil. Wooden did not want to be pressured by "helpful" fans as to who to select or recruit for his teams, but he was cooperative to some extent, and of course, always friendly.

Wooden, in 1982, pondering his relationship with J.D. Morgan, commented on the role of athletics to a university: "I think J.D. would feel that athletics are important to the overall academic side, just as I think he'd say that the faculty club is important toward the academic side. What does a faculty club have to do with academics and the university? What does having a recreational swimming pool and recreational buildings have to do with the academic? There would be those that say they have none. I think they do have, just as I think athletics have, and I think J.D. felt probably the same as I do along those lines. I think he thought that a band has something to do with the overall program and not just the music program. I think it serves people other than just the music department. If athletics were for the athletes alone, I feel—and I believe J.D. would feel—that they're not worthwhile. You don't need them. You can take care of all that through intramural and physical education programs. If it's just for the athletes alone it's not worthwhile. I think he felt it serves the student body in many ways. It serves the alumni who support the university, and whose support is vitally needed in many areas."

"Collegiate basketball and intercollegiate athletics are good," Coach believes, but "the management of intercollegiate teams is not always good. When I speak of management, I speak of the coaches and people above the coaches, the department as a whole and maybe the administration as a whole. I think the ills are all in the management, not in the sport itself."

Asked about those who suggest athletes be paid, Wooden replied, "nobody feels that way except those who are very envious of athletics" and it just gives "writers something to write about."

Morgan, Drake and Norman were the flying wedge, the unifying force who with Wooden coordinated and comprised the UCLA coaching machine. These were dedicated, serious, smart, hard working, focused, innovative, highly motivated men who wanted to and did work as a team with Wooden, though Norman ultimately moved on in 1968 to follow his own path, and Drake retired in 1972. Notably, Wooden continued to win despite the loss of these assistants.

In 2002 it was suggested to Wooden by the author of this book that "it all came together" with the combination of Morgan, Norman and Drake. Wooden replied, "it all came together when Pauley Pavilion opened," and commented on the difficulty of not having a home court.

Together these four men presented the ultimate management team, a team to manage teams, in which each performed his function well, communicating with ease and regularity amongst themselves, each deeply respecting the other, all while having an enormous amount of fun doing so. They loved their jobs and competed with themselves to be at their best. Each basketball team was under the wing of the ultimate role model of a team as exemplified by these talented, disciplined men. They knew what they were doing and they taught their formula. Playing basketball for John Wooden and UCLA was as good as it could get for any young student-athlete. Players learned how to play basketball, got to travel and play in exciting matches, but were shown and could observe the bigger picture, that there was life after sports, that egos need to be kept in check, all of which was done in an egalitarian atmosphere. The sport existed at the campus to develop young men (and ultimately women), the revenues earned for the university were a byproduct. There were no player contracts to negotiate.

They had some disagreements. Once, Morgan wanted stars Curtis Rowe and Sidney Wicks to play in a game when Coach had benched them during the first half for being late to a training table meal. Wooden went to Morgan's office the following Monday and told him, "If I have to let you tell me how to discipline, then you don't need me!" Morgan told him he had 100 percent confidence in Wooden, yet Wooden, who was right in that situation, today blames himself for being "irritated." Wooden got along with everybody, and he was fortunate to work with the best.

THE MAN AND THE LEGEND

The public, especially in Southern California, adores Coach. To give an idea of Wooden's popularity, from March through July 1974, the Los Angeles Museum of Science and Industry created an exhibit to salute him, an act unprecedented for a then-active coach. If you wrote to Coach Wooden when he was coaching, he always responded, often with a signed Pyramid. One of the biggest avalanches of mail came in response to Coach's comments when UCLA's incredible eighty-eight game win streak was ended by Notre Dame. Wooden recounts, "The game was on national TV and the first question I was asked was, 'Well, you must feel quite badly, don't you?' I said, 'Yes, I'm disappointed but this is the anniversary of the day a truce was declared in Vietnam, and it is also the birthday of one of my granddaughters.' I hadn't thought that out in advance. It just came out of me because I meant it. People apparently liked the way I approached defeat and I received many kind letters and telegrams."

Wooden's eighty-ninth birthday was a front-page news story on the sports section of the *Los Angeles Times*. He was at the time, and even more so today, respected and admired. Here's what a rival coach said about him in 1969: "He's got a dignified aloofness that rubs some people the wrong way. But in all the years I've known him, he's never said an unkind word about me. He's needled me, of course. He's honest to a fault."

The Wooden era ended in 1975. After winning the semi-final for the NCAA championship against the University of Louisville in the last seconds of the game, whose head coach was his former assistant coach, Denny Crum, Wooden hung up his coaching shoes. Always the sportsman, he told his players after the game, rather than at half-time, when UCLA trailed by four points, because "I wouldn't want to use a thing like that to hype up a team. I don't believe in using artificial things like that." Naturally, the team won the following game for the national championship. Wooden said when he retired that he did so for "lots of reasons, no single one."

Wooden said that his decision had been made after reading that morning's papers, and "over the previous four weeks, coming to a head in the last few days." He added that he felt better that he announced his retirement because he had not been "able to completely honest and truthful with friends."

In December of 2000, Wooden commented further on the decision to retire to PBS interviewer, Charlie Rose: "I would say—most people have a little difficulty believing this, but no one knew I was going to do it. I didn't know it. My wife didn't know it. No one. I decided, as I walked off the floor after [that] semi-final game . . . for the first time ever, I just—I didn't want to go meet the press. And I've never felt that way. And just to myself, I thought, 'If I feel that way, it's time to get out.'" Wooden added that he didn't want to overstay his time in the arena: "For example, I was a great admirer of Willie Mays, and [didn't like] to see him hang on to the last when he would misjudge a fly ball and the bat was too slow to get around. And I would like to remember him as he was. And we see a lot of that, I think in athletics, where they just stay around a year or two too long, and I—I hate to see it."

At that press conference, Wooden, after announcing his retirement, skillfully changed the subject away from his retirement, "The important thing here is the basketball tournament. I'm delighted to be here and have a team playing for the championship. I appreciate your questions along that line, but I'd appreciate it more if you kept it along the line of the basketball tournament, the reason we're all here." During the Q and A that followed, Wooden offered his analysis of the sport of basketball: that it is not who controls the boards that matters, but who has fewer turnovers, more field goals, and better percentages on those. He was complimentary of his Kentucky opponents, the Wildcats, another example of gracious sportsmanship, noting that they "take shots with confidence. [Coach Joe B. Hall] hadn't taken away their initiative, and yet they're under discipline too. I think they're an outstanding team."

As to his desire for another championship, Wooden commented, "I don't want it any more than any other one. Since the first one, I've wanted them all the same but I wanted the first one. When we finally got the first one, that's like a weight off your shoulders. You got one now and the rest following that have been like icing on the cake, so to speak, so no one has really been more meaningful to me, nor did I want any one following that anymore. And just because this would be my last year of coaching, no it doesn't mean I would want more for that reason."

UCLA won that contest 92-85, and the pleasant, sometimes jovial Wooden at the news conference afterward, was matter of fact as to his immediate plans: he would go back to the office and catch up on work, so the man who would replace him would not be burdened. In the dressing room after the victory, Wooden told the press, "I told them how proud of them I was and I tried to tell them it was a tremendous basketball game but keep it in perspective. Now that the game is over and they won a national championship [they can] be very proud and happy about it but there's other things coming up now."

Then, it was time to go, with these exit lines: "There's sadness in leaving the youngsters and all the associations with people I've been with over the years, you men [the press], my players, and other coaches and players . . . I'm sad at getting out but I'm going out pretty happy too." Wooden said in 2000, he has missed "the teaching. I miss the practices. I loved to teach, and I love to plan my practices. And it'd take us a couple hours to plan my practice, and the practice would never last two hours, and usually not one hour and a half. I enjoyed that, and that's the only thing I've missed. I haven't missed the games . . . the folderol that goes with it, the media."

Wife Nell "was worried about me, and I was worried about her." As for the final championship team, "Do I feel fortunate, yes, you bet I feel fortunate. But it's not a question of luck. We were fortunate to win, but we would have been unfortunate to lose."

To those who follow greatness, such as Gene Bartow, who succeeded Wooden as coach at UCLA, Wooden advised in 1975, "You cannot be concerned with what has gone on before you. You must not let the things you have no control over affect you. You must work with the things you can control." This notion Wooden attributes to having learned from his father. Wooden provided this interesting analysis of that issue in 1998:

Life isn't fair. Life isn't fair in any way. The only thing that matters is to think of yourself, nothing else matters. If you let the things over which you have no control affect you, whether they are good or bad, they will affect you in only one way and that is adversely. I used to tell my players early, "This year you are going to get praise that you don't deserve and you're going to be liked by everybody. You are going to get criticisms at times that you deserve and criticisms at times that you don't deserve and you won't like it any way. But your strength, your absolute strength as an individual is going to depend on how you react to both praise and criticism. If you take both praise and criticism with a grain of salt, it will be a great weight off your shoulders. Just make the best effort you can. In my six point creed, one thing is "take each day as it is something over which you have control." I tried to use that one—make each day your masterpiece, and I tried to get that across to the players. Do what you can, you're not doing for somebody else. You'd like to be well-thought of, of course, but to me, the main thing is what you think of yourself. What others see is what you are perceived to be. You are the only who knows what you are. Do the best you can, make mistakes, but don't make them over and over again.

Responding to a student's question, "What makes a winner?" before the UCLA student body in 1971, Wooden's advice was equally sagacious. To him there is no secret formula. Coaching alone is not the ingredient because no coach wins "unless the material is there. No one wins without it, not every coach wins with it. Assuming you have it, we've all been trying to get the most out of the material we have available—and you never get it all out of them."

Success and winning are two very different concepts, he explained to the students: "Success is not necessarily based on winning. I know that's the criteria that most of you would use if we win our games, but we're not all created equal. Teams aren't all equal. Some are bigger, stronger, faster . . . but we all have the same opportunity of making the most of what we have and to improve ourselves to the best of our abilities under the circumstances that exist for us." Wooden never speaks of "winning," "beating," or "defeating," rather a team "outscores" another. "We were able to outscore opponents so often because I never stressed outscoring opponents," is a typical comment from him.

"Winning isn't everything, it's the only thing," is the famous phrase popularized by legendary Green Bay Packer football coach, Vince Lombardi, though it originated with Red Sanders, the UCLA football coach in the 1950s. This philosophy is the antithesis of Wooden's. While Lombardi may have been a great, clever, charismatic coach with many fine qualities, David Maraniss' superb biography, *When Pride Still Mattered: A Biography of Vince Lombardi* (2000) established that he was no Wooden off the court. Lombardi spent far too much time at work and away from his family, not leading a balanced life, not taking care of himself physically, especially by smoking too much.

From 1959-67, Lombardi was the head coach and general manager of the Packers, who through discipline and strategy renewed and revived them and the nation by leading them to five NFL championships (1961, 1962, 1965, 1966, 1967) and victories in Super Bowls I (1967) and II (1968). In 1969, he took over as coach, general manager, and part owner of the Washington Redskins, resulting in the first winning season for that team in fourteen years. Sadly, he died the next year at the age of fifty-seven. Although comparisons between sports may be misguided, Lombardi's dynasty years are half of Wooden's. Wooden's dynasty lasted twelve years with ten national championships, Lombardi's dynasty lasted seven years with six championships, leading one to believe that Wooden's record is more compelling, more difficult to emulate.

THE PYRAMID OF SUCCESS

Wooden's greatest influence as a coach was Piggy Lambert, his coach at Purdue, to whom he credits being instilled with the idea that conditioning, a knowledge of and ability to execute fundamentals, and team work, along with the two foundational blocks in the Pyramid of Success, industriousness and enthusiasm, are essential to winning teams. "You have to be in condition whatever the game might be, and you have to be more than physically conditioned. You must be mentally conditioned. . .and you can't be physically conditioned unless you're morally conditioned." Wooden believes you can't reach "perfection but you try for it. I tell players at the beginning of the year that I want them to be in better condition than any team we will play. I don't say 'as good.' I want better. Whether they are as good, I don't know, but if they think they are, it'll help."

In 1969, Wooden explained: "The other team may be in better condition, but my job is to get our players at least to *believe* they are in no better condition than the team we're playing—and to keep applying pressure, both on offense and defense.

"Next to condition is the knowledge of and ability to execute the fundamentals. That's the coach's job. You have to teach them the fundamentals, and there's more to it than knowing the fundamentals. They must be able to execute them properly at the right time and quickly. Quickness is the most important asset in athletics in my opinion. If you can't do it quickly it doesn't do any good. If you can't get a shot, it doesn't do you any good to be a good shot. You have to be able to do both. The same thing is true in playing defense or rebounding or whatever it might be.

"Above all, if you won't put it together for the use of the team then your lot is a failure. We're all selfish in many ways, and it's a human trait. We have to fight ourselves not to be. I suppose it's natural in many respects to fend for one's self and consider one's self first, but when we stop thinking of our neighbor and stop thinking of our teammates, then we're not going to do as well as a group. There are various means I use to bring about team play, a lot of little things that you might not notice. For example, I never want a player to score if after scoring as he heads for defense he doesn't turn to the man who gave him the pass and give him a nod, a wink or a smile. And he'll get another pass. Once in awhile, a player will say, 'What if he's not looking?' And I say, 'I guarantee he'll be looking at you.' We all like to be patted on the back. . . I get a lot of criticism. I hope I can take criticism. We must be able to take it, and the players certainly have. You have to take it, and you can learn from it. I've always felt that commendation is a great motivator and I try to use it as much as possible with my players."

As to motivation and discipline, Wooden has distinct opinions. "One of the greatest motivating factors we have is a pat on the back," Wooden says. "But sometimes the pat has to be a little lower and a little harder."

In the incident with Wicks and Rowe which resulted in friction between Wooden and Morgan, who were eight minutes late for a pre-game dinner, Wooden told them they would each sit on the bench for eight minutes. When one protested, Wooden advised that they might sit out the entire game, and did bench them the entire first half, necessitating a come-from-behind win.

Wooden has written that "I don't lead through fear, and would rather have a Robert E. Lee or an Omar Bradley in charge than a George Patton (although in wartime I'd want Patton on my side). As Lincoln has said, 'there is nothing stronger than gentleness.'"

He used to require players to wear jackets all the same color, but he stopped insisting on that, just requiring jackets. Wooden's teams also looked like a million bucks on the floor.

UCLA star Marques Johnson commented, "It's funny, we didn't have a dress code on the road. We had Bill Walton and Greg Lee, who liked jeans and casual clothes, we'd look like bums coming to the game. But we'd all look neat while we were playing."

Sartorially, Wooden wore conservative clothes picked out by Gilbert's in South Bend, which traded him clothes for commercials he would make for the store. "I haven't picked out a suit, a tie or a shirt, I guess, since I've been married," he told a reporter in 1972. However, when one writer said he dressed like an undertaker, Nell insisted he stop wearing only blue suits and he began to wear sport coats and blue and yellow shirts. Today he is still well-dressed, as if out of a catalogue for Brooks Brothers

He used to have bed checks when the players were on the road, but by 1971, he would ask his players what time was a reasonable curfew and would usually agree with their proposals. One amusing bit of UCLA lore tells of the time when trainer Ducky Drake discovered an empty bed, so he climbed in and was awakened by the wandering player.

In 1986, Wooden offered these views to the *Christian Science Monitor*, "Having worked with young people all my life, I can tell you for a fact that today's kids are crying out for discipline and most of the time they aren't getting it. They aren't getting the direction they need at home or from most of their teachers. And until we give them the proper standards to live by, we will continue to be a nation whose young people will be in and out of trouble. Sometimes I wonder if most people even know what real discipline is. The purpose of discipline isn't to punish but to correct. It's not there to be used to antagonize an individual, but to help and improve him. It's not yelling at someone, because that kind of approach never gets you anywhere. You can only get the response you want by acting fairly and rationally." Wooden said in 1969 that, "When I got older, I became more tolerant. I realize I'm not as strict as I used to be, but society isn't as strict, either . . . Perhaps, I've erred in some respects. But who can say for sure? At least, I'd rather make the mistake of going too far (in permissiveness) than not far enough. . .."

At the commencement of each season, Wooden's players would receive a letter from him in which he would lay down the rules. A sample from 1972:

> *Forget last year. We must work together if we are to measure up to our potential. Your lot is certain failure without discipline. I am very interested in each of you as an individual but must act in what I consider to be the best interest of the team for either the moment or the future. Your race or your religion will have no bearing on my judgment, but your ability and how it works in my philosophy of team play will.*

Mustaches, goatees and long hair were not permitted, Wooden explained in 1972, because, "When it gets too long, it can get in the way in the court. It can flop down in a player's eyes, and it is an unnecessary handicap." At that time, he admitted he could not make as good an argument for prohibiting mustaches, sideburns, and beards, but that "It's just something I feel. I think that it brings the team closer together as a unit, though. But I know that these men have to live off the court, too, and sometimes they take pressure from their friends, so I have relaxed my standards a little," and was then allowing contemporary length sideburns. By 1978, three years after his retirement, he no longer required coaches at his summer clinics to have short hair and be clean-shaven. He said at the time, "Now I hardly notice whether they are or not. If you ask me how many of them have beards and mustaches, I couldn't tell you. Two years ago I could. I didn't want them. "Basketball is a privilege, not a right. They don't have to be out there and if they can't go along with the one in charge, I feel they would be better off if we part company," Wooden declared in 1972.

In the early 1970s, a reporter traveling on the first road trip memorialized Wooden's extemporaneous talk to his players on a bus ride to Corvallis, Oregon: "We didn't have a meeting about this before we left, but because this is our first road trip, I hope you will act as gentlemanly as you do in your homes. You're always to be on your special best behavior with those you come in contact. And I want to impress upon you to keep your rooms neat, even after you check out. This is directed at two of you—and you know who you are—who had to be called back to your rooms last year."

In 1972, Wooden told a reporter, "I don't want to invade the player's privacy. I will seldom go into their dressing room at practice, but occasionally I will and they don't know when I'm coming. I like to make spot checks on lockers and see they're not getting slovenly. Wherever we are, we will leave our dressing room every bit as neat as when we came in. There will be no gum wrappers on the floor. No tape scattered around. No orange peels. They'll all be placed in a container. And I don't expect our manager to be the pick-up man. Our players understand this. I help. If I start picking up things, the players soon join in. We'll have equipment managers around the country tell us no one leaves the dressing room like we do. Well, I think that's part of better basketball. Now I'd have a hard time proving that, but I think it is. I think it gives us a little more unity, a sense of doing things together, of showing consideration for the other fellow. The waitress at the hotel here said this was the finest, best-behaved group of athletes she's had. Our players complimented her on the way she'd been serving them. She could hardly believe it."

Yet another example of Wooden's unique take on the conduct of his team, occurred after winning the seventh national championship against Villanova in the Astrodome, where Wooden told reporters that "two things that reflect the character of our seventh championship made me very proud. Several reporters told me they were amazed at how quiet and unassuming our players were after winning the championship. I want each of my players to be able to accept victory and defeat with grace and I think they did well. The other thing that pleased me the most was when the manager of the Astrodome to me, 'Your team leaves the locker room cleaner than any team we've ever had in here.'"

Wooden told his players they were not to carouse, and at one point would kick a player off a team who smoked or committed a serious infraction of the rules. "One rule we insist upon on the road, is that players—if they're going out shopping or for a walk—go in pairs, especially if we're in a big city, such as Chicago or New York. We believe in the buddy system for personal safety. I want to know all I can about them, but I don't want to invade their privacy. I make no threats. All I have is a list of expectations. Also, I tell our players, 'When you come to practice, you cease to exist as an individual. You're part of a team.' Sure, some players might say I'm harsh, but look at it another way. They're looked up to by others and receive a great deal of adulation. Is that a hardship? They're getting a grant-in-aid for their college education. Is that really a hardship?"

Wooden had three main rules, part of his list he called Normal Expectations: "Be on time, do not use profanity at any time and never criticize a teammate." As to the latter, Wooden would instruct with this pleasing tease: "That's my job. I'm paid to do it, pitifully poor, but I'm paid to do it." It got the laugh as it made the point: it was always in all ways a team effort and that required respect for the others. To demean was to divide.

Anyone who ever played for Wooden got this handed to him:

NORMAL EXPECTATIONS

Our chances of having a successful team may be in direct proportion to the ability of each player to live up to the following sets of suggestions.

1. *Be a gentleman at all times*

2. *Be a team player always*

3. *Be on time whenever time is involved*

4. *Be a good student in all subjects—not just in basketball*

5. *Be enthusiastic, industrious, loyal, and cooperative*

6. *Be in the best possible condition—physically, mentally and morally*

7. *Earn the right to be proud and confident*

8. *Keep emotions under control without losing fight or aggressiveness*

9. *Work constantly—improve without becoming satisfied*

10. *Acquire peace of mind by becoming the best you are capable of becoming*

11. *Never criticize, nag or razz a teammate*

12. *Never miss or be late for any class or appointment*

13. *Never be selfish, jealous, envious or egotistical*

14. *Never expect favors*

15. *Never waste time*

16. *Never alibi or make excuses*

17. *Never require repeated criticism for the same mistake*

18. *Never lose faith or patience*

19. *Never grandstand, loaf, sulk, or boast*

20. *Never have reason to be sorry afterward*

The player who gives his best is sure of success, while the player who gives less than his best is a failure.

THE JOHN WOODEN PYRAMID OF SUCCESS

Wooden told the *Daily Bruin* in 1998 that a player for him needed to be "very courteous and polite and well-mannered and will never do something on or off the court to bring discredit to him, to his team, to his family, to his coach, to his school. I try to get this idea across to all my players." Wooden said in 1975, "Politeness and courtesy is one of my sayings. Courtesy is a small price to pay for the good will and affection of other people."

For Coach, the most important word in the English language is "love," followed by "balance." Arguably the third most important is "dignity," what Coach insisted his players show to all whom they came in contact. He was outspoken about this requirement, advising Marv Dunphy, who was questioning him for his doctoral thesis on the coach, that when he criticized players, "I never wanted to bruise the dignity of the individual being disciplined."

Other teams were never ridiculed or demeaned. Greg Lee, a sophomore guard, after a victory against the Citadel in the early 1970s referred to the school as "comparable to a very good junior college team." Wooden took him to task for the comment, just as he fired away at the local sports press around the same time for similar comments about UCLA's adversaries. He spoke at the Southern California basketball writer's luncheon, "Yes, I'm upset. Very upset. I've never believed in demeaning and belittling others, and I have no respect for people who do." Wooden's rules required that players never challenge the integrity of the referees. "It's just that they're all different, which, of course, is to be expected. And they do things subconsciously, mainly because of the crowd," he said in 1969.

Another example of his concern for dignity, as well as tradition, was his refusal to allow numbers to be retired while he was coaching because "What about the fellows who wore the number before?"

Coach Wooden has always been a master of diplomacy. In hundreds of newspaper articles and in many interviews over the last half-century, including interviews with him and others for this book, we never saw evidence of, or heard of, Wooden being cruel or unfair to others. On the rare occasions when Wooden is asked to comment in a critical way of a person, the interviewer must turn the tape recorder off, and the story recounted is "off the record." He is very careful of what he leaves for posterity. Of the two dozen individuals interviewed for the oral history project on J.D. Morgan, Wooden was the only one who extensively edited and corrected his interview.

Wendell Phillips, who played softball with Wooden as a young man in Martinsville and was around the family a lot, says it started early, that Coach, "very seldom ever says a bad word. He was remarkable in that he never did speak ill of somebody."

Simply put, what comes through repeatedly are Wooden's character traits for kindness and forgiveness. In 2002, Wooden spoke of those in the public eye, "We hear so many bad things about the bad things, we don't hear as much about the good things. Might be in the past we didn't need to hear so much about the bad things."

This wisdom is worth incorporating into our own lives, with special meaning for those, such as journalists and attorneys, in a position to tear down the reputations of others.

He is crafty with his usage of language, and is the best exponent of his policy of never comparing others. Consider his answer in March 1998 to the UCLA student newspaper concerning who was the best coach in college ball.

I would never attempt to say anyone is the best. Generally speaking, I would say, "I have never seen a better one," or I would say, "He's as good as anybody else," or "He's among the best, I could go on and on." But there are many great coaches, and coaches are really only teachers—in places that you've never heard of. But they're doing a better job than many of these coaches you hear about all the time. It's just like the Thomas Gray Elegy Written in a Country Churchyard, *one verse in there says:*

Full many a gem of purest ray serene,
  The dark unfathom'd caves of ocean bear:
Full many a flower is born to blush unseen,
  And waste its sweetness on the desert air.

Is the flower less beautiful then because nobody sees it? Or the gem any less beautiful because it's on the bottom of the ocean and nobody sees it? Well, now there are many coaches that way—wonderful teachers in places you have never heard of and they may be doing a better job than the more publicized coaches, I will say without pinpointing. I have been impressed with the team play through the last number of years I have seen from Roy Williams and the University of Kansas. I think his team plays beautiful team play. I'm not saying he's the best coach of all, I just don't think I have seen anybody play better team ball.

In 1971, Wooden made another adjustment. "I always referred to my team as 'my boys.' I don't know how you could have a closer term of endearment than that unless you called them your sons. But they don't want to be called 'boys.'

So I try not to refer to them 'my boys.' Yet, at times, they can hardly be referred to as 'men.'"

October 14, 1975, marked the day of John Wooden's retirement party. With Bob Hope as the master of ceremonies, 6,800 well-wishers, friends, fans and over 100 ex-players sang "Happy Birthday" (it was his sixty-fifth that day) and "Auld Lang Syne," and gave tribute to the man who created the legend and dynasty of UCLA basketball. Wooden was deeply moved by the ceremony, and by the gifts he received (paid for out of the night's receipts), which included a brand new Mercedes and a gold watch with ten diamonds inset, one for each NCAA championship. Wooden told the assemblage, "The two great loves of my life are my family and UCLA, and all that goes with the school and makes it up." After reminiscing about his life at UCLA, including the stuffy, noisy, old Men's Gym that they shared with the wrestling team and the girls on the trampoline in their leotards, and thanking all who had helped him along the way, Wooden departed with this adieu, "Nell, come down here and stand beside me. You have always been with me since I would see you up there in the high school band holding a trumpet. This is the most memorable evening of my athletic career. Never before could I pick out one moment. Now I can. I thank all of you, but next to my family, I feel closest to my players. I am sorry if I ever hurt any of them. I never meant to. There is no player I haven't loved. I haven't retired. I've left coaching, but I will never leave UCLA."

Wooden received a letter dated March 28, 1974, from Walter Byers, the executive director of the National Collegiate Athletic Association, who eloquently put into perspective and words what everyone believed:

Dear John:

Looking back over the more than twenty-five years I have been associated with intercollegiate athletics, I recall what seems now to be an unending parade of great championship teams, outstanding coaches and superb college athletes.

In all that time and considering all the sports on the college calendar, there has not been an institution or a coach who has approached the success of UCLA and John Wooden in the sport of basketball.

Your ability to have achieved that success is remarkable. The fact that you were able to sustain it at a championship pace for the unprecedented period of time that you did is an unexplained sports phenomenon—probably never to be duplicated again. The problems that you had to overcome in achieving this unparalleled success can only be speculated upon by an outsider, but they obviously have been difficult and their demands upon you as a person must have been consuming and at time exhausting.

Considering all this, however, the most important aspect seems to me to be the unique position you occupy as a result of this. You stand today as the sport's most respected coach.

Great players made this sting of victories possible? Of course. But the thoughtful coaches of the nation have told me throughout your years of success that the manner in which you coached and motivated your players and planned your games was the result of a genius talent.

Even more important from my viewpoint has been the manner in which you have worn the mantle of championship success, both on and off the floor. I have shared pride in your accomplishments as a coach of NCAA champions because of the type of man your are.

Finally, you leave the role of champion—temporarily I am sure—with respect of your peers and colleagues in the intercollegiate family for having achieved your record through superior management and leadership, not as a result of questionable tactics for which some coaches are known within the fraternity. . .

Of the many critiques over the years by writers about Wooden, there are two he especially remembers favorably. The first is, "If there is a paradox in the career of John Wooden, it is that he gained his fame by winning yet never succumbed to the cult of winning." The other observation is "Wooden was more than games or streaks; he was the essence of doing the best to be the best without letting it ruin you."

As to criticism, Wooden said in 1974, "Whenever you lose a game, you're going to have your critics. Everyone has their critics. A doctor is criticized for losing a patient. A dentist is criticized for losing a patient's teeth. A salesman is criticized for losing a sale. No coach has a corner on material. No coach has a corner on brains. For every winner there is a loser. But some people forget that. I've even heard people criticize the Mona Lisa." In 1991, Coach had this to say, "You can't let praise or criticism get to you. It's a weakness to get caught up in either one. Some criticism will be honest, some won't. Some praise you will deserve, some you won't. You have to take both in the same light." On another occasion, Wooden commented, "I can honestly say that I received more criticism after we won a championship than I did before we won one. That's why I've always said I wish all my really good friends in coaching would win one national championship. And those I don't think highly of, I wish they would win several." In 1995, Wooden was proud to be able to say, "You always have your critics. That I can honestly say doesn't bother me."

Wooden has some regrets. Edgar Lacey was a star athlete whom he benched during the Game of the Century at Houston. Lacey thereafter quit the team and school. In 1995, referring to the Lacey situation, Wooden said, "I'm not wrong in what I did. But if I had known what was going to happen, I would have handled it in some other way. I'm sorry I handled it the way I did—although I don't know how I would have handled it. I'm not wrong. I wouldn't apologize for saying what I did because that's exactly the way I felt."

In 1995, he articulated his other two major regrets: "One was in high school, when I had a player who worked hard, but he didn't get enough playing time. We had certain regulations— they had to get so much playing time to earn their letter. Well, letters in those days really meant something. Today, they don't. They don't even pick up their letters now, half of them. And this young man, he'd worked hard, and the coach had the privilege of recommending someone for a letter who didn't quite meet the requirements. And almost always the board would accept the recommendation. I'm not sure I had made up my mind a hundred percent, but it was pretty close—I was going to recommend. Well, his dad came in and asked if Joe was going to get a letter."

I said, "Well, I'm considering it, but he didn't quite meet the requirements."

"Yes, I know!" he says. "But if he doesn't get his letter, I'll have your job!"

I was young. I invited him outside and told him pretty clearly what I thought of him. I did not recommend the boy. I was perfectly justified. He didn't qualify. And I regret that as much as anything I've ever done.

"Another thing in high school, I had a rule—no smoking. It was automatic dismissal from the team. And my star player—a player who was going to get a scholarship got caught smoking. I dismissed him. That was my rule. He quit school. Never graduated. Never went to college. Nothing wrong with what he did. I think he ended up a common laborer or whatnot. I'm not putting them down, but here's a player who was going to get a college education, to have a better chance, and it was all because of my being perhaps too stubborn. But I saw no middle—it was either black or white. There was no gray area. And there is a gray area on many things. So that bothered me."

In 1992, Wooden was asked for this book about his "misses" in life.

What if any professional disappointments do you have?
That I didn't do better.

What, you should have won fourteen?
No, I am not talking about winning championships. That's not what I am talking about at all. Mistakes I made with individuals here and there.

You just handled the situation wrong?

I did what I thought was right, but what I thought was right at the time wasn't always right and I am sorry. But I am not sorry that I did what I did because I thought it was right. I'm just sorry that it didn't work out. I'll tell you something I learned from Wilt Chamberlain. When he came to the Lakers they had a press conference announcing that I was invited to attend that and at one point one of the writers said, "Do you think that Bill Van Breda Kolff [coach of the Lakers] can handle you?" He said, "No one handles me. I am a person, I'm not a thing! You handle things—you work with people." Shortly before that my book had a chapter in there entitled "Handling Your Players." I came home from that and crossed it out and put "Working With Your Players," and every other place I put it in, there. I called the publisher on the next edition. I wanted it all eliminated and when you stop and think that perhaps it is a little thing, but it might not be little to somebody else and apparently it wasn't with him. And that's what you do [if you] stop and think about it. You work with people.

Edgar Lacey was a disappointment.

A great disappointment, I believe there is another thing that Hazzard mentioned about him that was all wrong. [see Hazzard interview] I never dismissed Edgar Lacey. Edgar Lacey quit, and I'm very sorry that a player quit on me. But I didn't dismiss him at all. I wanted him back and tried to explain to him how he was making a mistake but I wouldn't lie. He wanted me to retract what I had said and I couldn't retract it because I had said it. I couldn't put him back in the game because he gave me the impression that he didn't want to play. When I told Jerry Norman, my assistant, to get him and he said "look at him." He was on the other end of the bench not looking at the game at all. Not paying any attention at all. Afterwards, the press asked why I didn't put Lacey back in. I said, "He gave me the impression he didn't want to play." I'd taken him out originally because he wasn't defending [basketball great Elvin Hayes, the star of that game]. I don't know if anybody could have defended Elvin Hayes in that particular game, but there's a way I wanted him to try and he said he couldn't handle him, so I put somebody else in. The other fellow, trying it my way wasn't more effective and he wasn't as capable as Edgar. This was in the paper that I made that remark and he came in and talked to me and said if I didn't retract, he was going to quit. I said "I can't retract it, but you'd be making a terrible mistake," and I even had Lewis try to talk to him. But Edgar was an unusual person, a nice person, a good person, a quiet person. His name, players have a way of naming their teammates and he was "The Phantom," you never saw him. Bright, good student, no problem academically in anyway, polite, but this little thing bothered him. I take it was because the fact that he realized as a sophomore for us he was an All-American forward on our championship team, did a tremendous job for us. [He was] in the championship game against Michigan in '65 and then started out real well the next year, but very early, first conference game, he broke a kneecap. And he's out for that season and all the next season and he came back, but he wasn't the Edgar Lacey of old at all. He wasn't nearly the player. But when he came back, I was starting him even though I thought our team was better without him. I wanted to. I didn't want to hurt him, and the situation, the team we had. I thought, we are not going to be hurt and I can bring somebody else in, so I started him and this happened and so I lost him, and I'm sorry about that, I'm really sorry.

Did you ever reconcile with Lacey?
Nope. Nope.

Is that a regret that you have that you haven't made up?
I tried. Oh yes, it's a regret but I know I tried. I talked to his sister, the lovely girl who was a Playboy bunny (laughs) and she'd say, "Well, you know Edgar." He was about the same way at home, they hardly saw him at all. Yes, I'm very sorry. He's a good person. But to say that I dismissed him, no, I did not.

Interestingly, Coach Wooden was never asked to coach the Olympics. his explanation being, "I was never a part of the 'in group' of the coaching fraternity. Remember, I never drank, so I never went to those cocktail parties where everyone made their political contacts. When I went to a coaches' convention, I'd go with my wife, attend a meeting, and then go back to my hotel room." Wooden did admit to the *San Diego Union* in 1974, that during his college years, in Prohibition times, "I went out with the guys one night and drank some home-brew and got sick. I've never had a drink since."

There has been little published regarding professional jealousy among coaches of Wooden, though there is one recent example. Tex Winter coached at Kansas State University during the dynasty years. His team, the Wildcats, were eliminated early during the Final Four in 1965, losing to UCLA. Winter went on to be an assistant coach working under Phil Jackson during the championship reign of the Chicago Bulls and Los Angeles Lakers. In *More Than a Game* (2001), by Laker coach Phil Jackson and Charley Rosen, Winter asserts (in a section written by Rosen) that Wooden was not well-liked by his contemporaries. Winter, elected to the National Association of Basketball Coaches' says the board of directors during some of the period that Wooden coached, often gossiped about those who coached the sport.

Said Winter, "I got a real insight into several of them. Johnny Wooden, for example, who has another side that most people don't know about. Among his colleagues, Wooden wasn't very popular, and he was never voted to the board of directors. That's because he was kind of arrogant. He'd never let his UCLA players participate in the coaches All-Star game, and he never went out of his way to help anybody."

Wooden, queried about Winter's comment in 2002, said that he cannot remember Winter ever coaching a team that beat UCLA, and that his antipathy is probably professional jealousy. As far as being on the board of coaches, Wooden said that "I'm not a politician, didn't drink, and I didn't deal with the coaches who went to conventions without their wives and went to a lot of parties," nor did he lobby to be on such board.

Former student assistant and lifetime close friend, Ed Powell, thought Wooden did not like the politics in the coaching profession, but "being one himself, he did all he could to elevate coaching standards so that others would feel it to be a worthy profession."

Gary Cunningham told Marv Dunphy in 1980, that Wooden "realized there are good coaches, average coaches, and poor coaches; but, by and large . . . he viewed coaches as good people, as people that he liked to be associated with. He enjoyed sitting around the table exchanging stories and ideas on basketball. He loved to talk with younger coaches."

Wooden didn't put on airs and wanted to be treated as an ordinary fellow. Former assistant coach Frank Arnold recalls an occasion during the dynasty when Wooden, despite repeated prompting to cut to the front, stood in line for an hour and a half at the National Association of Basketball Coaches to pay his annual dues.

Coach Wooden is not entirely happy with The John R. Wooden Award, created in 1976 and given to the best athlete in college basketball each year. In 1998, he amplified why, "When that originated, I wanted it to be a well-rounded player. On the trophy there are five players. One is playing defense, then the other four are on offense—which I don't particularly care for. I wanted in the middle of that to be one player in a cap and gown. I wanted it to go to a graduating senior. I didn't want this trophy to be for the best basketball player. I wanted it to be for the best *graduating* basketball player, and I went along with it. I am sorry I did. And they know that. But I did get one thing in, and they have followed it the way I wanted them to and that is the best player who receives it must be making normal progress to his college degree, whatever year he is in."

Teenagers who bypass college and go directly into professional sports are of deep concern to Wooden. In 2002, he commented, "In the vast majority of cases it is a terrible mistake for a youngster to go right into the NBA, not 100 percent percent of the time—I like to never say never. For a vast majority of youngsters it would be a mistake in many ways. They are getting the immediate against the future. Most would say some of the happiest days of your life were your schooling. That's when you are associated or mingling with others of approximately your age with your same interests. When you throw high school youngsters into the pros, their lifestyle is a lot different. They're not ready for that, losing out on something extremely important and meaningful in their life as a whole which is more important than the short time. It's like passion and love. Passion is temporary, true love is enduring." Wooden lamented that some from the inner city did so because of economic necessity or "incorrect pressure from their parents."

During his retirement years, Coach Wooden has kept busy as a speaker, giving motivational lectures, and speaking at sports camps (he particularly enjoys third through sixth graders). The first year after Wooden retired, Morgan "arranged not exactly an office but a desk in another office over on the other side of the building for me to come in and use for a while," Wooden recalled in 1982. "That's where I made one of my greatest mistakes . . . I went along with his desire to have me stay for a while, feeling that I could be helpful to [my replacement Gene] Bartow, and Bartow indicated I could. But in retrospect, I don't believe Bartow really felt that way. I think he was uncomfortable with my presence. For a while I was right in the same office with him. I had a desk in the corner until they got something worked out on the other side of the building. It soon became apparent to me that Bartow never had any questions to ask about situations. I think I could have helped him if he'd come to me, not in coaching his team but in other areas. I should not have stayed, even after a place was made for me on the other side of the building. I seldom ever saw Bartow."

Wooden's policy is never to comment on UCLA's basketball teams during the season because he doesn't want to interfere publicly, to seem to be in any way divisive. Instead he writes private notes to the Bruin coaches, such as this missive to current coach, Steve Lavin, during the 2002 season: "I was severely criticized when I permitted Notre Dame to score the last 12 points to overcome our 11-point lead and break and an 88-game winning streak. I was told that if a hummingbird had my brains in his tail end, it would still fly backwards. Others could not understand why it took me fifteen years to have a national championship team and why I did not do many things that all knowledgeable basketball fans knew."

Wooden did not have a career as a commentator, explaining why in 1982: "[T]his is not my cup of tea. I've enjoyed doing it . . . I don't think I provided what the networks or stations wanted because I refused to be extremely critical of coaches or players. I would make comments if I thought a player forced a shot when he should have passed, or failed to thank a teammate for a pass. I would point out fine plays. But I am primarily looking for team play, not individual play, and I didn't try to use any showmanship and get fancy with my vocabulary. So I would say that commentary is the area that I was the least competent in as far as what I think the broadcast people—I am not sure about the general public—wanted."

RETIREMENT

As the years have passed, the legacy has continued and grown. *Wooden*, published in 1997, and written by Coach Wooden with Steve Jamison, is a delightful book containing advice, stories, thoughts and other maxims from Coach, that has consistently sold and been widely praised. That book engendered *Values, Victory and Peace of Mind*, a television broadcast in 2001 on PBS (available on video tape), and is essentially the video version of the Pyramid of Success lecture and an opportunity for all to see Coach close-up.

What Wooden enjoys most of all is his family. His two children, Nancy Anne and James Hugh, have produced seven grandchildren in whom Wooden delights. Wooden is now eleven times a great-grandfather, and joyfully boasts of them. All in the family are doing well in life. If you are fortunate to visit him at his Encino, California condominium, where he moved from a Santa Monica apartment after retiring, he will show you proudly, with a twinkle in his eye, the picture book of the many great-grandchildren prepared by his eldest great-granddaughter, Cori Bernstein. Finally, Wooden is readying for private publication of a book of one hundred poems, twenty each under the following rubrics: Family, Faith, Patriotism, Nature, and Miscellaneous. Wooden has always been a poet, having written hundreds of poems over the years, and says he can "seldom fly without writing some verse."

Nell attended the Final Four in 1984, in her wheelchair. After a lengthy illness, she died peacefully on March 21, 1985. Wooden was by her side throughout, and during the long vigils at the hospital, player after player would make an unannounced visit to keep him company. By all accounts, Nell Wooden was a fireball, who fought for him, including sticking up for him to UCLA Athletic Director J.D. Morgan. She felt at that time that Coach Wooden was exploited to some degree by UCLA; his salary in 1975 was a mere $32,500 that year. Wooden's salary in 1961 was an anemic $12,500, $16,500 in 1966, $19,500 in 1968, $21,000 in 1969, $23,000 in 1971.

Wooden, however, did not believe he was underpaid, commenting in 2000, that, "Maybe I didn't have a million-dollar contract like (Los Angeles Laker superstar basketball player) Shaquille O'Neal, but he'll never know what it was like to get a good meal for twenty-five-cents." Today, the head coach at UCLA makes over $575,000 per year. During the Wooden era, salaries for coaches were commensurate with those of college professors, but as sports became big business, universities were forced to be competitive to some degree with those paid in professional sports, and certainly were no longer pegged to those paid professors. Too much money was at stake; it has been that way ever since.

NELL

Family always played the most important aspect in Wooden's existence, and Nell's loss is a tremendous burden upon him, the most difficult blow he has faced. In Wooden's den, inscribed on his copy of the Pyramid of Success is, "For my wife, Nellie, who has been 'my life' all my life and without whose patience, faith, understanding and love, I would be lost. As ever and forever, John." Another plaque, given to him by Nell, reads: "God never closes the door without opening another one." After an initial and lengthy period of depression due to Nell's death, Wooden has rebounded and leads an active life.

In 1990, Wooden discussed his feelings. "Nellie and I were married for (almost) fifty-three years. We were sweethearts for sixty. When I lost her, it was difficult, and I didn't want to do much for two or three years. I was not what I perceive to be a recluse, but bordering on that, perhaps. Not from my family, but I didn't care to do things. Anything. I just sort of existed." There were several newspaper articles about his sadness and how he did his best to cope with it. "I miss her as much now as I ever have," he said. "It never gets easier. There are friends who would like to see me find another woman for companionship, I wouldn't do it. It would never work."

Jim Powers, who played for Wooden in high school and at Indiana State, encountered Wooden at one of those low moments, and remembers "that time that we were together at Indiana State. We were up in his room, and he was getting dressed. He came out of the bathroom after shaving. Tears came to his eyes, he said, 'I really miss her. You know, she just did everything for me. I can't even pack my own bag.'"

In 1992, Wooden said he was able to overcome his depression because "I had a lot of help from my friends, ex-players. Here were a lot of players that came and sat with me in the hospital on those days. I was sitting there all day long and my children and my grandchildren. The coming along of the great grandchildren was a blessing. But having so many wonderful friends and ex-players—they were great. For a year or two I wasn't interested in much of anything." Sometimes before he goes to sleep, he whispers to himself these lines of Wordsworth:

She dwelt among the untrodden ways
Beside the springs of Dove.
A maid of whom there were none to please,
And very few to love.

A violet by a mossy stone,
Half hidden for the eye,
Fair as a star when only one
Was shining in the sky

She lived unknown and few could know
When Lucy ceased to be
But she is in her grave, and oh,
The difference to me

In 1993, Wooden told an interviewer, "I try to dwell on the good times. She's the only girl I ever went with. There were good times and you try to treasure the good times. You try to be positive about things. I try to, and sometimes it's hard. Life is a short period of time." He continued, "It's the things after. . . they're eternal. And we shouldn't, in my opinion, worry about that. We should look forward to it. I look forward to it more since I lost my dear wife. I would say, prior to that, I had some fears of death. I shouldn't have, nor should. But I did. Now I have none at all. It's my only chance to be reunited, and I feel that way. This is the life you lead. You'll be judged, and it'll be a fair judgment. It won't be the judgment of people here. I believe that."

Wooden is at peace with his mortality, having learned from a master philosopher who confronted the issue in 399 B.C. Wooden, in 2002, addressed it as follows: "When Socrates was imprisoned and facing death, he had tremendous serenity. His jailors could not understand that at all. His jailors asked 'why aren't you preparing for death?' Socrates' answer was 'I've been preparing for death all my life.' He had huge serenity, peace inside." In 1998, Wooden wrote with equanimity, "A man or woman who strives conscientiously to become the best that he or she is capable of becoming can stand tall on Judgment Day. That person will be judged a big success regardless of whether he or she has accumulated riches, glory or trophies."

When Wooden sends checks to family members, he sends it in both their names because, "That pleases Nell." After Nell's death, Wooden refused to attend the Final Four tournaments because it reminded him too much of happy occasions. He and Nell had attended thirty-six in a row. He did attend—and it was national news—the 1991 tournament in Indiana, where he was feted (and really could not refuse to accept the accolades bestowed in his home state), and

THE JOHN WOODEN PYRAMID OF SUCCESS

the 1995 tournament in Seattle, when the Bruins, led by Coach Jim Harrick, won the NCAA Final Four championship, the first since the dynasty ended. He has since attended every tournament since, and in 2002, "An Evening with John Wooden," with tickets at twenty-five and fifty dollars was one of the highlights of the event. He speaks to Nell every night, visits her grave on Sundays, and still goes to the same church in Santa Monica which he has attended for the last fifty years. "My life, since losing her, is for my children, as she would want," said Wooden in 1989. When he was feeling low, he wrote this poem:

At times when I'm feeling low I hear from a friend and then
My worries start to go away and I am on the mend.
No matter what the doctors say and their studies never end
The best cure of all when spirits fall is a kind word from a friend.

On the 21st of each month, Wooden writes his wife a love letter and lovingly places it among a stack tied with a yellow ribbon on her pillow of their bed. In his missives, written on the monthly anniversary of her passing, Wooden remembers the good times, reminds her how she is missed, and brings her up to date on the doings of their progeny. Nell's robe is laid on the right side of the bed, where she slept, along with two framed pictures of her and flowers. At the foot of the bed is Nell's old license plate, "MAMA 7"—what she was called by her loved ones—which sits atop a UCLA blanket embroidered with "John and Nell." Wooden refuses to leave the condominium he and Nell shared, nor replace the drapes and furniture, which are starting to wear. His den, where he spends much of his time, is filled with memories of basketball, Nell, his family, and the award he is most proud of, his Big-10 Award for Proficiency in Scholarship and Athletics.

In 2000, Wooden agreed with interviewer Charlie Rose that Nell still lived in his head and heart, and added to that suggestion "and in every room in my place. And we have ten great-grandchildren, and seven grandchildren within fifty-five miles of where I live, who I see regularly. But I see her in all of 'em." If he has any regrets, "it would be that I didn't do more for my dear Nellie. I think she was always doing for me." He regrets that he never learned to dance, as she enjoyed that activity, or that he preferred to go to ballgames when she might have liked to go to a play. He says he lost Nell—physically—in 1985, making it clear by what is not said that her spirit and memory remain a big part of his daily existence.

THE CAMPS

Anyone who attended Wooden's basketball camps—adult or youngster—shares an unforgettable experience. In 1983, one sportswriter wrote in amazement at having watched Wooden pick up thirty soda cans which had been littered, and then go to the restroom to obtain a paper towel and clean the water faucet of gum. Just as he mopped floors for seventeen years before every practice in the Men's Gym, no job was too menial for Coach to do, so that perfection could be achieved. For example, when the Bruins went on a road trip in 1972, while Wooden was in the middle of his reign as the King of Coaches, he would assist the bus driver in removing the bags from the compartment.

Until 1991, Wooden coached four clinics a year, three for kids, one for adults. He loved doing so, and in 1978 he averred that, "Kids aren't harder to teach now. Oh, you'll get some malcontents, just as you do in classrooms or organizations. But that's been true for ten years. I've found in my camps youngsters still are eager to learn. I think they're more troubled than they were because society is as a whole. All youth of today have been though are wars—Korea, Vietnam. And they've observed so many scandals, times of violence, the hippie era, the Manson era, so many things. . ." In his last interview before curtailing involvement with the camps in 1991, he said, "I tell the parents not to send their boys to camp just to get rid of them for a week or two. My camps are to teach, not to entertain. If they want to be entertained, I tell them to go to camps run by pro players—not coaches. When you have a basketball camp for adults, it's different than those for youngsters. Here we give them ideas that will let them enjoy the game more as spectators or participants. We give them fundamentals, not endless drills. If they just wanted to play games for three days, they would go to the YMCA."

Max Shapiro organized the events and tells about the basketball camps:

"We got started in 1972 with our first camp, the John Wooden Basketball Fundamentals Camp, and had 900 kids the first year, the sixth year we had 2,100 kids—300 kids a week for seven weeks, who'd come and stay for a week, Sunday through Friday. In 1983, the first John Wooden Adult Basketball Encounter was held at Pepperdine University, and we held one every year since, the average attendance is from 30-40. It's $1,695 for the weekend, which includes an authentic UCLA uniform, a videotape of highlights of the game and a great weekend with Coach. We run the gamut of attendees. We've got a sixty-six-year-old business executive who had open heart surgery, and some in their twenties. Some are serious players, but most are not. Many have never even played organized basketball, but went to UCLA when Coach Wooden was there, which means they were around a lot of national championship teams. They just want to find out what makes him so special."

"Wooden had a real positive effect on the kids at the first camp that we did," Shapiro continued. "When he got done with his last lecture on Friday, the kids gave him a spontaneous standing ovation. Kids don't do stuff like that—adults give people standing ovations. The lecture was just about basketball. He was finishing up. They could sense and feel how much he had given to them and how important it was what they received. For junior high aged kids, twelve to fourteen, to stand up and give someone a standing ovation without anyone prompting them to do it is really special."

Shapiro was quite surprised that Wooden went to UCLA every afternoon during the summers until his retirement. "He was preparing for the next season, answering correspondence, whatever needed to be done," relates Shapiro. "The camps made a big difference in the lives of some of the campers. Kids, as a result of learning the Pyramid, did better in school, got along better at home with their parents. We have many repeat campers and we've had the children of past campers come to camp."

Shapiro loved working with Wooden because he "is as close to sainthood as you can get. He doesn't say bad things about people, doesn't carry any animosity around, thinks of others first. He's honest and cares about people."

In the summer of 1991, Wooden successfully underwent a hip replacement operation, which has slowed him down, but he is still on his feet when he needs to be. With his fierce and indomitable spirit, he remains the most youthful nonagenarian in existence. In 1991, Wooden told a reporter that the last book he'd read was *Abraham Lincoln: the Man and His Faith*, and when asked if he could change places with anyone in history, he responded: "Jesus, Abraham Lincoln, Mahatma Gandhi, Benjamin Franklin."

Wooden has aged with grace. He candidly discussed in 1992 how he did so:

How difficult is it for you to handle the aging process? To have a diminishment of your physical faculties. How do you deal with that?
I am disappointed that I can't get around. I enjoyed doing my daily walks. I am sorry that I can't get down on the floor and romp with my great grandchildren. But, I can do a lot of things. Yesterday I had my newest in my arms and gave him his bottle. [The Impelmans], my granddaughter and grandson-in-law, are driving down today because they are moving down here now. Then I will have them all very close and I am very happy about that. I have been blessed so many ways with family that I shouldn't complain about getting old. It's much better than the alternative.

Were there times in your life where you felt rage or anger or depression and did you mask that?
Perhaps depression. I don't think rage or anger during the terrible, terrible

long sickness and suffering of my wife. Yes, I was depressed at times. Like when she was in a coma for ninety-one days. And sitting there, such exhilaration when you hold her hand the first time she gives you a little pressure, then you know. Depressed but not anger. I've read some of the transcripts and I was very disappointed in one or two that I have read. One where a player [see Walt Hazzard interview] talks about my ranting and raving of throwing things and kicking lockers. That never occurred, absolutely never occurred. I don't believe anyone has ever heard me yell and scream. Raise my voice of course. I raised my voice, but it's entirely different from yelling and screaming and throwing things. I don't know if I ever threw anything. I think I have a reasonable degree of serenity. I think my father and mother, myself and my three brothers don't get uptight over things which you have no control. There are certain things that you just have to except. As my dad did. I saw him go through many things and I saw my poor mother having to work harder than she did. [I] never saw dad upset never heard him use a word of profanity. I don't think I have since I did one time when I was in grade school, [when my] older brother threw some manure in my face from one stall into another. Never after that to the best of my knowledge.

The man is a perpetual volunteer. In 1996, at the age of eighty-six, he visited Childrens Hospital in Los Angeles, spreading good cheer. He's now in his nineties, still attending basketball games, still in good cheer, still making appearances and giving the Pyramid lecture. In April 2002, he autographed books by and about him for long lines of admirers for three hours each on two days for the *Los Angeles Times* Book Festival held at UCLA. In 2002, Wooden delivered the Pyramid lecture on fifty occasions, an extraordinary feat considering his age. In February of 2002, Coach participated in Southern California in two day-long seminars on his philosophy. This author attended the first lecture with 125 others of all ages and from all walks of life, each paying $400. The John Wooden Course is the brainchild of Southern California marketing executive and Wooden admirer, Lynn Guerin, who spent two years obtaining Wooden's cooperation and preparing with him the course materials. The seminar is a touching, life-affirming, heartwarming, and moving experience, which includes written exercises taken throughout the day (to be completed at home) enabling the attendee to analyze his or her life, experience and goals in the context of the Pyramid of Success.

Wooden, in 2002, remains at the top of his game: articulate, funny, wise and in all ways wonderful, though he was taken aback by the heaps of praise, causing him to announce at the second lecture that he "wasn't dead yet" and requesting that the eulogies cease. For an hour and a half, Coach taught the Pyramid, recited poetry from memory, and answered questions on all subjects. Former player Swen Nater, who flew in from Seattle, spoke of how Coach had changed and focused his life, read various poems he'd created which honored Wooden, and accompanied himself on guitar while singing a version of *The Wind Beneath My Wings*, the lyrics tailored for Coach (see page 199). Andy Hill kept the audience's attention with stories of Wooden as coach and mentor, and told how what he'd learned had guided him as a television executive. Craig Impelman, grandson-in-law of Wooden, taught how he has integrated the Pyramid of Success into his business, of all things, a collection agency. There, the stated goals are to make the world a better place and to empower the employees to achieve the goals of the Pyramid of Success, one of which is at every work station. Coach's values and philosophy are literally part of the corporate culture and taught to all employees.

The enthusiasm of Nater and Hill became all the more contagious as one realized as they spoke that they sat on the bench during most of their time at UCLA (though Nater, who played behind Bill Walton, went on to become a first round draft pick and successful NBA athlete who set rebounding records, which shows how talented Wooden's teams were near the end of the dynasty). The evaluations by those attending the seminars unanimously indicated it was a worthwhile experience, and they were pleasantly surprised to find that although the Wooden approach can be applied to virtually all business models, promoting efficiency, teamwork, and effective management techniques, it resonates at a deeper level affecting one's "inner self," core human values, and morality, having a deep, almost spiritual quality.

Wooden is still growing, changing, evolving, bettering himself and even his philosophy. The Pyramid of Success credo underwent a subtle change at the turn of the millennium. No longer is success defined as "Peace of mind which is a direct result of self-satisfaction in knowing you did your best to become the best you are capable of becoming," but its author now defines it as "Peace of mind that is a direct result of self-satisfaction in knowing that you *made the effort* to become the best you are capable of becoming." (emphasis added).

Wooden stated in February 2002 that he believed the Pyramid had helped him become better, and that "twenty-six years after retiring, it pleases me that I still send out as requests for the Pyramid, over 1500 a year. That it could help somebody else is good because anything we can sow or do which is meaningful to another is helpful, particularly when it was done when there was no thought of getting something in return, and that is true, and it seems to have helped others in many ways."

In 1998, Wooden wrote on a website about the Pyramid that it provided him "with a guide, a standard of preparation and performance, that brought me the greatest peace of mind in all areas of my life." Curiously, the website is sponsored very subtly by Arthur Andersen LLP, the accounting firm which imploded in 2002 because of the failure of its Houston office to adequately and honestly audit the Enron corporation, which resulted in one of the biggest bankruptcies and business scandals of any generation. A few bad apples spoiled it all for Andersen, which did top-flight work since 1913 and was one of the Big Five accounting firms in the world until the debacle. It is now in ruins.

Andersen, which has sponsored Wooden for years, posted this letter written in early 2002 to President George Bush, on its website, written in the hand of the Coach, the way he always writes his letters, in neat, cursive penmanship that would bring joy to any schoolteacher:

Dear President Bush,

As a common man who attempts to stay true to his beliefs, I sincerely believe the indictment of Arthur Andersen by our Department of Justice is a miscarriage of justice for several legitimate reasons.

Enron stockholders are being hurt again. I believe that the Arthur Andersen indictment places the business at grave risk of failure. This also means that they maybe be able to pay on a fraction of the $750 million, the settlement they offered to shareholders before the indictment.

Furthermore, 28,000 men and women stand to lose their income which will vitally affect thousands more who depend upon them as well as further during an already unstable economy. Well over 99% of the people had nothing to do with Enron or the problem.

Is it right to punish an entire firm for the possible errors of a limited few? One should never discipline all those under their supervision for the misdeed of one. That would not be logical, fair or productive.

It appears that Andersen has been convicted without trial which may have caused irreparable harm and that our government is more interested in Andersen than the Enron managers who ran the company and have never been formally charged. Is that right?

Mr. President, time is running out and this is a matter of principle and principled people need to act. Please intervene and help resolve this indictment and permit the innocent people of Andersen to continue servicing thousands so clients as they have so honorably in the past century.

Respectfully yours,
John Wooden

By this letter, Wooden demonstrates loyalty, one of the blocks of the Pyramid, standing up for an institution and those who comprise it. One cannot think of a more unpopular and saddening financial disaster and apparent fraud than that of Enron, but Wooden is right in lobbying for the entire Andersen team, virtually all of whom were blameless, although the firm was perhaps on a doomed voyage given other audit failures in previous years of Sunbeam, Waste Management and and the Baptist Foundation of Arizona, the latter being the largest non-profit bankruptcy in American history. After the Enron scandal broke, Andersen was further tainted by disclosures that its public audits had failed resulting in the gigantic bankruptcies of Worldcom and Global Crossing.

The irony strikes as this is the same kind of monstrous misconduct that happened to an American president in the early 1970s, when the Watergate scandal toppled the government of President Richard Nixon, who was forced to resign and many of his senior staff and Cabinet officers were jailed. Wooden twice visited in prison H.R. "Bob" Haldeman, President Nixon's chief of staff. Haldeman had been a Bruin Hoopster, part of the alumni and fan organization that supported UCLA basketball, and had led the fund-raising for Pauley Pavilion. They had been friendly since the 1950s, and though Haldeman was vilified by the press and the public—indeed, it is hard to think of someone more despised at the time—Wooden did not turn his back on a friend, someone who made grievous mistakes and paid his price to society. Wooden still saw the good in him, just as he sees the good in the rest of the Andersen team, also victimized by a few.

Sticking up for those at Andersen is another brave act by Wooden; would others facing similar situations do so? Finally, at ninety-one, he writes with such lucidity, strength and poise. Whether one agrees with his position, his letter elegantly provides pause for thought.

In June 1998, Wooden gave the Pyramid of Success lecture to a class on sports psychology at UCLA. There is now a new discipline of study called sports psychology, and Wooden, of course, would have to be deemed the dean thereof. His knees are in bad shape, he can't stay on his feet long and needs a cane. Though the body is frail, his mind is perfect. He reads a lot; answers mail; talks on the phone; visits with family, friends and players; goes out for meals and generally has a grand old time. Until his hip operation, Wooden walked five miles a day, and after his morning walk he alternated between Winchell's donut shop and a McDonalds where he would sit with different groups of men who gathered at these locations.

His cute, thoughtful, playful and active nature was shining in August of 2000 when, to the surprise of American swimmer Lindsay Benko, who was trying out for the Olympic team, she was tracked down by Wooden. Wooden advised her that she would go all the way (she did go on to win a gold medal) because she "had good genes." Wooden knew this because he had coached her grandfather in basketball at Indiana State back in the 1940s. This is yet another example where kindness, class and style meet whimsy and fun.

In October 1999, Adidas, the sporting goods manufacturer, began a major sports marketing campaign around Wooden, to promote Wooden's philosophy, built around the slogan, "The spirit of excellence, the spirit of UCLA." Adidas believes that the present generation of youth will readily take to Wooden as they become aware of him, and that he was chosen to promote the university because at UCLA, "all roads lead to Wooden."

In March, 2002, giant retailer Costco featured Wooden on the cover of its magazine, which is distributed to all its customers, along with a lengthy and laudatory article about Coach and the Pyramid. The article invited customers to purchase *Wooden*, the little blue book of his sayings and philosophy. In May, 2002, banners hung from every light pole up and down Wilshire Boulevard in Westwood and West Los Angeles, promoting UCLA Extension, the continuing education program, with Coach's aphorism properly attributed to him, "It's what you've learned after you know it all that counts."

Bill Walton, in 1999, agreed that Wooden is the patriarch of UCLA: "UCLA can easily claim an endless list of people who have changed the world. In sports, that list would include Jackie Robinson (who integrated baseball), Arthur Ashe (tennis great), Kareem Abdul-Jabbar, Rafer Johnson (Olympic decathlon champion who also played for Wooden), Jimmy Connors (tennis great), J.D. Morgan and Ducky Drake. But of all the legends who have given so much, it is John Wooden, the former basketball coach, who had the greatest impact on the largest number of people. John Wooden does not have the physical prowess that enables so many to others to dominate their sport. Nor does he have a dominating, overwhelming personality to give him complete control over his world. What he has is a heart, brain, and soul that put him in a position to inspire others to reach levels of success and peace of mind that we could never dream of reaching by ourselves."

Since John Wooden retired from UCLA in 1975, no team or coach has approached within striking distance any of the records achieved by him. Some records may fall. Records are made for that purpose. Even Babe Ruth was not invincible. As to Mr. Ruth, Wooden, in 2002, had this sagacious comment: "You may suggest that Babe Ruth achieved greatness even though he broke training in every sort of way over and over again. But just imagine what he might have done if he had focused on bringing out the best that he had within him? He may have achieved greatness in the eyes of many, but did he have his own personal greatness? Did he try to be the best he could be?" Unlike Wooden, Ruth was suicidal after his baseball years ended and died a heartbroken man.

Perhaps a coach some day will beat the astounding eighty-one consecutive victories on UCLA's home court. The rules of the sport may change, better players may come along, but for his time, John Wooden was the best at what he did. Doing his best, he became the best. Wooden discussed his basketball accomplishments in 1989: "You have to measure a player's success or a team's success against what others did in the same era. It's impossible to tell how someone from one era would do in another. Would Ty Cobb be a great hitter today? Would Honus Wagner be a great shortstop today? Would Red Grange be scoring touchdowns today? Would Joe Louis be knocking out all opponents today? Who knows? Still, I'll say this much, I think our teams would have been quite competitive today. I'd like to think any team with a Kareem Abdul-Jabbar on it or a Bill Walton on it would be able to hold his own against anyone."

Wooden's contribution to this planet far exceeds the realm of amateur athletics. With the Pyramid of Success, Wooden has donated to humanity a philosophy for living, loving, achieving and understanding the human condition. John Wooden's courage, understanding, decency, dedication and guidance have affected many. His wisdom, teachings and example will withstand the tests of time and have made this world a better place to live. "I'd rather be remembered as a good person than as a good coach. It's hard for us to keep things in perspective sometimes," Wooden once said, and as the Pyramid lives on, his wish will become reality. In 1980, 1,100 guests and 104 former players showed up at Pauley Pavilion to honor Coach Wooden for his seventieth birthday, and to announce the construction of the John Wooden Recreation Center. Wooden told the crowd, "I want to be remembered as a teacher. Only as a teacher can you have such splendid company."

What we see when we examine the life of John Wooden is consistent wisdom, plainly spoken common sense. This was Wooden's closing advice to the UCLA student body in his 1998 interview in the *Daily Bruin*: "Just to the student body, remember why you are at UCLA. It is for the education, and I said the same thing to my players. But support your various other activities, whether it's athletics or music or whatever. But whatever it is, support them, and don't be too critical. Criticism eats on you. Forgiveness sets you free."

ON TEACHING

All four of the Wooden brothers became teachers. Daniel J. Wooden became assistant superintendent and business manager at Alamo Gordo in New Mexico, "Cat" Wooden was the principal at West Covina High School in

Southern California, and William Hugh Wooden taught at La Porte, Indiana.

Wooden loved being a teacher, explaining why in 1998: "Teaching is the most wonderful profession. The two most important professions in the world are parenting—that's the most important—and teaching. . . You don't have to treat all alike, that's being unfair. If you treat them all alike, that's showing prejudice. You have to try to give everyone the treatment they earn and you listen to them if they want to be heard."

Wooden certainly knew how to teach. In his textbook, *Practical Modern Basketball*, Wooden emphasized that it was necessary "to understand the learning processes and follow the laws of learning," to be able to "explain and provide a demonstration," to "have the players imitate the proper demonstration, constructively criticize and correct their demonstration, and have the corrected imitation repeated and repeated until the proper execution becomes automatic." A teacher, he continued, must also use and take advantage of all possible teaching aids, be a student of psychology and constantly make use of the results of his study, praise as well as censure, be patient, firm and forceful. He understood how to build and maintain a team without sacrificing the individuality of a member, succinctly explaining that: "It is natural for a player to want to score and I want every player to want to score, but not at the expense of a teammate or the team. If a player tells me he doesn't like to score and that he would rather set up plays or play defense, I immediately tell them that he is either lying or he must be abnormal and I want neither type on my team. I want every player to enjoy the thrill of being called team player and derive pleasure from playing defense, but I do not consider it natural to actually enjoy those fine qualities more than scoring. False modesty is not a virtue."

The key to being a good teacher, Wooden said in 2002, is patience. "No two cases are identical, but the teacher must always have patience. And you have to listen to those under your supervision. I think anyone in a position of supervision, if they're not listening to those under them, they're not going to get good results. The supervisor must make sure that all of those under his supervision understand they're working with him, not for him. I think if you work for someone, you punch the clock in and out and that's it. If you're working with someone, you want to do more than that."

Bill Walton, in 1999, observed with characteristic enthusiasm, "Our practices, our lives are constantly structured around the four laws of learning, explanation, demonstration, correction and repetition. And repeat we do. Everything, everyday until we have become John Wooden ourselves. But that is not his goal, for he knows that the strength of the team is the strength of the individual. And that when everyone thinks alike, no one is thinking. That is what and how he teaches. Rarely telling us what or why, but rather showing us how and letting us come to the rest of the answer on our own. He never talks about winning and losing but rather about the effort to win. He rarely talks about basketball but generally about life. He never talks about strategy, statistics of plays, but rather about people and character. And he never tires of telling us that once you become a good person, then you have a chance of becoming a good basketball player or whatever else you may want to do."

Wooden wasn't just a teacher, but also a leader, the ideal he preached in his textbook: "The coach must never forget that he is a leader, not just a person with authority. The youngsters under his supervision must be able to receive proper guidance from him in all respects and not merely in regard to the proper playing of the game of basketball."

He was also a leader with judgment, who said in the same book, "The coach much be extremely careful in his judgment and consider all matters in the clear light of common sense. He must have a sense of discretion and tact comparable to that of Solomon. A sense of values in regard to men, games, techniques, and training is a must for him."

Wooden habitually made lists, including what personal traits and abilities a coach should have:

Primary Traits	Secondary Traits
1. Industriousness	1. Affability
2. Enthusiasm	2. Appearance
3. Sympathy	3. Clear, firm voice
4. Judgment	4. Adaptability
5. Self-control	5. Cooperativeness
6. Earnestness	6. Forcefulness
7. Patience	7. Accuracy
8. Attentiveness to detail	8. Alertness
9. Impartiality	9. Reliability
10. Integrity	10. Cheerful, optimistic disposition
11. Teaching Skill	11. Resourcefulness
12. Discipline	12. Vision
13. Floor Organization	13. Consideration for others
14. Knowledge of the game	14. Desire to improve

LASTING RELATIONSHIPS

Wooden is in regular communication with many of his former players. In 1991, he discussed these relationships—so uncommon for their breadth and deepness—with some approaching seven decades: "Some of my closest and dearest players are ones who never got to play too much. I think I made a more conscious effort—because they weren't getting to play too much—to establish a rapport with them than I would with my players who got to play a lot. I had a heck of a relationship with managers and from what I hear, I never let my managers be servants to the players. I didn't want them picking up after the players. I didn't want them to have to go in the showers and pick up clothes, or pick up soap that might be on the floor, or turn the showers off, or pick up towels all over the place, or gum wrappers, or orange peels, or things of that sort. I said that they're there to help, but they're not your servants. And I think our managers always appreciated that. I'd say I had a better relationship with all of my managers through the years than I had with the players. With all of them."

From the foregoing information, we see yet again how everyone connected with the team, including managers, was important to him at the time. Coach remains interested in them, their lives, what has become of them.

He even remembers the parents of players. Carl Krausher in 1980 told this typical example: "One very personal incident occurred in 1969 when my parents went to their first game in Pauley Pavilion . . . the first game they had attended since I played in 1950. I was not with them, but as they entered they walked in back of the UCLA bench. Coach Wooden saw, recognized, and greeted them after period of almost twenty years. Needless to say, my parents were on cloud nine after that occurrence."

Because Coach is always tending to his garden of friendship, the fruits forever grow and ripen. We thus learn another lesson, the great teacher is constantly rewarded with the recurring benefits of attention and affection after the schooling is over, and it has a ripple effect, encompassing and including those who are close to the student.

Consider Wooden's self-effacing comment to a reporter in 1995: "I'm no legend and I'm embarrassed about that . . . I don't like false modesty. I'm proud of the fact that I was fortunate to have a lot of wonderful players who brought about national championships and that I'm a part of that . . . but I'm also realistic and I know without those players it wouldn't have happened. No coach wins without them and not every coach wins with them." His humility has always been part of his charm. This is how he began one luncheon speech in 1986: "I hope the good Lord will forgive my introducer from overpraising me, and me for enjoying it so much."

In January 1966, *Look* magazine, then one of the major weeklies, ran a three-page article entitled, "Shooting is the Least Important Part of Basketball," which is quintessential Wooden and written by him:

> *There are plenty of jokes about coaches and character building, but I'm not at UCLA to operate a farm system for the professional league. I'm here as an educator, and I try to teach decency through intercollegiate basketball. Furthermore, the better the character, the stronger the basketball effort. Virtue cannot be learned from a playbook or from chalk talks by the coach. It comes from example. . . Good character isn't antithetical to outstanding performance. It is not sissy to be a well-mannered athlete.*
>
> *. . .One thing I never do is talk to my boys about winning. I don't believe I have ever used the word "win" before a game. Fight talks only build temporary enthusiasm. The last thing I tell kids is, "I'm not concerned with the other team, I'm concerned with you. Just be able to say 'I did my best.' By dedication, you may be able to beat a better team."*
>
> *. . .By taking the emphasis off shooting, I think you strengthen the ideas of team play and make boys not only willing but eager to sacrifice themselves for the group. A raise in pay, like a basket, makes for temporary joy. In life, I think if you stop to consider your very happiest moments, practically every one of them has been the result of doing something for a parent, a brother, a sister, or wife— or for the team as a whole, the 38 minutes you're not shooting.*

Wooden knows he is loved by his players, some of whom used to gripe. "Wasn't it Mark Twain who said when he was a boy at fourteen his dad was so stupid he could hardly be around him? And when he became twenty-one, he was surprised how much his dad had learned," Wooden has said. "I think that's how these players felt about me." He's so right, as you will see when you read further. He's still a tolerant man. The bond with his players is special. Wooden observed in 1969, "The thing I like about coaching athletics is that you are dealing with boys on an emotional, mental, psychological plane, as well as physical. When I taught English, I never reached my students in this many ways. I never got as close to them as I do to my players."

In 1998, Bill Walton marveled at the evolution of the relationship. "Coach Wooden is like your dad. You talk to him about everything. He is such a terrific person, such a terrific friend. When you're playing for a great person, he can't really be your friend, because he's got to push you, drive you, ask more from you than is really there from you. [Now] the relationship we all have with him is just so special because he has so much to offer; he always has that great perspective." What Wooden taught, Walton says, "is that it takes a lifetime to get good at something. There are no shortcuts; there is no one word, no one speech. It's an accumulation of everything."

The players are the lucky ones, they learned not second-hand, but up-close, and all the players knew—even those from his high school teaching days—long before Wooden became the acknowledged wise man in the pubic eye—that he and what he taught were worth hanging onto. That deep respect from his boys, which he earned, thrills him to this day and is what ultimately motivated him, Wooden says: "When I was in the service in World War II, at one time I didn't get any mail for several months. Then I got eighty to ninety letters at one time, and the vast majority of them were from players, not just youngsters that I had as students in English, but players from my basketball team or my tennis team or my baseball them. These letters came from all over the world, from ships on the high seas, from Northern Africa, from the South Pacific, and some of those individuals never came back. Not a single individual in the letters I received was pessimistic. They were all optimistic and I feel that maybe athletics helped in some way and maybe I had helped in some degree."

Jack Tobin, who wrote with Coach, *They Call Me Coach*, in 1987 succinctly described Wooden as a "maker of men." Wooden helped turn boys into men, and when they looked back at the experience, they were ever grateful. In December 2000, Wooden proudly reported that "recently on my ninetieth birthday, I had a card from—signed by fifteen men that I think of as my boys that played for me in high school in the 1930s."

In 2002, Wooden acknowledged the powerful bond between him and his players: "Next to your own flesh and blood, they're just like your family. Their joys are your joys, their sorrows are your sorrows."

Wooden still writes poetry; here's one he wrote one morning in 1989:

The years have left their imprint on my hands and on my face:
Erect is no longer my walk, and slower is my pace
But there is no fear within my heart, because I'm getting old:
I only wish I had more time to better serve my Lord
When I've gone to Him in prayer, He's brought me inner peace
And soon my cares and worries and other problems cease:
He's helped me in so many ways, He's never let me down:
Why should I fear the future, when soon I could be near His crown?
Though I know down here my time is short, there is endless time up there
And He will forgive and keep me ever in His loving care.

THE JOHN WOODEN PYRAMID OF SUCCESS

Page 469 of this book contains the "Stairway to Heaven," which Coach, as one of many celebrities, created circa 1990 as his contribution to the fund-raising for the American Heart Association. Like the Pyramid of Success, it is perfection exemplified.

In March of 1999, Wooden wrote in his hand on a Pyramid to one admirer who inquired of his thoughts of being an American: "To me, the American Dream means a desire to become the best of which you are capable of becoming in a manner that will earn the respect of all who know you. To reach your Dream, you must never give up. You will encounter many obstacles and failures along the way, as did a great American, Abraham Lincoln, who, perhaps, was our greatest President, but he never quit and became a model of consistency."

Swen Nater, who has written many poems about and in honor of Wooden, said simply in 2002, that Wooden was a "role model" "who walks the walk."

Wooden has led such an accomplished life. Few players of the year in any sport, as Wooden was in basketball at Purdue in 1932, go on to greater, notable, public achievement, as Wooden has with his unequaled championships and records—which first and foremost belong to him, as the teams kept changing. The only champions—and they weren't players of the year—comparable to Wooden who went on to truly historic greatness after their college and professional careers are Bill Bradley and Byron White.

Bradley is the three-time All American basketball player from Princeton University, who delayed his pro career to be a Rhodes Scholar at Oxford University. He then starred for the New York Knicks on their championship teams in 1970 and 1973, and beginning in 1978, served in the U.S. Senate for three terms. He ran unsuccessfully for the Democratic primary for President of the United States in 2000. In 2000, Wooden rated Bradley as one of the ten greatest college players in the history of the game (excluding college players who did not complete their eligibility in college—for example, Michael Jordan and Magic Johnson—and UCLA players, whom he would not rate.)

Byron "Whizzer" White (who like Wooden hated his nickname) passed away in April 2002, and was a college football great at the University of Colorado, where he was class valedictorian. He also played basketball for the Colorado team that lost the championship game in the National Invitational Tournament in 1938 at Madison Square Garden. White, also a Rhodes Scholar, earned the highest signing bonus paid up to that time for the National Football League, and led the league in rushing in 1938 and 1940. He graduated first in his class from Yale Law School—while playing professional football—followed by a career in private practice in Denver and then the Justice Department in Washington, where he played a senior role in the enforcement of civil rights.

White was appointed to the United States Supreme Court in 1962, where he sat for thirty-one years as a highly respected, conservative jurist. White and Bradley always comported themselves as gentlemen, with modesty, and are leading figures, indeed legends, in sports and their subsequent professions, who deserve and have earned their accolades and our continuing respect.

Compare Wooden's life with the Joe DiMaggio of Richard Ben Cramer's biography, *Joe DiMaggio: The Hero's Life* (2000), a scary, disheartening, sad portrayal of a miserly, unpleasant, hostile, self-centered man, whose public image as one of the greatest sluggers in the history of baseball was opposite to the private one. Joe DiMaggio was about money, a man who would not leave his house unless there was a buck in it for him. Wooden, from beginning to end, is about love. John Wooden on the outside is the same inside. The public man is no different from the private man. Both were heroes on the playing field/court. DiMaggio, after baseball, made of career out of being a hero. Wooden's post-UCLA career has been almost exclusively to talk about basketball and dispense wisdom, usually gratis. He gets paid, sometimes substantially, for his talks on the Pyramid, but has always given many talks for no fee. The Pyramid is Wooden's gift to the world; other motivational speakers do not act similarly. The money he has made on *Wooden*, and *Be Quick But Don't Hurry*, the two most recent books of which he is a co-author, is an afterthought to him. Wooden just wants to get the word out that life can work out fine, that all should be striving to reach their full potential. Wooden is the consummate hero, recognized for his work on the court, but even more for his life outside of it. What makes him particularly special is that he is a hero with brains and class. Everybody loves him and with good reason.

Former player and author Andy Hill loves to say, "There is no one who doesn't like Coach."

Basketball great Bill Russell, in 2000, praised Wooden for coaching "always with dignity and honor," noting that Wooden ignored the jealousy, but instead did it his way, and "it turns out he was 100 percent correct."

Wooden is "pleased"—one his favorite words when he expresses happiness—that others enjoy his accomplishments, but reveling in them is not, and never has been, what he is about. He would never think of marketing himself as a hero, and is very careful about allowing his image to be used. He gives most of the money he makes to his family.

Wooden started teaching high school in Kentucky, reluctantly having to leave his home state, after being recognized as the nation's best basketball player, and then spent eleven years coaching high school athletes. It took him fifteen years, 1948-64, at UCLA before he won his first NCAA championship; the penultimate achievement, his Mount Everest. He was fifty-three years old at the time, thirty-two years since his last glory year at Purdue—a long time for anyone.

The doggedness, discipline, craft and craftiness, so finely honed, refined and applied, ultimately paid off so that UCLA became the sports equivalent of Old Faithful, winning with such regularity for over a decade that no one was surprised, rather it was expected. As the dynasty continued, respect for Wooden escalated as he remained calm as ever, treating each victory, each championship, with the same equanimity, where substance met style, character met reputation, demonstrating the zenith of sportsmanlike conduct on and off the court. Sports contests are frequently won by inches, seconds. The same goes for the business world, products and services are very competitive. An industry leader may become such because of better marketing, tighter budget control, asset and personnel deployment, and many other factors which, when cleverly utilized and closely monitored, will result in that competitive edge.

Litigation lawyers face such competition constantly: is the proper argument marshaled, the next witness ready and prepared, the necessary objection timely made? For sales persons, do they know and understand their product, their competition, their customers? Do they adapt to meet the needs and challenges of the marketplace? The winner of any competition in business, like sports, prevails because of that extra bit of preparation, hustle, and ability. Wooden demonstrated that victory could be achieved on a continuous basis, year after year, notwithstanding the changing variables, because he knew how to organize and supervise that over which he had control. Just when you thought he and his teams could not get any better, they did.

Wooden maintained a personal full-court press on learning. Every win and loss was thoroughly analyzed.

Coach discussed in 1980 his philosophy about learning in from all games: "The statement has often been made that we learn from adversity. However, to say that you can't learn through winning is wrong. You can learn as much through winning, in my opinion, as you can in losing, if you'll analyze it carefully. In games that you win or lose, if the score is close, probably about the same things prevailed; you made about the same mistakes, did about the same things correctly and incorrectly in the games that you won or lost. I think subconsciously if you are doing too well, a loss can perhaps bring you back to normal, get your feet back on the ground.

"There is a tendency, and I think more so among young people, to get carried away when they win or lose too much. Just like too much criticism, either one, if you get them out of perspective, it is going to affect you. If you keep them in perspective, then it will not. Sometimes a defeat, as far as a score is concerned, can bring a group back to the proper level. I think that is where you learn more than anything else. You are not going to learn more from a technical point of view. A defeat, more often than not, occurs because the other team is better than you are. What are you doing to do about that? Are you going to learn from that? Think it will help make you all better? Maybe, but you can also learn from that teams that you defeat. I have heard the statement made that the only way to learn is to get whipped. Well, I don't believe that. It is not the only way. It is a way and I think you can get stronger through adversity by learning to accept things better and to keep things in better perspective. It is important to realize that we are not all perfect. Most great inventors tell us they fail 99.9 percent of the time. Edison said that over 99 percent of the things that he tried failed. Some of our greatest people came from a background of failure. We learned from failure in sports, but we can also learn from close games and games that are won handily."

During the dynasty, the level of play of college ball was extremely high in the NCAA. Teams were competitive, but UCLA led the pack continuously for twelve years because Wooden kept tinkering with and improving the formula, just as any business must do lest it become stale. The competition was excellent, first class, but Wooden was just that much better, sometimes so far in front that the lead was staggering. Change is constant, good, and necessary, and Wooden didn't just keep up with the times, he improved upon and sometimes tested popular convention.

As Federal Express has been to delivery, Polaroid to instant pictures, Microsoft to the development of computer operating systems, Wooden's coaching of UCLA teams had the same impact and left the same imprint on the sport. Polaroid, however, failed to keep up with the times and technology, and to maintain a level of competitiveness, while Federal Express and Microsoft continue to pull a strong share of their markets. (Microsoft, in an antitrust trial, was sued in 1998 and found to have obtained such position, in part, by anti-competitive behavior, a decision ultimately upheld on appeal.)

By the time Wooden left coaching, college basketball had national importance and prominence. Wooden is the leading figure responsible for this catapult. America became obsessed with him and his teams, which became annual cultural and entertainment diversions. When he left coaching, there were no mars on Wooden's forty-year coaching record.

The Daily Bruin, the UCLA newspaper, in a souvenir issue commemorating the first national championship in 1964, wrote, "The NCAA basketball championship usually gives class to the winning coach. This year, the winning coach gave class to the NCAA basketball championship."

THE JOHN WOODEN PYRAMID OF SUCCESS

That sums up Wooden's life in basketball, how everyone feels who knows anything about him. His footprints in the sands of time will be evident long after most. Wooden's story is history, in part because of the records, but more importantly for how he achieved those records—fairly, squarely, with unerring cleverness, tight discipline, and coherent goals. He unified team after team into working units of preparedness, and was a champion who knew how to pick and supervise others.

Wooden is a teacher-philosopher. At the opening of Pauley Pavilion (it was even called "John Wooden Day") in 1965, Chancellor Franklin Murphy called Wooden "a whole man, a man of honor, a man of dignity, a man of achievement. At the same time, he is a man of abiding humility and great personal charm . . . and a legend in his own time."

The beauty of Wooden is the way he has always handled himself. Former assistant coach Denny Crum notes the self-control: "He is a very intense competitor, much more so that his appearance would be to the average person. This ability to "disagree agreeably" makes him stand out as the consummate gentleman.

Former assistant coach Frank Arnold describes Wooden as "absolutely fierce. One of the greatest competitors I have been around. I think I learned [from him] that you can be a nice guy and gladiator at the same time. He was the epitome of both."

Wooden knew how to and did maximize his opportunities and utilize his assets, he could and would drive a truck through the smallest weakness in the armor of the opponent because he and his teams were prepared and conditioned to do so when opportunities arose. This is the way he was from Martinsville High School on, and what he had been preparing for and thinking about all of his life—how to maximize opportunities and how to minimize deficiencies. That spirit and philosophy he distilled and then instilled in his players, and they had meaning and impact far beyond the basketball court. The players learned that learning and teamwork can be not just enjoyable experiences, but are fundamental for true achievement. The experience of learning his technique of basketball was the best course one could get in learning how to grab, enjoy, and understand life at its fullest. He didn't want his student-athletes to obsess on basketball, but to have balanced lives, filled with all the other experiences—social, educational, and recreational—that come with university life. But when they suited up for basketball, Wooden was all business. He taught them the fundamentals so well that when it came time for them to learn and then execute nuance, as so gloriously demonstrated by the full-court press in 1963-64, Wooden's canny coaching lifted basketball to an entirely new level of attention.

From then on, everyone was intrigued by the unprepossessing gentleman. What would he do next? Could he keep it up? How did he keep it up? Nobody could be as square as he was, so square he became cool.

Because he chose well-rounded young men, both for their athletic abilities and their maturity as persons, they didn't let him down. Off the court they comported themselves as gentlemen, There were very few occasions when they deviated from social norms, where alcohol and drugs (marijuana is the only drug during the Wooden era that presented a problem) were involved, or their behavior that was inappropriate, rude, nasty or condescending. That there have been virtually no public embarrassments by the players post-UCLA is another tribute to Wooden.

That Wooden was not a braggadocio made him and UCLA all the more appealing. After a game, Wooden and the team did not "blow the victory" by stupid or inappropriate comments, rather the attitude displayed was almost studied diffidence. That glory period reminds one of *The Magnificent Seven*, when a team of skilled cowboys, working as a team, rousted outlaws from a village, with Wooden as Yul Brynner, masterminding how to "outscore" the opponent at the inevitable shoot-out. There was and remains esprit de corps of the first order among anyone who played or worked (for example, managers) with Wooden. The players, going back to the days of Dayton, Kentucky, still want to please him. The team spirit crosses over teams, over generations of men who played for Wooden.

THE FINAL MEASURE

What does Wooden think of his accomplishments, such as the eighty-eight game win streak? In 1985, he commented, "I don't want to belittle it, but that gave me more satisfaction at the time than it does now. My greatest pleasure is seeing the players do well and I'm not just talking about the ones who played professional basketball. We've got twenty-six ex-players practicing law in California. There are doctors, teachers, businessmen. I find myself reflecting more on how well they are doing rather than the championship." In true Mr. Chipsian fashion, he told the *Sporting News* in 1971, "My greatest coaching joy is seeing my players go into the working world, into society. Their joy became my joys and their sorrows, my sorrows. After they have left his supervision, Wooden admitted in 1972, he wondered "if I have contributed to their successes and failures." What could be more rewarding?" What is Wooden's greatest accomplishment? In 1985, Wooden answered, "The close relationship I have with my players after they have gone is most important to me. There's the pride I have from . . . all those who have accomplished something long after they've gone from under my supervision. I like to feel that I had a little bit to do with that. Maybe I didn't, but I like to feel that I did." Wooden delights in knowing where all but eight of the one-hundred-eighty players he coached are today and what they are doing.

The measure of Wooden is not those hallowed victories in sports arenas throughout the nation, but the knowledge and ideology he passed on to every-one else, the relationships he made and formed. As seen in the preceding pages and those that follow, almost without exception, the relationships initiated vir-tually always paid off. Players became lifetime friends with Wooden and their fellow athletes; his strategy for life took hold and rooted itself in the psyches of those under his tutelage. Those who played for Wooden are members of a gold-en circle, as lucky and rare as astronauts, fortunate just to have made the team, for they had the honor and the pleasure of being instructed by this special man whose main goal and desire was to teach them. The players grew and adapted into life and made something of themselves. In 2000, Wooden was asked what was most rewarding about coaching, and replied: "The fact that almost all of the players that I had in my twenty-eight years at UCLA graduated, got their degrees, most of them in four years. And practically all have done well in their chosen professions. I think there's thirty—over thirty attorneys. There's eight ministers. There's ten or eleven dentists, ten or eleven doctors, a lot of teach-ers—but the vast majority probably just in business of one sort or another. And that—that makes you feel good."

A basketball coach, of all persons, taught them that the key to happiness was doing one's best, not just on a basketball court, but everywhere, and that doing so besides being the honorable and intelligent methodology, could be fun and self-satisfying. It goes to show that anybody, no matter the profession or calling, can set an example, lead, and have an effect that will last the lifetimes of teacher and student. Wooden taught a form of physical education, but he real-ly taught Life 101. The words and acts of a great teacher can resonate and rever-berate a lifetime; mentors are found in all sorts of circumstances. Actions speak louder than words, and when the words are intelligent, and the guidance by words and conduct of the first order, all things are possible. Wooden provided rationality. The championships were not the product of magic, it was hard work created pursuant to the Wooden formula, which stressed fundamentals. But, the formula was continually modified to keep up with the times and the talent with whom Wooden worked.

In the history of sports, we remember great teams, great players, great plays. Not often do we remember great coaches. It is one thing to be at the top of one's profession, but how long does that reputation last? Wooden has been out of coaching a quarter of a century. His reputation has only increased, and what we appreciate is the man behind the records.

Why shouldn't a consideration of the philosophic and moral underpinnings of what we do in our everyday experience be a part of the teaching and understanding of those participating in the endeavor? Wooden's grandson-in-law, Craig Impelman, requires incoming employees at his debt-collection business to become familiar with the teachings of Wooden and his overall concept of how to live an honest, fulfilled life and to be a valuable member of a team. This is followed by regular discussions about fundamental values, and should be implemented in every business. Put bluntly, the Pyramid of Success is a money maker: it promotes team work and individual accomplishment, a complex idea presented in deceptively simple packaging. It brings inner and outer peace. Put it up at you workplace, where you play, where you live. Do it now.

Life is a complex experience requiring one to deal with spirituality, emotions ranging from love to anger to distaste, to one's physical condition, to self-esteem and how to relate to the rest of the world. To examine and consider Wooden's life is delightful because of the results he achieved in dealing with these issues we all face. It is such a happy ending on all fronts and what an amazing journey, from small town Indiana to not just the big time in sports, but the winner's circle year after year, where his family life did not suffer, where his progeny all turned out well. Wooden's precious love for Nell, so poignant and tender, and his family life, where he found, and still finds, balance and joy, is inspiring.

"The person who had the greatest influence on my life was my late wife," Wooden said in 1988. "[She was] the reason for staying in school when things were difficult from a financial point of view, and [my] support through all my years of teaching." Wooden today is at peace with himself while still trying to change the world for the better.

An optimist in world of naysayers, how many nonagenarians are still doers, as Wooden has continued to be since his retirement? Despite his frailty, Wooden keeps what would be a grueling schedule for anyone his age and he loves doing so. In a world filled with resignation and malcontents, Wooden has been and is a bright light, a human gyroscope who simply brings out the best in himself and in others. He is a man who never lost or loses his cool, who always knew, and still does, how best to handle any situation. He is a giver more than anything, an ascetic who gets a bigger kick out of life than most, who is and has always been actively involved in life from all its varied angles—philosophical, humorous, romantic, physical, artistic, spiritual. He has earned our respect. Greatness is not measured in records and books, but rather in measured steps. Through tens of thousands of acts of kindness and continued thoughtfulness throughout a lifetime, Wooden has come as close to perfecting the art of living as one can.

Our paths have been illuminated by the Coach of Love—who Wooden truly is, and the appellation he most greatly deserves. Considering his class, style, intelligence, integrity, longevity in the winner's circle, importance to basketball as an innovator and teacher, worldwide influence as a philosopher, lack of marring on his record and life, Wooden is the premier example of an all-around, supremely well-adjusted, "good guy." Coach John Wooden comprises a league of his own.

He's just so good, so impressive, so highly evolved. "He stopped coaching UCLA twenty-five years ago," Bill Walton said in 2000, "now he just coaches the world." Says Bill Walton of Wooden nowadays, "He is more John Wooden today than ever. He is a man who truly has principles and ideas. He is more interested and involved than ever. He is on top of everything. He didn't teach basketball, he taught life." That he is so modest about it makes him all the more endearing.

How has he kept himself from getting so big-headed asked an interviewer in 1975? Wooden knew whom to thank: "I think my dad helped me. My father impressed upon all of his sons: 'You're as good as anyone, but you're no better than anyone, and don't forget it.'" Wooden never has, he surely believes it, the rest of us don't. Few approach him as a man, and then, of course, Mother Teresa and Abe Lincoln never coached basketball.

Chapter Three

John Wooden's Pyramid of Success Lecture

Soon after I had entered the teaching profession, I became somewhat disappointed, disillusioned and surprised by the pressures that were put on my students in my high school English classes. It seemed that their parents wanted them all to receive A's. We all know that the good Lord in His infinite wisdom didn't create us equal in intelligence, physical appearance, size or the environment into which we may have been born. Not everyone could earn an A, and I felt I had youngsters who received the mark of C who were every bit as successful as students who received the mark of A. It seemed as though, in my early years of teaching, that parents felt that if their youngster received a B that the teacher was perhaps young, inexperienced, that he might improve over time. If the youngster received a C, which was the average mark, most parents thought that was proper for the neighbor's children, but for their own, they did not quite understand.

It did bother me about the students in my English classes, so I began searching for something that might help me become a better teacher. We all want success—but I'm not sure that we would all define success in the same way. I went to the dictionary and found out that Mr. Webster defines it as "the accumulation of material possessions or the attainment of a position of power, prestige." I believe those are very fine accomplishments and certainly indicative of success—but not necessarily so in my opinion. I wanted something different, so I finally came up with my own personal definition of success. My dad, on the farm, had taught me and my brothers that we should never try to be better than someone else, but that we should always be learning from others and never cease trying to be our best. A professor of mine had discussed success that also contributed to my thinking, and about this time I came across this simple verse:

At God's footstool to confess
A poor soul knelt and bowed his head.
"I failed," he cried. The Master said,
"Thou did thy best, that is success."

That's all I ask—the effort—from my English students, my players, under the conditions that exist which won't be the same for anyone, doctor, salesman, whatever the calling, but you are all equal of having the opportunity of making the effort. I choose to define success as:

THE JOHN WOODEN PYRAMID OF SUCCESS

Peace of mind which is a direct result of self-satisfaction in knowing you've made the effort to become the best you are capable of becoming.

No one can do more than that, and we each owe ourselves that and we owe each other that: the effort to make the most of whatever we have. We are all the same in having the opportunity to make the most of what we have, whatever the situation. Anything stemming from that success is simply a by-product, whether it be the score, the trophy, a national championship, fame, or fortune. They are all by-products of success rather than success itself, indicators that you perhaps succeeded in the more important contest.

After coming up with that definition, which I thought would help the youngsters under my supervision—and me as a teacher—I wanted to have something more concrete which one could see, rather than a somewhat abject definition one would only hear about, and I came up with the concept of a "Pyramid of Success." I started working on it in 1934 and finished it in its present form when I was discharged from the service in 1948. When I went to Indiana State University, prior to coming to UCLA, I brought it to its present form and I haven't changed it much since then. I've never changed the cornerstones, although many other blocks have been eliminated or changed position within the structure. If any structure is to have any real strength and solidarity it must have strong cornerstones, a strong foundation. "Industriousness" and "Enthusiasm" are the cornerstones of the Pyramid of Success.

"Industriousness." Industriousness is the most conscientious, assiduous and inspired type of work. You can work without being industrious, but you cannot be industrious without work. There is no substitute for work. If you are looking for the easy way, the short-cut, the trick, you may get something done for awhile, but it will not be lasting and you will not be developing your abilities whatever they may be. Worthwhile results come from hard work and careful planning. Perfection can never be obtained, but it must be the goal, and must be sought by determined effort.

Grantland Rice I consider to be the greatest sportswriter of all time. He was a positive writer who wrote about many things, not just sports. He wrote many things in verse, including one entitled, *How to be a Champion*, that I truly enjoy:

You wonder how they do it, and you look to see the knack,
You watch the foot in action or the shoulder or the back,
But when you spot the answer where the higher glamours lurk,
You'll find in moving higher up the laurel-covered spire,
That most of it is practice and the rest of it is work.

There is no substitute for work.

The other cornerstone is "enthusiasm." Your heart must be in your work if your are to learn more. You must truly enjoy what you are doing, otherwise, you can't force yourself to work as hard at it as you are capable of doing. If you are a leader, you must influence those under your supervision and you must be enthusiastic to do that. Enthusiasm brushes off on those with whom you come into contact. It stimulates others. If you are not enthusiastic, you won't get support from those under your supervision. I'll never forget my first year at UCLA when I attended a meeting at Royce Hall. I heard a gentleman speak about a topic about which I had absolutely no interest. Why was I there? Perhaps the same reason some come to hear me speak. Somebody said that I should be there and I sat close to the front so that I would be seen. It was my first year at UCLA and I was trying to get established and I wanted to do well and to please. I'd hoped the speaker would not go on for a long time, but soon after he began my whole attitude changed, primarily, I think, because of his enthusiasm. Of course he had another quality that also helps: he knew his subject. I was sorry when he brought his remarks to a close that particular evening. Some days later, after I had been over to the administration building on the UCLA campus and was returning to my office, I passed by the library and, with no thought of doing so, found myself inside and searching the stacks to find some additional information about a topic which just a few days before I had no interest whatsoever. The speaker's enthusiasm had brushed off; he opened doors to me on a subject that's given me a lot of pleasure ever since. We must have enthusiasm if we are going to make the most of our abilities in any area.

Between the cornerstones of the structure I have three blocks, all very similar because they include and require others. Anything that truly includes others must be worthwhile, must be meaningful. These three blocks are "friendship," "cooperation," and "loyalty."

"Friendship." We must work at friendship. We must have a sincere liking for all. Too often friendship is taken for granted. We think friendship is something nice that someone is doing for us. That is not friendship. That is one-sided. Friendship comes from mutual esteem, respect, and devotion—"mutual" being the key word. You have to work at it, just as you have to work at marriage or it won't be successful. You have to give. Be a friend and you'll have friends.

Some years ago I was speaking in San Francisco at an IBM convention and a gentleman from Indianapolis whom I'd known for many years was there.

Afterwards he came up to me and said, "Johnny, people in California sure aren't as friendly as they are back home, are they?" I replied, "What do you mean?" He says, "For example, coming over here I met a lot of people and not one of them spoke to me, not a single person." I asked, "Did you speak to them?" He said, "No, I didn't know any of them." I smiled and he said, "You have a point there." If we wait for the other person to speak, it may never happen. It takes two.

"Cooperation." We must be cooperative on all levels with our co-workers, with everyone. Listen if you want to be heard. Always strive to understand the other point of view. Be interested in finding the best way, not your own way. It is such a small world in which we live today and it is getting smaller everyday. Modern science and technology are amazing. We can get places through jet travel before we leave, although, of course, the time change might have a little something to do with it. We have people landing on the moon. We see things happening today on the other side of the world, as they are happening. When I was of school age it took us a long time to receive news. And while we might hear or read about an event or see some still pictures about it, we did not see it as we do today. It's all changed with television. Our neighbors constitute the world. When you think of the food we eat, our means of transportation, the clothes we wear, the beautiful churches and temples in which we worship, there is one common denominator: others are involved. We need others in every way. The surest way to have cooperation of others so that we can make the most of our own abilities is to be cooperative ourselves.

The third block in the base of the structure is "loyalty." I don't see how anyone can truly make the most of his or her abilities without expressing loyalty at all times to the people, institutions, and principles that are important in one's life. Maybe it's our supervisors, our co-workers, our family. Loyalty means keeping your self respect, knowing whom and what you have allegiance to, giving respect to those with whom you work. Respect helps produce loyally. Loyalty is very important when things get a little tough, as they often do when the challenge is great. Loyalty is a powerful force in producing one's individual best and even more so in producing a team's best.

On the second tier of this structure are four blocks: "self-control," "alertness," "initiative," and "intentness."

"Self-control." Practice self-discipline and keep your emotions under control. Good judgment and common sense are essential to maintain the delicate adjustment between mind and body. Regardless of what we are doing, if it is a physical act or a mental decision, if it is done with self-control, it has a chance to be workable, to be productive. If emotion takes over, reason usually flies out the window and the decisions that need to be made, the acts performed, are not likely to be nearly as productive as they should be. If it's disciplining children, it must be done with reason, and if it is done so it can produce desirable results. But if we lose reason when disciplining them, it will not be productive. Children want and cry out for discipline, to correct, help, and improve. They don't want punishment which oftentimes antagonizes. It is difficult to get positive results when one antagonizes. Denial of privileges is one of our best methods of discipline.

You cannot antagonize and influence positively and that's what you do when you lose reason. The loss of self-control will profoundly and deleteriously impact your physical and mental abilities. Life is full of peaks and valleys, but that does not mean our emotions must ride a roller coaster. Recognize and enjoy what is wonderful about being alive, be satisfied as goals are realized and accept and understand the traumas, pains and sadness that cross your path. Never wallow in self-pity: for every disappointment there is a joy. We must maintain our self-control at all times if we are going to function anywhere near our level of competence.

The second block is "alertness." Abraham Lincoln is my favorite American. What a great and gentle human being he was. I continually find things that he wrote or said that are so meaningful, oftentimes because of their elegant simplicity—which proves the value of simplicity. He could say so much in so few words. I've often said that the game of basketball is a very simple game, although coaches can make it complicated. It is the little things that count. Abraham Lincoln once said that he "never met a person from whom he did not learn something." Then he said in his humorous way, "Of course most of the time it was something not to do." But that's learning just the same. We must be alert, observing constantly, seeing the things that are going on around us. Otherwise, we are going to miss so many things from which we can improve ourselves. We must be alive constantly. By doing so we can improve ourselves and take advantage of the errors of others. Watch for anything that can help or harm you and be eager to learn. Stay open-minded.

The next block is "initiative." We must not be afraid to act. If we are afraid to do something, for fear of making a mistake, we will not do anything and that is the worst mistake of all. Realize that the road to achievement could be difficult, but don't let the difficulty deter you from making the effort. We learn and get stronger through adversity, something we should not dread or fear. It will only make us a stronger, better person. Someone once said:

When I look back, it seems to me,
All the grief that had to be,
Left me when the pain was o'er,
Stronger than I was before.

When it is a physical act, we get stronger physically through adversity. We get stronger mentally through adversity. We must not be afraid to fail although we are going to fail at times. Face adversity. Sometimes, we, as parents, deprive our children, the ones we love the most, of the development of initiative by making decisions they should be making in certain areas, thinking we know better because of our love and concern for them. Sometimes we are hurting them, rather than helping them. Lincoln said, "The worst thing a parent could do for his children is doing the things that they could and should do for themselves." Give them the opportunity to fail. Let them learn from it so that they won't make the same mistake over again when you are not there telling them not to act so. We must have initiative. The courage to make decisions. Don't be afraid of failure, but learn from it.

The fourth block in the second tier is "intentness." I might have used "determination," "persistence," or "perseverance." Intentness is not giving up, but the ability to resist temptation and stay the course, to concentrate on your objective with determination and resolve. Impatience is wanting too much too soon. Intentness doesn't involve wanting something. It involves doing something. Set goals that are realistic. Idealistic goals that are unattainable can be counterproductive. Goals should be difficult to achieve because things easily achieved, attained, or acquired usually aren't meaningful or don't last too long or are not worthwhile. Set goals that are difficult but in the realm of possibility.

If necessary, change the method of attack, go around, under, over, back up, look the situation over, try a different method. Be intent on reaching that realistic objective. Concentrate on achieving your goals and resist temptation that hinders your way. We must maintain our self-control at all times if we are going to function anywhere near our level of competence.

On the next tier are three blocks, what I call the heart of the structure. One is "condition," the next is "skill," and the third is "team spirit."

"Condition." We must be conditioned for whatever we are doing. As an ex-basketball coach, one would probably surmise that I mean physical conditioning. How can you have physical conditioning without spiritual conditioning, moral conditioning, and mental conditioning? There is no way. You cannot have moral conditioning without spiritual conditioning. These characteristics are a matched set and they operate in an integrated manner, otherwise the entire system is out of kilter.

Rest, exercise and diet must be considered. Moderation must be practiced. Dissipation must be eliminated. When I was teaching at UCLA, around the first of October each year I met with the prospective candidates for the team, and one of the things that I would tell them was, "We are going to be in better condition this year than any other team against which you will participate. That is, of course, if you live up to your responsibilities and I live up to mine. I have great responsibilities. I must study you carefully, I must analyze and realize that no two of you are alike, although you may be similar in many respects, no two of you are identical. I must devise drills to meet the needs of certain individuals. I must know where and when to use these drills in practice. I must know how long to use them each week, each day, and how long to continue as the season progresses. I must watch carefully, analyze, judge, evaluate and continually come up with new ones so that monotony will not set in. So I have to do a lot. I must not treat you all alike either because I want to be impartial in my treatment and the surest way to show partiality is to treat you all alike." There was a time in my early years in my coaching when I said, "I'm going to treat you all alike." And I did treat them all alike, and I used to say, "I like you all the same." Some of them I could hardly stand. As the years went by I stopped saying that. I no longer was fooling myself. I would say, "I won't like you all the same anymore than you'll like each other the same or you'll like me all the same, because you won't. It isn't natural. I hope I will be strong enough that I won't permit my personal likes and dislikes to enter in to who's going to play and who isn't. But I won't like you all the same and I won't treat you all the same."

I'd like to be able to say that I had the philosophy of Amos Alonzo Stagg, who had the most beautiful philosophy of any person that I knew in that type of position. He was a football coach for many years. He said he never had a player whom he didn't love. He had many that he didn't like, many he didn't respect, but he loved them all the same. Well, that's what we should do. We should love all those that are under our supervision as well as those that aren't under our supervision. And I'm glad that Alonzo Stagg was strong enough to do that. Others aren't quite that strong. I used to say, on occasion, that, "You know there are some of you that may start every game for me and play most of the game until the game is won or lost. But if I had an eligible daughter at home, I wouldn't let you near the place. There may be others among you that may sit on the bench most of the time and not get to play very much. But you could come calling any time. Don't expect me to like you all the same. So there are many things that I must do that are necessary if we are going to obtain and maintain the type of physical condition that I desire. But you have a responsibility, too, young man. Your responsibility begins when practice ends and until you come back to the next practice because you can tear down more between practices than we can build up during practice. You can tear down by lack of moderation, by dissipation, by your moral conduct, so you have a responsibility, too. And if each of us live up to our responsibilities we are going to be in as tremendous physical condition as possible as the type that we want. So let's try to live up to it."

At the center, if not the heart, of the structure is "skill: "the knowledge of and ability to, not only properly, but quickly execute the fundamentals." Skill means being able to execute all of your job, not just part of it. As much as I value experience, and I value it greatly, I'd rather have a lot of skill and little experience than a lot of experience and little skill. You must have that in any profession. I had some basketball players at UCLA who were great shooters, but they couldn't get any shots. Then I had some players who could get the shots, but they couldn't shoot. You have to be able to do so quickly. A surgeon must have it. He must not only be able to perform delicate surgery, but he must be able to do it quickly, because he may lose the patient if he can't. An attorney must not only have the skills, he must be able to react quickly in certain situations that come up in the courtroom or he may lose the case. It is true in almost every profession that you must not only be able to know what you are doing, you must be able to do it quickly. Moreover, in addition to quickness, we must use our skill at the proper time. Finally, we must be thorough, covering every little detail, if we are to have true mastery of our endeavor. Little things do count. It is important to be prepared for any situation. We must have the skills in whatever we do.

The third block in the center of the structure is "team spirit," which is simply a genuine consideration for others, an eagerness—not just a willingness, which doesn't mean you want to—to sacrifice personal interests or glory for the welfare of all. Every family and every business requiring two or more individuals is a team. Selfishness, envy, egotism and criticism of each other can crush team spirit and ruin the potential of any mutual endeavor. If the heads of state and people in important positions of leadership throughout this troubled world of ours today truly had more consideration for others, the problems in this troubled world of ours would not be nearly as serious. They could be worked out.

What a sad commentary it is that so many wars in civilization have been fought, and lives lost, because of religious reasons or racial reasons. We must do something every day to alleviate prejudices. Criticism is like jealousy or envy, it doesn't hurt the ones of whom you are feeling envious or jealous, rather it hurts you and can become cancerous within you. Coming back from a trip on a plane during the war in Viet Nam, I came across this, written by an infantryman in World War I, who saw the horrors of war and during a lull in one terrible battle wrote *The Two Sides of War.*

All wars are planned by older men in council rooms apart
They call for greater armament and map the battle chart
But out upon the shattered fields where golden hopes are gray
How very young the faces are where all the dead men lay
Portly and solemn in their pride, the elders cast their vote
While this or that or something else that sounds the warlike note
But where their sightless eyes stare out and gone are all their joys
I've noticed that nearly all the dead were hardly more than boys.

It was said that the average age in a battalion was eighteen. Considerably older people were sending them to their death. Perhaps it was necessary, I don't know. I just wish there was more consideration of others among those in the upper echelon who have to make decisions affecting others. We must have consideration for others if we are going to develop our own capabilities. Without team spirit, there can be no team. Respect and dignity for all is mandatory.

Above those three blocks I have two blocks: "poise" and "confidence," which you cannot have without the other elements. Poise is much like self-control, which is why many people over the years have asked why I keep poise in the Pyramid, and it's a good point. I don't consider poise to be quite the same as self-control. I have my own definition for poise: "Just being yourself." You're not acting, pretending. You're not trying to be something you're not. You are yourself. Therefore, you're going to be able to function closer to your own particular abilities.

Next, you must have "confidence." Not over-confidence, and not whistling in the dark for confidence either. We want solid, valid confidence, respect without fear, but not cockiness. You must believe in yourself if you expect others to believe in you. Confidence and poise both come from being prepared and are vital requisites for being a good competitor. Failing to prepare is preparing to fail. Those who lack confidence in themselves are certain to be lacking in poise. Can we have poise and confidence that is real and valid? Yes. Easy? Not at all. It's very, very difficult. How can we acquire it? By being prepared and keeping all things in their proper perspective. By being industrious, enthusiastic, friendly, cooperative, and loyal. By maintaining our self-control. By being alert and alive and observing and not getting in our own narrow tunnel-vision. By having initiative, and not being afraid to fail, because we know that we are not perfect, and that we are going to fail on occasion. By being intent, and persistent on reaching the realistic goals that we set for ourselves. By being conditioned—spiritually, morally, mentally, emotionally, physically. By being skilled. By knowing what we are doing, being able to do it, and doing it quickly. And by having consideration for others. Then you will have poise and confidence, and it will be real. You will not be whistling in the dark at all, and it will make you competitive.

The next block, and the last block in the structure, just above "poise" and "confidence" is "competitive greatness." What a wonderful thing competitive greatness is—enjoying it when things are difficult. What fun there is to be derived from being involved in a difficult situation. There is truly no fun, no joy, no pleasure in doing something that anybody else can do. The great competitor loves and looks forward to a serious challenge, being implicated in something that is difficult. "When the going gets tough, the tough get going." You don't have to outscore anybody, you know that you love being in a difficult situation and were enabled to execute at your own particular level of competence. Grantland Rice wrote *The Great Competitor*, which captures this goal:

> *Beyond the winning and the goal, beyond the glory and the fame,*
> *He feels the flame within his soul, born of the spirit of the game,*
> *And where the barriers may wait, built up by the opposing Gods,*
> *He finds a thrill in bucking fate and riding down the endless odds,*
> *Where others wither in the fire or fall below some raw mishap,*
> *Where others lag behind or tire and break beneath the handicap;*
> *He finds a new and deeper thrill to take him on the uphill spin,*
> *Because the test is greater still, and something he can revel in.*

Running up and down the perimeter of the Pyramid is the mortar holding the blocks together. On one side is "ambition," "adaptability," "resourcefulness," fight," and "faith."

"Ambition" must be carefully and properly focused and have noble and worthy purposes. Never let ambition cause you to sacrifice your integrity or diminish your efforts on any other aspect of the Pyramid. At the same time, you'll never reach a serious goal unless you have the intention to do so.

Be "adaptable" to any situation. Change is constant and inevitable. Know about it, grow with and learn from it and by it.

"Resourcefulness" is simple to understand. Use your wits with proper judgment. The human mind is the most wonderful weapon for overcoming adversity. Use it to invent the solutions to whatever problems you face, whatever goals you seek to achieve. It's fun to create, to be clever, especially for worthwhile purposes.

By "fight," I mean determined effort. In basketball lingo, this means "hustle." I like to say, "Be quick, but never hurry." Be ready to move whenever opportunity arises. Stand your ground, grit your teeth, and dig in—with exuberance and gusto—when required.

Have "faith" that things will turn out the way they should. We must do the things we can to make that a reality. Sometimes we expect too much. For me that requires prayer. What's the point in attempting a goal if we don't think it can and will happen? Believe in yourself and all that is good in the universe.

On the other side of the Pyramid, as mortar, are these blocks: "Sincerity," "honesty," "reliability," "integrity" and "patience."

"Sincerity" makes and keeps friends. It is the glue of friendship and team spirit.

"Honesty" must occur at all times in all ways of thought and action. By being dishonest we deceive others as well as ourselves. By doing so we destroy our credibility and reputation and we lose our self-respect. We feel good about ourselves when we are honest. It's not only the best policy, it's the best therapy for our psyches.

If we are not honest or sincere, we cannot be counted upon as being "reliable," the next element on the Pyramid. Others depend on us so we must earn and create their respect. The first requirement for a job is showing up.

"Integrity" is purity of intention. Integrity speaks for itself. Sincerity, honesty, and reliability are components that encourage and lead to integrity. In Judaism, a man with this quality is referred to as a "mensch," one of noble character. We must strive to act with rectitude, character, and dignity. We must never sacrifice our morals or values.

Success is not easy to obtain, which is why "faith" and "patience" meet at the apex of the Pyramid. You must have patience and realize that worthwhile things take time, and should. Things that come easy, as a general rule, are not meaningful.

Finally, there is but one person who can measure your achievement of success: you. Forget what others think, ignore all accolades, you alone know the truth about your capabilities and performance. Winning is irrelevant, doing your best is what matters. Be more concerned with your character than your reputation because your character is what you truly are, while your reputation is merely what others think you are.

Purdue's "Indiana Rubber Man"

Chapter Four

Interview with John Wooden about The Pyramid of Success

*The following interview was conducted with John Wooden in his living
room on December 15, 1983. Fascinated by the Pyramid of Success,
I wanted to know more, such as how and why it came to be written. I was
fortunate to obtain an invitation to visit with him, which is when I peppered
him with the following questions, with the assistance of my friends,
Matthew A. M. Powell, and Jamie Cohen.*

What are some of the companies that have invited you to give your motivational lecture on the Pyramid of Success?

IBM is the one which I have done the most over a period of years. I have
spoken to them sixty or sixty-one times. Others include various insurance companies, computer companies, TRW, a lot of banks.

Why do they want you to give the speech?

Motivational purposes. Sometimes it might be an award ceremony for
salesmen. At these meetings they usually have a speaker. Why they like speakers I really don't know. I sometimes say that the speaker who received the greatest reception in history was a Chinese philosopher named Wang Chu. He was
at a big dinner, and after the presentations, he was called up to be the principal
speaker of the evening. He got up and said, "Why bother with a little wind
when you have just had a hurricane?" and he sat down tremendously well
accepted. I speak at a lot of sales meetings.

Have you ever been a salesman?

I have been all my life. What is a teacher if you don't sell your supervision,
whether it be an English class or on the athletic field?

You sell discipline, ideas.

There is more to it than just material.

**Why did you start giving the lecture? Was it because of the money or
because you were interested in expressing yourself?**

It originated primarily for myself, to help me be a better teacher. I didn't
like the idea of just basing everything on an A in class or a B or outscoring
someone in an athletic contest. I think there is a lot more to athletics. There is

a lot more to the subject matter that just receiving a mark. I didn't like the emphasis that seemed to be placed on just one area. Of course it's all right to want to earn an A, it's all right to want to outscore somebody, but I don't like the sense of failure when you fail to do that. Other people are just better than you are sometimes, and there is nothing wrong with that. I developed the Pyramid for my own education and to help me be a better teacher. To get ideas across to youngsters so that they could get satisfaction and pride and an inner feeling that they had done their best regardless of what somebody else might think—because nobody else knows. You are the only one that really knows.

You started working on this when you were teaching high school. Did you talk to your students about it after you had designed it?

I didn't complete it until 1948. I started it in 1934 and in the interim period, until I went into the service, I talked with the students about it. I developed the definition in 1934. I would give them the definition, and tell them, "This is what I want you to try to do." I had some of the different blocks. For example, in 1934, the two cornerstones—industriousness and enthusiasm—were some of the first things I talked to any class about. To basketball groups that would turn out, I would say, "You better be a hard worker and you better enjoy what you are doing. If you don't, you are going to fail." I don't care what somebody else thinks. It's like a reputation or character.

What was happening between 1934 and 1948; how many evolutions did the Pyramid go through?

Many. Many different blocks dropped out or changed positions within the structure. "Success" was at the top at the very beginning, and the cornerstones: "industriousness" and "enthusiasm." They never changed.

Then all the other elements gradually worked in. Do they all work together?

Oh yes, I think it's very important that the elements work in combination. And you must have certain things for the foundation and the cornerstones. The cornerstones must be the strongest of all: hard work and enthusiasm.

Is there any priority between the elements that line the perimeter of the Pyramid?

Yes, they're just like mortar in the sense they are holding the other elements into position. I could change the positions of them, but that's their purpose.

Do you regard "faith" as a higher priority than any other elements?

You must have faith. You won't work towards the apex if you don't have faith that things are going to happen. And you must have patience or you'll give up. Both elements could be placed lower on the Pyramid, but both are integral components. You could change the elements of the Pyramid around in various ways, and I suspect that none of us, putting in our ideas, would come up with exactly the same, but I like to have "success" resting on "faith" and "patience." There is a logic to the levels. Take "poise" and "confidence." You can't have poise and confidence without being in condition, having the requisite skills, being considerate of others, and blessed with team spirit. So "poise" and "confidence" rest on these elements. In turn, elements such as "skill" cannot exist without "industriousness" and "enthusiasm."

Is competitive greatness the proof of all the other elements?

I don't know if I would use the word "proof." It's a type of forging. There is no such thing as a great competitor, in my opinion, who doesn't have the other characteristics.

There is a negative side to being to competitive, where it is too important to win rather than play the game.

Don't mention winning. Being competitive doesn't mean winning, not at all.

But there is a negative side that comes out in people.

Being competitive is not winning. Being competitive is being able to do your best. You may be competing against a team trying to beat you, but you are going to play your very best against them even though in a sense, by the score, you lose.

So in a sense you are competing against yourself.

Absolutely. You are trying to make the most of what you have. Sometimes we get so concerned with the things we don't have, the things over which we have no control, that the things over which we do have control become adversely affected. I know I was guilty of that for a long time. I think most people compare. Don't compare. I don't want my wife to compare what other women have. My basketball players at UCLA, what did they compare? What the football team had that they didn't. I want to get away from material comparisons. I want you to make the best with what you have. I think I was consistent in my teaching about that. As a coach I have scouted opposing teams probably less than any coach in any major college or university. Probably less than most anyone. I did not want my players thinking and worrying about the other fellow. Why should I tell a player I have defending against the opposing team that an opposing player goes to his right? Then my player will be watching for him to go to his right. I don't want that. I teach fundamentals. If you are playing a person on the right side of the floor, you watch his right leg; if he's on the left side, you watch his left leg. That's what you teach, not having a player change because an opponent plays a certain way. I want good, solid fundamentals, offensively and defensively, because they are going to carry. Don't worry about the other fellow.

Do you set up a rating system where everybody is judged by the same criteria? Each person is different?
Each person is different. We are also alike in many respects. I saw my thinking change as the years went by. I used to tell my players, when I first started coaching, "I like you all the same and I'm going to treat you all the same." I never treated them all the same or liked them all the same. They never liked each other all the same. And yet I made it a point of telling them, "I like you all the same." Some of them I couldn't stand. I never would treat them all the same. They didn't all deserve the same treatment. They didn't all earn the right to be treated the same. There are some who say, and I hear it constantly, that you have to be impartial. The surest way to show partiality is to treat everybody alike. You're definitely showing partiality when you treat everybody alike.

What were your influences when you were designing the Pyramid? Was it just your own logic that created it out of nothing?
No one individual can be credited. I devised it because I was concerned because of parents who had spoken to me about their youngsters who were in my English classes.

Many of the elements comprising the Pyramid can be found in a wide range of philosophies and religions. Were you reading a lot on such subjects when you devised the Pyramid?
I have read a lot of philosophy, but I can't say that any one specific idea or concept influenced me. I have always read a lot, being an English teacher.

There are religious undertones in the Pyramid, but it seems non-secular.
Correct.

You do have "prayer" listed.
There is prayer in all religions. Elie Wiesel wrote a book wherein he discussed all religions and that the basic theme to all religions is the Golden Rule. Jamaal Wilkes, before he embraced the Islamic branch of religion, brought me a book to read. After I read the book, he asked me what I thought and I said, "The essential theme of the book is peace, goodwill toward your fellow man, and living by the Golden Rule. If that's what it is and what it means to you, and if you can live with that, that's great." I believe very much in Christ.

Is what you're saying that each person has to be inwardly reflective towards their spiritual growth and their relationships with other people?

I gave a talk on a several-point creed that my father gave me when I graduated from grade school. I always keep it with me. As a matter of fact, I have it in my pocket now. The first point is "Be true to yourself." I believe in that. Sometimes I stress other things in my talk. For instance, "Help others. Make friendship a fine art. Make each day your masterpiece. Drink deeply from good books, especially the Bible. Build a shelter against the rainy day," and "Pray for guidance and be thankful for your blessings everyday." Another is, "Four things a man must learn to do if he would make his life more true: to think without confusion clearly, to love his fellow man sincerely, to act from honest motives purely, to trust in God and heaven securely."

Is there much difference in educating athletes as opposed to business people?

Yes. Athletes are in the public eye, whereas businessmen are not. The businessman is, for the most part, interested in the accumulation of material possessions, while the amateur athlete is not, although he may be interested in that in the long-range. The athlete is interested in image, public acceptance, and publicity.

Are you received the same by people, irrespective of their age?

I find that the older people can understand a little more. Almost every college player that I had, some years after he graduated, came and talked to me about the Pyramid. They have said that they wished they could have understood it better and wished that they could have accepted it better. They see the importance of the ideas that come to them after they have graduated.

The Pyramid seems to say that there is a symbiosis involved in which one must be mentally, morally, physically, and spiritually in tune at all times. You can't really be a success if you have achieved some of the goals, and these goals must always be sought on a short-term as well as a long-term basis.

I think any teacher must be concerned with the long-range goals of teaching. Too much emphasis is placed on the development of character through athletics. Athletics can develop character. So can any number of other things. Athletics can also be detrimental.

You mean someone might become very successful and get overconfident?

Athletes can get false impressions of themselves and false impressions of what athletics are. I think it has hurt as many star athletes as it has helped. It does more good for those who never attain any degree of recognition.

Chapter Five

Essays, Woodenisms, Maxims and Poems

Coach Wooden gave motivational lectures for Medalist Industries, which sold sporting equipment and operated a lecture bureau during the 1970s and 1980s, and occasionally contributed articles for their newsletter, Medalist Sports News, *including the following three.*

NEED ONE KNOW WHY

It was a delightful morning, cool and clear, for my daily five-mile walk around the UCLA track. After this sixty-five minute exercise, I relaxed under a cool shower, and then enjoyed a leisurely breakfast before leaving for the Los Angeles International Airport to catch a plane for a trip across this great, wide, beautiful, and wonderful country of ours.

Even though I have flown hundreds of thousands of miles, I never cease to marvel at this jet age in which we now live. How is it possible to place several hundred miles an hour under complete control toward another destination? I simply cannot comprehend how such a thing is possible. As I thought about this, and gazed out the window at the beauty of the sea, the mountains, and the landscape below, I found myself caught up in a somewhat reflective and wondering mood about many things.

I wondered why—

- are there so many who want to build up the weak by tearing down the strong?

- is it that many non-attainers are very quick to explain and belittle the attainers?

- are there so many who cannot seem to realize that winners are usually the ones who merely execute better, at least on that particular occasion?

- is it so difficult to realize that you cannot antagonize and influence at the same time?

- is it that we are so slow to understand that failing to prepare is preparing to fail?

- can't we realize that it only weakens those we want to help when we do things for them that they should do for themselves?

- is it so much easier to complain about the thing we do not have, than to make the most of and appreciate the thing we do have?

- is it that so often we permit emotion rather than reason to control our decisions?

- is it so difficult to realize, at times, that nothing we can do will change the past, and the only way to affect the future is by what we do now?

- is it that it is so much easier to give others blame than it is to give them credit?

- is it that many who are quick to make suggestions find it difficult to make decisions?

- don't we realize that others are certain to listen to us if we first listen to them?

- aren't we more interested in finding the best way rather than having our own way?

- is it so difficult to develop the feeling that those under our supervision are working with us and not for us?

- is it much easier to be a critic than a model?

- is it so hard to disagree without being disagreeable?

- can't we understand that all progress comes through change even though all change may not be progress?

- is it that we often forget that big things are accomplished only by the perfection of minor details?

- do we dread adversity so much, when facing it is the only way to become stronger?

- can't we motivate ourselves when we know that results come through motivation?

- is it that some seem ashamed to let others know that they pray or read the Bible?

- is it difficult to give thanks, express thanks, or merely say, "Thank you?"

- can't we have patience and expect good things to take time?

- is it so easy to be quick to judge when possessed of only a few facts?

- is it so easy to see the faults of others and so difficult to see our own?

THE JOHN WOODEN PYRAMID OF SUCCESS

I certainly do not have the answer for these questions, but I feel that the more I am aware of the fact that they do exist, the better chance I will have to face up to and possibly make them less of a problem.

Since I occasionally dabble in various verse forms to express some thoughts, I managed to come up with the following before we safely arrived at our destination.

Need One Know Why

Man in Space
A sea of clouds,
Huge jet engines,
Who can understand?

A baby's cry,
A hungry man,
A woman's tear,
Who can understand
Or tell me why?

The East at dawn,
The West at dusk,
The stars at night,
The mountains tall,
The valleys green,
Need one know why?

Must we know why we are here on earth,
Does wealth or station prove one's worth,
Is appearance made in three score plus,
A way to measure one of us?

I truly want to find the way.
And know for this that I must pray,
And it won't matter what I say,
For He to whom I'll speak will know,
What is true and what is show;
To Him all things are very clear,
He knows exactly what we are,
And His judgment will be fair,
When we are called together There.

Need one know why?

JUST THINKING

It has been said that you will be hurt occasionally if you trust too much, but you will live in torment if you do not trust enough.

This statement could apply to both the youth and the adults in the uneasy society in our country today. Because of modern technology and the advances in all areas, our youth are more inquisitive than ever and this seems to scare their elders because they do not have the answers to the problems that our young people want solved—right now.

Youth is a time of impatience and they can't understand why the problems of society haven't been solved. They haven't lived long enough as yet to fully understand human nature and do not have the patience that eventually brings about more faith and better understanding. Good and worthwhile things take time and that is exactly as it should be.

On the other hand, older people tend to become set in their ways, fear change, and, quite possibly, become too patient for problems to be solved. They sometimes forget that, although all change isn't necessarily progress, all progress is the result of change.

Perhaps the breach between the youth and the adults of today is similar to the official-coach relationship in athletics. A few years ago I concluded an article in regard to this with the following statement: "In the final analysis, perhaps the main thing we need in all walks of life is more mutual trust and understanding of the problems of the other fellow. If we can acquire that, the coach-official relationship should no longer be a problem."

I am inclined to feel that our society as a whole has become so infatuated with material things that we have gotten away from the values that are everlasting. We are not seeking our happiness and we should remember one of the great quotations from the greatest book of all, "Seek ye first His Kingdom and His righteousness and all these things will be yours as well."

It is wonderful to see our young people so interested and so aware as they are today. They are truly concerned and are searching for answers to our problems. We older people should not judge them all by the few who get out of line through their impatience and immature judgment, but show the patience and understanding that should be the mark of maturity. As has been said, our young people need models more than critics. It has generally been proved that concrete example is usually a better teaching aid than word of mouth or written criticism, although there should be a place for all.

With all our problems, this should be a time of optimism, not pessimism. The very advances in technology and other areas that have contributed to many of our problems should eventually solve them. What the mind of man can create, the mind and heart if man should be able to control and, if advances in technology can be used for evil, surely they can be directed toward good.

I cannot presume to advise others, but I am confident that we all need help. Most of this we can get from talking to God through prayer and listening to Him by reading the Bible. We can get further help from others, if we will only be receptive. Although I fall far short of being what I should be, I am certain that the creed that my father gave me when I graduated from a small country grade school in southern Indiana has helped me to be a better person. *[See page 12 for a complete listing of the creed.]* It would be nice if I could feel that I live up to this creed, but imagine that I am more like the one who said, "I am not going to be, but am thankful that I am not what I used to be."

ON MOTIVATION

In my opinion, there is but little difference in the technical knowledge about the game of basketball among most experienced coaches, but there may be a vast difference in their ability to teach and to motivate. Knowledge alone is not enough to get desirable results.

This article will discuss an idea in regard to motivation.

Since young people of today are far more aware, inclined to be more openly critical, and more genuinely inquisitive than they used to be, leaders must work with them somewhat differently.

There was a time when the vast majority would follow blindly, even "into the shadow of death," but such is not the case now. Therefore we must always be on the alert for better ways to get ideas across and to motivate.

Every individual under our supervision is a distinct and separate person from any other as no two people are alike although they may be very similar in some or many respects. Therefore we should realize that we can not expect maximum results from each individual if we treat them all alike. Each one must be given the treatment that he earns and deserves.

Some players need and respond only to the "pat on the back" and public criticism will harm rather than help them, some need to be urged in a more stern or demanding way, while others need a concrete challenge in a competitive situation.

An important thing to remember is that criticism is not to punish, but to correct something that is preventing better results. Furthermore, test after test has proved rather conclusively that the "pat on the back" method is far more productive as a general rule than the "kick in the pants" or any method that causes loss of face before your peers.

There was a time when I gave all my players a rather extensive notebook.

Later, I decided that too many of them really did not study it, so I decided to pass out a little information at a time. I found the latter method to be more productive, but, of course, it was necessary to use good judgment not only in the material presented, but also in the timing as to when it when it was given to them.

Hand-outs pertaining to the following topics were passed out at what I considered to be appropriate times: Goals, New Rules, Training Suggestions, Practice Responsibilities, Player Essentials, Attitude and Conduct, Normal Expectations, Academic Responsibilities, Criticism, Game Competition, Individual Offensive Moves, Fundamental Hints (Shooting, Passing, Receiving, Rebounding, Dribbling, Stops and Turns, Pivoting, Individual Defense, Team Defense, Team Offense, When You Do Not Have The Ball, etc.).

Since I have been a collector of maxims, precepts, mottos, principles and the like, I made it a practice to keep some posted on our player bulletin board at all times. I normally would not keep any one up too long and would try to find several that would be suitable for given situations such as the following:

FOR TEAMWORK

1. Happiness begins where selfishness ends.

2. Politeness is a small price to pay for the goodwill and affection of others.

3. The best way to improve the team is to improve ourselves.

4. It is amazing how much can be accomplished.

5. Forget favors given, remember those received.

6. The main ingredient of stardom is the rest of the team.

7. True happiness, freedom, and peace cannot be attained without giving them to someone else.

FOR INDIVIDUAL IMPROVEMENT

1. When you are through learning, you are through.

2. I will get ready and then perhaps my chance will come.

3. Ability may get you to the top, but it takes character to keep you there.

4. Discipline yourself and others won't have to.

5. Do not mistake activity for achievement.

6. If you do not have time to do it right, when will you have time to do it over?

7. You may make mistakes, but you are not a failure until you start blaming someone else.

THE JOHN WOODEN PYRAMID OF SUCCESS

8. If you are afraid of criticism, you will die doing nothing.

9. The smallest good deed is better than the greatest intention.

10. The man who is not afraid of failure seldom has to face it.

11. Don't let yesterday take up too much of today.

12. Time spent getting even would be better spent getting ahead.

GENERAL

1. There is nothing in this world stronger than gentleness.

2. You can do more good by being good than in any other way.

3. When success turns your head, you face failure.

4. Love is the medicine that can cure all the ills of the world.

5. There is no pillow as soft as a clear conscience.

6. Revenge is the weak pleasure of a little and narrow mind.

7. A good memory is one that can remember the day's blessings and forget the day's troubles.

8. The true athlete should have character, not be a character.

9. Your reputation is what others think you are, your character is what you really are.

10. The future may be when you wish you had done what you are not doing now.

11. Failure to prepare is preparing to fail.

13. The greatest conquest of man is the conquering of himself.

14. Talent is God given, be humble; fame is man given, be thankful; conceit is self-given, be careful.

15. More often than we ever suspect, the lives of others we affect.

Once again, I want to reiterate, since no two players are exactly alike, some may not be motivated at all in this manner and very few to the same degree. However, it may help some and certainly should not hurt any. It might be compared to going to a coaching clinic or even going to church. You may not be able to put your finger exactly on where you were helped, but I am confident you would never be hurt by attending and always will be helped to some degree.

WOODEN'S MAXIMS AND WOODENISMS

The term, "Woodenism," was coined by Wooden's grandson-in-law, Craig Impelman, who compiled about thirty of these maxims, aphorisms, and truisms for his own edification. We've expanded the term to include statements, thoughts and reflections which evidence wisdom. They have been culled from interviews with, articles about, and writings and lectures by, Coach.

Some Thoughts to Consider

1. An unbeatable five consists of industriousness, enthusiasm, condition (mental, moral, and physical), sound fundamentals, and proper team spirit.

2. Never expect miracles. It is steady progress that we want and it will come with industry and patience.

3. Mental, moral, and physical individual and team balance are essential.

4. There is a wonderful mystical law of nature that the three things we crave most in life—happiness, freedom and peace of mind—are always attained by giving them to someone else.

Ten Helpful Hints

1. Be quick without hurrying.

2. Show me what you can do, don't tell me.

3. It is the little details that make things work.

4. The harder you work, the more luck you will have.

5. Respect every opponent, but fear none.

6. Hustle makes up for many a mistake.

7. Valid self-analysis means improvement.

8. Be more interested in character than in reputation.

9. There is no substitute for hard work and careful planning.

10. Is it hard for you to keep quiet when you don't have anything to say?

Many Things

1. Keep courtesy and consideration of others foremost in your mind at home and away.

2. Pray for guidance and strength to do your best and then have faith.

3. Although it may not be possible to determine what happens to you, you should control how you react and respond.

4. Try to have fun without being funny.

5. Never try for a laugh at another's expense. Try to laugh with others, never at them.

6. Our school will be judged by our appearance and our conduct. May we command the respect of all in both.

7. Good manners should control our actions at all times.

It's teams that win or lose games, it's not individuals or coaches.

You meet the same people on the way up as you meet on the way down.

The Golden Rule may well be the basic concept of every religion.

Life is a united effort of many.

The harvest of old age is the recollection and abundance of blessings previously secured.

Life is not all good, nor is it all bad. What mortal man can separate the many gray areas into good and bad?

Respect is something that has to come from how you treat the players, the game itself, and your preparation. It cannot be demanded from the players.

Probably the two most important elements in coaching are the knowledge that's necessary and the rapport, the company you have with those that you're trying to teach. They must be receptive and it is up to you to make them receptive. It is up to you to have the proper teaching techniques to be able to get it across.

If you're a great teacher and you don't have any knowledge, what are you going to teach?

There are no secrets. It is studying and learning all you can from all those with whom you come in contact, and that is not only other coaches, but all others.

The ideal level of motivation is nothing other than consistent preparation and execution that starts the first day of practice and is maintained at a constant level throughout the basketball season.

Quickness, not size, is the most important aspect of athletics.

I'd rather have talent than experience.

It's what you do during the week. There's very little you can do during the game. We coaches sometimes get carried away with strategies.

Those who have never suffered adversity, never experience the true meaning of success.

Although it would be great if we never had to face adversity, the fact is that it only makes us stronger—be it physically, mentally, morally or spiritually.

It takes a lot of little things to make one big thing.

You get ideas across better through listening and the pat-on-the-back method than you do with a kick on the pants.

Sometimes winning hides some problems but sometimes it creates some of its own. Whenever you bring together a group of intelligent, highly motivated individuals, you are going to have conflicts. My job as a coach is to convince the players that these conflicts cannot get in the way of what the team has to do.

I don't know whether winning is always good. It breeds envy and distrust in others and overconfidence and a lack of appreciation very often in those who enjoy it.

Serenity is ever with whose whom are considerate of and courteous to others.

Too much has been said about athletics building character. I think they can build character and I also think they can tear it down. I think athletics not properly supervised, not properly administered certainly can be detrimental to character, just as properly done it can serve as a character builder in many areas. I don't mean to infer that I consider it to be the only method of character building; I'm saying that it is one and can be useful in that area.

I think that we live in a world of hero worship to some degree and that we all have idols. It is the people in the public eye that become the idols, the objects of hero worship. They can be movie people, entertainers, musicians, politicians, or they can be athletes. If intercollegiate athletics are properly administered and conducted, they can be very helpful to the growing youth who are going to be running this country in the times to come.

I feel that any coach that has no concern over the moral conduct of his players, or any person that has no concern over the moral conduct of those under their supervision, shouldn't be in a position of leadership. Now that doesn't mean that you can change them. But you have to be concerned about it and I think you should try to set a proper example, certainly for youngsters of school age, and I'm speaking of college age also. It becomes less important as they become older because many habits have been set and are not going to be changed. You still have, in my opinion, a responsibility to set an example and their age should not change your concern.

Don't get carried away because you're a basketball player. That's the short period of your life and even if you play professional basketball, when that's over the vast majority of your life, the years of your life are still going to be ahead of you.

O, Lord, if I seem to lose my faith in Thee, do not Thou lose Thy faith in me.

There is no progress without change.

On the ingredients of a good leader:
One that doesn't try to be a leader. One that is not lost in himself, not consumed with himself, that's not a dictator. One that is deeply and vitally concerned with those under his leadership. One that is interested in finding about the best way to accomplish things rather than having his own way. One that makes every effort to make those under his supervision know that they are working with him to accomplish in the end rather than working for him. I think if you have someone working for you they'll just put in hours and punch the clock and that's it.

On the ingredients of a great coach:
One that's truly interested and concerned about those under his supervision, and more so than just basketball because basketball then will be a by-product of all the others. The understanding coach is a teacher that causes all the squad to accept the roles that he considers to be the most important for the welfare of all. That is hard, because they all want scoring roles, if that's at all possible.

On what makes a good official:
Having a good relationship with the coaches. I'm assuming that you know the rules or you wouldn't be officiating. You recognize what the coach's job is and he recognizes what your job is, and you have no animosity toward him in any way personally or otherwise. The officials that I might not like as well as others are those who were very officious in their bearing.

I have become more convinced than ever that our main problems are neither the rules nor the interpretation of the rules. Most of the serious problems seem to be the result of the administration of the rules by the officials and the lack of proper teaching of the rules by coaches. Too many of us do not teach our players to abide by the rules but look for ways to beat or get around the rules. In other words, we teach evasion of the rules and look for the technicalities that permit us to beat a rule rather than attempting to teach and live up to the spirit of the rule.

The four laws of learning:

The first is demonstration of what you want. The second is the criticism of the demonstration. The third is the imitation of the correct model. The fourth is repetition. Over and over and over until it becomes habit, where you don't think about it.

As to adversity:

Take matters in school. We don't start with calculus, but start with arithmetic and work up through algebra and geometry. We get stronger morally and spiritually through adversity. It's only going to make us stronger. We shouldn't worry about it.

The worst thing about new books is they keep us from reading the old ones.

Ability is a poor man's wealth

Adversity is the state in which man most easily becomes acquainted with himself, being especially free of admirers then.

You want the best player that you can get and then try to mold him into the type of player that will work into your particular system. I found out that seldom, on a squad that I had, the players that I considered to be the five best would make the best team. They wouldn't have what some people call chemistry. The best five players very, very seldom make the best team.

You cannot live a perfect day without doing something for someone who will never be able to repay you.

Things turn out best for those who make the best of the way things turn out.

It is what you learn after you know it all that counts.

Ability may get you to the top, but it takes character to keep you there.

Young people need models, not critics.

The great secret of life is to cultivate the ability to appreciate the things you have, not compare them.

A player who has given his best has given everything, but one who has given less than his best, regardless of how good it looks on the scoreboard has given almost nothing.

THE JOHN WOODEN PYRAMID OF SUCCESS

A player should not just be willing to sacrifice his own interest for the good of the team, he should be eager to.

When you are a coach, your greatest ally is the bench.

Wouldn't it be a wonderful world if everyone magnified their blessings as much as their sorrows?

To me, there's no such thing as an overachiever. I think we're all under-achievers to different degrees.

Honors are very fleeting, just as fame is; I cherish friendship more.

It is not what you do, but how well you execute it if it is based on sound valid principles.

Have courage and do not worry. If you do your best, never lose your temper, and never be outfought or outhustled, you have nothing to worry about. Without faith and courage you are lost.

In the final analysis, perhaps the most important thing we need in all walks of life is more mutual trust, faith, and understanding of the problems of others.

If I were ever prosecuted for my religion, I truly hope there would be enough evidence to convict me.

No matter how fine a person is at anything, he can always improve. No one ever reaches maximum potential.

You can't put dignity and personality into a person who doesn't have any.

Don't let making a living prevent you from making a life.

"I do it because he does it," is not a good reason.

If you are going nowhere, you'll get there.

Passion is momentary; love is enduring.

What is right is more important than who is right.

Never make excuses. Your friends won't need them and your foes won't believe them.

I don't like to be the guy in church who coughs loudly just before putting money into the offering plate.

There is no clock-watching when the leader has respect.

Pride is a better motivator than fear.

Fairness is giving all people the treatment they earn and deserve. It doesn't mean treating everyone alike.

Mistakes occur when your thinking is tainted by excessive emotion.

True happiness comes from the things that cannot be taken away from you. All material things can be taken away.

Never say never.

A winner never quits, a quitter never wins.

There is no progress without change, though change is not necessarily progress.

Be a gentleman at all times.

Never criticize, nag, or razz a teammate.

Be a team player always.

Never be selfish, jealous, envious, or egotistical.

Earn the right to be proud and confident.

Never expect favors, alibi or make excuses.

Never lose faith or patience.

It's not important who starts the game, but who finishes it.

Sports do not build character, they reveal it.

A man makes mistakes, but he isn't a failure until he starts blaming someone else.

It's impossible to do something for someone else without doing something for yourself at the same time.

A gentleman is one who considers the rights of others before his own feelings, and the feelings of others before his own right.

Courtesy and politeness are a small price to pay for the good will and affection of others.

Acquire peace of mind by becoming the best that you are capable of being.

It is amazing how much can be accomplished if no one cares who gets the credit.

THE JOHN WOODEN PYRAMID OF SUCCESS

The athlete who says that something cannot be done should never interrupt the one who is doing it.

Don't let what you cannot do interfere with what you can do.

Failure is not fatal, but failure to change may be.

A coach is someone who can give correction without causing resentment.

Don't measure yourself by what you have accomplished, but by what you should have accomplished with your ability.

Consideration for others brings many things.

You have success within, it is up to you to bring it out.

Bad times can make you bitter or better.

Consider the rights of others before your own feelings, and the feeling of others before your own rights.

There are many things that are essential to arriving at true peace of mind, and one of the most important is faith, which cannot be acquired without prayer.

It's the little details that are vital. Little things make big things happen.

If you lose self-control everything will fall. You cannot function physically or mentally or in any other way unless your emotions are under control.

If you keep too busy learning the tricks of the trade, you may never learn the trade.

People are usually as happy as they make up their mind to be.

Things usually turn out the best for people who make the best out of the way things turn out.

A man makes mistakes, but he isn't a failure until he starts blaming someone else.

Never fear failure. It is something to learn from. You have conquered fear when you have initiative.

Failure rests with those who stay on some success made yesterday.

The way you think will be the way that you will play.

It's not what you think you are, but what you think.

You cannot function physically or mentally unless your emotions are under control. That is why I did not engage in pre-game pep talks to stir emotions to a sudden peak. I preferred to maintain a gradually increasing level of both achievement and emotions, rather than trying to create artificial emotional highs. For every contrived peak you create, there is a subsequent valley. I do not like valleys. Self-control provides emotional stability and fewer valleys.

You use discipline to help, improve, correct, prevent, not to punish, humiliate or retaliate. When you lose control of your emotions, when your self-discipline breaks down, your judgment and common sense suffer. How can you perform at your best when your are using poor judgment?

To do better in the future you have to work on the "right now." Dwelling in the past prevents doing something in the present.

Complaining, whining, making excuses, just keeps you out of the present. If your complaints are constant, serious and genuine about your calling, then leave when practical.

Self-control keeps you in the present.

Quiet confidence gets the best results. Leaders shouldn't do all the talking.

If you lead a team as coach, parent, or businessperson, you must have enthusiasm or you cannot be industrious. With it you stimulate others to increasingly higher levels of achievement.

The goal is to satisfy not everyone else's expectations, but your own.

If you're too busy making a living, you're not going to make much of a life.

I used to tell my players at the beginning of the season that they were probably going to receive criticisms, some deserved, some not, as well as praise, but their strength and character will depend on how well they accept that praise and criticism.

Everything revolves around your faith, your family and your friends.

There is so much good in the worst of us, and so much bad in the best of us, there can hardly be room for any of us to talk about the rest of us.

Love is the most important word in the English language, followed by balance.

Achieving love and balance isn't hard if that's where you put your priorities.

Make friendship an art.

Disagree without being disagreeable.

I've always cautioned my teams. "Respect your opponents, but never fear them. You have nothing to fear of if you have prepared to the best of your ability."

We all want to do well and achieve individual praise. That is fine if you put it to use for the good of the team, be it sports, business, family, or community.

Success is not perfection, which you can never obtain. Nevertheless, it is the goal. Success is giving 100% of your effort, body, mind and soul to the struggle. That you can attain. That is success.

What is so important to recognize is that you are totally in control of your success—not your opponent, not the judge, critic, media, or anyone else. It's up to you. That's all you can ask for, the chance to determine your success by yourself.

You can always get help from one book (the Bible), and friends, but you have to have faith.

Team spirit begins in the home where it must and then extend out to all other areas throughout the world.

Consideration for others is team spirit. You might think as an individual you can't do much alone. That may be true. You are not alone. We are many but are we much? No, not until we together collectively try to be more considerate of together and do things good for the welfare of all.

Most of the things we do in our daily lives, most anybody could do. Whatever we do we should be trying to do the best of our ability. The joy will come from doing the more difficult things.

Kindness in words creates confidence,
Kindness in thinking creates profoundness
Kindness in giving creates love.
  -Lao-Tse

Learn as if you were to live forever.
Live as if you were to die tomorrow.
  -Matahma Gandhi

Count your blessings instead of your disappointments.
  -Abraham Lincoln

There is nothing stronger than gentleness.
-Abraham Lincoln

Toward the end of the Civil War, reparations were being discussed in the White House. Abraham Lincoln was told by one of his advisers who favored punishing the South. "Mr. President. You're supposed to destroy your enemies, not make friends of them!" Lincoln replied, "Am I not destroying an enemy when I make a friend of him."

It's better to trust and be disappointed occasionally than to distrust and be miserable all the time.
-Abraham Lincoln

The worst thing you can do for those you love are the things they could and should do for themselves.
-Abraham Lincoln

The best thing a father can do for his children is to love their mother.
-Abraham Lincoln

Most anyone can handle adversity, but to test a person's character, give them power.
-Abraham Lincoln

It is one of the most beautiful compensations of this life that no man can sincerely help another without helping himself.
-Ralph Waldo Emerson

Those that mind don't matter and those that matter don't mind.
-Perle Mesta

Forgiveness sets you free.
-Mother Teresa

JOHN WOODEN'S FAVORITE POEMS

When we fail to give our best,
We haven't met the test of giving all and saving none,
Of playing through when others quit.
Not letting down.
It's bearing down that wins the cup,
Of dreaming there is a goal ahead,
Of hoping when our dreams are dead.

Of praying when our hopes have fled.
Yet losing, not afraid to fall
If gamely we have given all
For who can ask more of a man
Than giving all within his span?
Giving all it seems to me,
Is not so far from victory.
And so the fates are seldom wrong
No matter how they twist and wind
It's you and I who mark our fates
We open up or close the gates
On the road ahead or the road behind.
  -George Moriarty

Stubbornness we deprecate,
Firmness we condone,
The former is our neighbor's trait,
The latter is our own.
Remember this your lifetime through –
Tomorrow, there will be more to do. . .
And failure waits for all who stay
With some success made yesterday. . .
Tomorrow, you must try once more
And even harder than before.
Success is never final
Failure is never fatal.
It's courage that counts.
  -Winston Churchill

Enjoy the present hour,
  Be mindful of the past;
And neither fear nor wish
  the approaches of the last.
Dare to be Daniel!
Dare to stand alone!
Dare to have a purpose firm!
Dare to make it know.
  -P. P. Bliss

The crowd on each they soon forget the heroes of the past
You know they cheer like mad until you fall
And that's how long you last.
Four things a man must learn to do
If he would make his life more true;
To think without confusion more clearly,
To love his fellow man sincerely,
To act from honest motives purely,
To trust in God and heaven securely.
  -Reverend Henry Van Dyke

WHAT WE GIVE

It's not what we give,
    but what we share,
For the gift without the giver,
    is bare
Who gives on himself
    of his alms feeds three,
Himself, his hungering
    neighbor, and me.
  -James Russell Lowell

When you get what you want in the struggle for wealth
And the world makes you kind for a day,
Then go to a mirror and look at yourself
And see what that guy has to say.

For it isn't your father or mother or wife
Who judgment upon you must pass?
The feller whose verdict counts most in your life
Is the guy staring back from the glass.

He's the feller to please, never mind all the rest
He's with you clear up to the end,
And you've passed your most dangerous difficult test
If the guy in the glass is your friend.

You may be like Jack Horner and "chisel" a plum
And think you're a wonderful guy,

THE JOHN WOODEN PYRAMID OF SUCCESS

But the man in the glass says you're only a bum
If you can't look him straight in the eye.

You can fool the whole world down the pathway of years
And get pats on the back as you pass,
But you final reward will be heartache and tears
If you've cheated the guy in the glass.
   -Author Unknown

A bell isn't a bell until you ring it
A song isn't a song until you sing it
And the love that is within us was not
      put there to stay
Love isn't love until you give it away
   -Author Unknown

THEY ASK ME WHY I TEACH

They ask me why I teach,
And I reply,
Where could I find more splendid company?
There sits a statesman,
Strong, unbiased, wise,
Another later Webster,
Silver-tongued,
And there a doctor
Whose quick, steady hand
Can mend a bone,
Or stem the lifeblood's flow.
A builder sits behind him –
Upward rise
The arches of a church he builds, wherein
That minister will speak the word of God,
And lend a stumbling soul to Christ.

And all about
A lesser gathering
Of farmers, merchants, teachers,
Laborers, men
Who work and vote and build

And play and pray
Into a great tomorrow
And I say,
"I may not see the church,
Or hear the word,
Or eat the food their hands will grow,"
And yet—I may.
And later I may say,
"I knew the lad,
And he was strong,
Or weak, or kind, or proud.
Or bold, or gay.
I knew him once.
But then he was a boy."
They ask me why I teach, and I reply,
"Where could I find more splendid company?"
-Glennice L. Harmon

GOD'S HALL OF FAME

To have your name inscribed up there is
    greater yet by far,
Than all the halls of fame down here and
    every man-made star.
This crowd on earth, they soon forget the
    heroes of the past,
They cheer like mad until you fall and that's
    how long you last.
I tell you, friend, I would not trade my name
    however small,
If written there beyond the stars in that
    celestial hall.
For any famous name on earth or glory that
    they share,
I'd rather be an unknown here and have my
    name up there.

THE ROAD AHEAD
OR THE ROAD BEHIND

Sometimes I think
    the fates must grin
As we denounce them
    and insist
The only reason we
    can't win
Is because the fates
    themselves have missed
Yet there lives on
    the ancient claim
We win or lose
    within ourselves
The shining trophies
    on our shelves
Can never win
    tomorrow's game
You and I know
    deeper down
That there's always a chance
    to win the crown
-George Moriarty

No written word,
    no spoken plea
Can teach our youth what
    they should be
Nor all the books
    on all the shelves
It's what the teachers
    are themselves

I carry a cross in my pocket,
A simple reminder to me of the fact
    that I am a Christian wherever I may be;
This little cross is not magic, nor is it
    a good luck charm,
It isn't meant to protect me from every
    physical harm;
It's not for identification for all the
    world to see,
It's simply an understanding between
    my Savior and me;
When I put my hand in my pocket to bring
    out a coin or a key,
The cross is there to remind me of the
    price He paid for me;
It reminds me, too, to be thankful for any
    blessings day by day, and to strive
    to serve Him better in all that I do and say;
It is also a daily reminder of the peace
    and comfort I share with all who know
    my Master and give themselves to his care;
So I carry a cross in my pocket reminding
    me, no one but me, that Jesus Christ is
    the Lord of my life if only I will let Him be.

I am not what I ought to be,
not what I want to be,
not what I am going to be,
But thankful that I am not what I used to be.

WIND BENEATH MY WINGS

(Adapted by Swen Nater)

"You must be quick,
    but don't you hurry."
We can still hear it
    ringing in our ears,
You were content to make
    us shine, that's your way.
You always walked
    a step behind.
So we were the ones
    with all the glory,
While you were the one
    with all the strength,
Teaching us how to play
    and live, for so long.
Showing us how
    to love and give.
Did you ever know
    you're my hero,
And everything I
    would like to be?
And I can fly higher
    than an eagle,
'Cause you are the wind
    beneath my wings.
It might have appeared
    to go unnoticed,
But I had it all here
    in my heart
You worked much harder
    than the rest,
Just so that we
    could be the best.

Chapter Six

Interviews, Recollections and Comments

HISTORIANS

MARV DUNPHY
Malibu, California

Marv is the men's volleyball coach at Pepperdine University and did his doctoral dissertation on Coach Wooden. In 1994, he was voted into the Volleyball Hall of Fame at Holyoke, Massachusetts.

I'd done my master's at USC (University of Southern California) in leadership, cohesion and competitive team success. I went to Brigham Young University mostly because the coach there was going on sabbatical and he talked me into getting my doctorate. I was getting a degree in organizational behavior, motivation psychology and administration. I was trying to prove that A might be better than B in leadership styles within athletics. I was at the point where I was somewhat bored with the process, and it had become circular. I knew what all the research had said and I was basically jumping through the hoops. I went to my chair and I said, "Give me some other avenues."

He said, "Why are you here, what do you want to learn?"

I said, "I would like to learn how the great coaches coach."

We thought of a few designs, and then he said, "You might consider a historical study on somebody like Rockne or Naismith or Wooden."

I didn't want to do a purely historical study. I wanted to know the coaching process. Not the content, the x's and o's of any sport, but the process. I wanted to know his philosophy on every item, on every aspect of coaching and what he did or didn't do and what his assistants did with him to implement his philosophy. I went to the dissertation abstract to see if anybody had done anything on Coach Wooden and there wasn't anything.

I prepared an introductory paragraph or two and introduced myself to Coach Wooden. I had a page to make sure that he knew who was going to be writing this on him and working with him, and also where I wanted to go. He stopped me right off the bat, I couldn't even get through my introduction. He said, "Marv, I know who you are, we met out at the pool at Pepperdine. Congratulations on your national championship. Frankly, to be honest with you,

Marvin, I'm honored that someone of your caliber would like to do this on me."

I then proceeded to make up about a hundred items in coaching, perhaps a couple of which were related to basketball. I sat and documented all of his philosophies on tape over several days, had that transcribed, then I met with all his former assistants from 1948-75 and sent out questionnaires to some athletes. Then I wrote *John Robert Wooden, The Coaching Process*, my dissertation.

It starts for me a little bit further back. Everybody has a John Wooden story. Coach Wooden, excuse me. I would never call him "John." Throughout the sixties, when I was a youngster, I grew up watching UCLA athletics and basketball. For some reason, even when I was in high school, I was watching the coach and the coaches.

When I first started to coach, I was a little bit Marv Wooden, and I found out early on that didn't work. You have to be yourself, and yet you can borrow from others and learn from others. And I think I did. Now there'll be situations, not every day, but hard issues, and I'll say as my standard, "What would Coach Wooden have done in this situation?" Then I'll say that I've taken the right course.

I found out in my short career that sometimes when I get closer to an individual who I have heard or read about, that individual isn't quite as good as I've heard or as I've read. It was 1,000 percent opposite with Coach Wooden. The closer I got, the more awesome he was. "Awesome" is overused I realize, but in his case it's not. When we sat down, I had roughly one hundred items that I wanted him to comment on, and five tapes. By the end of our first day, roughly 9 a.m. to about 3 p.m., we hadn't finished. He hadn't finished answering the second question. I had ninety-eight plus more to go! And I was a full time student, and I just said, "How much time am I going to spend here? How many tapes am I going to have? How much money am I going to have to pay to get these transcribed?" From then on, I would say, "Coach Wooden, could you briefly comment on these things?"

I'm smiling because he really knew it. It wasn't somebody else who did it. J.D. Morgan had a role, Ducky Drake had a role, everybody had a role, but I knew who was steering the whole thing.

I took the dissertation to Coach Wooden as rough as can be. It was triple spaced, and I said, "Conceptually, what are we looking at here? Just give me some feedback, and if there's anything in there that was transcribed incorrectly or that you would like to alter, please let me know and just give me a call."

A couple days later, I get a call. We go to his apartment and he invites me in. I sat down in his den, and I look over and see all my work and all these red-lines, and I'm going, "Oh, no."

He handed it to me, and goes, "Here it is."

I looked through it, and here are all these grammar marks. Correct, punctuation marks. He had corrected about 850 pages of triple space. He had dotted every "i" and crossed every "t." I was so embarrassed, and said, "Coach Wooden, I didn't mean for you to do this."

He said, "Oh, Marv, it was my background and I enjoyed it."

You know how it is for a doctoral dissertation. They want you to go through "Here are your orals, here is your defense."

I said to my adviser, "Here's what I've done. Get the committee together tomorrow. I'm getting a flight and I'll be up there."

He said, "No, that isn't the way we do it here, we do it this way."

I said, "Do me a favor and just do it." I went in and sat down and I looked at all these guys and they're sports and athletic fans along with teachers and educators. They were like kids in a candy store.

They said, "He did this?" and were looking through it. They got a little bit of composure and they just basically stamped it.

I invited Coach Wooden down to speak at the USA Volleyball Awards banquet. There were 500 people there. It was sold out max, the only sell-out we had. Five hundred people had John Wooden stories. Not just a couple. Everybody there had a Coach Wooden story.

I've seen how everybody wants a piece of him at all times. I try not to be one of those people, and yet I'll be sitting here in this office like I was a few years back, several years after my study. It was a Saturday morning. Monday through Friday, I'm a teacher and a coach, and I meet with all kinds of people, so I don't get a lot of quality time to write thank you's and to do the special things. I've always come in on Saturday morning. I just pull the curtains here and look at the ocean, and I won't even turn on the light and I would do that quality work.

It's about 8:30 on a Saturday morning, when somebody comes in and taps me on the shoulder and says, "Marv, how are you doing?" It's Coach Wooden and I haven't shaved. There's a standard there. He's clean-shaven and not a hair's out of place.

I said, "Coach Wooden, what are you doing here?"

He said, "Marv, I start my camp, I heard you might be up here and I just wanted to say hello."

All I could think of was that I haven't shaved and what's he gonna think of me? That's where I am with Coach Wooden.

I picked John Wooden to write my dissertation on because when I was a young student athlete in the late sixties and seventies there was one dominant coach in sports, and that was Coach Wooden. The opportunity to go back five years after he retired and study his philosophies and the process was the opportunity of a lifetime.

I am no one to judge Coach Wooden or to even attempt to rate him. We're getting a lot of coaches who have a style that we would say would be comparable to Wooden's style, but what he did is that he did it his way, before anybody else. It's difficult to be the first of the new. Once that's established, there are people who always jump on the bandwagon to be second. He set a standard that is a really high standard for coaching in the United States and in the world.

Coach Wooden, and probably any good coach, given some technical expertise, could coach any sport. Coach Wooden, if he had some football knowledge, would be a great football coach. He'd be a great baseball or volleyball coach. Some things transcend coaching. Coaching is not necessarily knowledge. There are a lot of knowledgeable coaches in sports who can't coach a lick. He had both knowledge and the process. Sometimes you're a little bit more knowledgeable than you are with your relationships with the players, or vice versa, but you can't be lopsided. You have to have some knowledge and you have to have a little bit of the process. He had high levels of both and that was confirmed.

Also, he was consistent. You can't be sarcastic or witty as a coach. You have to leave your sense of humor out of it because some people will get your humor and some people won't. The great coaches, the great leaders, the great parents, are consistent. And he was consistently John Wooden.

Wooden knew the game, he knew the process, and he was an elite athlete. I was talking to an elite musician one time, and he ended up being a taxi cab driver. And I said, "Why is that? Why didn't you teach?" And he said he did, but within an hour he kicked the chair out from under a student because they didn't want it as much as he wanted it. They didn't respect it.

John Wooden was and is a master psychologist. He knows what makes people tick. The one comment that I heard over and over again that just (and I'll use this word one more time) was "awesome" was shared by two or three assistant coaches. They would be in the locker room, uptight as you could be before a national championship. The players, assistant coaches, had all the butterflies and were filled with anxiety. Coach Wooden would walk in and within ten seconds everybody knew just by his presence that they were going to win the national championship.

You hear that over and over again. There's a tremendous presence there. It's not something that's given. It's earned. If you're an expert and you have a reference source, if you're a good person and you have the relationship with the individuals, you know what makes them tick and if you're real and sincere, you're going to have some influence. He had a tremendous influence on people.

He was so principled and so talented and so comfortable. The great ones are so comfortable with who they are that there's no baggage. So you feel comfortable with that because they're comfortable with themselves.

Wooden was the most important coach of the sixties and seventies, in any sport, without question. It was not only the accomplishments, but the way he accomplished it. You can't have worthy ends with unworthy means. He did that. He focused on his own team. All the things that you would read about or listen to him talk about on the Pyramid, he believed. He was a sportsman.

He didn't say to this me, but I always told my kids that ability and class are the things that intimidate me, not somebody who's yelling and screaming. His teams always had a high level of ability and a high level of class. Look at sports today. I see some professional sports and even some collegiate sports that are a little bit closer to wrestling and roller derby. His teams didn't do that. His teams were pure teams. The acknowledging of the outlet pass. The guy who puts the ball in at the end turns around and acknowledges the other guy. He started doing that and having his players do that before other people. Now it's commonplace.

I interviewed all his former assistants. That was a dissertation within a dissertation. I put Coach Wooden and the time and things he offered me in a separate category. A couple things stood out. One question was how competitive was Coach Wooden? Gary Cunningham talked about how in those days coaches did things that I don't think our society lets happen now. They used to go camping together, all the families. He spoke about Denny Crum, how Denny was like Coach Wooden. They'd go fishing, and it would not be to relax and fish, but to see who could catch the most. So if it was pool, cribbage or whatever, Coach Wooden was always competing. I asked Denny about that, and he got a big smile. He wouldn't say a lot, but I could tell there were competitive battles won or lost. Denny would have something to say about Coach Wooden, his competitiveness, then Coach Wooden would say, "Well, I always told Denny that from the tip of his nose to his chin, he was the best goofy player around."

One thing that stood out was preparation. Wooden challenged his coaches, "Why do you believe that?" He wanted you to stand up for what you believed in. If you didn't say it and document it, if you weren't fully convinced that this was the way to handle, say offensive rebounding or to press, then you didn't have much to say. You couldn't just throw something out to Coach Wooden without having it be well thought out and the ability to back it up to the hilt. Anything would go, according to his assistants, behind closed doors. Then once they went out, they went out together.

I have the Pyramid of Success in my dissertation as a page, but that wasn't my mission when I was looking at the process. I've heard him talk on his Pyramid of Success. It's something that's worked for him and for others. I didn't play under him and I've learned to be Marv Dunphy, not Marv Wooden. When I talk, I share the things that are important to me and I do well. It's nowhere near his Pyramid of Success, but as you go along, you have the things that work for you, so I am somewhat independent of the Pyramid of Success.

When I was young, I watched all sports teams play, yet his team was a true team. I didn't know why, all I knew is that it looked great and I liked his style. He wasn't ranting and raving. I was a basketball player until I changed and became a volleyball athlete. I've worked pretty hard to make sure that if I'm going to be leading a team that we're all pulling on the same end of the rope. That's important. Team play was important to him and little things were important.

There's a tendency, I think, for teachers to teach the way they were taught, for athletes to coach the way they were coached. Early on, my ears were open and I was listening to what others were saying and doing. Just about everybody who finds out I did my dissertation on Coach Wooden, says something like, "Did you get the magic and now you have it?" If someone were to read my dissertation, they would say, "Oh, I do that!" It confirms some of the things that you're doing.

As the U.S. National Volleyball Coach in 1985-88, we played about eighty matches a year all over the world. There wasn't a country that we didn't go to where there wouldn't be a John Wooden story. When people would read the program or the press release, or perhaps ask how I got into coaching. Coach Wooden's name would come up, and the first question asked was, "What did you learn from Coach Wooden?" People always ask me that. "Did you pattern your style, your philosophy after Coach Wooden? Is that why you were successful?" I always give credit where credit is due. He deserves part of the credit for where I am and where I'm going and I'll always be grateful for that.

In the United States, we have coaching effectiveness programs that are the trendy thing to do. He, to me, was a coaching effectiveness program.

It is mostly people in volleyball whom I come in contact with, and they are very familiar with John Wooden. If they were in coaching or sports, whether it's Cuba or China, they'd know about Wooden. I remember spending days in Tallinn, the capitol of Estonia, talking with coaches from Tarta University, and they were asking me my coaching process. And I'd say, "Okay, here it is."

As I was speaking, one of them said, "Well, that's somewhat comparable to John Wooden at UCLA, the famous basketball coach." They had studied Coach Wooden in Estonia in the Soviet Union in August of 1987! Snow flurries in

Russia and there I was sitting in the lobby of the hotel talking about Coach Wooden.

Walking in to meet Coach Wooden caused a lot of anxiety because I didn't know how it was going to go. It's like going into an Olympic gold medal match. If you know how it's going to go, and you have a plan like we had in 1988, you feel pretty good about that. The plan and your talent that you have and your history lowers that anxiety level. Going to meet Coach Wooden was more than a first date could ever be. I was always on my toes, but about halfway through that day and the following days I just felt better and better. It was Coach Wooden who was making me feel better.

Great people have a sense of security about themselves. They're exactly what you see. There's no excess baggage. They feel comfortable about themselves and they have a presence about themselves and they have an air about themselves that they're not afraid to stand up for what they believe in and what they say. There's a tremendous sense of integrity. Their words match their deeds and their deeds match their words and they have no problem with that.

You feel that automatically with Coach Wooden. My five-year-old feels that. It's a sense that animals have about other animals and people and that people surely have about other people. My daughter could have that same feeling that the athletes had in the locker room. Anxiety, what's gonna happen? National television, national championship, professional careers, dollars, and within ten seconds, his presence, they knew that they were going to win. My little girl, within ten seconds of contact with him, feels at ease and is sitting on his lap and is telling him about her day. There's just a presence there that people are attracted to.

Swen Nater says that the athletes don't go back to Wooden because they want to relive the national championships or look at the banners or rewards but because they know where love is. That's a great statement. In some way, shape or form, coaches and teachers are going to have an impact on the athlete. It could be positive, it could be negative, but an impact either way. You can see the tremendous impact that Coach Wooden had on the lives of the people that he coached and the people that he touched.

If you go back to where Coach Wooden was in Indiana, he basically got his values from the farm. So if a young person were to say, "This Friday I'm going out with Susie Q," the rest of the boys would say, "No, no, no, you're only fifteen. You wait until you're nineteen. You've gotta work on this farm." You got a lot of values from your family, from that close-knit society.

Now we're a little more transient, and I don't know if they get as much from the families and that sense of community we used to get. Kids today get a lot from some of their heroes, some stars and some teachers, but I think there's not that emotional experience with the teacher as much as with Coach Wooden. He had a tremendous impact on the athletes that were around him. They got a lot of their guidance from him. Some of them came with their own and would challenge him on his principles and on his values, but they know what he stood for and I think that they learned from him. And I'm sure that at times they would disagree, but I think the further they get away, the more they respect what he believed in, what he stood for, and how he treated them as people and as athletes.

This is what Coach Wooden wrote on November 5, 1981 on my ten copies of my dissertation:

Thank you, Coach Marv Dunphy for considering this retired teacher/coach a worthy subject for this doctoral thesis. I hope that the project will prove to be beneficial to you personally and to all those who will review it. Growth is the result of the things that we experience and our study of the experience of others and how we react to both good fortune and misfortune. May the parts of my philosophy that you have presented in this study help others lessen the time gap in the development of their own personal philosophy.

Best wishes to you and yours.
Always in all ways, John Wooden 11/5/81

RON NEWLIN
New Castle, Indiana

Ron, at the time of this interview in 1991, was the executive director
of the Indiana Basketball Hall of Fame.

People are crazy in Indiana about basketball. One of my goals for this museum was to address that issue, not to take it for granted. This is the state with such a great, certainly high school, basketball tradition. The numbers certainly bear it out. We draw over a million fans a year to the state tournament and have sold out the state finals seventy years in a row—forty thousand people in the Hoosier Dome for a high school basketball game! There are solid historical reasons why of all the states, Indiana became the hotbed of basketball. Of all the sports, basketball was the one that Indiana latched onto.

There's no other state basketball hall of fame anywhere, although I'm aware of a number of them which are getting started now.

Compare the state of affairs in Indiana at that time to, for instance, Ohio, right across the state line. Ohio at the turn of the century was a state of small cities that had the critical mass that's necessary to get groups of young men together to play football. Indiana at the same time was a state of small towns and was a rural state. There were a thousand different high schools in existence in Indiana in the nineteen-teens, the vast majority of which didn't have enough boys in the school to make a football team, but they all had enough to put together a basketball team.

Then, because we were a rural state, the fall football season was harvest season. Winter was the only season when people had the opportunity to get together. Not only the opportunity, but perhaps even the need to congregate in the small towns around the high school gyms on Friday nights. The boys were available to play basketball and the fans were available to come out. There are demographic and historical reasons and perhaps even an inevitability that Indiana would become a basketball state as opposed to a baseball state or a football state.

There are also aspects about basketball that made it appeal to the Indiana character that weren't necessarily found in other sports. There are no other team sports like basketball that reward solitary practice in the way that basketball does. It's hard to practice baseball or football by yourself, but you can practice many of the basic basketball skills by yourself in a barnyard, which was the experience of so many young people growing up.

Basketball's a very egalitarian sport. In football, certain players can't touch the ball. In baseball, the pitcher has certain rules that apply only to him that don't apply to other players. There are different levels of responsibility and even rights under rules of other sports, but in basketball, the rules treat every player equally.

When you think of basketball, it's easier to think of a great individual instead of great teams. When you think of basketball history nationally, internationally, three of the top names in basketball history at any level of the game anywhere in the globe are John Wooden, Oscar Robertson, and Larry Bird. There is not another state, another area, another region in the country that can claim a trio that good.

Wooden was the basis of it. Wooden was not only one of the first people inducted into the Indiana Basketball Hall of Fame, but he was part of the first class inducted into the Naismith Basketball Hall of Fame in 1969, which is only three years older than this organization. He was inducted as a player. In 1959, John Wooden was one of the greatest players who had ever played, who had gone into coaching and gone out West and had some success, but San Francisco was the great program out there. In 1959, and in 1962 when we inducted him into this Hall of Fame, he was inducted because people remembered him thirty years prior as one of the greatest basketball players in the first seventy years of the game, not as a great coach. He was one of the five greatest players in the first seventy years of the game. And then on top of that, he became undoubtedly the greatest coach in the history of the game.

I've heard Wooden be asked the question on several occasions about would it ever be possible for that type of run to be made again. Sometimes the question is asked in a back-handed way, like the expectation is no, it can't ever happen again. It was a great accomplishment, but times were different then. There were only sixteen teams in NCAA tournaments. The talent is spread so much more evenly today that no, Wooden couldn't have won ten out of twelve if he were coaching today. That's the implication in the question. John Wooden is a tremendously modest man, but I pictured the wheels turning in his head when that question was asked. He answers it by saying that if in fact the talent is spread more evenly today, if it was more possible then than it is today, then how come Cincinnati never won it with Oscar Robertson? How come Kansas never won it with Wilt Chamberlain? How come those great Ohio State teams only won one national championship?

I think that the impediments to winning a string of national championships, which were evidently just as great in the fifties and sixties as they are today and witnessed by the teams I just mentioned. UCLA managed to win the figure used before, not just in all the regular season games, but from 1966 through 1973 they won thirty-eight consecutive sudden deaths. In sudden death NCAA tournament competition it doesn't matter who you're playing. Under that type of pressure to win those types of games consecutively means that there is something more than just the talent. That speaks not just of the talent of the players but to the entire system.

One of our most important exhibits here at the Basketball Hall of Fame is a talking mannequin of Coach Wooden who gives a very brief summary of his philosophy of the Pyramid of Success. From an educational standpoint, I told someone just the other day that if we did nothing else here but review game scores, that exhibit alone would allow us to qualify as an educational institution. It is a tremendous statement of Hoosier values.

There's something mystical, if not mythical, about Wooden's involvement with basketball. I'd like to share with you about how that exhibit came about. First I wrote to and called Coach Wooden to get his agreement to allow his image and his words to be a part of the exhibit, and he did. He asked me to draft the presentation and then he wanted to edit it. My first draft was taken almost entirely from various excerpts from published sources and quotes from him. It was something more conversational than the final presentation. Coach Wooden edited it into a little more of a formal presentation than what I had first drafted for him. He was very interested in making sure of what he wanted to say. He had an appreciation that this was significant and his thoughts would be shared with visitors for posterity.

He prepared the script and knew what it was going to consist of. Then we transcribed it on cue cards for him. He came to Indiana in September of 1989 for this and a couple of other appointments. While he was here we filmed the presentation. The technology consists of shooting a Super 8 film loop of the person speaking onto the sculpted head of a mannequin and the mannequin head has to be sculpted so that the cheek bones match. It's not that complicated a technology, but what makes it difficult to film is that the subject has to remain completely stationary while they're reading.

John Wooden, in 1989, who was eighty years old at the time, walked into this studio where the film crew's all set up and they put him down in a dentist's chair and clamped his head shut. He wore a black turtle neck, in front of a black shroud so there was nothing on the film except his face. The rest of the frame was completely black. His head was clamped so he couldn't move his head while he was talking or otherwise his eyes would move back and forth on the mannequin. On top of that, we had to take his glasses off of him and ask him to read cue cards.

He sat there in this chair, had all this done to him, and we asked him to read through it once without the cameras running. He did a very good job, but we had some suggestions. We thought he had read a little bit too fast. We asked him to enunciate a little bit more clearly. We asked him to emote a little bit more at key places. In a rather intimidating situation we asked him to read through it once and said, "Okay, that was good, but now do these three things differently, and remember, don't move your head." And they started the camera rolling.

In a three minute presentation, he has a couple of minor stammers, but basically he just nailed it his first time through. And at the end of that time, he took things off his face. Obviously, he wasn't going to do it again. The presentation was almost perfect on the first time through. The production company that does this type of technology for us on a regular basis usually uses trained actors. They're used to doing five or six takes to get the one they want. They were just amazed that Coach Wooden, at age eighty, would be able to sit in that rather uncomfortable situation, reading cue cards without his glasses, and be told, "Make these three changes, Go!" He did it on command. They were amazed.

I hope I haven't embarrassed Coach Wooden with some of the things I've been saying, but they're all true. Now don't get a fat head, Coach.

[The Coach Wooden exhibit is still an important part of the museum.]

MARK MONTIETH
Indianapolis, Indiana

Mark has a great interest in Indiana basketball, is an author of books on sport, and currently a sports writer for the Indianapolis Star.

John Wooden is the greatest basketball figure ever to come out of Indiana, and probably the greatest basketball figure in the history of the game, next to John Naismith, who invented the game. Consider everything that John Wooden has done as a player and coach. He came out of Purdue in 1932 as probably the best guard in the country. He undoubtedly was one of the best players of his era. He was an Indiana all-time scoring leader, and at Purdue was an all-time scoring leader on an undefeated team.

Had there been professional basketball then as there is today, he would have been a great pro player. As it was, he played professionally on the first professional team in Indianapolis. They played one day a week, on Sundays. He got paid fifty dollars a game and drove up from his teaching job in Dayton or down from South Bend. That was just a moonlighting activity at the time.

People who follow basketball now know what a great coach he was, I think a lot of people forgot what a great player he was. Until Oscar Robertson came in the 1950s, you could argue that Wooden was the greatest player Indiana ever knew.

I've interviewed Wooden several times. For a man who's accomplished all that he's done, he was a very down to earth person and always cooperative. When I would hang up, I would always feel like it was almost a cleansing experience to talk to him on the phone. He's an intelligent, decent, precise person. You just feel that you've talked to a great person. It's an uplifting experience to have a conversation with him.

His reputation amongst the press is very good, although I've read that he could be volatile and temperamental like a lot of coaches, that he wasn't always the gentle personality that his image portrayed.

The Kautsky Grocers of Indianapolis started in 1931 as an amateur team. They won the state amateur championships that year, and from that Frank Kautsky had the bug to turn the team professional. I have the impression that one of the main motivations for turning it professional was that Johnny Wooden was coming out of Purdue and he was such a popular figure that he had an instant drawing card.

Wooden was also contacted by other teams. He wanted to teach, though, so he took a teaching job in Kentucky and played for Frank Kaustsky.

THE JOHN WOODEN PYRAMID OF SUCCESS

Wooden played, off and on, for about eight years. He played continuously for the first few years. After two years in Dayton, he took the teaching and coaching job at South Bend and continued to play for a year's period there. He played for a team in Whiting, because it's closer, but then he didn't get along with the owner in Whiting and came back to the Kautskys.

He would drive down every Sunday from South Bend. Today it's about a three-hour drive, so I can only imagine what it was then. The roads weren't really good then. They might play in Detroit or Cleveland or Akron, and on a Sunday evening, he would drive straight back to Dayton, Kentucky, or to South Bend. A lot of times he'd drive straight through the night, get home say at six in the morning and then go teach at eight that next morning.

All the players had that kind of schedule. A lot of them were coaches and teachers. But fifty dollars, that's not too bad. Wooden's first teaching job paid him $1,800 a year in Dayton, so you can imagine a fifty-dollar bonus each week was a significant amount of money.

The other players were making as little as ten dollars, maybe twenty-five if they were much better players, but there seemed to be no sense or bad feelings about it. Wooden was the star. A typical game with a league team at the Armory in downtown Indianapolis held 2-3,000 people. They'd sell it out occasionally. A typical crowd might be 1-2,000. Then they would play the New York Renaissance, and they would play here at Butler. Sometimes they would draw as much as 9-10,000 people, so they had a huge crowd.

It's ironic. The Renaissance won eighty-eight straight games through a three-year period. Wooden's streak at UCLA was eighty-eight games. The final scores in those days were like 32 to 30. Wooden might have ten or fifteen points. That was when they had a center jump after every basket before the game got wild. It's hard to exaggerate his greatness as a player for his era.

At the Kautsky's game, the players sometimes took the tickets at the door. The first game against the Rams drew something like 7-8,000 people, and took everybody by surprise. They actually ran out of tickets. They didn't have that many printed. The ticket takers were giving tickets back to the ticket sellers, they'd kind of recycle them. That wasn't working, so they just told fans, "Give us your money and come on in, don't worry about a ticket." Once word of that got out, fans started coming in, said they had paid their money, and they say Kautsky lost who knows how much money because he wasn't able to handle the crowd.

When he was at Purdue during the Depression, Wooden worked his way through school. At that time, if you made the honor roll, you got a free semester's tuition. He was always on the honor roll so that was taken care of. He lived in a fraternity, and he worked on the kitchen crew there to help pay his bills. He helped clean the football stadiums, and bandaged ankles at football practice. His business enterprise was to buy grocery items from Murphy's in Lafayette, like apples and souvenir things, and ride the train with the alumni to away football games and walk the aisles. [Wooden in 1965 admitted that Piggy Lambert gave him a letter of introduction and that town merchants donated ham, cheese, bread and other things so "it was all profit."] He'd sell these food items, and he would buy black ribbons and make a ribbon that the women might want to wear on their lapel. He called it "walking to Chicago" because the train would go from Lafayette to Chicago, say, to play Northwestern or at that time, the University of Chicago. He made a good amount of money that way. He also had a program for the football games. He would buy the programs, and hire other students to help him sell. The profit on the programs was ten-cents, and Wooden would split that with the salesman.

He paid his way through school. One of the doctors in Lafayette found out what Wooden was doing to pay his bills and knew that he came from a poor background. He had taken a liking to Wooden as a player because he was so good. Before Wooden's senior year at Purdue, Purdue's coach, Piggy Lambert, called Wooden in and said, "This doctor here really likes you and he wants to help you out. He is offering to pay all your bills for your senior year to help you out. He doesn't want anything in return, he just wants to help."

Wooden asked him, "Who is this guy and what's the story behind it?"

Lambert said, "There's no catch, he just wants to help you out. You think about it and come back next week and tell me what you think."

Wooden thought about it, and decided he was making it okay on his own and didn't feel comfortable taking money from somebody like that. He went back and told Piggy Lambert that he decided he'd go on his own.

"I knew you'd say that. I had confidence in you that you would," Lambert said. "When you get out of here, you'll owe nobody nothing because you'll have made it yourself. Hard work never hurt anybody and you're gonna be okay. You don't need to take any money from anybody cause you're making it on your own as it is." Wooden likes to tell that story, because you can imagine the great players in college basketball players today have scholarships and don't have to do anything. There were only academic scholarships then. When he came out of high school, they didn't have real intense recruiting battles at that time. He'd gotten a call from Piggy Lambert at Purdue, from Tony Hinkle at Butler, from Everett Deed at Indiana, from Phog Allen, one of the pioneers of basketball, and a few other coaches. They would call and express their interest in him and tell him that they would like him to play for them, but that was pretty much it.

Wooden told me he got more calls from various fraternities at schools asking him to rush at their house than he did from coaches.

He went to Purdue because he liked Piggy Lambert a lot and thought he was a man of high principles, and because he wanted to major in engineering. They had a civil engineering program that was very good and he decided that was what he wanted to major in. But when he got up here and enrolled, he found out that the engineering majors had to attend a summer engineering camp, that was part of the curriculum. Wooden could not do it because he had to help out on the family farm in the summers. He simply did not have time to go to engineering camps in the summer, so he immediately had to change majors when he got to Purdue. He wound up in English.

Wooden said that had he known the requirements for engineering majors at Purdue, he may very well have gone to Indiana, because Nell, his girlfriend and the woman he married, stayed in Martinsville, and he could have gone to Indiana and stayed closer to her. So it was really a break for Purdue that Wooden didn't know the requirements for the major. Guidance counseling wasn't an institution then like it is now.

He had bad luck at Christmas when he was at Purdue all four years. Wooden missed all the games because he had either had an injury or an illness. His sophomore year, they played at Butler. It was a big game. Butler had a nationally recognized program, Wooden was well known. It was a game everybody looked forward to and it had a lot of coverage. The day Purdue's team was to leave Lafayette to take the train here, he was walking downtown to the train station. A man driving a cleaning truck was driving by, recognized him, said, "Hey, hop on, I'll give you a lift." The roads were icy. Wooden was on the back of this truck, and they were on a hill, and a car came from behind and slid and hit Wooden's leg. He broke bones and had bad bruises and was in the hospital for a couple weeks. I looked up the game on the microfilm in the library and it was the headline, that he was injured. In later years, he suffered an injury during practice, and had his tonsils out one Christmas.

Wooden gets his proper just due and recognition in Indiana. Because he's been out of coaching so long, he's faded into the background, although I doubt that it bothers him. He comes back occasionally and everybody here who follows basketball is well aware of his contributions to the game. Personally, I question Purdue's not having paid greater tribute to him. I've heard various reasons. There's no animosity at Purdue on Wooden. Perhaps some bad feelings have come out of when Purdue played UCLA for the national championship. Wooden was disappointed when they built a new basketball arena and they named it after Brett Mackey, who was the athletic director there, rather than

Piggy Lambert, who was Wooden's coach. There are not bad feelings, but there aren't close ties between Wooden and Purdue. I've always thought Purdue should bring him back and honor him and name something after him. He was one of the great figures in college basketball and Purdue should feel fortunate that he came to Purdue.

I'm familiar with his Pyramid of Success. It's great, and obviously something that you just don't come up with in an afternoon. If you sit down and look at it and think about it, it makes a great deal of sense. It's the common sense type of things that could lead anybody towards success. I don't have it memorized, but it's one of many things I've read that has been an inspiration to me. You don't hear about it much in Indiana, but people who have heard him speak and have read about him are familiar with the Pyramid of Success and it's something that has had a lot of influence on a lot of people.

John Wooden has been inspirational to many other people. His success is going to be the first thing that catches your eye. But beyond that, he's obviously a man with high standards. In one article, I referred to him as the unofficial conscience of college basketball. All the things that go on today, the dirty things of college basketball, Johnny Wooden was far from that. If more people and more college basketball coaches were inspired by Johnny Wooden, the game would be a lot better off. He had his priorities in the right place. He was competitive, emotional about the game, but he had his priorities in the right place.

I greatly appreciate his basic sense of decency. He's an inspirational figure for all of college basketball and I hope I help spread the word of his accomplishments.

Harry Keller, Wooden and Coach Ward "Piggy" Lambert
at Purdue in 1930.

THE JOHN WOODEN PYRAMID OF SUCCESS

JACK TOBIN

Jack co-authored with John Wooden They Call Me Coach.

Pete Newell (who coached U.C. Berkeley) told me one time, "Playing John Wooden is no problem. He gives you a road map and says, 'Here I'm coming, try and stop me.'" Newell did the best job of stuffing him. He won more games than he lost coaching against John Wooden, but later on, Wooden became a much better defensive coach than he had been. When he put the press on, it was a magnificent sight. I saw UCLA score nine points in six or seven seconds to win a game. Impossible, but they did.

Wooden resisted my writing the autobiography, *They Call Me Coach*, with him. He's a humble man who didn't think his achievements merited a book that anybody would buy. I said, "Coach, you're so wrong you won't believe it." The book still sells like mad, and it was published in 1972! He hasn't been on a basketball floor since 1975 in San Diego, but you can't go anywhere with him, bam, they're there in thirty seconds, with shirts, handkerchiefs, menus, and that is at any restaurant. We used to walk down to lunch. If you had a one o'clock lunch date, you had to leave by 12:15 because you weren't going to make it by one o'clock because he'd run into faculty, students and businessmen, who stopped us every ten feet. He's a very friendly person who will sign autographs until his hand drops. I don't know how he does it. I sat with him at a bookstore where he must have signed books for six hours. Have you ever tried to write your name for that amount of time? It's tiring for your arms, fingers, hands.

I've known John Wooden for fifty years and never found any flaw. Some in the sportswriter community don't like what they perceive is a holier than thou facade, but he's for real; some believe that deep down he's not this goodie two shoes, but he is the same way as he is on the veneer.

We never had an argument, except once in a while on politics, where his views are very conservative. *[Wooden told the author in 2000 that he was a life-long Democrat but always voted for the right person irrespective of party affiliation. He recently told former UCLA player Andy Hill that he was a Democrat because his father was.]* He is a basketball coach who is really a philosopher and political scientist. He loves to talk politics, and is a very observant, well informed, well read person. He talks politics in an agreeable manner, his diplomatic skills are very high.

I never saw a man who was more crestfallen, depressed and demoralized after he buried Nell. That went on for several years. He was not a suicide candidate, he's too strong, but I did think he might wither away from not eating properly. I know damn well he doesn't eat properly now. The great-grandchildren saved him.

Wooden took UCLA basketball from the pits to the pinnacle. Wooden and J.D. Morgan made the NCAA, not because of that incredible streak they had, rather they were so entertaining to watch, even in defeat. Once the game was over, win or lose, the players had better walk out of there with their heads high and their eyes sparkling, because he said, "Remember, it's just a game."

There was much professional jealousy of Wooden. All kinds of coaches thought his success was because he had all the talent in the world especially when they had Alcindor. Los Angeles was a non-basketball town until Wooden arrived. USC was the dominant basketball team in Los Angeles and the dominant basketball team in the Pacific Ten Conference under Sam Barry. Once Wooden arrived there was a complete reversal. He took a team that was dead last and won, which had a great impact on the whole of Southern California and the whole damn nation. He took college basketball from a sport that was not high on the radar to a multi-million dollar a year program. The dollars generated from the NCAA Final Four go right back to John Robert Wooden.

He had a $500 scouting budget; they spend that much in a week now, but he seldom spent any of it. He didn't believe in scouting. He would watch a team warm up, might take a look at a film, but he wasn't looking at the team, he would look at the idiosyncrasies of the men. He wanted to know the nuances.

The initial attraction to John Wooden is his success in sports, the long run attraction is the man. To meet him is to realize that he has great depth. He always has the perfect saying to illustrate a point, and is a writer's delight, as it is impossible to have a dull interview with him. Every time I talk to him he says something new. There's no one in the world I work in who I have spent more time with than Wooden, hundreds of hours, and I always come away with my spirits improved, feeling better for the effort I've made to see him and what he had to offer.

Sports should play an ancillary role in society. Professional athletes are given this opportunity to assemble more money in a month than the average male American will make in a lifetime and they throw it away. So many of them end up broke, degenerated, drunks, narcotic addicts, gamblers. I say to my sport agent friends, "Can't you get it across to the people what they have accomplished?" I read that the average male American will make $500,000 in his life time. Some of these guys are making that in a month, and end up with nothing. What was also extraordinary about Wooden was how many of his players turned out fine, virtually all graduated.

Athletes should be given the right to have a basic preparation course on how to write a check, how to balance a checkbook, what credit is, what revolving credit is, what a mortgage is. I've had kids tell me when they got into the pros, they didn't know how to book a plane reservation, how to get on an airplane, how to get off one.

From John Wooden, we should learn about family management, that a game is only for an allotted space of time, a very incidental part of your life, that you're going to have to do other things besides bounce, kick, or hit a ball, that you have to prepare yourself to go out into the world and succeed. Wooden's graduates have gone on to have remarkable records.

I am most proud in my career of having written *They Call Me Coach* with him. Most books are perishable but that one is going to be forever. When I'm long gone, the odds are that my son will receive royalties on this book, so rare in writing about sports.

When Wooden's high school team won the state championship, it was headline news.

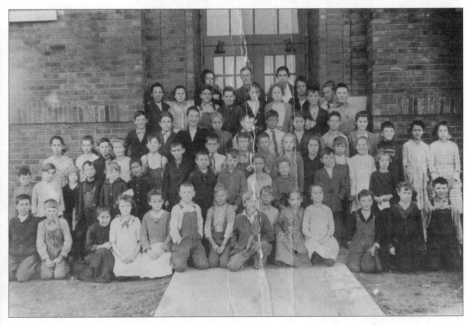

Third grader John Wooden, sixth from left, first row at Centerton School, Indiana.

FAMILY

CARYN BERNSTEIN
Los Angeles, California

Caryn is John Wooden's second oldest granddaughter.

I found out I was pregnant with my daughter Cori about three months before my grandmother died. Being the first great-grandchild, she came at an important time for him.

He spent quite a lot of time with my daughter. I went back to work when she was nine months old, and when my sitter couldn't watch her, he would. Picture this seventy-six-year-old man down on the floor with a year-old baby, crawling around and playing with her; he just absolutely loved it. They developed a real special bond early on. He absolutely loves kids, and not just those he's related to.

My daughter adores him. It's funny. She never met my grandmother, but Papa talked to her about my grandmother and showed her pictures when she was very young. She's always had this special thing for "Mama." She would talk about Mama and just get tears in her eyes, though she was someone she's never met, all because what my grandfather had told her about her. She has things that my grandfather has given her that she says, "Mom, I love this. . ." I was taking her to her dad's house on Saturday, and she was in the car and said, "Mom, this is my favorite doll."

And I said, "Do you remember who gave this to you?"

She said, "No."

I said, "Papa gave that to you."

She said, "I love this doll the most, cause anything Papa gives to me I really love." She was six. She doesn't see him as much now as she used to, but they spent a lot of time together.

I'll try and get him to come out and spend the night, which he'll do on occasion. It's hard because of the stairs. The last time he came out, he said, "Do you mind if I sleep on the couch?" because the stairs are kind of difficult. He slept in the living room and Cori slept in a sleeping bag next to him because she wanted to sleep by him. She bugs me all the time to spend the night at his house.

My grandfather is a very mellow type of person. I don't see him being extreme one way or another way. He doesn't fly off the handle at a situation immediately, like I probably would. He sees the situation, thinks about it and handles it in a calm manner. I'm more reactive.

Papa has a wonderful sense of humor and he can tell stories. The kids love to hear him tell stories about when he was a kid. He tells them about when he was growing up and life on the farm. My grandparents were always around when we were growing up. I'm the middle daughter. We have a special bond. I was very ill as a child. When I was three or four years old, I was just very sick and dehydrated to the point where the doctor came to the house and they thought I was not going to make it through the night. The only thing I wanted, and I was delirious, was my Papa, sitting there with me.

He's not one to give advice where it's not wanted. If you ask for it, he will give it to you, but otherwise, he more or less wants you to do what you feel is right in a situation. That's how he's always been with my mom.

I was a normal, rebellious teenager. I had my own mind and I was going to do what I wanted to do. Having divorced parents made me a little more rebellious. We had a lot of talks.

I took care of my grandmother after she had her surgery. I spent a lot of time at the hospital with my grandfather. My ex-husband and I would go every weekend to the hospital. Eventually, when we knew my grandmother was going to be coming home, we were thinking about getting a nurse because of Papa's traveling, and she could not be home alone. I told him that I would like to be there to take care of her. When she came home, I quit my job at the time and I came over every day. I bathed her and stayed with her, and when my grandfather traveled, I spent the night with her. I went with her when she went to the doctor's appointments.

I don't think I'll ever forget when we were taking her to Orthopedic Hospital for a checkup on her hip and she was not feeling well at all. Driving down the Hollywood freeway and Ventura freeway, she was starting to really sweat and was in a lot of pain. When we arrived I let them know that she was having a lot of problems and they took her over to emergency. That was something my grandfather and I went through together. He was driving. I always went because it was hard getting her in and out cause she was in a wheelchair. In those moments with him, we bonded very close, because we were together through a lot of the hard times with her. She never really got better after the original surgery.

He was wonderful to her. Did you know that my grandmother Nellie called him "John Bob"? I think something he regrets more than anything is that he spent so much time at the hospital, but she died in the middle of the night when he wasn't there. That was very hard on him. He had great patience with her. She was very hard of hearing. She used to watch soap operas, which she loved. I'd sit with her, and we watched them from eleven in the morning until three in the afternoon. She'd sit in his den, on the couch, and have the TV on full blast because she couldn't hear. Well, somebody would call Papa. I don't know how he could hear who was talking to him, but he never, ever would ask her to turn the set down. He would talk on the phone with this TV blasting.

He loved her company, even when she was ill. They had a very great romance. They teased each other. He would tease her, and she'd say, "Oh, John!" She'd get angry and frustrated with him when she was sick, but he would have all the patience in the world for her.

He'd try and cheer her up. He would be so happy if she felt like going out for dinner, because she never really felt like it. If she wanted to put on a dress and go out to dinner, that was wonderful. It was very difficult for him with her being so ill to still do things. He still traveled, and because I watched her he was more comfortable doing that.

Papa watched sports and we used to play cribbage and cards. He's a channel flipper. With that remote in that hand he flips through the channels. He likes Westerns and sports. *Goodbye, Mr. Chips* is one of his favorite movies.

When people come over and he's here, my daughter Cori will say, "Did you ever meet my grandfather? This is the great John Wooden." She's funny. One morning I put in the tape that Pepsi Cola made on his life. I was upstairs with the baby and after the tape had finished, she came in with tears in her eyes, and said, "Mom, that tape was so good it just made me cry." There's definitely a bond. When she dies she wants to be put in the wall where my grandma is and my grandfather will be.

I like my grandfather for the person that he is. I've never felt like I had to answer to him for my actions in my life. I never felt that I couldn't talk to him about things and have him criticize me or tell me I was doing something wrong. He's not judgmental. And I am.

I don't ever remember not having a good time just talking with him. He is very funny, he has a great sense of humor. I shared a lot of close times. When my grandmother was ill, just spending time with him at the hospital. A lot of it was quiet time where we really didn't talk. We just sat together.

I'm fortunate to have him as a grandfather because of who he is, not because he's John Wooden. When people find out I'm a Wooden, there are different reactions. Some people don't know who he is, have never heard of him. Some people say, "Oh, it's John Wooden, wow!" I've probably been treated differently from some people than I would have if they hadn't found out that I was related to him. Some people want to know about him, when they when realize I'm related. He is a pretty famous person, but he doesn't come off like a famous person in any way.

THE JOHN WOODEN PYRAMID OF SUCCESS

He's great with kids. He's an unmerciful tease. I used to get mad at him when Cori was little. He'd tease her to the point where she'd really start to whine. I'd say, "Wait a minute, she's not coming home with you. Stop! Enough!" He doesn't get bored around kids.

He's very caring, non-judgmental, basically a very nice person. He brings a lot to a lot of people, and people who do that are wonderful people. People come up to him and say, "Boy, you really have influenced me." It's almost a daily occurrence, someone saying that he inspired them. He just takes it all in stride, a very down to earth person.

I am very lucky to have him as a grandfather, to have somebody in my life who I can go to and talk to without worrying about him being judgmental.

Wooden and great grand-daughter, Cori, October, 1990.

CHRISTY IMPELMAN
San Vincel, California

Christy is John Wooden's oldest grandchild

My earliest recollection of my grandpa is going to UCLA with him when he was coaching. The athletic department was in bungalows, and we used to walk from his office into Westwood and have lunch. As we walked down the street, any time he'd find a bobby pin laying on the ground, he'd pick it up and stick it in a tree. He always told me that was for good luck. I was three or four years old.

The first time my grandparents took me to Estes Park, Colorado, I was six years old. On the way back we stopped in Las Vegas, where they were going to take me to a dinner show. We checked into the Desert Inn Hotel and they had a gift shop there and a little stuffed dog that I wanted, which was priced ten times as much as it should have been and I said that I wanted it. My grandfather said that he just didn't have enough money to get it

That night when I went to bed the dog was sitting on my pillow. I still have the dog. It has no hair left. I didn't know it at the time, but they didn't even know if they had enough money to stop in Las Vegas overnight. I didn't cry when he said that I couldn't have it, but he just saw my eyes were so sad. He told my grandmother that he was going to go buy it for me. We almost didn't have enough gas to get home. But he thought that I really wanted that dog. That was really special.

I first began understanding the game when I was ten and during Kareem's year as a sophomore in 1967. Then we won the national championship every year until 1974, so I just expected that's what happens.

Between the ages of three and ten, he was just my grandfather, not a famous coach. He is the best grandfather there is. He is a much better grandfather than a coach. He just had a way with people, children especially. They seem to be drawn to him. He has a genuine interest in people, no matter what age, that makes you feel very important. He's interested in everything that's happening in your life. He was always there for me as a role model. When my parents divorced, he was more of a father figure. I was sixteen. He and my grandmother were both very supportive and really helped my mom a lot. I always felt very close, that I could tell him anything, and he would never prejudge me. He might disagree with me, but he would never tell me that his opinion was correct and mine was incorrect. The subjects cover all areas, not so much morals, but mores.

My memory of my grandmother is that she was always sitting by my grandfather. I remember when he was coaching, she always wanted to have a red car, but when he coached at UCLA, it was always light blue and gold, UCLA's colors. Finally, when he retired, he bought her a red car.

She quit taking the *L.A. Times* because she'd get so mad when she'd read articles after the game. I remember when we'd win by too much, they'd say, "UCLA was a boring game, they won by too much." She took it very personally. Papa would come over to my mom's house and read the paper because he didn't want to get my grandmother aggravated. She'd say what she thought.

She never really had outrageous opinions, she was just very loyal to her husband and her family. That was her first priority. It wouldn't matter what you would do to her, but don't do something to her family and cross her family. That would make her angry.

Obviously, my grandparents had a very special relationship. That was just how I was brought up, and how things should be—to have a caring relationship and be supportive of each other. I didn't realize until I became almost an adult how rare it is to find that one right person with whom you want to share everything. They fit so well together, they were almost like one person. They always did everything for each other. Now I especially realize it.

My grandmother was always really open, and always inviting players to come into her home. When I was younger, a lot of the players from out of town were invited to spend the holidays with us. Kareem was terrific with all my little cousins. He was always portrayed as quiet and rather aloof, but with the children he was just wonderful.

The players came back to see us after they graduated and went on to other things. Bill Walton calls him about once a week. Maybe as you get older and go out on your own, some of the things start sinking in that maybe were taught. I've never met any of them who have a bad thing to say about him.

The first game I remember losing was in 1968 at the Astrodome with Elvin Hayes. I used to get sick if we'd lose. My mom was the worst. She would have to go to the ladies room, especially if we were playing USC or somebody like that. She couldn't handle it. I couldn't eat. I'd get really keyed up and nervous. When we lost in Houston, it was like (gasp). It was just terrible. Then when we beat them that year in the semi-finals of the Final Four, that was the greatest. His teams were always just so much fun to watch because they played as teams. Everyone played so well together, it was fun to watch.

I didn't discern any noticeable change in him from 1967-75. My grandfather was the same. What happened was that we couldn't go out and eat somewhere without people interrupting us during our meals. They wanted autographs. He had become much more in the public eye, but that did not affect him at all. He was the same.

I remember when we won the national championship and about to go to dinner at a coffee shop. It was nothing fancy. We were at their apartment in Santa Monica with my uncle and his family and my family and the phone rang.

Grandmother said, "Don't answer the phone, we're going out to dinner."

But he answered the phone, and I heard my grandfather saying, "Well, I can't hold on, my family's leaving," and then he changed his voice and says, "Oh, well in that case I guess I can hold on." It was the White House calling. President Nixon got on the phone and the first thing he did was tell the President, "Well, my grandchildren are here, and this would be something they would always remember. I'd like you to speak to them." And he had all of us get on the phone and talk to President Nixon.

Anyway, here's Nixon asking me, "Now what year of school are you in, my dear?" And he had just called to congratulate my grandpa.

"Well, thank you sir, thank you, sir. Now, could you please talk to my family?" He was always thinking about us and not himself.

My grandpa had a lot of influence on my life. I learned a lot from him without being told to do this or that. I would hope that I learned a lot just from seeing how he lived his life. He's really special. He lives his life very close to how you should follow it in the Bible, and he really is concerned for others and puts others before himself. I learned from him in the way he always stressed team play. That's even helped me in my career with what I do now. I'm in management and I try to have everybody work as a team. I remember things now as I get older and I appreciate what I think I really have learned from him.

He does things for the right reasons. He has a special talent for getting people to work together and getting the most out of them. He has a very special way of communicating with young as well as old, and getting his ideas across. A lot of people have good ideas or have good intentions, but they don't have the ability to share that with others; he does. He's always been a very good influence on me.

As a grandfather he was always very fair with me. When I wanted to buy a car, he helped me buy one, but I had to save up money and then he would match what I saved. I learned the value of earning.

I got my first copy of the Pyramid of Success when I was about nine years old. He autographed it for me. It was on old parchment paper, but I didn't understand everything that was broken down. I never even heard him speak on it until last year. It was very interesting. It can be applied in everything you do. I appreciate it more now being in business and dealing with people everyday. He got a standing ovation for five minutes after his speech. There were probably about one hundred fifty people. Senior managers.

People mention the Pyramid of Success to me. I have a couple of employees who would like some little cards of the Pyramid of Success on it and have asked me for it. In business meetings I've had people mention it. I managed a lighting store in San Francisco and I gave each of the staff a Pyramid. We had a Saturday morning meeting and we touched on the creeds and briefly on the Pyramid. I gave them all a little card. It's funny, some of the guys will notice, "Oh, that was Coach Wooden." They're more impressed with that. The females were more impressed with the information.

When we go out anywhere to lunch or dinner, people are always saying, "John, John, Johnny." I finally said to him, "You know so many people. How do you know all these people? Who is that?" And he said, "I don't know, it's just another one of my friends, I don't know his name." That's how he referred to all these people, who would walk up to him off the street. He had the same demeanor with anyone and would never refuse. If somebody came over and interrupted his dinner and wanted to talk to him, he would always be courteous.

I feel lucky that I am John Wooden's granddaughter. To spend time with him does you good. It can only make you better.

The young married Woodens.

CRAIG IMPELMAN
San Vincel, California

Craig is married to John Wooden's granddaughter, Christy. Since the interview, he has become the general manager for American Agencies in Torrance, California, a collection agency where Wooden's philosophy is taught to the work force and integrated into the philosophy of that enterprise.

My relationship with John Wooden actually goes back to when I attended UCLA. The reason I went to UCLA was because of UCLA basketball teams.

I was an okay basketball player. I tried out for the freshmen team at UCLA, with the Walton group. We had sixty guys try out. We had seven guys on scholarship. It was down to eleven and I made that. Gary Cunningham was the coach. Then, about two weeks before the regular season started, I got cut, myself and one other guy. They kept nine guys on the freshmen team that year. I thought that was the end of the world, my last shot at UCLA basketball. Later, of course, I ended up coaching the same team that I got cut from.

I wanted to be a basketball coach after I got out of college. The decision to cut me from the UCLA team was made by Gary Cunningham. Coach Wooden wasn't involved. The next year I wanted to try out for the varsity team. I was an awful player. I should no more have been trying out for the UCLA varsity at that time than I should have been trying out for the Lakers. But of course as a player, you think that you're the greatest.

I went up to the athletic offices, and I wanted to make an appointment to talk to Coach Wooden. He made the time to talk to me and I went into his office and sat down. I don't remember exactly the gist of the conversation in terms of what he said. What I do remember is that he made time to talk to me and he talked to me eyeball to eyeball. He just explained to me very honestly that there were not going to be any walk-ons trying out for the team that year because the positions were filled by scholarship players, but that he appreciated my interest. He makes the time for everybody and he treats everybody with tremendous respect. It had a tremendous impact on me, that this guy who was the greatest basketball coach ever would take the time to talk to me. He didn't have one of his assistants talk to me. He was so straight-forward about everything.

I got interested in him. I used to go watch the UCLA teams practice all the time when I was a student, because I knew all the guys on the team and I loved basketball. His organization, the way he teaches, was very striking. A UCLA practice was like clockwork [snapping fingers], it was drill to drill to drill to drill. Then, at the end of the practice, the team scrimmaged every day for half an hour. They kept complete statistics of the scrimmage and posted them on the board afterwards.

I became a basketball coach. I was a part-time assistant to Gene Bartow. I also assisted Larry Farmer, the junior varsity coach at the time, who tried to run all the drills and everything else exactly the same way that Coach Wooden did when Larry played for him, because Larry believed that was the best way and the only way to do it.

In the process of doing that, I got very interested in the Woodenisms, Coach Wooden's motivational material. I used to go on the road during the summer and speak at a lot of camps all over the Northwest. The camps could put in print that a coach from UCLA was going to be there. UCLA was such a big name that if one of their coaches was there it made a big difference.

The first time I went to do a camp I thought, "What am I going to tell these guys?" Larry told me what drills to do, and how to put together a package to teach a particular skill. But in terms of communication, I also wanted them to understand the type of attitude that it would take for them to be the best that they could be. That went right back to the Pyramid and all the Woodenisms. That's when I became a student, and read all the things I could get my hands on that John Wooden had written. I just kept collecting them and reading them, and I used them to help the youngsters understand the kind of attitude I was trying to get across. Eventually, the way I ran the camps was based entirely on Woodenisms, telling them to the kids.

When Coach communicates, he says, "as fine as" or "as insightful of a thing." And he's so considerate of other people and their feelings, he never wants to say anything that could be construed the wrong way or is going to offend them.

I always felt that if I knew all of John Wooden's basketball drills, and I knew his philosophy of life, and I knew his teaching techniques, that if I could do everything the way that John Wooden did it, I could get my teams to play the way John Wooden's teams played and we could all go home happy and win national championships. That was always the cue—if we weren't winning like Coach Wooden did, then there must be something we weren't doing like he did. And I wanted to learn exactly how he did it so I could reproduce it.

Coach Wooden has incredible charisma and presence. And he's so humble, sometimes you forget how charismatic he is. With all these youngsters, who didn't know who he was, when he started teaching basketball it was like watching somebody conduct a symphony. He started slowly, with his voice at a low level, so those in the back were leaning forward to hear him. Over the course of two hours, it built and built and built, and the end of it, it was like a crescendo. I'm a gym guy, I'm a basketball guy; symphonies and operas, I don't do that, he got kids seven years old in perfect balance. They were hanging on every word that the man said. He blows the whistle and they're there, quick and on balance. You could have dropped a pin in the gym. Every youngster was unbelievably totally focused. He had complete control of the whole group. He put them through drills. He was teaching them. You don't learn sitting on the floor.

I remember seeing him speak about the Pyramid at the adult camp. I was watching him do the Pyramid for the ninth or tenth time, and I was crying. He's talking about God's Hall of Fame and doing the speech. When he was done, I realized at that moment that I had just heard one of the truly great Americans of all time speak. Sometimes you have a great appreciation for a moment, sometimes something great happens to you but you don't realize it for a long time. I've never seen Papa do the Pyramid and not get a standing ovation. Every time it ends the same way, with everyone standing up and applauding. It's truly a great speech. You're sitting there and he's not only talking about the Pyramid, but when he touches on each building block in the Pyramid he alludes to a poem and recites the poem chapter and verse. It's an incredible presentation.

The reason he was such a great coach is because he taught by example. That's what his players got. He was always quick, but never in a hurry. And he didn't mistake activity for achievement. And failing to prepare is preparing to fail. He was always prepared. If you watch him teach basketball, when he demonstrates how to do things, he's in perfect balance when he does it. He doesn't ask other people to be kind to each other, he gives them thoughts that he has about his expectations of a UCLA player: be a gentleman at all times.

Other coaches think John Wooden is the greatest ever, period, end of conversation. I've been all over the United States, and done basketball camps everywhere. People who really know basketball say he's the greatest basketball coach of all time. What they ask is, "Why was he so great?"

Where do you start? He's a great teacher, with a great understanding of the game, who paid incredible attention to detail, yet had the ability to still keep it simple. When you look through the Woodenisms, you see many little things, and he did them all.

To give you an example, a UCLA basketball team-playing defense when John Wooden coached was special. There were a lot of different players over the years, and they were all good, but other coaches had good guys, too. UCLA basketball teams never gave up the baseline on the dribble; the other team never dribbled around you on the baseline side. And every time the ball was shot, somebody got a hand up and contested the shot.

Now that may sound kind of funny, and not sound like a big deal. But when the UCLA players got out of basketball or got into coaching and went into other programs, they saw other defenses. A lot of teams, when somebody beats you on the baseline on the dribble, they do what's called "rotate." A player comes over and helps, and there's a whole defensive rotation. The UCLA players who became coaches were saying, "I don't get it. Why do we need a defensive rotation? We never got beat on the baseline."

I'll tell you a great story. This is typical. Coach Wooden asked me what I'd like him to do the last day of camp. I told him it would be great if he spoke on the Pyramid of Success. He said, "Oh, fine, okay." Now here's Coach Wooden, he's speaking at this camp, and of course his only requirement for him speaking at the camp was that I not pay him. When he sat down with Christy and me up in Utah, he saw I had a camp, and he said, "Craig, you have this camp coming up, I'd like to speak at it every day. You can advertise that I'm going to do it, but there's one requirement—you're not going to be allowed to pay me." So here he's doing this camp as a freebie for our family to help us out. It's the last day of camp and Coach, unbeknownst to me, gets a hundred parchment Pyramids, takes them home that night, and signs them all individually "Best Wishes, John Wooden." Coach Wooden says, "I didn't know if your youngsters would be interested in this, but I brought this." He's got a paper bag. "Craig, they may want these." I take them out, and there are all the Pyramids that he had gone home and signed for every camper.

Wooden was able to put it together at that high a level for so long. That's what was so interesting, he had that consistent winning streak. Unbelievable. Best teacher of all time, with great players. You look at Michael Jordan as a rookie with this great raw athletic ability but it's not fine-tuned. He gradually becomes a team player. Then you've got the whole package, where he's really pretty sound most of the time. With Coach Wooden, you've got this incredible teacher with this great consistency. It's phenomenal to understand. When you think Michael Jordan, you think phenomenal athlete, a great basketball player. And when I say John Wooden, you think phenomenal teacher, an unbelievable coach. You can see Michael Jordan jump, but you can't see John Wooden teach.

I was at a basketball camp, a superstar camp in Santa Barbara, and I was talking to another coach. I was coaching UCLA at the time, and he said to me, "What's so great about John Wooden?" or "What makes him so special?"

And I said, "Well, the most amazing thing is that he's a better person than he was a basketball coach."

Someone interrupted and said, "No, you don't get it. The reason he was such a great coach is because he's such a great person."

What John Wooden taught as a basketball coach translated into the lives of his players so that they went on to have successful careers. And the Woodenisms, the positive attitude—be thankful for what you have, not what you have not—this way that he lived, this way that he projected himself, carried and transmitted to his players, and his players translated that to their work situations. It set them apart from the masses, and rubs off on other people and creates a happy situation.

It was unbelievable to marry into the family. Christy has so many of her grandfather's qualities in the way that she acts (one of the reasons that I'm madly in love with her). She's a great person. And the other Wooden characteristics which you see with her mom and with her and with her grandfather is that they're incredibly well-organized. It just gets done beautifully, it runs like a clock.

Going back to Coach Wooden's coaching style, his daily work day included a staff meeting at UCLA for the coaches from ten to twelve every day. Period. End of conversation. He did his correspondence at a certain time every day. One of the most debilitating things in getting anything accomplished is task interruption. As a teacher and as a manager, that's the one thing that Coach Wooden avoided. You just didn't have it. If they had a staff meeting from ten to twelve, it was ten to twelve. There were no interruptions, no phone calls, unless it was a family emergency.

After Christy and I were married, we went to Weber State, where we had a bad season, lost twenty games, and I ultimately got fired. We were in the middle of that season when Coach came up and watched practice. When I got back to the house, there he was, sitting at the table. It would be an overstatement to say that he was waiting there for me with pencil and paper, but when we sat down and talked and I said, "Coach, what did you see?" he was pretty direct about what he saw and what we could do better. It wasn't the old, "As fine as. . .", it was, "Now Craig, I think this will. . ." He was as pointed as he could be in his advice. Now that I was officially his grandson he had gotten a little more direct. The other side of him that I saw that I had never seen was his incredible sense of humor. Sharp wit. The way he would tease and the limericks.

When I was the graduate assistant coach at UCLA for Gene Bartow my first year, I was making $156 a month. That's what I got because that was the scholarship check that they gave to the players. I lived in a room in a house. A lady had eight cats and five dogs. I had a 1960 Volkswagen, and I washed dishes from 6:45 to 9:15 a.m. That's where I got my meals, and then I went to practice.

A pretty famous coach named Bob Polk—the head basketball coach at Rice University—was good friends with Gene Bartow, and told him, "Hey look, I've got an opening for a full time assistant coach, do you have any recommendations?"

Coach Bartow said, "Well, Craig Impelman would be great for you, you ought to hire him." So Bob Polk called and wanted me to come down to Rice, and with Gene's blessing, leave UCLA to become a full-time assistant. It was going to be $19,000 a year with a car and an apartment, which looked like a lot compared to what I was getting. Polk wanted me to fly down there and check it out, which I didn't want to do unless I had a sincere interest in accepting the position. I didn't want to lead the guy on a wild goose chase.

I went to Larry Farmer, and in true Wooden style, Larry wouldn't tell me what to do. Where did he get that from, right? I was in a quandary, I didn't know what to do.

I told Coach Polk that I couldn't make up my mind and he said, "Well, you talk to Johnny Wooden. He'll tell you what to do."

So I talked to Coach. I didn't know him. I knew him from telling me I couldn't try out for the varsity, and I knew him from being a guy who was always walking around the office. That's as well as I knew him.

Coach first asked me what my goals were. I said, "Being a basketball coach." And then, of course, he told me that he couldn't tell me what to do. I felt like saying, "Yeah, Larry told me that, Coach!" It's all the same thing.

Coach Wooden says, "Well, you know, Craig, take a look at the head coaches in the Pac-8." He named all the head coaches in the Pac-8 and he went through their coaching records, where they worked before they became a head coach. He pointed out that they had all gone from one winning program to another winning program to another winning program. I didn't need a diagram, Rice at the time was struggling. He didn't have to draw the rest of the diagram up for me. I got done with that meeting, called Coach Polk, and thanked him for his interest but I was going to stay at UCLA.

I left coaching because I couldn't find another coaching job I wanted. I did it for nine years, and the first seven it went great. Win, win, win, win, win. The last years we lost, lost, lost. This was at Weber State in Ogden, Utah. To make a long story short, I didn't want to pack up my family and go to anywhere in the United States to get another coaching job. I wanted to develop other skills.

Coach never acts like he's better than anybody else, although he's a phenomenal celebrity. He stops and talks to everybody.

He gave me a signed photograph with a poem, I'm going to read it to you. I stop and look at this sometimes and I get tears in my eyes.

"For Craig Impelman on a very important day of your life in May of 1986." That's when our son, John Impelman was born.

A Little Fellow Follows Me

A careful man I want to be
A little fellow follows me
I do not dare to go astray
For fear he'll go the self-same way
I cannot once escape his eyes
Whatever he sees me do, he tries
Like me he says he's going to be
The little chap who follows me
He thinks that I am good and fine
Believes in every word of mine
The base in me he must not see
The little chap who follows me
I must remember as I go
Through summer sun and winter snow
I am building for the years to be
The little chap who follows me.

The original of this was presented to me in 1936 upon the birth of my son
and has been kept nearby since then.

John Wooden, UCLA

On the occasions that I've heard Coach allude to his father, the thing that I remember him talking about is how his father was a masseuse, and how kind and gentle he was about what he did. He never complained about what they didn't have. And I think that as Coach Wooden describes his father, he truly became the little fellow that followed him.

My parents, of course, and John Wooden before I knew Christy, shaped the philosophy around which I try to do things on a daily basis. My personal relationship with him since I married Christy has been great. It's great to see him with my son, Johnny. It's phenomenal, it's the best. It doesn't get any better. That's all that I can tell you.

NANCY MUELHAUSEN
Reseda, California

Nancy is John Wooden's daughter.

It was never difficult to be the daughter of John Wooden. I first realized that my father was something special in the eyes of other people when he was coaching at Indiana. He did very well in Indiana, which is a real basketball state. There was a lot of enthusiasm and excitement about him. He was thought of very highly. I was in junior high, seventh and eighth grade.

He didn't bring basketball home much. I always loved basketball since I was introduced to it at a very young age but I don't remember it dominating our home existence. We'd talk about a particular game but never anything in depth. Basketball never took Daddy away from family times together.

When we were very young, in South Bend and when Daddy was in the Navy, one of the highlights was every Sunday we went to Sunday school and church. I remember very special Sundays. After Sunday school and church we'd go to this little chicken place, called Howell's Chicken in the Rough, and had pieces of chicken, french fries and hot biscuits in a basket for fifty-cents. Then we would go to the Palace Theater in the afternoon. It was always something what we would now say was G-rated, never anything objectionable for the whole family.

When we came out here, the family liked to play together at little pitch-and-putt golf course in Holmby Hills. During basketball season we were pretty wrapped up with the games. That was when we played every Friday and Saturday night, so that would take care of a lot of our weekends. If they weren't here we would be by the radio. I had a social life of my own, but the games were just a part of my life. I wanted to be there, and I genuinely enjoyed watching basketball. There were times when my mother would be angry—if UCLA lost a game if she didn't feel we got a fair shake. Daddy never felt that way.

I don't remember ideals being laid down verbally by my parents; it was a matter of how they led their lives. Sometimes you read that people who are the children of famous people have difficult lives because of the fame of their parents, but that's not applicable in my situation.

One story that stands out in my mind was the only spanking I ever had. Daddy was stationed in Georgia during the war and I was in the fourth or fifth grade. We were over at the PX one time and I had seen a wrist watch that I really wanted. I don't know if I asked for it, but I had a feeling I was going to get this wrist watch.

A few months later, Mom and Daddy had some friends over for dinner. They handed me a little box for my birthday. It was a cameo ring. I thought it was going to be the wrist watch. I was very upset and I took it and I threw it and said that I wanted the wrist watch. (He had bought the wrist watch for me for Christmas.) Then I headed for my bedroom with my father on my tail. He came in the bedroom and closed the door and gave me a whack on the seat of my pants. Then he took a hold of my arm and told me how disappointed he was in what I had done, and that I was to go in and apologize to my mother and everybody at the table, which was the hardest thing in the world for me to do. I could have handled him just spanking me more than I could having to go in and apologize, but I did.

I never did get the wrist watch. Daddy took it back. And it was a long time before I got the ring back. I was robbed here about five years ago and the ring was taken, but I still wore it and loved the ring.

My father wasn't a particularly stern disciplinarian. I've heard that in families where there's a son and a daughter, the mother leans toward the son and the father is more lenient with the daughter and that was the case. There was discipline, it was just balanced out. Mother was stern with me and Daddy was stern with Jim. I know he's always honest with me. He's never told me what to do or how to live my life. I hate to disappoint him, but not because I'm fearful. I can't really explain it but I've thought about it a lot.

As I look back and see what my father has accomplished and the kind of satisfaction that he's had in his life, it's amazing. He's always very patient with everyone. I get very impatient sometimes when we're interrupted. My mother used to, too. But Daddy's always very patient with everyone and he said, "I don't mind doing this." I get tickled, too. Sometimes, it's amusing to sit back and watch. When we go to basketball games at Pauley, people will line up after the game if we stay, before the traffic is out. They want just to touch him or get an autograph or say "Hello" and "I knew you when" or something like that. I'm a great people watcher anyway and I can see them coming. As they get up a little closer they're going over what they're going to say. Then they get up there and you can see that they didn't say what they had planned to say and the look on them, saying to themselves, "Oh, dumb, dumb, he must really think I'm dumb. Why did I. . ." It's like the scene from *The Godfather*, when that character was practicing his speech.

He's almost mobbed when he goes out, and he certainly was when he was in the limelight and was seen on television. People still recognize him. We took him recently to the doctor's office for his checkup. They sent the paper work in and then the technician came out and said, "Well it is John Wooden." So evidently he'd seen it and thought, "Well, it can't be *the* John Wooden." And then he comes out, "Well it is *the* John Wooden." He was just flabbergasted.

Daddy gets a tremendous amount of mail. You can't let a day go by with his [mail] box. You've gotta go there every day or you'll never be able to get it in. And it's from all over the world. He gets fan letters from people who have followed his career. What amazes me is that there probably are as many women as there are men who write. He gets a lot from coaches asking questions.

Many people would ask for autographs and they wouldn't enclose any return envelopes. For a long time he put the postage on and would take it to the post office, but when he became more limited in his ability to get to the post office, he said if they didn't send something to return it in then he wouldn't take care of it.

He never talked to me about the Pyramid of Success. He might offer some advice that related to the Pyramid of Success, but not word for word. The Pyramid did affect me and there are certain aspects of it that I try to follow. I'm not always successful, but it's in my mind A lot of it makes sense. The creed that my grandfather gave me, makes sense, too. But it was never anything that was taught to me; I became more aware of it in later years when I've heard him speak.

My mother's family adored Daddy. They were very close and mother came from a very close family. I never knew her father, but my mother's mom lived to be in her eighties. She and Dad had a great relationship and my mother's sisters were very close with my Dad.

If I could change anything about my father, it would be his way of thinking that he's an imposition on us. We're settled in now and we love having him over for dinner or whatever we can do for him. That's what family is all about. I have no criticisms of him except I think he's hard on himself, which I don't think is justified, but you know the way he believes. He makes sure everything's always the best that it can be.

I can't remember Mother ever telling me why she married my father, other than it was just one of those things. She was attracted to him and grew to love him. In high school she signed up for the band, and played the cornet so she had good seats for the basketball game. Daddy would kid her, "You don't play that, you just hold it up to your lips."

I don't know if she played or not. She was very good on the ukulele, though. She was musically inclined and a very good dancer. Daddy never really liked to dance, and he has regrets sometimes now, as you always do, that he should have danced more because my mother loved it so. Daddy has very good rhythm, but mother used to turn and say she always felt like he was dribbling the ball. It was one of those chemistry things. They just hit it off and they were right.

He's a big tease. Sometimes he carries it a little too far, but he is teasing. He has a great sense of humor, we have a lot of fun. With his hip surgery, we kept the fun really light. We rented the movie, *Misery*. My husband, Dick, and I sat there on the bed with him the first week we brought him home. He'd say something to me and I'd go, "Listen Mr. Man, I bring you the pills, I put on your. . ." You know, we go through this routine. We have such a lot of fun.

And he'd say, "Oh, you kidder, you're such a kidder."

The extended family when they get all together is a great occasion. As my daughters keep having more and more children, it is hectic. I think Daddy handles it better than I do. I sometimes I think I'm going to run out for a walk or something because we've got all ages and it's a zoo but it's a lot of fun.

Daddy was a deacon at the First Christian Church in Santa Monica. The deacons served communion and passed the offering plates. He was a deacon in the church in South Bend as well. He also taught Sunday school. I see acts of kindness from Daddy every time we've gone out. He's very kind, very interested and patient. It's way he is. I don't see it as any particular, "I think I'll do an act of kindness" kind of thing. It's just the way he lives his life. He's just kind to people and considerate.

If he had a day all to himself to relax, he would probably go out to the cemetery, which we haven't been able to do for awhile. He'd write – he's working on a few things. If he hadn't seen some of the great-grandchildren in a few days, he'd want to see them. He'd catch up on his correspondence.

The greatest loss he suffered was when my mother died. The single biggest factor in his recovery was the birth of Cori. She was the first great-grandchild, and Mother knew that Caryn was expecting before she passed away. Jim and I were very concerned about him. He was very despondent. For a brief time he lost his will to live. We talked to Dr. Gary Kaye, who's a noted heart surgeon. Gary said, "Your dad would never take his own life. He's too strong a person." But Jim and I were concerned. That thought went into our head. The turnaround was when Cori was born. The day she was born, I was working at UCLA at the time and Caryn called me about five-thirty in the morning and told me that she thought she was in labor. As soon as it was nine o'clock, she was going to call her doctor and see if he wanted to see her.

So I said, "Well, honey, call me when you go to the doctor and let me know what's happening." And I hung up the phone. And then I thought, "I'm not going to work today, this is crazy." So I called her back, and I said, "Honey, Mother'll be right over." I took her to the doctor and the hospital was next door, and she had Cori three hours later. I called Daddy, who was speaking downtown, and he got there before Cori was born. We were very excited, and Daddy was very emotional. He is very close to all three of the girls, but Caryn particularly because Caryn was Mother's caregiver for two years after she came home from the hospital. She came every day and helped her with everything so there's a real special bond there.

I finally came home later in the afternoon. I was dating someone and Daddy said, "Well, I'll take you out to dinner to celebrate." We were getting ready to go out and the phone rang. It was Daddy. He said that he had a little problem, an accident on the freeway coming home from the hospital. His car was totaled, a big truck had hit him. I went right over and spent four hours over at Tarzana emergency while he was x-rayed and examined. The funny thing about it was Daddy said he was driving from the hospital, he was so pumped up, he was so excited, and as he stopped on the freeway he saw this big truck barreling down on him from behind. And he said, "Do you know the first thought that went through my mind. . ." At that single minute, that was the turnaround, he really wanted to live again. He said the thought that came through his mind was, "Well, a new one came in and an old one's going out."

From that time on, it changed. He wanted to live. He's also been enervated by the ability to go out and continue to speak to people and give his motivation talk. That's been very important, because he is a very, very active, vital person. He likes the feedback he gets from people. In his later years it means even more to him. He feels, "Well, I have done good." What he's always said is that he's a teacher getting feedback from his players. You don't appreciate the value of things when you're younger. His players have said that over and over again. It isn't until later, until they're raising children or pursuing a career or they you can start to think, "Yes, he really made sense." Fortunately, those things stick with you, they're still there, so the turnaround will eventually come. You haven't really lost it, you've got it and it's been there all the time, but maybe it wasn't very important to you until later.

My girls love Daddy, but there's more to it than that. There's a very profound, very deep respect for him. Cathleen was the last of the girls to have a baby, and she and Paul had wanted to wait, but she just said, "I want a child and our children to know my grandfather. I just don't want anything to happen to Papa. I want them to get to know him."

I had my father's parents and my mother's. It was really very special because I had friends who didn't have grandparents. I have close friends now who my mother and dad were grandparents to their kids. My friend Amy's father had passed away, and her children never knew their grandpa, so Daddy took over that role, too. Children have always loved him. When I was a little girl and I was with other children, they always loved my dad. He took an interest in them.

Children know when someone genuinely likes them or is putting it on. The next door neighbors' kids were always at our house. They couldn't wait for Daddy to come in the driveway. He truly enjoys the simple things in life, which includes playing with kids or talking to anybody anytime. He can get something out of almost any conversation. Cori and John, climb up on him and say, "Papa, let's talk about the old times." Some of it'll be fact, some of it'll be fiction, and they are just mesmerized with the story telling. They love to hear about the old times. I like to hear about the old times, too. Whether it's close, long-time friends or just the family, we love to go back and reminisce, and surely it doesn't have anything to do with basketball.

I can remember what a wonderful, gentle man my grandfather was. Daddy'll say over and over again, "Grandaddy never had an unkind thing to say to anyone. Nor did he ever complain about anything." You would ask him how he was and he'd reply, "Just glorious, just glorious," and his face would just beam. He passed away when I was in high school. He was a very good person who worked very, very hard, a lot. He was an attendant at the Homelawn Sanitarium in Martinsville where wealthy people came for mineral baths, and his salary largely depended on tips, which is why my dad is a very generous tipper. And, of course, Daddy put himself through school, by being a waiter.

One eccentricity about my father is that he refuses to stop and ask for directions. Finally, he'll realize he's lost. Another is driving on the freeway. He tries to see how far he can go in the car on a tank of gas. I don't know if he ever runs out. And he is scared of big dogs.

My parents were both non-economically oriented. Daddy said one time he and Mother both had a fear they never wanted to ever be totally financially dependent on their children. Of course, Jim and I laugh that they didn't want that because they'd starve to death! I never thought of us as deprived. We didn't have a whole lot of things materially, but we always had money. I wanted to take piano lessons, and they had money for that at the teacher's college I went to. They furnished the instruments and I played the violin.

Roxie Wooden, my grandmother, didn't pass away until after I was married. She was a real good person. Daddy said her heart was broken. Daddy had two sisters who did not live. One died at birth and one died when she was three years old. Daddy said over the years that he doesn't think grandma ever got over losing her daughters. She was a good mother. That's the only thing I really remember him ever saying. He was close to his mother. Uncle Cat was the oldest, and Daddy was next. There was three years difference. Daddy said that he weighed twelve pounds when he was born, and only weighed fifteen pounds when he was a year old because Cat was born first he was still nursing, so Daddy kids that he didn't get much.

Nancy Muelhausen, Coach's daughter, 1991.

CATHLEEN TRAPANI
Los Angeles, California

Cathleen is another of John Wooden's granddaughters.

My earliest memories of my grandpa—we call him "Papa"—is that he's always been there. I still see my father occasionally, but my dad left when I was young and my grandparents were always there. He had a big impact on my life. He's always been very giving and loving and positive. He never says anything bad about anybody ever. Never. When I would get mad about something, I'd hear, "Honey, now that's not nice. If you can't say anything nice don't say anything about them." He finds everybody's good points but not the bad. He's never said a harsh word about anyone that I've ever heard. I've seen him get mad, but he's very calm and he's very patient. Mad wouldn't be a good word, I'd say maybe slightly irritated. I've never really seen him angry. Never.

Most people know who he is and most people admire him. He gave me away at my wedding and I have a picture of it in my office. There was a guy in here recently who was enrolling his daughter at the nursery school I supervise, and he said, "I saw him up at Coco's and I sat down and joined him for his lunch and he was just so nice. I just couldn't believe I saw him." They know who he is. People know of him because of being a coach, but as they know more of him, it's just because of the way he is.

He never brought coaching home. I think he lives by the Pyramid of Success. What he has written on it just fits him to a T, but he never sat down and talked about it. At home we talked about family and what was going on in our lives. He didn't talk about the games. The games weren't important to him. He enjoyed the practices much more than the games.

He won his first championship the year I was born. When he was winning during those years, he was always calm. My grandmother and my mother would be nervous and uptight during those times and during games. I don't think my mother watched half the games because she sat with her hand over her eyes and her knees shaking through the whole game. When it was an important game, she didn't watch. We all sat together. My grandmother, when she was watching the games, would get irritated. I've seen my grandmother mad. She was very feisty and Papa used to call her that. I remember him telling her, "Oh, Nellie, calm down. It's okay, Nellie, it's okay," and patting her constantly.

She'd say, "Oh, that just makes me so mad!" And he would tell her it was her Irish temper. But she was the one who would get real upset and he was always the calming person. Always.

She was pretty quiet during the games. We'd hear about it after the game, how unfair it was, and my grandpa would say, "Well, you know, Nellie, I think it was pretty fair. That's their job and that's why there's more than one ref."

When I was little and used to go to his practices, he'd take me to a 31 Flavors and we would have lemon custard ice creams and go sit on the grass under the trees and eat them. I will always remember that. That was such a special time.

He's always been so proud of us, his grandchildren. There are things that we've done that I know he hasn't agreed with. I lived with Paul before I got married. Both my sisters had done the same thing. It was our life and he never said a word. You'd know what would disappoint him so you don't want to do it because he would never say that it bothered him.

When Paul and I lived together he would come over to the house and say, "Oh, honey. . ." We bought the house in January and we got married in August. We were engaged before we lived together, but we got married on my grandparents' anniversary, on August 8th. My grandpa gave me away. My grandmother had already passed away. We had asked him if that would be okay if we got married on their anniversary. So every anniversary we spend with him.

He would come in the house and he would say, "Oh, everything looks nice," but he would never go in our bedroom. He wouldn't even peek in there. He wouldn't say anything. He'd say, "Oh gee, Paul, are you sleeping on the couch?"

When we were married, we'd gotten back from our honeymoon and he had my niece, Cori. He used to watch her quite a bit for my sister when my sister was working. He had her the whole day and drove out to our house. We had been married about two weeks. He came over with Cori who was two at the time and was just a ball of fire. He said, "Oh, I'm just exhausted."

I said, "I'll take Cori and our dog and we'll go for a walk, Papa. Why don't you lay down?" So Cori and I went for a walk and I came back and I looked in the living room and he's not in there. I'm looking all over and he's not anywhere. I go in my bedroom and he's asleep on our bed. And I said to him, "Oh, now that we're married you can come into our bedroom."

And he said, "Yes, honey, now you are married I can come into your bedroom."

It was a tremendous blow when my grandmother died. He was very sad, still is I think. I think he always will be. I've never seen anything like that, the bond they had, the attachment that they had. Because my sister was pregnant at that time, that's what kept him going. That was with Cori, to whom he's got a special attachment. It was something he had to look forward to. His family is pretty much everything. He just loves his great-grandchildren.

My mom was pretty much the disciplinarian. Papa didn't live with us, but he was there to take us to do things that like we didn't get to do with my father. He spent a lot of time with us.

I remember when he was coaching, we had a lot of players over at our house and at my grandparents' house for holidays. There were always players around the table at Christmas and Thanksgiving, mostly because they couldn't afford to fly home. One of them was Kareem. I was real little because he gave me a shoulder ride and I had to go outside. He had to duck to get in our house.

Papa is a big tease. He'll tease all the time. I would get my feelings hurt and cry and my grandmother would say, "John, you just tease too far and you just upset the girls!" He would tease, tease, tease, which is why he and Paul get along. It runs in the family among the men.

When the family all gets together, Papa pretty much sits in the background and watches. He enjoys seeing everyone together.

We were at a restaurant one time with my mom and my grandfather, and a man walked up and said to him, "You look a great deal like John Wooden. I don't know if anyone's ever told you that, but you really resemble him. I'm a really good friend of his and I know you're not him." And he walked away.

I was laughing so hard, and I said, "Well, why didn't you say something?" He said, "Because he's a good friend of John Wooden."

It was just like grandpa to kind of nod, never saying, "That's me." It was just hysterical, we were laughing so hard.

We never saw much in the way of ego from him. He never expected anything. He never would say, "Oh, it'll be nothing to win this championship." He used to always say, "Failing to prepare is preparing to fail." He says that all the time.

I wasn't a big basketball fan when I was growing up. I used to go and draw pictures. We did an interview one year with the whole family, and they asked me what I did on Friday and Saturday nights.

I said, "I color with my crayons." And they went, "Cut! Wait a minute! That's when they play the basketball games."

And I said, "Well I am at the games, but I color with my crayons."

The guy was going, "Cut! Cut! She can't say that!"

And my grandpa said, "But that's what she does." You know, what's the difference? I was little. But I didn't really watch. I didn't get interested until I got older and would go to the games with him. And we still go with him to games. When we go, he's very quiet. He doesn't say anything. My husband usually sits next to him and asks, "Why this, why this?" It's hard for him at the games. He is just bombarded with people. My grandfather would never say no to anyone.

THE JOHN WOODEN PYRAMID OF SUCCESS

If they ask him for an autograph or ask to speak with him, he never says no.

One time I got up to go to the bathroom and I came back and there was some man sitting in my seat, so I scooted over a little next to him cause the guy sat there the whole game. And I said to my grandpa, "Who was that?"

And my grandpa said, "Honey, I just don't know."

"Well what was he doing there?"

He said, "Well, he was just visiting with me."

I mean, the whole game he sat there! He never asked him to leave, he just wouldn't. I'm thinking, the guy's talking and he introduced himself to me, I don't remember his name, but he shook my hand. So I'm thinking, "Oh yeah, this must be an old friend."

There haven't been any real crises he had to weather other than my grandmother's death. I've seen him handle the advancing of age and what comes with it. You see a lot of people get frustrated and I don't see that in him. He used to walk five miles a day. He did that rain or shine, wherever he was. He was walking at Balboa Park at four o'clock in the morning one time when my grandmother was in the hospital, and the police pulled him over and made him get in the car and took him home. They told him not to walk around Balboa Park at that time in the morning.

They said, "Coach, get in the car."

And he said, "No, no, no, I'm doing my walking."

And they said, "Get in the car. This is not safe. You don't walk about Balboa Park at four in the morning." So they took him home. They said, "If you're gonna walk, walk around your complex."

I don't ever see him in a bad mood. Since my grandmother died, I'll see him sad, in a depressed mood, but not grumpy or grouchy.

WILLIAM HUGH "BILL" WOODEN
LaPorte, Indiana

Bill is John Wooden's youngest brother.

I'm twelve years younger than John, and the youngest in the family. I was about five when he was in college. As a freshman, he had to wear a little green beanie cap. And as soon as he could get rid of that cap which I envied, he gave it to me. My folks thought just as highly of him as they did of the rest of us. He didn't stand out amongst the family though because of the basketball success. If Brother Cat were here, he'd be glad to tell you that he was a much better ball player than John was. They were both outstanding.

What I find interesting about my brother is his influence on other people. He never tried to put on airs or showed off. He was more interested in other people than himself. He made them feel important, willing to do their best. He had concern for me all his life. His freshman numerals letter I admired so much. Mother was always doing something trying to make extra money. She was an excellent seamstress. She took his freshman sweater and cut it out for me so I could have a sweater to wear to school. I was proud of that. I have a picture of myself in the second grade, and I have this black sweater on. I have a picture of our third grade class, and I had that sweater on. I have a picture of our fourth grade and I had that sweater on. So I wore it all through elementary school. Mother made whatever adjustments and patches where needed. I wore it for years. I must have worn it every day, 'cause every picture that was taken, I had that sweater on.

I've tried to live up to [John's] standards. He always showed a lot of concern for the family and made many sacrifices. All four of us Wooden boys married our high school sweethearts. We all grew up in Martinsville, all eight of us. And our wives were in the band and we'd be there at the games together.

John and Cat put on a show all the time. They'd go to a carnival, and they'd have these "shoot the free throw" contests. They'd make an awkward pass. The fellow would persuade them to invest their money, and then they'd take their coat off and sink free shot after free shot. After they got prizes for everybody, finally the guy would try to get rid of them.

Dad and I and Dan, if he was available, would go to Indianapolis and see the [Kautsky] games. The players were very large in those days , most were bigger than John was, and played just as rough in those days, if not rougher. They'd try to take John out early because he was a prolific scorer and if they could eliminate his scoring potential, they'd have a better chance of winning.

John couldn't find a teaching position in the whole state of Indiana. This is 1932, the Depression. Schools were not hiring new teachers. They weren't even paying the teachers they had. Here he was, an All-American three years running, the first three year All-American ever. He set Big-Ten scoring records playing as a back guard, who aren't supposed to score. He was captain of his team. He had an undefeated season, and his team was national champion. He had offers. I remember people coming to our house and trying to talk him into these various jobs and to do commercials. Lucky Strike cigarettes always had a big name. A baseball player would win the game by hitting a home run, then they'd say, "After a home run, I always light up a Lucky." They wanted to use John's name in a commercial and he absolutely refused. He didn't smoke. He felt it would be the wrong example for his players, so he turned down the money. Hollywood offered him a job. They wanted him to make a picture on basketball. He turned that down, too, 'cause he wanted to teach.

Many of the college athletes went on to star. He talked to Piggy Lambert about it. Piggy told him, what did he get his education for? So he could teach. He answered his own question about what he should do, but he couldn't teach in Indiana, so he got a job at this little school in Kentucky.

When I was in the sixth grade, during the Depression, Martinsville discontinued all sports except basketball. They wanted to have a sixth grade basketball team. The school didn't have any equipment. They said, "Well, we'll have to have uniforms." They cost something like four dollars for the basketball pants and four dollars for a shirt. If you wanted to be on the team, you had to buy your pants and your shirt. That was more money than my dad made in a week. He made one dollar a day, working twelve hours a day. I peddled newspapers and that sort of thing. I mowed grass, but then we'd only get a quarter or so for mowing the yard. And I couldn't afford it either, so I was beside myself.

Lo and behold, Brother John came through with that money so I could be on the basketball team. It's been that way all my life. I was plagued with a bad throat before I could talk, just a baby in my mother's arms. I had my first siege and my throat would swell bigger than my head. And it would be infected with tonsillitis. They despaired for me. When my mother was holding me, the blood and the pus burst out through my skin and dribbled out on her shoulder. The doctor said I was fortunate. If it had burst on the inside, I never would have pulled through. I still have the scars on my neck. Every year I'd get this bad case of tonsillitis and become delirious. I'd just be out of it and I'd miss school every year because of it. That displeased me because I liked school. It was the one thing I could do, and I did well in it. When Brother John went to South Bend, he talked to a man about my condition. I never worried, it was just something I put up with, that I'd had all my life. The man said he'd have to examine me, and that probably my tonsils and adenoids should be removed. So Brother John came to Martinsville and brought my mother and me back up to South Bend. We go see the doctor and he convinces me that I can get rid of those bad throats if I'd let the doctor take care of it. I didn't know what I was getting into, but I reluctantly agreed. I had second thoughts as I was being given the ether though, and Brother John said I gave him a black eye, then they belted me down to the operating table so I couldn't resist anymore. The doctor cut out my tonsils and adenoids. Oh, I had the sorest throat. I'm perhaps a freshman in high school at this time. I wasn't interested in food of any kind, and the only carbonated beverage Nell had on hand was ginger ale. So I'd sip a little bit of that. It was horrible stuff, and to this day I don't like the taste of ginger ale. That was just an example of how John was looking out for me, but he does that for everybody.

On another occasion, when I was an elementary school student and he was in college, I was playing with some friends at a house that was being constructed. Some older boys walking down the alley decided that we were on their turf. They picked big stones up out of the alley and threw them half a block away to the corner where the house was being built. Everybody dashed for cover so that we could hide as the missiles flew through the air. It was to them probably just a game, but unfortunately, one of them hit me right in the mouth, broke off my two front teeth and cut my upper lip so that I don't have control over it today because of all the scar tissue on the inside of it. Brother John came home that weekend and they went looking for the boys who were responsible for that. If they'd caught them, I hesitate to think how it would have turned out.

At the elder hostel where I just visited, when they discovered that he was my brother, they wanted to talk about John. They were from all over the country. Whenever I mention my last name, people say, "Are you?" and I say, "I am." And they say, "You're not!" They want to know if he's as nice a fellow as they think. And of course I couldn't say anything bad about him. None of us ever used profanity of any kind, which I think is rare among the coaching fraternity. Can you imagine Bobby Knight—opposite person, completely. Yet he's had success. Of course he's driven many other people away. Larry Bird, started at Indiana University and transferred to Indiana State in Terre Haute. Indiana University is in Bloomington, which is only fifty miles from his home, but he didn't want to put up with [Bobby Knight] and didn't have to, so he went to State and took them to national prominence.

I can recall John coming home because Dad and Mother never had a car, and I was too young to drive. They'd come home whenever they could and take Dad and Mom wherever they wanted to go. Before she died, Mother wanted to go back to North Carolina and trace her roots. One summer they took us out there. When John would come home, he and Nell would get my room, and I'd sleep on the floor on a pad the way I did for years, because we always rented out the bedrooms to try to make some extra money.

I never felt any jealousy because he had such success and fame. Heavens no, when I was around him you couldn't tell he was successful. I didn't know he was famous. No, indeed, he was just my brother. Glad to be around. I never saw him brag. The worst time he went through was the death of his wife. Nell was a buffer for the outside world. John would stop and talk to anybody at any time. Whatever they wanted, why John would go to it. Nell would realize that they couldn't do that, and was a buffer to move him along. He missed that. Nell went to every game he ever coached. When the team went, Nell went. She'd go on the road. She packed his suitcase, and told him what clothes to wear. From Dayton on, she saw every game. That's one reason why [for many years] he never went to a NCAA tournament after Nell died. He'd be alone, and that would bring back all those memories of when she was with him on the road.

They had great fun when they went on the road. They never smoked, never drank. The hotels where they stayed would have a complimentary basket—he'd like a bowl of fruit. It got so they'd always have a bowl of fruit for him. When we'd come to visit, "Here, take some fruit," he'd say.

I don't think my seven kids realized how important he was. He was just a member of the family, just like any one of their other uncles. Brother Cat was far more of a showoff than John was.

All the brothers were close and would always try to outdo each other. Brother Cat ended up as principal of West Covina High School. Brother John would come storming into the office, "Who's in charge of this school?"

The secretary would cower, "Well, Mr. Wooden is!"

"Well, I want to see that so and so!"

Brother Cat would come out of the office to see what the racket was, and they'd laugh over it. Brother Cat would reciprocate when he'd go to UCLA. He'd give the girls in the outer office a hard time. The girl offered to see if Coach Wooden was available but who should she say was calling? Brother Cat said, "Tell him that the oldest, the smartest, the best looking of the Woodens is here." That was when Brother John came out and said, "He got one out of the three right." John and Nell and Cat and Thelm were out there in California so they would do a lot of things together. If they went to a carnival, Cat and John would vie with each other to see which one could hit the hammer the hardest or whatever it was. They loved playing pool, too. They'd slow up a little bit until somebody would challenge them to a game. Then they'd get down and dirty.

Our father was his biggest influence on him, and on all of us. He was just a man of outstanding talents and ability. Very intelligent. He would work a crossword puzzle—they were so easy for him that he'd dream up new ways of doing it. For instance, he'd do it in a spiral form until he'd end up putting the last letter right in the middle of it or something like that.

Any game you could mention he could play. I watched him play checkers, and I was no challenge for him. He would give away most of his men and then beat me. For recreation, after a day's work, they'd either gather in the back end of the funeral home around the card table or in the back end of the fire station where firemen sat out on chairs on the hot summer days with the card table. Dad was always welcome because he could play any game they were playing.

Dad was not much of an athlete. He was taller than any of the boys. He was over six-foot, the only one. I was the shortest one of the bunch, five-foot-nine in my prime, and I've shrunk since then. Brother Dan was about an inch bigger, and Cat and John were about an inch bigger than him. They had bigger hands than me. My hands are shaped just like my father's, but his were two inches longer. He was a farmer, but he did many other things besides farming. Brother John could palm a basketball. I never could. Usually it takes a big man to do that.

Father was not frustrated by not having made more money. Money wasn't important. Be happy with what you've got, that's the saying. He'd lost the farm in bad luck, cholera wiped out the hogs, drought got the crops, but he just picked himself up and went on. In Martinsville, he got a job working for the sanitarium. The sanitarium was like a health spa. This mineral water boiled up in Martinsville. They were drilling for oil in the mid-1800s, and instead of oil they got this foul smelling water. They left it and an old racehorse started drinking it, so they decided, "Well, it might be all right." [The horse] got invigorated and acting up, and they started racing him again. They decided, well if it's good for beasts, it ought to be good for man, so some enterprising fellow built a hotel there and invited the people in. They had literature about the invigorating waters. It's still going. At one time they had nine of these sanitariums flourishing, but they've all burned down now, there's not a one left.

The Homelawn was the largest, for the most affluent guests. They had their own dairy farm and their own garden produce, a staff of four doctors on the premises, a beautiful cafeteria, a bowling alley in the basement, landscaped lawns, stained glass windows, a beautiful lobby. All four of the girls who married Woodens worked as telephone operators at the Homelawn. Isn't that a coincidence? And Dad ended up there. It was the last one in business.

Dad never complained about his work. I never heard him complain in his whole life. Mom always had complaints, and many of them were based in fact. She had internal troubles and had operations and very bad feet. She couldn't afford shoes, so she'd wear shoes that somebody else would give her and they wouldn't fit her feet, so her feet were deformed and very uncomfortable.

The summer he died was 1950. Mom wasn't feeling good, and so they put her in the hospital. Dad was so weak that he couldn't climb the steps to go in the hospital. He couldn't drag himself up those steps. He was the one who should have been in the hospital rather than her, but he never complained. He wanted to work until he died. And he almost made it, but not quite.

I went down that summer and stayed with him. We were in and out of the hospital, and the doctor said it wouldn't be long. I told my brothers, and they all dropped whatever they were doing and came to Martinsville. We all were there when Dad died. It was one of the few times after John had gone to California that all of us were together. When mom died nine years later, in 1959, that was next time that we were all together. Nan, John's daughter, thought we ought to get together at a happier occasion instead of a funeral, so she invited us to her house. Cat was just a few miles away, but I drove to New Mexico and picked up Dan and Phyll, and we went to California together and just had a ball. We were trying to outdo each other. Poor Nan was beside herself, trying to put up with us. She declared absolutely never would she have four Wooden boys in the same house at the same time!

The funniest Wooden brother, no doubt about it, is me. And they'll all say the same thing. Oh, John possibly could be. We all have a good sense of humor. Here's a typical anecdote. Cat and John stopped at this big restaurant in Texas. For the first time in their lives, they saw a urinal mounted down at a lower level. As they were using the man sized levels, they look at that one, and finally one said to the other one, "They must have some pretty short men around here." And the other one looked over and said, "Yes, or else some mighty big ones." It was always that type of thing. Each one trying to outdo the other one. One would make a funny remark, and the other one would top him.

The legacy that Brother John has left to basketball is be a nice guy whether you win or lose. You don't have to put aside your ethical and moral standards just for the sake of winning. John Wooden is an unusual man with outstanding accomplishments. He seems so normal and natural. There's nothing outstanding about his appearance. His language is quiet and well thought-out. He has a wonderful vocabulary and expresses himself well. In short, he's a model that if more people emulated, we'd have a better world.

CARLEEN WOODEN
Irvine, California

Carleen is married to Jim Wooden, John Wooden's son.

John Wooden didn't mean anything to me before I met Jim. He wasn't really famous at that point. That's before all his championships and I wasn't really a sports fan at that time.

I met my husband in 1961. We were married the next year. Jim really didn't say much about John. He was a regular dad. He just said he was a coach for UCLA.

When Jim and I started to date seriously, I met his dad and his mom and we had dinner at their house. Jim brought me over to say, "This is my girlfriend, and I like her a lot." It was a very home-cooked meal. My mother-in-law made you feel very at ease. So did my father-in-law. It was a family get together, and I felt very comfortable. She had early American furniture, it was very warm.

His mom checked me out pretty seriously. She drilled me pretty good. I became pretty good friends with her. She was a very likable person. We felt very comfortable. I was impressed by the very homey environment. They were easy to talk to, very poised and polite and interested in other people. I was a little nervous when I went over there but they put me at ease.

Nell would occasionally have a glass of wine, like Nan and I and Jim. She needed to relax. She was on the hyper side, let's put it that way. She'd tip the glass. That was it. She wouldn't have more than that. She would enjoy it at dinner occasionally.

Having John Wooden as an in-law is exciting. For not liking sports, I really got into it over the years. I decided I liked it, with the family cheering and the whole bit, getting upset if we were behind and excited if we were ahead. It was really great.

Nell was very nervous at a game. So was Nan. When I first experienced one of the really close games, sitting there, I could smell this strong odor. It was smelling salts. I thought, "Where is this coming from?" Nell would sit right next to me and I would see her sniffing on this, and I thought, "What was happening?" She was afraid she was going to faint, so she's smelling the salts. Nan in back of me would be hiding her face in her lap. I just felt, "Is this what I want to go through?" Nan would cover her face instead of watching the game. She was so afraid of losing I guess. I was a little more at ease, but when we got to the championship games I could see where it would get to you if you really want to win.

It may have been difficult for Jim to be in the shadow of John Wooden. He went into the Marine Corps right from high school. He might have been compared, and I think it was hard. He may not admit it, but I really think it was. People expect you to follow in the same footsteps if your dad has a big name.

I know the Pyramid of Success. We've got copies in our den and the children all have them, personalized. They try to follow that as closely as they can. I think he's given them all that impression. The children don't all go to church, but Dad is a very religious man. To me, you don't need to go to church every Sunday to prove that you're a good person.

Dad has always been very close to the family, especially after we had children. He was so proud of his first grandson. He wanted to carry Greg all the time and tease him. He loved to tease the kids when they were little.

John Wooden was always generous, but he saved and worked hard. He always expected you to work hard for what you have. Industriousness. Jim is too much that way. He's a workaholic, my husband. Too much like his dad in that direction because he overworks. He puts too much time in. He'll always quote and say, "Well, Dad said it takes hard work to get where you want to go."

Jim's a family man, and he gives all the children time. He's always understanding, and a little hot-headed like his mom. They're Irish. My mother-in-law was very sweet, but she did, on the spur of the moment, get a little riled up over games. Dad Wooden is more mellow. He takes things a little bit laid back, and is not as feisty.

The only time I ever saw John Wooden lose his temper was at the basketball games. I've never seen him lose his temper at home. Dad Wooden is a little more patient than Jim. Jim takes things a little harder, more so than his dad.

John Wooden is an extraordinary man, a very warm, loving and caring person. He gives his all, and he's a real family man. You feel comfortable being around him. There's something special about him, his reliability, stability and overall kindness. He's a very kind person, very gentle. He has a very soft-spoken way about him. To a certain degree he's almost a shy person. That shyness somehow makes him warm. He's a very respectable man. He never says anything bad about anyone. I had no idea when I married Jim Wooden what I was getting into. It's nice to have a famous father-in-law. It's been exciting, that's for sure. When we visited Indianapolis for a Final Four tournament, we went to Elmo's Steak House, a hangout for all the athletes and all the fans noticed Dad Wooden was there. After dinner as we left, each room of diners and everyone in the bar gave him a standing ovation as we walked out. The entire restaurant just clapped as hard as they could and kept yelling, "Coach! Coach Wooden!" He just took it with a "Thank you." I think the family was more impressed.

He means so much to so many people. You don't realize until you're around sports fans, especially. He's well loved. It's because of his poise, his being a coach, and he's not prejudiced, he treats them all the same. It's because of his love for the game, his love for the players, and not just in sports. Each player means a lot to him above sports. He's so impressed if they become a lawyer, a minister, and if they're happy. He wants to know, too. He likes to follow them. He just wants to see them happy, to believe in God and be a good person. That's what he wishes for his family and friends.

It was interesting to watch my kids realize who John Wooden was. They're impressed, that's for sure. Now when he comes over to visit, they really enjoy talking to him and talking sports. They could spend hours in front of the TV. Sometimes I like to visit and he's just watching television, all the sports, whatever's on. He loves baseball, too. When we visit Jim's Dad's house, he'll have the TV in the den and we'd be talking there and the sports would be on, football or baseball, clicking it back and forth to other games.

I can see a lot of Dad Wooden in Jim's ways. My husband works too hard. That's part of Dad Wooden in him to a certain degree. There's no substitute for work. The harder you work, the better. Marriage to Dad Wooden was a real closeness, and I feel my husband and I have that also. We're very close and family oriented. Jim Wooden puts his family first. He's always treated me with respect and we've always been real close. I think that had a lot of influence there. They talk a lot.

When I mention my name, people say, "Oh, just like the Coach."

And I'll say, "That's my father-in-law."

And they say, "Oh no, it can't be." They're real excited, and they come out and say that he's a great man and that they're really proud of UCLA, so it's nice.

It's like being part of a dynasty. In Las Vegas in the lobby of the hotel, Dad Wooden was visiting with Jim and I, waiting for Nan to come down. We were going to have lunch. There were so many older persons who would stand and look and try to get the courage up to come over and say "Hi" or shake his hand. When they shake his hand they say that they've followed him over the years and they're very impressed to meet him, and want to find out how he's feeling and how he's doing.

Another man came over who wanted to promote sterling silver coins with Dad Wooden's face on it. Dad said he's just not interested. They go on and on, "Well, you know, we could make some money doing this," but he goes, "Nope, not interested." A lot of people want to promote his name. In a sense it's sad that everybody's trying to use his name. And John Wooden's not trying to promote his own name.

THE JOHN WOODEN PYRAMID OF SUCCESS

DANIEL J. WOODEN
High Rolls, New Mexico

Daniel was John Wooden's younger brother.

I'm seven years younger than John Wooden, my brother. I was a little squirt who tried awfully hard to play basketball but I was awfully small. I didn't get to grow up too much with him. I took care of my little brother, Bill, who is five years younger than me. He and I were together most of the time and John was with Cat because there was only three years between those two. By the time I got up to any size at all they were all gone.

Over the years we had a very good relationship. He was always looking after his younger brothers. I always thought he was going to go off to have the success that he had because of our upbringing. And he had the natural ability of an athlete. Our upbringing was very Christian. Our father was a person who never spoke an ill word against anyone at any time. He never cussed a word. He chewed tobacco a little. He smoked a cigar every once in awhile. We all attended church.

I remember my brother falling in love with Nell. He started leaving chewing gum on the side of a building every night if he saw her, spelling out her name. My younger brother started doing the same thing when he got up old enough to do it. Her folks were very nice people.

When John came home from school he mostly worked. When he graduated from high school and started college he was between five-foot-ten and five-foot-eleven, weighing 180-185 pounds. He worked during the summers, unloading coal cars and cement out of boxcars, and on the highway. He was industrious. He never got into trouble much as a kid, none of us ever did. When the family got together, we played cards primarily and visited with each other. Back in those days it was Euchre and what they called 7-Up.

I can remember one instance when the big boys weren't home. This was after I was married, but we were at my mother's house on Sunday evening in the summertime and the Baptist minister came by. All the windows were up because we had no air conditioning in those days, and we heard the Baptist minister preaching against the evils of playing cards on Sunday. It made my mother very unhappy, because she said at least she knew where her boys were. They were at home with her.

My parents were very proud of John. My dad was the one who gave John much that he lived by and taught—which he did to all of us, of course—and that was that you always tried to help everyone. You never did anything against anyone. You never tried to be better than anyone. He told us to just try and be the best we could be. John did not have an active social life as a kid. He was concentrating on his school work and working and being with his family.

Everyone looked at me and wanted me to be the same thing, and of course you can't. People expected me to be just like him and I wasn't. I couldn't be. I wasn't the size and didn't have the natural ability that he had.

His Pyramid of Success is very good. Many people have wanted it and I have written for them to him and he has sent it to them, and they appreciate it. Once in awhile I run into somebody and the first thing they come up with, is "Wooden, are you any. . ." and I say, "Yes I am." That's about as quick and as fast as you can get it.

My brother is a good Christian person who is always trying to do something for someone else. There's nothing about him I would change. He was very devoted to Nell, but that's no different from the rest of us. We were brought up that way. We take care of our wives. They're the best things of our lives.

The Wooden family in Martinsville had a pretty happy home. We didn't have much, but we were happy. The two older boys got to go to college and get degrees on athletic abilities. My younger brother got a sports scholarship, then switched to academics. Billy got his degree through academic scholarship. And I went to school working and on a Lion's Club scholarship.

Cat was the first one out, because he was three years older than John. He went to Franklin College in Franklin, Indiana. He graduated from there and coached basketball in two small schools, in southern Indiana and went from Ben Davis High School in Indianapolis to New Mexico State Teachers' College in Silver City, as the basketball coach. He wound up there in 1949 as the registrar. Then he went to California, where he was principal of the West Covina High School, which was a new high school that had just started when he died. He and John were very close. They were together most of the time every summer.

JIM WOODEN
Irvine, California

Jim is John Wooden's son and youngest child.

My earliest recollections of my father are when we lived in South Bend before the war, when Dad was teaching and coaching at South Bend Central. I remember our house, our neighbors, and when the war broke out and Dad joined. I was born in 1936 and Dad joined in 1941, so I was five years old. We moved. We followed Dad every place that he went in his service career. He enlisted. He thought it was the thing to do, and he went to officers' training. The first place we went to was Iowa City, Iowa.

Dad joined the Navy. He ended up being involved in training pilots, not to fly, but physical training. He went from Iowa to Williamstown, Massachusetts, where he was in training and in school. His first duty station was St. Simon's Island, Georgia. We lived through a hurricane. We lost the family house during the war because he couldn't make the mortgage payments. It got tough. The people they'd rented it to were reneging on the payments. He went back once and they'd sawed the stairs down that went down to the basement and just literally destroyed the house.

His last duty station after Georgia was Chicago, Illinois. He was based on an aircraft carrier on Lake Michigan. The U.S.S. Sable was an aircraft carrier used for training. He didn't want us living in Chicago so he moved us back to South Bend. Mom and I and Nancy lived in a little place behind a house. It was basically a kitchen, a bathroom, a bedroom, and a little bit of a living room.

We didn't see much of Dad during the war because he was in Chicago and we were in South Bend. When the war ended, we ended up going to Terre Haute, where he took a job at Indiana State Teachers' College. He was real busy then, too. He was the basketball coach, baseball coach, and athletic director.

We lived right across the street from [the college]. When he was there, he also was going to school and getting his master's. He would take me to ball games and we would do things, but he was always pretty darn busy. I felt I got enough time from him, though. We were close. Our whole family was close. Before and after the war, we took vacations and we went up into Michigan.

I don't think there has been a handicap being the son of John Wooden. If there was any, I would have put it on myself, but it really wasn't there. When I was in high school, he hadn't won any championships but he was coaching at a major university and people did know who John Wooden was and that he had won tournaments. As a matter of fact, it was great. I and some of the team members used to go up and watch practice when we could. My mom used to make a pre-game meal for us when we were playing, like a training table for some of my friends. Dad could never come and see me play, because his practices were always basically the same time our games were, and my Dad didn't miss practice very often. Also, in those times, the only time they could see high school teams play was during tournament play.

He saw me play in one tournament. It would have bothered me to know he was there, because I was real self-conscious. I was a decent basketball player, but nothing outstanding, and I did play regularly for two years. We had good basketball teams. I went to University High and we won the city my senior year. I had some good genes helping me. At the first house that Dad bought in West Los Angeles, we put a backboard up and used to have some good games out there. We almost had a half-court in our back yard. We shot a lot of hoops.

A lot of people ask the question, "Oh, are you related to John Wooden?" And I'd say, "Yes." And then a good majority of the time, it's, "Oh." It's not that I've encountered many situations when I felt people were unfairly talking to me in an attempt to get through to my father. Naturally I am very proud of my Dad and even more proud of him as a man than as a coach. Many times when people would connect the two and find out I was his son, the first thing would be, "Why are you doing what you're doing? Why aren't you a coach?" My reply always is, "Well, my dad's dad was a farmer. Why wasn't my dad a farmer?" I'm just doing my own thing. It would have been very hard if I had been a good basketball player and had the grades to get into UCLA, so in a way I was fortunate not to have to followed his footsteps.

My father is an extraordinary person because of his ways and the way he's modeled his life. I don't know anybody who practices what he preaches more than he does. He just doesn't say it. He does it. That's really extraordinary.

I never felt that it was too much to live up to. I really wasn't a rebel, a bad kid. I was a mediocre student, but I wasn't in trouble. I did things that normal kids do. When I graduated from high school, instead of going right to college, I joined the Marine Corps. That could be a type of rebellion because at the time a lot of people were asking, "Where you going to college? Are you going to play college basketball? What are you going to do?" A lot of people knew that I wasn't good enough and a lot of them were friends of my family's or people who weren't interested in me. Maybe you would call that rebelling, but I don't ever regret what I did. I joined the Marine Corps for four years, got out, went on with my life, went back to school. That naturally surprised everybody, number one, me going in the service and not going to college. Number two, why the Marine Corps? I wouldn't want my kids to go in the Marine Corps if any of them chose to go in the service because I think it's the one that's gonna teach you the least. Now it's better, but at that particular time I enjoyed it. I grew up. I just knew that was the right thing to do. I spent 3-1/2 years overseas, totally away from home.

It must have been frustrating for my father that I wasn't a good student, but he never actually let on that it was. He always backed me on everything I did. He didn't punish me because I didn't get good grades. I've always said that my Dad had a whole bunch of sons because he took his players in almost like they were sons. The ones who were trouble he gave more time to. When Dad had practice and then training table, he would be home late, not extremely late, but his week was pretty well filled. I just didn't see him a whole heck of a lot. It's a shame, and I think we all realize this, that we don't really get to appreciate our parents until we are older and then sometimes it's even harder to get together with them.

It does surprise me that I was born the son of John Wooden. Of all the families in the world I could have been born into, of all the times and the places, this is my Dad and everybody else wants him to be their dad. Sometimes I think (and I've never ever said this to anybody) that, "God, could I be adopted?" Why don't I love this game of basketball like other people? I mean I love it, but why didn't I love it enough to pursue it as a career? Why didn't I try harder to play harder? And I have said, "Maybe I'm adopted. Maybe my genes aren't there." I've never even said that to my Dad, and it's just silly thinking because in a lot of ways I'm a lot like my Dad, but I'm also a lot different. It's the same with our four kids.

I'm definitely dissimilar to my Dad because I drink. I enjoy drinking, and I've been in sales. I very seldom drink in front of him. I'm sure it bothers my Dad, but he never said it. He'd prefer that none of his family drank. My mom never did either until later in life when we convinced her to drink some wine once in a while to try to settle her down and she enjoyed that.

My drives are different than my Dad's. I was more of a hard worker with my hands than doing things with my mind. I didn't really get into books and studying where my Dad did. He truly is an intellectual.

I think I'm similar to him in the way I deal with people, that I don't like to hurt anybody. I like to make friends easily. I don't say bad things about people. The way I feel about my family is the way he feels about his. I put my family first.

It almost seems that I've given out more Pyramids than my Dad has. People ask for it. People always ask me, "Have you modeled your life by the Pyramid?" Well, I wish I could say I have but, no, I haven't. I like to relay to people that this is something that he started when he was in college and he's added to it and he has really stuck by it. The Pyramid is important to me.

It was hard and yet the love was always there and there was no doubt of that. After the kids came along, Mom and Dad's Sunday was to go to church and then come and visit the grandkids. I could be working in the yard in grubbies, but Carleen, naturally being a woman, always wanted to look good, and you never knew when they were going to come by. You didn't know if they were going to my sister's first or come to our house first. You never knew who they were going to bring with them, because there was always going to be another couple from church. I think that was hard on Carleen for awhile.

The household that I grew up in had a tremendous amount of love. They were both so much alike, they'd grown up together and Dad never let anything get out of control. Nothing ever went to his head. The main thing that I tell people, is that he is a far greater man than he was a basketball coach, and I don't think my dad's success as a basketball coach is because he knew so much more about basketball. It was because he knew how to deal with people and he knew how to get the best out of the people he had. And he had great people. He had people who were very talented on a physical level, but he knew how to really motivate people. He knew how to control them, too. Take for instance Lew Alcindor, Kareem Abdul-Jabbar. He got blamed for a lot of things that he had promised Lew's parents he could do, and that was keep Lew away from the press. His parents wanted Lew to stay on a low mode and not get his head blown out of proportion. If Lew had played on other teams he would have been scoring fifty, sixty points a game. Look at LSU (Louisiana State University) with Press Maravich and his son Pete. He led the nation two years in a row in scoring but what did LSU ever do? They never won a tournament.

My father was the same at home as he was on the basketball field, a calm fellow at all times. His emotions were always under control. He never really showed any of them. It's the truth that after a game, win or lose, if you hadn't seen the game, by his emotion you wouldn't know whether he'd won lost. After games, we'd go to Ships and have chili, hamburgers and malts. As the family grew, more people went, and more friends. There were sometimes twenty-five people and Dad never let anybody pay. He always wanted to pick up the tab.

I honestly never saw a change in my dad from one championship to ten championships. I've heard him say many times that all his good friends who are coaches he wishes would win one national championship—and the ones that he doesn't like so well he hopes they win more. He means that when you do win one, they expect you to win it all.

One of his eccentricities is the 3" x 5" cards in his index pocket with all these sayings that he can pull out at a moment's notice. His pocket gets thicker and thicker as the great-grandchildren grow because it's mostly pictures now. Again, that comes from being organized, because he normally has pretty much his whole schedule in there. And that's one thing that I have seen in the past years, sometimes he gets a little mixed up on some of those.

I think what he's done as far as his championship records will never be beaten. I don't think there was a greater coach ever in any other sport, but Dad would be the first one to disagree with that. I don't think it'll ever be beaten and it's easier to do it now than it was when he did it. It's easier to get in the tournaments now. But again, what I say to so many people is that I look at him as the man, as the person, which is even far greater than the coach.

My criticism of my father is that he doesn't come here enough. I had some hopes that when Mom passed away that he might (and we talked about it) want to come and move into Leisure World or something like that and be close. It's harder for me, because I work long hours, to get together. A lot of times I go into the office on Saturdays, so I don't see him. Naturally, I want to be with my family on Sundays, which he understands.

One thing really touched me during the time my mom was so sick. My sister was going through a divorce, and she was spending a tremendous amount of time with Dad at the hospital. I would go in probably three, four nights a week, plus the weekends. Dad just never gave up hope, even when we were told that if she did come out of the coma—she was in the coma for three months—she wouldn't know any of us. The chances were she wouldn't come out of it, but she did and she knew us all. It was as though he knew that it was going to happen. It was the total devotion. He was at that hospital every day probably at least twelve hours a day. What hurts me is the fact that he blames himself for not doing things that Mom wanted to do that later on in life, when he could afford to do it, they still didn't do it. For instance, going to Ireland. Dad's being unfair to himself.

When I was in Marine Corps boot camp and when we were allowed to have visitors, my mom and dad would always come down. I was at San Diego, and they came all the way. And they were so good to my friends, too. When I could have liberty, I always brought two or three friends home with me.

My dad and my mom were very simple. It didn't take much to make them happy. Nothing fancy. They didn't need fancy cars, they didn't need fancy clothes, they didn't even go to fancy places. They had each other. They entertained, but they didn't entertain near as much when my mom started feeling bad. They had people in, but remember now, neither one of them drank. A lot of the people who were their friends did. I imagine there was a lot of things they didn't go to because they knew there was going to be liquor there. If you went to Woodens' house, you didn't have liquor served and people still came over.

We were quite concerned when Mom did die. First of all, we thought it would make it easier now because of all that he had gone through and all of us had gone through. It affects everybody. It affects in my life because I was spending so much time there and my wife is worried about me, and it affects my sister and her marriages and my dad, naturally. Then, after Mom passed away, he just didn't care whether he lived or not. We were really concerned. There was a time when I think—I've never said this to Dad, I've never even said it to my sister—that I would possibly have liked to see him remarry. There's no way. We even talked to the doctor a couple times about his state of mind. We were concerned, but there's not a whole lot you can do in a case like that. He made it clear when I said to him that I hoped he'd move out here, that he would probably never move out of the condo. That's what Mom wanted and then he just didn't even want to change it. If you talked about, "Why don't you take the drapes down? Why don't we put the shutters up, Dad? The shutters last and drapes rot." No way, come on, are you kidding?

His biggest problem is he feels he's putting this load on Nan and Dick. What bothers him more than anything, and what his biggest fear is, is that he's going to be a load on somebody, that something's going to happen to him, that Nancy and Dick are having to devote a lot of their time to his recovery. And they're more than tickled to do it. Fortunately they're in a position where they can do it because Dick and Nancy are retired, and financially they don't need to work.

Dad's biggest fear is being troublesome to someone. He's always said that.

The only time I ever heard my mom and dad arguing was when he balanced the checkbook. He would balance it once a month. He told me later on in life that he always kept a lot extra in there because Mom never entered checks. My mom would write checks and forget to enter them. So he always kept that extra and then he'd try to figure it out. "Honey, come here a minute. What's this? What's this check?"

"Oh, I didn't put that in there, dear." That's the only time I'd ever hear them really, really argue.

There was a time if my dad had endorsed a shoe it would have made my mom happy. Mom was in support of that because everybody else was doing it. Denny Crum was making ten times as much as Dad was making, but that never bothered my dad. Remember when 3M came out with the Tardon Basketball Court? They offered it to him at that time. Oh it was a tremendous amount of money, to endorse it. He said he didn't know if he liked it. And they said, "Well, we don't care whether you like it or not, endorse it."

He said, "I can't do that." He was happy. And it didn't take a whole lot to make him happy, nor my Mom.

What makes my Dad happy is that he knows that all of his children are happy. If he knows that his loved ones, regardless of what they're doing, are happy, that makes him happy.

Jim Wooden, son of Coach, 1991.

MARTINSVILLE

FRANCINE ABBOTT
Mooresville, Indiana

Francine is the daughter of Carl Warriner, who was John Wooden's basketball coach in grades four, five and six.

There weren't words to express Dad's feelings toward John. In the last years of my dad's life, John really made him feel good. He was so good to my dad.

He wrote about Daddy in his book and no one will ever know what that did for my dad. John did things like this before people passed away and they got the enjoyment out of it. He made sure they knew what an impact they had on his life.

There were no stars in my dad's eyes. All he could think of is who you were, how good you were. It took everyone to play his game.

My father was the principal of the school, which is twenty miles from Martinsville. I first heard the name John Wooden around 1940, when John was in the service. My mom and dad owned a swimming pool here in Mooresville and John made a special trip here to see Daddy and talk to him. I can still see him standing there in his uniform. Daddy just worshiped the ground John walked on, and there were many boys or girls who he taught who came back and stayed in touch with him. John is a special person, a kind person, loving and considerate. A godly person.

I have a check written January 14, 1967. My dad wanted some tickets to go to the Notre Dame game. Daddy had done this before, written checks for John, but John would never accept money from Daddy. This time, Daddy sent a check and signed it and left the money for him to fill in the amount of dollars. He expected John to fill it in with the amount of money that he owed for the tickets. John sent the tickets back and the check with it, and where it was for the dollars to be stated, John had written, "Friendship far too valuable to be measured in dollars." My dad thereafter carried this check around with him all the time.

Over the years Daddy heard from him quite a few times. Whenever John would be within this area, he usually stopped in at our house because my Dad was living with us. In 1967, friends of ours and their three girls and my husband Jack and I, went out to California and we stopped by UCLA to see John and talk to him. He was just the most gracious man. "Why, come on in!" he said. He sat down and talked to us for quite a while. He took us over to Pauley

Pavilion and showed us around there, then he went in a locker room and came out with three huge basketball jerseys, and gave these three little girls these jerseys for them to take home with them as souvenirs. Those girls are married and have children of their own now, and each of them still has that jersey. He took us all over the campus for at least a couple hours and then took us to dinner and would not have it any other way.

The most interesting quality about John was his love and devotion for Nellie— they were just perfect. He dearly loved that girl. Before any ball game that went on, he'd stand up and look around. When he saw Nell, the ballgame started.

He had the boy in him, but he was not mean.

On April 19, 1966, on University of California stationary, John wrote my father.

Dear Earl:

There is something especially heartwarming about hearing from very special people, and so it was with a great amount of pleasure that I received your letter. I am glad you enjoy the brochures and hope you enjoy the book. Neither would have been written had it not been for what you taught me during my first years in school. It may have taken me longer than it should have to realize this, but it did happen.

This last school year has been a very rough one as far as both my family and my team were concerned. We had a fine time that would have had an excellent chance of repeating this year, but sickness and injury kept us in bad shape all year long. Our most important series found us in the worst shape of all with only one really sound player of our top six and two completely out. However, I have had so many blessings that I do not want to complain.

Here's a card from May 16, 1988, he wrote in his hand,

Many thanks for your note. Your words were very kind and deeply appreciated. He may have been Earl to many, Pop to many more, but he was always Mr. Warriner to me and I loved him for what he was and for what he did for me. I would be proud if it were possible for me to feel that I had touched as many lives in a positive way as I know he did.

John did so much to make the latter years of my dad happy that he's just precious, and he means so much to me because of that. My dad had lost his wife, too. When you live with someone so many years and lose them, you're lost. John came along and picked my dad up.

John Wooden is a very humble person. He has a lot of knowledge about people, and how to handle them. He believes in Jesus Christ and his God. And I think he really lives that way.

His Pyramid of Success is just great. What it says there about faith, success, patience, integrity, all of these are John if you really get right into it. If you drove right down his Pyramid of Success, that's John. Any way you look at it—poise, confidence—he has it all. Fantastic person.

Wooden's touching writing on the check from his first mentor, who sought tickets for the play-offs: "Friendship far too valuable to be measured."

LARRY MAXWELL
Martinsville, Indiana

Larry is a football, track, and basketball referee with the Indiana High School Athletics Association.

Over the last few years I've talked to a lot of other high school referees about John Wooden because of my acquaintance with him a few years ago here in Martinsville. It was very well publicized state-wide that Coach Wooden was coming to town, and I happened to be co-chairman of the committee that brought him back. Johnny Wooden is so much more than basketball.

Let's go back to 1963, which is when I graduated from high school, the year before Coach Wooden won his first NCAA championship. The speaker for my graduation from Martinsville High School was a fellow who had graduated in 1932 and was coaching basketball at UCLA and no one in high school really had any idea who this fellow was. They were bringing him back from California. We were seventeen and eighteen-year-old kids, and Wooden had not been that prominent a name. Oh, his picture was up in the gymnasium and people around town mentioned John Wooden, but he didn't have that name recognition that he had a few years later.

That was my first path crossing and I did not speak with him at that time. I was like most of my classmates, sitting there in my cap and gown, wondering if this fellow was going to finish his talk so we could get out.

The gym was packed that night. It was hot. There was an awfully large crowd there for graduation. I remembered more of what he said a year later after he won the NCAA championship. Then I thought, "Hey, this guy was just here and talked to us."

My first contact with Coach Wooden was five years ago. The basketball program was as low as it had been for a number of years. The school principal said, "We've gotta do something to bring people into the gym."

I said, "What do you have in mind?"

He said, "Let's bring Johnny Wooden back to Martinsville."

My niece was writing a paper for her English class and she was supposed to be doing it on a famous person from Martinsville, so she was writing a paper on Johnny Wooden. I was able to acquire Coach Wooden's phone number, and we called him and she interviewed Coach Wooden on the telephone for her term paper. This is an indication of the type of fellow he is.

He talked to her on the phone and answered some questions that she had written down for him. I asked him at the time, "Coach, if we were to do something here at Martinsville, would you possibly be willing to come back to Martinsville for a high school ballgame."

"Well," he said, "if my health would permit it." So I left it at that. A few months later, I was riding with the Martinsville High School basketball coach, who was going to speak at a basketball camp in the northern part of the state. And he said, "Maxwell, why don't we rename the gym after Coach Wooden and bring him back from California? We'd pack the gym."

I said, "Well, okay, my class is having their twenty-fifth class reunion this summer, and he spoke at our graduation, so let me take it to my class." So that summer, in 1988, at our class reunion, I mentioned it to my classmates, "Let's start a drive and put some money together and see if the 1963 graduating class can't do something for the high school, and name the new gymnasium after John Wooden." We passed the hat and collected about $500 that night. In August of that year, I went to the school board and told them what we wanted to do. I had the backing of the high school principal and a lot of other people, and they gave us permission to go ahead.

We set a date with Coach Wooden that he could come back and that got things going. That was when I really got to talking to him quite a bit, setting arrival times and, "This is what we want to do, and is this okay?"

Coach Wooden said, "You bring me back. Whatever you like, I'll be willing to do whatever you like." He was the most gracious person I know. That weekend was as rewarding a weekend as I've had. You just wanted to shut up, which is a hard thing for me to do, and just listen.

My graduating class reacted to him a lot differently twenty-five years later. A lot of people of the graduating class of 1963 made quite an effort to get back to see Coach Wooden and be a part of the dedication ceremonies at the high school. For a bunch of people from a small Indiana community, we felt we'd pulled off a very nice program in bringing Coach Wooden back. We had *Sports Illustrated* here. *USA Today* had an article about it. Two or three weeks later we got a front page of a sports page in Oklahoma City sent to us and it had a picture of Coach Wooden giving a clinic here at Martinsville High School. We accomplished an awful lot in getting Martinsville's name put back into prominence in the basketball picture that one weekend.

We had a press conference when Coach Wooden was here for the dedication. This was prior to the basketball game where we had dignitaries there from different universities and so forth where Coach Wooden had been associated. At the press conference, one of the reporters asked him what he felt might have been the highlight in his coaching career or in his basketball career. He stopped for awhile, and he said, "I've accomplished a lot, and a lot of people would say it was my tenth NCAA championship or my first NCAA championship, the undefeated years we had." He said, "Winning the high school championship in Indiana, now that's something!" And it was just the way he said it, in a very sincere way. He wasn't saying it because of the situation he was in, it was something he genuinely believed. I read somewhere that one of the biggest disappointments he had in basketball was his senior year in the state championship when a fellow hit a shot from behind the ten second line to beat Martinsville by one point in the championship game. Being an Indiana basketball fan, that means a lot to me because high school basketball is almost bigger than life in Indiana.

My wife's two girls rode to the airport to take Coach Wooden back for his plane to California. He would not sit in the front seat with me. He said, "I want to sit in the back seat with these two girls." Well that's fine, so he rode with them. Three days later, the girls got a letter from Coach Wooden, and he had written a poem about them. In just the short time from Martinsville to the airport, which is forty-five minutes to an hour at the most that he had been with them, he had captured their feelings, their emotions, the types of individuals they were. One of them is very shy, not really outgoing. The other one is full of life and bubbly, and he had captured these things and it was put into verse, and it means an awful lot to us. I know it's something that we're hanging onto to pass onto the girls. And he bought them a gift once he got to the airport and gave it to each one of them. Now they correspond back and forth. When I call Coach on the phone, it's not, "How are you Larry?" It's, "Well, Larry, how are the girls getting along?" So, they made quite an impression on him. And he on them. The girls were ten and six at the time.

Here's the poem:

For Amy and Molly from John Wooden 1/28/89

Dear Molly and Amy:

Molly and Amy are an eye catching pair.
So sweet and so pretty
And so willing to share.
Shy Molly, one who wants to hold close and squeeze
But know right away
She is not one to tease.
And beautiful Amy is too eager to please.
Our meeting was short if measured by time
But in my memory

You'll stay like an immortal rhyme.
It is true that I may never see them again
But I know in my heart they will forever remain
And I pray that the future will bring them no pain.
The joy that Molly and Amy can bring
Is better than wealth or any material thing.
May each ever be like a sweet, gentle dove
May their actions e'er be tempered by love
For that will insure being blessed from above.

Love, Coach Wooden.

It says so much and it was such a short meeting with those girls. Throughout that weekend, Molly grew so attached to him. She's very shy. At the clinic he gave at the high school, there were hundreds of kids sitting up here in the stands, and he had been trying to get Molly to come to him. Like he said in the poem, she's one of those you just want to take and squeeze. And he looked up and he said, "Isn't that right, Molly?" This was during the clinic. Those things mean a lot to us, and I know that Coach Wooden means a lot to these girls. As they grow older and are able to read and comprehend a lot of the accomplishments Coach Wooden has made on his own, I think their association with him is going to mean a lot more to them. I don't think they realize the scope of John Wooden at the present time.

They give a John Wooden Mental Attitude Award at the high school to a senior on the high school basketball team who has demonstrated a good mental attitude toward the game of basketball. Last spring when we went up to the gala Pepsi put on, Willie Naulls, who played for Coach Wooden in 1957, said he felt it was appropriate that they were honoring [Coach] on Easter Sunday because the church and God had played such an important part of Coach Wooden's life. He said it was a fitting day to honor Coach Wooden, a day that we think about Jesus. That day there were a lot of people in Indianapolis also thinking about Johnny Wooden. And they have a very close relationship, Jesus and Johnny Wooden.

Coach Wooden wanted to make sure he had seen the girls that weekend. He said, "We we were at Poe's Cafeteria for dinner that day." Well, I had no idea. I thought he and his son and daughter and their families, and his brothers and their daughters. . .well, here's Bill Walton, Willie Naulls, Swen Nater, this whole entourage, three stretch limousines come pulling in. All the people in Martinsville are wondering what's going on, but he took time out to visit with

Amy and Molly. They had taken him Easter cards and their school pictures from last year and he was genuinely happy to see them

He's much more than basketball. People think basketball when you talk Johnny Wooden, but if you live a life the way he has lived it, you're gonna be rewarded. It's not so much what he's accomplished but how he's accomplished it all.

I took him by the farm at Centerton when we were coming in from the airport. He says, "Oh, the house hasn't changed much." He said, "Now there used to be a little milk house out in back. Now the outhouse is gone. Now there was something special about it since it was a three-holer!" We got a big kick out of that.

The weekend that Coach Wooden was here we were fortunate to draw *Sports Illustrated* into it. They were doing another story on Coach Wooden, and Alex Wolf, who is one of the senior writers for *Sports Illustrated*, was doing the story. He and one of the photographers came to Martinsville on Friday and went to the banquet on Friday night. Saturday they followed us around all day. On Friday they asked Coach Wooden, "Tomorrow morning, can we do this and this and this?"

He said, "I don't know, you'll have to check with Larry or Mr. Rest to see what my itinerary is. I'm at their disposal this weekend." That impressed me that he wasn't going to let *Sports Illustrated* take anything away from us. If they could work in with what we were doing you know, that was fine, but he wasn't going to cater to *Sports Illustrated*.

Saturday he asked me if we could leave early enough on our way back to the airport on Sunday that he could go by the cemetery at Centerton where his mother and father were buried. That was no problem at all. When I got to the hotel to pick Coach Wooden up, the two gentlemen from *Sports Illustrated* were also there. And they said, "Well, Coach Wooden said we could follow you back to the airport and stop at the cemetery." That's somewhat of a private thing.

We're on our way toward Centerton and Coach Wooden said, "I really wish they weren't going to be here, but I've got to try to accommodate them." We got to the cemetery, where he and his brothers had set a trust up to maintain it. It's a very small, rural cemetery, and very well taken care of. There is a chain-link fence with a gate in front of it.

That morning was overcast and there was almost a misty rain. A very dreary day. This was January 27th, so it was not snow, but the sky looked like it could have snowed. When we got to the cemetery, I pulled up in front of the gate, and Coach Wooden got out quite rapidly and went around the back of the car, through the gate, closed the gate behind him, and put the latch back on top of the gate. I sat and watched this elderly gentleman walk back through this cemetery. There's were no leaves on the trees, you could see the limbs outlined. It was such a moving sight to see this man going back to visit the gravesite of his mother and father. It's a very, very touching moment. He came back, and it took him a few minutes for him to compose himself, as it would any of us.

The *Sports Illustrated* guys kept their distance. They stayed at the fence and tried to shoot from there as best they could. They respected his privacy. When he closed the gate, that was his time then. As well it should be. It's a very private thing. It touched me as well as. Amy and Molly, the girls, were in the car waiting also. And each of them had a tear in their eye when he got back in the car also. And so did he.

I'll never forget it. I have a tear now, yes I do.

EARL WARRINER

Earl Warriner was John Wooden's Jr. High School principal,
and recorded this interview in March, 1973 in Indiana.

There were three rooms at Centerton. I had the upper room. The other two rooms had three grades, and my room had two. I taught Johnny and basketball in the seventh and eight grade. I was the principal and coach. For uniforms, all they had was the top to pull over their overalls and they were lucky if they had shoes.

We played outdoors. We called it a basketball diamond. We worked on it until we could play basketball within a half an hour after it rained on account of the type of soil. It was a sandy clay. On Sundays there were so many boys gathered down there that you'd hardly get a chance to play. We didn't have any scheduled number of games, and probably played four or five during the season.

Wooden was a class dribbler, and not only could he play basketball, he was equally as good a baseball player. We didn't have a lot of plays, maybe one or two, but the plays didn't amount to too much. Johnny says what helped him the most was the desire to play. He wasn't a bully, and neither was he a sissy. He had the grit to stay in there and fight.

That he got from me, he claims. He said, "I got the fire, the vim, the desire and the grit from Warriner. I got the polish from Curtis." He didn't think too much of the girls. They didn't bother him any. He'd rather tease them and get them mad. That was his heart's delight, to get one of them mad at him.

He was an A student. If there was anything going—I don't care where it was—on the playground or anywhere, you could bank on John being in it. He was popular among the students. Even the girls liked him, but he didn't pay any attention. Didn't interest him.

There's the story about when I didn't start him one game. It was Friday afternoon and had been raining that morning. John lived a block and a half east from the school. He went home for lunch, but it was raining. During the noon hour it cleared up, the sun was shining and the whole sky cleared off and I knew we could play. So I called the other team and told them to come on over. John came back at noon, and the boys were all ganged up around me and talking basketball. Johnny told this story to 300 people in Indianapolis at the Old Timers Club. He said: "I stood there and I got a chance to talk. I said, 'Mr. Warriner, I can't play this afternoon.'"

He turned, looked me right in the eye and I said, "What's wrong, John?"

"Oh, my suit's out home."

John said to the audience, "Mr. Warriner said, 'It would take you five minutes to run out there and get it and back.'"

"I said, 'Oh, Pa wants me to come home just as soon as school is out.'"

John said he remembered looking me right in the eye. In about three seconds John turned to a little fellow standing beside him and said, 'Freddy, you got a suit over there?' He just lived across the street. John said, 'I'll go get mine.'

Wooden tore out of there like mad, ran all the way home, got his suit, which probably wasn't any more than a top and a pair of tennis shoes, ran upstairs, changed his clothes, came down, and sat down on the bench. Wooden said, "When the game was over, I was still sitting on the bench. We lost the game. I got up, walking towards the building with my head down. Mr. Warriner stepped over, put his hand on his shoulder, and said, 'John, we'd have won that game with you in there, I know we could. But after all, there's just a little bit more to this basketball than just winning.'"

He stood there and he thought a little bit, and he looked over the whole crowd, he said, "Gentlemen, John Wooden learned early in life that he was not a necessary article. It didn't make any difference how good he was in sports, business, or anything else. If he didn't put out, he wasn't worth a dime." He said, "Gentlemen," and waved his hand over the crowd, "that's been my goal ever since. Of all the things that I learned in grade school, high school or college, I learned it right there."

I didn't have any serious trouble with him, mostly mischief. One winter day it was turning cold, and I told him, "Go down and ask the janitor if he'd fire up." About ten minutes later I glanced at the monitor and it was still down three or four degrees. I called another name, I said, "Would you run down and ask the janitor if he would please fire up." And he did. About ten minutes later I began to get cold, and I knew [the students] were. I looked at the thermometer and it was still going down. I thought, well, I'll take care of this little situation myself.

I went down the stairs and I got about halfway down and the janitor met me halfway. He says, "Coach, what in the world is wrong? I just don't understand what's wrong. I fired up," and he reached back and pulled the door open.

I said, "For goodness sakes, leave that door open, you're gonna burn this place down." He was a fellow who got all nervous and excited and they liked to tease him. That's the only reason they did it, to tease him. And he began to vibrate, and I said, "Now wait a minute." I looked all around the furnace, and I just looked up the popes and the damper in our room was just turned square off. And I reached up and turned it on. I said, "You want to find out who did it?"

"Sure I do."

THE JOHN WOODEN PYRAMID OF SUCCESS

"Just don't say a word. Whoever turned that off is going to have a bit of fun out of it. He's gonna have to tell it. When he tells, I'll know who did it."

"All right," he says. So we finished the whole year and didn't hear one thing about it. Next year, they moved to Martinsville when John was in eighth grade. They invited the wife and I and the family out there for Christmas dinner. Herbert Orr was a big buddy of his, and John and I were going across the pasture after the cows. They both got into an argument over this. When they got through talking, I said, "By the way, John, who helped you turn the heat off."

He turned around and looked at me and said, "Well, how did you know?"

"Oh," I said, "Don't you remember. . ." We had outside toilets and he'd gotten a little piece of chalk. Even though he had gone to Martinsville that year, he wrote all the way across it, "I turned the heat off, Guess Who!?" With an exclamation mark and question mark. Well, the minute I saw it, I knew who turned it off, but I didn't say to him a word. I was waiting for the right time.

And I said, "Do you remember when you wrote on the wall?"

He said, "I should have known better than that. I'd have known you'd recognize my handwriting." He'd done it just to get the janitor all souped up. Boy, he could do it, too.

I was twenty-two when I was the principal there. I always went to his high school games. When he went to Purdue, I didn't get to go too often. Several friends and I visited him there and he took us all to dinner at this hotel and wouldn't let us spend a penny. My friend says, "I'll never forget the time I went up to Purdue and saw Johnny there."

When he first got out of the service, he came to visit me at the swimming pool in uniform. I was busy working and I glanced up and saw that there was a Navy man coming up, and I went ahead working. Just before he got to me I looked back again and he had his head down. When he saw me he looked up, and he grinned. I said, "Come on, John, you couldn't fool anybody." I saw him the next year, after he went to Indiana State, and met him in Indianapolis. He said, "Mr. Warriner, I may be in bad down there."

I said, "Oh, John, why?"

He says, "I'll tell you what it is." He'd taken his high school team that was runner-up in the state down there with him, and "I kicked off seniors and juniors and I'm playing my freshmen team this year. I've got to win. I'm gone if I don't win. I've got to win."

I says, "John, I think you'll do it." And he was runner up in the NAIA the two years that he was down there with that team. Then he went off to UCLA.

I've known him since he was six years old. He had one of the finest daddies, and his mother was nice, too. His daddy was very active in athletics. Got out and played baseball, basketball, anything else. He just thought his daddy was it.

I remember when Wooden was asked "What about long hair?" Some of his players at UCLA wanted to wear that style. John grinned and said, "Well, I haven't seen Wicks all summer. He came into the gym last week. I just stood there and looked at him. He walked right up to me, and when he got close enough to me, said, 'Wicks, what are you trying to be, a black Santa Claus?'"

He says, "Listen, Mr. Wooden, first practice I'll have that off right there.

Johnny says, "Did you get a letter last week?"

"Yes sir, Mr. Wooden, I got a letter."

John says, "Then I advise you to go home, read that letter again. Then when you come back, I'll be the judge."

John says, "I noticed a boy standing there. It was one of his players. He was studying, so I didn't pay any attention to him."

So he said, "Mr. Wooden, what have you got against beards?"

"Oh," John says, "Really nothing. I like my players to look as neat as they can. John noticed that didn't satisfy him, but he didn't say anymore. The player stood there a little bit and said, 'Mr. Wooden, don't you know Christ had a beard?'"

"Oh," John says, "If you're gonna be Christ, you come right on, I'm gonna need you this year."

When he sent me the tickets I requested with the check filled in, in place of the number, it said, "Friendship far too valuable to be measured in dollars."

My daughter, when she read it, said, "Daddy, how in the world does he ever think of all the nice things he said?"

"Oh," I said, "Franny, he doesn't have to think. That's just a part of him. He lives it every day, and he does."

At the dedication at Pauley Pavilion, he mentioned three or four people who molded his life, and the program at the top in large black letters said, "The four most important men in my life." First, the way it should be, was a picture of his dad. It was the nicest tribute to any dad that you ever read.

Second, then, was mine and a tribute. And I recall just now one statement in there, "There's no stars in his eyes." And that word "stars" was in quotations. Third was his high school coach, Curtis. And a very nice tribute to him. And fourth, Piggy Lambert, and a tribute to him.

When I show you that book of the dedication of Pauley Pavilion, you'll know why I never go anywhere without some fellow who will come up to me, introduce himself and say, "I believe you're Johnny Wooden's coach."

THE JOHN WOODEN PYRAMID OF SUCCESS

PURDUE

BOB KING
West Lafayette, Indiana

Bob, at the time of this interview in 1991, was the associate athletic director at Purdue University, and had been an opposing coach when John Wooden was at UCLA.

I was assistant basketball coach at Purdue from 1960-78. Those were the years that we played UCLA. I knew John Wooden. I was very fortunate to watch him play when I was in high school. The best way I can describe him would be perpetual motion, constant pressure all the time. He ran at one speed only and that was all out. He had a great knack of driving to the basket. Many times his momentum would run him right out of bounds into the students, who threw him right back out onto the floor, here at Purdue. John personified fast break basketball. He was quick, unnaturally quick almost, and a tremendous competitor who went for forty minutes just as fast as he could go.

Wooden was somewhat of a folk hero here in Indiana. He was a tremendous competitor. He was a guy you had to kill almost to beat him. That went along with his constant quickness, constant speed, ability. He never walked at anything. He ran all the time. And as a result the teammates ran. Purdue ran. As a result, Purdue won. His reputation as a sportsman, as a deity if you want to call it, of basketball, began earlier, but it culminated in all those years at UCLA.

I'll tell you a story that has never left me. We had a big seven-foot center named Chuck Davis who dislocated his shoulder against Marquette in the regionals, and could not play in the finals. So we're down at Louisville in the final game against UCLA. Both teams are warming up and I'm standing there talking with John, and Chuck, who cannot play and is not in uniform, came out of the ramp and down to sit on the bench in his street clothes. John was talking to me. He said, "Bob, excuse me just a minute. I want to go talk to Charles." The guy's name was Chuck Davis, but that's the way he would call him— Charles. Just like he called Lew Alcindor, Lewis. That's just his way of talking.

I was close enough to hear him. He went over to Chuck and he shook hands with him, introduced himself, and he said, "I want you to know that you gave Lewis more trouble than any center that he's played all year. I really feel for you to work all your life to get to this game and not be able to play." Now, he didn't have to say those things, but it always stuck with me. That was the kind of guy he was. And Chuck has never forgotten that either.

Simply on performance alone, record alone, you have to say he would be the number one college coach, because John did something nobody's ever done or ever will do again. Now people say, "Well, there's so many more teams today than twenty or thirty years ago." I don't care who you were, how many teams were competing, you still had to win. He had the ability to find good players. Secondly, he had what I think was his biggest ability, he created the team concept. There were great stars, but it was still UCLA, it was not Alcindor. It was not any particular player. It was UCLA. And third, he created a feeling of organization, never letting anything go unchecked or taking anything for granted.

I'm the executive director of a basketball coaches association and we've had John as a speaker at our clinics. That's always one of the things the young coaches want to hear. "How did you develop this Pyramid of Success? Did it really contribute to your success at UCLA? Could I use it and be successful, too?"

And John always says, "Yeah, but you've gotta have players, too," which is obviously true.

John Wooden is not a name that's kept in front of people all the time, but the minute his name is mentioned, people from Indiana are very proud to say, "He's from Indiana. He's not UCLA, he's Indiana." Every time he comes back to the state, and when we've had him back here for things at Purdue, the turnout's just swell because he's one of a kind. Although he worked in a different arena at UCLA, he's never gotten away from being a Hoosier.

John's philosophy, although he never said anything to me, was that if a coach can't control himself, how can you expect the kids to have much control? My memories of him are a rolled up program, sitting on the bench, tearing himself up inside probably, but exhibiting a very calm demeanor. I have to think that helped UCLA on many occasions. He gave them the same picture I think he gave to all the public. "I've got the answer to what's going on. You do what I tell you, we'll get it done." That was one of his biggest strengths.

I'm a director of the Indiana Basketball Hall of Fame, and he and Oscar Robertson are our two prize exhibits over there. The contribution that Wooden has made to basketball is to establish some levels that probably will never be achieved again, the other legacy he's left is excellence. He was an outstanding coach at every level. He's created goals for other coaches to try to emulate.

There's nothing I don't like about John, other than he'd win those damn championships so often. It was unbelievably frustrating for all the coaches across the country during that time. Part of coaching is recruiting, and as his legend grew, he was able to recruit the players you need. But you've still gotta do something with them. To do it for all that many years in a row, nobody's ever been able to even come close to that, and I don't think anyone ever will.

THE JOHN WOODEN PYRAMID OF SUCCESS

SOUTH BEND

ED EHLERS
South Bend, Indiana

John Wooden was Ed's high school baseball and basketball coach. Ed went on to play pro sports, and then was extremely successful in his insurance business.

I played for John Wooden from 1938-41 at South Bend Central High. I played basketball and baseball. In basketball I was a guard, in baseball I was a third baseman. Baseball was fun for him, not that basketball wasn't fun, but Coach Wooden was a lot more relaxed and free. We really enjoyed playing. It was a lark after the basketball season, and he was a good coach. He'd participate and play second base. We won the championship, and the majority of our games.

The difference from other high school teachers back then would be that he was with you 24-hours a day. It wasn't just in the classroom or on the floor. He wanted you to succeed 24-hours a day in any endeavor that you chose.

He talked about how you can be better than what you are. My parents and I loved him dearly, but I don't think my parents had finished the eighth grade. I had the opportunity to turn pro in baseball in 1941 for the Red Sox, paying me $4,000, which was more money than my dad made in two or three years. My dad wanted me to sign to turn pro, and Wooden told me I should go to college and get a degree, then I could sign when I got out and I would have a college diploma. I did, and the Yankees gave me $10,000.

When he was teaching summer school, he would give me the keys to the gym and a ball, and I'd go work out all by myself. He was with you continually. He had a sincere desire to help people and he was a great role model.

Wooden was very controversial in this community. He was not accepted by everyone by any means. I remember a lady calling my mother and telling her not to let me play for him, because her son had played for him and he was a very poor influence. [Apparently] this boy, and two other fellows who were stars on the team, had broken training and Wooden kicked them off the team. One boy's father was the assistant principal, but they had gone to a dance when they should have been in training.

In the stands, people got all over him. He was a great player at that time, but he hadn't proved himself as a coach. Ultimately, he came to be accepted, but not overnight. He worked very hard at it.

People here remember him with a great deal of respect, not only for what he did here, but what he did after he left here. The gymnasium at Central High School was very small. We practiced at the YMCA, which has a bigger gym. We had to be there at 6 and we practiced until 9 a.m.. It was in the day before school buses, so we walked or rode our bikes, through the snow. Wooden was always there. He'd wrap our ankles himself. He was the trainer. He was everything.

He got us vitamin pills because he didn't want us to forget them. We'd never heard of vitamin pills. I kept getting my nose broken all the time and couldn't breath, and one day a doctor showed up at the front door. He said, "I want you to come to the hospital, I'm going to operate on you." And he operated on me and straightened my nose out, and I never paid a cent. I never knew who set it up, but I know Wooden did—he's just that type of person.

Nell was feisty and terrific. One time we were going to a ball game at Riley High School. They had beaten us, and a kid (who was pug nosed and looked like a bulldog, and he was tough) was walking down the street with his South Bend Riley sweater on. As we went by, she rolled down the window and she said, "You no good little bulldog, you!" Wooden grabbed her and pulled her back in. I mean, she was feisty.

John Wooden still has an impact on my life. Wooden says, "Remember this your whole life through, cause tomorrow there'll be more to do." And, "Failure rests with those who stay on some success made yesterday." That gets me, over and over again. He's always out there, helping somebody. If not for him, I probably would have never have gone to college at Purdue.

When we were playing in the state championship, we had a bad first half. I never was chewed out like he chewed me out after the game. He broke the door down, because the door wasn't open to our locker room. He was a fierce competitor. The janitor wasn't there to open the door and we were standing out in the hall. And he wanted to talk to us. So he broke the door down, he and his assistant coach. They went in there and chewed us out like I'd never been chewed out before, and we went out the second half and just kicked their ass. He had the great sense of timing, when to get on you, when not to get on you. I didn't think I was doing too badly, but he thought otherwise. And the end result was we won.

All the things that are in the Pyramid he's been doing all his life. Even when he was all over me, he never swore. His whole life was devoted to the Pyramid of Success. When I watched UCLA play, they used the same offense and defense that we did in high school. He just refined it. The same way with the Pyramid of Success—he lived that. He just wrote it out and refined it.

I was drafted by three pro teams. The Boston Celtics drafted me in the first year of the draft in the NBA, and I was the first college player ever drafted. Baseball was the big thing then. The Yankees paid me a real nice bonus to sign. I was in pro baseball five years, but I never made it big. Then I was drafted by the Bears to play football.

I'm in Coach's book, *They Call Me Coach*. He gives me credit for naming the book, cause I couldn't call him anything but "Coach" because I had so much respect for him. I couldn't call him John. Nobody called him John. It was always "Mr. Wooden." After high school, I couldn't call him "John." It makes me very uncomfortable, even today. Not many of his players will from our generation.

Life is a remarkable experience. He was unique then and his success does not surprise people one iota. Some of it rubbed off on me, apparently.

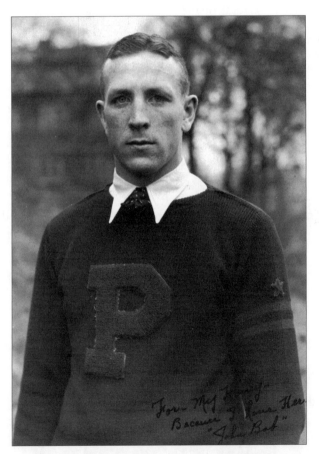

Wooden in college. The inscription reads, "To My
Honey, Because I Love Her. John Bob."

STAN JACOBS
Baltimore, Maryland

Stan was a student manager of high school and college basketball teams that were coached by John Wooden.

It took me a long time before I called Mr. Wooden "John"—he finally told me to when I was about forty. He still refers to me as "Stanley."

I went to South Bend Central Junior/Senior High School. It was all in one building. I was a little, tiny fellow. I'm still short, but a little stouter. I had a tremendous interest in athletics that I expressed by being a fan. I even had been a manager in elementary school

When I got to junior high, I walked up a steep flight of wooden steps to the gym office where several of the coaches had their wooden desks in a rather small cubbyhole of an office, including Mr. Wooden. I walked in and said, "Is there any kind of a place that you could find for me to help with the basketball team, as a manager, not as a player?"

I had read and knew enough about sports that Coach Wooden was a real hero to me, certainly a local hero. He was able to find a way to set me up as one of the managers of the junior high school team, so I became a glorified water boy as it were. I was in seventh heaven. I was involved with the basketball team. I thought Mr. Wooden was old. He was probably about twenty-eight at the time, but he was old to me. I was fourteen. This would be about the fall of 1940.

The senior manager of the basketball team was somehow dismissed from his job. John Wooden was really a stickler about training rules, smoking was absolutely verboten by anybody associated with his team. That is, if he found out about it. Somehow, Mr. Wooden found the senior manager smoking and said, "You're done!" so everybody moved up a notch, and even though I was in the eighth or ninth grade, I got moved up to be the third ranking manager. Then, misfortune struck another man who was a manager. His father died suddenly so I moved up another notch. By the time I was a sophomore, I was the head manager. It was just great. Without going into detail, I came out of a rather disturbed home life. I was an only child. My parents were together. In those days, people didn't get divorced, especially Jewish people, but I came out of a home fraught with what today would be called abuse. I wasn't abused, except verbally.

Whatever good values and standards of ethics that I might have today I attribute to my association with John Wooden, and looking at his values and learning from him, the standards he's set, the character he acted out. What he not only spoke about, but acted and lived, have held me in very good stead. I could never fit into his shoes, but I have a sense of ethics and values that I attribute very much to him. He was my father image. I've said that to many people.

My parents had a second-hand store and flea market. I'd been around the store, so I had a little business sense and that held me in pretty good stead counting jock straps and sweat socks and keeping inventory.

I'm smiling as I say this because South Bend Central didn't have a gym that we could practice in. We practiced at the YMCA in downtown South Bend about three blocks from the high school, early in the morning. I had the key to the lockers. Sometimes I overslept, and Mr. Wooden would call my house, "Stanley, where are you?" I can hear him now. I was late. I'd get on my bicycle and zip down there. It was about eight blocks from my house.

We practiced during what would be homeroom and first period for the other people that were at school. I was living my sports life vicariously through Mr. Wooden. Sport is extremely important in the societal pecking order of high school in Indiana. I found a way to channel myself. That's the fairest statement I could make about it.

I was really carrying out an important function. I was on the glory trail. I found out a little about girls in those days, but nothing was too important to me except sports. I was a decent enough student, I did my schoolwork and got A's and B's, but basketball was everything. And Mr. Wooden was my father and my idol.

Today, with my maturity and adulthood, I can look back and say I had some inner voice that said I was in the presence of one of the great ones. That may sound overly dramatic, but he was my idol. He was above other people. The more I got to know him, the more I loved him. It was a deep admiration and respect.

I was around was some terrible language as a child in my parents' home. John Wooden never uttered a curse word in his life that I have ever heard. Not only did he not utter a curse word, but his English was beautiful. He spoke well, he wrote well.

I started to see some things. We went on a basketball trip. You have to know a little about Indiana, which is a long state. The southern part of Indiana then and even today, is pretty Southern in attitude racially. We traveled quite a bit for a high school team. We used to travel to all parts of the state. I remember going on a trip. We would walk into a restaurant with the two or three or four black kids we had on our team, always, because we were an integrated school and had an integrated team, and being refused service for the black kids on our team.

John Wooden took the whole team and walked out and we went to a grocery store and bought bread and lunchmeat, and we sat by a park and ate. Often, he stood there, debating with Southern Indiana small town restaurant owners, saying, "Look, it's a free country." And we would sit down and eat. I remember him in his polite, beautiful English, telling people that it wasn't going to hurt to have his team eat there with one or two or three black kids eating there. He didn't argue, he never got abusive with people, but that stands out for me. It fortified my views on racial equality. I was a minority myself in the Vatican of the United States, South Bend, Indiana. In those days, it was not uncommon for me to be called, "Hey, Jew!" I guess you could call me an early liberal of some sort. I never saw the example. I certainly didn't see it in my parents, who had a rather derogatory term for black people that they used in our home. I didn't have the example that John Wooden set for me of treating people as equal human beings. I didn't have it even from friends. So, I got it from him. I learned about civil rights that way, long before there was ever such a term.

I used to talk to him some about my personal problems. He never tried to preach to me from a standpoint of religion and convert me. He talked about a higher power, God. He was a very staunch lay Protestant. He was involved with his church. I had never been around anybody like that, with such a value, who was so genuine about it.

From working closely with him for three years, I learned to be honest, to be fair, to be tolerant of different kinds of people. Although I didn't always carry it out then and now, I always try to speak well of other people and not hurt other people, not to harm people with words, to try to be a giving kind of person. It's bragging on myself, but my wife tells me, and others, that I to this day often think too much of others and not enough of my own self.

A lot of this came from those days with John Wooden. There was a strictness about him. He taught me how to eat some foods I didn't know about, because in my home, my dad had a very bad stomach ulcer. We had very few vegetables, and a very bland and mundane diet. When we went on a basketball trip in high school, John Wooden ordered the pre-game meal, and even a manager had to eat the same dry roast beef and dry head lettuce and toast without butter that he ordered. You had to eat the vegetables. I had never eaten a bean in my life. He was very concerned about nutrition, and he was very careful about food and what we ate. He had very strict training rules compared to other coaches of that day. Today, there's just no comparison. He was strict about all the training rules—rest and sleep and so forth. There were times that people slipped around him on it, but for the most part, he was able to keep his players in high school and in college towing the line.

THE JOHN WOODEN PYRAMID OF SUCCESS

I don't think at the time the other players and I knew that he was going to be as extraordinary on a national basis as he became, but most of them knew they were in the presence of somebody who was quite special. His reputation as an All-American at Purdue preceded him, and that he had won the Big-Ten award for having the highest scholastic average in the Big-Ten of any athlete was known, so he served as an example that one could be an athlete and a student as well.

We turn out a pretty great group of young men. Take *[high school and college player]* Lenny Rzeszewski, as an example. I know Lenny's whole family. There's no way Lenny Rzeszewski would have ended up in anything other than the production line at Studebaker's or Bendix like the rest of his family had it not been for John Wooden. When we went to Indiana State in 1946, when John went there after World War II, there were no scholarships at all, no financial scholarships. Lenny got out of high school with decent enough grades to get into Indiana State, not that he was any great scholar, but I often think of that.

A lot of people made more out of their life. There were some failures, too, who were disappointments to him, who drank, who didn't stick to training rules and who didn't get their academic work done and keep it up to par. Not everybody came out of their exposure to John Wooden and made the grade. He was very strict, and some people had a problem with that. He was very authoritarian as a coach, very disciplined. He was a perfectionist in drills. He kept people up on the practice floor beyond the regular time if they had a certain weakness that needed working on, and he would work with them individually. Then he'd make them drill and drill and drill. He was strong on fundamentals, even in college.

After coming back from UCLA after my one semester there, I worked at Indiana State as manager for his successor, John Longfellow, who was the total opposite of John Wooden in discipline, and practice was very laid back and casual.

John Wooden was strict about even style. I remember that he was strong on bounce passes at that time. He was a strong believer in the two handed underhand free throw even when people started shooting one handed free throws. Wooden did not allow his players to shoot one handed free throws for quite awhile. It held me in good stead, his strictness.

We were both in the Navy from 1943-46. I went to see him when I was at Pensacola Naval Air Station, working at the hospital, and he was a physical education instructor officer at St. Simon's Island, Georgia, which was not too far above Jacksonville. I spent a weekend with him. I wrote to him a lot. He was my father. We stayed in touch. I remember getting a weekend leave, and I spent the weekend with Nell and John at their home. It was a fond, wonderful weekend.

I eventually went overseas in the Occupation and he stayed in the States, but I very much was in written contact with him. People didn't call long distance as much in those days.

In the spring of 1946, I got out of the Navy. He'd gotten the job at Indiana State Teachers' College. I had applied and been admitted to Indiana University at Bloomington. When Wooden got the job and he started asking some of these South Bend young men if they'd like to go to Indiana State and play basketball for him. He put a team together, literally, from South Bend, about eight or ten of them. He asked me if I'd like to be his manager, no financial reward, just would I like to come and be the manager of his team? I jumped at it.

I ended up rooming with him some on trips because Indiana State could not afford an assistant coach full time. Eddie Powelski, who changed his name to Powell *[see interview]*, was from South Bend, and Eddie's legs were bad, so John made him the assistant coach while he was a student. If we couldn't afford enough hotel rooms or whatever, sometimes Powell didn't go along so I got to room with John. That was like rooming with the President to me. It was great.

One of my favorite memories is a very recent one, when Mr. Wooden honored me and did me the tremendous favor of coming to Baltimore for the National Convention of the National Association of College Stores. I happened to be the chairman of it that year. Six-thousand people came to that convention. We always try to have an inspirational speaker after one of our major luncheon meetings. John agreed to come for a very minimal fee as far as honorarium and expenses. He said, "I'll come as a favor to you."

I asked him on the phone ahead, I said, "John, what do you like to eat?" he says, "Well, I'm still a meat and potatoes person." Baltimore's a seafood town, but there's one great restaurant here called the Prime Rib. I had a reservation there. We walked in and we had to wait, even though we had a reservation. As we were waiting for the maitre d' to seat us, a party came out, and I recognized one was a man named Brother Conan, who had been the book store director at Notre Dame for about forty years. I knew Brother Conan both from my bookstore world and from my days as a jeweler in Indiana, after college.

Brother Conan and his entourage walked out of the Prime Rib, and walked right by us. And then a lady that was in his party came back in and turned to Wooden and said, "Aren't you Coach Wooden?"

He said, "Yes, I am."

She says, "Oh my gosh, Brother Conan would give anything to have your autograph." Brother Conan by this time had left. She took out a cocktail napkin, and John said, "Well, I've got something better than that." And he took out one of these little business cards he has that some savings and loan in Los Angeles has with his picture on it and his Pyramid.

And he said, "Here, let me write it. Who's it for? Brother Conan." He wrote that message. He took that little extra step to not write on a cocktail napkin. He took the time and he was so gracious about it.

The next day after lunch, he spoke and we set a record. He gave his Pyramid talk and people still come up to me and say that was one of the greatest things they've ever heard. He was besieged with people afterwards.

So many people wanted a copy of that Pyramid! We have a very nice *College Store Journal*, a magazine that comes out every other month. And John agreed to send a good copy of the Pyramid, and it was to ten thousand or more people, because there was such an unprecedented demand. People said, "Where can I get a copy of that?" To this day, people say that was one of the most inspirational things they've ever heard at our meetings.

What's in the Pyramid certainly was being taught to me in individual steps. If one can live by and practice the various steps, credos and ideas and ideals that are in it, one can achieve success, not necessarily in dollars or material goods, but success in life doing the best you can and being proud of what you're doing. I have it right here on my wall. It's more of an overall thing to me that if I live by some of those guiding principles and be true to myself and true to others, I can achieve success.

Since I went back to Indiana, my relationship with Wooden over the years has been a very warm one. I became an adult son when he told me I could call him "John." He's followed my life through some of my trying times. I talk to him a lot about personal problems, both as it related to my family, and when I was having some personal problems in my own life. We were some distance apart, but I would stay in touch and write rather, strongly personal letters to him and get back advice from him that always gave me examples of how to handle things. It's been kept up till this day. I call him a couple of times a year when I'm in California. I've gone to see him, but I don't see him as much as I'd like to.

Putting aside the personal value and worth that he was and is to me, I can say in all honesty, and a lot of important people have crossed my path, John Wooden has the highest degree of character and value structure of anyone. He lived by example what he taught and preached. By his example, by his word, he is so fair and equitable to all mankind and womankind above anybody I've ever known.

Nellie was John's biggest fan. She spoke out with criticism, not quite as politely as John did over the years, never with abusive words, but she was a pretty outspoken lady. She was the staunchest fan he could have had. And very devoted. They were rather, by today's standards, straight-laced. That was good for me, to see that a married couple could live by rather strict and conservative values, because I was coming out of a very tumultuous home. I've forgiven my parents for what they were and I love them in their repose, it was just a poor atmosphere. The good family memories I have, frankly, were when I went to John Wooden's home when I was in high school. I would be over there once in a while for a meal. And you know I'm not Christian, but Christian values were certainly instilled. I can have Christian values even if I'm not a Christian. And I certainly got them there.

My wife and some of my friends tell me I'm a pretty good guy, a pretty decent person. I give credit for the majority, if not all, of the learning of what's right and wrong to John Wooden.

SEBASTIAN NOWICKI
South Bend, Indiana

Sebastian played high school basketball for John Wooden.

I played for Wooden in 1937 and 1938, as a guard and forward, a swing man they call it now. He had a tremendous effect on me. I decided that I would like to become a coach. There were four other coaches in South Bend here. In the fifties, there were four large public high schools and one parochial high school. Four of Coach Wooden's basketball players in high school and one at a county school were coaching the high school teams.

Out of five major local high schools, all the basketball coaches had been trained by him. That's quite an impact he made. He taught us by his example of Christian attitudes. You could feel it in the man. Not only would he coach and teach us, but some Saturday evenings he and a friend, who was his barber, would meet at a bowling alley and bowl a few games. He was quite an accomplished billiards player. So we would play a few games of pocket billiards. Of course curfew would be 10 p.m. He's just an average bowler.

I'll never forget the poem he gave us. Once we were in practice a week or so, he gave us a poem entitled *Mr. Meant To.* I've committed that poem to memory. It is:

Mr. Meant To has a comrade,
And his name is Didn't Do.
Have you ever chance to meet them?
Did they ever call on you?
These two fellows lived together
In the house of Never Win
And I am told that it is haunted
By the ghost of Might Have Been.

Wooden helped me quite a bit teaching. And with a way of living I think that a person should live. I can't say exactly how, he was just there.

Wooden used to give us team principles. I don't remember all of them, but one of the main ones was "The way you think will be the way that you will play." He'd say, "It's not what you think you are, but what you think."

Southern Indiana is strong basketball country. We drove down there to play and stopped at Logansport. We were supposed to have a meal there. Pete Donaldson, a black man on our team, sat down, but they went to Coach and told him he had to eat in the kitchen. That's fifty years ago. And he says, "Let's go somewhere else." And we did.

ED POWELL
Los Angeles, California

John Wooden was Ed's high school English teacher and coach. Ed later served as Wooden's assistant coach at Indiana State and at UCLA. They are lifelong friends.

Coach Wooden was my high school coach. For two years I was his assistant at Indiana [State], and when he went to UCLA I went with him. I spent four years with him and then went to Loyola University in Los Angeles as the director of athletics, and the coach of basketball and baseball.

I had him as an English teacher in high school. He was a good teacher. To this day, you'll never hear him using a double negative or end a sentence with a preposition. He spurs you on, challenges you, to the point where I majored in English. How many athletes do you know who want to major in English?

One time in high school we had won eight or nine straight. You get pretty cocky. So Wooden said, "Today, we're not going to have a practice. We're going to have a little practice game. I asked some of the faculty to suit up and we're gonna have a little scrimmage." We had a supporting cast like Michael Jordan has, just a few of them would fill out five. He took us to task. We couldn't stop him. I don't think he missed a shot the whole game. He had us faked out of our supporters. It was a humbling experience, but it brought us back down to earth. You know that there is somebody better than you are just around the corner.

In high school, the kids on campus related to Coach Wooden the way it was in college. He was highly regarded, one that you would seek out for advice. Sometimes I think of John as a father figure, a brother, a coach, but always a friend. He'd go out of his way to assist you. He would work with you on schoolwork if it needed to be done. He insisted on excellence. That's the way he was.

When the Pyramid of Success was first used in college coaching, he really stressed three things over and over—fundamentals, conditioning and team spirit. He felt that if you could dribble better, rebound better, pass better, shoot better, all of that weakened the other team's defense. Conditioning had an awful lot to do with his success, not only his personal success, but his team's success.

While he was in college, while he played pro ball and when he played in high school, he was always moving. He would be passing, cutting, dribbling, moving. Whoever guarded him would stay with him maybe for a quarter or two or three, but then, towards the end, John would get one or two steps away, just enough to score the winning basket. He didn't do anything differently towards then end than he did during the game, except that conditioning paid off. He thought, "Once I go into coaching, if I had so much success as an individual, what if we had the whole team?"

We all are familiar with the terrific blow that he encountered when Nell passed away. She used to set his clothes out. When he got up, took a shower in the morning and shaved, there was his jacket, his shirt, his tie, his pants, his shoes, his socks. He didn't have to worry about color coordination or anything like that. No wonder he always dressed well. Very conservative.

Nell taught us a lot about social graces. My wife says she learned a lot about how to serve. To this day, she'll still say, "Well, Nell would do this." If someone in the stands started heckling him, they'd better not say that in front of Nell. If she heard it, she would tie into them. She was a tiger, a feisty Irishwoman.

I sensed long ago that he enjoyed practices. That goes back to teaching. The games are almost like exam time. I used to marvel at how he would devise a drill that would be game oriented. Once we had a game where a fellow was coming from the weak side, running towards the basket. His teammate gives him a pass that's around the knees or a little below it. By reaching down for it, he hit the rim from underneath, because he was off balance. We won the game anyway, but he remembered that. The next time we had a practice, we had a drill where you run full speed and the players would roll the ball to you. Now if you can go full speed and pick up a rolling ball and put it in the basket, there is no pass that is lower than a roll. And if you can handle a roll, you'll handle anything, because it's going to be that much easier. The next time there was a situation where the pass was low, we picked the ball up and put it in like nothing. Nobody in the audience would realize the reason he made that basket is because of a drill. Magnify that many times over and you see why he was such a success.

One time we were in Kansas City with Indiana State in a tournament. We were walking down the street and at that time, men wore hats. He stopped a stranger and he said, "How many people are here in Kansas City?" He said, 105,000 people or so. Wooden said, "Thank you," and went on.

I said, "What the hell was that all about?"

He took his hat off, and he had a pigeon dropping there. He said, "I just wanted to know what my percentage was that pigeon would choose me."

Did you know that John Wooden could name the players, the players' wives names, their children's names, all the way back to 1940? There isn't a player who played for him at UCLA or Indiana who he doesn't take a personal interest in their family life. And it's not, "Okay, you're graduating, you're no longer of use to me." That's why he has such a rapport and still corresponds.

I take great pride whenever he tells people that, of all the individuals that he's known, I know him better. I don't mean because of the number of years I know him better. I knew better what he wanted to put across to the team. We had a rapport that was almost frightening.

One time we went to Logan, Utah, to put on a clinic and John would get up and speak and I would get up and demonstrate whatever he was saying. He got a frog in his throat and he said, "Take over," and went to the men's room. I took over where he left off. He was gone five minutes. He came back and he took up where he left off, and everybody started to laugh as he's going along. He didn't know why they're laughing. What had just happened, almost word for word, example for example, was that he repeated what I had said.

Some of the coaches who were not in attendance were given a transcript of the whole thing. The secretary who did the transcript said, "You know what? We got so many calls, they said, 'You repeated six pages of the same stuff!'" I was losing my own identity. Nobody ever asked me, "What do you think the team's chances are this year?" They said, "What does Coach Wooden think?" Ninety-nine percent of the time it would be the same.

He was overpowering, a terrific influence. As an assistant I got my fair share of credit from him for my work—but you have a role to play. When you're an assistant, all you are is an extension of the head man. If you ever get to the point where it bothers you so much that you're not in agreement, then you move on. It's not fair to either one of you. You won't do a good job.

When we were at Indiana, we were on our way to a game with Notre Dame. You have to drive through Lafayette. I had my car, he had his car, and the trainer had his car and the players. Wooden said, "Once we get to Lafayette, let me lead because I went to school there and I know the city and I know the shortcuts."

As we got to Lafayette we slowed up and he tooted the horn and got in the lead. We were driving along thinking, "Great, he knows the shortcuts." Pretty soon, swish! Dead end! We had all these cars in the snow, trying to back up. And you know what? He made reference to it later. He said, "If you have any trouble finding your way, let me lead you."

He liked music. He was a big friend of Lawrence Welk, and played golf with him. He had terrible form. He swung it like a baseball player, but he scored well. He's still an avid sports watcher. He watches the pro games and the UCLA games. Sometimes I say, "Did you watch the game?"

He'll reply, "Ah, I tuned in and out."

But then I'll say, "Well, you know this happened."

And then he'll correct me, "No, that was when he was running. . ."

I know he watches a lot more than he lets on. He's an avid reader.

THE JOHN WOODEN PYRAMID OF SUCCESS

ED POWERS
South Bend, Indiana

Ed played basketball for John Wooden in high school.

I played for Wooden in 1937-38, and 1938-39 at South Bend Central High. I was a center at six-feet, because we didn't have any big, tall guys then. He came to Central in 1936, and was the assistant coach under Ralph Parmenter. He really didn't coach very much then because he was playing with the Indianapolis Kautskys, a semi-pro team out of Indianapolis. Wooden used to be gone two or three days a week. We thought he was a rich guy. He got forty dollars a ball game plus expenses, which back in the Depression days was a lot of dough. So Wooden we didn't see much of. He taught his classes, but he would leave at least a couple days a week, maybe three times, at two-thirty in the afternoon when the next to last class would be over. Then he would go to Fort Wayne or Hammond or Indianapolis and he played ball. Then he would come back that night and the next morning he would be teaching.

I never had him as an English teacher, but I know he's an expert on Shakespeare. He worked Shakespeare and the poets into all his athletic programs. He doesn't show a great deal of emotion, but boy he is sharp.

Parmenter got fired and Wooden was named the coach in 1937 and 1938. The prior teams were very poor. Their record for ten years was lousy. When Wooden came in, the first year we were 15 and 5, which we really thought was great. The next year we were number one in the state the whole year. We beat Elkhart. We played a ball game at Notre Dame in the field house, which was unheard of back then because you never drew crowds like that. But we filled Notre Dame's field house, which held 4,800 people, which back in 1938 and 1939 was unbelievable. And we beat them.

So we were number one going into the tournament. We'd lost two ball games, we were 18 and 2. Then we lost in the sectionals in the finals. I never saw Wooden so dejected in my life. He was sick, because he thought he had a team that was going to go all the way. But we just weren't meant to be.

There are a number of reasons why he was able to turn the team around. To give you an example, when he came in to be coach, you never even had the ball in your hands from October 15th until about November 1st. The season started November 15th. He had you running up and down the stairs in the school, three flights high. You'd get on a basketball court, but he never had you shooting the ball, you were always playing three on two, two on one, one to one, but you never shot the ball. It was just ball handling. The defensive guys were doing the same thing, playing defense.

After you did that for two weeks, then you finally got to play basketball, but the fundamentals were there, the pivoting, the passing, everything. So all of a sudden, he made everybody on the ball club a good ball player. Some were better shooters, but everybody fundamentally was strong. They were good ball handlers. They knew how to pivot, how to guard, how to block. They passed off if they never had a good shot. You never took a bad shot. If you did, you'd better hit it, because you do that twice in a row and you're on the bench.

He never was mean, ornery, drank, or smoked. He was just a super man. I never heard him swear but once. We were in Mishawauka, that's the town next to us. We were the big rivals, South Bend Central and, back in those days there was only Washington High School and South Bend Central. And Washington was new so they weren't really predominant. We at that time were number one in the state and we went over to play a ball game late in the season and we beat them. Their coach after the ball game came up and I'm close to the scorer's bench, and he said, "You fixed those G.D. officials, didn't you, John?"

John says, "What?"

He said, "You fixed those referees." And we're playing there, not at South Bend, we're playing at Mishawauka.

And Wooden says, "I don't know what you're talking about."

And I'll never forget, he says, "You're a G.D. liar." He called Wooden a "Goddamn liar."

Wooden reached over and grabbed him, and he says, "Don't you ever say that again you son of a bitch," and grabbed him. Man, I'll tell you. He was mad. So we go in the dressing room, we take our showers, we're ready to jump on the bus. We're waiting until the crowd clears out because everybody's down there, they see this. So they think that Wooden's a real S.O.B. Finally, a half-hour after the ball game's over, we come out and they had about five or six Mishawauka cops to put us in the bus. That's the only time I ever heard John Wooden swear. *[When asked in 1992 about this incident, Wooden retorted that Powers' recollection "is entirely wrong. That fellow called me that name. That is true and the next Monday he was barred from coaching for life." Did you ever call him an S.O.B.?, Wooden was asked. "No, I did not. No! And I think you can talk to the people that were there. It didn't happen." Did you grab him by the lapel? "I did! I hit him! That's true. I hit him."]*

The first year he came as a coach, there were four or five kids who lived across the river, on the East side. Half our team lived on the West side, which was Polish and Hungarian, and some lived on the East side, and we were all Irish or Italian. We used to play Friday and Saturday ball games. On a Friday night, there were about four of us guys walking home and we're gonna meet our girls on the other side of town just as we crossed the river. We were going to go to one of their houses to have some fun after the ball game. Not fun like today, it's different as you know.

A car came pulling up by us and a voice says, "You boys want a ride home?" We look, it's Coach Wooden.

"No, no, Coach, we're going home."

"Why don't you want to ride with me?"

"Well, we just want to walk."

And he said, "No, you boys get in, I'll take you to your houses."

The girls are waiting down there about three or four blocks down on the corner and we're going to go to this one girl's house. He found out. I don't know who squealed, but somebody told John Wooden. As he dropped us off, he says, "Fellows, you know we've got a ball game tomorrow night, so you get to bed real early now and have a nice night's sleep."

That was back in 1937, or so. We knew we couldn't go on a Friday night after a ball game and meet our girlfriends. So you think Wooden wasn't thinking even back then? That made us realize that this guy knew. . .we'd better not try to fool him or lie to him, cause he knew us better than we knew him.

Two years ago, our teams were invited to an assembly of Christian athletes. They had all of us come down who'd played on the first teams that Wooden coached. There were ten of us who went down. When we went into the arena, people gasped because here are these old jocks coming who'd played for him fifty years before. They honored Wooden with an award. He didn't know we were there. We were in a room and every station in town was shooting interviews with him, when all of a sudden, he came into this room saying, "What are you guys doing here?" He was dumbfounded. He knew every guy. Every one of us couldn't believe it, after all those years and coaching, all those games and all the national championships. Some he hadn't seen in fifty years. He knew every guy by their first name, which we thought was amazing. At that time he'd have been seventy-eight. He's got a sharp mind.

ROBERT W. PRIMMER
Muncie, Indiana

*When John Wooden was in high school, Robert played for a
neighboring team. Robert went on to become a coach.*

I have known John Wooden for many years. When he was a player at
Martinsville High School (my hometown is Frankfurt, Indiana), we were rivals
in basketball.

I shall never be able to repay John Wooden for what he did for me. John
recommended that I take his place as basketball coach at South Bend Central
when he went to Indiana State. That was in 1945. When we came home from
the service, we had sold our house, and John and Nell had an apartment. John
and Nell asked me to come and live with them in their crowded conditions until
we found an apartment. I'll always remember that and be very grateful. John did
me and a lot of people a lot of favors.

I did well as a coach. I have his Pyramid of Success in several places. It's
one of the examples of the great detail person he was, he was a great philosopher. A lot of people have the idea that he was a strict disciplinarian, but he had
a big heart.

This is what I received from him upon my retirement.

Mr. Robert Primmer
Ball State University
Muncie, Indiana

May 7, 1976

Dear Bob:

May 19 is the day, they say,
You stop all work and begin to play.
Since I went this route one year ago,
There are some things I think that you should know.
Make sure that Lavone understands,
That she must accept the fact that home you will be,
Much more than you ever have been before,
And must not complain when you're in the way,
But continue her duties with nothing to say.
She must take care of every household chore,
Mow the grass and go to the store.

Do the washing and ironing too,
And cheer you up when you feel blue.
Plan every meal with a favorite dish.
Be alert to respond to your every wish.
Mend your clothes and shine your shoes.
Take care of the bills and pay all dues.
Keep your clothes all neatly pressed.
Rub your back, and then your chest.
Disturb you not when you are taking a nap,
Keep cold drinks handy from the refrig tap.
Rake the leaves and shovel the snow.
Keep the fireplace logs aglow.
Fetch your slippers with loving care,
Have the paper unfolded at your easy chair.
Wash the dishes and mop the floor.
Turn out the lights and lock the door.
In fact, Bob Primmer,
It will be seen,
For you things will be as they have always been.
Providing, of course,
If you've convinced Lavone for her your retirement means carry on,
*   carry on.*
I must confess, yes, I must tell,
I never got that across to Nell.

That poem means a great deal to me. I received quite a few letters from my former players, but this is on the first page of my retirement book. He's had a great influence on my life as far as coaching is concerned, and in helping me with my values in life.

LENNY RZESZEWSKI
South Bend, Indiana

Lenny played basketball for John Wooden in high school and in college.

I played at South Bend Central High for John Wooden for senior year; I played with the B team the year before that. At one time, Wooden wanted me cut from junior high team. I was a small individual, about five-foot-five in the junior high. When I graduated, I was only five-foot-eight-and-a-half. Now I'm six-foot-two-and-a-half.

I also played for him at Indiana State from 1946-48. He helped me in many ways. He was a great man. Every time he would come to play the Fighting Irish, I would call and go see him. He would always give me a ticket.

He showed us the Pyramid in high school. He was strict. He wanted you to do certain things. You couldn't step out of line. If you did, you wouldn't be playing. He would work on you as an individual to keep going.

We were on a trip to play and we had with us Clarence Walker, a black ballplayer. We stopped at a restaurant in West Virginia, and everybody ordered. They saw that we had Walker, and wouldn't feed him. We decided that everybody would walk out. And we did.

Whatever he preaches, he believes in. And if you don't want to do it that way, you might as well forget about it.

When I got out of the service, he asked me if I would like to go down with him to Indiana State. I didn't know where Indiana State was. If he didn't do that, I probably would have never been in college. He wanted to see me advance, and that's the one thing I'll never forget about him. He wasn't doing it for himself, he was doing it for me and for other individuals.

He said, "You have the potential." So there I was. You've gotta love the man.

INDIANA STATE

DWAYNE KLUEH
Terre Haute, Indiana

Dwayne played college basketball for John Wooden,
and went on to a career as a pro player and coach.

I had read and heard about John Wooden during his time at Purdue and when he was coaching at South Bend Central. When I got out of the service, I decided to go to Indiana State. At the time I got out, the coach at Indiana State decided to leave to coach professional basketball, and the replacement was John Wooden. And we, I say "we"—several other fellows who were planning to go out for basketball—were pretty excited about that, knowing that he was an All-American player and a great player at Purdue.

Terre Haute was quite a ways from South Bend. I didn't know a great deal about him as a person. In the summer, he moved to Terre Haute, and the gym was always open, so we got a chance to meet him and talk with him a little. He was a very impressive individual, to say the least. I could hardly wait until practice began. We had 150-plus players report the first night. He talked to us in general terms for maybe ten or fifteen minutes, and then he said, "I want all you people who think you're guards to get in these two lines, and forwards in these lines, and centers in this line." And then he just peeled off teams, one by one.

He said, "All right, we're going to scrimmage." The scrimmage went on from three in the afternoon until everybody had a chance. That was pretty late in the evening as I recall. He would run games cross-court, so there would be two games going on at the same time. We did this for, I suppose the better part of a week but slowly but surely, there would be fewer people coming back each day.

He was gentle about cutting guys. I don't think he relished that part of the process at all. It was pretty hard for him. Fortunately, he had two people that he could sort of use as sounding boards on this, who were also watching, including Eddie Powell, who came down with him from South Bend. Cutting players from a team is tough for all coaches. I don't know of any coach who likes it. And many coaches on various levels will say they never cut a kid. They'll keep him and they won't promise him he's gonna get to play or even practice a great deal, or that a lot of attention will be paid to him, but he will stay on the team. Wooden was a lot like that. Now, you can look back at some of the squad pictures and so forth, and find that we had 18 or 20, which was quite a lot.

He impressed upon us that if we were going to be a good team and a team that would win games, we would have to be in good condition. Then he talked about himself and the fact that he was just like every other player in the Big-Ten, he thought, through the first thirty-five minutes of the game, but the last five minutes he was darn sure he was going to be in better shape than the other players. He said, "If you look back in the records, a lot of the damage I did was in the last five minutes of the game. We want you guys to be in shape to play the full forty minutes, and not just thirty or thirty-five."

So he set us up. I used the same type of practice arrangement when I was coaching. He set us up in fast break drills every night at practice. Practice was at 3 p.m., but it wasn't just a kind of general time. We had to be dressed and on the floor at five minutes past. And if you weren't on the floor at 3:05, you weren't going to get on the floor that day, so everyone was very quick about getting all their things done and getting their ankles wrapped and so forth, so you could be out there ready to go.

At about ten after, the whistle would blow and he'd say, "Three lines." That's three lines underneath the basket, one basket. And then we had at least two dozen ways, three people at a time, with various kinds of configurations and passes and cuts, to take the ball to the other end. You would have wave after wave, maybe six groups going to the other ends, six coming back and so on. They were very innovative drills for the time, and he created them. We would do this thirty minutes. Some coaches probably would really frown on that, but he spent thirty minutes with us going up and down the floor at full tilt, and trying to be as careful as possible about passes you make and the shots that you take.

After that, when your tongue's hanging out pretty well because you've been moving, then we would get onto some offensive and defensive work. Coach Wooden was not a coach who spent hours and hours working individual or two-man (although we did some of that) or three-man. He realized that the game was played with five and that the more time you spent with five people working against five, the more realistic that is, the more game-like, and the better it would be.

In the two years at Indiana State, he won 47 ballgames and lost 14. There was a pretty good spread between the winning score and the losing score. Much of that I think can be attributed to being in good shape and being able to run and to go with the ball.

The other players and myself, at various times, have been together and talked about the man. We agree that we knew we were playing for somebody pretty good, pretty special, that he was aware of what he was doing and he was very competitive and wanted us to be that way. We knew we were playing for a good coach.

The Pyramid of Success was a part of what you talked about and learned from him about coaching. The initial Pyramid of Success, however, wasn't as detailed as it is today. I remember hearing about it and it made sense. I still think it makes good sense. The foundation and those key items that form the foundation, such as conditioning and so on, are all important. If you don't have one of them, up the ladder it's going to crumble a little bit. You won't be as good.

John Wooden had a very substantial impact on my life because as a result of playing for him at Indiana State I had the opportunity to decide and determine that I wanted to go into coaching. I had the opportunity to delay that a little bit and play professional basketball in the NBA for a couple of years. All of that has had a significant effect on my life, and where I've lived it and how I've lived it.

John Wooden is a competitor, he may not always show it, but there's a fire there when he's involved in a contest. What he used to stress to us in his coaching courses, and clinics, and practice, and locker room talks was paying attention to detail. I'd never heard that expression before I played for him, and that made an impression on me. No matter who we were playing, he was not worried about them. He'd say, "This is the team I have something to do with, and I'm worried about you guys and what you're going to do."

He's very special to me and to all of us who played for him.

UCLA

KAREEM ABDUL-JABBAR
Los Angeles, California

Kareem Abdul-Jabbar was the greatest offensive force in basketball history. His number at UCLA, 33, is retired. He was elected to the Basketball Hall of Fame in 1995. Playing varsity during 1967-69, he led the Bruins to three consecutive NCAA championships with a record of 88-2, and is the only player ever selected in the Final Four as Most Outstanding Player three times. He is a three-time College Player of the Year, a three-time consensus All-American. He holds the record at scoring average (26.4), ranks second with 2,325 points and 1,367 rebounds (15.5 average) and third with his .639 field goal percentage. He was the number one draft choice for the NBA in 1969, and played for twenty years for the Milwaukee Bucks and the Los Angeles Lakers, where he was selected as MVP six times and the only NBA player to do so, won six NBA titles (five with the Lakers) and holds the league scoring record with 38,387 points. He is a charter inductee to the UCLA Athletic Hall of Fame.

When I was playing for Coach Wooden, the influence wasn't as strong as now. I learned more after leaving UCLA just by judging the events in my life and comparing them to the examples that he set. He set an incredible example and you don't really realize exactly what he was doing until quite some time later.

It came in increments in my first couple of years out of UCLA. I really appreciated what he knew about basketball as opposed to the other coaches. As I got older, I appreciated what he did as a man, the example that he showed us and the opportunity he gave us to do something significant with our lives.

As a basketball coach, he didn't have any equal. They say Adolph Rupp of the University of Kentucky was a great coach, maybe he was, but I don't think that he had the knowledge of game that Wooden had. Red Auerbach coached in the professional level. They're coaching adults and it's more or less keeping people motivated.

College ball is not the same as pro. College guys are between boys and men, and it takes a totally different mindset to deal with it. You have to deal with maturity and lack of knowledge of the game. Coach Wooden had all of that together and in place before he even spoke to me.

Coach Wooden and I didn't have that close personal relationship in college. I had a lot of respect for Coach and I listened to what he said to do, and I did it. It made our relationship very simple. He figured out what I needed to do to improve my game and I saw my game improve, and we were very successful. It was like they say, "If it ain't broke, don't fix it." We never had any fights to resolve.

I definitely enjoyed playing for Wooden. There were no aspects of the relationship that I didn't like. I wish we had training table [food] more often, that was about it, *[he laughs]*. I didn't have any complaint with the people in the athletic department or the coaching staff; they were great to me. I did what I had to do, I listened to my great advisors and I got out in four years. They made it really easy for me, and I was able to take advantage of them.

Wooden made sure that all of his players got an education at UCLA. If you didn't really have it together in your mind mentally to cope with academic life at UCLA, you wouldn't have been able to play for him. That was all part of how he used your potential. You had to be intelligent enough to do what he said to do.

Wooden set by example. It wasn't a direct one to one, "I think you ought to be this, period." There wasn't much of that at all, he never proselytizes about anything. He would try to get you to read the Pyramid of Success, but that was about all. Most of that doesn't have any meaning to a young man. You have to go out and experience things to really understand what that is about. But as an adult I can see what he did, working like he did to get through school, getting his degree in four years during the depression, marrying his wife and raising a family in a miniature apartment, and moving several times while he was in the Navy.

When I first saw the Pyramid of Success, I had my own ideas about success but I respected Coach Wooden and I listened to it. Now, I think it's a very effective blueprint for life. Most people can't deal with life like that.

As to Nell, it is quite obvious the bond that they had. It was always obvious to everyone. I have not been so fortunate to meet a woman I feel that way about and who feels that way about me. As an adult, I envy his good fortune, but it wasn't something that he tried to promote. But it was there to be seen.

He had such a subtle touch in the way he would impart certain things. I remember during my second or third year at UCLA, I had done real well on my finals and my grade advisors were real happy with me. I was feeling full of myself. He just said to me, "That is why you came to UCLA, to get an education." My attitude was, "I can take these pats on my back." He didn't want me to be beeping my own horn so hard and emphasizing that this was what was expected of me.

The way he trained me really helped me play the pro game, the fast-paced game, which was how he liked to play. That is always the way to win a basketball game, when you can beat the other team up and down the court.

He helped me play in the pros. Being able to adjust to your teammates is always a key to playing this game. As far as movement of the ball and passing, if you don't catch the pass, he would want to know was it a bad pass or were your hands not right? Keep your hands ready and bring your tips up and above your waist. The habits that you develop during practice every day are some of the key things of learning how to play for him.

His method is a fundamental way of winning when you can outrun your opponents. If you understand how to do that, it gives you an advantage. It makes you easy to coach in the pros. You know how to dribble the ball. As a setter I learned how handle the ball and do things that the guards do, plus I enjoyed the challenge, and it made me a better basketball player. In the pros they were invaluable skills.

One of the things that commentators have said about me over the years and about Wooden in general, was that he could take someone who was talented and bring out the best of them even further. He did that to me. Definitely.

Bill Walton had great running teams. My team was a great running team, but UCLA emphasized me in the post a little bit more to build his team. That was just John Wooden, fine-tuning with talent to soup the main player and he knew how to feature them and get them off. When Gail Goodrich was there, he was able to get a lot of nice seventeen and eighteen-foot jumpers. John made people look for that because that was his strength. When they had Hazzard running the break, the other guys filled the lanes, and they couldn't get the lay-ups. He knew where to tell people to go, to do your thing and not constrict them, not get them into a system. He did not make his players fit the system. He made both of them adjust. He adjusted the system and he made the player adjust, working with other people to get the maximum out of both.

Wooden instituted, not necessarily a gag rule, but he restricted press access because they never had the volume of requests when I arrived. I agreed with it. I wanted to graduate, and I knew if I got caught up in the press, it would hamper that. They could have done it differently. With hindsight they should have done it differently, because the give and take with the press, and being pulled at by the press is something you have to deal with at the pros, but before me they never had that type of demand.

When I was playing for him, I appreciated that he wasn't the type of guy who was always screaming and had his own show and his own car dealership. They get that out in the Midwest where the coach takes over the whole basketball program. He was totally against that. He didn't want people giving him gifts.

I always appreciated the lack of pretension about him. What people don't understand about John Wooden is that he is a very tough individual. He likes to win and he plays hard to win, he does not give up. He was a lot less of a gentlemen than people wanted him to be. He was a hard-nosed guy, but he did it by the rules and he respected the rules and his morality to the point where he didn't let it twist him away from the way things should have been.

I've written about redemption in sports. Just having failed to get the prize, you still have another chance this next season, the next game, where you can get it all together and come out with the result. If not in getting the prize, then at least with your effort in what you are able to do with the opportunity that you had.

I remember a bus trip we took in the Midwest when we discussed religion with him, as a group discussion. He is the mentor of a group discussing view points. We were exchanging information. I was very much into learning about Islam about that time. One or two guys on the team were Jewish. Wooden accepted different religions and he was interested to know how you felt about it and what effect it had on your life. A lot of people would say they believed in whatever it is, and then their lives are just examples of greed and selfishness.

I've had discussions with him on many topics other than basketball and got to know him well. We'd talk about everything. I enjoyed talking with him about things unrelated to basketball because that's all I was ever able to discuss. I talked about politics, events. We went through some very tumultuous years. Nineteen sixty-eight would qualify just beyond what happened on the basketball court. Although the student unrest at that time didn't really affect us and didn't get into the athletic department at all.

He was always working on improving himself and maintaining whatever improvements that he'd already made. I had a simpatico temperament with him. I think our natures are similar. I was very competitive and quiet about it, but I had the same burning desire to win. That was something that he wanted to see in everybody who played for him. Learning how to control and focus that desire is the key to being a good athlete, and I think he saw that in me and really saw someone he could help mold.

I had that desire coming in, but he saw it there and he helped me develop it. You can't put it in there.

Wooden influenced me much in my life outside of basketball. Coach Wooden has helped me with my children. After knowing how he dealt with us, and seeing the lessons, I understand that if you implant them in a young person's mind he'll learn them down the road. He had that figured out. As a teacher, he could see what that was about. It's really helped me with my children.

When I was in Milwaukee, it was very difficult to stay in touch with Coach Wooden. Since I have been in town, I get with him every so often and anytime they give a function for him. I never went to Wooden with any particular problem, I never had one to approach him with, but we've conversed on very serious issues. I learned to be non-emotional playing in [high school in] New York, just keeping it all inside. Anytime you got upset, you just used that to help your concentration and your desire to win.

I went to UCLA because if anybody knew their way through the turns and bumps and bruises, he did, and I trusted him to be the person who would. He knew what he was trying to teach inside and out and he knew what was important to your life. My freshman year, I went from one level of playing to another. That's really tough. I worked with the varsity the first year, so I had to really get into another level of conditioning. The freshmen weren't giving me any challenge, so I had to work against varsity players.

Wooden is from another era. People don't understand that. He's one of those boy stories in sports. He's not from the modern era with all the money and height.

Other than my religion, there are no other theories or philosophies that I've had taken an interest in. I learned a lot about self-discipline in high school and it continued with Coach Wooden. He took it to another level.

He could be tough with somebody but that really wasn't where he was at. As a kid from New York City, with all these people trying to get in your door all the time, he just encouraged me to keep my eyes on my goal, which was to get my degree. As long as I did that, everything else fell into its rightful place. That was one of the key reasons I was able to graduate and have as good a basketball career as I could.

Wooden was a constant teacher and role model. I really appreciate his morality and what he was able to impart as far as how to live your life, how to enjoy success, and not let fame destroy you. I got that first hand. Success destroys a lot of people. Fame and glory and money came with the success. It never had a chance with him. That to me says a lot.

He still calls me "Lewis" on occasion. It's an ingrained habit. He respects my conversion to Islam. It took my mother a couple years to call me "Kareem." Some of my friends whom I've known since grade school still call me "Lewis."

I remember what it was like to be on the other end, of being defeated my freshman year in high school. We didn't win the city championship. We lost a couple games. I looked bad in a number of games. I remember what that was about so when I had people in the opposite position I didn't get too much of an arrogant posture, because I'd been on the other side.

I was courted by a number of institutions, but I appreciated the way [Wooden] carried himself, and the total lack of pretense and arrogance. Other coaches, like Adolph Rupp, were very high profile, flamboyant. They didn't have the appeal to me that John Wooden did.

THE JOHN WOODEN PYRAMID OF SUCCESS

CARROLL ADAMS
Palos Verdes, California

*Carroll played basketball for John Wooden at UCLA
and went on to coach at the high school level.*

I started in 1949 and played one year of freshmen basketball, then I went in the service for three years, and came back and played 1954-56. I left with a year's eligibility to go but I was married and had two kids. I was a twenty-six-year-old service vet playing with the youngsters. Because I was a little older, I think he treated me a little different than some of the youngsters.

He told me one about his first high school job. There was this youngster who was kind of the school bully. This one guy would bully everybody—teachers, other students, other athletes on teams. One day it came to a point where John was confronted by this guy who was testing him, and John with one punch decked the guy. From that point on that guy was his buddy. Naturally that individual lost his clout with the rest of the kids, but he was John's buddy from that point on. It was the irony that he was relating.

I went into coaching after I got out of UCLA and I coached at the high school level for approximately ten years. I patterned my whole coaching philosophy and techniques after John. I even went to the 3" x 5" cards that were so infamous with him. I still have them, I'm sure he still has all of his, too.

His Pyramid of Success has changed over the years. He keeps refining it all the time and those were tenets that I tried to live by. Not only are they good for playing basketball, but also for everyday life. You can live your life that way. He used to pass the Pyramid out at the beginning, once he made his cut and had his solid fifteen. He would go over it and constantly refer to it during the course of the year. We all kept a notebook with all of his little tidbits of wisdom in it.

He did one thing I thought was unique. He always said that not necessarily your five best players make your best team. After several weeks of practice, prior to the start of the season, he would take us into a room and tell us to write the three teams as we saw them, placing ourselves where we felt we should be.

He said, "I'm not gonna make my starting line up out of what you guys determine, but it's just an indication as to how everyone feels about who should play where." He'd never let us see the results, but he always said it was so close with his thinking, it just goes to show you how democratic sports really are. There were always one or two players who would maybe be a third-teamer, yet they'd have themselves up in the first team, but Wooden said that you have to discount that.

I thought it was a good tool because it gave the kids a feeling, "Well, gosh, I've got a say in this team. I'm not just a body out here trying to make a slot. I have some vocal input, too." This was a good technique, in fact, I incorporated that in my coaching too, and got the same results. Kids basically are honest and objective.

In the 1955-56 season we had really a good club. That was Willie Naulls and Morris Taft, and I was the other guard and we had Al Herring and Conrad Burke. In 1954-55, they started that Holiday Festival Tournament, which was played over the holidays. It ran through Christmas and New Year's, and we played in the first two. We played in 1954-55 and didn't do real well. LaSalle won it that year, beating Duquesne in the final and us in the semi-final game.

The following year was right in the middle of University of San Francisco's reign with Russell and K.C. Jones. We played them in the final at the Garden on New Year's Eve. There was a line around the Garden (that's the old Garden) that just went completely around the block. That's what brought, in my opinion and I think a lot of L.A. sportswriter's opinions, West Coast basketball into the national spotlight. Prior to that time we were some silly guys who bounced the ball and shot with one hand. Eighteen-thousand people stuffed in that Garden to see two West Coast teams was unbelievable.

The night before the big game, two of our leading stars stayed out after curfew. Ducky Drake always used to sit in the hotel and wait to see who was coming in and make sure everyone was checked in by the time they were told to be in. He and John were down in the lobby that particular evening and it was after curfew and these two (our best players) came in after and John said, "Okay, that's it. You guys are going back home." And he purchased airplane tickets and had them gone.

The next morning at breakfast he told the team that they were leaving and we were going to have to play USF minus these two, and he was very adamant. Ed Irish was the impresario of the Garden back in those days. He came in with a cadre of New York writers and they took John into a room and were in there about 2-1/2 hours. It was very tenuous, but they finally convinced him and reluctantly he did let them play. What they impressed upon him was that this was West Coast basketball getting its chance to be aired nationally. I don't know if that's a weakness, but it shows compassion.

We were playing Kansas State back in the old gym back in '54. It was our first or second game of the year. And at that point, blacks weren't really integrated yet. A few teams had them, but I know the year before when John and the team went to Kentucky, the black kids couldn't stay in the hotels, so when Kansas State came out here, we had Johnny Moore, Willie Naulls, Morey Taft,

Nolan Johnson. We had three or four blacks on our teams and they started call-ing us "nigger lovers." Right on the floor. The fans couldn't hear it, but they kept making disparaging remarks to our black kids. And our black kids took it real well. They just let it slide off their backs and didn't let it really hurt them.

I wasn't in the game, I was on the bench sitting next to John. And there was a loose ball right in front of our bench, laying on the ground, and Johnny Moore jumped on it. And then three Kansas State guys jumped on him. They weren't going after the ball, they were going after him. That just pissed me off. I jumped up, grabbed one of the guys, popped him and sat back down. And after, you know, there was a lot of turmoil and chaos going on at the time. And the refer-ees calmed everything down.

And I'm sitting on the bench going, "Oh, my hand!"

And Coach says, "What's wrong with your hand?"

I said, "I think I broke it when I hit that guy."

He said, "Hit that guy? You never left the bench."

I said, "Yeah, when that started and he jumped on John it made me mad and so I just grabbed him, I jumped up and grabbed and hit the guy."

He said, "Oh, come on."

So the next day in the films, when we saw the films, there it was! Me jump-ing off the bench. But nobody saw it. It was that quick. I just jumped up, grabbed the guy, popped him and sat down. But I did break my right hand, my shooting hand.

We had a lot of good times, but a lot of times I was calling him a lot of names too. His practices were very arduous and repetitive. That's what made him so great. He just drilled you on the strict fundamentals and when that situ-ation would come up in a ball game, you would handle it because it was just second nature with you. He never allowed you to fool around on the free throw line. I see kids nowadays, just throwing the ball up, or they're going up for lay-ups and they're doing all kinds of dipsy-dos. You never missed a lay-up with him. If you shot a lay-up funny you'd be running laps after practice. He just stressed basic strict fundamentals and that's what won for him. That's what won the close games.

DR. DON ADAMS
Playa Del Ray, California

Don was, for a time, John Wooden's physician.

I took care of Nell Wooden principally for a period of time and then was John Wooden's internist on a rather irregular basis. When he got into his heart troubles and his hip or orthopedic troubles he had other people that he went to for that.

When he got Jerry Norman as assistant coach and Jerry did the recruiting is when Wooden's success really took off. A lot of people have said over the years that Jerry Norman really got him started in the recruiting business and was the kind of personality who could go out and really recruit players. He really added from then on to the kind of success that Wooden had. Jerry Norman I've known for many years too, as a personal friend, and I think he was quite important in UCLA's successes.

I have great admiration for Wooden as a man and a person. He was always a straight-shooter. He never would tell you what wasn't really real. Wooden is a very quiet person, not a bubbling personality. He doesn't make long conversation. He's friendly, he remembers things, he's sincere in the way he responds to your questions, but he never appears nervous or anxious or worried. He seems to always be under control.

Nell was a very anxious person. She was a little more vocal and a little more active. Wooden was the attentive husband when he brought her in. They were a very, very devoted couple and he always came in with her when she came to the office. He'd sit there in the waiting room very quietly. At that time, of course, he was retired. People in the waiting room would sit around and say, "Hey, gee, there's Johnny Wooden." It was nice to have a celebrity sitting in the office waiting room. He was always friendly to people and our staff.

In his earlier days, when he really didn't have the success he had, we used to have the basketball games in the old men's gym. He used to get a little wild. He was a little less under control with his emotions. He'd yell at the players a bit, but he never used a foul word, "Gosh darn it!" is his strongest statement. He used to really get after the players. I suppose this is youth and his new position. There was really a change after he got better control of his assistants. I remember a few times when I was really surprised because he was sort of the model Hoosier, and he had some pretty rough, but not foul, language, chewing (players) up and down. He changed with time and age and experience.

RAY ALBA
Sherman Oaks, California

Ray played basketball for John Wooden at UCLA.

I played Wooden's first years at UCLA, 1948-50. I was rebellious and I had been playing for Wilbur Johns, the coach before Wooden. He was somewhat permissive. We were losing but he was a good guy. All of a sudden Wooden came in, and here's this martinet who makes us do basic things. The workouts were very difficult. At first I was angry, and said, "What the heck is this guy. . .?"

It took me through the years to realize that he was a master teacher and marvelous person.

I utilized the Pyramid in my life, subconsciously. Since UCLA, I went to work at the studios and I'm a film editor. I've been doing that my whole life. A nice middle class life.

I used to run into the Coach when he used to walk at UCLA, that was another amazing thing. Here I hadn't seen the Coach say in, I don't know, twenty years, and I say, "Hello, Coach." And right away he says, "Hello, Ray."

And I said, "I'm Ray Alba from 1949. . ."

And he says, "I know, Ray."

And I thought, "My God, out of thousands of guys that have been through the mill with him, he remembered me." I'm sure he remembers most of the people's names.

One time I was jogging at UCLA, he said, "You're doing about a 7-1/2 minute mile aren't you?"

I said, "Yes, I am." I was amazed, and I said, "How can you tell Coach?"

He said, "Well, I can tell by your stride just about how fast you were running."

I learned from John Wooden that it takes hard work and perseverance to get what you're going after. If you and somebody else are going after something, you have to have more training or perseverance. Success is a lot of hard work. It isn't something magical that comes along or that you get a lucky break. It's you working for the break and working very hard.

It helped me in my career as an editor. We had a training program when I was starting. I was an apprentice and they were going to see who was going to make editor and so on. They would pit one against another. The guy that hung in there and worked hardest usually got the promotion. He helped me that way.

LUCIUS ALLEN
Los Angeles, California

Lucius played basketball for John Wooden at UCLA and went on to play pro ball. He was inducted into the UCLA Athletic Hall of Fame in 2000.

I played for John Wooden from 1965-69. It was a time that I call "the good old days." There were all types of exciting things happening politically. UCLA had just won a national championship so the campus was very excited about basketball.

Pauley Pavilion, my freshman year, was newly built. The school itself was starting to receive notoriety, not only academically, but athletically. It was a great place and I formed a lot of really good lifelong relationships.

I went to Wyandotte High School in Kansas City, Kansas. Jerry Norman recruited me, but I had seen John Wooden in my senior year at a Fellowship of Christian Athletes basketball camp. I'll never forget it. Bill Bradley was the keynote speaker. Jerry Norman had been in contact with my coach, Walt Shulbolm, who in the Midwest is a very renowned high school coach of basketball. We won state championships in high school. When we didn't win it, something was wrong. That's the type of coach he was.

He was in contact with Coach Norman and told him that he thought he had an athlete out here that might fit into their style of play, so Jerry Norman came out to see me practice a couple times. Then John Wooden, my senior year, came out and saw me play at the Fellowship of Christian Athletes camp.

It was the summer of 1964. He had just won his first national championship, at Kansas City, Missouri that year, so I had been witness to this style of play that was unbelievable—they were full-court pressing. The basketball that I had seen was from the Hank Iba school of basketball, which was pass the ball around until you got a lay-up. If you didn't get a lay-up, it had to be a four-foot jump shot and nobody shot the ball until you got a good shot. With the full-court press, they didn't even have a center; the biggest guy they had was six-foot-five.

This was a new, exciting thing to me as a high school basketball player who thrived on quickness. I didn't have a whole lot of "shake and bake" moves, but I was gifted with a talent of quickness, so I really liked the UCLA style.

The full-court press was extremely radical. Nobody could believe it. All of a sudden there was a new way of looking at basketball. If you feel you have superior athletes, you could actually control the tempo of the game, which was just unheard of in basketball. You thought anybody who played basketball this way was not going to play winning basketball.

We looked at full-court pressing as something that wasn't structured; you do things a certain way all the time in ordinary, mechanical-type basketball. The press relied a lot more on quickness and jumping ability and athletic ability as well as the ability to be in great physical condition.

When I met Coach Wooden, I was a Baptist, so this was a great experience in religious terms. Coach Wooden, being a very pious man, taught lessons and spoke and was a big part of this camp. I got a chance to speak with him from a consultant's point of view, and then of course we shared his knowledge of the basketball court also.

It seemed like the Pyramid was always being discussed in one way shape or form, but that was not the focus at that time. As long as I've known him, it's always been around in one sense. He would talk knowledgeably about the Bible as well, and to this day can quote you scriptures, I'm sure. If you were to talk to him tomorrow about his knowledge of the Bible, he'd astound you in that arena.

Bill Bradley, who the year before had averaged about fifty points a game in the NCAA Final Four, a Missouri boy and a legend to us guys in the Midwest, was helpful and put on clinics. It was almost in his name that they ran the camp, so it attracted an awful lot of high school athletes.

Wooden was not as big a draw. He was a West Coast coach and he had just won an NCAA championship, but he wasn't Johnny Wooden at that time. I was in awe of him and so I was very shy and didn't have a whole lot to say. I was intimidated by the man, because I really looked up to and had a lot of respect for him.

I had considered going to the University of Kansas, which was traditional basketball and had cultivated a relationship with me, and Northwestern University, which told me I could be a big star on a big team—and I liked that.

Then I visited UCLA, in California. Everybody was looking at TV in those days, and California was the place to be. You had the ocean and the mountains and the swimsuits out there on the beach. The sun shines 360 days a year. After I came out and saw the University, there really was no contest as to where I was going to go because I wanted to get out of the Midwest and I wanted to play fast basketball. I didn't want to play slow down Hank Iba type of basketball, which was typical of Big-8 basketball in those days.

My freshmen team at UCLA played the varsity. The varsity had just won the national championship, so there was this big game between the incoming freshmen and the national champs, and they lost on their home court to the freshmen!

That was really a phenomenal thing. Kareem scored fifty-six points that night. We were opening up Pauley Pavilion. We just won the national championship. There was heavy pressure. A lot had been written in the papers about Kareem and these other talented freshmen, and now they'd get a chance to showcase these guys in the game. There were lots of bets on campus. When we played in our practice games six, eight weeks prior to that, everybody was coming in. Everybody wanted to see Kareem and of course they had a chance to see us other players on the team and see that we're gonna be all right here for a while cause we kept beating those guys.

The old guard said "Yeah, but the freshmen, they have to mature, blah, blah, blah. . ." The new kids are saying, "Hey, these guys are great." There was a lot of tension on the campus and a lot of excitement. And when we go in there's a lot of press. It was the first time in Pauley. Kareem was just phenomenal; he just dominated the game.

We weren't astounded when we won—we kind of expected it. We knew we were pretty good. We knew we were pretty good because there was nobody who could stop Kareem. Here's a seven-foot guy who can jump quick and pass (he didn't have much of a jump shot in those days), and he was so physically intimidating. You couldn't score on him and you couldn't stop him.

We knew we were pretty good just having him around, but there were other things that we had: people couldn't zone us because we had Lynn Shackelford and myself. And the team really couldn't concentrate on double teaming because Kareem was an excellent passer. Kareem picked them apart with his passing ability that night. And all we did was throw the ball into him and then he either dunked it or passed it.

The varsity did not win the national championship that year. I think that freshmen game shook their confidence in their ability to win. They ended up taking a second in the Pac-10 that year.

At UCLA I lost one game to Houston. Without Coach Wooden I probably never would have been a professional basketball player. Coach Wooden used to have Kareem and myself, when we were freshmen, in order for us to get to know each other, playing together against the varsity.

Wooden had special drills for Kareem and me. Everyday before practice I had to pass the ball to Kareem and Kareem had to play one-on-one against Jay Carty. I was getting special training because I could not dribble the ball. I thought I was a pretty good guard, but I needed work. I did not have the ability to handle the ball that I thought I had. He had me doing all these funny things with my ankles like walking on the side of my ankles which was supposed to strengthen my ankles. I've never had a sprained ankle in my life.

Coach Wooden was teaching Kareem how to shoot jump shots and play one-on-one basketball. Kareem was a great dunk artist and he had a little bit of hook, but he couldn't do anything else. So Kareem learned how to put the ball on the floor, how to face the basket, how to operate and perform turn around jump shots. He learned all these one on one things that went on to make him a great basketball player.

We hated our special practices. We decided we were leaving. This guy was working us harder than he was working everybody else on the team and we didn't have to take that crap. And we were gone. We talked about it, this dirty stuff. Everybody else comes in an hour after us, we're already tired, and now he expects us to go out there and do it with these people—we don't have to take that! "Where do you want to go? Well, let's go to Michigan State. They know how to treat their athletes out there." We were gonna go.

Willie Naulls got wind of our dissatisfaction, and came and talked with us, and so all of the sudden we had a buffer who had gone to UCLA. We formed a nice relationship with Willie, and he introduced us to a few of the alumni and we started to win. We kind of forgot about all our "problems." Those things that he had me doing in those years, those were the only tools that I had to keep me in professional basketball. I'm indebted to Coach Wooden for what he taught me.

I played pro ball for ten years. I was on a championship Milwaukee team, and played with the Lakers. I played eight out of my ten years with Kareem. Seattle and Kansas City were the other two teams. I have a very special bond with Kareem, without me making those great passes to him, he never would have got 30,000 points, maybe just 25,000! We had a lot of fun together.

When I graduated from UCLA, I had the fundamental skills to play basketball as a profession. When I got to pro ball, I was a solid fundamental player. You could tell watching me in ten minutes of play I had instinct (knowing where to be on the floor) and the ability to make the proper decision out there. It was all that Johnny Wooden training.

It became automatic. I was a solid player. I knew it and they knew it. And I didn't make a lot of mistakes out there, and that's what rookies do. Compared to other rookies, by far and away I'd had the best coaching. It was a huge advantage for me. I was an All-American two years. My third year I did not play with the team because I had got into all types of personal problems. I did not play the third year and therefore was not eligible. All the years that I played I was an All-American. I ended up turning pro a year early. I was one of the first ones to turn pro a year early. With my situation at UCLA it was probably the best thing. I was not doing well in school and I got arrested for possession of marijuana.

Wooden had his Pyramid of Success and there were several principles on there where I had let him down and not fulfilled my obligation as a UCLA basketball player. This is what he expected, this is what he preached. I knew it, he knew it and everybody else knew it on the basketball team. He was very bothered by it. He just sat down and said, "You know, we aren't all perfect. We'll have to do something. I don't know what it is that we're going to do." That meant that I would probably have to red shirt a year or sit out a year.

It would have been my senior year. At that time, I had professional basketball potential and wanted to play, so it was the best thing for me to do. I didn't speak with him personally. We never got to that point. Had I talked with him, being the man that I know that he is, he probably would have discussed with me and said, "Your education is more important," and pushed me in that direction.

I was a rebel in those days. I was out from under my mother's hand, without her permission, and learning about life. There were a lot of influences that were going around at that time. I wasn't a bad kid. Also I was a star on campus on the biggest team of all time. It impacted professors in how they perceived me and it impacted me on how I perceived myself. I thought I was a big man on campus and that I was not going to have to do as much work as the other students. But, by God, the professors were going to make sure that I did at least as much as all the other students. They would focus in on me and it was very important that I do more than my fair share because they were looking at me. We had 30,000 students there in those days and the classrooms were pretty big, but they weren't big for athletes like me.

On a human level, I've learned discipline. I didn't have it. I've learned how to relax and yet always be alert. Concentrate no matter what the situation is, be it a social situation or an athletic contest. He has given me a lot of direction as far as spiritualism is concerned. I really am a spiritual person at this point in time. What I believe is not a so-called Christian religion, I'm a Science of Mind, and Jesus, of course, was one of the greatest prophets ever.

It's hard to put into words all the different ways Coach Wooden has had an impact on me. He is a shining example of what you can do if you keep yourself in shape and treat everybody well around you—good things will happen. He was one of those people who was not very dollar oriented. He could be like some of these other coaches, always demanding and have a lot of things, but that's never been his way. I really appreciate and hope that I never get so engrossed in things that they become more important to me. That's what he taught me.

He's a great speaker. He comes across very humble and he's very funny and he generally makes fun of himself, so there's a dichotomy there. Everybody's looking at this great, great man who's telling them he's not so great. He has a tremendous impact on students of the game, students of life, and of course all the folks who are interested in basketball.

What I remember about Coach Wooden is that we never prepared for anybody else. He was never really afraid of anybody. He figured that if we did what we did best that we didn't have to worry about anything else that an opposing team might try to do to us.

Organization. I remember going in and talking to the Coach and saying, "Coach, I can't believe how tired I am! But you know, I didn't think I worked that hard."

And his comment was, "Well, you were too busy having fun, weren't you Lucius?"

I said, "Yeah, that was fun."

He says, "Well, you know what? A couple of other guys have come in and told me that." So he took me back into his file. . .and we're talking ten years ago on the same date, the same practice that he had just taken us through.

He said, "I can just show you right here, every practice minute that I spent for the last twenty years." And that was just so impressive to me that he had that to fall back on.

And, oh boy, the Pyramid of Success! I was fighting the Pyramid of Success. Like I said, I was a rebel in those days. Coach Wooden was tuned in. His focus was to make an All-American person out of me first. And if I happened to be an All-American basketball player, well, that'd be real nice. His primary focus was to make a person. But my primary focus was to fight that, it seemed. So on all levels I was losing this battle because of that darn Pyramid of Success. Coach Wooden was very good at the methods that he used to control you.

Take a basketball situation. I used to like to take the ball and throw the ball behind my back because I had the ability to do it, but that was not the proper way to make the pass. The proper way was to make a crossover pass and bounce the ball on the floor. And we'd get in a game and I'd make my behind the back pass and the crowd would go crazy and we'd score the lay up. I'd be feeling great about the great play that I'd made and the horn would sound and I'd come out of the game. So as soon as I came out of the game (we'd been through this scenario before) I'd get a pissed-off look and I'd go sit at the end of the bench. And the first half would go by and the second half would be half-way through. And pretty soon I'd mosey my little old self on back up to Coach Wooden and he wouldn't look at me. He'd say, "Well, you ready to play basketball now, Lucius?"

"Yeah, Coach, I'm ready to play." So I learned. That was the way I learned not to throw the behind the back pass. We didn't have to say anything, I knew what I had done and he knew what I had done. All 20,000 people in Pauley Pavilion knew what I had done. They all knew what he was doing to me.

He was very effective in his means of controlling us, getting us to do what he wanted us to do. The guy was a master of psychiatry, psychology, whatever you want to call it. He was one of those kinds of people who know what buttons to push when.

The Pyramid did affect me in later life. All of sudden these things started to fall into place for me. I realized that I was a professional basketball player because I had obtained certain skills at UCLA. That was my goal. I would meditate on the Pyramid and look at it on occasion. We got all the books and little trophies of the Pyramid. I had a crystal version. I would look at it and I understood that it was more of a philosophy than a punishment. Things actually started falling into place and it started making a whole lot of sense. I can relate to it and say that I agree totally with it and try to live by a lot of the things that his philosophy brings forth in the Pyramid of Success. I talk to young kids all the time about it. The Pyramid of Success is what I base my talks on, depending upon what sector of the community that I'm talking to. I speak sometimes to underprivileged areas and other times at the basketball camps.

I didn't get my degree at UCLA because I left early. It bothers me sometimes, but in the business that I'm in it really hasn't affected me. Getting arrested for marijuana caused me financial problems. I wasn't able to get the dollars that I would have been able to coming out of UCLA after another championship. If I hadn't had a "cloud" hampering me, I would have earned more. Nobody brings it up anymore, but it was a real big deal at that time. I played pro ball for ten years. After the pros, I had my own construction company, and did that for years.

At that point, I moved back to California and became a sales consultant. I train sales people and I tell them about the Pyramid, we go through the whole nine yards. There's a certain way of looking at life and what you're going to go out and accomplish that day as a salesman.

I'm very happily married. I've got two kids. We think they're basketball players. One is going to UC San Diego and is going to play basketball down there. This marriage is four years old. My previous wife committed suicide. The tragedy was incredibly difficult to overcome. It makes you look within and you grow from those types of things. Some of the things I learned from Wooden helped me through that period.

Everybody thinks that it's so glamorous when you're a professional athlete, but we're people like anybody else. I've had my ups and downs in my private life, and I've been fortunate to discuss this with Coach Wooden.

The UCLA players I'm close to feel that he's a great teacher, and a great philosopher. As far as the real person-to-person, father-to-son type interaction, he is not that. What the problem is that because he's who he is and we all want to be so close to him and he's only got so much to give—he is the professor and the professor can only get so close to the student, so to speak.

As to the talk about some players over the years having received improper compensation, I don't think he would let anyone tell him. He would control that situation so that he could honestly say that he didn't know. I really think that he was astute enough to keep himself and be general enough with his discussions with his staff so that he could honestly say that he never knew.

Coach Wooden is a very philosophical, intelligent type guy that you just wish you could hug all the time. He's one of those type of people that gives far more in relation to what he gets back. He's an exceptional guy you can profit from by observing. You look at his family, he's a perfect role model for me to design my family and my relationship with my wife.

He was remarkable for his color blindness, especially because it was a new thing in college athletics at that time. Mike Warren and I, when I was a freshman, were supposed to be pretty good jump shooters, but Coach Wooden would bless us with his presence on the court and challenge us to a shooting game. Mike and I had heard that Coach would always take the guards out and just let them know that, you know, "You guys might be pretty good players but old Coach here is still the best shooter out of anybody that ever blessed the halls of UCLA." So Mike and I, we vowed that we were going to retire him. Needless to say, I don't know if anyone finally succeeded, but it certainly wasn't Mike and myself. He just whipped the crap out of us. He was at least forty-plus at the time, and probably fifty. He certainly had some of the wrinkles that he has now, cause I helped put some of them there. But he used to take us out and beat us and talk to us the whole time he was beating us.

"Now listen guys, this is how you shoot a jump shot, okay? Watch this release and oh, that went in, didn't it?" He always was intimidating us. See most people don't realize that Coach Wooden would be rolling up that little program, they'd say, "Well that seems a little thing." But while he was rolling that up, he's steadily talking trash. Most people didn't understand that Coach Wooden can talk with the best of them. He could really intimidate you with his funny remarks.

ART ALPER
Los Angeles, California

Art played basketball for John Wooden at UCLA.

I played for the Coach the first three years he was at UCLA, 1948-51. He was very well organized. His practices were run in a specific manner. He was good teacher. He rarely ever really chastised anybody. He used the principles of teaching. Both my mother and all my mother's sisters were all teachers, and in those days a teacher had a lot more respect. As a result of that you listened. And all the time he'd stop a practice and show you what you were doing wrong.

I thought he was different. Fortunately, the coaches I had in high school used a lot of the same fundamentals that he did so I didn't have to pick up a lot of that but I was amazed at the footwork I learned.

One thing that I appreciated was that he didn't chastise anybody. It was a teaching experience rather than an upbraiding. It was a positive reinforcement. That's what you really learned out of this and it's a tragedy that the high school coaches today don't use that kind of approach. A lot of them have not participated in a higher level of sports and as a result they're frustrated and they take it out on the kids. In a college level, Wooden was the first coach who had himself under control. He knew what he wanted to accomplish. When you see that, you listen.

He was also very strict in regard to his conditioning. Some of the principles we use today are entirely different. You couldn't drink any water. We were always standing up, moving. He was organized, and you absorbed a lot. As you went along, you realized the system wasn't that difficult. You had to learn that there was a place for you in the system. Either that, or you weren't going to play. And nobody was bigger than the system. If he didn't feel that you were playing within yourself or if you were out of control then he'd sit you down. He'd sit you down or pull you out. He wouldn't just yank you. I mean there was a reason for it. He'd indicate to you what you were doing. You learned to put out. You learned there's a price to pay for winning and that's dedication and living within the system.

If you were a so-called star in high school, it didn't matter. There were no stars effectively at UCLA because somebody was going to rise to another level. Everybody was in there to contribute. The system wasn't designed around one man. You felt that if you were in the system, you were contributing.

I still carry a lot of the principles, whether it's on the Pyramid of Success or just a learning experience. I learned a lot about teamwork, and that nothing comes easy and that if you're willing to pay the price in most cases it's going to happen for you. Wooden was able to motivate his team, they had a positive mental attitude.

I'm in the insurance business. When Kareem's house burned down, although Kareem doesn't know it, Sam Gilbert, of all people, was concerned about what was going to happen and was making sure that it was taken care of properly. So I arranged to get the adjuster out there and the right people to help him so that he could get the maximum that he was entitled to under his insurance contract. It was a major loss for Kareem, but I don't think he even knows who did it. Lucius Allen was working for a bank and we tried to put some money in his bank and buy CDs. Over the years, we tried to help the guys out.

If they need some direction, we definitely would call and sit with them and find out what they might be looking for a future and explain what the insurance business is. The Pyramid of Success had an effect on my life. I use a lot of that. I've owned several companies that I've sold to public companies. I've formed a savings and loan (along with Jerry Norman, I might add, and several other UCLA athletes). That turned out very successfully. Most of the fellows in our earlier group have been very successful with whatever endeavor they wanted to do, whether it be coaching, business, medicine, law or whatever they chose.

For most of these people, Wooden had a profound impact. I think part of that is that you pay a price for everything and if you're willing to do that, work hard, with honesty and integrity and all the things that are on that Pyramid, things are gonna happen.

Over the years my relationship with Wooden was somewhat strained. It wasn't real close. He had a lot of marvelous assistant coaches. One of the things that's maybe perturbed me a little bit is that nobody's ever really given credit to those assistant coaches. [Alper is primarily referring to Jerry Norman.] They did a marvelous job. No question Wooden was an outstanding teacher, but these other coaches were outstanding recruiters, strategists, including his first coach, Ed Powell, who he brought from Indiana with him.

Although it was a little strained, I always had a great deal of admiration for him, and he has been very loyal. For example, he used to have these camps where he was integrally involved, and my boys went there. He made them feel like they were special. He always called everybody "my boys" and still does, and I still call him Coach when I see him. When these young kids went there, he made them feel like they were something special and that really made me feel good. It's not been an intimate relationship but we're friendly, and, if there's any strain, it's on my end, because maybe I felt a little guilty not getting closer.

GENE BARTOW
Birmingham, Alabama

Gene was an opposing coach when John Wooden was at UCLA. Gene also followed John Wooden as UCLA basketball coach when Wooden retired.

I coached against John Wooden in the Memphis State/UCLA national championship game (losing to UCLA in 1973) and I followed him as the UCLA coach in 1975.

John Wooden will go down in history as the best basketball coach at any level (college, professional, high school, whatever) who has ever coached the game. He just had a great feel for the game and a great feel for getting the most out of the players that he coached. A lot of us in the coaching profession feel that he certainly was the best. Nobody else had ten national championships.

Wooden's legacy to basketball is that he's a very good person who had great winning teams and national championship teams, yet still was a very kind and humble man. I was a high school coach in St. Charles, Missouri in the late fifties when I first heard of John. The first time I ever met John, I was a graduate assistant/assistant coach at California—Santa Barbara. I was watching a high school game in the Los Angeles area in 1960, and visited with him that night, and he made a great impression.

When I coached at Valparaiso University in Indiana, he had a brother living in LaPorte and we convinced John to come back and speak at our clinics there once or twice during that six year period, and I got to know him a little better. I became aware of Wooden through his coaching clinics, and through his coaching at UCLA. UCLA was a great university and he was doing a good job.

John has influenced all of us in coaching to a certain degree. There's no doubt that some of the different offensive sets out of the high post that he ran at UCLA for many years I've used as a part of our program since those Valparaiso days. He's had an influence from the basketball technical standpoint on many. Because he's a very good human being, from that standpoint, he's influenced a lot of people, including myself.

When I went to UCLA, I'd given some thought to the problem of trying to follow a legend, but I just felt very confident that I could have a very good program there and make it all work. And I think we were making it work pretty well, but I just couldn't get real relaxed about the situation and felt the pressures and stress of that job more than I had in my Valparaiso and Memphis State college situations. I wasn't having a lot of fun and that's the big reason that when these people from University of Alabama and Birmingham came at me with a lot better financial offer, I thought, "Gee, I believe I'd go back and see if I could have fun again." And it's been great.

The pressure was a combination of a lot of things. I probably put most of it on myself. You get the feeling you need to win at every game. We only lost nine, but there's a great microscope on certain jobs. Take Notre Dame football— they're still following Knute Rockne there in many ways. Same thing, Kentucky basketball and Adolph Rupp. We've got it right here in our state at Alabama, with Bear Bryant's football programs.

Following John Wooden at UCLA is a different kind of job, and not a completely normal job. Maybe "ever" is too big a word, but it may be a hundred years before that job will be completely normal again. You've got so much media attention on it. There are certain expectations from many of the alumni that are used to nothing but great teams and complete excellence. From the media and alumni and even students and fans and friends in those situations—like Alabama, Notre Dame, Kentucky and UCLA basketball—there is almost an unfair expectation and it takes a very, very special person in coaching in those jobs to really be happy and enjoy it. Certain people perhaps can. I couldn't.

John was a great friend while I was at UCLA and I visited with him on occasion. We played golf a few times. We asked him to help us visit with prospective players at times when we were recruiting and he did whatever we asked.

John and I talk once in a while and we've had meals together on two or three occasions since I left. We talk about basketball, my time at UCLA and our families. I know his children and he knows mine. We visit as friends might. I like him because when you're a basketball coach and a person has had his record, you are in awe of his success but moreover he's just a very nice person.

As to the Pyramid of Success, my son's got a copy of it up on his office wall and I've got a copy of it. It's something that John came up with that was his philosophy of life and it's excellent.

DR. JOHN BERBERICH
Seattle, Washington

*John played basketball for John Wooden at UCLA and went on
to play pro ball before becoming a clinical psychologist.*

I didn't play high school basketball, but did in junior college. I was fortunate enough to play well against UCLA and USC and had offers from both. I played center from 1959-61, and professionally for a year.

I always had good coaches, but Coach Wooden was by far the best. He was an organized, caring, thoughtful man who prepared you to play your best game. He just stood out. He had a lot of character.

He lived up to his Pyramid of Success and I have it in my office. He sent me a signed, large copy of it. I have it not where people can easily see it because it's so hard to live up to and I don't want to imply that in order to be a success in my office as a clinical psychologist you have to have been a success like John Wooden. Wooden truly is and was a great man, there's no question about it. It was a great honor to play for him. I learned a great deal about being a human being from playing with him.

A lot of people notice the Pyramid. I've never used it as a way of saying anything except that I know a man who lived up to this. People look at it and they're impressed. For athletes, I make sure that any athlete who I see gets a chance to look at it and they understand what it says. They strive for the things that are there, not all of them, but many of them. The Pyramid is very impressive. What more can anybody say? From bottom to top, it lists the kinds of characteristics and qualities of truly fine people, the kind of qualities that John Wooden showed.

When people ask me if I played at UCLA and if I played for Wooden, I of course take a great deal of pride in saying I did. He taught me, perhaps more than any other coach that I had, to try hard to make use of what I had and never look down if I did the best that I could. I brought that into my own life after leaving UCLA when I raised my own children. People would lead more fulfilled existences if they meditated on and tried to adhere to the principles of the Pyramid. The characteristics are almost religious. One would want to avoid guilt in the presentation of those kinds of things and have people look at them with the idea that if you can, adopt these kinds of things, they can take you a long way.

Guilt is one of the main things from which people suffer. Wooden never presented the Pyramid to anybody saying, "You should be this way," or "You have to be this way to meet my needs." He just lived that way. In a religious sense, the person preaches the best who lives as an example rather than trying to preach to other people about how they should be. He lived that way. As far as I'm aware, he did it consistently and he reached the top.

I'll tell you a story about him. We were at the airport once and he had wandered over to the newsstand. And all of a sudden, he turned around and the players were all standing around him. He had in his hand a *Playboy* magazine. The centerfold was entirely open, and he looked over his shoulder and saw that everyone was looking at him, and he said, "Oh, look, blue shoes!" referring to what the model was wearing.

Another time we were on a horrible trip. We were in Kentucky and driving to Lexington. We had to go by bus because the weather out of Chicago was so bad. There was a drunk on the bus, who was not a person associated with the team. I'm sitting behind this guy, and he falls into the aisle out of his seat trying to reach Coach Wooden. And he looks up from the floor and says to Wooden, "Say, Coach, are you drunk?"

Coach looked down at him. [The drunk] had already introduced himself as Jim Ledbetter. Coach said, "No, Jim, I'm not. Do you know anyone who is?" This got the entire team roaring.

We had a brawl riot with the Air Force Academy in Colorado. The stands came down. We were behind 18 points in that game at the half and we won by one point. The game was called for the riot. The referees defaulted us and disqualified us and gave the game to the Air Force Academy. The general there said, "Oh no, we'll finish the game." And we, of course did, and won.

The riot came about because the referees were badly homering us. The players were smaller than we were and were taking advantage of the referees' unwillingness to call fouls against them for body blocks, elbows and all kinds of stuff, even after the whistle. Wooden came out on the floor and demanded a technical foul in a very quiet way. He said, "All right, give me a technical," and told the referees to stop pointing fingers at the players. Well, that set the fans in a bad mood, and the referees gave him a technical. The fight ensued after that.

Coaches sometimes ask for a technical foul when they feel their team is getting a bad deal. It was a protest, but it was designed to let his team know that he was behind them and he, too, knew what was going on and that he was going to do what he could to even things up and make sure the referees couldn't get away with it. It was his way of noting to everyone in the stands that he had enough of this kind of homer refereeing. And we did win the game.

We were not able to get our team together, and I think that was one of the saddest things for Coach Wooden. In his career, because we had the kind of team that could have gone far, it's hard to say why it didn't work. One sopho-more was a loner, a guy who never quite fit in. He happened to be a friend of mine, and a very fine ball player, but he played without thinking, like a sopho-more does. He was resented on the team because of his defiance of Coach Wooden a couple of times in not taking direction and walking off the practice court. We just never came together in the way that one would hope. As the years go by, you look back and you think about what could have been and what you wish would have happened.

John Wooden is intensely competitive, very proud and very smart. He's a compulsive man, and by that I mean extremely well-organized. He's a keen observer of people and situations, a better pre-game coach, if you will, than a game coach as I observed him. He had the capacity to prepare his players for a game so that they would play their game.

Once the game started you played your game. He was loathe to change the game plan. He figured that what he had prepared his team to do and what his team was prepared to do would make them play their best and if a team was going to beat them, they would beat them with UCLA playing their best.

His development of the zone press and the press mechanisms he used came after I was with him. It is an example of a person making absolutely maximal good use of his team and each of its players. In terms of his philosophy of bas-ketball, it made the game go fast and it made everybody play his pace, which was the way he liked to play basketball—fast. When we would play the University of California with Pete Newell or Oklahoma State it would drive you up a wall, because they would pass the ball for ten minutes and then final-ly take a shot that they'd passed up seven minutes ago.

In business, what they would say is he controlled the agenda. He dictated the outcome by making you play on his court in the way that he could beat you because he was better conditioned and he could play the game fast. His teams always could play the game fast. On top of being able to go fast, we were orga-nized and you don't see that year after year after year with teams, but he did it—because he knew how to prepare people.

Wooden was a father figure to me. Just having the success of being able to play for him on first string, to do well, and play on a strong team was great. He taught me a lot of self-discipline, a lot of things about personal pride and doing one's best and much I'll never forget and I hope that I pass on to other people.

THE JOHN WOODEN PYRAMID OF SUCCESS

PETE BLACKMAN
Los Angeles, California

*Pete played basketball for John Wooden at UCLA between 1958 and 1962,
became a high-powered lawyer, and is now the Administrative Vice
Chancellor at UCLA, the man who makes the University run.*

I grew up in a UCLA family. Both of my parents graduated from UCLA on
the old campus in the last class, 1928, before it moved to Westwood.

I met him originally when I was a high school kid at the home of mutual
friends. Bill Barnes was then the football coach at UCLA, and his wife was an
elementary school teacher. My mother was a school principal, so I met Coach
Wooden in that kind of setting. In those days I was three, four years away from
playing, about fourteen. I remember him very well even from that point in time.
He was warm and thoughtful, very acute, very perceptive, intellectually precise,
and an intriguing human being. That's what struck me from the very outset, and
it was true whatever the subject was, whether it was English literature (which
we share with a great ongoing interest) or analyzing a set of defenses. Whatever
it happened to be, it was that same focus of precision and organization.

He is clearly a man of great control and a man of the church and a man of
a lot of other qualities that we don't necessarily associate with being a tough son
of a bitch basketball coach. But I never dealt with many people then, nor have
I since, who had more fiber, more clarity of vision in terms of where they were
trying to go, more focus on it, or more ability to understand precisely how to
motivate the people around that could get to that goal. I'm talking about business people—it doesn't make any difference what their particular walk may
have been—lawyers, others that I've dealt with and have had contact with since.
He had that extraordinary clarity and firmness of goal orientation and drive
toward it. It was very clear.

People would say, "How did he get to be a several time All-American at his
size?" or "How did he achieve all of these things?" A great deal of it had to do
with not only that clarity of perception, but an awful lot of it was guts and drive
and toughness, mental toughness. He's an extraordinarily demanding person,
but understanding of people in the sense of knowing what they could reasonably give. That was a good combination, and it paid off.

He affected me, mostly in post-play time. Just having played for Wooden,
I enjoyed playing for him but that's now decades ago. My senior year was the
first UCLA team that made the Final Four. We lost to Cincinnati by two in the
semi-final. That was a remarkable experience for me because it was the first

time I had ever confronted anything quite that dramatic. It was a dignified loss and like a lot of things in life over the years. The fact that you lost that particular game has evolved away in terms of any sense of real negativism, and the participation in such an event has remained with me as a glowing, marvelous experience of a lifetime. We won the conference. We got off to a terrible start.

He had great comprehension and organization, drive, toughness, and the ability to understand that different people are motivated by different things—to understand that I might treat you in one way to get the best result from you and a different way to get the best result from another. There were other kinds of very fundamental, stylistic approaches to problem solving and interchange with human beings. I learned from his honesty that being tricky with people or cutting a corner in the long run just simply does not get you anywhere.

He would come forward with lines that I still remember, such as "I just simply am not going to like all of you the same." That's a tough thing for a coach to say. But he was honest about things like that. He had many very brisk ways of getting fundamental concepts across. He was willing to take on tough issues of communication with you. Those processes would ultimately show value. I learned from his extraordinarily detailed organization. He was fantastically prepared, literally every practice was planned down to the minute. You don't lose track of lessons like that.

When you're preparing for a major business presentation fifteen years later, you look around and you're probably the best prepared person there. Well, why is that true? Because people like that proved to you at an early stage of development that the time spent in preparation will pay off. Seventy percent of what you did in preparation probably will turn out to be irrelevant. Unfortunately, you just don't know which portion you have to prepare for, right? We've all been through this. He was great on those counts.

He drove everybody, but within a conception that always had value. Make yourself as good as you can be. Always. There was very little emphasis on the opposition, very little scouting, very little attempt to understand what they were going to do on the theory that if you do the best you can do, we're going to statistically come out well. These are lessons of a reasonably profound nature. Focus on yourself, your own values, doing things correctly. Develop a plan of sound strategy for yourself and pursue that plan, recognizing how it's affecting others, but handle criticism from the point of view of the source. Understand the source of criticism and try and determine what the problem is with the source of criticism before you jump to the conclusion that you need to react to it. Those are all lessons that in many ways I learned from Wooden, both from watching him operate and in retrospective of recalling how he had operated.

THE JOHN WOODEN PYRAMID OF SUCCESS

I found myself five years out of law school in the middle of a downtown law practice, under what I thought in those days was a reasonable amount of stress, and trying to juggle twenty-three things at the same time. I'd say, "What kind of lessons have I ever learned that would help me cope strategically with this seemingly intractable set of circumstances." And I'd find myself going back to these lessons trying to find that sort of solid, simple executable strategy that would get me through the muck. Those lessons were very valuable.

The parts of the Pyramid that I've come to know were all displayed, but more in just day to day circumstances. I think it is a very elegant manner of displaying a set of evolved ideas over an extended period of time, which he organized and which is a very valuable tool. I think we might have all benefited tremendously had it been displayed to us more aggressively. But, people dropping Pyramids of Success on you when you're a twenty-year-old undergraduate doesn't work as well. I'm more willing to accept the lessons in the Pyramid itself at the age of thirty than I would have when I was trying to shoot hoops at nineteen. When you're out there running up and down the court worrying about whether or not you're going to get your ass kicked on a Friday night, you don't feel like sitting there reading something quite that philosophical.

People talk to me about the Pyramid all the time. People often ask me about what it was like to play for Wooden. He's a famous guy, particularly to my jock interested friends. In a business context, I'm constantly encountering people and "What did you" or "Oh, I remember." More likely, somebody will introduce me as having played. And then the first question is, "Well, what was it like? What's Wooden really like? What was it like to play for John Wooden? How about the Pyramid of Success?" He's linked to the Pyramid of Success in a significant way. It's become a statement of his philosophy in a public sort of a way. People are intrigued by it and corporate heavyweights read it and say, "That's interesting, I'll use it as a motivational tool," and so forth. It's got real significance.

I went in the Navy for two years, and shot hoops there. It was between Korea and Vietnam, so there was a lot of ball being played. Then I came back and graduated from UCLA Law School and, went to work for a large downtown-based law firm. I did finance work there for about ten, eleven years, then moved to Europe and ran the European office in Paris.

Before coming back, I got talking to Chuck Young, the chancellor to UCLA. They were looking for somebody with a real estate, commercial and not necessarily legal, but transactional background, to restructure the way the business of capital project development takes place on campus, so I got involved.

My communications with Wooden over the years since I left UCLA have been extensive. We get together for lunch about once every three or four months. I'm a fan of his and will be for a lifetime. He's been a resource to me and I like to talk to him about hoops and what's going on there. As my own kids have come up—they're both competitive athletes—he was a resource in the sense of somebody knowledgeable to listen to my questions about how you handle father/son relationships as they're developing. He's a serious father figure to me along with my own father who is a fabulous guy, still alive and kicking and a great resource, too. Coach Wooden is the number two influence in my life from the perspective of an advice giver and a person of real dignity in terms of intelligence and judgement and experience.

I venerate him to the degree that when I do something of which I am proud I want to tell him about it. He tolerates that. But that's the way fathers act.

He and Nell were exemplary. He was very solicitous of her. It was clear that she was a tremendous resource to him. When you're eighteen, nineteen, twenty years old, it's nice to see people sharing the stresses, sharing the successes, in a traditional family value kind of way. I found that good to see. She was tough in her own right, and she was behind John 100 percent.

One of his real skills and attributes is diplomacy, always, and most evident in the years after he left here as coach. He's very bright about knowing he had great skill, but he always had some great ball players and some good luck.

In any event, the point is that he knew you don't always have a perfect ending the way he did. He was very cautious not to be a source of undercutting the people who came after him. It was tough enough as it was, perhaps too tough no matter what. But he sure didn't contribute to that and I think everybody thought well of him. That was consistent with the kind of style with which he approached pretty much everything.

There was a special period of greatness athletically that took place at UCLA that will probably never be recreated in college basketball, maybe never in college sports. It's almost a non-paralleled achievement, ten out of twelve national championships. I believe that the part about it that everyone around here is most proud of is that not only was it well turned out, but there was an aura about those teams that made them really true champions.

There was nothing cheap about any one of those teams. By and large, the ball players who played on them were bright kids who went on to success in the pros or in other endeavors. It was a period of extraordinary quality in terms of both great championships, and also the generation of classic student-athletes. He had a lot to do with that. He represented that balance himself, because he himself is a tremendously tough competitor, but at the same time, clearly, an intellectual. Anybody who knows him knows that the intellectual side of life has been a dominant theme for him from the get-go.

THE JOHN WOODEN PYRAMID OF SUCCESS

He has a very firm set of principles from which he does not waver. People say, "What sets him apart? What were the. . ." It was the fundamentals, the simplicity. The Pyramid of Success is a very apt reflection of why this guy was special, because building from a base of fundamentals is the concept of the Pyramid of Success. You don't leap from here to there, you build it up and you "pyramid," figuratively and otherwise, to a successful pinnacle.

When we went to the Final Four, to play Cincinnati, we were running the same drills to warm up and the same drills on a repeat basis at the beginning of practice that we did when I was a first year, first practice freshman. Why? Because there were things that you do and they're going to be ingrained to a point that you just continue to do them and we're going to execute better than the next guy.

These lessons translate into real life. I wrote my kids the other day, and I said when you turn fifty, you start looking around and say, "What are the values that I look for in people who work with me?" or "What are the values that I find in friends and others?" And many of these harken back to lessons I learned from Wooden. There was a day when I was younger when I would have said that intelligence or perspicacity or other kinds of things material. Now I find myself leaning toward ideas like relentlessness and loyalty. Maybe that's being fifty, or maybe it's because I'm older and have learned something. Most tough problems don't evaporate just because you have one bright idea. People who have simple but penetrating ideas, ideas that can be well applied and extended in a consistent way, tend to get more done in the long time. That's fundamental to the kind of thing that Wooden taught us. Do the basics right, and do as well as you can with what God gave you, and you will be surprised at how far you can get in life.

I've met many people who have played for him at other times, and we have an instant camaraderie. Invariably, we end up discussing Wooden. The interesting point is a lot more in what it meant to play basketball for him than it is who beat who and when.

I'm thinking about a personal Wooden story. It's on me and on Hazzard. Walt came out of Philly and was a great player, the best player by far. As a sophomore, he walked in, was prepared to run the team, run the shop and make us into a national contender when we weren't even close to being one. We had a bunch of Southern California beach guys who could shoot, maybe the jumpers and that was about it. We were going to be playing all these tough teams from the East, but Walt wasn't going to take no for an answer, and he was and is very tough. Walt liked to score like anybody likes to score, and Walt could score, but it became clear to him from the outset, and became sort of the watchword of his career, that if he dished it off, everybody else would score more in the ball club and we'd do better. Even though he was a younger player—I was a senior—he could have taken over the team and scored a lot more points. Instead he scored about thirteen or fourteen instead of the twenty-one he could have scored.

This was the 1962 season, Gary Cunningham, John Green, Slaughter, Hazzard and yours truly. And he dishes it off, and you've got guys like Mecell who couldn't get a rebound to save his soul, but I could run on the break and fill a lane, let's say. It was only because of Walt's tremendous ability to see the court that we ended up with a ball club after a very rocky start that won the league and came within a move to get to the final national ball game.

Walt had scored eight in the game, but he'd had twelve assists and basically won the game for us. He was sitting in the locker room looking at statistics and he says, "God, I've only scored eight points." And I was sitting there next to him and I said, "Walt, yeah you scored eight, but you didn't score eight, you scored thirty-eight. Now look, I had fourteen tonight, and if you look there I've got ten of those fourteen on assists from you. You're the one who won this basketball game. Every time you flip the ball to me, that's what's winning ball games for us and those points are all being scored by you. They're not being scored by me. All I do is catch it and stick in the hole." And there was a little hyperbolic quality about that, but not a whole lot.

He went away musing, "Yeah, well maybe that's true." Wooden overheard this, and he's often told the story on two points being made. One was that he said I'd be a lawyer someday because I thought of things like that. He uses it as an example to talk about how the dynamics of team play start to emerge in a team when the chemistry is right; when you find people who are seeking opportunities to reinforce each other and ways to validate each other's skills. Instead of saying, "I got mine," say, "Hey, you're really doing your job." Wooden would grab an incident like that, as instinctive or colloquial as it might be, and he would run with it and use it and he would find a way to reinforce his concept.

I have another remarkable personal recollection, partly because it says something about the evolution of sport in our country. We played University of Houston in 1962 at Houston, which, five years later with Elvin Hayes, made a real run at the national championship. In 1962, Houston had no black players, which says something about how phenomenally the sport changed. We went down there to play and we couldn't find a hotel because we had Walt Hazzard and Fred Slaughter and Larry Gower, who are African-Americans, so we stayed in a dormitory, which was fine. We were all buddies. We could care less.

The stands were fundamentally segregated. I don't know if they were literally sectioned, but it was de facto segregation in the stands. I've been hammered a few times, but never like this. We walked out and Walt and Fred started the game, and they had four fouls in two minutes. It was quite clear that you weren't going to come into Houston and play against the white Houston ball club with your black guys and compete. It wasn't going to happen.

It was so flagrant that we lost that game. We got killed. So the next night we were playing Texas A&M, which was actually a better ball club. Wooden sat the black guys down. He said, "I'm not going to put you in a position of being treated this way. It's inappropriate. You're our starters, but we're going to play this game without you." It was a silent protest. He didn't articulate it quite that way, but said, "I am not going to subject my ball players to that kind of treatment."

So we played Texas A&M. And Dave Waxman and a couple of guys come in there, and I'll tell you, before the game, I've never seen a group of players in the whole time I played more committed to win this silly ass game against Texas A&M, which didn't count for anything much anyway. But by God, if we didn't do anything else the rest of our lives, we were going to win that game.

And we went out there and we just went nuts and beat them by sixteen or something like that. And afterwards we all gathered around and it was pretty emotional. And I got to thinking later that win or lose, what Wooden did for that ball club: he welded us. And it turned out to be interesting later that as a group we became extraordinarily close. That was one of the welding experiences. He took a risk. Maybe that could have been read differently, but this was 1962 and a lot's happened since then. It's a tough story to tell and fully comprehend. All I know is that it did work, and it welded that ball club together in an extraordinary way.

Wooden was only willing to have his name used if it was a facility that would benefit the general student population. There was always discussion to build a "Wooden something" that would clearly be the kind of focal point to raise a significant amount of money to benefit intercollegiate athletics. He was not in favor of that. The first thing he said was that he didn't think that you should name buildings after people who are still around, but beyond that, if you were going to do it, he wanted it to be a facility that would benefit the general student population, not just intercollegiate athletics. So you have the Wooden Center, which is exactly what he wished it to be. It's a fabulous place for the general student population to engage in club sports and other kinds of athletic activity, with a weight room and all the rest of it. It indicates something about his ongoing sensitivity to the nexus between intercollegiate athletics and the true undergraduate experience, of which, I think he always felt quite critical.

DENNY CRUM
Louisville, Kentucky

Denny was the head coach at University of Louisville for thirty years, retiring in 2001, and was enshrined in the Naismith Memorial Basketball Hall of Fame. Regarding this award, Wooden stated, "He's the only player I ever had that, while he was playing, I knew he was born to coach." In 1995, Coach said one of the reasons is, "He would question everything we did—in the right way—he wanted to know the reasoning about every drill." Crum's teams won two NCAA championships (in 1980 and 1986) and played in six Final Fours.

I played at UCLA and graduated in 1959. I played two years, and I played two years in junior college prior to that. When I graduated from UCLA, I was doing graduate work and I was assistant freshmen coach there, like a graduate assistant for two years. Then I left and taught junior high school for a couple of years and junior college for six and came back to UCLA in 1968-69, Kareem's senior year, as assistant coach.

I had wanted to go to UCLA out of high school but they didn't offer me a scholarship, so I went to junior college there in the valley, Hearst Junior College. My college president, Dr. Shephard, knew Coach Wooden and he told him how badly I wanted to come and invited him to come watch me play. And he did, and he liked me, and he offered me a scholarship.

The team used to eat in the dining hall at Kerckoff Hall. He took me in through the back way, past all the garbage cans and through the kitchen. He didn't put on airs about anything. That was just his nature. We chatted awhile. He dragged over a trainer who ate with us. We chatted, said hello to the players, and when we were done, he hadn't said anything about scholarship, but he told me of UCLA's interest so I assumed that's what they were going to do. Then he said, "Well, are you coming or aren't you?"

And I said, "Well, yeah, I guess I am."

I loved my college days. If I had to live them over again, I would. The great experiences, the competition—it was the time of my life. The practices were organized, regimented and fatiguing.

Wooden influenced me professionally in what I've learned about basketball and his whole basic idea and philosophy of how and what to do came from him. I learned from him how to organize and to be patient. I learned that most of what happens in the game, the win or loss, is about how you practice and what you do in practice. I learned how to deal with people—treating kids fairly—not necessarily equally, but fairly. Basically my whole philosophy about coaching, about dealing with people, learning, and teaching started from him. All those things influenced me professionally, and a lot of them I think carry over into personal life, too. Dealing with people is part of life. That's probably the one thing that helped me more than anything else—learning to be patient.

He used to have the Pyramid of Success on his desk, and on his wall also. I knew about it as a player because it was right there in his office, but he didn't push it on us. I have a copy of the Pyramid on my desk and I refer to it. Anybody who knows Coach Wooden or ever heard him talk knows about it. The Pyramid is quite well known in athletics, and certainly in basketball, and its well known outside athletics because of his public speaking over the years. It's the primary basis of what he talks about. He was great to have as a boss.

He's a very intense competitor, but it doesn't show outwardly. What impressed me about him more than any other thing, when I came back as his assistant in 1968, was that he was very open to suggestion and change. This was unusual given the success he'd already had to that point. One advantage I have is I played in his system and helped coach in it, and then I went out on my own where I had an opportunity to make changes and adjustments. I learned within the same framework and structure some things that I thought were very effective.

When I came back to work with him after that, I brought them up to him when it would come up within the framework of our practice planning or evaluations I'd say, "Well, here's what I was doing and I think this works a little bit better."

And he'd say, "Well, show it to me," and then I'd show it to him on the blackboard and we'd talk about it. And he'd never say "Yes," he'd never say "No," he'd say "Let's try it. We'll try it in practice and see how it works. If it works, we'll put it in, if it doesn't, we'll take it out." For someone of his stature, background, knowledge, and experience, it was remarkable for him to listen to a rookie college coach.

The assistant is not there to get credit. I got the Louisville job because of my experiences with him and what he taught me and because I had the opportunity to work for him. Credit to me was not important. The only thing that was important was that I had an opportunity with Coach to play under him and to work for him and to learn from him.

I went straight to Louisville after UCLA. We've had a lot more than our fair share of success.

Most of what I learned about coaching came from Wooden. I played for a good high school coach and a good junior college coach, and had some very good experiences. When I got to Wooden's level, I really got to thinking a lot about it because I wanted to be a coach. There's never been a better college coach. You can't compare him with pro coaches because he never coached in the pros, but he's the best coach that ever coached in college

We're very close. You've gotta call him. He's always there when you need him. He's not just a great coach, he's a great person.

He and Nell had probably as totally complete a relationship as any I've ever seen. They were inseparable. I could rarely get him to go out and watch the recruits play cause he wouldn't leave Nell. That was just the way he was. He wanted to be home and with his family. He didn't want to spend time on the weekends away. I never saw him anywhere without her.

I never went to Wooden for personal advice over the years, but I wouldn't hesitate to if I thought it was necessary. He is the wisest man I've ever met in my life. One incident that I won't forget is when we played UCLA in San Diego in 1975 in the Final Four. They beat us and he announced his retirement and after our game they were playing Kentucky in the championship game, and that's when they beat Kentucky. I remember him, coming from the press conference back and walking and I was going the other way. I was waiting there so I could congratulate him. One of the boosters grabbed him by the arms and said, "Great going, congratulations, Coach. You let us down last year, but you came through this year," which shows you how spoiled they were out there. *[Wooden frequently mentions this story, noting that the previous year, 1974, UCLA had lost the championship in the final game in double overtime!]* When he'd won as much as they had, they expected it. When he didn't win they felt let down. It was that kind of thinking, that kind of pressure which caused him to retire. It wasn't as much fun for him, not that he doesn't enjoy the game, but all the other stuff that goes with it. Of course he did enjoy winning.

He talked a lot about his dad, about what his dad taught him and what he'd learned, the values that he had, his upbringing. He was a great teacher. Some guys coach and teach certain kinds of kids. He taught all different kinds, different sizes and shapes. When he formed his teams—he won with all of them. That is quite unusual in that he was winning as much as he did. He won national championships with different kinds of teams. What puts him apart as a coach and a person is his ability to teach, his ability to organize, to plan, and his willingness to change. A lot of people, when they're that successful get steadfast in their ways, but the game changes and you've got to change with it and keep up with it. He was always willing to do that. You rarely saw him in a bad mood. He was always nice, and polite and fun to be around with. A real good sense of humor.

If someone came up to him who was bothering him, he just found a polite way of excusing himself from the situation. People don't know that he's really an intense competitor, but he's also very level-headed. I never saw him get out of control—upset, but never out of control. If you ever saw any films of him playing, he's a tough, hard-nosed guy, a very intense competitor. I've played other games with him—snooker and card games, and he's very talented in a lot of ways, and quite intelligent. He knows how to do things, how to win.

I had a lot of interesting conversations with him on the road and socially. We went to lunch together almost every day and spent a lot of time together. He's so well-read. It was amazing to me his memory. He's got a tremendous memory for poetry and things he'd read.

I've seen him remember names over and over again. People would come up and they'd say, "My name's so-and-so."

He'd say, "Yeah, you're so-and-so, and your dad's name is such-and-such and I remember your aunt. . .." He's unbelievable. He never forgets anything.

Above: Wooden in his classic pose, with the rolled-up program.

Right: The cross Wooden clutched during games.

MARC DELLINS
Westwood, California

*Marc is the sports information director for UCLA and
was a student reporter when Wooden was coaching there.*

My office publicizes all twenty-one of UCLA's athletics teams. I have five full-time assistants and some interns. We try to create media interest for all the teams, be it men's basketball, football, women's soccer. I came to UCLA in the spring of 1972 as a student, worked for four years as a student in the athletic department and the school newspaper, the *Daily Bruin*, graduating in June of 1976. I was hired in August as the third person in the sports information office, and have been here ever since.

I covered basketball for three years, and for the last two years I was one of two sports editors, so I went on a lot of the basketball road trips. My junior year was John Wooden's last year. What you remember most about that time was that it was taken for granted that UCLA was going to the Final Four. Fans would call the sports information office, asking, "Where's the Final Four this year, because we need to get our ticket reservations." It was a different world then. There weren't as many teams in the tournament. It wasn't up until the last year or two of Coach Wooden's career that it changed. The West teams stayed in the West and the East teams stayed in the East, and you won two games to get to the Final Four. Now you have to win four games to get to the Final Four. But conversely, only league champions, and certain at-large teams that were independents got in the tournament. You couldn't finish fourth in the league and get in the NCAA tournament. So even though you weren't playing as many games, you were playing cream of the cream when you were in the NCAA tournament, because they were all league champions.

I will always remember late March of 1975. We were playing in the Final Four, as we always did at that time, in the San Diego Sports Arena. We played an overtime game against Louisville in the semi-finals, and we beat Louisville. I'm in the pressroom where all these reporters are, a junior in school, writing for the school paper. Coach Wooden gets up and is answering questions, and someone asks him a question about his favorite team, and he said, "I'll always have a special feeling for my first UCLA team and for my last UCLA team."

That kind of sits for a minute, and someone says, "Your last UCLA team?"

Wooden responds, "I've just informed Mr. Morgan that I'll be retiring after the game on Monday night." All hell broke loose. Everybody then rushed to the locker room to talk to the players.

The school paper wanted to do a special section on him, so I asked him if there was any chance that I could get some time, and he said, "Well, I'm going out to dinner with my family, but call my room." At 9 p.m., I call his room and he says, "Come over." I go over, I've got my tape recorder and my notepad, and I'm sitting alone in the room with John Wooden. He's got his feet up on the table, and isn't wearing a tie.

I think, "What am I doing here?" This person who has had so much written about him, by so many people, and it's just the two of us.

There wasn't a game during my first three years in school, his last three years, where you went into the game thinking, "There's a chance we're going to lose." And, of course in 1972-73, we didn't lose. My second year, we lost four times. Students would camp out for two or three nights before a game to ensure seats. They were loud, "We're UCLA!" I probably never heard it louder than January of '74. We had lost at Notre Dame the week before, and they came back and played here the next week, and we beat them by twenty points.

The media shared the feeling that they were seeing something special too. But they were, as the media was apt to be at time, still critical. *Sports Illustrated* inferred that Coach had lost control of the team in '74 when they lost two games in Oregon, as if nobody could lose two games in a row. But it's hard to be too critical of somebody winning five, six, seven championships in a row. How can you be criticizing the greatest coach that ever lived? But there were those who tried.

The other schools didn't hate UCLA, though Digger Phelps was hell-bent on beating UCLA. He wrote a book, basically because he beat UCLA, and talked about practicing cutting down the nets because he had this feeling that they were going to win the game. Come on, we were twelve points up with three minutes left! We didn't score again at Notre Dame, and they won the game by one point! That was the highlight of his career! A couple of years earlier, Notre Dame had come out here, and we had beaten them pretty good back at South Bend, and the *Herald Examiner* ran a picture of a gas chamber on the front of the sports page, "Today's Execution," and I thought that was a little much! Poor Bob Boyd coached terrific teams at USC, and could never get out of the shadow. In 1972, they were 24 and 2, and the losses were to UCLA, and they couldn't get to the NCAA tournament!

There's still a lot of interest in Wooden. People call all the time. I just got a call the other day from the station that does our men's basketball and football games, and they've got a client who they want to keep happy, and they said, "Is there any chance we can get a John Wooden autographed basketball?" Coach has been retired almost thirty years, and people still want stuff. I have my John Wooden autographed basketball, and my perma-plaque.

We still run The Pyramid of Success in the media guides. [All these] years later we still run a bio of Coach Wooden. He comes to most of the games, and sits in the second row behind the bench. People still line up to get autographs. Event management has to make sure there's some security there so he's not bothered during the game.

Wooden and UCLA are synonymous. Adolph Rupp of Kentucky, Joe Paterno with Penn State, Bear Bryant with Alabama, are similarly linked to their schools, but they're few and far between and nobody ever approached what he approached. When you're talking about seven straight NCAA championships, that'll never happen again. Even though Coach says, "Well, it happened once. It could happen again if all the right things are in place," it'll never happen. As a sports aficionado I am staggered by the exceptional record, compared to any sport. The Boston Celtics won eleven championships in thirteen years, but they basically had the same players, Bob Cousy would leave, and then John Havlicek would come in, but there was always a basic four. Coach Wooden always had a different team.

I don't recall too many times ever seeing him get off the bench, except when it was time to go the locker room, or during a time-out to get up to talk to the team. He didn't jump up. He didn't run around. I've heard the "goodness gracious, sakes alive" once or twice myself, and there was an edge to it, you knew he was unhappy. When you watch college basketball today, there's a reason that the TV cameras are always on the sidelines watching the coaches. Because they're up and they're jumping around and they're squatting. And he sat on the bench. I always get a thrill talking to him. It's John Wooden. Who wouldn't?

Wooden at his first coaching job at Dayton High in Kentucky, 1933.

THE JOHN WOODEN PYRAMID OF SUCCESS

DICK ENBERG
Rancho Santa Fe, California

Dick is a nationally-known sports announcer.

In the 1966-67 season, I was working at Channel 5, KTLA-TV in Los Angeles, doing sports on the early evening and late evening news, boxing from the Olympic Auditorium, and I was the Rams radio announcer. KTLA came up with this unique idea, which had not been tried before anywhere in the country, of televising UCLA games on the road live, but at home, delaying them three-hours and playing them back at 11 p.m., after the evening news. This puzzled many of us at the time. We wondered, "Well, who in the world would want to watch a three-hour old basketball game where you probably knew the score?" In those days with UCLA, you knew the outcome. It was just a matter of what the score would be.

There was this growing interest in UCLA basketball. They won two titles in the years previously, but now with Alcindor (later to become Kareem Abdul-Jabbar) being in the picture, they thought this was a highly marketable item. The ratings were really outstanding; they would beat *The Johnny Carson Show*, and other late-night programming in Los Angeles. People would go to the games, get home by eleven and watch the replay of the home games. Others were interested in seeing it as fresh drama and would not listen to the radio. My dad wouldn't answer the phone for fear somebody would call him with the UCLA score because he wanted to see it from the top at eleven o'clock at night.

I was the television announcer for UCLA basketball all through the Wooden wave, up to the last 1975 game. I often referred to my assignment as being the announcer for "The Bruin Ballet," because you knew the ballet, you just didn't know quite how it dramatically would unfold. But they always won.

When I started, Wooden had already won two national titles and everyone in Los Angeles knew of his tremendous coaching talent, though we were not expecting it to go on to ten championships in twelve years, and all the various streaks.

J.D. Morgan, the athletic director at the time, was one of the pioneers in that role of understanding how to market collegiate sports, football and basketball especially. Since UCLA was enjoying such enormous success, it became a national buy, if you will, a national attraction, even with the disadvantage of being three-hours delayed from New York. A game over in Los Angeles at 10 p.m., is 1 a.m. in New York. The scores don't even get in the paper the next morning. So there's a real disadvantage in every sport of being on the West Coast. But even with that handicap, as with any dynasty, people tune in to see if someone can beat the dynasty. And actually, you create a whole audience that roots for UCLA, but perhaps an audience just as big on a national level that roots to see if someone could beat UCLA. It was a team difficult to root against. They weren't exactly villains, just a tremendously talented team with the greatest coach in the history of the sport. But once you got away from Southern California and the fan base of UCLA, as they became a national power and nationally covered, part of the attraction of tuning into the UCLA game was to see if the underdog could win. It was no different than the Yankees, Green Bay, Celtics and their dynasties. As a team becomes so good that no one can seem to beat them on any regular basis, then the national instinct of sports fans in every country is to root for the underdog. You would get another whole audience that would tune in for the underdog understanding that it would be a rare time when UCLA would lose.

The biggest rated games and the most memorable games in that period of time—the ten years that I covered the Bruins—were the games they lost: the UCLA-Houston game in 1968 in the Astrodome, at that time the largest crowd ever to see a game, which really marked the coming out of collegiate basketball, when everyone finally realized that college basketball was a highly viable television sport. If you ask a long-standing basketball fan the most memorable games in college history, that game will make the top five list every time. Notre Dame's ending the eighty-eight game streak ending at South Bend. North Carolina State's ending the thirty-eight straight games in tournament play in '74. UCLA was so dominant, and it was such a rarity for them to lose that those became the big ones. It's sad, but it's realistic that those were the games that the average fan would remember.

Wooden had, without even trying, an aura about him, even a mystique because he (1) seemed so much in control, (2) had the appropriate answers during game coaching, and (3) his approach seemed so simplified. By not demanding winning or threatening not to lose, Wooden provided a platform after a game where his team might have won handily, but didn't play well, that he could read them the riot act and work them much harder the next practice. On the other hand, in the rare times where they might have played, but lost, he could go in and embrace them and tell them they were a terrific team and he was proud of them. So simple, and yet so much a part of his genius.

What fascinates me about him is that he's a total man. There were a lot of great and good basketball coaches, but he was a great basketball coach and a great man. I've made this statement publicly that other than my own father, he's the one other person in my life where I can honestly say I've rubbed shoulders with greatness. How fortunate I am to have been associated with his teams, and being close to him, to travel on trips to watch him work, how he behaves, his manner. Always in control. Always a gentleman. Always interested in improving those around him, himself first and those around him.

I remember a bus ride from Spokane across to Washington State. Wooden turned and yelled back to me and said, "Dick come up and sit by me."

I thought, "Wow! I'm finally going to actually sit for a couple hours next to the Coach, I'm going to really get some insight into what he's going to do against Washington State, and I'm really going to pick his brain."

When I got there, Wooden turned to me and said, "Do you like poetry."

I was going to fake it no matter what, so I replied "Yeah, I enjoy poetry."

"So how about Edna St. Vincent Millay?" and so he spent a half-hour talking about her and the poems that he appreciated most from her pen. That is a classic example of so many coaches and so many of us in any profession being so involved with that activity and yet there is time to expand and enjoy all that is around. That was the case with Coach Wooden. He loved to read. He was a student. It's reflected that at his age he has such an active mind, and still is looking ahead, not looking behind. He's the best ever, as far as I'm concerned. There is no one who has accomplished what he has as coach. When you combine what he means as a man, you've got a crown on his head.

While Coach was very religious and lived by a high moral standard, he didn't impose that around people that were with him. As an example, while he didn't drink, he didn't cluck his syllables at you if you ordered a glass of wine with a meal. He understood that was all right, as long as you maintained behavior that was appropriate. He didn't go to church and say, "Well, you better go." He respected those around him for their individual lifestyles as well. And all the while, those of us looked at him in wonder that somebody could really be so good.

Has anybody brought up the *Raindrops Keep Falling on my Head* incident? In 1970, UCLA was the defending national champion, and they opened their Pac-8 season at home against the University of Oregon. At the time, there was no rule preventing a team from stalling. Once you got over the mid-court line, you could put the ball on your hip, and didn't have to play. Now, as soon as you do that, they count five seconds, and make you generate action. Steve Belko was coach at Oregon, and he knew he had no chance to beat UCLA and the score was, let's say 10-4—something of that sort—early, four minutes on. He ordered that the ball be dribbled over the half-court line had them just stop and not play. The guard had a ball on his hip. Wooden motioned his team to go back into a zone defense.

There I was—no color man—the only announcer, describing nothing. I did everything. I recapped the scene, "and there's thirteen minutes left . . . and . . .

look forward to the upcoming schedule. . .now there's twelve minutes left." Then I'd talk about all the great championships for UCLA and the great players and all the banners there. . .and now there's eleven minutes left." I'm running out of material, and as a former teacher I finally was honest with my audience. I said, "Hey, nothing is happening, as you can see. It's still 10-4. He's not going to take the ball off his hip, and UCLA's not going to come out defensively. And besides that, I've got a song going through my head. It's a rainy night, and I've been hearing this song all week, and I don't know the lyrics to it, but it goes kinda like this." And so I go, "Dum, dum, dum, dum, dum, dum. . .." It was just when *Raindrops Keep Falling on my Head*, the Burt Bacharach song in *Butch Cassidy and the Sundance Kid*, was out.

The next night when I arrived at my broadcast location, just above the student body, across from Wooden's position, there must have been ten different students who came up to me with the lyrics to *Raindrops Keep Falling on my Head*. That night they played Oregon State, which had a very good team, and in fact, came close to beating them as I remember. I think it was 71-70. John Ecker, a reserve, banked one in to win for UCLA. It was really a stunning game because at that time UCLA had not lost at home forever. We're on delay 'til 11 p.m., and didn't get off until a little after 1 a.m. actual TV time. So I figured it was innocent enough, and I looked down at the lyrics and said, "I tried to hum this song last night—and I appreciate these lyrics—they apply to the opponents of UCLA. Just like the guy whose feet are too big for his bed. Nothing seems to fit. Those raindrops keep falling. . .just as the losses keep falling when you play UCLA. That must be how they feel." And I said, "If and when UCLA wins the title this year, I'll sing those down at center court. . .and good night." I thought was innocent enough. It wasn't contrived. Well, they finally did win the title, and I had to go out in the middle of Pauley Pavilion. I stalled for a half hour after the telecast, I sang once in public, and 12,000 people suffered with me! Coach had some fun with it. He still gets a smile when he talks about Dick Enberg trying to sing *Raindrops Keep Falling On My Head*. The punch-line to the whole story is that three weeks later I got a letter with UCLA stationery from a professor of musicology, who introduced himself and said that he was a big basketball fan. He's always enjoyed my work. He knows I'm a former college professor. He just wondered if in the pursuit of advanced academics, if I ever were in Westwood, would I drop by his office. He just wanted to quiz me about two notes that he had never heard before in thirty years of. . .."

Two or three times a year something brings us together, either in person or by phone, and it just reaffirms all of the wonderful feelings you have about the man. He's truly remarkable. He doesn't age. His body may be a little slower, but it almost seems as if his mind is quicker.

THE JOHN WOODEN PYRAMID OF SUCCESS

I get asked all the time about UCLA because they know of my relationship with it through those glory years. But there was another side in Los Angeles, which was basically a University of Southern California town. They were there first successfully and athletically, and most all of the writers came out of the USC journalism program. It was a little difficult for some of the hard-core Trojan fans to accept this UCLA dominance. There were those who called him "St. John" in a derogatory way, that he really wasn't as perfect as we were all making him to be. There were those who wanted to convince fans that he swore at officials and that he misbehaved like every other coach. There was never any real evidence of that, but I heard it and others did. It was very difficult for hardy USC fans to understand this. Finally, there was another university in town with a great athletic program. I can remember in those years some unkind things said about him, not always directly in the press, but innuendoes. I can't imagine a man being as perfect a gentleman as Coach Wooden. He just seems to have no Achilles heel.

It was really my great fortune to have been with UCLA. Almost all of the announcers who have gone on to reasonable success had a team or a moment that catapulted them forward to better things. I had UCLA, the platform that attracted the networks. At first we just did games in Los Angeles, then a small independent network called TVS did a regional Game of the Week on Saturdays. That led to doing Notre Dame games, which led to the UCLA-Notre Dame game. [TVS] produced the UCLA-Houston game, as UCLA had a powerful national image, and they televised them as much as they could. While I was doing those games, NBC hired me to do college basketball. That all traces back to UCLA. If I hadn't been the right guy at the right time, and lucky enough to be at Channel 5 when they decided to do UCLA basketball, who knows? Thanks to Coach Wooden, it was the opportunity that gave me the opportunity to be seen locally and nationally, and led to many great years with the network!

Now I do Wimbledon, the Olympic Games, NBA games, the French Open, the golf tour of the U.S. Open and other golf events. I've done World Figure Skating Championships. Just about any sport, you name it. I did the Angels for twelve years in Los Angeles.

In closing, as to John Wooden, I'm not sure that if I had another lifetime, I would meet a man any more impressive or more outstanding in his field.

Wooden and Dick Enberg, 1972

GAIL GOODRICH
Santa Monica, California

Gail led UCLA to the NCAA championships in 1964 and 1965, and was an All-American in the latter year. He played fourteen years in the National Basketball Association, was on the 1972 World Championship team, and played in five NBA all-star games. He is a charter member of the UCLA Hall of Fame and inducted into the Basketball Hall of Fame in 1996.

The Pyramid that hangs on my office wall was given to me for Christmas by a friend who took it from the New York Times cover. It's made out to:

Gail Goodrich, One of the best who ever played with best wishes from your old coach at UCLA, John Wooden 12/25/86

John Wooden to this day has influenced a lot of my thinking in terms of how I handle business and hopefully every part of my life. It has to do with preparation and a lot of trying to follow those characteristics that basically lead to success, or his definition of success. It's looking yourself in the mirror and asking yourself did you really do the best you could? What I learned from him on the basketball court I've been able to transfer to the business manner in which I approach things.

In my personal life, it's helped. I played for UCLA in 1963, 1964, and 1965. I graduated in 1965 after the second championship win. In 1964 and 1965, my last two years at UCLA, we won the NCAA championships. My sophomore year we got beaten in the regionals. I was a guard. My freshmen team was the first undefeated team in UCLA history.

The Pyramid was introduced at a team meeting at the beginning of the year. In college, it was introduced but the impression wasn't there. The substance wasn't there. I think that the substance really hit home after I graduated. Fortunately I had played professional basketball fourteen years and was able to play under a number of different coaches. At that time, the tenure of a coach wasn't as long as it is today, so I went through a number of different coaches. As a result, I was able to appreciate John Wooden even more than I had appreciated him when I played for him. Looking at that, the Pyramid and the characteristics that make one successful made me stop to think and look back. The impact was greater when I was a professional player and I would give clinics and different basketball camps for kids. When you teach, and that's what John Wooden is, a teacher, you break the fundamentals down. I was able to shoot the basketball, but I could never figure out why I was a good shooter. When I was teaching youngsters I'd break it down and then understand the fundamentals. That's the Pyramid—understanding the fundamentals. After graduating, I began to understand what it took to be successful.

I started to really think about the Pyramid later when I was teaching the basketball camps and started to understand those individuals who were successful. I've talked about the Pyramid of Success to youngsters at camps and at banquets.

There has always been, with the success, an interest in Coach Wooden and why or how he was able to be so successful. There have been a lot of people—players, coaches, particularly college coaches—who've asked questions. The greatest aspect of his coaching was his ability to communicate with his players. Yes, he had a great knowledge of the game, better than most; and yes, he was able to look at players and evaluate their skills, but his greatest asset was his ability to communicate with the players and motivate them. He took players from different environments and motivated them to work together as a team and to understand the roles within the team and ultimately to be successful.

He has a masters degree in English. He understood how to motivate one individual as opposed to another. He was a good psychologist. Another thing is that he is a perfectionist. He was a firm believer in fundamentals and execution. Basketball is a game of habits, and you would practice those habits over and over. When we went out there on the court, we were prepared. In basketball, if you look at most of his teams, they never lost their poise. When it came time to execute, you had been there before.

What I learned in college basketball helped when I went in to pro ball in terms of preparation. Coach is an extraordinary disciplinarian. You did it his way, and if you didn't do it his way, as he used to say, he had the biggest stick that he could carry and that was playing time. If you didn't do it his way then he would suggest that you sit over here and watch a little bit and then maybe you would understand that his way was the way it was going to be done. You got that message real quick. He had his ways of letting you know he was in control. On the court you quickly came to understand, especially as we got more and more successful, that his way was ultimately the best way.

It wasn't hard for me or my teammates to handle the adulation that came, although we were on his first team that really went through the roof. The first year our biggest player was six-foot-five and we were always the underdog, but we were a team. We were 30-0 that year, but *Sports Illustrated* at the beginning of that year didn't even rank us, and picked us as a surprise package. We were always the little guys coming up. The next year we lost a couple players and we lost the first game, but we ended up 28 and 2. We were always a small team.

We had a couple players who were a little bigger but not much. It wasn't like the teams of later years with Alcindor and Walton where they had the dominating center. With those type of players Coach became a lot calmer. He crossed his legs and had the rolled program. He was a lot calmer because sooner or later they would win because they were dominating teams. Our team was not a dominating team. We had the zone press and that was the first time he had introduced that. We were always fighting and he was a lot more vocal. And he was a lot tougher I think on our team than in the later years.

The zone press was a lot of fun to execute. I think that the more we did it, the more confidence we gained from it. One of the great things about our team was our confidence that bordered on cockiness. We knew that sooner or later we were going to force the other team to turnover to the pressure of the press. That was the characteristic of a lot of our players, we were very confident. As Coach would say, "Always be confident but never cocky," so it was bordering on that.

We enjoyed doing something that had never been done before, or since. What it did was set a trend for years to come as to how the game should be played. I don't think we really honestly realized that at that time, as much as it was fun. It was an up-tempo game, that was really the reason it was designed, because most of the teams in our conference were slowing the games down. With our size, we had terrific advantage if we made it a transition game as opposed to playing on a half-court basis.

I was not a great student. I became a good student my last year, but up to that time I had some difficulties. I did not have good study habits, which Coach continually stressed. I can't say that the Pyramid helped me in school. After school, it helped and it is something that I practice today in my business approach.

I never have heard the man swear, but when you heard "goodness, gracious sakes alive" you knew he was upset. There were a couple of times he kicked me out of practice. I had some differences with him, but the man had great foresight. I didn't understand at that time. Before the 1964 final game, he asked the question, "Who finished second last year?" And no one knew. And he said, "They don't remember who finished second, so go out there and play the way that you've prepared to play." And that was his pep talk. Basically if you go out and play the way we prepared—zone press, fast break—play the game on a ninety-four-foot basis, by the end of the game we'd be able to hold our head high and we would be all right.

The way I got to UCLA is somewhat unique. My dad played basketball at USC, was captain of team in 1939, and an All-Coast player. All my life, until my senior year in high school, I wanted to go to USC. I went to Polytechnic High School in the San Fernando Valley, which is in the L.A. City system. I used to sleep with my Dad's SC blanket. I ended up being City Player of the Year, and John Wooden was one coach who was really interested in me. When I came to UCLA at the beginning of the year I was very small. When I graduated from high school I weighed 135 pounds.

I'm six-foot-one now, but I was five-foot-eleven at this time. I was a scrawny little kid. Wooden invited me out to UCLA. I saw the campus, he offered me a scholarship. He, of course knew my dad, and he didn't put any pressure on me. He just said, "Look, I'd like you to understand the situation. We'd like you to come to school here, we have a scholarship available if you want it." It was a really low-key selling point, and then I saw practice. Interestingly enough the two things that really stood out in my mind even then were the organization and the practice. I was totally impressed by the way practice went and the teaching and the coaching. He was the only one who was interested in me and I figured I ought to go where someone was interested in me and wanted me to play. That's why I went to UCLA—because of John Wooden. He then went on to see a couple of my games in my senior year.

I was awed by Wooden probably until my junior year. He was "up here" and it was sort of hard to talk to him. He didn't fraternize with the players. That's not what head coaches do. The assistants bridge that gap.

Wooden would be the first to tell you that one of the reasons he was so successful was because he had great players. He selected well. The selection process was a key element, and he would get players that met certain roles that were necessary to meet certain goals. He made it clear in communicating with the players the importance of each player in contributing to the team. You could get benched if you didn't acknowledge the other guy's pass.

When I came to UCLA, I was used to having the ball in my hands. At the high school level, I was the best player on the team and I was a good scorer. I could always shoot the ball. When I came to UCLA and was playing my junior year, when Walt Hazzard was playing the other guard, Hazzard was the passer, the playmaker, the ball belonged in his hands. One of things he said was, "What are you going to do for me if you don't have the ball?" He was helpful in realizing the ball was going to be in Hazzard's hands because he was the better passer. If I would work hard without the ball to get open, then I would get the ball in a position in which I would be a bigger threat offensively to shoot the ball and score. He made me realize the ability to work without the ball, and made it clear that we want to keep Walt happy, because if you keep Walt happy, thank him and make him feel terrific, he's going to pass you the ball more.

JOHN GREEN
Hesperia, California

John played basketball for John Wooden at UCLA.

My relationship with Coach Wooden was more than coach and player. It was almost like a second father. I played for him between 1959 and 1962. He taught us values. He is a very Christian man and he taught us morals. He taught us to conduct ourselves in public to be a good citizen above all else.

I've got several copies of the Pyramid of Success; I got fifteen copies for a friend who used it to motivate his staff at Rocketdyne.

In 1962, I made All-American my senior year. Whenever anybody found out I played ball for Coach and that I made All-American, they didn't ask me about my basketball experience or how it felt to play in the Final Four. The one question that always came up is, "Is it true that Coach Wooden is really as good a man as they make him out to be?" They always wanted to talk about Coach, as the individual, as the greatest basketball coach ever. He's as good a person as everybody says, and probably better. He is a tremendous man. I've moved around quite a bit and every time that I do, I've gotta let him know where I am. He cared as much for the fifteenth man on the team as he did for the star.

We were more than just players to him. We were individuals and he really cared about us. There was no doubt about it. What an experience, playing for him. He was tough. He didn't mess around in practice. He got us in shape. He once said that we may not be the best team, but we'll be the best-conditioned team, and he wasn't kidding.

We played USC one night and he played just the starting five. The next night, everybody thought we'd be tired. No way, we were ready to go. I remember a comment that Curt Gowdy made in the Final Four. "Well, UCLA will probably be tired tonight because they played such a tough game last night and the starting five had to play the whole game." I sat back and said, "Curt Gowdy, you definitely didn't do any homework. They'll be just as tough tonight as they were last night." Coach Wooden was so dedicated to the game of basketball and to the individual that it's just amazing. I enjoy when someone finds out I played for UCLA. The first thing they ask, "Did you play for Coach Wooden?," and man, my chest just goes out and I say, "You bet I did!"

What made him such an outstanding coach was discipline, first of all. He was the boss. There was no messing around, no matter who you were. You did what he said. You respected him. He just demanded it and got it.

I heard a story about when Bill Walton went into his office after his junior year and said, "Coach Wooden, what are you going to do if I turn pro?" Coach just looked at him and said, "Well, Bill, I'm gonna coach UCLA basketball next year." And that was that. So he came back. There was never a dull moment in practice. He had it planned from beginning of the practice to the end of it. And he may work ten minutes on a certain drill, and let's say we didn't get it. He didn't dwell on it. We went to another drill. The next day we may have fifty minutes on that drill until we got it right.

Before he had the big centers, we played a high-post. Most of his teams played a high-post. He used the same plays year after year. Everybody, especially in the league, knew it, but there was no way they could stop us. We knew where to go, where to be and we'd better be there. It's just amazing that they all knew what we were going to do, but very few could stop us, all because of going over and over it and getting it right.

He had the desire to get the most out of each and every player. And he did. He didn't let you waste your talent. He got it out of you.

I'm originally from Minnesota, and my family came out here in my junior year in high school. Coach knew I'd grown up in Minnesota. My sophomore year we were playing the University of Minnesota at Minneapolis. I was a starter, but sophomores are never captains. It's always the seniors. He never elects the captains until the end of the year, and he always switched captains. I had all my high school friends and relatives at the Williams Arena in Minneapolis and the referee comes up to me and says, "Number 45, John Green, you're captain." And I said, "Well, you've gotta be mistaken." And I looked over at Coach and he had just the biggest smile on his face. He knew all my family was there and even though I was a sophomore, he made me captain that game. That's just the type of man he was.

He treated practices like it was almost the Final Four. You worked hard and you did things that he thought was best. And they were. That's obvious. We never had a losing season.

It's amazing the reputation that he has developed throughout the basketball world, and the community. He was much more than a coach, he was a teacher. He didn't coach us, he taught us. The example he set by example. He didn't tell us anything that he didn't do himself. He didn't say, "Well, I didn't do this but I want you to do that." He set an example for us to follow. And what an example. He was a good Christian, a good citizen and a good family man.

Even if Coach Wooden weren't such a great basketball coach, I'd want my son to have the opportunity to meet the man and be next to him for three or four years. He'd learn so much about life and how to conduct himself. You were at UCLA to be a man. Second, he wanted you to get your education. And somewhere around third and fourth, if you've got time, we'll play some basketball.

He gave us an opportunity to get an education and develop into a good citizen, a good American, a Christian.

Wooden, 1967

THE JOHN WOODEN PYRAMID OF SUCCESS

H.R. "BOB" HALDEMAN
Santa Barbara, California

The former Chief of Staff of former United States President Richard Nixon, Bob was forced to resign and was imprisoned as a result of the Watergate scandal. John Wooden was a true friend to him.

I got interested in John Wooden when I was active in the Bruin Hoopsters, then a very small group when he first came to UCLA. I was very much impressed with him as a man. We got to know him pretty well because in those days it was a small organization. Over the years we stayed friendly.

I went to UCLA partly because I knew a number of the guys on the team and secondarily because it was, especially in those days, a very personal sport. We played in Men's Gym and we sat on the edge of the floor and you had a chance to really be involved in the game on a close up basis. I found it an interesting game, and had been a basketball manager at Harvard High School in the San Fernando Valley.

I became chairman of the fund-raising drive for Pauley Pavilion. Wooden was an attraction in helping raise money because he was regarded so widely as a very fine man, as well as a great coach. Even though we were not into the stratospheric results, things were going well and people saw him as a good coach. We had some good years back in the Gail Goodrich time and all that built interest in UCLA basketball even though we didn't have the string of championships.

I began to develop a personal relationship with Coach Wooden starting in 1948, and would see him mostly at Hoopster events. I had a dinner in conjunction with Pauley Pavilion, and one in my home that he attended and in later years we had a closer, personal relationship in which we usually talked basketball. He's a wonderful guy and I count him as one of the people I've been extremely fortunate to have had the opportunity to know over my lifetime. He has been a role model.

He and Nell visited me in prison, and that says something for his loyalty. Wooden was a true friend. He came up to the prison visiting area and we chatted about baseball and world conditions or whatever came to mind. His visiting me in prison is the thing that impressed me the most, because it was something that there was absolutely no need for him to do. He did it, as far as I know, totally of his own motivation and at his own instance and I think it's about as clear a picture of John Wooden as you can come up with.

The guy is as close to 100 percent good as any human being can be. If you're trying to shoot someone down, you have to have some target area to shoot at to do it effectively and I don't think there is one with John Wooden.

He's an unbelievably fine man and you can only describe him in super, glowing terms. He's an outstanding individual. If I had a son playing basketball, I would have been delighted to have him play under John Wooden and can't imagine wanting him to play under anybody else. He brought an enormous amount of stature to the University at a time when [the University] was acquiring it in a lot of areas, academically and institutionally. It was a fortuitous coming together, that he and Franklin Murphy were around at the same time because both of them contributed a lot to the University, beyond the direct contributions they made as part of their job.

What you see is what you get with him. There's no dissembling.

I talked to [former President Richard] Nixon about Wooden. Nixon had absolutely no interest in basketball, but he was an avid sports fan in a general sense, and he was enormously impressed with John Wooden from what he knew of him by reading and hearing of him. He was interested in knowing whether John Wooden was really for real, which is what people wonder. He is for real.

Wooden's kindness to Haldeman in his time of need is a fascinating, poignant example of kindness and friendship to someone who deeply needed such. Haldeman had fallen from the highest mountain, and the man who came to comfort him was the one many consider to be the master of rectitude and integrity, John Wooden, who in the mid-1970s was at his most prominent peak of fame and glory.

Wooden explained his feelings towards Haldeman (who died in 1993) for this book in 1992. For history and Haldeman's legacy, it is fitting that one person saw and remembers the good in him. (Ask yourself if you would be there for a friend in a similar crisis?)

You knew Bob Haldeman. Why did you visit him in prison?
I knew Bob from UCLA. He had written me different times. Nice letters. He was concerned about me as an individual. I am not condemning Bob Haldeman or his family. I think he is a good person, an extremely bright person, but politics is a difficult situation.

Had he been in touch with you while he was in the White House?
Yes, I had heard from Bob.

You went to see him because you were his. . .
Friend.

He was your friend and he was a friend in need.
I contacted his wife and went with her and my wife. I don't care what happened to Bob Haldeman. He is a good person. His wife is a good person. A good family.

THE JOHN WOODEN PYRAMID OF SUCCESS

WALT HAZZARD
Los Angeles, California

Hazzard's jersey, number 42, is retired. Playing 1962-64, he was a two time All-American, and in 1963-64 led the Bruins to the its first NCAA title and an unbeaten season. That year he was the Most Valuable Player of the Final Four. He won a Gold Medal in the 1964 Olympics in Tokyo, played ten years in the NBA, and went on to become Head Coach of UCLA from 1985-1988. In 1987, he was Conference Coach of the Year. At the time of this interview, Hazzard was associate vice chancellor of student affairs at UCLA, working on a program called Young Black Scholars, doing public relations, attending career days, seminars, and speaking at school districts for blacks. He later suffered a stroke and is now wheelchair bound. He is a charter inductee to the UCLA Athletic Hall of Fame.

I was a high school All-American from Philadelphia and had been recommended to UCLA by Willie Naulls. Coach Wooden had not seen me play. Jerry Norman called me, and we made arrangements to send my transcripts. At that time, the admissions requirements at UCLA were very high and very strict for

John and Nell

out of state students. You had to have a 3.5 GPA in the A to F categories, your solid subjects. I didn't quite reach that criteria. I decided to come anyway. UCLA was very attractive to me because of the long legacy of African-American athletes who had an opportunity to participate in sports, going back to Ralph Bunche who was not only a great athlete, but one of the great men in the history of this country.

I had a friend named Woody Salisbury who was Rookie of the Year in the NBA in 1957 who was from Compton. He'd gone to Texas Southern, and had gone to the Globetrotters. From there, he went to the '76ers, the year before Wilt Chamberlain joined the team. I used to babysit for him and he became like my brother. He was always talking about California, UCLA, and John Wooden being a coach on who had a different style of play as compared to most teams out here. It was a more wide-open game, and UCLA was a great school.

Then I met Willie Naulls who was with the Knicks. Willie saw me play in preliminary games for the Philadelphia Warriors at Convention Hall. That night I had forty-nine points or something like that. He called Coach Wooden and told him I was student body president, came from a great family, and had a great father. He thought that I was the kind of person he would want in his program.

Willie, who has his first nickel, said, "Well, if he can't make your team then I'll pay for his scholarship," and Coach Wooden knew that was pretty strong, coming from him, so I came out right after I graduated and played summer league. I was here two days and Jerry Norman, who is a very dear friend and a great basketball mind, took me to some of the games and Coach met us there. I didn't start, but when I came in the game things started happening.

When the game was over, I was headed to the locker room and Coach Wooden was at the door. He said, "I promise you that I'll give you a full scholarship to UCLA next year." He wanted to make a deal, to make sure that I was committed. Wooden didn't go out and recruit much, but when he did, he moved if he wanted something.

I went to practice every day, and from that point on, I started studying consistently, so by the time I walked in the court the next year, I understood it like the back of my hand.

Everybody respected Coach Wooden. Off the practice court, he was a nice man, but put that uniform on him and on that bench, he's real tough. The man I lived with most of my life was my father. He's the best in the world and I think Coach Wooden's very close to him. Coach Wooden and I had a good relationship; we had a lot of disagreements, but we were always friends. He has a thing about contracts—once you sign a contract it's a contract—no renegotiation. That's a different time, a different world. If he had signed a contract for twenty thousand dollars and everybody else around him was making a million, according to his standards he wouldn't renegotiate.

We got into a lot of philosophical discussions. I'd say Coach Wooden is a conservative liberal. Many times he's very conservative about a lot of issues, but very liberal in his treatment of people. He would base his relationship with people on the merit and the character of the individual he's dealing with, but underneath that is a philosophical foundation that's very conservative.

THE JOHN WOODEN PYRAMID OF SUCCESS

He's the best basketball coach who ever lived. He's the finest teacher of the game of basketball and his system of playing basketball is the soundest of any system I know of. He played modern basketball with match-up zone defenses, motion offenses, passing game and flex offenses. Wooden's system is sounder than any of the others, because it puts you in a high percentage situation when it comes to playing. Nothing's left to chance. I agree with the principles of his thoughts about basketball, and agree as to the spiritual qualities involved.

His emotional approach to the actual playing of the game was a little more esoteric than anybody else's in that everybody talks about intensity and he substitutes that word with enthusiasm. There's a difference. There's a joy involved in enthusiasm. There's a harshness involved with intensity.

He talks about honesty. That's the very base of the Pyramid of Success in that first we have to be honest with ourselves. The pre-game speech was not, "You have to run over them, and do all this and kick butt and blah, blah, blah." It was, "At the end of the game, everyone here should be capable of walking to the mirror and looking at themselves and saying to themselves, 'I did the best I could.'"

Every year we had a session with the Pyramid early in the season. We listened. When you look at the caliber of the individuals in terms of student athletes, and the character of the individuals on the teams I played on, we had high-level people who had already demonstrated that they could be students. Their thought processes went beyond just rebounding the ball and trying to play basketball against the pros, because the pros did not represent a lot of opportunities with only eight teams in basketball at the time. He had a captive audience that understood what he was talking about and the depth of what he had to say went somewhere, not just into the air.

The Pyramid had some impact. He gave us the foundation. He gave us a certain cold, calculated kind of demeanor when it came time to perform. There was not a whole lot of rah-rah. There was always the balance, the physical and the mental balance, which was something that he talked about all the time. Balance was the key to what you did physically on the basketball court. And mental balance and self-control was the key to poise and self-control in the game.

If you hear these ideas for three or four years, they become a part of your behavior pattern and a part of your emotional makeup so when you win championship games, you're a little more excited than subsequent championships.

I was on the first championship team only and on three conference championship teams. I was on the team my sophomore year that lost in the semi-finals, in the Final Four to Cincinnati, the team which eventually won the championship. They beat us by two late baskets in the late seconds.

When we won the first national championship, Coach Wooden was very excited. He had a lot of anxiety, especially in the regionals. He was more uptight in the regionals than when we got to the championship game. In fact, the championship game was the easiest we had of the four. Our first game, we played a very good Seattle team in the regional court in Dallas. Tough game. Bob Wood was the coach. He had some outstanding players. He had John Treszant (who played in the NBA for a long time), two excellent guards, Charlie Williams and Apollo Phillips, and a guy named L.J. Weidler who was a big, six-foot-ten guy. We had nobody big, so he was a problem for us. It was a close ball game, where we ended up winning the game by five or seven points.

At the end of that game we went to the locker room. We were in the regional championship game and if we won the next game, we're in the Final Four, we're going back to play for everything. In those days there were sixteen teams in the tournament. There were four regionals—the winner that came out of those regionals went to the Final Four.

The next night we were scheduled to play USF, a very good team. The last game that we'd lost was to USF in a consolation game at the Western regionals the year before.

John Wooden came into the locker room. I had twenty-six points. I played well, the way a senior was supposed to play. I'm in the locker room sitting down, I'm tired. I don't think I left the game. I played the entire forty minutes. I'm happy we won and I'm relieved mentally (and that's where I'm more tired than anything else). I'm sitting with my legs crossed and a towel around my shoulders drinking a soda when I hear this noise. There's a commotion at the door. I see trash cans flying over the room, locker doors being kicked, people screaming and it was John Wooden going nuts. He's screaming, "You bunch of fat cats! Look at you, just sitting around just satisfied as you can be! No way that you're gonna win that game tomorrow night with your attitude tonight!"

I said to myself, "I know he's not talking about me," so I just turned my head, and he moves all this mess down here in front of me, and stops right in front of me.

I look up, and he said, "You're the main one."

So I turned around to see who he was talking to. He says, "You're the main one. If you ever play like that again, you'll never play at UCLA again."

So I started talking to myself, I said, "Right, okay, I'm seeing if we lose, I will not be playing here again. I understand that." And I said, "What are you talking about Coach?"

He said, "Shut up!"

And I said, "What?"

THE JOHN WOODEN PYRAMID OF SUCCESS

He said, "Don't say another word" and he started screaming at me.
I said, "Well, tonight, I'm not shutting up." I stood up, "Now what's the deal?"
Ducky Drake came in and separated us. Coach is still screaming like a madman, just going nuts. He kept telling me to shut up. I said, "Hey, I've taken this for three years and I'm not taking it any more. I've had it and I'm not shutting up. . ." He just kept going and going. Finally, Ducky got him out of there. About five minutes later, I walked into the bathroom. Coach Wooden is in there and he's smiling at me. And I said, "This man's really gone nuts. He just went nuts." What he was trying to do, was to keep our guard up, keep us sharp, keep us mentally alert, keep us hungry. It was trick psychology. Excellent. *[Wooden denies the foregoing occurred, including trash cans "flying." In 1966, Hazzard said he was "a helluva man. Tough but fair. He used to chew me out in front of the team just to get me mad. He knew I had to be mad to play my best." Hazzard, in 1989, told a journalist, "Coach was always good in terms of psychology. Some of it I agreed with and some of it I didn't. But he was just brilliant." In 1998, Wooden was the guest of honor at a charity gala promoted by Hazzard and held at UCLA which many of Wooden's players attended.]*

The next night we played USF. He's gone through all these shenanigans to keep us psychological and mentally ready, right? We start the game against USF. The score's 18 to 2 in favor of USF. The great psychology didn't work. The half-time score was tied and we went on to win. We had two tough games and the third game was against Kansas State. We were behind most of that game. We never had the lead until the end of the game. One thing about that particular team, the smallest team in the history of the NCAA championships, was that once the team got a lead, it never lost it in thirty straight games.

Before we won the championships, nobody in Kansas City expected us to beat Duke; Coach said they didn't think we were big enough, that we were lucky to be there. It was the easiest game we had. He was very happy after the first championship, very excited but not jumping up and down. We'd come a long way.

We played the NCAA tournament three years in a row. My first year was the first time he'd ever won an NCAA game in his career. He was like 0-13 up to that point, he'd never won a first-round game.

I think the best thing that could be said about Coach Wooden as far as his leadership is that he was a consummate competitor. He is one of the most loyal people that you could find in the world, which is a part of the Pyramid.

We were always well-prepared for the games, but we weren't prepared for the opponents, we were prepared for ourselves. There was never a real concern about what the other team was doing. Maybe that wouldn't hold true as much today because you have facilities and technology to make those things easier. It makes you more accessible. We had little information about other teams, but we knew when we walked out on the basketball court that we were in better condition than anybody in basketball, with maybe the exception of the Celtics.

We were mentally conditioned because those of us who played before Pauley Pavilion played in the Men's Gym. There was no air conditioning. He would close the windows and turn the heat up. He put us through the real test.

On the practice court he was a tyrant, one of the worst people in the world, but I loved practices. It wasn't hard to me because it was basketball. Basketball was always a joy. I enjoyed the challenge of the drills, and I used to make my teammates angry because they used to tell me to slow up, and I said, "Keep up." That was my role. My role was to make the team the best.

My major motivation to play basketball was to win, for the team to win. I've been blessed with having the good fortune of playing with great players whose major concern, if not only concern, was for the team to win. My high school team had four All-Americans. There, the players combined played about forty-five years of NBA basketball. In high school we won sixty-three games in a row. At UCLA, Wooden continued that philosophy. It was a tradition, and at the top of the tradition is Wilt Chamberlain, who embraced all of us.

Wooden really formed us. He taught us the fundamentals of basketball, but it's more than that. Basketball is a game that is physical and non-verbal. He created a system that facilitated communication. In his offense, which to me today is still as sound an offense as there is, there are physical keys. You don't come to the court calling numbers. You might give a sign, if you're running the 1-3-1, which was the offense that was created out of the high post offense to take advantage of the physical talent of Kareem and Bill Walton down on the block. Instead of a two guard front, you had one man out and just spread the court. You put them down there, and say, "Stop them." There are automatic counters and the automatic overplay on the forward where dribble toward him. He'll go backdoor. Everybody knows where they're supposed to go. It's all orchestrated. Because when you physically rehearse and practice these things on daily over a long period of time, it becomes part of behavior. You know exactly what the response is. On defense, they can go in the gym, they can read the book. It was almost, "Here, this is where we're running. Okay, stop us." We had no secrets.

What happened in the profession because of John Wooden's tremendous success was tremendous jealousy about him and about UCLA. Even today (1991). There's tremendous criticism for those of us who are proponents of his system, saying that we haven't caught up with modern basketball. At every level, pro, college, or high school, you'll see some part of that system being executed.

THE JOHN WOODEN PYRAMID OF SUCCESS

There isn't anybody really in the sport though who doesn't really respect Wooden and truly considers him to have probably been the greatest college coach of all time. They'll say it, but they don't like saying it. There's the Pete Newell school of basketball. There's a tremendous rivalry between those two people. Pete Newell is a great basketball coach.

I was very disappointed with the level of coaching proficiency at the pro level. I left UCLA and went into the NBA. It was a major drop-off. The coach didn't understand the concept of winning basketball. I know he didn't, because he kept losing to the Celtics. Red Auerbach understood it, but nobody else in the league did, with the exception maybe of Alexander who was at St. Louis.

My pro career was from 1964-74. I played for the Lakers, Seattle, Atlanta, Buffalo, Golden State. I tried to suggest some of what I'd learned to them. The response was, "That's college basketball. That doesn't work up here."

When Wooden would hear comments from the team, he would integrate them in if he felt it was a valid maneuver or technique. He would listen, even if it sounded stupid. He's very articulate and bright.

He and Nell had a very strong relationship. A lot of coaches resented the fact that Nellie was with him, because he'd always take her to the championship. He wasn't a carouser or a drinker. In those days, part of the coaching profile was after the game was over to meet in the bar. He just wasn't part of that.

The man was one of the most superstitious people I ever met. In thirty straight games, we'd line up for the scrimmage and everybody would go right to the floor but me. I would just stand there on the sidelines in front of him. Then he'd reach in his pocket, get a piece of gum and unwrap it and hand it to me and pat me on the butt and I was gone. That was part of the ritual. Then he'd turn around and look at Nellie and do something. What you see is what you get. There was never a hidden agenda. The honesty was right there on his sleeve. He would tell you the truth even if it was painful. You have to give him a lot of credit because he made a lot of mistakes that impacted some people. And now, you know, in the late stages of life, he's just trying to figure out a way to rectify them.

The Edgar Lacey incident was one. He threw Lacey out. Coach had a real temper. He regrets what happened to Lacey, because he didn't realize at that time the power that he possessed in the field.

The story is about the University of Houston game. They were playing against Elvin Hayes, who had twenty-seven at half time. During the first half Edgar and Coach had a disagreement on how he should play Elvin. Coach wanted him to deny him the ball. It didn't matter, how Lacey played that night, he was not gonna stop that guy. The guy really was just a superior athlete. It was tough for Lacey to do anything to change what happened with Hayes' individual performance that night.

At one point during the game, Coach told Norman to tell Lacey to get ready to go in. Norman looks down, he says, "I don't think Lacey wants to play," cause he had his head buried in a towel.

And so he said, "Well, forget it" and he didn't play. After the game, he was asked why he didn't play Lacey. He said, "Because he wasn't playing well." Then Lacey went off in the paper about how he'd been treated. He just didn't agree with him, thought he was wrong. So Lacey got suspended. He came back home and they met, but about two days before that meeting. Lacey said the same thing to another reporter and it came out the day after the meeting. They had apologized and he was reinstated. Then it came back out in this paper and Coach Wooden told him to get out. Well, he ruined the boy's life. He just destroyed Lacey. If he had thought about it, he wouldn't lament it at this point. I've talked to Coach and he wishes he could get back on good terms with Edgar.

He suspended Edgar because you're not supposed to be critical. It was an unwritten rule that you had to be careful about what you said to the press. You had to be very cautious about what you said because of the impact to the effectiveness of the team. You don't give them information about what's going on with the team, which is not what happens today. What happens today is coaches criticize players in the newspapers. Players criticize coaches and teammates.

The right way is the original way. I don't think as a coach I would ever shift the blame on the outcome of the game on a player. I don't think your teammates (pro, college, or whatever) should ever have a word to say to the press about the team. I don't care what the circumstances are. Maybe I'm old fashioned.

Edgar had a very short professional career in the American Basketball League. He was never given an opportunity to try out for a professional team. He's somewhat bitter about that experience, and rightfully so, because he was a very gifted basketball player. [Wooden says Hazzard has his facts wrong, he did not dismiss Lacey. See pages 130-131] When Walton came to the team, Wooden dropped his guard. It was not the same tight ship that it had been. He treated Bill, who was involved in the peace movement, with a bit more deference.

I was in the pros, but I still talked to Coach Wooden on October 14th, every year. That's his birthday. Every time things are in torment, I talk to him. Before I played the first game in the pros, I talked to him. I paged him in arenas and talked to him before championship games. It's just our relationship. I have a very special bond with him. I'm as bullheaded as he is, but I love him very much. And I like him. But I don't agree with a lot of things that he's done.

I've been to his house many times. I've talked about a lot of things, for example, religion. I have definite convictions about that. He's a Christian, I'm a Muslim. The differences are not as drastic as they seem. I've asked for advice on my life, and about the coaching profession and about our team.

When I was coaching at UCLA, I tried to get him involved. He came to practice quite a bit, and spoke to the team. It was great. I found his comments helpful, but you're dealing with different kids today. They're video game kids, it's hard to keep their attention. I don't think they really get involved in the history of the game as much They don't understand how everything got to this point. Without UCLA being involved in college basketball, it would be just another game, but the NCAA basketball tournament is the biggest show in town, the biggest game of the year. Wooden dominated it.

The NCAA tournament, as far as college intercollegiate athletics is concerned, has more impact than football. You crown one champion, and one school has totally dominated that arena. Those are two things that have never been before. There was a team involved—John Wooden and J.D. Morgan. J.D. Morgan's ascension to athletic director at UCLA was a turning point in college basketball because he was a businessman and he created an environment where John Wooden's talent could flourish. He gave him a full-time opportunity to coach.

J.D. Morgan was a businessman, the business manager of the institution. He gave Coach Wooden his first full-time assistant coach, so Jerry Norman did not have to teach and work another job to make ends meet.

I've heard criticism that Wooden did not give enough credit to J. D. Morgan and Jerry Norman, but I think it's more public promotion than anything. When they started to win championships, he didn't call himself the Wizard of Westwood. I was originally the "Wizard of Westwood," and then he became the "Wizard of Westwood." That's what they called me when I played at UCLA. He didn't call himself "St. John." He didn't make himself bigger than life. He maintained his humility. He stayed humble. He had to, just to continue to put teams on the basketball court that performed the way they did. He kept his mind fresh by always trying, always coming up with new wrinkles to make his team better.

Jerry Norman pushed the 2-2-1 full-court zone press, and the 1-2-1-1 full-court zone press. It's common knowledge—everybody knows that. But Coach Wooden doesn't dictate what the press says. The press is just about what everybody listens to. He gives J.D. plenty of credit. I've always heard him praise J.D. The turning point in college basketball was the Astrodome game between UCLA and Houston. That's what generated the interest of the network in intercollegiate basketball. Over the years that I've known him he did give credit where it was due to coaches and players and staff.

In dealing with personnel and people, you get hung up on some things.

We're talking about the 1960s. Attitudes were real different. Wooden is from Martinsville, Indiana, anyway you cut it. He's liberal, but only to a certain point. I don't think he was really in favor of the demonstrations back in the early sixties when there was civil disobedience. I believe he felt they should obey the law.

Other than my father, Coach Wooden would be the next person who most influenced my life. My father had to get Coach Wooden straight about dealing with me. He had to straighten him out. My father has a doctorate in theology. I came from a very highly motivated family, a lot was expected of me.

I was going to leave UCLA. I was tired of being yelled at and he benched me. And he was right to bench me, because I had missed a pre-game meal. I didn't intentionally miss the meal, I just put myself in the position where I missed it. When we got to the Sports Arena and got ready to play Ohio State, I didn't start and we ended up losing.

I don't think that he would be ecstatic if his daughter married a black man. I don't think he saw color, but there was a difference, a very implicit kind of thing. He would not yell at Gail Goodrich, but he'd yell at me. His explanation was that Gail couldn't take it and I could. That's a personality thing. That's his evaluation. I didn't look at it that way. I saw it another way. It has to do with perceptions. I wasn't always against it. I didn't like it. Anyway, I called home and told my parents I'm leaving. I said, "I'm out of here."

My parents said, "Where are you going?"

I said, "I'm coming home."

They said, "You're not coming home. There's no place to come."

They talked. Wooden said, "Well, I can't get him under control. He's making all these fancy passes, throwing the ball behind his back. . ." I was a sophomore. But understand, I had been raised in the playgrounds by professional basketball players. I'd been taught all these tricks. Some of it was a little over-creative and you had to get a certain balance to that, I agreed with that point.

I [finally] just showed up at practice. I didn't even talk about it. The main problem that existed up to that point was we were 2 and 7. I had a lot of turnovers, but turnovers were coming because I was hitting people in the face with the ball. I was hitting people in the hands with the ball. They had lay ups, they weren't ready to catch the ball. When the ball would come to them, they'd be looking somewhere else. So he keyed in and said, "Anytime you're on the court, make sure that your hands are in position and your eyes are on the ball. Because if you're not ready, the ball may come to you."

We ended up 19 and 4 the rest of the year. Two of the losses for that season were in the NCAA championship Final Four. We lost to Cincinnati on a jump shot. They eventually beat Ohio State the next night. We could have beaten Ohio

State because we were strong. Really, we were 19 and 2. We ran off thirteen wins in a row. We had clinched the conference with five games left in the season.

It wasn't an impossible task when I coached UCLA. I'm still confident to this very day that if left alone for just one more year that we would have had our noses in at least one championship. I played ten years pro ball. The only level I didn't win a championship was in the pros. I played for some interesting coaches. I made an okay living. Then I became a coach at Compton Community College, Chapman College, and then to UCLA.

I use the Pyramid of Success as one of my motivational tools in teaching basketball and developing team play as a coach. I think that most of the people who were students and coaches have used it. But then again, the rest of the industry is so jealous they'd rather not use it. The Pyramid has been a very good supplement to what I was taught, as a son and in my own family structure. It gave me a tremendous philosophical foundation for my coaching style and for my coaching development. The Pyramid is very simple, very clear, and it makes sense. It's a tremendous motivational tool for self-esteem, personal development, it's a human development tool. I use it when I go out in peer leadership.

John Wooden is one of the great men of our history, one of the great teachers, a great family man, a leader of men, undoubtedly the greatest basketball coach that will ever be seen in college athletics. I know how lonely he is at this point in his life without Nell. I was at the hospital many days with him. He handled it as he's a religious man. He has faith, he prays. He calls on the Creator and the Creator gives us strength when it seems like it's the darkest of all times.

At UCLA I often led the prayers. We prayed every night before we went on the court. When I was a player, I was Christian, but as a coach I was Muslim, and even then we prayed, but it was a style of meditation rather than praying. You have to have faith. There are spiritual qualities to this game, to life, that changes things. When we were playing in the semi-final against Kansas State, a kid came off the bench who hit four jumpers in a row. He started a fifth and I swear, the ball was already through the net and it went back up through the basket and came out. I said at that very moment, "It's our game."

That's one of those moments where the Lord says, "It's your game." The year before, we were playing a game at Arizona State where they made seventeen shots in a row, missed the eighteenth, tipped it in. They were 23 out of 27, shots that we wanted them to take. Jump shots, coming across half court, just firing the ball, twenty-five-foot jump shots. Bam! Bam! Bam! Bam! We tried to lead down the floor. Joe Caldwell takes a shot, backboard, front of the rim, it rolls in. "We're not getting out of here tonight. It's their game." That's another one of those spiritual moments.

KENNETH HEITZ
Los Angeles, California

Kenneth played basketball for John Wooden at UCLA.

I played for UCLA from 1965-69, on three championship teams. John Wooden was a major influence during the three years that I played for him, and a lot of the things that made him great would be translated in some way to all of us as a result of the experience.

The Pyramid I found really useful. I had the Pyramid when I was in high school being recruited by UCLA. I thought it was an interesting way of looking at things. It was part of the UCLA recruiting strategy. I don't remember him ever saying anything about the Pyramid in the context of coaching the team. What made him as effective as coach was discipline, attention to detail and absolute belief in a system. He's the best practice coach in the history of the game.

We had a great feeling of success as a team but most of us, if you weren't one of the superstars, were in a constant battle for playing time. A lot of us felt not so successful at UCLA. A lot of us were high school All-Americans and great scorers who were relegated to role players before the term role players was introduced. Most of us found in our experience playing at UCLA a great sense of accomplishment at a team point of view. We were grateful for that, but on an individual level most of us found it a struggle, so we weren't exactly going around thinking we were major successes and reveling in personal glory. We were wondering why we were only getting twenty minutes of playing time.

I understood it while it happened. We had an abundance of talent. I'm very fortunate. I averaged twenty or twenty-five minutes of playing time a game while I was there. There are guys I know who were sensational players who averaged two.

I'm a lawyer and the job of lawyering is to think and analyze. If you think and analyze in a basketball game, somebody beats the tar out of you. What you spend your time doing on a basketball court is learning to think from your ears down, because if you stop to think, then the game is over. The genius of a John Wooden is to be able to turn all of those players into thinking players—what everyone in the stands perceives as thinking players—but you're doing a set of muscle memory things. You are thinking out there, but in my judgment, athletic experience, except in learning how to cope with pressure, has very little to do with the real world. One's a game, the other is life, so I think you learn how to cope with adversity, how to deal with pressure. You find out whether you're the kind of person that steps up when things are on the line. Those all translate, but it's a very strange set of intangibles involved.

THE JOHN WOODEN PYRAMID OF SUCCESS

There is much curiosity about my experience with Wooden, and I get asked about it often. He is probably, and always will be, regarded as the preeminent coach. Wooden has an image of someone who is a very moral, upright, American kind of role model who succeeded. It's a correct image.

Anybody who's a coach has certain players who think that in a certain game they should have played or they should have been treated in a certain way, but I don't think that's really a coach's job. A coach's job is to coach the whole team and to succeed. Nobody did it better than he did.

Coach Wooden isn't what you call a colorful or interesting character. He's a very solid disciplined person. I've talked to players who have gone on to coach with him on a student/coach, or assistant coaching level, and they all say he's a completely different person when you're functioning as a kind of peer. When you're playing for him, there's a particular kind of John Wooden he wants you to see and respect and play for. It's a very distancing kind of relationship. Coach is not funny when you're playing for him, he's a very serious man.

We had wonderful players. He has a well-deserved reputation for coaching teams, and he takes care of all the little things, things that are important in the game. There's a way to do everything. You could take players from different UCLA teams, from entirely different eras, who have never played together and in 15 minutes they'd be a functioning team because they would all know what the other guy was going to do, how he was going to react to a particular situation. There was a tremendous stability and uniformity, an unbearing emphasis on unselfishness. It was a sure way to get benched if somebody passed you the ball for a basket and you didn't acknowledge the pass. There were plenty of things that you could find yourself being screamed at about in practice, but it could happen in a game. It didn't matter if you were Kareem, or me. Nobody thought about it. It is a natural thing to do once you are made to understand that the guy who is important is the guy who passed the ball, not the one who scored it.

I had a high discipline level when I got to UCLA and I give my folks that credit. What I give Wooden credit for, other than grounding me in the fundamentals of basketball, is that he had an exceptionally good set of values that translated to me. When you hear Coach Wooden say things like he didn't care whether his teams won or not, that he was concerned that they play up to their ability, he's not kidding. When he says that there was an emphasis on keeping things in perspective, family and education, and that they were more important than basketball, there is no doubt about that. Nobody kept track of graduation rates in those days, but if you look at his teams they're like the Duke teams today or the Notre Dame football teams, virtually everybody graduated.

After UCLA I went to Harvard Law School. I work at a major law firm, Irell and Manella, in Los Angeles, and became a partner.

FRED HESSLER
Los Angeles, California

Fred was UCLA's sports announcer during the John Wooden era.

I began as a radio announcer in the mid-thirties. I got into sports simply because I loved them. I announced UCLA games in 1960-61, and did until 1983.

I knew John when he first came out. I broadcast some of his games in the old "B.O. Barn" as they called it, the old Men's Gym. I met John when he first came out, his first year, 1948-49.

I had been aware of John Wooden before he came out to UCLA. I saw him play in the thirties in my hometown of Sheboygan, Wisconsin. He played for a semi-pro team and was very quick, very fast, a great ball handler. I remember walking off with another sportscaster after UCLA had played their first game in the Men's Gym, saying, "Well, it looks to me as though Coach Wooden can come up with a pretty good team. He's got some good material."

He said, "Ahhhhh, won't win a game!"

Being the primary announcer for UCLA basketball was one of the highlights of my life. I've known a lot of coaches in my life, but he rates as number one and not just because of the wins. I really got to know him. We'd be waiting around at the airport talking. Occasionally, I would eat with the team in the early days.

My job wasn't to be an impartial announcer. I came from the school where you rooted for the team. I rooted for UCLA. I tried not to be too obnoxious in it. If anyone is traveling with a team consistently, how can you feel otherwise? How can you feel anything but downcast if, let's say, a Gary Cunningham who never missed a free throw, missed a crucial one. You suffer. It's in your voice. You don't have to say anything. The people listening to you who know what you sound like and know what you say are definitely aware that you're suffering or elated.

Coach was mad at me one time. I don't know to this day what it was, but he didn't speak to me except very coldly. This was not our normal relationship. I didn't say anything. I thought well, if I've done something, he'll tell me. Finally, I did ask him. I had said something that offended Nell. She was upset and I apologized to her. Another time, he came to me after he had been very cold, and he said, "I owe you an apology."

I said, "What for John?"

He said, "I owe you an apology because somebody told me you had said something that you did not say. It was not true. They lied to me. I'm sorry I believed them and I want to apologize to you for it." That I won't forget.

John is a good man. I said this once and I'll say it again. While he was not Jesus Christ, I think he tried more to be Christlike than anybody I know. You don't always succeed in every way, but he came as close to it I think as you could come.

Wooden used to get upset with a few referees, but he toned that down in the sixties. There were a couple whom he felt he wasn't getting an even break with. He was probably right. But when we used film more extensively than in the early days, he admitted that he'd looked at a lot of these and he'd discovered that perhaps the official was right after all in a given call that he really thought the official blew. His sense of fairness was always there.

He got a kick out of a lot of people. He enjoyed people and other coaches although it got to the point where they hated to see him win. Nobody except UCLA fans enjoyed the winning streak. The win streak of UCLA made college basketball, no question about it. A community benefits from and is uplifted by following a winner. UCLA was an attraction to all the young people who hadn't gone to any school or didn't have any affiliation. They affiliated with UCLA mentally by following them.

One of the things about Coach Wooden that people don't realize is that money didn't mean anything to him. One time he asked me, "You're from Wisconsin. Do you know Wayland Academy in such and such a town?"

I said, "Oh yes, they're quite a well to do."

He said, "Well, they've invited me to speak there and stay over night at a cottage on a lake nearby. I can take Nell. But if I handle it right and don't stay, I can go down to Arkansas. There's a friend of mine at a small college down there and I can do a clinic for him. He can't afford to have me otherwise." That's the type of thing he would do. He would cut short things and try to get somebody else in the action.

He also took the basketball team in those early days to help programs, such as Indiana State at Terre Haute, Indiana, which didn't necessarily produce the revenue that UCLA's athletic director was looking to.

Wooden never had any relationship with Sam Gilbert, who apparently loaned players money. One coach told me once at another school, "You know, Fred, every school has a Sam Gilbert." What he was referring to was someone who did things that were not what the NCAA would want.

The most dramatic moment for me with Coach Wooden was when he announced that he was going to retire before that last game down at San Diego. He had told me earlier in the year that this was going to be his last year, but if I said anything on the air he would deny it. And I said, "Well, stick with me John. Whenever you do, I'll be ready for it." Well, I was not ready for it. When the moment came, I was talking to then assistant, Frank Arnold, who later coached over at BYU as the head coach. I was interviewing Frank and suddenly a great big lump got into my throat and I couldn't speak. I was overcome with emotion and tears for almost a minute. That moment overwhelmed me—the knowledge that he wasn't going to be there anymore. UCLA basketball was not going to be the same without this man.

When I first saw the full-court press effectively utilized in the early sixties, it was pretty devastating and a lot of fun. It made it exciting, and particularly after the winning streak got going and you had NCAA records. People would tune in at half-time to see whether anyone was giving us a game or not. That's what it amounted to. When I say us, okay, make me a homer.

I co-hosted a television show with Coach Wooden and he used the Pyramid of Success on it quite a bit. He did it all over the country, and it was very much in demand. It inspired a great many people as a new discovery. They'd say, "Gee, caught the show with Coach Wooden last night, isn't that wonderful, the Pyramid of Success."

I said, "Yes, it is." And somebody else would pick it up. So you'd get a new audience. It's the type of thing that certainly lent itself well to addressing any organization that you want to inspire. I was fascinated with the Pyramid, and I certainly heard it a number of times. I heard new meaning and thought new thoughts each time I heard it.

UCLA won more clutch games under Wooden than the average team did. Usually the better team may not do as well during the course of the game, while their opponent, trying to get the upset of the century, is going all out. Near the end they realize they've gotta put out a little bit more and then they usually do and wind up winning.

Our Southern California Sports Broadcasters group, boy, if there's one man that they idolize, it's Coach. They always ask me because they know I keep in touch with him, "Gee, how's Coach Wooden getting along? What a wonderful man!" That's what I hear from my fellow sportscasters. The coaches who followed him blamed him for the problems that they had. They said he was too good. His record perhaps denied them the opportunity to be themselves, but I think a lot of them put themselves on the spot more so than the fans did. I think each of them has to be accepted for himself. Fans have to be educated to know they can be a visitor to the Final Four occasionally, but it's almost impossible for anybody to even repeat as champion these days, and that's what's expected of a UCLA coach. John Wooden brought them a championship every year.

One of the great experiences of my lifetime is having known John and doing the Bruin games all those years. I loved them all with him.

THE JOHN WOODEN PYRAMID OF SUCCESS

BILL HICKS
Ventura, California

Bill played basketball for John Wooden at UCLA.

I played for Wooden from 1958-61 as guard. I have the distinct advantage of being able to see him and talk to him quite often. I get his cars for him, and keep them serviced so I do have the advantage of talking to him quite a bit. He was very admirable when his wife was dying. It was such a trauma for him that in order to keep his mind altogether, every day he would go down to the hospital, and he kept copious notes on every single thing that was said and done. I found them in his car one day, and he'd literally written down every word the doctor had said, what TV program she was watching at one o'clock, everything that happened to her. That's the way he kept his mind occupied. It was just typical of him.

I've been taking care of his cars since the early 1980s. I gave him a brand new Mercedes for his seventieth birthday. He had that Mercedes until about 1985 and then he got a new Ford Taurus. He knows a little about cars. He likes to have a nice car, and he likes to make sure it's right. He's always carrying all his paraphernalia in the back. He's always got his sneakers and all his Pyramids of Success. His car's always loaded with good stuff.

As a partner in a Ford dealership, I've been economically successful, beyond my wildest expectations. From day one at UCLA we learned about the Pyramid. I've got a signed copy right on my wall at the office. People often come and ask for it. I just run them off. I use it in my sales meetings all the time, and it works excellently. This Pyramid, other than religion, gives you some guidance if you want to be successful. It's what it takes.

He's one of a kind, a national treasure. There'll never be another one.

ANDY HILL

Andy, a former Bruin player, wrote a memoir of his relationship with Wooden entitled, Be Quick, But Don't Hurry, *published in 2001, which is now in its third printing.*

To be with him every day is unique, in that you see the real coach; there is no "coach behind the curtain." He's like that with the public, and when you're alone with him. That is consistent with his philosophy, and what is so impressive is that he is a living example of his philosophy. He is such a great teacher because he models everything he says.

We did thirty or so promotional appearances, and he obviously is someone people take incredible joy in meeting. At UCLA's book fair, a fellow handed Coach and me a letter saying that reading *Be Quick, But Don't Hurry* inspired him to meet Coach Wooden and shake his hand. Coach Wooden asked, "Where are you from?"

He said, "I'm from Charlotte, North Carolina."

Coach asked him if he knew Joe who owned the drugstore behind the park, because Coach knows somebody from every part of the country. The man said he didn't know Joe, and turned to walk away.

Without thinking, I asked: "When's your flight to Charlotte?"

Over his shoulder, the man replied: "I'm driving." That this man was driving back to Charlotte, North Carolina with a signed book feeling that this was one of the highlights of his life demonstrated to me the kind of respect and admiration Coach engenders.

He enjoyed the appearances. I would have thought at ninety-one he would have signed so many autographs and shook so many hands, it would have been routine for him, but Coach always talks about this idea of doing something for someone else without any thought of getting anything back. He feels the happiness that he gives others and it turns into happiness for him.

Except for a few players, Coach was fairly stern taskmaster; in his classroom, he was all business and guarded. After graduation, my fellow players had a chance to connect with a really sweet, genial guy, who he really is away from the classroom. You can't spend a lot of time with Coach without being struck by his charm and humor. Whatever our feelings about him as a male figure in our life, he was the best basketball coach we ever saw. We felt neglected when we didn't get to play, but underneath were all those feelings of admiration. My book is about reconnecting with him as adults, when none of us were on the bench anymore but all in the game of life using his lessons everyday, which really came in handy. A lot of the other fellows felt the same way.

My book ultimately became an act of reflection on how the players felt. We had a reunion several weeks ago at the home of Ken Heitz where twelve solid guys gathered who were doing well in their own lives, were really happy to see each other and who have evolved into a group which feels really warm and close towards Coach. He obviously feels great joy in that.

Until writing my book, Coach and I had never really sat down and talked for nearly twenty-five years. Coach is someone who has the rare ability to look at his life with honesty, and his re-connection with John Ecker (who had negative feelings towards Wooden), which I write about, really changed Coach. Today they are wonderfully close.

Coach has so many people in his life that his phone rings off the hook. He is the happiest ninety-one year old man I've ever met. There is no person more universally admired than Coach.

I wrote my book because I felt that Coach's philosophies not only led to success and personal happiness, but were based on values and morality that ultimately reflected the best this country had to offer. Young people were feeling that you had to make a choice between success, and making the right choices and living a moral life. The real strength of this country is not about greed, avarice and Enron, but about the kind of openness, honesty, and excellence of John Wooden. If we don't pass on his ideals, they might be forgotten.

Evidence of greatness, more awards than any coach, anywhere.

RALPH JOEKEL
Las Vegas, Nevada

Ralph played basketball for John Wooden at UCLA.

I was a member of the first two teams at UCLA. Over the years, I've always kept in contact with Coach Wooden. I usually see him every other year. The last time I saw him, he came to Las Vegas. Coach was in a suite on the top floor of the Golden Nugget downtown. He and I spent some time together and he insisted that I got to a banquet with him, and I just hung out with him.

After the banquet was over, I went up to his room and I think we finally broke it up at two or three o'clock in the morning. We have a primary common belief, that the Bible is the true word of God. He reads from the Bible, I read from the Bible. He has certain quotes that he likes. He reads poetry and we talk about each other's family. It's extremely personal, almost like father and son. My dad died in 1980, so he's sort of like a father figure to me, except not in terms of everyday closeness because although we're only three hundred miles apart, it might as well be three thousand.

I'm a graduate engineer here in Las Vegas. One of my pet peeves when I went to UCLA was the media. When I got out of school in South Gate, I had just turned seventeen and then the following September I was on the varsity team because all the guys were gone to war. The only people there were some 4-F guys and some guys that were in the B-12 program. It wasn't that we were so good. The *Daily Bruin* would just plaster us. They would belittle us. It lowered your self-esteem. They were trying to break you for some reason that I never could figure out. So I always used to say, "When I graduate, I'm out of here." And that's what happened. My relationship after that was strictly with Coach Wooden.

Wooden in 1962, with assistant athletic director Bill Putnam, who also worked with him, on the left, and Jerry Norman, his assistant coach, on the right.

THE JOHN WOODEN PYRAMID OF SUCCESS

ANN MEYERS-DRYSDALE
Huntington Beach, California

Ann Meyers-Drysdale is one of the greatest female basketball players in history. Her jersey at UCLA, number 15, is retired. She was inducted into the UCLA Athletic Hall of Fame in 1988 and to the Basketball Hall of Fame in 1993.

I was the first woman to get a full athletic scholarship at UCLA. I was on the team that won the Silver Medal in the 1976 Olympics, the first year they had women's basketball. I was on the UCLA basketball team that won the national championship in 1978, and I'm the first four-time All-American. I was also on the UCLA team that won a national championship in track and field. I played two years of volleyball at UCLA. I was the number one draft pick in the Women's Basketball League in 1979, but I did not go because I wanted to stay amateur for the 1980 Olympics.

I signed as a free agent in 1979 with the Indiana Pacers—I'm the only woman to have signed an NBL contract. I've played against guys my whole life, so what I was doing was nothing different. Sam Nassi was then the new owner of the Indiana Pacers, and it was obviously a publicity ploy for him. I had a very big name at that time, and he thought it would get a lot of attention. People in Indiana were not happy about it, especially in the organization. "What are you doing, bringing a girl in. You're going to embarrass our organization."

Although the Pacers released me from my playing contract, I had a personal services contract with them, and did other work for the organization and as a result got into broadcasting. I went back into the WBL (Women's Basketball League), and played for the New Jersey Gems, in the 1979-80 season, and was MVP of the league. Then I competed in the television show, *Women's Super Stars*, which is where I met Don Drysdale, who was a broadcaster for ABC. We eventually married and raised three children.

I come from a family of eleven children. My dad played basketball at Marquette, and all of us were involved with athletics. When I got to UCLA, Title 9 (equal opportunity for women in all categories), was causing lot of changes in women's sports. UCLA out of the blue offered me a scholarship, which was great, because I was very family-oriented. I wanted to be close to my brother, David *[see interview with Dave Meyers, which follows this]*, and I was still close enough to see my family on weekends. I had a lot of interaction with the men because the Women's Athletic Department was located in the Men's Gym, and I was Dave's little sister.

I feel very comfortable around Papa. Even today, it's hard for me to call him "Coach Wooden," he's just always "Papa" to me, though obviously that didn't come until later. He became very much a part of my life. My mom was real close to Nellie. They would get real nervous and she was a smoker. At half-time they'd go smoking.

In the first interactions I had with Papa, I observed just how much in control he was. The practices were broken down, and there was no time wasted. I am amazed to this day how a lot of coaches—in any sport—do running drills, suicides. When I was on the Olympic team in '76 we did a lot of lines, gut wrenches—they have lots of different names for running—for conditioning. Papa's drills were never about that; he never made his team run as a punishment, yet they were always the best-conditioned team in the country.

What was interesting about his practices was the intensity of each drill, whether it be two or five minutes long. Everyday they did the same thing. The first fifteen to twenty minutes were taken up with stretching and for the warm-up lines where they'd jog and run backwards. Then they'd do change-of-pace: get in four or five lines of three guys, and do the jab step-shot, or take the shot or go up for the rebound, pivot, and pass the ball out. This was all done without the basketball. Then there were imaginary rebounding and shooting, and defensive slides. Gradually he would add the basketball, and a player would dribble, change hands, dribble, change hands. It was change of pace, with and without defense.

David told me about his experience with the triple-threat position. You'd get the ball, catch it with two hands, and then fake with two hands and move the ball around. David had big hands and once in practice he held the ball in one hand, as Connie Hawkins, who was a big guy in the NBA back then would sometimes do. Papa stopped practice and said, "Mr. Meyers we don't take the ball like that. We take it with two hands. This is not the NBA. This is UCLA, and this is how you will do it. With two hands." From then on, David was a pretty fundamental guy.

When I was a freshman, I went into Papa's office a dozen times and talked about basketball, school and family—he always asked me about family. That was the comfort zone, it put us on the same field. As I got older, my sister Kathy became best friends with his granddaughter, Christy, so our families intertwined.

The big deal in the '70s, when they hit their peak, was basketball camps. Papa had his, and a big name in basketball. I was a counselor and coach at his basketball camps, which were co-ed. My relationship with Papa got closer when I started doing his camps, and I just loved hanging around him. What impressed me most about his camps was that he didn't keep score in the scrimmages with the kids. You want to play because you love the game, and it shouldn't matter what the score is. Today, camps are completely different, all they do is play scrimmages, games. Papa's camps were about teaching, not only the fundamentals of the game, but how to treat your opponent—to have respect for them. He wasn't into jeering guys, in your face, and air ball like kids do today. At his camps, not keeping score in the games made an impact. One team could dominate another and know they were winning, but the other team didn't feel quite as defeated, whereas today all they do is play games and keep score.

Papa was always so humble, and he always gave other people credit. God has blessed us on this earth with him because there are not many like him. He is a religious man, but he doesn't preach it to people all the time. He lives his life that way. You know this man is here for a purpose. He's had a lot of tragedy in his life, a lot of hardship, but continues to go on . . . for others. It's how he gives that really reflects on many people, and a lot of people admire that, some ridicule it, and some don't understand it, so they don't accept him, which is fine, whether it be in the basketball world or any other side of life. Basketball is a small part of any of our lives, a sport that you can play and compete in—but you learn from sports about what life is about.

It is fascinating that he had such an insight on everybody. I feel like I'm part of the family. I'm not at all of the family functions, but I do go to some. Look around my house and see the things that he writes to me, which I've framed. When my husband, Don, passed away, Papa was very important in counseling and comforting me. There's a love about him. He has become so much a part of my life, that although I don't live my life as he does, I strive to. He's taught me so much, and the bottom line is that he's always a teacher. Of all of his awards, he's proudest of winning the teaching award from Disney. He makes you understand that it's okay to fail, to make mistakes, because that's how we learn from them. This is a man that cares about others, who cares enough to try and reach everybody that takes the time to reach him.

The Pyramid of Success, which I've got on my kitchen wall, is about life. I feel really fortunate that he has been a big part of my life, especially since I've gotten out of college. I probably didn't understand how much of an impact he had on me in college. Papa's influence changed my brother, obviously, in his fundamentals, but also in confidence in himself, so that there's a quality of leadership about us. But there's also a quality of "maybe we don't always believe we're that good," which may be why we fight and play so hard. Not just to prove to other people, but to ourselves that by hard work, which is what we've always been taught by our parents, we will accomplish a lot.

Sports are a privilege. First and foremost were our grades. Though I didn't always get good grades, I never got in trouble either. I had an enormous amount of fun. I was a part of UCLA basketball and in that inner circle, which meant a lot. There was something magical about going to UCLA games. Walter Matthau, the Jackson family would all come. It was so packed that people would come for the freshman games. I remember one game when Lee Majors and Farrah Fawcett walked in late and all of a sudden everybody's heads in Pauley Pavilion literally turned to watch this couple take their seats. It was a crack-up, but that was the place to be, Pauley Pavilion.

Ann Meyers-Drysdale and Papa at Wooden's Sportscamp, 1991.

DAVE MEYERS
Temecula, California

Dave played basketball for John Wooden, and went on to a pro career. He was inducted into the UCLA Athletic Hall of Fame in 1992. Dave Meyers is one of three players to have been named captain during a whole season.

I played in 1973, 1974 and 1975. I was captain of the 1975 team that played with Wooden. Playing for Coach Wooden was quite an experience, all four years. It was a basketball factory. Anybody knew that in the high school ranks, because all they talked about was UCLA's unbelievable system. As a teenager, I was one of those players who got better every year. I knew I wasn't ever going to go to UCLA, but I always was a telephone call away from them and [the call] came and I ended up going there.

They had a freshmen team at UCLA, which I was very happy about. The next year the freshmen could play on the varsity. It was a great experience for me just to play basketball and not have the pressure that the varsity had. Walton's sophomore year was my freshman year. They had tremendous pressure. They were all so young but it didn't bother them. It gave me a year to get assimilated and then I had my next three years with Coach, where I felt like a little kid all the time around him and didn't say much. I was in awe of him.

I remember being the captain and I had two or three sitdown discussions with Coach, and all of them were after we lost games. I would go to his office and apologize to him for playing lousy. It was funny because he wasn't about winning and losing, it didn't bother him at all, but I would feel bad because he always taught us in his Pyramid about how success is always trying your best. You always have bad games, win or lose, but it's funny, when you lose them you think about them more. Those were the only times I really sat down and had a heart to heart talk with him, because I, even being twenty-one years old and being the leader of the team, was very shy about communicating with him.

At those times, Coach always had that little sparkle in his eye. He'd been through all of this before, and I'm sure there was a time in his life where winning was very important, because you get involved in that with sports. Success breeds victories. And yet, through the latter stages of his steaks that he had, the seven titles in a row and college basketball, the eighty-eight game winning streak, Coach put everything in perspective his last five or six years of coaching. When he did that, he portrayed a sense of stability and balance to his team and his players. He'd never let you get way high or way low.

That's why we're an unusual group of people at UCLA, because he did not talk about winning and championships and "You're wonderful." He talked about growing up, being kind, treating people with respect, being appreciative of the abilities you had, and utilizing them for the good of others—not for yourself. That probably fell a lot on deaf ears at UCLA, because being nineteen, twenty years old, you think you're on top of the world and you're so important. But he always balanced everything with his own personality and his own lifestyle.

I gave him everything I had. I played hurt my last month of the season my senior year. I was in a lot of pain. Both my legs. I sprained an ankle. My quickness was gone. I just played completely on heart. A lot of that was because of what he gave me on controlling my emotions and going out there and trying to be a leader for the team emotionally and not worrying about my physical assets, which inhibited my abilities.

We ended up winning the championship and that brought a tremendous amount of respect for him from my part, because I realized now that life was a lot more than just a game. He always brought that to our attention, so that now that as I look back, I'm happy for the memory, but I'm happy with what I do as a husband and now as father with my children. Basketball was just a part of me that I refer back to, but I don't make standards by it.

Coach had a system and you played within that system. I saw him take delicate, glass-like personalities and come close to cracking and breaking some of them. Coach coached a lot of years. There were a lot of personalities that came through that school. You would hear the old adage, a Coach Wooden type player. And I think a lot of the players felt, "Well, I'm a Coach Wooden type player."

He was not into flash. He was not into the glide, the finesse. Coach was really into hard working cooperation from a team so that we looked like an orchestra or a symphony. You didn't look at any one of the people out there in the violin section going, "Boy he really can play the violin and that one is a little slow there." He was working at unifying us. Some of the players it affected greatly because they wanted to be a conductor out there. They wanted to be a Sidney Wicks, an Andre McArter, a Walt Hazzard.

Someone wrote an article on our 1975 team in the *Oregonian*. He traced what happened fifteen years later on the starting five. It was interesting as I hadn't kept up with Richard [Washington, Jr.], Marques [Johnson], Andre [McArter, Jr.] and Pete [Trgovich], and it gave me a twinge of sadness to see there was an underlying loss of those years at UCLA and how terrific they were. It's a great memory but sad to see some of them weren't settled in their lives now, as Coach really tried to teach all of us, that family was important.

Believe me, this was not a perfect organization. Players had their problems, and Coach was a wonderful man in dealing with the problems, but the media back in the sixties and seventies was not as hungry as they are now. Coach protected his team. When Coach left, the floodgates opened up. People were allowed to go into the locker rooms. We never had that. We were always protected. It was more of a guarded time period for us, as far as media exposure.

But well it should. That's the way families should be run. I mean neighbors shouldn't know you spanked your kid and sat down and talked to him about something he did. Yet that's what the media wants to hear today. Coach kept that all under control. And what a fine example for all of us as we've gotten older.

After UCLA, I played in the NBA for five years. I had a couple of serious injuries. I played for the Milwaukee Bucks, and after my five year contract was up, I retired, which surprised a lot of people because I was a starter on the team. I turned down a lot of money cause I was already making a lot of money. I became a Jehovah's Witness during my NBA career. I went into sales for five years, and then became an elementary school teacher.

I don't have favorite stories that I tell about Wooden. Every day was an event. The way he led his life. A quick reflection are the days on the road, on the bus to the hotel, to the pre-game meals, to going to bed at night on curfew after a game, it was just amazing to see his example. What's sadly lacking today with so many people is they don't set a good example. He set a fine example for his players, and that's why so many of his players I'm sure to this day try to imitate him, and if they come close they've done an excellent job.

I write him letters, I drop cards in the mail. Every time I write, I thank him for the association I've had with him and that I've had a part of my life with him. I've always been appreciative of that. Coach always loved poetry and I love poetry. I've sent him poems in the mail. I've sat down with him and had long talks. I almost wrote a book about that last team. I decided against it because people just like to talk about the soap-opera stuff. I just said, "Forget it."

AL MICHAELS
Brentwood, California

Al is a nationally known sportscaster.

I'm a sportscaster for ABC. In 1973-74 and 1974-75 I was a sportscaster for the Bruin games on television. It was a great time, Wooden's last two years. The team reached the semi-finals of the NCAA tournament that first season, when they lost to North Carolina State in double overtime, and then went on to win the national championship against the Navy.

When I first saw the Pyramid of Success, I had my own ideas about success but I respected Coach Wooden and I listened to it. Now I think it's a very effective blueprint for life. Most people can't deal with life like that.

Frankly, I can't think of anything that's more impressive than winning eighty-eight straight, especially since a lot of those have to come on the road where it's unbelievably difficult to win. It's harder for teams to win games away from home, much harder. You feel like you're alone. That was one thing that was driven home to me as I traveled with the Bruins during those two years. There was one entirely different set of circumstances at home as opposed to what you saw on the road. You felt very comfortable at Pauley Pavilion, the fans were behind you, there was a feeling of invincibility, whereas when you went on the road, they hated you. It wasn't as if just some ordinary opponent was coming in to face their team, it was UCLA, and they couldn't wait for UCLA to get there. They hated UCLA, and they lived for the night that UCLA came to their building. You could feel it even as a broadcaster for the Bruins at that point. When I did my scene-sets in those buildings, people would throw things at you, they would yell at you, they could curse at you. If you were affiliated with the Bruins they just didn't want you to be a part of the scene. And it always astonished me how you could just feel it. It permeated the building. Anywhere they might go on the road, you'd feel this tremendous antipathy toward UCLA. A lot of it, I think, was born clearly of jealousy. The fact that the Bruins were able to win eighty-eight straight, and have to win on the road in the neighborhood of about 30-35, is astonishing to me.

We did the home games on tape delay. The games would start at 7:30 or 8 p.m. at Pauley, and they'd play 'em back at 11 pm on Channel 5, and they'd get enormous ratings. We'd do most of the road games live. Occasionally we'd do a road game on tape delay. It was extraordinary for a college team to have gotten that kind of coverage at that time, but it wasn't just any college team. They were royalty. This was the greatest dynasty in the history of college basketball. You could feel it, you knew it was something special.

THE JOHN WOODEN PYRAMID OF SUCCESS

I'm not in awe of too many people, but I was awed by Wooden's presence. He had everything down to a science. Nowadays, there are a lot of coaches who have every moment of every practice accounted for, and who are right on top of things. But when you talk about what went on twenty-five, thirty years ago, there may have been only one man who was that good at everything he did. You knew when he was there. He commanded incredible respect from everybody in his presence, and yet he didn't outwardly demand it. You just knew you were with somebody who was special, extraordinary, unusual, and unique. I learned a lot from him in observing how players reacted to him, and in being around him and that whole situation, enough to be able to see what it's like—when a group of people so totally respect somebody. It's not that he had to demand their respect. It was just that he was so damn good at what he did that if you didn't respect him you were just stupid, and he didn't have any stupid people around him.

He was very smart about the people that he needed to recruit, who would be good for UCLA, and good for him to work with. I'm sure that there are some guys who played for John who felt that they probably could've done other things at other schools and maybe been more of an individual star, and might've been drafted a little higher in the NBA. But I think ultimately anybody who had a chance to play for John Wooden and those great UCLA teams and doesn't really appreciate it, really has no understanding of what life is about. Very few people get to work under masters. It doesn't matter whether it's in the computer industry, business, law, medicine, or sports, there are people who are masters. John Wooden is a master.

I wasn't a team member, but I was around a lot, and I was extremely fond of him. Obviously, I had a tremendous amount of respect for him. And I really wanted to learn as much as I could from him. Just observing and listening to him was quite an education. I couldn't have gotten a better basketball education from anybody, and in how to deal with college athletes. To this day, I think back and see how John did it and make comparisons to others and how they handle it. At least, I was able to do that up until the mid-eighties when I was doing college sports. Since then, I haven't been around the college scene very much. He was amazing. Never ruffled, he was always in command. He always knew what he was doing. In the two years I was around the Bruins, there was never anything you could've labeled as a blow-up, or something that could've torn the team apart. They never came close.

He was a pretty good interview. It was a different time, the early seventies, and what you expected from somebody then and what you expect from somebody now is quite different. Now you're always looking for the controversial side. Well, not always, but you're not afraid to explore the controversial side, in fact, it's incumbent on you to do that. I think I'm very good at that, and I've never shied away from it. At that point, though, in the early seventies, it was a different type of a situation.

This is my craft, and when you announce for a team—at least in my case—you want to see them win because it's easy for you, and it's better for you, and the ratings are going to be better, and more people are going to pay attention to it. So in that regard, you want to see the team win. But do you live and die with it? Nope. I don't, and didn't, and never will. Clearly, as the voice of the Bruins, and knowing that if the Bruins were able to keep this streak alive, were to be in national championship contention, the better they did the more people were going to watch and the more exposure we were going to get. I definitely wanted to see them win.

It's been years since I really studied the Pyramid of Success. I know a lot of people think it's sensational. They've gotten great results from it. Clearly, it works, and I've heard people rave about it. John Wooden is a master, and if you can't learn from him I'm not sure you can learn from anybody.

My difficulty in trying to announce a game and provide color commentary would occur when UCLA would just wipe out the other side in the first seven minutes of a game. It happened all the time, especially when they would play Pac-10 foes. When they were playing the Oregon States and the Washington States, or the University of California, or Stanford—some of the teams that weren't particularly good at that time—at Pauley Pavilion, ten minutes into the game UCLA would be out in front 30 to 8. And not only would they be out in front 30 to 8, they would have been out in front in five of their last six games by 30 to 8, and maybe in the other they were leading 28 to10. So here you are with twenty-five or thirty minutes of game left, which translates to over an hour of television time, and not a lot of places to go. I mean, all of a sudden, strategy is out the window, people already know about the Bruins—it got to the point where I relished when the Bruins would meet a formidable team, and normally that would have to happen on the road. Very few of the games I did during those two years went down to the last ten or twelve minutes of the game, because the Bruins had the kind of team that would either totally destroy you, and it would be reflected on the scoreboard; or the game would be somewhat close. In other words they might only have a twelve-point lead with twelve minutes left in the game—but it wasn't a contest, and you knew it. The other team had no chance. It was impossible. They might as well have been leading by forty. Those were the Bruins of the early seventies.

Wooden was extremely important to the game of college basketball, which

THE JOHN WOODEN PYRAMID OF SUCCESS

really began to take off around that period. What the Bruins did was so extraordinary it captured the attention and the fancy of the fans around the country. This was royalty, and I think that anybody who likes sports understands that when you have a situation like this it's a once-in-a-lifetime deal. To win nine titles in ten years, seven in a row, thirty some odd post-season victories in succession, eighty-eight wins in the regular season; to do it over and over and over and have the stars that they did. . . Just John's presence—John was UCLA, he was there. Alcindor was there, and Walton was there, and all of the other guys, but they came and they went. John was the one constant. You could always count on him being there with a rolled up program. In their own way, I think what the Bruins did was really make college basketball a much more important sport, a much more visible sport, a sport that captured the fancy of a lot more people when UCLA was finished than before they started. It's pretty much like what the New York Yankees did for baseball.

Around the country everybody knew about UCLA. It was a phenomenon. It really was. I'd put 'em up there with the Yankees and the Green Bay Packers during that particular period in the early sixties which helped make pro football what it is today. The Boston Celtics helped to do it for pro basketball, and the Montreal Canadians did it for hockey. That's where the Bruins fit in—they're right there with the great, top of the line dynasties of all time.

A favorite memory is when we were up in Pullman, and the team had played in Seattle on a Saturday night and we traveled cross state to get into Pullman on Sunday night for a Monday game. There was a workout at the Performing Arts Coliseum, which had just opened that year. John had put them through their paces as usual, and we go to the locker room. It's very cold outside, and we've got to walk from the Performing Arts Coliseum a couple of blocks to the hotel, and he goes around the locker room making sure that everybody's hair is completely dry. He doesn't want them to catch a cold in the night air. It tickled me so much. I thought, here's John Wooden, so loved, so admired, so respected by his players, and clearly a man who's a father figure. And he's not only a father figure, but he's going to be their mother, too! I can picture that as if it happened yesterday. And I thought, "Boy, he doesn't miss a thing."

John didn't have to say anything in a loud voice. John could always speak in a very normal voice and you better believe that, even if they had to strain to hear him, they made sure they heard everything he said. I rarely heard John raise his voice, and if he did it was just half an octave or something. He would just speak at a normal level.

With Wooden, every second of practice was accounted for. I remember going to a number of practices where they'd be scrimmaging, and John would be sitting in the second or third row of the bleachers, and he would call one of the players over, and the player would come right over and he would sit down next to Coach. Coach would talk to him, he would tell him exactly what he needed to say, but he never took his eyes off of what was happening on the floor. And once in a while he would stop and he would say, "Richard, you have to be over here," and then he'd go back to his conversation. He'd look back out on the floor. "Greg, you've got to look for the opening over there." You know, boom-boom-boom, he just didn't miss a thing. He was just incredibly observant.

Nell was a terrific woman; I got to know her fairly well during those two years. I found her to be very bright, very witty. She was John Wooden's wife, but she wasn't going to throw her weight around. I just found her to be extremely pleasant. I had some nice conversations with her on road trips, in the hotel lobbies and the rest of it . . . just a very caring woman, a modest woman, but very, very smart. You could tell there was an extraordinary bond between them, an extraordinary love between them.

He is truly special. Hey, everybody has warts. If you want to go looking for John's warts I'm sure you can find them. God knows I've been around people who've been overblown and overstated and over-glamorized and over-respected and all of that, but not John. This man gets everything he deserves. And if people start to take off after him and say he wasn't as good a guy as he looked and all this stuff, to me that's just somebody with an ax to grind. Hey, nobody's perfect, but he's damn close.

Wooden and Al Michaels, 1991

THE JOHN WOODEN PYRAMID OF SUCCESS

DENNY MILLER
Ojai, California

Denny played basketball for John Wooden at UCLA.

I played at UCLA between 1953-54, I then went to Korea and came back and played for two years, 1956 and 1957. I dated Wooden's daughter, Nancy. She was a lovely lady, but I couldn't take all the guff I got from my teammates. Our relationship was short-lived. He was a typical father. I'm going through the same thing now that my daughter is eighteen, sizing up the guys that come to the door. He was very nice, and by the time I was being coached by him, the relationship had come to an end. We had a good time. We'd go to Crumpler's and have a malt and go home. I made sure I got her home on time, I'll tell you that. He was a stickler for that.

John is a gentle man. He's an enigma (sadly) in the sports world. He's a poet in the locker room. Wooden made me appreciate putting effort into something. I've been in acting now for over three decades and it's a team sport. Even if you're doing a monologue you have to work with lighting and directing and everything else. They even use some of the same terminology. There's the star, supporting players, and role players. The director is the coach. You perform in front of an audience and that's the same as team sports. I always liked his insistence upon sharing. If you had a shot from fifteen feet and there was a guy in the open at ten foot, you would hear about it if you didn't pick him out and give him the ball.

The Pyramid of Success is important to me. I've given a few talks about it. I always get a favorable reaction unless there's somebody in the audience from USC.

I've been a screen actor, In the beginning I was kind of hero type on *Wagon Train* and played heroes. Some years ago, I convinced somebody that I was real dirty mother, and I've been playing heavies ever since. I'm dead or in jail by the second reel. I only play despicable characters now. If I asked for a date from John's daughter now, he'd turn me down flat. I play rapists, and I'm not too bad at it. My size has helped me. I've been beaten up by all the stars. Charlie Bronson who comes up to my arm pits, he's beat the hell out of me. And Tom Selleck. I make them look great because I'm usually bigger than they are and if I'm not, I wear lifts, and then they just stomp the hell out of me and walk off into the sunset and I bleed to death. It's a silly way to make a living for a devout coward. I've never been in a fight in my life.

One of my few claims to fame was that I was number twelve in the long line of Tarzans. There's now been nineteen. I was in the book, *Tarzans of the Movies* under the chapter heading "Tarzan the Worst." In the film that I was in, they stole footage from everybody from *King Solomon's Mines* and I think from some of the Shirley Temple films. Anyway, it was just terrible.

From Wooden, I learned how to play with pain, not that he wants you to hurt yourself. I'm never aware of the fact that they gave pain killers to anybody. I learned from him the cumulative effect of training. And I train to this day. I work out almost every day of my life and I now teach relaxation and stretching, I teach it for the Navy over at Port Hueneme to their weapons designers who get uptight about what they do. Until recently, I had my own gym and would teach individuals or small groups fitness.

The Wooden clan, late 1970's.

RENE MILLER
Raleigh, North Carolina

Rene was a student manager for John Wooden.

I was a senior manager for Coach Wooden, and I managed for him in 1953, 1954 and 1955. I was on a baseball scholarship and I got hurt. A job they gave me in connection to my scholarship was to sweep the steps from his office down two floors (which nobody ever checked). I liked to do it just to drop in and talk to Coach Wooden and catch Ducky. I got to know him before I really got hurt at school and before I became the manager.

My first job was to tape the Pyramid of Success up in all the lockers of all the guys at the first day of practice.

Later, I ran sports clinics for the Air Force and brought Wooden to Europe in 1972. The people overseas were civilian coaches from Holland, Germany, Belgium, Switzerland. They all knew of John Wooden. He's a diplomat, a good spokesman for his country.

One of the most important things I learned personally and saw was when he gave a half-time talk. One of the things that really hit me one day when we were at Stanford was when he got everybody quiet. You could hear a pin drop. He said, "You're the only one." He's talking to all of them, "You're the only one who really knows if you're giving 100 percent. Some of you aren't. You know. I can't tell if you're giving 92 percent or 100 percent or what. You know. And I expect each of you. . ." He tried to get them to internalize their desire to win and to succeed. He really hit them between the eyes. I've always remembered that. I've used that because you are the only one who knows how much you're giving. You can fool a lot of people and you can go through the motions but you're the only person who knows what you're doing and what you're giving. I used that all the time. I used that for seven years. When I told my wife about this book, she said, "Make sure you tell them that you made me read that darn thing (the Pyramid of Success) on our honeymoon." And that's the honest to God truth. She tells that story wherever we go. She says, "Well what was he thinking? Well, he had this darn thing and he made me read this."

Since I left UCLA, I've been pretty successful in what I've done, and most of it's been with the military. When I was at Medalist, they had a speakers' bureau. I had Wooden, Barry Switzer, Dan Gable, Ernie Banks—we had the top people.

Wooden was always well-received because he's got such a reputation that people are there to hear the oracle. At Medalist, he was their bell-ringer. He was the best they had.

Managers are sometimes looked down upon, not respected. I got a lot of respect from him, but when I was the manager, you've got to be big enough to handle it. They threw the towels at you and things like that.

Coach Wooden was the most influential man in my life, hands down. He's a role model for anybody in coaching. It's just too bad that we don't have more intelligent, more articulate people in the coaching business. He was a man apart. He could fit in with anybody, and yet he remained aloof from the standpoint that he wasn't a wise-cracking, hyper, cigar-smoking type that was preeminent in the coaching business. He's a super person.

He's not underrated. He was underrated when I worked for him, but he certainly got all that he deserved.

THE WHITE HOUSE

WASHINGTON

April 2, 1975

Dear Coach Wooden:

Warmest congratulations to you and to all the members of the UCLA basketball team on your 1975 NCAA championship! It was an exciting climax to an outstanding tournament and I want to add a special note of congratulations to you for having coached ten National championship basketball teams. The sports world is filled with records of all sorts but the one you and your teams have set in tournament play is truly impressive and may well permanently endure.

You have said that the first National championship will always mean the most to you. Yet I would imagine this last one is almost as satisfying in many ways, coming as it does on your retirement. Although you will be leaving the active coaching ranks and will be greatly missed by sports fans throughout the country, you have left all of us with an unsurpassed legacy of excellence that is an inspiration to young and old alike, in and out of sports. Perhaps of greatest importance, through your personal integrity and dedication to a pyramid of basic principles of living, you have set an example for success which all of us can follow with confidence whatever our calling in life.

Again, congratulations and warmest good wishes to you and your family in the years ahead for all the continued happiness and success you so richly deserve.

Sincerely,

Jerry Ford

President Gerald Ford's letter to Wooden on his retirement.

THE JOHN WOODEN PYRAMID OF SUCCESS

ALGENE MOORE
Los Angeles, California

Algene was married to John Moore,
who played basketball for John Wooden.

My late husband, John Moore—they called him Johnny Moore—played for Coach Wooden from 1951-55.

I remember Coach Wooden as being a tremendous caring man. My husband had great respect and admiration for him. I saved a newspaper article from the *Post Tribune* from Gary, Indiana where my husband was from. Here is what my husband said about Coach Wooden: They asked, "What were Moore's feelings toward his coach, the legendary John Wooden?"

John said,

I thought he was a great man and a great coach. His record bears that out (620-147). He showed interest in his players even after they graduated. He remains close to all of his former players. And I thought this was just wonderful. He's never too far away and I will later go on to explain that statement.

His philosophy is what still inspires me. He believes that when you do the best you can, nobody can criticize you. His only criticism of his ball players was that they were not doing as much as they were capable of doing. He recently lost his wife. I visited with them while she was in the hospital. I also talked to him after her death.

Coach Wooden was the first coach who arranged for a black player to stay on the UCLA campus or in the Westwood area. This was in 1951. John Moore had been quite a highly respected basketball player in the state of Indiana. He had also received scholarships to Michigan State and some of the other leading colleges who would allow black players to stay on campus. But at that time, UCLA was not as liberal, so John was having to stay in town. He was very unhappy because he said it was so cold and he had to travel in this little car from wherever black people lived in Los Angeles.

Johnny talked to Coach Wooden and said, "I'm unhappy and I want to leave because I have to travel so far, and it's so cold in the morning, and I have to study and I want to do well on the basketball team." So, Coach Wooden went around, and he got my husband John a place to stay with the Zeta Beta Tau Jewish fraternity there at UCLA. And my husband was the first. You see how times have changed. John was so happy about that, and incidentally, a great friendship was formed with all the Jewish guys there. In fact, most of them came to John's funeral. After then, since John was staying at this Jewish fraternity house and he didn't have to travel so far, Coach Wooden arranged for Willie Naulls to stay at another Jewish fraternity house.

My husband was an All-American basketball player. He was the first UCLA basketball player to score 1,000 points in his career. And during those times, guys didn't shoot as much! John was voted Most Valuable Player in his sophomore and senior year.

My husband went on to become a bank manager. Then he left the bank and went to a savings and loan association. Coach Wooden, whenever John received recognition or any type of celebration, would attend.

John Wooden had a tremendous impact on my husband and my family. I loved his wife. With my being black as well, when I would go to the basketball games, it was a different environment for me. They always acknowledged and made me feel good at home there in the basketball gym. It was just a very good feeling. Color didn't matter to the Woodens. My husband just loved him. He was such a wonderful example. John Wooden came and spoke at John's funeral. He recited some poems and I could see that he was deeply moved. He wrote on the program, he signed his name and said, "I love John."

We tried to pattern our life after Coach and Mrs. Wooden. We were married for thirty-two years. Nell would always talk to my friends and me, as females, and would admire our little clothes or whatever that we had. She would talk about her husband and we'd talk about our boyfriends at that particular time. She was always receptive to us, and a lot of the other basketball players' mothers were as well and they were white. They were very warm to us and it was just a wonderful experience for me getting to know them and going out to Westwood and to UCLA.

Some of the boys were rough, but Wooden set such a great example for them, they all respected him. They wanted to please him, to make him happy. He's just a great man.

FRANKLIN D. MURPHY
Los Angeles, California

Dr. Murphy was the Chancellor at UCLA from 1960-68.

Pauley Pavilion was built during my tenure. I had a deep motivation to try to bring athletics onto the campus when I got to UCLA. Basketball was played all over town, in Santa Monica, in the Sports Arena and so on. There were no track facilities, no baseball facilities. There were no intercollegiate athletic facilities at UCLA. The first thing I set out to do was to try to get a multi-purpose auditorium for basketball and for major events—a 15-, 16-, 18,000—seat type pavilion. I got then Regent Edwin Pauley to put up some money. The state was willing to put up the money for a portion of it because of academic—in those days we were small enough to have graduation there.

We started playing basketball there about the time that Lew Alcindor, as he was then called, had come from New York. Of course that was not John's first NCAA championship. John won his first NCAA championship in my third year. He had been promised that he was going to get an arena within a couple years, but it took fifteen or so. It showed a lot of "stick-to-itiveness" to stick it out and have to play around almost like pickup games in different arenas around town.

It was a great thrill for me to be chancellor of the University when your team won the first national championship. Then I got to know John more as we began to conceive of Pauley Pavilion. I spent time with John and the architect because we wanted John's ideas built into it. It's half underground and half above-ground. It's the convenience of getting in. You come in the middle and you can either walk up or walk down, whereas if you had it all above ground, you'd have to walk all the way to the top. That was architect Welton Beckett's idea. He spent a lot of time going over how the floor was laid out, and the dressing rooms and where they were located. But most of all, the idea of having a 13,000 seating-capacity facility was the really meaningful thing to John.

John proved that he could win once he got going with any kind of a team. And he proved that he could win under adverse circumstances without even having a stadium. That had a lot to do with how successful your recruiting would be. I suspect that he would never have been able to recruit Kareem from New York or Bill Walton from San Diego without Pauley Pavilion or something like it. But he did pretty well before, so who knows?

I did get to know John well. I used to go to most all the games, and I'd see him about. It was clear that one of the main reasons John was successful as a coach was that he was a real disciplinarian. No nonsense, and the boys knew this.

I noticed an appreciable effect on UCLA because of Wooden's success as a basketball coach. When I first came to UCLA in 1960, I came from University of Kansas. I grew up in Kansas City, Missouri, though I was educated in the East, at the University of Pennsylvania, where I got my doctorate in medicine. Living in the Midwest and the East, whenever you said, "University of California," it meant Berkeley, automatically. When I came out here and was asked to take on UCLA, a lot of my friends in education in the East and the Midwest, said, "Don't do it because the UCLA campus is run by Berkeley. You won't have any authority, you'll have minimal responsibility." That was almost a challenge.

But in 1960 I came because I sensed that it was a place that had the potential of taking off. At that time there were maybe 15,000 students. But, we didn't have a school of architecture, didn't have a school of dentistry, the school of medicine had barely gotten started, and the graduate programs were not large or extensive. During the eight years I was there, there was enormous growth in student population.

Shortly after coming to UCLA, I remember calling my office one day and the operator answering, "University of California." Well, that infuriated me. So I went to the office that day and gave instructions that I wanted the phone answered, "UCLA." I wanted those four letters to become identified. And the great thing that John Wooden's teams did—right at the time that we were making a concerted effort to get UCLA recognized as an entity, out from under the umbrella of the University of California at Berkeley—was that he started winning these championships. And we had Pauley Pavilion. You started reading in the paper about UCLA this, UCLA that, Pauley Pavilion. A ticket was one of the hardest tickets in Los Angeles to get.

UCLA's success in basketball played a consequential role in getting UCLA identified, nationwide and internationally, as an entity. When you had people like Kareem and Bill Walton and these other fellows who came along, that even identified the place more so. The Wooden tradition did more to catapult UCLA into becoming an entity unto itself than anything that happened during my time.

I sensed a tremendous *esprit de corps* on campus during those days. Little brother became big brother in two ways. Up to that time, the city was athletically owned, as it were, by USC; and the University of California was owned by Berkeley. Then all of a sudden little brother came out of nowhere and began getting recognized as an equal. Everybody on campus was beaming during basketball season. It was a tremendous morale booster for just that reason. We were no longer little brother, we were no longer the doormat. We were in there with the big boys.

THE JOHN WOODEN PYRAMID OF SUCCESS

Plus it was an exceptional style of basketball. John was innovative in what he was doing. Although the average individual doesn't worry much about technique and how the game's played, John's teams were always lots of fun to watch. Never a dull moment. He didn't believe in stalling.

Winning basketball led to a growth in revenue. The basketball program was always well funded. It generated surplus funds, which then went to help some of the minor sports

Over the years, I've been queried about John Wooden a great deal. He's a living legend. I think most people regard him as the single greatest figure in college basketball history. And there have been some great ones—Adolph Rupp, Phog Allen—but none of them have even come close to approaching the stature, the quality of the record that John had.

Wooden dealt directly with the athletic director, J.D. Morgan, most of my time. I appointed J.D. after a couple years. J.D. and John got along extremely well, and I really didn't have much to do with athletics. After appointing J.D. as athletic director, he did such a superb job I didn't have to worry about it. And my liaison with J.D. in the athletic department was increasingly through Chuck Young (who later became chancellor). Morgan had enormous respect for John. Fierce loyalty. He would unhesitatingly state that he was the great figure in the history of college basketball. I think there was even a little hero worship.

Other chancellors and colleagues in higher education used to joke quite a bit. The joke would always be, "You know, Franklin Murphy's unique among university presidents."

And the other guy would say, "In what respect?"

"Well, he's the only university president you know who ever has recruited three seven-foot All-American basketball centers: Wilt Chamberlain, Lew Alcindor, and Bill Walton."

I'm familiar with Wooden's Pyramid of Success, though I'm not sure that I could reproduce it for you. What the Pyramid of Success says is that you are successful by applying common sense. I don't think John discovered any magic formula. All the pieces are there.

People reminisce a lot about those teams and those days. Those were exciting days. When the freshmen team beat the varsity, it was hard to believe. But to see Lew—Kareem—the first time he went up to dunk one of these things, you could hear the entire crowd groan, sigh. He was two feet above the basket when he dropped the ball in.

The pressing defense I just loved. The press wasn't easy, because it took people with enormously quick reflexes. Those were wonderful days and nights. Not only did John Wooden play a major role in getting UCLA on the map, but he played a major part in putting college basketball on the map.

Phog Allen was for many years the coach of Kansas. And, of course Kansas is where Dr. Naismith was, the inventor of basketball. He had come from Massachusetts—where he invented the game with a fruit basket. Phog Allen was the basketball coach for many years and was, in his time, the most prominent basketball coach in the country. Playing on his teams were Dean Smith of North Carolina, and Adolph Rupp of University of Kentucky. Phog was the one whose insistence finally got basketball into the Olympics. Up until John Wooden's appearance on the scene, Phog Allen was the best known figure in college basketball in the country.

With television, you were in everybody's front room. The televising of some of these games brought in a lot of extra money that was then spent on minor sports at UCLA. Wooden played a major role in developing the consciousness of college-ball sports aficionados. After the first couple of years when he won, '64, '65, it turned from a streak into a dynasty into something that was extraordinary.

Nothing succeeds like success, because you can't win without good basketball players. You've got to be able to get the manpower. John was not a particularly avid, active recruiter, but once the ball got rolling, people wrote and wanted to come to UCLA to play for John Wooden. He could pick and choose.

Because of the growth of Southern California, UCLA—regardless of John Wooden or Franklin Murphy or anybody else—was predestined to become a major university, just by virtue of its location and by being part of the University of California. UCLA's growth mirrors what's happened in Southern California; the cultural explosion, art museums. In 1960, when I arrived in Southern California, you didn't have anything. You didn't have the Music Center, the Getty Museum, the Norton Simon Museum. UCLA was a small, not very well known institution. There were no professional sports of consequence. Walter O'Malley hadn't brought the Dodgers out from Brooklyn yet. You didn't have professional basketball. The Lakers were in Minneapolis. There was an explosion of sports and an explosion of cultural life—theater, music, art—and an explosion in the quality of higher education. And UCLA was right in the center of all that.

John Wooden was an absolutely exemplary human being. He's the prototypical example that good guys do finish first. [Baseball manager Leo Durocher is most famous for the quote "Nice guys finish last," though he actually said, "Nice guys finish seventh," referring to the baseball standings.]

THE JOHN WOODEN PYRAMID OF SUCCESS

WILLIE NAULLS
Los Angeles, California

Willie played basketball for John Wooden and went on to a career in pro basketball. He was inducted into the UCLA Athletic Hall of Fame in 1986.

I was at UCLA from 1953-56. I went to San Pedro High School. Coach Wooden saw us play the last two years. After evaluating all my options, I decided to go to UCLA. I went out to see them play, and was really impressed with his talent, the fast break, the aggressive style of play.

He scouted me. I was All-City two years, and was a good student, too. Looking back on it, the more success I received in basketball and baseball in high school, the more success I had in academia. There's a confidence and a warmth about Wooden. He never made jokes about it. He just said he'd like to have me at the school. I went because of him.

My parents really fell in love with Coach Wooden. I was impressed with Coach Wooden's style of play and the fact that he didn't make any promises. At the time, Westwood was closed to blacks. You literally couldn't rent a place there, so I rented a room in a fraternity. It was a great experience. I met a lot of people who are friends right now. It was a mostly Jewish fraternity. It was very open and giving and I learned a lot.

When you reflect back over anybody's life, you can tell what type of life they've had by the seeds that he's planted. As far as I'm concerned everything is seeds. You plant those in a person and the person, their lives are an expression of the fruits of that seed. And you look at all the athletes who played under Coach Wooden and most of them have been successful. He built up the confidence. He developed the theory of no pain, no gain. If you put a good effort forth, you get a good result.

On top of that, his attitude toward teaching basketball is applicable to the rest of your life. We learned lessons about how to deal with racial prejudice. We learned in Kentucky in integrating the first hotel, the University Hotel. We went to a movie theater downtown and there was no fanfare.

I was supposed to play freshmen ball my freshman year, but Coach said he'd like me to play varsity. I was the last one on the team. That's the way I looked at it. Everybody else had been on the varsity the year before, and I was the only freshman. I was first string before too long in the season. That's the way he was. If you proved that you could play, you survived on your own merit from day to day. He didn't play favorites, and since he didn't, you got confidence that your individual production and level would be rewarded.

I gained confidence, a philosophy of success. A philosophy of not getting high and low about the situation, just being on an even keel. Preparation is important. Preparation gives you knowledge about what you're doing. You learn the system, get an understanding of it, and then you learn about all the alternatives that you can do in that system.

You'll never plant those negative seeds in me and have them grow. I spend my time dealing not with planting, but growing. It was always a very giving place. People gave, not only because you were an athlete, but people really became friends. Most of my friends were ahead of me.

At UCLA I did very poorly, I don't know why, but I learned a lot. I eventually went back and got a degree twenty years later in sociology.

I heard about the Pyramid at our high school banquet. It contains spiritual characteristics. It's a tripartite theme. You have a soul and a mind and a body. The spiritual characteristics are what a man actually is and does. It's controlled by his will to do whatever he decides to do.

The mind is in the soul and the will. John Wooden's spirit and mind are related like blood and water. Those characteristics define a person's actions. Those words on the Pyramid are descriptive adjectives of a person's actions, and the mind decides if the body will function depending on what your mind is programming, whether you are lazy, under productive, or giving 101 percent effort. It's what you tell your body to do.

If a person is ever increasing and working on those characteristics willfully, that man is going to be successful. He's accountable, he's loyal, he's good with kids, he serves. John Wooden is a servant. You almost feel uncomfortable you have so much respect for him, yet he wants to serve you all the time. That's truly a man of God.

My motivation was very selfish. I wanted to be great. I wanted to be recognized. First of all, I came out of the ghetto. Watts is pretty rough. I wanted to get out of there and I wanted to be recognized. At the time, there was not a lot of television. We certainly didn't have one. So, I wanted to be the best. I loved baseball, it was my best sport in high school. I was a pitcher and first baseman. It was me against somebody else. Our team was in the projects. It was all black.

When I moved here from Dallas, Texas, I was about eight years old. We lived in a very segregated community. We moved to Watts and then we moved up to San Pedro two years later to an integrated project. I had the freedom to go to the park and practice and not worry about somebody grabbing and killing you, a feeling that was very real in Texas. When I got to UCLA I had the same freedom. There were no racial problems when I was playing basketball.

I consider Wooden like my father, he gave us that standard that we were to achieve in basketball and in our lives. He always had rules and regulations, and as much as you might have disliked him, that was the difference in our program.

After UCLA, I followed the games and, I wrote him during the ten years, I played professional ball, but I didn't really keep close contact. Since I retired, I call him. I had very serious conversations with him when I retired and once before I retired. We talked about my future and he gave me advice.

I was drafted by the [St. Louis] Hawks and when the season started I was traded to the New York Knickerbockers. I spent half a season with the Warriors with Wilt Chamberlain in the group. That was my seventh year. Then I played for the Celtics and we were world champions. When I left UCLA I had the scoring and rebounding records and was an All-American three years. The last two years we won the conference championship. That was a thrill.

Coach Wooden had a philosophy about developing men. He felt that if he could get every player to reach a peak of performance every year in a team concept, that the team would do as well as it could do. He was a benevolent dictator. His personal life was that of a minister almost, a very devoted man to his wife. He built on those beliefs and he altered the personnel, but never on what he expected of the personnel, and that was to give it their best.

Mastery of fundamentals allows you to function in your creativity. I played against UCLA over the summer out of high school. These guys ran us off the court with little simple plays—backdoors here, passing there. He taught us how to play. He broke the game down—dribbling, passing, boxing-in and rebounding. Shooting was the last thing that he worried about. It was rebounding and that tenacity, always being ready. You go in for a lay-up on a fast break and you lay the board on the backboard and hit the ground. You don't stand and wave at the fans, you hit that ground and get back in there in case you missed the shot or to be in your position for defense. Back in there. Anticipation. It was marvelous. When you get to the pros, you're just ready.

I've been asked about Wooden a lot in the last twenty, thirty years. Wherever we go, people have so much respect for him. They ask what's it like to play for him, what type of man is he? And a lot of them have heard him speak and they have their own thoughts. It's an affirmation generally. He was a great family man, an honorable man, a particular man, a teacher. He loves all of us. We were his boys.

My last year of pro ball was 1967. When I was a professional athlete playing in New York, Kareem asked me about UCLA, before he went there. He was in high school and I was playing with the Knicks. Coach Wooden was the reason he went to UCLA. Wooden took Kareem Abdul-Jabbar and molded him into a team player so that he made everybody else better.

After the pros, I returned to UCLA for a year, was an assistant there on different classes, and I got my degree. Then I went into the nightclub business, opening a non-alcoholic club with dancing. Then I went into the franchise food business. I negotiated contracts for professional athletes for a while. Then I built single family homes. Recently, I've bought a Ford dealership.

Now, I live in a beautiful home in Westwood. It's a sweet irony to be where you couldn't move in the 1950s. Sometimes I sit around and think about how I got where I am and through the gentle hand of God I'm still alive. It was the prayers of my mother and all the things that I learned. I've stayed a Christian and have a beautiful family, and a wonderful wife. She's a physician. It's my second marriage. I have four kids, who have all done great.

The striking thing about Coach Wooden is that he was a corporate executive in charge of basketball at a major institution. They criticized Coach Wooden because UCLA lost after their seventh year. They'd won seven championships in a row and he was criticized. They said he was getting old! Through it all the Coach was there, dependable, doing his job. Every year he came out and had a set of new players, new circumstances. Everybody is after the NCAA championships. But he never changed.

My children went to Coach Wooden's camp. He sat with them, not only my kids but everybody's kids. He took pictures of every kid in camp, And he talked to them, and sat with them as if they were his children. He'd talk about basketball and afterward he'd read a poem. He's somebody who found out that stability and strength comes from inside. The things he'd tell us made sense. When you walk out of a game you shouldn't be able to tell whether or not you won or lost, it's simply a circumstance in life. Don't react like a ping-pong ball. Develop characteristics and goals and knowledge of yourself and a plan. And execute it. The circumstances try to get you off this track.

I was ready to leave professional basketball. I could have played three more years, but I was tired of it, and of being on somebody else's schedule. I didn't think I wanted to coach, but I wanted to try it anyway. I worked with Coach Wooden. It was a good, calming period that helped make the transition. I traveled with him and looked at some ball players. His life with his wife was a good example showing our children what love is. He just loved the lady. *[Since this interview was conducted, Naulls has gone on to a new profession and is now a minister.]*

PETE NEWELL
Rancho Santa Fe, California

Pete was an opposing coach when John Wooden was at UCLA.

I was the basketball coach at the University of San Francisco from 1941-50, then I went to Michigan State for four years, and came to UC Berkeley during the 1954-55 to 1959 season. John and I are about even on a win-loss basis. We won the conference—'56, '57, '58, '59, four straight years and we went to the finals of the regionals all those years, and two of the years we went to the Final Four. One year we won it, and the last year we were beaten in the final game.

John was a tough coach to play because he came from different background of basketball. West Coast basketball was a walk-up kind of game, a half-court game, and we were probably behind the rest of the country in the quick-up game, as in the fast-break in college today. John played a running game, and he brought a different style of basketball that really helped quicken-up our game and the first time we were really exposed to fast break basketball. We brought to him solid defense that we played out in the West.

He never expressed frustration, personal difficulties or anger in those years when I was beating him, just the opposite. When I had announced my retirement in the middle of the 1959-60 season, he told me that he wanted to sit down and talk about defense in the summer. I told him I would be happy to. I ended up coaching the Olympic team in Rome, but my assistant, Rene Herrerias, who later became the head coach, discussed strategies with his assistant, Jerry Norman, who sold John on the full-court press. We were one of the first proponents of the press defense out here in the West. A couple of years later, when Wooden won the first NCAA championship, he did so using a press defense with one of the smaller teams in modern times that ever won the NCAA.

We weren't social friends; John and Nell were not as close as the West Coast coaches were with each other. We each had a great deal of respect for the other as a coach. While we are different, we stood for the same thing: a disciplined team, able to play with planning, education, and being conditioned. When I was at Berkeley, we were determined we weren't going to call a first time-out. John and I believed the same thing about time-outs, that it was a white flag, a last resort, almost an early surrender. At Berkeley, playing for the conference championship, the first of the four that we won, neither one of us called a time-out in the first half. In the second half, with three minutes to go, UCLA called a time-out, because we "got them" and we were pressing them the whole time. This was a number of years before they ever pressed. We won that game, but we both felt that we were better conditioned than the opponent and we always tried to use it as the weapon.

It's hard to win a championship, but it's even harder to repeat it, because to keep players motivated is not an easy task. It's easier to motivate players when they haven't achieved, than after they have.

I was the athletic director of UC Berkeley until 1968. During that period, the UCLA dynasty, when Wooden was playing the press, I knew he was great. Let me give you some background on the press. The press defense did not become a part of basketball until after the war in about 1946-47. The reason is that prior to the War, until 1937-38, the game of basketball was played differently. There was a center jump and after any basket you came to the middle and there was a center jump, so there was no continuity as we know it today. The other team would take it up and bang them right back at you. There was no opportunity to press because everything started with a jump ball. When World War II came along, not much was happening in basketball. You couldn't travel during the war because of troops and competition was local, so there were no chances for the coaches to make the best use of this new rule that was being used instead of jump.

I played it in 1947-48, not because I was trying to invent anything, but I had a five-foot-seven guard who was a very good player, and smarter than I was. I wanted him to be a guard, but the way the game was played he was front line on defense and he had to play offensive forward. I also had a guard who couldn't dribble, was six-foot-four, a good jumper and rebounder, but I could only play him on defense because he got the basket. During one spring practice, I decided to do something different so I could use them both. I kept my guard, who was out in front, at guard and offense and used my forwards like they use them now to play back-line on, to get from basket to basket, on defense and on offense. It meant a lot of running, but it was different and that is how we started the press. We were giving advantage to a lot of people, including my little guards who were able to take up their bigger guards on the back court because opposing teams were not used to encountering.

John started playing the press in 1963-64, differently than we played it, and with something that I advocated in my thinking on the press, that you have a complementary press. He'd make an adjustment as needed. When an opponent would reply to his initial press, he'd then counter that move.

When my wife passed away in 1984, he called me and I really appreciated his thoughtfulness. Since I retired, we've continued to respect each other, and because we no longer are playing each other, have been able to mingle more. For a few years we worked together doing clinics for other coaches, and they're very successful. We don't try any one-upmanship. Sometimes we're totally in agreement on the way we approach a basketball issue.

THE JOHN WOODEN PYRAMID OF SUCCESS

JERRY NORMAN
Los Angeles, California

Jerry played basketball for John Wooden at UCLA, was one of Wooden's assistant coaches, and was inducted into the UCLA Athletic Hall of Fame in 1986 for his contributions as a player and a coach.

I played for Coach Wooden from 1949-52, and I was his assistant coach from 1960-68. I was in the Navy at the tail end of the Korean War. When I got out, Coach Wooden had gotten hold of me wanting to know if I wanted to coach in high school. His brother was the principal of a high school out in West Covina, so I went out there and decided I would take the job. I stayed out there one year and came back to UCLA the following year.

He coached in an era that is so different from today, it's hard to compare him to what the coaches are today. Unfortunately, today the coaches don't have a lot of control over the players. The era when he coached was a totally different era. He's fundamentally a good person.

If he was just starting out today, he would have the same difficulty as all the other coaches today. If you've already established yourself, like a Bobby Knight or like Wooden had, you have a pre-cast image which the players know they're coming into. You can exercise a fair amount of control, but, if you're just this new coach starting out, it's very difficult to become established in today's environment.

Wooden changed somewhat when all of the success came, most people would. When everybody tells you that you walk on water, it's easy to start to believe it.

The Pyramid of Success had no effect on me. Initially it was something that his college coach started and Wooden added a bunch of bells and whistles to it. The players were never really involved in that aspect of it. I never focused on it as a player or even as a coach. Most of the players I know probably didn't even know it existed, though a lot of them do after they played, but we never startled the season saying "You ought to do this, this and this..."

I don't know what I got out of the experience of working with Wooden. I have had people asked me about Wooden, sure. People are always curious about somebody who has any kid of notoriety. He's very different from what his public image is, and I don't necessarily mean that derogatorily; it's too long a dissertation to go into, I'm probably not the best one to ask and I'm not interested in harming his image. Fundamentally, he is what everybody probably perceives him to be for the most part.

He's an outstanding coach. It's difficult for anybody to rate coaches unless you're looking at it from a macro standpoint. The people who played for him haven't played for anybody else. Being in the coaching profession myself, I think his strengths were as a great practice organizer and as a great practice coach. He knows how to relate to the players for the most part. He's a great fundamentals coach.

I attribute the remarkable win streak to the players. I don't mean to sound derogatory, but if you look at Wooden's record, he was at UCLA fifteen years and never won anything. He won the conference five times. I played on two of those teams that won the conference. You'd normally say, "Gee, you had five shots at beating somebody in the NCAA tournament, we ought to be able to outsmart somebody once, right?" And we didn't. Then you say, all of the sudden we started to win. Why did we win? Overnight he became a genius?

It was pretty much the same stuff over and over, but you're telling it to different players. He started attracting better players and then ultimately it all worked once he got the players.

He treated me well. We got along very well and gave you a free hand to do what you could do. He had not done real well in the late fifties going into the early sixties. The program was really on a downtrend. He's a very intelligent guy and he realized that he needed help. Up until that time he never really had any true assistants. He had guys who were helping him part time. I contributed primarily to the technical side of the game, and the strategies that we used. From the basketball standpoint, it would have to do more with the strategies of what was employed. The other side would be the recruiting.

The full-court press was my idea. He gives me credit for it. It wasn't a tough sell for me to make to him. When you do something that's a dramatic change from what you're doing, you obviously do it on a trial basis. You don't go in saying, "Hey, we know this is going to work," that "we're going go with it for the next three years." You're gonna go with it for what you feel is an appropriate time frame to see if it is giving you the kind of results that you're trying to get. The intent was to go in and give it a full shot trial. How many games that would be, no one would know. Probably at least five or six anyway. It worked better than we thought it would work. In retrospect, at that time, most of the coaches in coaching were not as knowledgeable in the technical aspect of the game as they are today. A lot of them couldn't figure out why we were even pressing them. It's pretty difficult to counter something when you don't know exactly what you're trying to counter. That was really the position that they were put in. The reasons why a lot of teams weren't successful against us is because they were incorrect as to the reasons we were doing.

THE JOHN WOODEN PYRAMID OF SUCCESS

Therefore, they were employing the kind of strategies that really weren't countering what we were trying to do. We were doing it to create tempo in the game the best we could. We wanted to spread the court out because we didn't have size. They thought we were trying to do it to take the ball away from them.

I don't know how much Wooden's success had to do with his ability to be a psychologist, or to handle the players as individuals. It was probably the same as any other coach. Every coach is faced with that problem. Each of them handles it differently. You can be a Bobby Knight and kick Larry Bird off your team, which he did. He handled interpersonal relations.

Based on Wooden's basketball record, you've gotta say he's certainly one of the outstanding coaches of college basketball history. Like most things, you look at somebody's record and that's what they have to go on. They have to look at his record. He had a very, very good record, particularly the last fifteen years he was in coaching.

All in all, for me it was an enjoyable experience. It's just difficult to walk out in the middle of something that great. Coaching is an addictive kind of a thing. I was at the age I had to make a decision whether I wanted to stay in coaching or get out.

I had a family then, I was thirty-eight. I felt I either had to make a decision to stay in coaching, or wait around until Wooden retired at UCLA. I could have gone somewhere else, but I happened to be born and raised in Los Angeles. When you first get into something, you'll go anywhere to do it. The longer I was in coaching, the more places I wouldn't go. It's terrible on family life. You don't get home until 8 or 9 o'clock at night, gone weekends, recruiting, and playing during the season, it's just terrible hours; there were no letters of intent then, so I was recruiting year round.

The last year I was there, Notre Dame called the Coach and wanted to know if they could talk to me. I was asked if I'd be interested in talking to them. And I said, "Well, it'd be nice, and it'd be an honor and all that, but in all reality, I don't want to come, I don't want to live in South Bend, Indiana."

Every year that I was out of it, the happier I was. I was happy when I was in it. I'd have done the same thing again. I enjoyed it. I loved working with the kids we had. They were fabulous.

There's always a degree of uncertainty when you go into business, but at that time, coaching was paid so poorly. You could stumble around out on the street and make as much money as you would in coaching. Nobody was in coaching for financial rewards. When I left UCLA, I was the second highest paid coach in the conference. The only guy getting paid more than me was Coach Wooden.

I was getting paid peanuts, $14,000 a year, and Wooden was getting $17,000. Don't forget, Walt Hazzard went as the number one pick in the draft and I think Gail Goodrich went behind Bill Bradley. They signed contracts—one for $16,000, the other for $17,000.

Today, it's a whole different perspective. In later years, it was a different situation and people were happily getting paid. But in that era, anybody in business who could do anything was going to make more than we were making.

You've got to realize that when I played for UCLA, at that time the coaching was pretty minimal in this part of the country. It was a beginning sport. If they sent you out to coach volleyball out in Indiana, you'd be the only guy who knew anything about volleyball. Wooden in the earlier years was a far better coach than any of the guys out here. Together we put it together. Along with the players. It takes the players. It was really a team effort. He had skills and I had skills. Maybe if he hadn't had me there nothing would have happened. Strategy

is not his forte. When he learned the game and he came up as a coach and a player, they didn't have those things. When I played, we didn't have any strategies and neither did Coach Wooden nor did the other teams we played against. Nobody had strategies. They just went out and executed the fundamentals and that was it. Things evolve, and all of a sudden, some team started coming up with different ways to do it.

Wooden on his early morning walk at the UCLA track, July 1974.

THE JOHN WOODEN PYRAMID OF SUCCESS

BILL PUTNAM
Encino, California

Bill was an assistant coach for John Wooden.

I along with Eddie Powell was one of John Wooden's first assistants when he came out to UCLA. He inherited me from Wilbur Johns.

He was third or fourth choice. A couple guys turned it down. When I met him, I thought he was a very nice guy, very straight forward, clean cut, no horsing around. No swearing. He smoked some. Never drank. Just a hell of a good guy. I thought he was just great, the kind of guy who would do anything. With the other coach, Eddie Powell, and I, he sprinkled water on the floor and mopped the floor before every practice.

I worked twelve years with him. It was nothing but great. He's so adamant about liquor. Once, he had a very bad case of hemorrhoids in Peoria playing Bradley. We had to get a doctor for him, and he said, "I think I can bring you some relief. Here, take some of this."

He was getting ready to take a sip of it, blackberry brandy, and he put it down and he said, "No, no I can't take that." He would not touch it.

Coach Wooden always listened to his assistants. He would give his assistants time before the game and during half time, and he'd say, "Bill what do you have to say?" He'd ask whoever else the other assistant was what they thought. Then he'd sum it up and we'd go out for the second half. And he always was careful that we both had enough to say. It varied of course the way the game was going. It could be pretty coarse and pretty hard or it could be just very down to earth, good stuff. There wasn't any definite pattern, but he always took care of letting us in on the half-time talks and I thought that was fine.

I think I got treated better than most other assistant coaches. His treatment of me and his other assistants was 100 percent. I feel he gave me enough credit to other people for the work I did, although we never got that much credit, but he was always careful to say, "and my assistants." He would never say, "Myself." When Red Sanders was coaching football at UCLA, he'd stay, "I and the staff." Wooden was always, "The staff and myself."

He was on the officials in a nice way, but with a very forceful manner. He figured out the way to do everything for the game and he tried it. He knew which referee he thought he could get a little more from, and those he couldn't. He didn't ignore that part of the game.

BEN ROGERS
Anaheim Hills, California

Ben played basketball for John Wooden at UCLA.

I went to UCLA as a freshman in 1953 and 1954, then I red-shirted (played in scrimmages in practice but was not on the varsity team) in the 1954-55 season with Connie Burke and Bob Wills. I played 1955-58. I played center most of the time.

My first encounter with Wooden was awesome. Even at that time he had a very good reputation. The offices were over in some temporary buildings off Westwood Boulevard. I thought of him as my favorite uncle. He had a very good rapport with people—very staid and concerned as far as your own personal being. He was just somebody that I enjoyed being with.

I got married at the end of my sophomore year in college. Just prior to that I had some real difficulties in terms of maintaining eligibility and I actually lost my eligibility the second half of my sophomore year because of grades. It was inattention. I felt terrible about it. John was very understanding and helped me work through that. I felt I'd let the team down and let myself down and a whole bunch of other people.

John stayed with me on that and helped me do all the things that were necessary as far as getting back my eligibility. He did that by having an open office door, and if I had a question or a problem or anything of that sort I could always see John and he always made time available. He never made you feel like you were wasting time or that you weren't important enough to be attended to or anything of that sort.

The Pyramid is something that John believes in and lives essentially. I recall as an incoming freshman I got this note in the mail, a rather fat packet of letters and materials and the Pyramid was part of it. You look it over and give it some passing significance. Each season we got that same packet of information. It's something that John had internalized and had been exposed to as a player himself. If you ask me what was on the Pyramid of Success, I couldn't tell you. The main [idea], I could tell you.

John and his wife Nell made my wife feel very comfortable at the games. They did some very positive things to make us feel part of the basketball family. Every time that we saw John and Nell, they always called us by and knew Mary Lou's name and were just pleased as anything to see us. The kind of life that John lives and that Nell lived was something that you could point to and say, "I want to be like that."

Since I left UCLA, I went into education and I'm still teaching. I'm the president of our teachers association in Fullerton. I teach Economics and American Government. I'm still married to Mary Lou—for thirty-five plus years. John's example of stability and commitment didn't hurt me at all.

To describe Wooden, I would not put basketball foremost in that description, but as a teacher in the truest sense of communicating. Not basketball, but principles to live by in terms of giving your best to things that you do and not being satisfied with what you've accomplished but trying to push a little further.

The experience of playing for Wooden gave me a lifetime of memories. It's one of those moments like when Neil Armstrong put his foot on the moon. It's just something that's with you. I'm not one for nostalgia particularly. I don't have my yearbooks out, but it is one of those little journeys that you've gone through that absolutely nothing can take away from you. No matter what happens, you have that experience and it's something that is considerably more precious than any kind of material thing you might have gotten out of your college experience.

One of the things about traveling is that there's a lot of dead time so you often would be sitting in a waiting area. Bill Putnam and Ducky Drake were much more talkative than John, but every now and then John would give you a little insight as to the way things went on in his life. I know he had some problems. I don't know that it was as much John's problem as it was his son, who I think had some expectations. He maybe felt that he had expectations from his father that he should have been an outstanding basketball player. I know that caused John some anguish. He felt a little estranged from his son. That's something that I recall him sharing on one occasion. I would imagine that's something that they've resolved at this point.

It would be tough not to put that kind of pressure on yourself if your father is a famous coach and three time All-American. You may be an All-League or something, but you're not in that same category and since you've got a different yardstick, or at least you feel like somebody's putting a different yardstick against you. It makes it tough. I'm sure it's not something that John applied to his son, but I know from brief glimpses of conversations with John, and then with other people close to John that there was a kind of estrangement between the two of them.

When we were on the road he used to take us to movies. We would go as a group. I'm sure some of the local citizenry always wondered, "Well what's this group of towering people walking around with this little short guy in front? What are they up to?" Often we would be in the Midwest or the Northeast and it would be freezing cold, so we'd all have topcoats on and hats. Probably the shortest person other than John would be maybe six-foot-one or six-foot-two and then going up to myself at six-foot-seven. Walking down the sidewalk, people would sort of step off to the side when they'd see us approaching. He's a great fan of westerns. We probably saw a dozen Randolph Scott films, some really terrible cowboy films, which he loved. He's probably read everything that Zane Grey has ever written. Maybe he caught the bug back in Indiana. That's one thing I never quite followed up on that John did. I've never been a great Randolph Scott fan.

LARRY RUBIN
Santa Monica, California

Larry is a former UCLA Bruin sports writer who in 2001 was elevated to sitting as a Justice on the California Court of Appeal.

I first became aware of John Wooden in 1954 when my father took me to a basketball game at the Men's Gym. I was eight. As long as I've been aware of any sort of memory, John Wooden's been one of the more important names. I went to a lot of basketball games growing up. My dad had season tickets and was a president of the Hoopsters, a support group, a couple of times. My first exposure to sports was UCLA basketball. My dad was such a big fan probably because he was short and couldn't play basketball and wanted to. He had gone to UCLA and graduated in the first class that spent all four years at the Westwood campus, after they moved over from what is now Los Angeles City College.

I went to a few of the Bruin Hoopsters events. It was mainly just to say we care and we like basketball. The coaches would speak every month at their meetings, and they'd probably have a practice session during the year where the members of the Hoopsters could watch. Maybe they'd have a player speak. It was a way to get a little closer to the game.

At that time it was a small operation. The basketball was not what it is now. We're talking about one assistant coach, one freshmen coach. Wooden was one of the main reasons I went to UCLA. I started at UCLA the summer of 1964. They had a championship in '64 and '65. I went to a number of the games. They were at the sports arena at the time. Then they moved over to the Pauley Pavilion the year after the second championship. I remember listening to the radio the year we went to the semi-finals, in 1962.

His basic credo, the Pyramid of Success and measuring success based on your own abilities and not in comparison with other people, is emotionally very healthy and is something that I, as a young kid, thought a lot of. My father impressed that upon me. I remember my father talking to me, as fathers do to sons, about what life is all about, and his telling me how John Wooden measured things.

My father was impressed by Wooden and he was a fairly impressive fellow. He was a major lawyer at a major law firm and at that time president of the State Bar, so he was not someone to be influenced easily. I grew up with the presence of John Wooden, even though it was not as if I saw him a lot and spent a lot of time with him.

We're talking high school. By the time I got to college, when I was on the

Daily Bruin as sports editor from 1966 to 1968, I would see him fairly regularly. As a writer covering the team and going on a number of trips, I was exposed to him on a fairly regular basis.

Being the sports editor during that era was wonderful. We had John Wooden and Tommy Prothro, the football coach. Two wonderfully successful coaches. It was a great time, a lot of good athletes. I think everybody, as you look back, wants to paint an earlier age as one of innocence, but athletes were very approachable then. I remember lots of conversations with people like Mike Warren and Kenny Heitz. You could talk to them whenever you wanted to. And this was true even though they were national champions and there was certainly a lot of exposure for them. It was a very good time.

They were all affected by Coach Wooden. I'm sure they told me that at the time. Talking to them afterwards, they'll tell you that very plainly. What makes Wooden so different and special are two things. One, he was a man guided by strong principals, a deep religious philosophy. He knew who he was and he knew what he wanted to accomplish, in a human sense, not just as a basketball coach. And he was not out for the media gratification. He had a place in this life that transcended basketball or momentary victory. And his philosophy was certainly more important to him than any immediate gain.

The other thing is he views himself as an educator first. Being the basketball coach was the device by which he could impart that he wanted to educate others. But he would have been just as successful, though not as well known, as a teacher of any other subject that he was qualified to teach in. I'm sure he would have been as good an English teacher as there ever was if he would have stayed with it. Nobody would have known him, but he would have been great. If you look at other coaches now, either college or pro, you don't see people like that. They're good at what they do, but it's different. They're just not like him.

I remember the full-court press when it was utilized effectively for the first time in the early sixties. It had two effects. One, players didn't get a chance to rest. You're always up, you're always working. It's the opposite of a traditional zone defense where, to a large extent, you don't run around a lot and you get lulled into a sort of slowness in the game. From the first moment on offense you're moving. The minute you score a basket, you immediately turn around and you're playing at one hundred percent efficiency as well. If you have well-conditioned athletes, as he always strived to have, you're going to do well simply because you're going to be pursuing and the other team's going to get tired.

That first group of Slaughter, Hirsch, Erickson, Goodrich and Hazzard was amazing because nobody was more than six-foot-five and somehow their arms seemed very long because there were never any open spaces on that basketball court. The other thing it did is it got the fans really involved in the game.

When your team scores a basket, the fans are usually at its loudest, the peak, the big cheer. What you find is that the fans were so involved with the press and yelling so much that the audio level does not increase when UCLA scores. It's just a constant din. And as I'm talking right now I'm getting goose bumps just listening and remembering the feeling . . . it was just a roar. And it would go on for two or three minutes and the team would be out of the game, and that was it. The game was essentially over.

During those two years, the first year more than the second, you would find that there was a point in the game, almost always in the first half, where the game just ended because of that press. It was amazing. Students of the game and fans of the game were dumbfounded by the press. No one had ever seen it utilized like that. And since then, of course, people have used it off and on in different times. But it's never really had the success that he had with it. He just knew how to teach it very well.

I found him accessible as a coach when I was writing about him on the school newspaper. I had a deference that a younger person would have to an older person. I certainly didn't think it was my right to impose upon him too much. I don't remember any times when I wanted to talk to him about something that he wasn't available.

The student body at that time collectively thought of him just as most people do, as an amazing person of great moral strength who was a wonderful leader. It really uplifted the campus. It absolutely makes you feel better and different than any other person. It wasn't that other coaches and other educators weren't good people and weren't competent coaches, but John Wooden was John Wooden.

After I graduated from college, I went to law school at UCLA. The major force in me staying at UCLA rather than going to Cal or Michigan or some other place was the basketball. I didn't want to miss any ball games.

I remember being fascinated by Wooden's ritual of rolling the program and turning to either Jerry Norman or Gary Cunningham and touching one, looking down on the floor, pulling up his sock and then looking over to Nell and winking at her. It was so amazing. In this high-pressured situation, with all these fans, this man has the presence of mind to take a time out and think of a family moment and recognize what he said in the past about family coming first before your profession. With all the pressure, that would certainly excuse someone from not saying a final word to your wife before the game starts, yet he still would always remember to do that.

Over the years I've stayed in touch with him. I try to see him once a year.

I've talked to him a few times on the phone or dropped him a note, or sent him something that I thought he might like. I don't think my kids will ever appreciate the man he is, because I think they're too young and he's not as public as he was. I want to make sure that as I try to convey to them as they grow up what type of person he was, that they will know they were exposed to him and met him and they have that connection which is helpful in teaching and in talking about someone. We will never see anybody like him, there is no doubt in my mind, in the world of sports in terms of his sportsmanship as opposed to championships. If you look at all the people who've come since then, you can't think of anybody who reminds you of him. At least I can't.

I have three Pyramids: one in my office, one in my oldest son's room, and one I keep on my wall.

I've talked to my older son, who's nine, about it a lot. I've introduced him a couple of times, but generally I don't talk about the Pyramid a whole lot. It's very interesting, because I help coach his hockey team and I certainly could use it as an example, as an opportunity to talk to some of the kids. But because some of them on the team are as young as six, I don't think maybe they'd understand it.

John Wooden was an educator who cared very much about all the students that he came into contact with, with the hope that in his brief time in their lives he would have made an impact on them. I told him once in a letter that other than my family, there's been nobody who's had more of an influence on my life than he has. And I'm very grateful and even though we've never spent a whole lot of time together one on one, the success I have today is in large measure due to what I learned from him.

LYNN SHACKELFORD
Santa Monica, California

Lynn played basketball for John Wooden and in the American Basketball Association before going on to a career in broadcasting and as a businessman.

I played for UCLA from 1966-69. I was a member of a championship team my junior and senior years. Any time you are on a team like the one we had, your whole life will be affected for the rest of your life. People still come up to me and say, "Lynn, I used to see you play at UCLA."

I was doing women's pro beach volleyball in Reno, and the announcer kept announcing that, "The ESPN crew with Lynn Shackelford will be coming out in a few minutes." I had people coming up to me all the time and talking to me about UCLA. Here it is more than thirty years later. When people would ask what I majored in at UCLA, I would say basketball. How could you not be thinking about basketball all the time when you are the number one team in the country, and expected to go eighty and nil over your three years?

With regard to Wooden, he was a very difficult coach to play for in a lot of ways. He was very demanding, and had strict principles and what he believed in. He used to say that "There are probably some of you that I'll like better than others, but I'm going to treat you all the same." I think he did a good job of that. If there were two guys tied for the seventh player on the team, and he only wanted to play seven during the season, he'd pick one and the other guy would sit on the bench. He wasn't afraid to make that decision, not afraid to do what he thought was best for the team. If that hurt somebody's feelings, that hurt their feelings. That's unfortunate, but that wasn't really his primary concern.

His primary concern was to field the best basketball team he could, and that made it tough. For example, my senior year I had lost confidence and I was tired of being there. It's a very demanding, high-pressure situation. He says that pressure is what you put on yourself, but you're in the limelight of the whole community of Los Angeles. We were on TV all the time with very high ratings. It does wear you down mentally. Bill Walton lost the championship his senior season. I felt that team was not as good. I felt that the Bill Waltons and the Greg Lees and the Jamaal Wilkes were tired of being there. I was tired of being there as a senior. I felt that our team was limping in to the season because we had a lot of seniors.

We had a very talented young man by the name of Sidney Wicks, who was pushing me for the starting position. He was very frustrated, he knew that in a one on one game there was no comparison in talent, he was far superior, and I knew that. At the same time, I wanted to finish on a nice note as a senior.

I was being pushed, and I felt that with my experience at a key moment, I was the best player to have in the game. I was a forward. Midway through the year, I could see that Sidney's playing time was increasing, I would still start until about ten minutes to go in the first half, and then I would sit for a long time. I went in to talk to Coach and he gave me the same line that he had given to many people before. He told me that, "It is my job to field the best team that I can. So Lynn, there will be times when I think that it is better to have Sidney in the game than you. He's a better rebounder, he has more size, etc., etc. There are going to be times when I think you'll do better. You're a better outside shooter. You have experience. You have knowledge. He's a sophomore and I want him to get some experience for the future." That's the same thing I would do if I was the coach, but it was frustrating for me as a senior. I felt I had paid my dues. I had lost my confidence and here's this guy who's pushing me, and how do I get my confidence back? If I know this guy is ready to come in the game the first time I make a mistake, that's a fact of life. It's a high-pressure situation.

I think if I were in John Wooden's shoes I would have done the same things. And if Lynn Shackelford gets his feelings hurt as a senior, than his feelings get hurt. That's one thing about my experience at UCLA. UCLA is a really tough place to play basketball and that makes what John Wooden did even more amazing when you consider all the people he had to keep happy—if not happy, at least satisfied, and if not satisfied, at least still on the team or in the school.

You're talking about guys like Kareem and Lucius Allen who want to transfer after one or two years. You're in a very competitive situation. You've got the Dodgers, Lakers, all these teams. You must field an exciting competitive team or you don't draw. What's happened there the last few years is that they don't draw unless people think they have some glitter or some big name high school star. For Wooden to survive this with different personalities, Lew Alcindor, the kid from New York, Bill Walton, a wild hippie (for lack of a better term) from San Diego. To not only survive it but to field championship teams is amazing.

I don't think people really realize what goes through playing at UCLA. I think the greatest influence he's had on me, and I keep telling people in business that our philosophy at UCLA was to not worry about the opponent. It was to go out and do the best job that you could as a player and as a team. Prepare yourself in practice, get ready to play your game, and play your best. If that meant that you were going to win, if that meant that you weren't going to win, then that meant that there wasn't much you could do otherwise. I've gone through with that philosophy in life.

As between me and Sidney Wicks, it was very frustrating and it wasn't a friendly type competition. Sidney and I are friends now, and he is much more mature, but he was very frustrated. There would even be passing comments about the fact that I couldn't jump and run and this and that and that he was much superior. What he didn't realize was that I was a much smarter player in pressure situations. Sidney was a wild, untamed horse. As John Wooden would say, "He's spectacular. Sometimes it's good and sometimes it's bad, but he is always spectacular." One time we had a semi-final game against Drake and it was my senior year. He put Steve Patterson and Sidney Wicks into the game in the first half. We had built up an eight-point lead and I felt we were starting to pull away against a bunch of little short guys who were really playing hard. I was sitting there in the bench and we gave up the eight-point lead just like that. Cunningham said to Wooden that he had to get the seniors back in the game, meaning me and Heitz. We did, we got back in the game and it was a dogfight the rest of the way. Wooden told me that he never really felt we were going to lose that game. We could have lost it, we only won by one point. I think I made two free points after the buzzer to make it a three-point game. I felt that he was putting Steve Patterson and Sidney Wicks into that game to get them NCAA semi-final tournament game experience. It was risky, but I think he was looking ahead to the next year.

I'd lost my confidence. I just got tired of playing basketball. The only way I broke out of it was when I went to rookie camp in June for the San Diego Rockets in good shape, and I really played well and impressed them enough that they invited me back for the fall. I was the seventh-round draft pick, and had a lot of comments from them about how I was a good player. I got a good taste of basketball back in my mouth. I just wanted to finish the season. When you have that in basketball, it's not a good attitude. It's like playing a round of golf, saying I just want to finish the round. You should be finishing like, "I want to play another eighteen, I think I can birdie every hole."

Wooden says that pressure is something you put on yourself, and I was a guy who put a lot of pressure on myself. He always said that I worry too much. I worried about what people were going to think, what my teammates were going to think, whether I was going to wake up in the morning and still be able to hit a twenty-foot jump shot. I was the kind of guy who worried a lot and put pressure on myself and just wore down.

What I learned from John Wooden about life is the basic faith that things in the long run will work out. If you have principles, stick to them even if they cost you some in the short run. They will help you in the long run and it will be for the best. It may not be a good example, but he would pick out somebody whom he thinks is going to be a good player and in December that player may be making turnovers or missing shots, but that player in February will be a star.

He saw the long run of the season or the long run of the player's career. He had a great knack for making a decision on a player in a matter of a few weeks where the player was now, where he would be in a year from now, and where he would be in two years.

It's a combination of having confidence in your principles of not wavering on making a decision on a player and not wavering from that point on. If a player proves you wrong in practice, he was willing to make changes. Through the years of following basketball, he acquired a great knowledge of where a player's physical skills were and where those physical skills could fit into the UCLA program. He was willing to have the patience and was confident that he could develop the player.

I don't think playing basketball at UCLA was fun. I'm not sure it's fun at very many places. There are some aspects of it I enjoyed, but it's a little overwhelming for someone who's nineteen, twenty or twenty-one. I'm glad I did it because of what I got out of it. I got some lessons in life which have made me a better person. I can endure anything. It's almost like going through war. I'm sure people who have been through war would laugh at me, but you are in a very survival type situation—luckily if you don't survive it's not death. You're coming out of high school with this pride of being the best athlete and everyone's competing; it's very competitive.

To me, the Pyramid of Success is embodied in Coach Wooden's statement that success is doing your best, not winning or losing. I believe that's true. I've been around sports too long not to believe that. There's a great quote over at Wimbledon by Rudyard Kipling or someone like that over the doors, "Treat victories and losses the same. . ." I don't know the rest, but it's the same philosophy.

The last road trip we took when I was a senior before the NCAA tournament was up in Washington. Everybody was cutting loose after the game in Seattle. Everyone was having fun and partying. We had an early bus the next morning and Wooden said we would have a meeting in the locker room. So we get in the locker room and he's very serious and he says, "There were some things going on last night that we can't have going on. I won't tolerate that on this team. Anybody who had girls in their rooms last night I want to stay here in the locker room, everybody else get out on the court for practice." Sidney Wicks started to get up and walk out and he goes "Sidney, there's a lot of things I'll tolerate, I won't tolerate a liar." Sidney turned around and walked back in and sat down. That's the kind of guy Sidney was, he wanted to be a big stud guy, but deep down he wanted to be John Wooden's friend and a good person.

I've probably cheated life a little bit. Being so famous at UCLA has made life a little bit easier for me compared to most people. I feel very fortunate. It opens doors, but you have to produce. There are a hundred of ex-athletes who are trying to make it as announcers. I got the name because of my association with UCLA, and I had to keep it because I was competent. It has helped me get jobs, there's no question about that.

People liked watching John Wooden teams, they were a pleasure to watch. They knew that they were well coached, they were fundamentally sound. It was basketball at one of its purist forms. People adopted UCLA from all over the country. Our society doesn't balance things out. You shouldn't care that much about UCLA basketball that this guy who is twenty-five years old can tell me who we beat in the championships in 1967, 1968, and 1969. Maybe I picked up some of that from Wooden. Those things aren't the most important things in life. It's more important if he gets the most out of the talent and blending together. I as a player get the most out of my talent, it doesn't matter if I win the championship or not. When the NCAA tournament came around he tried to win, but before that he had this idea to develop the best team. Winning will take care of itself. That is true. No matter what you are doing in life or any other sport, winning will take care of itself. That's what the Pyramid is about.

By watching and interacting with the man, his principles rubbed off. Decades later I can still recite the Pyramid credo. The other thing is we all try to complicate life too much. Wooden is far ahead of everybody in those things.

I get questioned about Wooden everyday. People ask what made him special. My answer is he kept things simple. He didn't complicate it. Basketball is a simple game. It's not meant to be complicated. It's a game of reaction. By the time you think, the guy has gone by you. We never put plays on chalkboards. You have NBA teams who chalk everyday. Keith Erickson and I used to laugh because we've got guys on our team who don't even know our plays. I remember playing on some teams where a guy would go by me and I would remember that I was warned about that. What Coach Wooden would do is get you to play with good basic fundamentals and good defense. His offense is done the way it should be, regardless of the defense. The guy had a masters degree in English and could say in one or two sentences what it takes most coaches five minutes to say. A great example is when I was a 75 percent free throw shooter in high school. One day after my freshman year he comes up and says, I should be a better free throw shooter because I could make every jump shot from the same spot. He told me not to take too much time bouncing and dribbling. Just do it. I would make every one. I was over 80 percent most of the next year.

He always says the first championship was the most satisfying. I remember the first time we lost after winning something like forty-three in a row. We lost to Houston. He came in the locker room smiling. I think he was relieved. He never thought the first year we'd go thirty and nil. He told me he was surprised that with four sophomores and a junior that we went thirty and nil. He was almost happy we lost. It made us a better team. I don't think he enjoyed the idea of winning every game. J.D. Morgan was a great athletic director, but he was a pusher, he wanted success in everything. John Wooden had more of an emphasis in practice. To him, a game was a test of how he had taught during the week. He used to tell me that. He really enjoyed working with kids in practice and teaching them how to play basketball, and seeing a team come together. His preference would to be just to watch the game with a rolled program. He would tell us we had to take two time outs because of TV, and he would rather take no time outs. Today you have to take four time outs. He thought two was a lot. That's why he never took a lot of time outs at the end of a game. He felt there was nothing more to learn.

John Wooden is a real different kind of guy. There are a lot of things that he didn't care about. He had these principles and that's what he lived by.

EDDIE SHELDRAKE
Santa Fe Springs, California

Eddie played basketball for John Wooden and in 2000 was inducted into the UCLA Athletic Hall of Fame.

I played his first three years. I graduated in 1951. Ducky Drake was my junior high school coach. I ended up going to UCLA before Wooden came.

When Wooden came in 1948, I didn't know much about him. I started a lot that year. I was a fair player. I think I helped the program because I was very tenacious. I didn't have a lot of skills, but I could run all day long, and the rooters felt comfortable with that. With our fast-break, we were in great condition. It was unbelievable the condition we were in. Wooden said, "I'm not giving you training habits or telling you what to do," although he did tell us one or two things. He said, "You're gonna have to work out so hard at practice that you're not going to be able to feel like doing anything." That's the truth.

When he first came, he tried to get me to learn how to shoot two-handed, and he worked out with us. He's a tenacious, tough, hard-nosed, vicious competitor. When he was coaching, he was the same way. He's a gentleman—he's honest, straight, he's not going to do anything to cheat you, but he's gotta do everything he can to beat the hell out of you. He looks like a preacher, and acts like a preacher, and he could be a preacher cause a lot of preachers are that way, too, but when you look at those beady eyes, and that pointed nose and you get him on you, he's wiry. Let him guard you for a game, and you'd wish you never went on the basketball court. That's the truth.

His competitiveness is what made him want to win. He wasn't afraid of a job, because he wasn't getting paid much. He could have made that much being a good teacher, and he would have been a great teacher. He was a great teacher.

I stayed in touch with Wooden over all these years. There was a time there when I had a lot of personal problems, and Coach and Jerry Norman were always there. It was really great because I could call up and say, "I don't have a ticket for tonight's game," and I was alone, and they'd say, "Hey, there'll be one at the door." I felt part of the family. I was a contributor. In the early years I actually felt part of their success. Some of us who are inferior like to be associated with people who are great. Maybe that's what carried it on later.

I talk to him on the average of once a week or once every two weeks I'll call him. He calls me, but not near as many times. He'll say he hadn't heard from me and am I pissed or something? He wouldn't use that word. He doesn't have to, he says great, sensational lines. That's just like us cussing.

In the early days, he would stick to his standards. If a guy broke a rule he wasn't going to play. He was punished, whether we would win or lose. I really respected him for that.

A famous story was with Lou Stringer, an official and a good guy, who tells the story of when Wooden was really complaining about a call that was made, and he was really chewing at him and calling him in front of our team. Lou came to the Coach, and said, "You might not like that call, but they sure like it at the other end."

He was very serious. He couldn't sleep after games or before games. When we were on the court, he wanted us to be well-mannered. You didn't fool around with Wooden.

There are a lot of coaches who hate Wooden because of his success. Wooden's contribution is far bigger than basketball. Basketball is very small. Through basketball he's contributed a lot to what most Americans would like to do. He's bigger than basketball.

Wooden was part of the team, and he didn't try to take all of the glory and act as if everything revolved around him. That's the smart thing to do as a coach. Had Wooden wanted to, he could have but did not develop the "cult of Wooden." He never set out to commercialize himself.

Whatever happened was a by-product of where he was. It was his goal to succeed. I asked him what would he do if he had money. He said, "Well, I only want one chauffeur. I don't need two. I only want one big limousine." And then he goes on and on. He'll tell you about one housekeeper to do this, and one to do this. He never cared about money. He was very happy in himself for what he was getting done. There are a lot of people like that. We want to make a living and we want to be able to take care of our families. What he accomplishes, what he did was important. He succeeded in his mind. He could have lost and still have been successful in his mind, in my mind.

Winning all those championships was a lot of talent, a lot of the team (not counting players), and a lot of luck. And a lot of God on his side. A lot of games were decided in the last seconds—the ball could have gone in or out.

I learned good habits of time management from Wooden and I'm learning them now. Productivity is so important. When you set a time for a meeting, you have the meeting. He had a meeting with his assistant coaches every morning at ten. That meeting was going to go on. It didn't matter. You could be the President of the United States, Wooden was going to have his meeting. And his guys knew he was going to have his meeting and they were going to be there.

GEORGE STANICH
Gardena, California

*George played basketball for John Wooden, and was inducted into the
UCLA Athletic Hall of Fame in its second group in 1985.*

I am a physical education teacher at El Camino College. I coached the basketball team from 1955-70, but I continued teaching from 1970.

John Wooden influenced my life a great deal. He was my second coach at UCLA. I came there in 1947 and played in 1947 and 1948 for Wilbur Johns and John Wooden 1948, 1949 and 1950, my junior and senior years there. He had a tremendous impact on me.

I was a hard worker and I knew what I wanted, but a lot of times I had strong beliefs. I'd lock horns with anybody, including Coach Wooden. A lot of times what I believed wasn't the proper thing. I needed guidance and at that age we're all seeking and looking for what we want to do with our lives. So he really did have a positive and tremendous impact on my life, as the other coaches did too. Once you became a part of Coach Wooden's team, you became a part of his family, and so he not only took care of me and all of his players there at school, but he helped us after school was out, too, so he never quit looking out after us. There were many incidents after school where I would come to him for advice at different crossroads in my life and he was able to help me tremendously. When I was looking for my first job, and he was in his early forties and he had a young family, he took me all the way to Oxnard to a job interview. I didn't get the job. It was a full-day trip, and he did everything he possibly could to get me the job. In retrospect, I didn't realize what was going on, but as the years go by and you have your own families, this was a sacrifice, and he was doing it for one of his boys. The effort was there and all through my life, whenever there came any crossroads I knew I could pick up the phone and he would always give me the time of day. I would head over there and we'd talk and he would never tell me what the answer to my questions were, but after the talk I knew the decision I had to make. It was just nice to have somebody like that to go to in a time of need. I really was one of his family men as far as extension of his team.

The Pyramid also had an effect on me. When I was a senior and starting to get into graduate school, I was looking for a Master's thesis. I talked to Wooden and he was interested in somebody like myself to work on it and develop it a little bit more. I eventually decided to do my thesis on another subject but in talking to him about it I understood where he was coming. As I got into teaching I got into similar things and I became more interested in and more involved in his beliefs and the Pyramid of Success became my belief too. A lot of the things that he believed in you incorporated into your life and your own beliefs. The idea as far as the winning and what success means I incorporated into my own philosophy and my own life. Getting down into the heart of the Pyramid there were three things I may have not known, but I lived it at the time because one of the things I believed in was conditioning. Being a first year coach, he was trying to get everything into his team in a short period of time. He was trying to get his offense, his defense, and he only had a month's time. From my perspective, I believed that he was trying to do too much with us, and he was trying to get his whole philosophy into us.

Our second round of games we went up to San Francisco and played USF and Saint Mary's. We won the ball games up there, but not by much, and we weren't in too good of shape. I'll never forget when we came back from the trip—he more or less forgot about his philosophy of offense and defense and just went back to hard work from the beginning of practice to the end of practice. I know we weren't in shape those first two weekends of games so he felt in time we would be in shape.

I've shown the Pyramid to my whole family and our playing teams so its been part of our lives. I'm not sure whether he originated this value I have, but one of my strong beliefs in my coaching was to work harder with those who didn't play than the ones who did.

If the starters let down, the other guys were ready and they never felt they were neglected, that they weren't part of the team, and they got my attention, but in doing so, it took a lot of effort and time.

He has been a part of my life and he knows my three children and wife.

I would say that he, along with the other coaches, was one of the most important people in my life who had an influence on me as far as basketball, and for all the philosophies because of the beliefs I took from him.

[One time] I was coming back for a function on a plane from New York. One tall black young man was looking at me and I'm wondering why he is doing so. He said, "I know you. You're from El Camino,"

I said, "Yes." He played football at El Camino, so I went back to sit with him.

He made the comment, "You know, I don't remember my English teachers, I don't remember my history teachers. I remember my three coaches. They really touched me." I think coaches do touch students more. You're with them more. You're putting a lot on the line.

I've heard Wooden say this, "You're putting your emotional, your mental, your physical state on the line when you're playing." You have all your emotions there when you're playing and then you're also a competitor and you want to be the best in the world and here you've got a man who is directing you that wants to be this and you want the best from him, even though you may not like it. When this is all said and done, a coach has a tremendous impact on you, as Wooden has had in my life.

Announcement Tue., May 4/65

STATEMENT OF JOHN R. WOODEN

It should be no surprise to anyone who follows basketball that I am delighted that Lewis Alcindor *has announced that he* has selected UCLA as the university of his choice.

This boy is not only a fine student and great college basketball prospect, but he is also a refreshingly modest young man who shows the results of excellent parental and high school training. After meeting Mr. and Mrs. Alcindor, I could easily understand the fine impression Lew made on all of us when he visited our campus. Their guidance has enabled him to handle the fame and adulation that has come his way in a most gracious and unaffected manner.

He is a polite, well-mannered, intelligent, and unselfish young man who plays basketball at both ends of the floor in the best interests of his team. Everyone with whom I have spoken who has seen him perform has been as much impressed with his team play, hustle, and desire, as they have been with his physical ability.

Jeff Prugh

I'm very, very pleased that Lew Alcindor has announced that he has announced that is coming to UCLA

The original press release, May 4, 1965, in typically perfect Wooden prose, when Lew Alcindor came to UCLA.

JOHN VALLELY
Newport Beach, California

John played basketball for John Wooden, went on to both pro and coaching careers, and now owns a successful sporting clothes manufacturing business.

I played for UCLA in 1969-70 as a guard. I wanted to go to UCLA because, what Coach Wooden was doing in his basketball program, I admired a great deal. Obviously the teams were very successful. They had a great tradition at UCLA.

I had heard so many things about Coach Wooden, including the Pyramid of Success. I didn't really know what that meant at that point. The Pyramid of Success was discussed with the 1964 team because it was a part of his motivational approach. It was somewhat known in basketball circles.

Coach Wooden has had a huge effect on me as a person. What I learned at UCLA had much more to do with life than with the game of basketball. Other than my father, there's no doubt that John Wooden is one of the biggest influences in my life. Beyond that, the other source of inspiration for me would be my perception of who God is.

Wooden's foundation for life was something that I admired, although I didn't quite understand it when I came to school there. I'll never forget the first day in practice. It was a meeting over at the athletic department where he gathered the team together and told us basically what he was going to expect of us. And he told us that day, which shocked me, that he wasn't going to talk about winning or losing for the rest of the season. He said he was more interested in us becoming successful and his team becoming successful. He went on to say that he believes success was peace of mind, a direct result of self-satisfaction and knowing you did the best you could to become the best you're capable of becoming. He felt that if we could walk off the floor on every day that we played the game with our heads up knowing we had tried to acquire this peace of mind then we were successful. I looked up in later years to find exactly what "peace" meant, and it meant "absence of conflict in the heart." It's absence of conflict in the heart as it relates to your effort, who you are as a human being. I found that a great challenge when he said that he wasn't going to talk about winning or losing but was more interested in what was in our hearts and our souls.

I found that very motivating, that I really just had to deal with my own efforts, and who I was. That winning and losing wasn't to be a factor, except he did mention that he would love to win as many games as he could. I looked around the room and there was Sidney Wicks, Curtis Rowe, Lynn Shackelford and Kareem Abdul-Jabbar.

THE JOHN WOODEN PYRAMID OF SUCCESS

I thought that was not a bad philosophy. I really appreciated that. I had never heard anything like that before. I've utilized the Pyramid in my life often. I have had Coach Wooden come and speak to employees in my business about the Pyramid of Success and I have delivered it myself to my sales staff. I have used the Pyramid of Success in youth groups at my church. I followed the exact formula that Coach Wooden used. I've coached about twenty teams in the areas of soccer, basketball and baseball with my children and their friends. I opened the season of each of those teams with a demand on the parents that the parents come with their child and listen to the basis for which I'm going to teach them for that particular season. I would open up with the Pyramid of Success, and I would tell these parents and their children that I wasn't very interested in winning or losing, but I did want to win as many games as I could. I told them, "Kids, you know how when you go to school and you don't do quite the thing you thought you should have done, and you know in your heart when you get home a little bit of uneasiness in your heart? Well, that's called conflict in your heart. And I believe that peace of mind is something that we should go after, and that means when you don't have any conflict in your heart."

I've had wonderful reactions to the philosophy that I had embraced and which I was going to teach their children. I've had people come up to me afterwards and say, "Oh! It's so wonderful to run into a coach who is not crazy about just winning or losing!"

And I say, "But don't misunderstand me. I expect to try to acquire peace of mind as it relates to self satisfaction in knowing that we have been as industrious as we possibly could." That we would develop friendship. That we would go after a sense of loyalty to this team. That we would be cooperative and enthusiastic. And I said to them that I expect a certain amount of reliability. I expect that part of the loyalty for this team will come in having your kid on time at practice and not a minute late. That if you you're gonna be late, don't come at all. Either come on time or come early. Those are your two choices.

We had very successful teams. In one case, a woman told me that one of her children should go to a costume party four days before Halloween. I explained to the woman that what I was trying to teach was commitment and loyalty, and that there were going to be ten other kids at practice that day. I felt that it was really out of line that her kid would go off and do something as selfish as that when there were other children relying on her kid, that the very thing that I was trying to teach, she was undermining. She told me I was crazy. She said I was way out of line, and that her kid would never play for me again. Actually, this was the result of me having dug a little bit deeper and found out that she had made various commitments in the community and had not lived up to them. I suggested that her child was missing out on a very important experience, one that maybe she hadn't learned yet.

I was quite direct. I probably came across a bit as a zealot. Her kid never played for my team again. Another child was listening to me as I went through this conversation with this woman, and another parent listened to me. The parent called me up and said, "That was probably the most important thing that my daughter has ever heard—what you went through with that person." So, we lost one, but gained another. I saw the woman, a month later, and said, "I'm so sorry about what happened. Unfortunately, you and I will probably disagree on how things should be done, but the only loser in this deal would be your child, because the kind of principles that I was teaching I still believe in, and nothing would change as far as the direction I was going to go."

I called Coach Wooden about it. I said, "What do you think?"

And he said, "Well, nowhere in the Bible does it say it's going to be easy."

So I said, "Yep, I guess that's the way it is."

The Pyramid of Success has really helped me and that's just one negative reaction to the Pyramid that turned out to be a positive. It is a really valuable motivation tool. In the end, since it's rather truthful, it will stand the test of time. It has to do with my own faith. If there's a point in spiritual life that someone should explore, this really challenges any human being's effort in that area. It actually had to do with my development of a personal relationship with my God as I perceive him. I'm a Christian. My world changed some years ago. Unfortunately, my family had to fight through cancer with our twelve-year-old girl. [The Pyramid has] come in very handy, not only in my faith, but everything that we do in fighting back. We're actually out in the community doing a great deal with our oncologist, who happens to be one of the top researchers in pediatric oncology. We're not sitting on our hands and watching our child go through the therapy. We're doing the best we can to fight back, and it's part of our healing. I'm sitting on the board of directors of the Pediatric Cancer Research Foundation here in Orange County. My wife and I both are quite active in the program, as is my daughter who's fighting the cancer. She's very artistic and does a lot of work that way.

I've tried to raise my kids with [the Pyramid]. My little girl was in church (she was in remission at the time) and I was invited to go down to the local church and deliver the Pyramid of Success to the kids. I asked, "Gee, is there anybody in this room who has ever heard this before?" And two or three kids had heard of the Pyramid of Success.

And Ann says, "Oh gosh! I've heard this about a hundred times!"

I know that in time she has embraced it because she's been extremely successful in her academics and does very well with it. She plays the piano. My son is fifteen and playing on the varsity basketball team. He's heard about the Pyramid a million times. It takes the onus off winning and losing. It simply takes the person's soul and pushes it to greater heights in the sense that you're always challenging yourself, knowing that you can't lose. All you've gotta do is go out and do the best you can and become the best you're capable of becoming.

Even on a given day, when you lose the game, if you can look at yourself and say, "Hey, I did my best," (and some days you might not be able to say that), at least you know the difference. That's the point. At least you know the difference. You don't just live in some world of chaos. You live in some sort of organization.

Since UCLA, I still call him "Coach," but I talk to him like a close friend whom I don't get to see very often. He's struggled with the loss of his wife, which was his greatest loss in his life. He goes forward with certain inspiration and whenever I've had huge struggles in my life, I call and talk to him. We visit about all the things that count in life.

One thing that always blew me away was how he could remember people's names everywhere he went. We could go to Chicago to play a game and we could walk into a lobby of an airport or a hotel, and he always played the association game. He shared with me how he does it. I don't play it myself, but he's got the ability to associate something that causes him to remember names. I found it really admirable for a man in a high powered position and he was a coach, in business and a politician.

Another thing, of course, that had a big effect on my life occurred after I graduated from UCLA. I had signed a basketball contract to go play for the Atlanta Hawks and was a very young kid with what appeared a decent future. I had been dating this gal for about 3-1/2 years, and she was working while I was at school at UCLA and lived in Orange County. She would come and visit with me a couple nights a week usually and spent time there. [She] got to know Coach Wooden, and he got to know her. At twenty-two I didn't know whether I should get married or not. He looked at me right in the eye, and he said, "John, you marry that girl." I consulted with my father on this issue also, but Wooden had this way of judging talent. I'm still married to the same lady and am crazy about my relationship with her. She obviously endorses Coach Wooden. We've had a very nice marriage and we have a nice little family, and maybe Coach Wooden has his hand in that.

I'm twenty-some years removed from my experience at UCLA, and what I'm talking to you about are things that have to do with real life, not running around the basketball court in your undershorts. It has to do with commitment to people who count. And that was the example that the man set. Coach Wooden was a man who performed a job based on a foundation he had in his relationship with his God. He was continuing in his whole life as I knew him to search out who he was as a teacher and how to handle being that teacher.

There were some ego problems on our basketball team, not so much in the year that I played with Kareem (that year I was in the back court with Ken Heitz and Bill Sweek—they traded off on the other job—actually, Ken Heitz had it most of the time). Then I played guard full time, and we had Shack and we had Curtis Rowe. We were all real young except for Shack and Kareem. Kareem was obviously our leader, and he did it by example, so there wasn't much jealousy on that team. There weren't many mental problems, except from the standpoint that we got into a mode where we tried to keep from losing, instead of trying to win. And I use that word "winning." When you're kids in college, you really do want to win. But you hear this Pyramid of Success laid on you all the time—his half-time speech might revolve around loyalty or cooperation or enthusiasm or industriousness. He typically would talk about just an element of the Pyramid at half-time. Never about winning or losing. I never heard him talking about winning or losing after the first day of either season that I played there. It's an awesome experience when you think of it in those terms. We didn't have much trouble that first year, but we had some breakdowns. We didn't always perform up to the level I think we could have. We would beat teams by fifty points sometimes. We only lost one game—it was a 29 and 1 season for us and we lost to USC in a stall game. I can't even remember what the score was, but they beat us by two.

When I was recruited, my family held him in very high esteem because of what he had accomplished. He came down to my house and met my parents. He didn't do that very often. My folks were quite impressed that he would come. He and Nell came. Then I got to go up to the campus, and Coach Wooden showed me around and he took me up on one of the hills and we looked over the campus. Somehow the subject came up, "Coach," I said, "I just want one thing here. I want a chance to play. If I come to this school, will I get a chance to play?" That question turned out to be very important in my development as a player there, because I didn't ask him, "Would I start?" I didn't ask him if I'd make even the second team. He promised me, and that's why I went there.

He said, "You'll have a chance, but I can promise you nothing more than that." Some kids went in there and asked would they start when they were a junior or a sophomore or senior or whatever it was. Those were the kids he generally shied away from. So, it turns out, that he liked what he heard me ask. He responded with, "I'd have to earn it."

THE JOHN WOODEN PYRAMID OF SUCCESS

I realized that I was in the presence of an extraordinary man and began to really admire him on the walk around the campus that day. The way he walked and carried himself and the response that he gave me that day. He didn't give me any B.S. He told me the truth. He didn't give me anything that wasn't so. In fact, I don't think he's ever given me anything that wasn't so, at least as he perceives it. He may have perceived something incorrectly, but he's never laid anything on me that he wasn't telling me exactly as he perceived it. Integrity is what it translated into.

At UCLA, you weren't going to play unless you were eligible. He always made a big point that the education we got there was more important than what we did on the basketball court. He believed it. He was altruistic.

When you believe something, especially in the beginning you become a little zealous about it. Coach says, "Well, that's fine, John. But that's for you. Someone else may not embrace that." In the beginning, sometimes a Christian can get way out there, as far as their zealot belief. I've come around to his side. Each man is given his free will and choice and he must choose what direction he's going to go. Coach Wooden has simply shared with people a very heavy reflection. That reflection is what you hear out of his mouth, and what you've heard from him and seen him write. Here is the Word as he understands it. It's very important from my perspective, to know that his foundation is in his perception of God. I'm not gonna preach to anybody. I'm just gonna tell you that this man comes from that foundation. You and I have some other perception. We'll always be different, because we're just as unique as we can be. He recognized that in every person. He knew that they were created uniquely, with certain gifts and talents. He always encouraged people to develop those talents. He gave us some motivational tools to go about developing ourselves. He felt that if we addressed some of these issues, we might become successful, happy, whatever. That was his contribution and I think it's stood the test of time and will continue to motivate and help people.

I helped coach a freshmen basketball team and I called Coach before I took them up to a UCLA game, and said, "Coach, I'm bringing up these twelve kids from this little team and we're gonna be sitting in these stands, and we're going to come up early. I was wondering, would you mind coming over and visiting with us before the game?" I wanted him to come by so the kids could meet him. Here was truly a legend that, if they didn't know it now, they would know at some time in the future that this man was somebody whom they got to meet and visit with for a moment.

Coach said, "Well, I'll do my best. Nan takes me over there. Sometimes we don't get there just on time." When we showed up in the arena, I walked down the stairs in the corner of the arena, and I got to the bottom where there was this man with his cane waiting for us. It brings tears to my eyes because that's the kind of man he is in his commitment to first, his family, and second to his basketball family.

So we went over and sat down, and I turned to Coach and I said, "Coach, what could you share with these young people here? Maybe just a couple of things in your life that made a difference. What are a couple of words, or maybe a couple of phrases that you would use that might help these people as they go about trying to do what they do in their lives?" So he rolled his eyes for a moment, and he said, "Well, I think it was probably two words that really have made a difference for me. One of them is 'balance'—the other one is 'love.'"

When he was all done saying that, I said to the kids, "Let's think about what that is that he just got through saying." He left us. He didn't elaborate. That was just what he had been teaching me over the years. Balance. "All things in moderation," he used to say as it related to conditioning, or self control. He'd talk about drinking or going off too far in your business—let's say a person who fell in love with his wife and went crazy with his wife and became something strange in that area, but didn't have balance or let's say, he didn't have balance in his business. Maybe he works too much. Maybe you work too much.

Two big words, balance and love. Love of what you do—have a passion for the work that you do. Love for your wife—have a passion for her. Love of your children—how to raise them. Love of your God—how do you know Him? Love. An all encompassing word. Those were the two words he left us with. The kids had to think it over.

Coach and I have always had a great relationship. I mean . . . I *loved* going there. I *loved* the opportunity of getting to play for that man. I *love* what I learned from him. And the love's still there, and I just really appreciate our relationship.

*Wooden loves
young people.*

THE JOHN WOODEN PYRAMID OF SUCCESS

BILL WALTON
San Diego, California

Bill Walton, inducted into the Basketball Hall of Fame in 1993, is one of the greatest basketball centers ever to play the game. He is a charter member of the UCLA Athletic Hall of Fame. He played with the Bruins 1972-74, leading them to two NCAA titles, with a record of 86-4. His teams won their first 73 games, part of UCLA's record eighty-eight consecutive wins. He ranks first in career rebounding with 1,370 (15.7 average), second in field goal percentage, (.651), third in career scoring average (20.3) and tenth in career points (1,767). He was the number one draft pick for the NBA in 1974. He led the Portland Trail Blazers to the NBA championship in 1977, and played with the Boston Celtics who nabbed the 1986 title. He then went on to a career in broadcasting.

John Wooden had the most profound influence on me of any male person outside of my father; he's just an incredible inspiration. Once you're touched by greatness in your life, no matter what location it comes from, you're never willing to settle for anything less. He set such an incredibly high standard for himself, and for others, that I've just been forever chasing the level of excellence that he established.

I went to UCLA for a combination of reasons. Of course, he was a huge factor. I wanted to go to UCLA when I first started reading about it in the newspaper. We didn't have a TV growing up, and the very first game I ever saw of basketball in my life was the 1965 college championships, the Final Four between UCLA and Michigan. Michigan had these big, strong, very physical and athletic players and UCLA had these little skinny, scrawny kids, the kind I was. Before the game started, I didn't think UCLA had a chance, and it was just a masterpiece of UCLA, John Wooden basketball. Quickness, teamwork, conditioning, movement without the ball, and I said, "That's what I want to do in my life."

I was a huge fan. The way they played the fast break, the press, the teamwork, the defense, everything. And the humble way Coach Wooden always carried himself. When Lew Alcindor showed up at UCLA, that just made it the place to be even better, then they built Pauley Pavilion making it even more attractive. And Los Angeles is such a fantastic city, such a cultural, educational, financial center of the world. There was no other place for me to go to school, no second choice whatsoever.

I was recruited by him personally. UCLA was the very first school that contacted me. Denny Crum, the assistant at that time, was instrumental in organizing all the recruiting. They contacted me when I was a sophomore, and expressed their interest over the next three years even though I told them from the very beginning that I was coming to UCLA. They still did the most professional job of any school

When I was seventeen years old, I was so ready to leave home, I hit the door running and never went back. When I got to UCLA, I thought I was free, free, free at last. And there was Coach Wooden, standing there saying, "Come right on in here, you're mine for the next four years!" I thought my parents were strict disciplinarians, but Coach Wooden certainly took that to the next level.

I was a three-time Academic All-American, graduating in 3-1/2 years with honors, and I'm in the Academic All-American Hall of Fame. I majored in history. I love education. Both of my parents are college graduates who worked their entire lives in education.

The other schools offered me everything under the sun. Let your imagination run wild. Coach Wooden came into my house, sat down and said, "Look Bill, we don't do that at UCLA. We're not going to build the program around you, where you get all the shots, you're not going to set all the records. In fact, we're not even going to promise you that you will make the team! But if you come to UCLA and you work hard, you'll get an education." He talked education all the time.

I saw him every day, even in the off-season. I'd go in the office every day just to talk to him about what was happening, who was on the team, who was going to be playing. He was my buddy. I loved UCLA, and I spent all my time on campus. I wasn't going other places, I was just going to school every day and learning from Coach Wooden.

I was painted as a radical in college, but I was mainstream. I would test him sometimes, but I was just being normal. He was insistent on deciding everything about what we did. Our activities, dress code, everything. I didn't want him to tell me how long my hair should be, or what kind of clothes I should wear. Whenever we had any sort of disagreement, he would always end the conversation with, "You know Bill, we have enjoyed your time here at UCLA, but we're going to miss you," and he'd laugh. And that was the end of it, because there was nothing more important to me than being on the UCLA Basketball team. I never let anything get in the way of me being part of that dream, chasing my dream.

He never presented it as the Pyramid of Success, and it was never one talk, but a lifetime of leadership by example. We became aware of the Pyramid over time, but those were just things that he talked about on a constant basis every day. It was never in the context of the Pyramid, but what we were doing that day, and that's because he was, and still is, a teacher in the truest sense of the word, and he selflessly gave of himself to give everybody else a better life. He was not into self-promotion, or making himself rich, but only into improving everyone else's life.

The Pyramid was just the structure of so much of his teachings, but because he was with us every day, he never had to give us the whole thing at one time, just different parts when it was appropriate. From the very first day we thought so much of the stuff was nuts, and that he was crazy! He was sixty-five years old, we were seventeen, eighteen, nineteen years old. It was the age of Nixon. We were all from California, going to Dylan concerts, the Grateful Dead, Neil Young, the Rolling Stones, going to the beach, having a great time. The sixties and seventies were a wonderful, magic time, and here he was with all that stuff, and I said, "What is this all about?" Over time, it all made sense. It really takes root when responsibility comes into your life. When you're a college student on a basketball scholarship, you don't have a lot of it, you're just out there playing, going to school, having a great time, and it's fun. But as you get older, get a job, a career, and kids, everything changes in your life. When you are in a position of responsibility, then it all becomes so much clearer.

I have four kids. They've been listening to me about John Wooden their whole lives. Our house is filled with pictures of John Wooden, posters of the Pyramid. I'd write on their lunch bags his sayings, such as, "Be quick, but don't hurry." "Failing to prepare is preparing to fail." My kids looked at me like I'm some sort of nut, the same way we used to look at Coach Wooden.

I thank Coach Wooden all the time for everything he's given me, and I always thank him for his patience. A very special part of John Wooden is how willing he is to patiently deal with other people including people like me, I mean, mostly people like me.

We loved Coach Wooden. He was our hero because he made it so much fun, event though we had disagreements and differences. When I say he was a disciplinarian, it was not in a negative sense. He was never critical, he would never yell, never curse, never raised his voice, but he was tough and demanding, but always in a positive sense.

When I left UCLA, I was blown away because for the first time in my life I was in a situation not about the team, not about the joy, not about the specialness of what we have as a unit. When I first joined the NBA, I was so excited and so full of hope. But then it was the antithesis of what I knew good basketball to be, because it was all about the individual, about selfishness, about guys trying to make more money by scoring more points, about guys trying to get more publicity individually for themselves and it was terrible. It really just destroyed me.

I would talk about Wooden and try and use his technique, and I did that all the time. Most people, until they come in contact with Coach Wooden, can't believe that this guy is so special, because they've always dealt with coaches, teachers, or partners, who were self-promoters, who were interested in their own enrichment, who cared more about themselves then they did about the team. I would talk to them about Coach Wooden, how special he was, and how his only goal was us, the team. He never made commercials, he never did anything other than help the sport of basketball and help individual players. They just don't believe it. He taught us how to learn, how to learn how to do things. He was a teacher who gave you a strategy, a method to develop, but you didn't know it because he never sat you down and gave you an hour lecture. He never sat you down and explained everything. He taught as we did it. We were always doing it, were always active, always playing the game.

I socialize with him as much as possible. I call him all the time. I'm well aware that he goes to bed at 9:30 p.m. every night though, as he's an early riser like I am. He never calls me because he knows I'm going to call him. We have little reunions on a regular basis, with about fifteen to twenty of the guys, and more frequently since more of us have settled in Los Angeles. The effect he has had on me is shared by all of the players. At his last birthday party, it was unbelievable. We just went around the room and everybody was saying what I'm saying now. He's embarrassed about it. To him, it's just his way. He learned it from his father. One of the special things about Coach Wooden was that he had strong family ties and bonds, with good values, strong personalities and characters, who reflected what was good in the world. He did not go out and recruit a lot of punks. The only ones who ever talked bad about him were the guys whose dreams didn't come true at UCLA, who came here thinking that they were gonna be the man, that they were going to get all the shots, or all the playing time, and it didn't work. In the early years of that, it was very difficult for the guys, but over time they came back.

One of the neatest times involves my older brother, who also played at UCLA and knows Coach Wooden very well. Our youngest sons are the same age and play on the same team. Their coach is John Wooden's biggest fan. So one day, my brother and I gave him a surprise. Under false pretext, we got him here to Los Angeles, into a limo, and he ended up at Coach Wooden's house with the two kids, and we had a great time! I've taken all my kids over to his house, and sent them to his camps.

He taught us everything you need to know about the game of basketball, and about life—because the latter is what he really talked about. He rarely talked about basketball. Basketball was the vehicle, but it was really about life. To him, that was more important.

Coach Wooden is an incredibly fiery competitor, who really wants to win, to be on top, to do it the right way, and he just works nonstop. He loves the competition—and he taught us how to win, how to rise to the occasion.

You just cannot say enough great things about him. I like everything about him. He's got such a marvelous sense of humor. He's so quick. When we talk about the competition and the drive for perfection, it comes out in his conversation. He is very verbal in his competition. It's almost to the level of trash talking, and taunting, but in such a great, good-humored way.

It was never about him. It was fun being a UCLA Bruin. You just had so much pride, even today, about being a UCLA Bruin. To us, there is no other place, no other school. He was the guy who made it all happen for us.

It's so incredibly rare in any sport that a coach has this kind of effect on his players. Sports is an incredibly transient profession. You're here, there, changing teams, affiliations, and soon as it's over, the tie, the bond, is cut. Not so at UCLA, and not so for the Boston Celtics. That comes back to Red Auerbach and John Wooden and their ability to generate loyalty, to create a family. A coach's hardest job is to get people to go beyond normal limits of effort, or commitment, of sacrifice, of willingness to go over the edge to make it happen for the team. Most coaches can't do that. They don't have the ultimate respect of the players.

The glory was just the natural result of John Wooden's efforts. One of the things that happens with a lot of athletes is that they fall on their faces when they end their careers. The greatest testament to John Wooden is that those he coached are happy in their lives. Everybody had different levels of success, and you know what his definition of success is. He taught people how to work hard, enjoy working hard, and at the end of the day, it's over and you start all over, and you go out and do it again.

I get a phenomenal level of interest in Coach Wooden. Wherever I go they want to hear about him, Larry Bird, the Boston Celtics, and the Portland Trail Blazers. They want to hear about the greatness, why people are so special, about Michael Jordan, why Kareem Abdul-Jabbar was so phenomenal. John Wooden is right at the top of that list.

The Pyramid of Success has become the foundation of my life. It's what you base your life on. You look at it and it's so simple, yet so complete and so well thought out. Life is easy when the ball comes to right to you, but it's what you do when the rebound bounces the other way. That's where the Pyramid of

Success comes in. The ability to recover, the ability to overcome adversity and get to the next step, to the next good thing.

These days, I'm a television broadcaster for the NBA, college basketball, beach volleyball, and Olympic events. I also do a lot of public speaking. I'm very active in the business of sports. I'm busier than I've ever been before and having the greatest time. I have a lovely wife and four kids. They're chasing their dreams right now.

Wooden is at the top, an innovator, a creator. So many of the drills are in use today—amateur and professional—many of the actual practice elements, how you run a practice, how you think about basketball, are his creation.

I talk about Wooden at the beginning, at the end, and all throughout the motivational speeches I give. John Wooden is like UCLA: he's perfect, just what you would hope for, just what you would want. John Wooden is that coach that you dream about getting but you never really do unless you play for a John Wooden or a Jack Ramsey or a Red Auerbach, someone who is so special you just cannot believe how lucky you are. They're always a step ahead of you, teaching you, giving to you, and they're doing it because they want to. They created an environment where you can't wait to get up in the morning and get started. You go to sleep at night saying, "Boy, tomorrow I'm going to have the best day I ever had in my life." That's because of what they have created, in terms of the environment that you're in: [an environment] of joy, health, movement, sports, competition, life, and values. It's just a big circle that keeps growing. It's a big ball that never stops rolling forward.

Wooden and Walton.

THE JOHN WOODEN PYRAMID OF SUCCESS

SIDNEY WICKS
Los Angeles, California

Sidney Wicks is one of the all-time greats, whose jersey, number 35, is retired. He played on three championship teams, was Most Outstanding Player of the Final Four as a junior, was a ten-year NBA athlete and Rookie of the Year in 1972, and he was an Academic All-American in 1971. He was inducted into the UCLA Athletic Hall of Fame in its second class in 1985.

I played for UCLA from 1969-71, as center and forward. I was recruited by UCLA. I did well in high school and Johnny Wooden did the color the first year they had the city playoffs televised. My team was in the finals that year. We got killed but I did real well. A couple of days later I got a note from Johnny Wooden saying, "Hey, we're interested in you coming to our school. Here's a questionnaire, fill it out." I went on from there.

It was difficult for me my first year, not starting. I sat on the bench. I didn't really understand everything that was going on because I felt that I was better than the guy playing in front of me. I was sitting watching him play. We were winning and doing really well, but you have the competitive edge and it's hard to be watching. At a lot of the games I used to go in (unless there was foul trouble, or someone got hurt) at the ten minute mark of the first half, no matter what was going on. I would just go and check in automatically. A lot of time at the ten-minute mark, the game was over. We were up by thirty points, so you go in there and its hard to make an impression when you're up by thirty points, and everybody has cheered themselves out already. There aren't many cheers left. I was upset about that, but I weathered the storm and things got better.

I wasn't playing because I was a sophomore and I was making too many mistakes, which was pointed out to me. I went into the Coach and said, "Coach, just between you and me, I'm sorry, but I don't see why I'm not starting. Look at the stats. I average more points than this guy, more rebounds, more blocked shots, I play better defense, so why don't I start."

He said, "You covered all of the columns, Sidney, except for the last one. That's turnovers, mistakes, unforced errors, whatever you want to call them. I don't want to play you and have to depend on you and have the whole team depend on you, and have you make a crucial mistake for the only reason being that you are a sophomore, and an anxious sophomore." He would rather go with the senior who didn't do everything, but didn't make mistakes. He knew exactly how it was going to happen. "Plus Sidney, look at this, you play more time than he does. What do you really want? You average more points, rebounds, and more time, and you want to start too. You have any more questions?"

I said, "No."

He told me, "Next year you'll be the guy, but this year, see ya." I tried to store up all of this energy. I went in there all charged up, and I came out with my head hung down to my knees. I went home and told my brothers exactly the conversation, and my brothers told me that he was saying that I had to wait my turn. I went back to practice the next day and just killed everybody. I was so pumped to play that I did really well in practice, and he just gave me a little smirk. When I got to the NCAA tournament, the exact same thing happened. I go into the game when we're up by thirty points. We win. Next game, we're up by twenty-five points when I go in. In the finals, it was a close game and I didn't play. After we won the NCAA championship, I felt that I wasn't a significant part of the championship. So after the game was over we had a big dinner celebrating the tournament with all the boosters. My face was this long. Everyone would come up to me and say, "Hey Sidney, you happy you guys won?"

I'd say, "Yeah."

The Coach came over to me and said, "Sidney, smile. We just won the NCAA championship. You'll have your turn, you helped us get here. You played. We won. Smile."

The next year, there were two guys returning back from the starting varsity team. Curtis Rowe and John Vallely. On the first day of practice, you have pictures, and the Coach appoints a captain and you run. At most places, your coach picks your captain, the one who he feels is the most mature, who gets along with the players, and the one who can set an example. So the first day, he's saying, "I think we have a great team. We have an excellent chance at repeating the championship. We only have to worry about ourselves . . . and the captain of the team this year is Sidney Wicks. Any other questions? See you on the court at two." That's the first day of practice. Needless to say, I think I wore out two pairs of shoes. I was overjoyed.

I really toed the mark my first year, and that was paying off, but I wasn't really completely confident of what I could do as a player, and where I fit in on the team, and having him pick me as captain, told me what I was. I was going to be the leader. I was going to be the one who was going to be setting the example for these guys. He was telling me that there were people older than you, people who had started over you, who had played more time than you, but I want you to lead the way.

I was the captain for the next two seasons. More than anything else, it was his Pyramid of Success which influenced me. He breaks everything down in his Pyramid. Success and what it means to be a success, how to succeed. It just stuck with me. I've always thought of myself as a successful person, doing things that were successful, accomplishing some of the things that I wanted to in life. You can look back on your parents and a great home life, but there are other influences in your life.

Curtis Rowe and I had an early class my junior year. We went to the class every day but we skipped it one time. It was an eight o'clock morning class, and eight o'clock classes are tough! Our professor called Wooden and told him that we didn't make it to class. Curtis and I came to practice that day all happy, life was great, but Wooden said, "Hey, you guys, come here. I received an alarming telephone call from your music professor." Curtis and I knew that we were in trouble then.

We said, "Well, what did he say?"

"He said that you didn't make his class today."

"Oh Coach, we've been making the class, but this one time we didn't make it."

"This one time, are you sure?"

So we said, "Yeah."

He told us, "I don't want that to happen again. I want you to go to class, and get your educational background. You're here for education first, and basketball second."

The next class day, Curtis calls me up at six o'clock in the morning, and says, "Hey Sid, I stayed up late last night, I don't think I'm going to make it."

I said "Curtis, listen. If you're not going, I'm going. The professor is going to call, and I don't want to deal with the coach in a negative light."

Curtis said, "Come on, man." We finally agreed to go and Curtis picked me up at seven. We go walking to class and Johnny Wooden is sitting in front of the class. He told us that he just wanted to know if it was just one time or what. We walk into the class, and I asked Curtis if he realized what he almost made us do. There were no more classes missed, ever!

What is interesting about John Wooden is his ability to deal with people. He was able to get guys together from all different types of backgrounds, get them to suppress their egos, and deal with a common goal and direction. I've been around a thousand coaches it seems, both in college and pro, and the hardest thing is to understand and realize talent, and be able to bring it together from all different backgrounds and say this is the unit and this is how we're going to get it done. This is how we shoot, this is how we run, this is how we pivot, this is how we rebound. He was able to break it down to an elementary basis but let you use your God-given ability.

He was able to make you understand the game intellectually. The way things worked out, you always looked for the other guy first. When you got the ball, you looked for someone else. That's not a tradition in basketball, but it was there. That's why we won. When I got the ball, I looked to see what everybody else was doing. When you start looking to other people and trying to get the best out of them, it helps the team. I like to think that carried over into my life. You can ask my daughter. Wooden's philosophy or influence has helped me in raising my daughter, definitely, without a doubt. I learned patience, more than anything else. My mom had great patience, but he really emphasized that. He told me, "Sidney, I'm going to have patience because you want to do so well your sophomore year, and you've become an individual. You're looking for your shot or your move, instead of looking to see what the other members of the team are doing or what the situation is. That's why you're making the mistakes. You're doing things a little bit ahead of yourself. You need to slow down and see what is best for the team. Have a little patience." He always said his famous saying (which he drilled into my head), "Be quick, but don't hurry."

I coached at UCLA for four years with Walt Hazzard. We won the NIT my first year. When I went back with Hazzard it was the old school, but we had to deal with the kids of nowadays. The kids nowadays, pardon the expression, are bananas. There are many more distractions. There's the media. They schedule you around the media. When I was playing at UCLA, we played on Fridays and Saturdays. These kids now are being taken out of school on Tuesday, and we don't come back home until Tuesday. They miss whole weeks of school. Wooden wouldn't allow that. Our schedule didn't have it that way. All our games were on the weekend. The distractions are sexual, the hip-hop, the drugs, the bud, the booze, etc. We didn't have videos and stuff like that. Through videos my daughter has seen too much.

In the old days, I was no shrinking violet. I was having a good time, and wanted to be as exposed to the cutting edge of the time, but the exposure at that time was nothing what it's like now. I went out to have fun, but the limitations were much more than they are now. We sit around now and think that we could never do that.

I usually see Johnny at the games. I chat with him all the time, go over to see him. Johnny and I have this relationship which is special to me. As a player, I always tried to protect him, and me, from people thinking that I kissed up, that he liked me too much. We always had a close relationship. I think more than anything else, we respected each other. He respected all of the things that I could do as a player and as a person. I respected the things that he could do as a coach and as a person. He stressed family, which I really admire. He stressed religion, which I really admire. I'm religious now. I respected his ability to coach and have the respect of the players, to have a focus, and be a success, and to know how to deal with it. He knew how to recruit people into his system, and have them genuinely want to be there not only because of him, but the atmosphere that he has around him.

In high school, I did real well in all the sports and was well known not only for basketball, but my track and my baseball abilities. I felt good about myself, and when I went into the situation I was able to see how other people were handling the recognition and acclaim: Kareem Abdul-Jabbar (excuse me, Lew Alcindor), Lucius Allen, Mike Warren, Mike Lynn and Edgar Lacey. These guys were so laid back and so cool. When we went up to them, they asked us how we were doing, and these guys had just won the NCAA championship! I realized that the deal, they had cool people at UCLA. I also realized that this probably was a result of the Coach, so I focused in on him to see where he was coming from. He is such a sweetheart of a guy, and would never beat his own wagon. He would never mention any of his accomplishments. He would never say, "I won the NCAA last year, or I did that." He would just tell me, "We want you. People like you allow us to be successful in this program."

The black guys on the team didn't talk among themselves how cool Wooden was. It was understood that you were graded on your merits, what you did. He was truly color-blind, and the team was as well. It's not what color you were, it's how many mistakes you made on the court. If you don't make any, you play. If you make some, you don't. That's it.

I've heard little criticism about Wooden. The criticism is more about the situation. You can't blame them for saying that. You never say "Dang, I'm not better than that guy," but you do say "Dang, Coach doesn't think that I'm better than that guy." It's easier to go to sleep thinking that.

I did well at basketball and I graduated with a sociology degree. I went to play professional basketball for the Portland Trailblazers, got traded to the Boston Celtics, and then played for the Clippers. After that I went to play in Europe for a year.

In Portland, there was a vast interest in John Wooden. They were on the West Coast, and Pac-10 people would come up. My first year, I made a relatively large impact—Rookie of the Year.

My abilities allowed me to get on all of the teams. They didn't really care about where you had been, they were more concerned about where you were going, but when I got there everybody was interested. There was a lot of envy. In the league, everyone talks about college. There was a lot of envy when I went to the league because of how well UCLA had done in the past, and how I had done there.

European basketball was tailor-made for me. It was very rough, a little bit crude—the conditions, the travel. I went with an open mind. They paid me a gang of money. I said I was going to go over there with a good attitude. I went over there and "observed" the language.

I played in Venice, Italy. I observed Italian. There is a difference. I learned by listening. I had my mouth shut for the first four months I was there. I was listening. I asked different questions. I got to the point where I could respond and ask questions in Italian. Then I got to where I was flowing.

It was the most exciting thing that had happened to me in a long time, going to Europe and playing there. The Europeans love basketball. Basketball is their second sport. The first is soccer.

After Italy I came back here and my mom was ill. I went to UCLA to get some x-rays, and I saw Walt Hazzard. He had just been named the head coach of UCLA. He told me that he needed my help to coach his big men. I wouldn't get a salary and I had to pay for my own transportation.

I was a coach. I did that for the first year. We did exceptionally well, and I paid out of pocket for everything. Everybody was doing well, and we were successful. The next year they changed the format. They gave Walt an assistant coach who was paid, so that spot was given to me. I was able to be around the guys, give my advice, see it work, really get into enjoying coaching.

Now I'm in real estate. I own a couple of housing complexes. I'm doing well. I'm happy.

Here's my version of the "goatee incident." I had a couple of days growth and I asked Coach what he thought about it. He said, "Oh Sidney, I think it's beautiful. I didn't know you could grow your own goatee. It's great, but too bad everyone won't be able to see it as well as I can see it."

I, being clueless at the time, asked, "Well, why not? Tomorrow I'm going to be on national TV. Everyone can see it like you can see it."

He said, "Because you won't be playing."

"Why not?"

"Because you won't be playing."

"But Coach, you said you liked it."

He said, "Sid, let me tell you something. I like clean-cut kids. Clean mind, clean everything, I believe in it. Your goatee is cool but it isn't clean."

So I said, "I guess you're trying to tell me something."

He simply said, "I guess so, if there is a message in there, I guess so."

For some reason Coach and I clicked, we just fit like your best friend, your partner. I like to think that he is like a brother to me. My brothers and I have a famous relationship. We're always together. My mother always had us dressed alike until we were eight or nine years old. It was like we were triplets, but we were a year apart. To me, he was like a big brother to me, more than a coach. I really resented his authority, his putting me down, his suppressing and holding me back my first year, but then he said, "If you understand what I'm doing for you, you'll be a better player."

Without a doubt, he influenced my being able to recognize and relate to people. That has helped me. He allowed me to put the trust in the right people. You have to hear the right thing, and talk to the right person, and you have to believe the person. It's not so much their telling you how great you are, its more their track record, and being able to have the ability to do what they say they are going to do. They have to have the track record to let you know that they are not just blowing smoke up your behinds. It's all mental intelligence, being able to negotiate. I had to utilize all of that. I had to get investors for my projects. I had to be the salesman, the deal maker, a businessman. I had to sweat it out and wait for the years to go by.

I never had a problem with drugs. I've seen many athletes have problems with drugs. When I was growing up in high school and someone was smoking marijuana, they were the bad people. Now when you do marijuana at that same age, everyone says they're cool.

I graduated with a 3.1 GPA. More than anything else he stressed, his emphasis was God and family, more than education, than athletics. There was never an emphasis on himself, he never said, "I did this." He came to you and said that my emphasis is God. If somebody tells me family and God, I say you're batting a thousand so far.

A lot of the stuff I was able to grasp right away. My first year was so traumatic. I had to understand a lot of things immediately. Some of the things that I didn't like, or that didn't go the way I wanted them to go, I was able to understand with his help and I was able to reach the ultimate.

A good coach is able to communicate with his players and allow them to play and have them absorb what he said and implement it. Not many people are able to do that. Not many people have a guy tell you these are the things that you are going to do, and this is how you are going to do it.

Wooden did as well or better than you can do as a coach. He had the right assistant coaches around him, he had his system updated. Denny Crum and Gary Cunningham played for him and they went out and did the recruiting deal and updated themselves and found out the game as it was being played. They were able to bring it back to Coach and put their input as to what the game was doing and how one little thing might make him better. I saw them make these small corrections and then the program took off even more. What could he have done better? He had all the bases covered.

I couldn't imagine years ago when I was a freshman in college, accomplishing the things that I accomplished. Having the experience that I did enhanced what I have done and helped me get to where I am. My dreams were just to be successful. I just wanted to be a successful person and wanted to succeed and do well. Success meant to make my mark, for people to say, "He was here and he did well." I think I've done that. With Wooden's guidance, it made it a lot easier for me. My time at UCLA was enjoyable. Everything was working on every level. It never got that way in the pros. I wish it had.

Pro ball is different from college ball. It depends on who you were. In Portland, they were a second year franchise and they were struggling to be a viable pro franchise. I played there five years, and the next year they won the NBA. I felt that I got them prepared to win the NBA. I moved to Boston and we lost to Philly in the playoffs. That was my first experience in the playoffs, and I made the cover of *Sports Illustrated* my first year in Boston. Boston had a great tradition and it worked out great. San Diego was a new franchise, just coming from Buffalo, and we were struggling to get started. My first year we had a great team.

I want to enjoy my next twenty years. These twenty have been getting to where I am now, now I want to enjoy it. I'm not married anymore. That's one of the things. I have to find someone to, like Bo Jackson says, "slide" to the next twenty with.

Wooden, 1991, with (l-r) Willie Naulls, Bill Walton, Sidney Wicks, and George Stanich.

THE JOHN WOODEN PYRAMID OF SUCCESS

INTERACTION WITH PLAYERS AND COACH WOODEN AT CAMP

On June 21,1991, I visited Pepperdine University in Malibu, California, where Coach Wooden's basketball camp was in full swing, and conducted one of the interviews with him for this book. After a day of practice and instruction, a meal, and Coach Wooden's giving the Pyramid lecture, the attendees went back to the basketball court where Coach and four of his former players, Willie Naulls, Sidney Wicks, George Stanich and Bill Walton, answered questions, interacted and joshed with each other. You'll enjoy the give-and-take and a chance to observe the deep love felt by Coach for his players and vice-versa.

WOODEN: One of the truly great players that UCLA had, Sidney (Wicks) came there his sophomore year. He used to say to me occasionally, "You know, Coach, that I'm better than Curtis (Rowe) and Shack (Lynn Shackelford). You know I'm better than them." I said, "Yes, I do. I know it, and they know it. Too bad you're letting them beat you out."

I think . . . now, don't misunderstand me . , . I think they were awfully misunderstood about things of this sort that he was selfish. He was a very unselfish player. But the way he had played, the style he played, it just didn't work in. Well, in my opinion (and of course it was my opinion that counted, though he didn't necessarily agree with that). But I thought the next two years following that, that Sidney was the finest basketball forward, probably in the country. And he went on to a very fine pro career. I thought his pro career was cut short, because he finished up with players that there's no way a good, sensitive person could play for. He's a sensitive person, and he had a great career and now is a great friend.

This young man played for me my first two years at UCLA. Most unusual. George Stanich is a medal winner in the high jump in the 1948 Olympics. In 1950 he graduated and signed a nice contract with the New York Yankees. Played professionally for awhile, and was an All-American basketball player for me. And he gave everything he had.

But one of the things that I think about George, which typifies the type of individual he is, is that when I came to UCLA they had a rule in the conference that you had to put in seventy-five hours of work each month to get seventy-five dollars. That was his scholarship. You had to put in seventy-five hours of work. I'm not sure that there's ever been one person, an athlete that put in their seventy-five hours. George didn't want something for nothing. That's the type of person he was. All the other basketball players I had, they were looking every which way to get somewhere where they could just sign their name and get out of it. But George and Val, his lovely wife, have three (beautiful children), they wanted a family. I should also mention that Willie's wife (Mrs. Willie Naulls), his daughters are over here too. And I'm very close to them.

These are four of many wonderful people who are responsible for the fact that I'm here. If it weren't for players like this, I wouldn't be here. I wouldn't be wanted anywhere as far as basketball is concerned. A coach is no better than the youngsters they have under their supervision. And I was most fortunate to have people like this. And now, suppose that we'll just go right down the line. We'll start with George and then Sidney and then Bill and then to Willie and then start over again and keep going that way. I might interrupt you occasionally for some remark if you get out of line.

BILL WALTON: I think one of the real strengths of Coach Wooden is his ability to make each and every player believe in themselves that they are the best player. Willie Naulls I'm sure thinks he was the best player ever. Sidney Wicks and I *know* we were the best players. Coach Wooden's strength was building confidence in yourself as a basketball player, as a person. He brought people together from every different walk of life. I was a shy kid from San Diego, and I'm still very shy.

Coach Wooden broke it down so the players could master the fundamentals and therefore could play up to their full potential. That's the thing that I remember most about UCLA basketball. The practices were more important to me than the games. The games were like an exam. We knew what we were supposed to do, and if you didn't do what you were supposed to do within the context of the way it was explained to you and told to you, you would sit on the bench. Every aspect of the game was broken down. When we had a bunch of guys my senior year who couldn't have made the UCLA team the year before or the year after, they got better and better and better and better. I remember those simple fundamentals, about getting inside yourself, looking in the mirror and making sure that you did everything that you're supposed to do, and everything else would take care of itself.

GEORGE STANICH: I heard somebody comment that Coach was like a father to the team. And he certainly was to me. I grew up in Sacramento and our family was returning from a Fourth of July party and a drunk hit us and killed my dad, and put the rest of the family—a brother and a sister—in the hospital. So I grew up without a dad. I was about seven years old then. So all the coaches I came in contact with in my high school, the community college, to UCLA had a tremendous impact on me because I was a little wild here and I thought I was the best center in the world, and you name it.

What I liked about playing at UCLA more than anything was the camaraderie the players had with each other. As Willie said earlier, the practices were the most important thing. Doing the small little things. When we came to UCLA, they figured that you didn't know how to play basketball, so they would say, "This is how we do it here." They started out by showing you how to run, to change your pace, to change your direction. He showed you how you could come together and be like one unit—three ball players, up above the rim, passing the ball, sliding in between each other, a cohesive rhythm. Working off someone. It was preparing you to be able to take that and put it into the game of basketball. It was so important and so intricate.

It prepared me for like dealing with my daughter, for having patience in dealing with life, because a lot of things happened. Ups and downs. Going to UCLA and dealing with a lot of the things that happened there prepared me for other things that came along. I really enjoyed myself, but you don't really think about that while you're there. You're too busy having fun or living the experience to really appreciate it. I felt good about living the experience and having John Wooden to be like a father or mentor or someone who you could depend on, and to have the camaraderie of these guys. I felt I could always come back and give Coach a call and come and talk to him. His door was always open, and he did this not only for me, but for all his players, which made it a beautiful thing. When there is a crisis in your life, it's nice to have somebody to talk to.

Three or four times when things would come up, where crises in my family or my job came, and where I didn't know which way to turn, and I'd give him a call and the next day or two, I'd go to UCLA and we'd talk. And he never would give me the answer to my question. He didn't need to give me the answer to my question. After talking with him, on the drive home I knew what the right direction was to take. And as I say, there'll always be things, you know to come against a wall sometimes, or you come to a road where you didn't know which way to turn. And after the talk with him, I knew the path to take once I was driving home.

I went to Yugoslavia with my wife and my family about twenty years ago and coached a team there. The team I coached was fortunate enough to win the championship of Yugoslavia. One of the players I had over there was like a Kareem Abdul-Jabbar. And I'd never had a player like this at El Camino, and I didn't know too much about what I should do with him. I got together with Coach before I went, by the time I left he had written a chapter on the different philosophies of what he tried to do with Kareem there. It really helped me over there and developed me in what I tried to do and tried to work with the teams there.

BILL WALTON: At UCLA, Coach Wooden would come into the pre-game talk for every game. And at the beginning, we were all sitting on the edge of our seats. And he'd come in and he'd give this real simple talk, "Okay, we're gonna play the board again today. They've got a couple guys who are supposed to be good. I don't know, just go out and play your game. Just go out and play your game and we'll win. And remember when you're done, if you walk out of here. . ." He'd give this long speech. And it was the same speech every game. We had some wise guys—not me, of course, I would always sit there with perfect attention. The other guys would start mimicking the coach, and they'd start voicing over his speech. Finally, he would get so flustered with us, he'd say, "Get out of here! Go play ball!" And every year that we were there, he had this little ritual before the first game of the season where he would have Gary Cunningham, his assistant, go in and hide a penny in the corner. Coach would be pacing around and giving his pre-game speech and he would stumble across this penny and say, "Ah, good luck!" And he'd pick up the penny and put it in his loafer.

By our senior year we had caught on. When Gary Cunningham came in to hide the penny, we were watching him, and when he left, we got the penny. So Coach starts pacing around, doing his speech. He's looking for the penny and he's looking for Gary Cunningham, and he doesn't know where to go . . . and we all break out laughing. We said, "Let's go Coach. We're gonna win this game anyway."

WILLIE NAULLS: UCLA was a standard of excellence. Everyone could achieve it within the definition that Coach gave us for success. I remember living in San Pedro and going to the school and watching George Stanich play at UCLA. There was this urgency always to get it on. Let's get the basketball, and let's get the shots going, and let's get it on. I watched this, and I said, "That's basketball." I was an all-city baseball pitcher and all-city basketball player. And very selfish, now that I go back and think about it, because I wanted to be the best. I wanted to score more points than anybody, I wanted to get more rebounds than anybody. I wanted to win all the time. And nobody knew that, because I was also very quiet.

My senior year in high school, after the season, I played on a summer league team and we played against some of the guys who had graduated from UCLA, including Sheldrake and Jerry Norman. We came in the court, and we thought we were going to beat these guys by forty points. Well, they beat us by sixty. And it was the simple fundamentals. That's when I really learned to respect the strategy in basketball, the fundamentals of basketball, and the intelligence of basketball. That standard of excellence is what I learned. I learned how to play basketball, I learned how to box people out. Coach took that tenacity and that selfishness that I had and molded it into a team concept. I had to work my way up from being the last guy on the team.

I remember going through a process. I selfishly wanted to quit the team, because it wasn't going my way. I actually went home to Watts, and quit the team without anybody knowing it for one day. Then I realized that there were a lot of six-foot-seven, six-foot-nine guys walking around Watts talking about how great they were when they were younger. So I very quickly went back to UCLA.

Coach never changed and that's the strength that we all felt. He always had a standard. You did your best, in the classroom or anything else. I want to thank him for that consistency. A lot of the person I am today is greatly influenced by that. Having been so selfish, I found out that I could get attention by doing well in sports. I didn't care anything about anybody else. I remember once playing against Eddie White. We were playing for the championship for the small baseball league. His team was in a town called Harbor City, and I was on San Pedro's team. It was for the championship of the whole South Bay area. I was the pitcher, and about thirteen years old. When I went out on the mound, out of the twenty kids on the team, about fifteen of them called me a nigger. I was shocked and their coach was behind it all. For seven innings I pitched a perfect no-hit game, and I struck out nineteen of them. That's always been my response to racism.

When I went to UCLA, Eddie White was one of my teammates, and a great person. After that game, they all apologized to me, but they thought that was the way to get you riled up. And they riled me up, for sure. Coach took us places (and this standard of excellence again), where we never thought about racial situations. We went down South. We were the first people to integrate hotels, movie theaters. What I found out later is that he would not have taken us there unless the people had agreed to *his* standard of excellence—that is that you accept people for who they are. Again Coach, thank you very much.

Walton is asked to tell the famous haircut story.

BILL WALTON: Oh, the haircut. I showed up on the first day of practice my senior year and Coach Wooden had very strict hair standards. At the time, I had less hair than Sidney has now. And Coach walked in for an inspection, like when you're in the Army. Coach walked into the locker room, looked at everybody, looked at me, and he said, "Bill, that's not good enough

I said, "Coach, I got a butch."

He says, "No, no, that's too long."

I go, "Okay, I'll get it cut tomorrow. I want to practice."

He said, "No, you can't practice." We had just won seventy-five straight games, two straight championships, and it was the first day of practice. We were all excited about getting started again. He said, "No, you've gotta get out of here." So we argued, and everybody argued with Coach, and he says, "No, that hair is just too long." I swear that I had a butch haircut. He said, "No, I can't see the tops of your ears and I can't see all of your collar, so you've gotta get out of here."

So I jumped on my bike and raced down to Westwood, got a haircut and got back for the last fifteen minutes of practice. We liked that because everybody always knew where they stood. He had very strict rules and he didn't play favorites. We all wanted to play. If you didn't play really well, if you didn't put out everyday, you were on the bench and he would put somebody else in there. And that other guy was just as good and was gonna take your spot, and you weren't gonna get back in there. It wasn't like so many situations where a coach is forced to deal with players of different abilities and even if Coach Wooden had players of vastly different abilities, I don't think he would bend the rules for any of his players. He's not that kind of guy. That's why everybody liked him so much and everybody respected him.

WOODEN: I always believed in closing practice pleasantly. I didn't want to leave mad, I didn't want my players to leave mad. I wanted them to be looking forward to the next day. When I speak at coaching clinics, I tell coaches, "Always close practice pleasantly. And don't become mad. You're young, probably newly married. And you shouldn't go home mad newly married. When you get older it doesn't make any difference, but when you're young. . ."

SIDNEY WICKS: The pre-game was very simple. You had the guys' names on the boards, what positions they played, and you had a name next to it. Coach said, "Okay, Sidney you guard this particular guy. He likes to go to his right. He's right handed, he has great outside shots." Or something like that. "Okay, Curtis you have this guy, his name's so-and-so, he does this. Steve, you have this guy." And he'd go on down the line.

If the game was tight at half time, he would just come and say, "Hey, these are the things that we're doing wrong. We're making mistakes with this guy," and so on. Everything was very simple, to the point. It wasn't long, NBA style. He would just say exactly what was going on and what we were doing wrong. And he would talk it over with his assistant coaches.

Coach Wooden was very intelligent to have assistant coaches who had coached at other places and were able to update him on new trends in basketball. And when I was there, Denny Crum and Gary Cunningham were assistant coaches and these guys were unbelievable. When Kareem came there, they had this guy, a butcher, Jay Carty. He was a big guy. I saw them practice, and I'd see this guy really killing Kareem. I'd say, "Why is he doing that?" They tried to toughen him up because when he plays in the game, guys would hit him in the ribs, and push him and stop him from getting to post position. Things like that were an integral part of making UCLA very successful.

WILLIE NAULLS: My second year, he was getting into a new system and we're all new to him and he was new to us. Our third or fourth game of the year we went up to San Francisco and we played St. Mary's and USF. We won, but the games were tight and we weren't in as good of shape as I think Coach would have liked us to be.

When we got back from our trip up there, he went to work on us. I felt he was trying to put too much in. I think a lot of times new coaches do that. You want to put your offense in, you want to put your defense in, you want to put your plays and all that. And he neglected his conditioning. The heart of the Pyramid is you've gotta be in shape. In the last few minutes we want to be as hard and as strong as anybody and in as good of shape as anybody.

But we weren't in shape up there, and he realized that. When we came back, I'll tell you, he gave it to us and really worked us. We hated it, but we loved him for it. One of the things that Coach said was to respect the opposition but not to fear it. The opposition you encounter in the business world, the competition, you don't fear them. What I learned from my UCLA experiences was that I could do anything. As long as I did my best, if whatever I had wasn't selling, I just needed to go back and reassess whatever it was that I'm selling and evaluate the market. I've never had any fear of doing anything in business, with people, racism was never a problem. I never had to spend a lot of time talking to people about the color of skin.

In New York, the first time we went back there in the Holiday Festival, some of us went to a party in New Jersey. We were supposed to be home by 10 p.m., and didn't get in until 2 a.m. We got caught. The finals were the next night of the tournament. The next day we had a team meeting, and all of the players were there, and Coach said, "If it's up to me, I'd ship you guys out of here. I'm really disappointed. You're a captain of my team, and you're setting a bad example." He left it up to the players and he left the room. Finally, a guy named Allan Herring said, "Ahhhh, let 'em stay," but Coach gave us an out, because he knew that we were sincerely sorry about the situation. It was a learning lesson. Coach knew that I was afraid of my father, and every time I'd do something, he'd call my father.

BILL WALTON: I remember the games we lost, the Notre Dame game where we were up eleven with the ball and two minutes to go and we lost, two games up at Oregon that we lost, and two games at USC. They're the most memorable to me because we beat ourselves in those games, and that's what Coach Wooden had taught us every day, don't beat yourself, and we did.

SIDNEY WICKS: The most memorable game to me, was when I came off the bench of my sophomore year, and we played against USC in back to back games. First we played them over there at USC and they were stalling. The guy had the ball in his arm. Watching the clock, watching the time go by. Coach said, "Just play back and let them do what they're gonna do." We started pressuring them, and we were losing by one point. We had the ball out at half-court. We designed this play for Shackelford to stand under the basket and Kareem to set the pit for him and he comes running out, if you can shoot, shoot. If he tells him to pass him the ball, pass the ball. Shackelford turns around, catches the ball. He's thirty-five feet away from the basket and takes an all the way jump shot—he shoots just straight up in the air. When he left his hand up there, you know it's in. He left his hand up there and "Ahhhhhh" it went straight in. Everyone went crazy because we won the game.

The next day we came over to UCLA. They did the same thing, stalling. Guess who got the last shot at the last of that game? It was a fast break, they threw the ball, I caught it, and I was like twenty-five feet out. I pulled up and shot it and the buzzer went off. The ball was in the air. There's a big hush. There hadn't been a loss that year by the Bruins, and it hit the rim and bounced off. I was deflated. I was thinking of ways to kill myself, slashing my wrist, whatever.

So I was walking to the locker room and was totally dejected. Kareem runs by me, grabs me and says, "Man, it ain't that bad, it's gonna be all right." I said, "No, man, we just lost for the first time, and what are you talking about?" By his saying that and the rest of the players saying, "Hey man, forget it, don't worry about it. We lost the game, so what?" I said, "If that's the way those guys feel, I guess it's okay for me to stay alive!"

I went to a second year expansion team. It was very frustrating to me. They didn't have much coaching, much organization. The players were selfish and everyone was playing for themselves. They were telling me, "Hey, get used to it. This is professional basketball. This is not college."

There was a lot of jealousy from players from other teams, with me coming from UCLA and the success I had in college. I don't care what anyone says, your college is where you hold onto the most. The players were very jealous and anything I had to say was automatically heckled. "So what you are saying is that you have to play hard and stay consistent. We don't want to hear that, not from him."

Bill Walton came to Portland two years after I was there. He would say, "Hey, Sidney, what's going on? These people don't know what they're doing! They're doing so many things wrong!"

And I said, "Hey, Bill, you have to get used to it. You have to extract the most that you can do out of it and do what you can do and that's all you can do." I learned that the hard way. After a game we were playing in Chicago, I had said, "We're gonna have to do something different, because for the last five games we've been down by twenty-five points at half time. I think we should do whatever it takes for us to play better. I'm not saying . . . pointing a finger at anyone." Those were my exact words.

The next day, a player on my team said, "Oh, well he should look at himself and he should think about what he's doing and what he had done, or what he can do to make the team better."

And I said, "Well, that's what I said. We, collectively, should sit down and get ourselves together and find out what we can do to stop us from losing by twenty-five points."

It got out that I was saying negative things about the team. When we got back home, we had a team meeting with the president and the owner who were waiting for me at the airport. I got back, and I said, "Yes?" I said, "If you had a tape of it, you could have heard that's what I said, I didn't point any fingers. I didn't say any player, I said 'we' collectively. And I don't see why this whole thing is necessary. And I also don't see why that player (I'm not saying the name) said what he said. When you really think about it, this player is not playing team basketball because we're supposed to pass the ball around, and everyone's supposed to be involved."

They said, "Well this player is a good offensive player and he's not geared to pass the ball that much."

I said, "Well then, I'm wasting my time, right? Because we're going to keep losing by twenty-five, thirty points."

And they said, "No, we'll make changes." They fired the coach. That didn't make any difference. We still lost by twenty-five points the rest of the season. We only won eighteen games that year. That's a long NBA season—out of eighty-two games, you win eighteen. That's what you call getting your butt kicked. I was from UCLA losing three games in my total career at UCLA looking at the schedule and saying, "Loss. Loss. Loss. Loss."

Luckily, Bill Walton had me and I had him then to sound off, so I didn't have to get frustrated enough to say, innocently, "We should do better." We'd say

"Those people don't know what they're doing. Why don't we call Coach Wooden up and have him come up here..."

WOODEN: I think you feel why I got so close to the players and they become a part of your family. They are all individuals. You don't want to take away their individuality and I tried not to take away their individuality, but I wanted to put their strengths to use in a well-run team. That's not always easy, but I feel that I was able to.

John R. Wooden, 1994.

THE JOHN WOODEN PYRAMID OF SUCCESS

AFTERWORD

I grew up in Westwood, a few blocks from UCLA, and used to play basketball games with my buddies when I was thirteen and fourteen at the Men's Gym at UCLA. As an arena for spectators, the Men's Gym wasn't much to speak of for a big-time university. It wasn't until Pauley Pavilion was built that UCLA had a decent home to play its games. Occasionally, we'd get shushed off the court so the team could practice, and out would come a bespectacled, middle-aged man in white shorts and a navy blue warm-up jacket with gold letters on the front saying "UCLA Staff" who proceeded to mop the floor. I learned much later that it was John Wooden. My friends from that period were enthusiastic followers of UCLA basketball. I remember one friend commenting in 1964 that he had seen Coach Wooden give an interesting and remarkable talk about something called the Pyramid of Success on his weekly television show during the season, and that there was more to Coach than just basketball. As UCLA charged to the NCAA finals in 1963-64, my coterie of friends, Southern California, indeed the whole U.S.A., was abuzz with the talk of the full-court press. It was clear to most that Wooden was not only a genius in basketball, but special in how he conducted himself, that he exuded and exemplified class.

As a sixteen year old boy in 1966, I often studied on campus and passed Coach Wooden there one afternoon. He said, "Hello." I was amazed a man so important was so open and friendly. After my first year of law school in 1973, I briefly worked as a clerk at Campbell's Bookstore in Westwood, and Coach Wooden came in one day to do some business regarding *Practical Modern Basketball*, which the bookstore was helping to distribute. I stammered a greeting, and we chatted briefly. I was awed at meeting this man who was so down to earth, unpretentious, and friendly. UCLA basketball was a very big—if not the biggest—deal at the time in Southern California, if not U.S. sports.

I attended numerous UCLA games during the Wooden era, and although I did not have more than a passing interest at the time, I saw for myself the well-oiled Wooden basketball machine and was obviously impressed. Like everyone else, I came to expect, and enjoyed, seeing UCLA win year after year. It was the equivalent to the Beatles putting out a new album. You couldn't help but root for them, and appreciate their elan, competitiveness, intensity, skill, precision, and teamwork. UCLA teams made you feel good. It transcended the student body, capturing the citizenry of Los Angeles. We were all proud, and in a way, it gave us confidence in whatever else we did.

Other than the deaths of John Lennon and Elvis Presley, the most important cultural changing of the guard for me in the last thirty-two years was the retirement of Coach Wooden in 1975. It was the end of a fabulous era. It was sad to see him go, and I wasn't the only one who felt that way. Coach Wooden and UCLA were a touchstone, a unifying factor for all of America. We had gone through many troubled times, especially the divisiveness caused by the Vietnam War, and the emergence of drugs, rock and roll, and continued criticism of traditions in America. One thing we could all agree upon was that UCLA played serious basketball, that it was gripping to watch, and that Coach Wooden was the reigning monarch of college ball. We were interested in him, we trusted him, we enjoyed whatever we heard about him. There was always a well-chosen, intelligent remark from him, he brought out the best in his teams, in himself, in us.

In 1981, I was riding high and had achieved what I the thought was my most important goal as an attorney: to represent the biggest client in the music industry. At the age of thirty-two, my client list was topped by Yoko Ono Lennon and the estate of John Lennon. I had worked hard, knew my craft, and was making good money, but was confused and questioning my "success." On the wall of a house of one of my clients, Lon Van Eaton, I noticed an artistic rendering he had made of something called the Pyramid of Success, so I asked him about it. He had seen it somewhere, copied it down and hung it up on his wall. "Who did that?" I asked.

"John Wooden."

"The coach from UCLA?" I wondered.

"Exactly."

I was astounded. I knew he was a great figure in sports—but a philosopher too? I had a vague recollection of my boyhood friend mentioning it, but I had never before seen it. I was so enthusiastic about the Pyramid diagram that I asked Lon to make several copies, and I gave one to Yoko.

The Pyramid of Success intrigued, inspired, and motivated me and in 1982, I contacted the UCLA Athletic Department to see if I could meet with Coach Wooden. They put me in touch with him and I told the Coach I was interested in the Pyramid of Success and asked if could discuss it with him. He invited me over with my brother Peter, and Lon and his twin-brother, Derek (the same Lon and Derek who were on Apple Records). We showed him what Lon had done, and were all surprised to learn that Lon's version was not entirely accurate. Coach gently suggested we take a look at his autobiography, *They Call Me Coach*, where he had discussed the Pyramid. The encounter with the legend was thrilling to each of us.

I was so taken by the Pyramid and the effect it had on my life that in December 1983, I called Coach Wooden and asked if I could interview him about the Pyramid. I wasn't sure what I wanted to do with it, I just knew I wanted to interview him. Again he graciously consented, only this time I brought a tape recorder, and visited him with Jamie Cohen, a music executive acquaintance of mine and Matthew A. M. Powell, my employee and friend, at his home for the interview you read in Chapter 4. Jamie had dealt with lots of celebrities, but he was blown away at meeting Wooden. To this day we still talk about it.

In early 1984, I decided that writing about Coach Wooden and the Pyramid of Success would be a good and interesting endeavor. I called Coach, told him of my intentions and asked for his cooperation but he said, "Neville, I'm sorry, my wife is very ill and I haven't got any time for anything like this." Notwithstanding Coach Wooden's preoccupation, I found myself in the UCLA Research Library, looking up old newspaper and magazine articles about Wooden, and I wrote the first draft of the first chapters of this book. I attended a lecture on the Pyramid of Success, read everything I could about and by him, and in 1985 sent a draft of my manuscript. Several months later, the mail arrived with that draft red-lined and corrected by him. I wanted to finish the book, but time and money interfered: not enough of either, and for any lawyer, his clients' interests always come first.

In May of 1991, thanks in part to the guidance of the Pyramid, my law practice was thriving, and I began work again on this book. I attended the Wooden Fantasy Camp in July of 1991 and saw up-close the reverence and respect others had for Coach Wooden. While there, I walked up to Paul Trapani to interview him as a camper. I was delighted to learn that he was family—a grandson-in-law of Wooden's. He led me on the path to the rest of the Wooden clan, all of whom were shining examples of friendliness, courtesy and intelligence. This is a book about a man whose family is first in his life. They didn't have to open up their lives to me, but they did, and because of that we have this case study of the family life of the man behind the myth. They are each their own person, successes in their own right.

To my surprise, when I interviewed Jim Wooden, I realized that I had encountered him when I was a boy of nine or so when he did some yard work for my mother. I remember him telling me his father was a basketball coach at UCLA and my not knowing where UCLA was and being curious that there was such a thing as a basketball coach. Several months later, I saw Jim at the local market, I asked him why he didn't do yard work for us anymore, and he replied that he had gone into the Marines, and to tell my father, a former Navy man, that, "The Marines are better." It's funny about life, how some people you meet again under circumstances you least expect. It all came back to me when I met Jim, and I recalled with him an incident, which involved the family car and his high school girlfriend. Jim Wooden was somebody I really liked a lot when I was an adolescent, and was interested in knowing and wondering what had happened to him. Now this! He is a very nice person, and so is his sister.

To Craig Impelman, I owe many of the "Woodenisms," which he has collected and shared with me, and now you.

Special thanks go to Eddie Sheldrake who helped me find many players and persons who had been affiliated with Coach Wooden. Ann Meyers-Drysdale was right in insisting that I contact Pete Newell and Dick Enberg, and giving me their numbers. Meeting her, indeed all who I've met because of writing this book, has been a thrill. Some are particularly memorable. Walton insisted we watch a volleyball tournament at UCLA while I interviewed him, but the interview he gave was unbelievably focused and he was so enthusiastic about Coach that he could hardly be contained. Bill Wooden and his wife exuded whimsy and down-home charm. A gaggle of septuagenarians and octogenarians were lined up to talk to me at Poe's cafeteria in Martinsville; they all wanted to be heard, to give praise. I shed a tear with Larry Maxwell when he talked about Wooden going to visit his parent's grave. Kareem Abdul-Jabbar gave me all the time I needed at his house where each doorway accommodated his height.

I am especially grateful to those who allowed me to interview them, everyone was so earnest, gracious and welcoming. It is their stories that comprise the bulk of the book and they are as much authors as I am. I conducted more interviews than space allowed, and am sorry they could not all make it into the final draft. Fred Hessler, Franklin Murphy, Jack Tobin, Bob Haldeman, and Daniel Wooden have since passed away; I'm glad this book is part of their legacy.

I will not thank individually each of those featured in the interview section—they made the first team, but there were so many others who contributed to this book. I was grateful to interview in Martinsville sisters Judy Savournin and Mary Schnaiter. Mary was Nell's best friend from that town, and their father was the one who lent Wooden the money to get married. In Martinsville, we also encountered Merrill Cox, who also supplied us with a treasure trove of clippings going back to the late 1920s about Wooden; Ervin Cohen, who knew him as a young man; Wendell Phillips, who knew the family; Kenneth Watson, who was a few years behind Wooden in high school and considered him a hero; and Blake Ress, the principal of Martinsville High School.

Doyal Plunkett (University of Iowa), and Dr. Ben Miller (Indiana University),who played against Wooden at Purdue, offered us insights into Wooden as a player. Howard Fahrubel in Dayton, Kentucky, remembered his high school coach as if it was yesterday, and supplied us with the picture of that first team. Stan Steidel, the athletic director at Dayton High School, impressed on us Wooden's legacy and how he is remembered. Davage Minor, an African-American from Gary, Indiana, who played against Wooden's teams in high school, remembered how Wooden was color-blind and that it made a big difference at the time. Mary Dohn remembers seeing Wooden at dances at Purdue like it was yesterday. In South Bend, Indiana, Jim Powers and the others interviewed let their emotions flow freely as they spoke with warmth and gratitude about their mentor.

For the UCLA years, I also relied upon the stories and memories of Marjorie Ashen, Ralph Bauer, Bob Bell, Kenny Booker, Diane Bragg, Barry Chasens, Dave Greenwood, Jim Harrick, Brad Holland, Ralph Joeckel, George Morgan, Dan Saffer, Doug Sale, Gene Sutherland, Doug Thomson, Roland Underhill.

For the family section, I also interviewed great-granddaughter Cori Bernstein, grandson-in-law Gary Bernstein, and grandson Michael Wooden. Joe O'Brien, then executive director, and Wayne Patterson, then historian for the Naismeth Basketball Hall of Fame in Springfield MA provided helpful information and guidance. Max Shapiro was gracious in talking about the Wooden Camps. There were many others who shared all they could about coach and to a person encouraged me in this endeavor.

Sports Information Director Marc Dellins' assistance was tremendous in getting me names and addresses of former players, as well as letting me view the UCLA athletic department's archives on Wooden, and answering questions when I was stumped. Jeff Van Wagenen, then a student intern from the University of Southern California (and now a successful attorney in Riverside, California), helped organize and attended many of the initial interviews (and conducted a few of them). He also helped type the manuscript, and was a positive and warm-spirited force to have in the office. Ed Powell was a great help in finding players from South Bend. My enthusiastic and helpful friend, Mike Flint, and I followed "The John Wooden Trail" in Indiana in late October of 1991, tracking down the memories, people and places of John Wooden's past. Barbara Poe, owner of Poe's cafeteria, which has to be the best cafeteria-style restaurant in the world, said she was too shy to let me interview her, but she went out of her way to find local Martinsville residents who visited with us to share their experiences. All the inhabitants made us welcome, and the same can be said for those who assisted us in Cincinnati and Dayton, Kentucky. Bob Birge of Indianapolis responded to an author's query in the UCLA alumni magazine and arranged a number of interviews, which turned out sensationally well. Francine Abbot was kind in providing the taped recollections of her father, Carl Warriner, and I will always remember the pleasant afternoon spent in her backyard.

The sports information directors at Purdue University and Indiana State University were kind to allow me access to their archives, and the librarians knew just where to direct this researcher at the South Bend City Library.

I pored through several thousand newspaper and magazine articles to research and write the biographical section of the book. Obviously, the sports-writers who contemporaneously covered Coach during the heyday of UCLA basketball, and since then who have written about the man, first reported many of the quotes utilized, and I must give them tribute for thoroughness and intelligence in reporting. The *Los Angeles Times* has done a terrific job of covering its hometown hero, but it is one of many throughout the land that tried to understand the man as a coach and human being. It is rare that the life of a man in athletics has been so extensively examined off the court as well as on, and it was a pleasure to find and pass on the nuggets and news items concerning Wooden's life.

Debbie Budge, a former basketball player, helped type the first draft of the manuscript and encouraged me. Tim Cloutier, Sandra Russell, Denise Ganz, Tia Yasuoka, and Tonya Mertens also were a great help with the manuscript. Donny De Mers did great research in the UCLA newspaper and magazine archives about Coach Wooden; I am also grateful to the staff of the UCLA Undergraduate Research Library for granting me access to the special collection materials on Coach Wooden, J.D. Morgan and Ducky Drake.

I recommend highly visiting the Indiana Basketball Hall of Fame in New Castle, Indiana and The Naismith Basketball Hall of Fame in Springfield, Massachusetts, the national institution. They are a must for any fan, and provide a tactile and visual experience that will assist you in understanding the sport and Wooden, and as to the former museum, establish irrefutably that people are just plain crazy about basketball in that state.

I was impressed overall with the classiness of those who played for and know Wooden—so many genuinely nice people are in his world. The legacy of Wooden as a teacher is very real and genuine, as evidenced by the lives of those student-players and managers, who have gone on to make something of themselves, to achieve in accordance with Wooden's principles. I was fortunate to be able to interview so many who shared intimate moments and memories with Wooden going back to the 1920s that I have passed on.

My teachers at Loyola High School in Los Angeles taught me more than I thought I wanted or needed to know, and they did an excellent job. David Littlejohn, a professor at the Graduate School of Journalism at the University of California at Berkeley, gave me an important and wonderful education about writing and literature, and as an undergraduate I had no finer professor than he.

I trained under three lawyers of great integrity and skill who taught me to think and write: Owen J. Sloane, the late Walter L. M. (Mike) Lorimer and G. Keith Wisot, now a retired Superior Court Judge in Los Angeles.

This is truly a second edition; the book has been extensively rewritten and many new passages, facts, quotes, anecdotes, and analysis added. The biographical section has tripled in length. Dennis Bitterlich, the Archives Assistant at the University Archives of UCLA, was gracious in welcoming me in 2002, and excited to assist in tracking down whatever interested me, helped fact-check, and even assisted in proof-reading. I was given access to Chancellor Murphy's files on intercollegiate athletics, as well as archives and papers of the UCLA athletic department from the time of Morgan and Wooden. This edition benefits considerably from the oral history of J.D. Morgan, which UCLA documented in 1982, and a UCLA oral history interview with Ducky Drake done in 1979. I pulled quotes liberally from Marv Dunphy's excellent, thorough, 1981 doctoral dissertation, *John Robert Wooden: The Coaching Process*. For the second edition, I listened to press conferences by Wooden, discovered other print and filmed interviews with him, and found substantial additional information from numerous other sources. Consequently, this edition contains a rare inside look and the bigger picture of how the UCLA athletic department operated as a business, as a team of committed coaches, and as an integral part of university life.

Given this unusual opportunity to improve the imperfections of the first edition and to update and further concentrate on the life of Coach Wooden, I was pleased also in this edition to preserve Wooden's place in the pantheon of the brave leaders who caused the integration of basketball. I have tried as best I could to do justice to Coach Wooden, to give a fair, comprehensive perspective on the man without getting lost in the minutiae of games, seasons, statistics and the lore of battles long over. One of the reasons sports are popular is because of the instant gratification of seeing an activity where it is a given that one side will be defeated. We are always looking forward to the next contest. Most coaches, like matches won or lost, fade into oblivion, as they should. Few coaches transcend their chosen sport and have a deep, lasting cultural impact. It has been twenty-seven years since he retired but we are all looking forward to what he is going to say tomorrow. He's still teaching, and his teachings will live on after he is gone.

Garry Abrams, one of the top legal journalists in Southern California, ably edited the first edition, for which I remain deeply indebted. James Ryan, an associate at my law firm, assisted in editing the second edition; and the final edits were done by the highly skilled, and very nice, Lisa Wysocky of

Nashville, TN. Brian Perrin and Bruce Petersen were a great help at Cool Titles in getting the first edition of the book to the printer and the public. I'm grateful to J.D. Haas who encouraged me to get this edition out.

Over the years, many friends have offered encouraging words about my Wooden project. I am especially grateful for the kindness and friendship shown me by Karin McEvoy, Janet Pelliccio, Tom Petersen, Ashley Andrews, Claire Fullerton, Wayne Coleman, Matthew A. M. Powell, Kyle S. Morris, Dale Kawashima (who also assisted in editing and promoting the first edition), Lida Paukert, A.E.H.G., A.B.B. and A.A.P. Thanks to my friend and long-time basketball fan, Kevin Fitzsimmons, for commenting on the manuscript, and to Steve Ellis for his opinion. A special nod of appreciation must go to Luke Johnson, who exemplifies all that Coach Wooden teaches. He's been an enthusiastic supporter of the project since day one, and accompanied me on the last interview with Coach. Norman A. Levy, my great friend in New York, has always been a source of encouragement for the book and generally life. Brian A. Rishwain, my law partner, has been both encouraging about the book and understanding of my needs at various occasions to supervise its distribution and promotion while maintaining a busy and challenging law practice.

The two most important people in my life are Barbara and L. Richard Johnson, my parents. If it weren't for their example, courage and enlightened attitude, I never would have the impetus and ability to have produced this work. My father lived to see the publication of the first edition of the book, which made him proud, and I miss him every day. I also want to thank my brothers, Peter and Wayne Johnson, and my lovely sister Anne, who as a UCLA student took me to a lot of Wooden games, and who, with her husband, Greg Greaney, urged me on with this book.

Finally, of course, my deepest and underlying gratitude goes to Coach Wooden. I share Marv Dunphy's appreciation, the closer I get to the man, the more I learn about him, the more I am awed. He is an extraordinarily kind man, and this truly is a book about love in all its permutations and varieties. He was gracious enough to assist in the promotion of the first edition, and gave some wonderful radio interviews, including the national radio program hosted by Jim Rome. There were no restrictions placed on me by Coach to what I could write and whom I could interview and many required his permission before they would talk to me.

I conducted lengthy in-person interviews with Wooden in 1983, 1991, 1992, and 1993, and many shorter telephone interviews between 1991 and 1993, and was fortunate to meet with him at his home several times in 2001 after the first edition was released, when I again asked whatever I wished. The tape recorder was only turned off a few times and then only because Wooden did not want to publicly state anything that could be construed as negative about another person. In 2002, Wooden graciously answered questions on those lingering issues that needed to be clarified or fact checked. There were no questions he would not answer and I have no more to ask. In researching this biography and from my encounters with him, what impresses is his stability, gentility, calmness, kindness, trust in others, trustworthiness, friendliness, compassion, wit, modesty, intelligence, intensity, integrity, and decency. The man has heart, it shows and glows. He lives and exudes love. He has gotten nicer as the years roll by, and he was unbelievably kind to begin with. At the same time, he is nobody's fool, doesn't waste time nor allow his to be wasted. Life gets a full-court press from him. He distributed three dozen copies of the first edition to friends and family, and inscribed in my copy the following: "For Neville Johnson—whose persistence in completing this project endured through many years, with thanks for considering it a worthwhile endeavor. John Wooden."

The Pyramid of Success has always been a touchstone, a place for me to go for contemplation, advice, encouragement and nourishment. It always delivers. It just makes sense, good common sense. It has definitely helped me in my law practice. In 1999 I won a unanimous decision from the California Supreme Court vindicating the right of privacy for all Americans, the legal equivalent of the Final Four. When the going got tough fighting a corporate giant, the Pyramid was there on my office wall and in my bedroom to keep me motivated.

What fun it has been to write this book and to meet so many interesting people in so many walks of life, who all share a common appreciation of this wonderful man! The mark of any person is the wellspring of affection he or she leaves in his or her wake. In the case of John Wooden, there is a tidal wave of respect. His impact resonates at the most fundamental levels of all who have had the honor to know him. Tears of joy and respect were shed by many an interviewee. Virtually everyone I came into contact with was enthusiastic about the project. Those who refused to be interviewed are Digger Phelps of Notre Dame (no surprise), NBA coach Pat Riley (who later came out with his own motivational book), and a few UCLA players, but I could have interviewed hundreds more. As a litigator, I'm trained to look for the negative, to uncover half-truths, mis-truths, wrongdoing of any nature, and I have tried to do so with Coach Wooden. Hard as I tried, I couldn't find anything of substance. It's true, folks, Wooden appears never to have uttered a curse word on or off the court. He is an honorable man who deserves the legend and the accolades, who turns cynics into pussycats. What a joy it has been for me to write about an individual who brings out the positive at all times. He's solution-oriented, disciplined, organized, and follows through on every level. Would that we could all be this way.

I've often said that it could have been anybody in any profession who came up with the Pyramid of Success, and I might have written a book about him or her, but it was John Wooden, a basketball coach, who did. He would have been successful at anything he attempted, I believe. I began a fan of the man, and now I'm an expert on UCLA basketball. Life is amazing! I didn't have any choice about writing this book, I had to do it. Lincoln may be Wooden's favorite American, mine is John Wooden. And for those of you wondering about the subject of the lecture Wooden references in the Pyramid of Success lecture in Chapter 3, it was Lincoln.

I can verify John Wooden is often hilarious. I saw or heard about many occasions when he displayed his sense of humor, and was impressed with his quick and witty ripostes delivered with a twinkle in his eye. The man knows how to have fun. Wooden lived life to its fullest and still does.

If you are interested in reading more on Coach Wooden, I highly recommend his autobiography, *They Call Me Coach*, written with Jack Tobin, which contains much information about his early years and life. *Wooden*, subtitled "A Lifetime of Observations and Reflections on and off the Court" (1997), and written with Steve Jamison, deservedly keeps on selling and contains the essence of Wooden and many nuggets of wisdom. Andrew Hill's, *Be Quick But Don't Hurry* (2001) is a moving up-close and personal look at the impact and wisdom of Wooden from a former UCLA player. Wooden's textbook on basketball, *Practical Modern Basketball*, is worthwhile even if you are not interested in learning the fundamentals of playing and coaching basketball, because it offers much on the teacher-student relationship, how to be a person of integrity, and how to learn, teach and coach. You can see for yourself the practical application of Coach's principles. *The Bruin 100*, by Scott Howard Cooper, published in 1999, is a history of the 100 greatest games in UCLA history (almost all Wooden games), and made the bestseller list in Southern California. It's also got a complete selection of statistics and records. For an interesting overview on the difficulty of following Wooden at UCLA, a good read is Mark Heisler's *They Shoot Coaches Don't They*, subtitled "UCLA and the NCAA since John Wooden," published in 1996. The video, *Values, Victory and Peace of Mind* (2000), will allow you to hear and see Coach as he educates you about the Pyramid. In 2002, John Reger, a sportswriter, compiled various Wooden quotes into *The Quotable Wooden*, which is a quick and entertaining read of what Coach is all about. Interestingly, Wooden didn't know about the book until someone asked him to autograph it.

THE JOHN WOODEN PYRAMID OF SUCCESS

It is a national tragedy that Wooden has not been awarded the Presidential Medal of Freedom, the United States' highest civilian honor. Write the President of the United States and tell him there is a worthy candidate.

You have a duty now. Kindness and friendship comprise the blood of our social lives. For yourself, and all others, endeavor to spread John Wooden's ideas and values. Pass along the Pyramid of Success. Think about it. Talk about it. Practice its tenets. We are all here so briefly. By will and skill, by being sensitive and sensible, by acknowledging and adopting the knowledge of those who truly have achieved peace in their lives, each of us can likewise find harmony.

The Pyramid of Success was created by Coach Wooden as a manifestation of love. May you find and live its values doing so with balance. You can achieve anything you set out to do if you try. Look what John Wooden has done and continues to do, and how he's ended up a satisfied and respected man.

Go for it, your best. There is no other choice or way. You only live once. You have an obligation to yourself. You deserve to own that feeling of self-satisfaction that Coach has identified and analyzed. You can and should.

It's only fair to give Coach the last word to help you on your way:

No one is better than you in making the best effort of which you are capable of. We're not equal as far as size, or appearance or other ways, but we are all equal in terms of having the opportunity of making the best with what we have.

There is only one type of pressure that is important, it's the pressure that you put on yourself. I don't care what you're doing—whether you're a dentist, or surgeon, or a groundskeeper or whatever, it doesn't matter. The pressure you put on yourself is the only thing that really matters.

-Neville L. Johnson,
December 2002

*Coach Wooden with
author Neville Johnson*

THE WOODEN BASKETBALL LEGACY

11-Season High School Coaching Record

Year	Won	Lost	Pct.
Totals	218	42	.838

Two-Season Record at Indiana State

Year	Won	Lost	Pct.
Totals	47	14	.778

27-Season Coaching Record at UCLA

Conference

Year	Won	Lost	Pct.
Totals	316	68	.823

Full Season

Year	Won	Lost	Pct.
Totals	620	147	.808

40-Season All-Time Coaching Record

40-Seasons	Won	Lost	Pct.
Totals	885	203	.813

Wooden coached two seasons at Dayton High School in Kentucky and nine seasons at South Bend Central High School in Indiana. He coached two seasons at Indiana State, in Terre Haute, Indiana before going to UCLA.

LAST 12 SEASONS: THE DYNASTY YEARS

Overall record: 335-22
(.938 winning percentage)

Conference record: 158-11
(.935 winning percentage)

NCAA tournament record: 44-1
(.978 winning percentage)

NCAA titles: 10

Conference titles: 11

JOHN WOODEN'S
Stairway to Heaven

"What I spent, I had
What I made, I lost
What I gave, I have"

"You can give without loving, but
you can't love without giving."

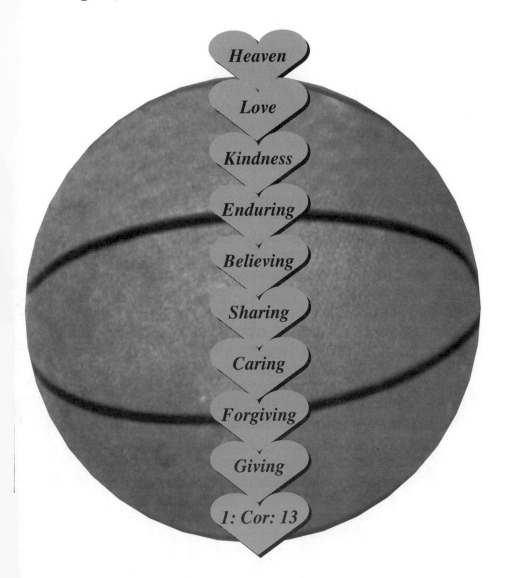

Heaven

Love

Kindness

Enduring

Believing

Sharing

Caring

Forgiving

Giving

1: Cor: 13

John Wooden's Pyramid of Success

FAITH through prayer

PATIENCE good things take time

COMPETITIVE GREATNESS
Be at your best when your best is needed. Enjoyment of a difficult challenge.

FIGHT determined effort

INTEGRITY purity of intention

POISE
Just being yourself. Being at ease in any situation. Never fighting yourself.

CONFIDENCE
Respect without fear. May come from being prepared and keeping all things in proper perspective.

RESOURCEFULNESS proper judgment

RELIABILITY creates respect

CONDITION
Mental-Moral-Physical. Rest, exercise and diet must be considered. Moderation must be practiced. Dissipation must be eliminated.

SKILL
A knowledge of and the ability to properly and quickly execute the fundamentals. Be prepared and cover every little detail.

TEAM SPIRIT
A genuine consideration for others. An eagerness to sacrifice personal interests of glory for the welfare of all.

ADAPTABILITY to any situation

HONESTY in thought & action

SELF-CONTROL
Practice self-discipline and keep emotions under control. Good judgment and common sense are essential.

ALERTNESS
Be observing constantly. Stay open-minded. Be eager to learn and improve.

INITIATIVE
Cultivate the ability to make decisions and think alone. Do not be afraid of failure, learn from it.

INTENTNESS
Set a realistic goal. Concentrate on its achievement by resisting all temptations and being determined and persistent.

AMBITION for noble goals

SINCERITY keeps friends

INDUSTRIOUSNESS
There is no substitute for work. Worthwhile results come from hard work and careful planning.

FRIENDSHIP
Comes from mutual esteem, respect and devotion. Like marriage it must not be taken for granted but requires joint effort.

LOYALTY
To yourself and to all those depending upon you. Keep your self-respect.

COOPERATION
With all levels of your co-workers. Listen if you want to be heard. Be interested in finding the best way, not having your own way.

ENTHUSIASM
Brushes off upon those with whom you come in contact. You must truly enjoy what you are doing.

THE PYRAMID OF SUCCESS